T0414097

The Eschatological Imagination

Intersections

INTERDISCIPLINARY STUDIES IN EARLY MODERN CULTURE

General Editor

Karl A.E. Enenkel (*Chair of Medieval and Neo-Latin Literature
Universität Münster*
e-mail: kenen_01@uni_muenster.de)

VOLUME 96 – 2025

The titles published in this series are listed at *brill.com/inte*

The Eschatological Imagination

Space, Time, and Experience (1300–1800)

Edited by

Wietse de Boer
Christine Göttler

BRILL

LEIDEN | BOSTON

Cover illustrations: (central image) Boëtius Adamsz. Bolswert, "Utinam saperent et intelligerent ac novissima providerent! Deuteron[omy] 32[:29]" (Oh, that they were wise, that they understood this, that they would consider their latter end!), engraving, 15.2 × 9.4 cm, from: Hugo Herman, s.j., *Pia desideria* (Antwerp, Hendrick Aertssens: 1624), before 107, fig. 14, New York, The Metropolitan Museum of Art, Harris Brisbane Dick Fund, 1939, inv. no. 39.33.1. Image © The Metropolitan Museum of Art; (background image) Hieronymus Wierix (published by Joachim de Buschere), The possible travels of the soul after death, 1563–1619, engraving, 13.2 × 8.9 mm, Amsterdam, Rijksmuseum, Rijksprentenkabinet, RP-P-1906-1825. Public domain. For further information, see chapter 1 by Wietse de Boer and Christine Göttler in this volume.

Library of Congress Cataloging-in-Publication Data

Names: Boer, Wietse de, editor. | Göttler, Christine, editor.
Title: The eschatological imagination : space, time, and experience
    (1300-1800) / edited by Wietse de Boer, Christine Göttler.
Description: Leiden ; Boston : Brill, 2025 | Series: Intersections,
    1568-1181 ; volume 96 | Includes bibliographical references and index.
Identifiers: LCCN 2024035729 (print) | LCCN 2024035730 (ebook) |
    ISBN 9789004688094 (hardback ; acid-free paper) |
    ISBN 9789004688247 (ebook)
Subjects: LCSH: Eschatology—History. | Future life—History.
Classification: LCC BT819.5 .E83 2025 (print) | LCC BT819.5 (ebook) |
    DDC 236—dc23/eng/20240904
LC record available at https://lccn.loc.gov/2024035729
LC ebook record available at https://lccn.loc.gov/2024035730

Typeface for the Latin, Greek, and Cyrillic scripts: "Brill". See and download: brill.com/brill-typeface.

ISSN 1568-1181
ISBN 978-90-04-68809-4 (hardback)
ISBN 978-90-04-68824-7 (e-book)
DOI 10.1163/9789004688247

Contents

PART 1
Cosmology and Eschatology

PART 2
Underlands and Netherworlds

Acknowledgements

The project that resulted in this volume was born during the early stages of the Covid-19 pandemic. While its central idea was conceived in prior years, inspired by recent studies on space and time in early modern culture, it took shape in a series of remote meetings held between the spring of 2021 and early 2022. For all the obstacles that stood in the way of research during that difficult period, the new Zoom platform allowed us contributors to meet and collaborate in the moment from the intimacy of our far-flung homes and studies. We would not exclude that the peculiar digital dimension in which we met unconsciously kindled our reflections on imaginative space and time. In any case, our intellectual community was most congenial and allowed us to fashion individual contributions from the ground up based on a common set of questions. Later in 2022, as conventional conferences returned, more advanced versions of individual projects were presented at the Renaissance Society of America meeting in Dublin and the conference of the Historians of Netherlandish Art in Amsterdam.

Most of the papers drafted during that time have now found their home in this book. Of the original members of our team, Byron Hamann, Chiara Franceschini, Theresa Holler, and Anna Pawlak were regrettably unable to contribute to the volume. We are nevertheless most grateful for their participation in the early stages of the project, as they helped shape it in important ways. Matteo Al Kalak and Antoinina Bevan Zlatar joined the group in 2022 and offered contributions on the cultural and literary history of hell which significantly augmented the volume's scope.

We wish to express our gratitude to our co-authors for their excellent contributions (and for their patience with us) and to the large group of anonymous peer reviewers who provided detailed feedback on the individual chapters. We are very fortunate to have worked once again with Jonathan Hoare, who, with his usual professionalism and keen eye, helped us create the index and review the proofs. Special thanks go to Karl Enenkel and the members of the Intersections Editorial Board, who once again supported and approved a project of ours with great enthusiasm. Last but not least, we gratefully acknowledge the expert and collegial editorial assistance of Gera van Bedaf and Ivo Romein.

Wietse de Boer
Christine Göttler
May 2024

Figures

Notes on the Editors

Wietse de Boer
is the Phillip R. Shriver Professor of History at Miami University (Ohio). His research interests are focused on Italian religious and cultural history between the fifteenth and seventeenth centuries. His publications include *The Conquest of the Soul: Confession, Discipline, and Public Order in Counter-Reformation Milan* (2001; Italian trans. 2004), *Art in Dispute: Catholic Debates at the Time of Trent* (2021), and seven edited volumes, including *Religion and the Senses in Early Modern Europe*, co-edited with Christine Göttler (2013), *Jesuit Image Theory*, co-edited with Karl A.E. Enenkel and Walter S. Melion (2016), and *La ghianda e la quercia. Saggi per Adriano Prosperi*, co-edited with Vincenzo Lavenia and Giuseppe Marcocci (2019). His book project, *The Windows of the Soul: Sensory Culture and Religious Conflict in Early Modern Italy*, is in an advanced stage of preparation.

Christine Göttler
is Professor Emerita of Art History at the University of Bern. Her research interests focus on collecting practices and collection spaces, the intersections between art, natural philosophy, and religion, the relationship between landscape and nature, and early modern notions of materiality and immateriality. She is the author of *Die Kunst des Fegefeuers nach der Reformation: Kirchliche Schenkungen, Ablass und Almosen in Antwerpen und Bologna um 1600* (1996); and *Last Things: Art and the Religious Imagination in the Age of Reform* (2010). Her twelve edited volumes include: *Spirits Unseen: The Representation of Subtle Bodies in Early Modern European Culture* (with Wolfgang Neuber, 2007); *Religion and the Senses in Early Modern Europe* (with Wietse de Boer, 2013); *Knowledge and Discernment in the Early Modern Arts* (with Sven Dupré, 2017); *The Nomadic Object: The Challenge of World for Early Modern Religious Art* (with Mia M. Mochizuki, 2018); *Solitudo: Spaces, Places, and Times of Solitude in Late Medieval and Early Modern Cultures* (with Karl A.E. Enenkel, 2018); and *Landscape and Earth in Early Modernity: Picturing Unruly Nature* (with Mia M. Mochizuki, 2022). She is currently working toward completion of her book, *Fluid Worlds: Art and Knowledge in Seventeenth-Century Antwerp*.

Notes on the Contributors

Monica Azzolini
teaches the history of science at the University of Bologna. She has published widely on the anatomical studies of Leonardo da Vinci, Renaissance astrology, and the formation and circulation of scientific knowledge, with particular emphasis on the relationship between orality and the written word, and the use of scientific illustration. In recent years her interest has shifted to the underground: she has explored the relationship between natural disasters and the cult of the saints during the Counter-Reformation. She is currently working on a history of the underground in early modern Italy. She is the author of *The Duke and the Stars: Astrology and Politics in Renaissance Milan* (2013).

Matteo Al Kalak
is Associate Professor of the History of Christianity and of the Churches at the University of Modena and Reggio Emilia. He has conducted research on religious history with particular attention to religious non-conformism. His books include *Gli eretici di Modena: fede e potere alla metà del Cinquecento* (2008); *Il riformatore dimenticato: Egidio Foscarari tra Inquisizione, concilio e governo pastorale (1512–1564)* (2016); *Mangiare Dio: una storia dell'eucarestia* (2021), and *The Heresy of the Brothers: A Heterodox Community in Sixteenth-Century Italy* (2022 [2011]). Further publications include several edited volumes and scholarly articles on the Inquisition, the Council of Trent, and the confraternities between the Middle Ages and the Early Modern Age.

Antoinina Bevan Zlatar
is a Privat Dozent and Lecturer in Early Modern English Literature at the University of Zurich, Switzerland. Her research focuses on the culture of the long Reformation with a particular interest in the late poetry of John Milton. She is the author of *Reformation Fictions: Polemical Protestant Dialogues in Elizabethan England* (Oxford: 2011) and two co-edited collections of essays: *What is an Image in Medieval and Early Modern England?* (Tübingen: 2017), and *Words, Books, Images and the long Eighteenth-Century: Essays for Allen Reddick* (Amsterdam: 2021).

Luke Holloway
is a postgraduate student at Clare Hall, University of Cambridge. He graduated in History at the University of Warwick in 2022, and his research interests lie in early modern British and European history, focusing especially on religion,

print, and society. He has recently co-authored research exploring Methodist correspondence networks and beliefs in the supernatural during the eighteenth century.

Martha McGill
is a historian of early modern supernatural beliefs. She completed a Ph.D. at the University of Edinburgh in 2016, and subsequently held postdoctoral fellowships at the Institute for Advanced Studies in the Humanities, Edinburgh, and the Warburg Institute, London. Since 2018 she has been a British Academy Postdoctoral Fellow at the University of Warwick, working on a project entitled "Bodies, Selves and the Supernatural in Early Modern Britain". She is the author of *Ghosts in Enlightenment Scotland* (2018) and co-editor (with Julian Goodare) of *The Supernatural in Early Modern Scotland* (2020).

Walter Melion
is Asa Griggs Candler Professor of Art History at Emory University in Atlanta, where he directed the Fox Center for Humanistic Inquiry (Emory's institute for advanced study in the humanities) between 2017 and 2023. He is author of three monographs and a critical edition of Karel van Mander's *Foundation of the Noble, Free Art of Painting*, co-author of two exhibition catalogues, editor or co-editor of more than twenty-five volumes, and has published more than one hundred articles. Melion is editor of two book series: Brill's *Studies on Art, Art History, and Intellectual History* and *Lund Humphries' Northern Lights*. He was elected Foreign Fellow of the Royal Netherlands Academy of Arts and Sciences in 2010 and Fellow of the American Academy of Arts and Sciences in 2023. He is president emeritus of the Sixteenth Century Society, current president of the Historians of Netherlandish Art, and a board member of the Print Council of America.

Mia M. Mochizuki
is a historian of Northern Renaissance and Baroque art (Ph.D., Yale University, 2001). She retired from teaching after holding tenured professorships at New York University Institute of Fine Arts and NYU Abu Dhabi, the Graduate Theological Union and Jesuit School of Theology at Berkeley, and the University of Chicago. Her eight books – including the prizewinning *Netherlandish Image after Iconoclasm* (2008), *Dawn of a Global Age* (2017), *The Nomadic Object* (ed., 2018), *Jesuit Art* (2022), and *Landscape and Earth in Early Modernity* (ed., 2023) – have treated the reformation of Dutch art, the global Netherlandish print, artistic exchange between Japan and the West, Jesuit visual culture, and the Northern landscape.

Laurent Paya

holds a Masters Degree in Landscape Architecture from the Agrocampus Ouest (Angers, France) and a Ph.D. in Art History from the Centre d'Etudes Supérieures de la Renaissance (Tours, France). As chief engineer of the Ministry of Agriculture, he teaches landscape architecture and garden design. As an associate researcher, he conducts research on art history at the Centre d'Etudes Supérieures de la Renaissance and the Centre de Recherches Interdisciplinaires en Sciences Humaines et Sociales (Université Montpellier III, France). His fields of research are the aesthetics of garden, ornament, decor and town in the early modern period. He has published a series of articles about the elaboration and the circulation of artistic, scientific and technological knowledge of the socialization of nature. He is the author of *Gouverner les plantes des parcs et jardins de plaisir au temps des humanistes* (2024).

Raphaèle Preisinger

received her Ph.D. degree in Art History and Media Theory from the Karlsruhe University of Arts and Design in 2012. She is currently Assistant Professor and Principal Investigator of the research project "Global Economies of Salvation: Art and the Negotiation of Sanctity in the Early Modern Period", funded by the European Research Council (ERC) and the Swiss National Science Foundation (SNSF), at the University of Zurich. While her current research centres on the global circulation of images and objects in the early modern period, she maintains a major focus on image and piety in the Middle Ages. Her first book is entitled *"Lignum vitae": Zum Verhältnis materieller Bilder und mentaler Bildpraxis im Mittelalter* (2014).

Aviva Rothman

is Inaugural Dean's Associate Professor of History at Case Western Reserve University. She earned her Ph.D. in History at Princeton University, and was formerly a Harper-Schmidt Fellow and Collegiate Assistant Professor at the University of Chicago. She is a historian of science with a particular focus on the astronomical and physical sciences of early modernity. Her first book, *The Pursuit of Harmony: Kepler on Cosmos, Confession and Community*, was published in 2017, and her second, *The Dawn of Modern Cosmology: Copernicus to Newton* (2023) is an anthology of edited and newly translated texts on the Copernican Revolution for the Penguin Classics series.

Minou Schraven

is senior lecturer at Amsterdam University College and associate fellow of the Amsterdam School for Religious History at Vrije Universiteit Amsterdam.

She is member of the research consortium "Mobile Matters of Religion. Devotional and Sacred Objects in the Early Modern World" at the University of Regensburg, and contributor to the project "Mapping Religious Heritage in Amsterdam", http://religieuserfgoed.amsterdam. A specialist in early modern art history and material culture, she has published widely on early modern funeral *apparati*, the ritual uses of coins and portrait medals, festival culture and processions, and the display of human remains in museums, especially issues of lifelikeness and likeability. The chapter on Juana de la Cruz is part of her current book project *Blessed and Indulgenced Objects in Early Modern Catholic Worlds. Materiality, Mobility and Anxiety.*

Anna-Claire Stinebring

is Assistant Curator of European Paintings at The Metropolitan Museum of Art. A specialist in early modern Northern European art, she earned her Ph.D. in the History of Art from the University of Pennsylvania. Prior to starting at The Met, she most recently served as Anne L. Poulet Curatorial Fellow at The Frick Collection. She is the co-author, with Salman Toor, of *Bruegel's Three Soldiers* (2024), a volume in the Frick Diptych Series.

Jane Tylus

is Andrew Downey Orrick Professor of Italian and Professor of Comparative Literature at Yale, where she also has a teaching appointment at the Divinity School. She is the author of *Siena, City of Secrets; Reclaiming Catherine of Siena*; and *Writing and Vulnerability in the Late Renaissance*, and with Karen Newman co-edited *Early Modern Cultures of Translation*. She has translated the poetry of Gaspara Stampa and Lucrezia Tornabuoni de'Medici, as well as Dacia Maraini's recent novel, *Chiara di Assisi: Elogio della disobbedienza*. Her book "Who Owns Literature?" is forthcoming with Cambridge University Press's Elements series. Tylus served as General Editor of *I Tatti Studies in the Italian Renaissance* from 2013–22.

CHAPTER 1

The Space-Time Dimension of Early Modern Eschatology: An Introduction

Wietse de Boer and Christine Göttler

Cosmology is an intellectual enterprise whose insights and scope have always been and continue to be subject to change. In a recent article, two well-known astronomers announced no less than a 'crisis in cosmology' provoked by the stunning discoveries made possible by the James Webb Space Telescope. Peering back into the remote cosmic past, the telescope revealed 'the existence of fully formed galaxies far earlier than should have been possible according to the so-called standard model'. As a result, this model, which describes the process of expansion of the universe after the Big Bang, would need not only serious adjustment (as has occasionally happened in the past) but might have to be abandoned altogether: it could 'require us to change how we think of the elemental components of the universe, possibly even the nature of space and time'. The complexity of this task, the authors suggested, is compounded by the nature of cosmology. For this scientific endeavour is itself part of the universe it studies. This raises questions both about the nature of space and time, and about 'the role of the observers doing the observations'.[1]

This reminder that cosmology, for all the spectacular advances of science and technology, remains a tentative, evolving, and anthropocentric venture, may be a good starting point for a volume on eschatological space and time in the early modern period. This is true not only (or not even primarily) because today's astronomers stand on the shoulders of their early modern predecessors – Copernicus, Kepler, Galileo – but because that period, too, was confounded by a crisis in the understanding of the depths, times, and material components of the universe, and by the place of humans in it. The "standard model" of the period was the cosmos constructed by medieval scholasticism – a model which, unlike its modern scientific iterations, proposed a seamless blending of astronomical, theological, and moral principles. In recent decades, historians of science have done yeoman's work to overcome simplified views, inherited from the nineteenth century, on the conflict between science and

---

1   Frank A. – Gleiser M., "The Crisis in Cosmology", *The New York Times*, September 3, 2023 (print edition), Sunday Opinion section, 8.

religion, and to refine our understanding of the complex ways in which the new science remained entangled in metaphysical premises. Our objective in this volume is a different one: we aim to study how expressly religious practices in Western Christianity – of theological reflection, devotion, contemplation, representation – engaged with the cosmic dimension of space and time, and how they evolved (or did not) as the scientific breakthroughs of the time became matters of common knowledge. This requires a different perspective from the one often adopted by historians of science. It assumes the mindset of those – the faithful in prayer, makers and beholders of sacred images, visionary mystics – who projected their spiritual imaginings, aspirations, and devotions in the here-and-now onto the vast canvas of eschatological space and time. Whereas astronomers today look back into the distant past, these worshippers had their eyes fixed on the *eschata* – the Final Things with which their past, present, and ultimate fate were closely bound up. What did they imagine that world to look like?

1   Spatiality

The early modern world inherited basic assumptions about eschatological space and time from high and late medieval Christianity. Space here refers to realms of the hereafter that were differentiated based on their intended functions, hence meanings. The heaven, hell, purgatory, and limbos (of the fathers and the unbaptized children, respectively) developed by scholastic theology were conceived as a coherent moral universe: these spaces were configured to serve as appropriate destinations of the dead, based on their moral and spiritual condition at the time of their passing.[2] While information in the Scriptures is sparse, there was a certain consistency in the iconography of heaven and hell, the joyful and terrifying destinations, respectively, for the virtuous and the wicked. Heaven might be represented as the Garden of Eden or 'the holy city, the new Jerusalem, coming down out of heaven from God' (*Revelation* 21:2), whereas hell could be shown as an underground cave or a giant devouring mouth (*Isaiah* 5:14).[3] There is frequently an emphasis on the doorways to these

---

2   For a basic introduction, see Ott L. – Naab E., *Eschatologie in der Scholastik*. Handbuch der Dogmengeschichte 4, fasc. 7b (Freiburg – Basel – Vienna: 1990). For visionary and literary accounts, see Gardiner E., *Visions of Heaven and Hell before Dante* (New York, NY: 1989) and, more recently, Pollard R.M. (ed.), *Imagining the Medieval Afterlife* (Cambridge: 2020).

3   *Isaiah* 5:14: 'Therefore hath hell enlarged her soul and opened her mouth without any bounds, and their strong ones and their people and their high and glorious ones shall go down into it'. Here and in the following we cite from *The Vulgate Bible: Douay-Rheims Translation*,

FIGURE 1.1   Erhart Küng, Tympanum with Last Judgement, ca. 1470. Central west portal,
Minster, Bern
IMAGE © WIKIMEDIA COMMONS

final destinations, the thresholds that must be crossed when entering the eternal worlds that have never been seen. The Last Judgement scenes that began
to appear in the tympana above the main west portals of churches in the early
Middle Ages vividly reminded men and women crossing the threshold of the
church of the dreaded threshold that would await them at the end of their
lives. A particularly interesting example is the late fifteenth-century tympanum at the Minster in Bern (Switzerland), which survived the 1528 outburst
of iconoclasm unscathed [Fig. 1.1].[4] Whereas the blessed, dressed in white, are
led in an orderly fashion through a beautifully carved gilded Gothic portal to
a realm situated above the starry sky, the damned – naked and much more
crowded – are tormented in all manner of ways and then pushed upward to be
hurled upside down through a funnel-shaped opening into a fiery hell.

---

ed. E. Swift, 6 vols. (Cambridge, MA: 2010–2013). Instead of *Apocalypse of St. John* (vol. 6,
1315–1405) we use the more common *Book of Revelation*.

4   Sladeczek F.-J., *Erhart Küng: Bildhauer und Baumeister am Münster zu Bern (um 1420–1507).*
Untersuchungen zur Person, zum Werk und zum Wirkungskreis eines westfälischen Künstlers
der Spätgotik (Bern: 1990) 42–68; Nicolai B., "Westbau und Westportal des Berner Münsters", in Nicolai B. – Schweizer J. (eds.), *Das Berner Münster: Das erste Jahrhundert. Von der*
Grundsteinlegung bis zur Chorvollendung und Reformation (1421–1517/1528) (Regensburg: 2019)
600–618, at 609–611.

The numerous printed images of the four Last Things that circulated at the turn of the seventeenth century suggest many continuities in the ways in which the world beyond death was spatialized and how these different spaces were thought to be connected. In a small engraving by Hieronymus Wierix the circular images of the four Last Things in the corners are complemented by a central oval image representing the Crucifixion and the instruments of the Passion – the warrants of salvation – and a purgatory in the form of an alchemical tripod standing on animal-like claws [Fig. 1.2]. The viewing process begins with the image of death at the bottom left, where various forms of dying (by violence, accident, illness, or old age) are represented, for 'it is appointed for men once to die, and after this the judgment' (*Hebrews* 9:27). From there, they can travel along three possible paths, one taken by the 'wicked', whose death is 'very evil' (*Psalm* 33:22), and two that pass through the image of the Crucifixion and lead either directly or by way of purgatory to heaven. The inclusion of purgatory is remarkable. Temporary rather than eternal, like heaven and hell, and therefore 'penultimate' rather than 'ultimate', purgatory differs from the traditional *novissima* in its three-dimensional form.[5] It is not shown as a final destination, but rather as a transit station through which the majority of the faithful must pass, those who have not built their lives entirely on Christ, but who 'shall be saved, yet so as by fire' (1 *Corinthians* 3:15).

The association of the purgatorial fire with the fire of the alchemists emphasizes its purifying and expiatory function; in an age of confessional polemics, Catholics promoted this third place as the road taken by the average Christian and defended its existence with reference to the words of St. Paul. Finally, the two quotations that frame the picture, *Deuteronomy* 32:29 and *Ecclesiasticus* 7:40 ('in omnibus operibus tuis memorare novissima tua' – 'In all thy works remember thy last end, and thou shalt never sin'), introduce a temporal element, reminding viewers that they should both 'recall' (*memorare*) the *novissima* and 'see [them] beforehand' (*providere*). This element, as Sigrud Bergmann has stressed, stood at the centre of the widespread 'art of dying' (*ars moriendi*): here, the imagination of the future was linked to the memory of the past: 'as all imagination is nurtured by remembrance, the past is also present in our images of the future, which again impacts on the present and one's imagination of the past'.[6] Since antiquity, as Pierre Hadot has pointed out, the 'art of dying' was an elaborate practice of self-examination and self-formation, and

---

5   Griffiths P.J., "Purgatory", in Walls J.L. (ed.), *The Oxford Handbook of Eschatology* (Oxford: 2007) 427–445, at 428.

6   Bergmann S., "What Images of the Last Things Do to Us: Introductory Remarks on Why Eschatology Matters", in idem (ed.), *Eschatology as Imagining the End: Faith between Hope and Despair* (London: 2018) 1–29, at 1. On the *ars moriendi*, see also chapters 13, 14, and 15.

FIGURE 1.2   Hieronymus Wierix (published by Joachim de Buschere), The possible travels
of the soul after death, 1563–1619. Engraving, 13.2 × 8.9 cm. Amsterdam,
Rijksmuseum, Rijksprentenkabinet, RP-P-1906-1825

it was within this religious form of introspection that an imagery of the other world was created that deeply affected the senses.[7] This imagery, which was both flexible and dynamic, extended the world beyond the horizon of death both spatially and temporally, linking universal and personal eschatology.

2　　　Temporality

Thus, as the *ars moriendi* suggests, if the spatial configuration of the hereafter was loaded with a dense set of assumptions, so was the temporal framework within which the Last Things unfolded. The imaginative projection of the self into the afterlife, in fact, assumed a comprehensive narrative that bound past, present, and future together. In it, the *eschata* or *novissima* formed the capstone of a salvation history that began with the Creation and Fall, and had its crucial turning point in Christ's incarnation, death, and resurrection, ushering in the Christian era. This was the trajectory onto which both human history and individual lives were grafted, giving them direction and meaning. Human existence was inherently dynamic, tending, as the scholastics said, towards its 'end' (*finis*).[8]

Yet the temporality this assumed was anything but simple or even unidirectional. Perhaps the clearest scriptural explanation could be found in the *Second Epistle of Peter* (2 Peter 3:3–13), where the author corrected the 'deceitful scoffers' who indulged their pleasures on the grounds that 'all things continue as they were from the beginning of the creation' and there will be no second coming of Christ. Not so, admonished Peter, for just as God's word had created the world from water and had already once submerged it in water, thus he held his next punishment in abeyance: '[T]he heavens and the earth which are now by the same word are kept in store, reserved unto fire against the day of judgment and perdition of the ungodly men'. When that would happen was deliberately left open: 'one day with the Lord is as a thousand years, and a thousand years as one day'. The eschatological delay that might be perceived as God's sluggishness was actually patience – the patience intended to give sinners a chance to repent. Then again, it was not endless: 'the day of the Lord shall come

---

7　Hadot P., *Philosophy as a Way of Life: Spiritual Exercises from Socrates to Foucault*, trans. A.I. Davidson (Cambridge, MA: 1995) 68–69, and passim. See also Foucault M., *The Hermeneutics of the Subject: Lectures at the Collège de France, 1981–82*, ed. F. Gros, trans. G. Burchell (New York, NY: 2005) 477–489.

8　Cf. Thomas Aquinas, *Summa theologiae*, Ia–IIae, q. 1, a. 2: 'omne agens agit propter finem' ('every agent acts towards its end').

as a thief'. In this state of suspense two elements were in tension: certainty (judgement will come) and indeterminacy (we don't know when). But there was a crucial third element: free will. It was about the faithful's response in the here-and-now. In this vein Peter asked: 'what manner of people ought you to be in holy conversation and godliness, looking for and hasting unto the coming of the day of the Lord, by which the heavens, being on fire, shall be dissolved and the elements shall melt with the burning heat of fire?'[9] In other words, it was in the present that the long-term scheme of salvation was to be engaged.

The temporal framework of eschatological expectations was much developed in post-biblical times but, despite the best efforts of scholastic theologians, not necessarily simplified. To be sure, some basic assumptions emerged. For individuals, the moment of death marked the separation of body and soul, and it closed their window of meritorious action – the opportunity to affect their spiritual fate – although others could still act on their behalf until the end of time. Based on their condition, souls were relegated to heaven, hell, or – in a way specified during the High Middle Ages – purgatory. Collectively, the end of the world coincided with the second coming of Christ and the Last Judgement. That was also the appointed time for the resurrection of the body and its reunification with the soul. This process, which was all the more dramatic for being collective as well as instantaneous, triggered the final sorting of the good and the evil, and their definitive dispatch to heaven and hell. Even this summary scenario raised difficult, even agonizing, questions. How long did the dead have to wait before hearing the final verdict? Did those still alive by the time of the Last Judgement have to die before proceeding to their final destination?

There were further complexities. A broad range of opinion – mainstream, prophetic, and/or suspect – speculated about the signs and events that, according to the *Book of Revelation* or other sources, might precede the end of history: a time of tribulations, the appearance of the Antichrist, the arrival of the millennium. But the most incisive factor that reconfigured the temporalities of the medieval afterlife was the elaboration of the scholastic doctrine on purgatory. Its history neatly exemplifies what was true for the construction of the afterlife in general: a presumed spiritual need or expectation required its own place and time – however defined – to be realized. In the minds of the devout the

---

9 Recent interpretations of this remarkable biblical passage include: Adams E., *The Stars Will Fall from Heaven: Cosmic Catastrophe in the New Testament and Its World* (London: 2007) 200–235; Frey J., "Second Peter in New Perspective", in Frey J. – Dulk M. den – Watt J.G. van der (eds.), *2 Peter and the Apocalypse of Peter: Towards a New Perspective* (Leiden: 2019) 7–74. The significance of this passage for late sixteenth- and early seventeenth-century discussions of a fluid, homogenous, and perhaps even corruptible heaven is addressed in chapter 2 of this volume.

long tradition of suffrages for the dead conjured up a holding place for those undergoing purification. Hence the origins of purgatory. That construct similarly raised questions of time. How long would the process of purgation take for each soul? How much could this time be reduced by the masses and prayers said by the living? Answering them could turn into a veritable arithmetic of salvation, which processed numbers of sins committed, suffrages extended, and time in purgatory already elapsed. The living thus engaged with purgatory on a quite different timescale compared to other parts of the world-beyond. They also knew that it had a unique place in the larger eschatological context. In contrast to the other spaces of the afterlife, as we have already noted, it was temporary: it lost its raison-d'être once the moment of judgement arrived, and in that awe-inspiring event it ceased to exist.[10]

Even the collapse of time itself did not resolve all questions of temporality. For, as Dante's *Commedia* demonstrates in the most sublime way, it proved impossible to imagine the existence of the blessed and the damned without associating it with speech, movement, sensation, and expression. This problem persisted well into the early modern period: a traditionalist theologian like the seventeenth-century Jesuit Gabriel de Henao (studied in chapter 3) – but also coeval mystics, poets, and artists – faced extraordinary difficulties in conceiving and representing the experiences of the glorified in a timeless universe.[11] How, indeed, could humans living in a finite world envision an infinite future time? One of the most widely read works that considered this question was *De aeternitate considerationes* (Considerations on eternity) by the German Jesuit Jeremias Drexel (1581–1638), a convert from Lutheranism and immensely successful author of Catholic devotional literature. Among the earthly objects Drexel recommended for creating (or 'painting', as he called it) a vivid image of eternal hell in one's mind were several marvels of nature that his learned readers were undoubtedly familiar with, such as the mineral asbestos, which, once ignited, was said to be incombustible, and the salamander, considered to be able to endure in fire.[12] He also warned his readers that even pleasant sensual experiences could become repulsive if they did not cease, illustrating this with the example of the murmuring running water of medicinal baths, which

---

10   Still relevant on these points is Le Goff J., *La naissance du purgatoire* (Paris: 1981) 388–391.

11   Visions of the afterlife are discussed in chapters 8 and 9 of this volume. Poetic explorations of the loci of the netherworld are discussed in chapters 5 and 6.

12   Drexel Hieremias, *De aeternitate considerationes* (Munich, per Raphaelem Sadelerum: 1620); within the space of a year the treatise appeared in German and French translations. We cite from the English edition, *The Considerations of Drexelius upon Eternitie*, trans. Ralph Winterton (London, T[homas] C[otes] for Nicholas Alsop: 1632) 26–29.

at first provide 'harmonious comfort', but in time become 'very loathsome and a torment unto them'.[13]

3   The Eschatological Chronotope

This observation confirms once more that the temporal framework of the afterlife, at any of its stages, hinged crucially on the present. That was the dimension in which spiritual exercises and devotional acts took place, when the faithful said their prayers, remembered their dead, venerated the cross, the host, or sacred images, and invoked the support or intercession of saints. The engagement with the great eschatological dramas – for individuals and communities alike – was thus embedded within the temporalities of life on earth: the seasons, the liturgical calendar, the feast days of the saints, and, especially for the sick and dying, the fear or prospect of impending death. The devotional evocation of the spaces of the afterlife – heaven, purgatory, hell – assumed them to exist contemporaneously: it was in the here-and-now, and amidst the challenges of daily life, that Christ and – depending on one's creed – the saints or the elect were imagined to be enthroned in paradise, hopefully receptive to the entreaties of mere mortals. This was, in fact, a necessary condition.

Mikhail Bakhtin's notion of the 'chronotope' may help us better to envision the intersections of ordinary human existence and the eschatological realms – to understand, that is, how the regions beyond earthly space and time were imagined, pictured, and engaged in devotional or meditative practice. Mostly written in the years 1937 and 1938, Bakhtin's long essay 'Forms of Time and of the Chronotope in the Novel', primarily aimed to explore time-space relations in literature.[14] It was one of the ways in which Einstein's relativity theory influenced the humanities in the prewar period.[15] Only when Bakhtin's works began to appear in English translations in the late 1960s did his methodological innovations prompt his broad impact and reception. His aversion to

---

13   Drexel, *The Considerations upon Eternity* 40–41. For an engaging discussion of changing concepts of eternity, see Eire C., *A Very Brief History of Eternity* (Princeton, NJ: 2010).

14   Bakhtin M.M., "Forms of Time and of the Chronotope in the Novel: Notes toward a Historical Poetics", in idem, *The Dialogic Imagination: Four Essays*, ed. M. Holquist, trans. C. Emerson – M. Holquist (Austin, TX: 2020) 84–258.

15   See, e.g., Novick P., *That Noble Dream: The "Objectivity Question" and the American Historical Profession* (Chicago, IL: 1988) 135–138; Bredekamp H. – Wedepohl C., *Warburg, Cassirer und Einstein im Gespräch: Kepler als Schlüssel der Moderne* (Berlin: 2015).

systematization further paved the way for the interdisciplinary application of his concepts, which has intensified in recent years.[16]

At first sight it might seem paradoxical to apply the term chronotope to the imaginative construction of the hereafter. After all, did that world – granted that it had a spatial dimension – not exist in a state of collapsed time? Yet Bakhtin himself already articulated the usefulness of his concept here.[17] Two elements appear particularly relevant for the essays collected in this volume. The first is the Russian critic's distinction of horizontal and vertical modalities of time. On the one hand, as we have seen, the contemplation of the afterlife was necessarily projected along the horizontal axis of historical chronology; on the other, the assumption of contemporary existence of the otherworldly spaces and many of its inhabitants (Christ, the Virgin, angels, and saints) constituted a vertical axis indispensable for devotional engagement with these spaces and those who dwelt therein. The resulting tension between the historical and the visionary underlies Bakhtin's analysis of Dante's *Commedia* – a vertical world whose 'temporal logic [...] consists in the sheer simultaneity of all that occurs (or "the coexistence of everything in eternity")'.[18]

A second important element is the idea of threshold. In 1973, two years before his death, Bakhtin added some 'concluding remarks' to his foundational essay, and it is in these later pages that he introduced several 'minor chronotopes' or 'motifs', including the road, the castle, the salon, the provincial town, and the threshold, all of which are defined by specific spatial settings that are themselves linked to particular types of narrative.[19] For our purposes, the chronotope of the threshold is crucial. Bakhtin defined this juncture as 'highly charged with emotion and value [...] connected with the breaking point of a life, the moment of crisis, the decision that changes a life (or the indecisiveness that fails to change a life, the fear to step over the threshold)'. According to him, time in the chronotope of the threshold is instantaneous, marking the moment when two different spaces or worlds are joined. Bakhtin did not list the end of life explicitly among the 'crisis events [...], the falls, resurrections, renewals'.[20] Yet early modern men and women certainly understood death, both personal and universal, as a threshold event that catapulted their souls into a world beyond earthly space and time. Bakhtin's theory thus helps

---

16   Bemong N. et al. (eds.), *Bakhtin's Theory of the Literary Chronotope: Reflections, Applications, Perspectives* (Ghent: 2010); Haynes D.J., "Bakhtin and the Visual Arts", in Smith P. – Wilde C. (eds.), *A Companion to Art Theory* (Oxford: 2002) 292–302.

17   See Bakhtin M.M., "Forms of Time", especially 146–151; for further discussion, see chapter 3 of this volume.

18   Bakhtin, "Forms of Time" 156–158, at 157.

19   Ibidem 243–258 ('Concluding Remarks').

20   Ibidem 248.

account not only for the peculiar space-time configuration of the *eschata* but also, and especially, for the imaginative, literary, artistic, and contemplative construction and engagement of that dimension.

4   The Disruptions of New Knowledge

How, then, did the eschatological chronotope evolve during the early modern era? As we have already suggested, important basic expectations and structural elements persisted. Yet this was also a time of profound disruption, if not crisis, in many areas associated with cosmology. How did this affect the eschatological imagination? Several chapters in this volume underscore the momentous effects of new technologies of visual perception. One example may serve to suggest how novelty and tradition could nevertheless go hand in hand. The first telescopes, "invented" in the early 1600s, news of which spread rapidly throughout Europe's expanding world, caused sensation and excitement similar to that provoked by the James Webb Space Telescope. Like all visual images, however, those that could be viewed through the new "eyeglass" posed interpretive challenges, arousing awe as well as scepticism and disbelief. On the one hand, the telescopes of the early seventeenth century were ascribed miraculous or even magical powers by contemporaries; on the other hand, they were being suspected of distorting long-established truths about a cosmos designed by God, the prime mover, as an ordered whole, a universe of space and time in which all phenomena are contained.

For this reason, the telescope did not represent in any way a clear rupture or an unambiguous triumph of the new science over a theologically founded cosmology. The urge to gauge mathematically the expanse of the universe was well established and even pervaded religious discourses. The Dominican Antonino Polti, author of a devotional work published in 1575, was one among many who drew on Ptolemaic cosmology to come to terms with the vastness of the Christian cosmos. Among many distances he sought to quantify, he estimated that between humanity ('us') and the ninth heaven to be 201,537,409 miles. Far greater, however, was the space separating us from the final two, namely the *primum mobile* and paradise itself, the empyrean. That distance also offered a measure of the immense size of those farthest heavens, 'because the greater the distance from which we see an object, the smaller it appears to be, and yet we perceive the heavens to be enormous'.[21]

---

21   Polti Antonino, *Della felicità suprema del cielo libri tre* (Perugia, Giovan Berardino Rastelli: 1575) 37: 'Sì che grandissimi appariscono i cieli dalla grandissima distanza, e particolarmente lo empireo, detto anco paradiso: perché quanto si vede una cosa da lontano, tanto

Conversely, in the following period of change and transition, which saw a proliferation of treatises on the physical nature of the heavens, the telescope could become a metaphor for contemplating one's ultimate fate and conjuring it up with greater immediacy. An example of such a telescope can be found in Boëtius Adamsz. Bolswert's striking illustration of the emblem 'Utinam saperent et intelligerent ac novissima providerent!' ('O that they would be wise and would understand, and would provide for their last end', *Deuteronomy* 32:29) in Herman Hugo's *Pia Desideria* [Fig. 1.3]. Dedicated to none other than the newly elected Pope Urban VIII, it was perhaps the most popular emblem book of its time. There is no mention of the telescope in the Jesuit's learned commentary, so its inclusion was entirely the engraver's idea. It was most likely inspired by two emblems in Giovanni Ferro's 1623 *Teatro d'Imprese*, also dedicated to the future pope (then still Cardinal Maffeo Barberini), which played on the instrument's ability to collapse or (if reversed) expand distances and thus stand both for the cardinal's foresight and his disregard for worldly riches. In the Novissima emblem, the telescope pointed by Anima (the soul) at the Last Things appearing at the end of a tree-lined alley emphasizes the power of the human imagination to draw the faraway future into the present – and like a telescope make distant things appear close by. The ingeniously crafted image showing Anima's bewilderment at the unexpected sight aptly captures the emotional involvement in visualizing death, judgement, hell, and heaven, the last and future things that will forever remain hidden from human sight. The fact that Bolswert's Anima gazes through the opposite end of the telescope further distances the eschatological world, which is at the same time imprinted upon the mind of the reader who would have been affected by the unique iconography.[22]

This telling emblem aptly suggests how early-modern scientific breakthroughs – including the mind-boggling results of global explorations – disrupted, but did not replace, age-old assumptions about the connectedness of the cosmos and the eschatological destiny of humans on a personal as well as collective level. In fact, these disruptions may have heightened apocalyptic anxieties and hence the urgency of pondering humanity's impending fate in light of new insights into the earth's shape and its place in the cosmos.[23]

---

minore appare, e pure i cieli si rimirano grandissimi'. Polti referred to the astronomical work of Alessandro Piccolomini (1508–1579) as his source.

22   For an extended interpretation of Bolswert's emblem see Göttler C., *Last Things: Art and the Religious Imagination in the Age of Reform* (Turnhout: 2010) 5–22.

23   Martin J.J., *A Beautiful Ending: The Apocalyptic Imagination and the Making of the Modern World* (New Haven, CT – London: 2022). On explorations of earth's 'underlands', see chapter 7 of this volume.

Vtinam saperent et intelligerent ac nouisfima prouiderent! Deuteron. 32.

14.

FIGURE 1.3 Boëtius Adamsz. Bolswert, "Utinam saperent et intelligerent
ac novissima providerent! Deuteron[omy] 32[:29]" (Oh, that
they were wise, that they understood this, that they would
consider their latter end!). Engraving, 15.2 × 9.4 cm. From: Hugo
Herman, s.j., *Pia desideria* (Antwerp, Hendrick Aertssens: 1624),
before 107, Fig. 14. New York, The Metropolitan Museum of Art,
Harris Brisbane Dick Fund, 1939, inv. no. 39.33.1
IMAGE © THE METROPOLITAN MUSEUM OF ART

5   Reformations of the Afterlife

The same may be said of the religious reformations that sundered the bonds
of medieval Christendom and produced numerous Protestant groups opposing the Roman Catholic Church and competing against each other. This transformation led to sharp divergences in eschatological theology, with profound
consequences for the religious experiences of individuals and communities
alike.[24] No doubt it left many with a profound sense of disorientation. We
think, for instance, of the radical changes in the liturgical calendar and the
broad tendency to spiritualize the world beyond death, that is, to understand
its loci increasingly as states of mind. But the most dramatic change in the
way men and women had been preparing for their lives after death was the
abolition of purgatory, the place of penance and purification that served as
the destination for most souls after they had separated from their bodies at
the moment of death. While doubts about this most recent addition to the
Christian afterlife persisted throughout the medieval and early modern period,
the consequences of its final dissolution – on which eventually all Protestant
denominations agreed – cannot be overestimated.[25] If there is no purgatory,
how could one ever achieve certainty or reassurance about one's own state of
salvation or the ultimate fate of the souls of relatives and friends? If the souls
of the dead could no longer be cared for by the good works of the living, such
as prayers, masses, fasting, and almsgiving, then the entire material culture
of religion centred on the Mass would become meaningless. This shift forced
many artists and craftsmen in Protestant countries not only to seek work elsewhere, but also to reconsider the value of their own products, which were suddenly suspected of being idolatrous.[26] And, finally, what was the true identity
of the ghosts and revenants who continued to appear to the living despite the
fact that the borders between this and the other world had been closed?

   Yet, as several chapters of this volume suggest, the afterlife was also undergoing major changes on the Catholic side. Purgatory was slowly transformed
from a place of physical punishment into a place of spiritual cleansing, and in

---

24   For theological introductions, see Kunz E., *Protestantische Eschatologie: Von der Reforma-
      tion bis zur Aufklärung*. Handbuch der Dogmengeschichte 4, fasc. 7c/1 (Freiburg – Basel –
      Vienna: 1980); and Schäfer P., *Eschatologie: Trient und Gegenreformation*. Handbuch der
      Dogmengeschichte 4, fasc. 7c/2 (Freiburg – Basel – Vienna: 1984). On the transformations
      of paradise, see Delumeau J., *Une histoire du paradis*, 3 vols. (Paris: 1992–2000). On Protes-
      tant representations of the afterlife, see chapters 9 and 12 of this volume.
25   The spiritual, intellectual, and literary consequences of the Protestant abolition of purga-
      tory are explored in chapters 4 and 11 of this volume.
26   This is further elaborated in chapter 11 of this volume.

the rich Baroque iconography it was relocated to a realm immediately adjacent to heaven.[27] However, despite the fact that the Roman Catholic Church created new instruments to aid souls in purgatory – such as the immensely successful 'privileged' altar for the dead, where one soul was supposedly saved with each mass – the number of requiem masses grew to unprecedented numbers, as if there were lingering doubts about their efficacy.[28]

In sum, the ways in which – and the stage on which – the final acts of the Christian drama unfolded, both individually and collectively, became more diverse than ever before. This diversity went hand in hand with shifting views about the architecture of the cosmos. Of course, this was hardly an absolute rupture: many had long realized that the hereafter was intrinsically unfathomable. It was impossible for mortals to know, as St. Paul had warned in an oft-repeated phrase, what 'eye hath not seen, nor ear heard, neither hath it entered into the heart of man what things God hath prepared for them that love him' (1 *Corinthians* 2:9). The scientific innovations of the early modern era – in natural philosophy and astronomy – no doubt opened the way to astounding new knowledge. Yet the cosmos, too, even when probed with the most powerful optical instruments, ultimately remained inconceivable to the human mind. And the new wealth of views from which to choose led to uncertainty, scepticism, and doubt. If the starry heavens were no longer unchanging and incorruptible, but changeable and perishable like the everyday world that surrounds us, how was it possible to draw reassurance and trust from the traditional imaginary of otherworldly places?

For the time being, this did not put an end to traditional habits of blending eschatological expectations with conceptions of the universe, at least as a metaphorical device or imaginative construct.[29] The connection between the two derived from a profound need: the wish to be assured that human existence, severely bounded in place and time for individual and community alike, persists beyond those confines. For all the new uncertainties, that

---

27 In the last three decades, there has been a steadily growing literature on the post-Reformation and post-Tridentine notion of purgatory. Relevant literature on the spatial and temporal imaginary of purgatory in sixteenth- and seventeenth-century European culture includes: Eire C.M.N., *From Madrid to Purgatory: The Art and Craft of Dying in Sixteenth-Century Spain* (Cambridge: 1995); Göttler C., *Die Kunst des Fegefeuers nach der Reformation: Kirchliche Schenkungen, Ablass und Almosen in Antwerpen und Bologna um 1600* (Mainz: 1996); Greenblatt S., *Hamlet in Purgatory* (Princeton, NJ: 2002); Malý T. – Suchánek P., *Images of Purgatory: Studies in Religious Imagination and Innovations (The Czech Lands, 1600–1800)*, trans. S. Roberts (Rome: 2021).

28 Eire, *From Madrid to Purgatory* 168–231.

29 For the metaphorical use of purgatory, see chapter 4 of this volume.

"world-beyond" – however conceived, but often conjured up in concrete, representable, even material terms – continued to be a source that gave life meaning and inspired hope, fear, or both.

Our premise is, then, that the early modern afterlife continued to be an imagined space-time dimension that allowed humans to process and project their deepest hopes and fears about their own mortality and, as Bakhtin intuited, to tell stories about themselves as actors in the historical and metaphysical drama of humankind. Accordingly, the essays gathered in this volume examine the construction, reception, and transmission of such extra-temporal and extra-spatial worlds. The focus is on the material, sensory, and affective components of these worlds and their multiple links with the actual world that created them. Besides the inspiration of Bakhtin's chronotope, our project builds on a wave of more recent studies on spatiality and temporality. But none, as far as we know, have begun to map out the eschatological sphere in these terms. Conversely, there is of course an extensive literature on the eschatologies of different religions, including the Christian tradition which is the focus of this volume. But no specific studies have examined the spatio-temporal configurations of this world-beyond and the ways in which these were embedded in religious and cultural practices here-and-now.

6   Eschatological Constructs

While the focus of this volume is on early modern Christian eschatology, we are aware of the rich material, visual, and textual cultures that emerged in other belief systems, shaping and interacting with early modern lives; some of these are currently being explored in parallel projects.[30] Even within the Christian realm, it would not have been possible, nor was it the aim of this volume, to provide a comprehensive account of the varieties of eschatological

---

30   Similar features of hell in different religious traditions have recently been identified by Proser A., "Telling Images: The Subject of Hell in Asian Art", in idem (ed.), *Comparative Hell: Arts of Asian Underworlds* (New York, NY: 2022) 15–21. See further the collections by Gardiner E., *Ancient Near Eastern Hell: Visions, Tours and Descriptions of the Infernal Otherworld* (New York, NY: 2007); *Buddhist Hell: Visions, Tours and Descriptions of the Infernal Otherworld* (New York, NY: 2012); *Zoroastrian Hell: Visions, Tours and Descriptions of the Infernal Otherworld* (2nd ed.; New York, NY: 2013); *Hindu Hell: Visions, Tours and Descriptions of the Infernal Otherworld* (2nd ed.; New York, NY: 2013); and *Greek & Roman Hell: Visions, Tours and Descriptions of the Infernal Otherworld* (New York, NY: 2019). For the ways in which Christian eschatological imagery was shaped by other religious and cultural traditions, see chapters 10 and 15 of this volume.

thought and imagination. Rather, our volume presents a series of case studies that revolve around specific space-time constructions of the eschatological world, including their physical, material, and sensory dimensions and their ties to historical realities in transformation. As detailed in the individual chapters, speculations about these hidden worlds were developed in a range of textual, visual, and performative media, from didactic and devotional literature to visionary accounts, paintings, poetry, architectural designs, and philosophical and natural philosophical treatises, aimed at different audiences and prompted by distinct interests and needs. They provide fascinating windows into the ways in which eschatological imaginaries and narratives were shaped by and responded to an increasingly global, but also increasingly diversified world exposed to frequently conflicting ethical and moral demands.

In recent years scholars specializing in the history of late medieval and early modern Europe have begun to question the claim by the German intellectual historian Reinhart Koselleck that European modernity, and with it a new understanding of historical time, began when expectations about possible futures were no longer defined within a Christian framework of eschatological hopes and fears.[31] With its aim of historicizing eschatological concepts and imageries of a world in transformation, our volume is a contribution to this critical reassessment of modernity. As amply documented by the authors of this book, eschatological and historical discourses should be considered as closely intertwined rather than separate from each other. The three chapters of Part 1, "Cosmology and Eschatology", attest to the persistence of the eschatological imagination and its astonishing ability to adapt to shifting truths about the universe, the earth's position within it, and the substance of the sidereal heavens. After the invention of the telescope, the cosmos could no longer be regarded as immutable and everlasting, as Aristotle had suggested. In her chapter on Peter Paul Rubens's *The Fall of the Damned* of 1621, Christine

---

31   Koselleck R., "'Space of Experience' and 'Horizon of Expectation': Two Historical Categories", in idem, *Futures Past: On the Semantics of Historical Time*, trans. and with an introduction by K. Tribe (New York, NY: 2004 [1979]) 255–275. For a recent critical reassessment: Weiskott E., "Futures Past: Prophecy, Periodization, and Reinhart Koselleck", *New Literary History* 52.1 (2021) 169–188; Kavanaugh L., "The Time of History/The History of Time", in idem (ed.), *Chrono-Topologies: Hybrid Spatialities and Multiple Temporalities* (Amsterdam – New York, NY: 2010) 91–124. While there is a growing literature on premodern conceptions of time and temporalities, the eschatological dimension is still largely neglected. See, however, Brix H.J. (ed.), *Encyclopledia of Time: Science, Philosophy, Theology, and Culture*, 3 vols. (Los Angeles, CA: 2009), DOI: https://doi.org/10.4135/9781412963961, especially the entries on "Eschatology" (Gregory L. Linton), "Eternity" (Carlo Filice), "God and Time" (Hans Otto Seitschek), and "Time, End of" (Betty A. Gard).

Göttler lays out the profound implications of this "new" astronomical truth for the eschatological imagination. With its references to 2 *Peter* 3:10, "the heavens shall pass away with great violence", a passage at the time frequently used as evidence of the mutability of the supralunar realm, Rubens's painting not only presented an engaged exploration of the universe's fiery end, but also hinted at the emotional turmoil resulting from the loss of celestial immutability.

While the telescope may provide a glimpse into the ethereal space of the upper heavens, where at the time of the parousia the dissolution of the old world was thought to begin, the instrument's optical power would never be sufficient to penetrate the walls of the empyrean, believed to be forever hidden from human eyes. Knowledge of this most sublime realm of the highest heaven prepared for the blessed could only be obtained by careful examination of the relevant biblical passages and their exegetical tradition: such was the argument of the learned Spanish Jesuit Gabriel de Henao in his *Empyreologia* of 1652. As shown by Wietse de Boer, the "novelty" Henao claimed for his massive neo-scholastic undertaking lies in its emphasis on the corporeal nature of this place and of the pleasures experienced by its inhabitants. Prompted by a surge in prayer practices at a time when, on the Catholic side, anti-Copernicanism had again become widespread, Henao's hitherto unstudied work also reminds us of the diversity of views on innovation and of the importance of studying projects that were seemingly out of step with contemporary trends.

Although purgatory had lost its reality as an otherworldly place in the Reformation, it lived on in allegorical and metaphorical terms, as demonstrated by Aviva Rothman in her chapter on Kepler's dream fiction *Somnium* (ca. 1608). Kepler chose the moon – the celestial body that marks the boundary between the terrestrial and celestial realms – as the site of a purgatory that cleanses scientific blindness rather than moral sin, recommending a lunar voyage as remedy for the unfounded belief in the geocentric model. But, as Rothman further elaborates, Kepler's heliocentrism, in which the earth once again assumes a privileged position, was also imbued with religious meaning, in that it centred on the brightest of the heavenly bodies and the one that most closely manifested the sublime existence of God.

Just as the space above the moon became the focus of both astronomical exploration and religious belief, the space below the earth's surface emerged as a domain in which a variety of interests competed and converged. The many intersections between religious and poetic eschatology, and among eschatology, metallurgy, and archaeology are explored in Part 2, "Underlands and Netherworlds". As Matteo Al Kalak suggestively argues in his chapter, hell was created to accommodate Lucifer and his angels who rebelled against God and were hurled down into an emerging abyss by the Archangel Michael; they thus found themselves at the farthest possible distance from heaven, but linked to it through sight. While Al Kalak is primarily interested in the spatial and material dimensions of this dark, fiery, and desolate place as described in normative and poetic texts and depicted in the visual arts, Antoinina Bevan Zlatar, in her interpretation of the hellscape of John Milton's *Paradise Lost* (1674), further examines how it is situated in the temporal history of salvation. Milton locates hell in 'outer chaos', thus anchoring it (in accordance with the sources analysed by Al Kalak) in primordial times, before the creation of the world and the first human beings, and before their fall from God's grace. That momentous event resulted in the construction of a bridge between hell and earth. Eschatology and the new cosmology converge in Milton's biblical epic, where Satan's shield is allegorized as the spotted, imperfect moon seen through Galileo's tele-scope. Ten years earlier, the prolific Jesuit polymath Athanasius Kircher, in his *Mundus subterraneus* (1664), drew on the model of Virgil's *Aeneid* to present his own exploration of the underworld as an epic journey through a hidden part of God's creation. As Monica Azzolini argues in her probing chapter, Kircher's underworld is multi-spatial and multi-temporal, the site of fossils and Christian archaeological remains, the habitat of giants, dragons, demons, and penitent souls awaiting their salvation, thus encompassing the whole of God's creation in a part of the universe that, despite its darkness, is still sub-jected to the animating power of the sun.

7 Lived Experiences

The construction of such eschatological space-times – in theology, astron-omy, natural philosophy, art, and literature – cannot be strictly separated from their engagement in self-reflective, meditative, and devotional practices. Yet evidence of the latter is vitally important as we seek insight into the ways in which speculations about or representations of the afterlife were embed-ded and enacted in lived experiences. Eschatological visions, the subject of the chapters in Part 3, richly document the ways in which they reflected the religious cultures and historical contexts from which they arose. The reported visions of the early sixteenth-century mystic Juana de la Cruz (discussed by Minou Schraven) do not dwell extensively on the spatio-temporal framework of heaven, but are all the more specific about its contents, both the structures that dot its landscape – the Narrow Gate, the Castle of Blood, the Hospitals of Mercy, the bridges to purgatory – and the community life consisting of proces-sions, pageants, and festivals of the blessed. Such visions are replete with scrip-tural and metaphorical signposts (the New Jerusalem, the Narrow Gate), but at a more elementary level they evince the contemplative's need for visual concreteness. This is perhaps not surprising for a Spanish mystic firmly grounded within the late medieval tradition of eschatological imagery. But the same characteristic re-emerges in the eighteenth-century Quaker and Methodist visions studied by Martha McGill and Luke Holloway. Notwithstanding the spiritualizing tendencies of their theologies and the vast gulf separating them from sixteenth-century Catholic culture, these visionaries in Britain and North America described recognizable landscapes, buildings, and people, even if they were simultaneously perceived as alien and transfigured. Traditional imagery is redeployed in yet another form in colonial Mexico. When, in the middle of the seventeenth century, an indigenous man named Juan Diego experienced visionary encounters with the Virgin of Guadeloupe, these events were interpreted as the realization of the apocalyptic visions received by St. John on Patmos. As Raphaèle Preisinger argues, the episode has to be understood in light of the millenarian expectations of the time. More specifically, the impression of the Virgin's image on the man's cloak turns the mission territory of Aztec Mexico into a providential space as the end times draw near.

Preisinger's essay calls attention to the seminal role of thresholds – here, the end of the world – in all human dealings with the hereafter. Such dealings, further exemplified in Part 4, are ultimately motivated by the prospect of death – hence, in Christianity as in most other religious traditions, the transition from life to afterlife. The border separating the two, along with a host of assumptions about what lies beyond, can thus summon the faithful to a reckoning with their life's balance sheet, good or bad, and also inspire a turnaround, even a conversion, intended to make the best possible use of one's dwindling days. This is, of course, the underpinning of the *ars moriendi* tradition referenced throughout this book. But it can also play out in a personal, literary, and artistic itinerary as extraordinary as Michelangelo's. As Jane Tylus shows in a perceptive essay (chapter 8), the ageing Michelangelo's reflection on his life and work in light of an inevitable if prolonged 'farewell' betrays – in contrast to the luminous medieval model of Dante – his questioning of an ingrained economy of salvation grounded in a works theology. It is a notable finding about an artist whose involvement with the reform-minded circle around Vittoria Colonna is well-known, but whose religious leanings remain notoriously difficult to determine. In a very different way, French Huguenots responded to their explicit break with the medieval tradition and the ensuing confrontation with their country's Catholic establishment by seeking places of heavenly refuge in this world, ahead of their eventual embrace in God's bosom. This, Laurent Paya argues, is the ideological programme underpinning two well-known garden designs, Bernard Palissy's 'Garden of Wisdom' and Duchess Renée de France's gardens in Montargis. Thus encoded, these plans reflected not only Calvin's understanding of the Christian's temporary condition in the world, but also offered eschatological lessons pointing to their final destination.

Landscapes, as recent scholarship reminds us, are indeed deeply imbued with meaning. In the early modern period they became privileged sites of meditation. Of this phenomenon the concluding chapters of this volume exemplify several modalities (Part 5). The desert, of course, had long been the paradigmatic setting of monastic asceticism. But in the hands of the Flemish painter Jan Sanders van Hemessen, the traditional image of the penitent St. Jerome in the wilderness also gains eschatological significance. As Anna-Claire Stinebring shows, the painting offers the devout viewer tantalizing glimpses of the heavenly rewards for those who submit to sensory deprivations in a barren here-and-now. In the Jesuit Jan David's spiritual emblem books, studied by Walter Melion, such penitential cleansing takes systematic form in spiritual exercises which train the votary's mental eye on a range of providential or eschatological sites. Among other things, the images examined here offer harrowing views of hell, confront exercitants with an imposing Last Judgement, and engage them with cosmic representations of the Virgin in glory. Thus they are invited visually and affectively to project their mind beyond the confines of the present world and to anticipate their ultimate spiritual journey.

Finally, three famous sites of martyrdom, foregrounded in Mia Mochizuki's chapter, bring together multiple strands of this volume. These stark images of the violent demise of Jesuit missionaries in Japan, currently in the Gesù in Rome, update the *ars moriendi* tradition of contemplating death. The scenes encapsulate the foreboding apocalyptic vision of an order that saw completion of its global missions as the precondition and catalyst for the universal conflagration with which this volume began. What is more, the author suggests, the Jesuit preoccupation with space-time – missionary, contemplative, and eschatological – was indelibly marked by the new optics, geography, and cosmology. It is another reminder of how age-old expectations of the *novissima* were scrambled by the changing horizons – intellectual, religious, and cultural – of a globalizing world.

Bibliography

Adams E., *The Stars Will Fall from Heaven: Cosmic Catastrophe in the New Testament and Its World* (London: 2007).

Bakhtin M.M., "Forms of Time and of the Chronotope in the Novel: Notes toward a Historical Poetics", in idem, *The Dialogic Imagination: Four Essays*, ed. M. Holquist, trans. C. Emerson – M. Holquist (Austin, TX: 2020) 84–258.

Bemong N. et al. (eds.), *Bakhtin's Theory of the Literary Chronotope: Reflections, Applications, Perspectives* (Ghent: 2010).

Bergmann S., "What Images of the Last Things Do to Us: Introductory Remarks on Why Eschatology Matters", in idem (ed.), *Eschatology as Imagining the End: Faith between Hope and Despair* (London: 2018) 1–29.

Bredekamp H. – Wedepohl C., *Warburg, Cassirer und Einstein im Gespräch: Kepler als Schlüssel der Moderne* (Berlin: 2015).

Brix H.J. (ed.), *Encyclopledia of Time: Science, Philosophy, Theology, and Culture*, 3 vols. (Los Angeles, CA: 2009), DOI: https://doi.org/10.4135/9781412963961.

Delumeau J., *Une histoire du paradis*, 3 vols. (Paris: 1992–2000).

Drexel Hieremias, *De aeternitate considerationes* (Munich, per Raphaelem Sadelerum: 1620).

Drexel Hieremias, *The Considerations of Drexelius upon Eternitie*, trans. Ralph Winterton (London, T[homas] C[otes] for Nicholas Alsop: 1632).

Eire C.M.N., *From Madrid to Purgatory: The Art and Craft of Dying in Sixteenth-Century Spain* (Cambridge: 1995).

Eire C., *A Very Brief History of Eternity* (Princeton, NJ: 2010).

Foucault M., *The Hermeneutics of the Subject: Lectures at the Collège de France, 1981–82*, trans. G. Burchel (New York, NY: 2005).

Frank A. – Gleiser M., "The Crisis in Cosmology", *The New York Times*, September 3, 2023 (print edition).

Frey J., "Second Peter in New Perspective", in Frey J. – Dulk M. den – Watt J.G. van der (eds.), *2 Peter and the Apocalypse of Peter: Towards a New Perspective* (Leiden: 2019) 7–74.

Gardiner E., *Visions of Heaven and Hell before Dante* (New York, NY: 1989).

Gardiner E., *Ancient Near Eastern Hell: Visions, Tours and Descriptions of the Infernal Otherworld* (New York, NY: 2007).

Gardiner E., *Buddhist Hell: Visions, Tours and Descriptions of the Infernal Otherworld* (New York, NY: 2012).

Gardiner E., *Zoroastrian Hell: Visions, Tours and Descriptions of the Infernal Otherworld* (2nd ed.; New York, NY: 2013).

Gardiner E., *Hindu Hell: Visions, Tours and Descriptions of the Infernal Otherworld* (2nd ed.; New York, NY: 2013).

Gardiner E., *Greek & Roman Hell: Visions, Tours and Descriptions of the Infernal Otherworld* (New York, NY: 2019).

Göttler C., *Die Kunst des Fegefeuers nach der Reformation: Kirchliche Schenkungen, Ablass und Almosen in Antwerpen und Bologna um 1600* (Mainz: 1996).

Göttler C., *Last Things: Art and the Religious Imagination in the Age of Reform* (Turnhout: 2010).

Greenblatt S., *Hamlet in Purgatory* (Princeton, NJ: 2002).

Griffiths P.J., "Purgatory", in Walls J.L. (ed.), *The Oxford Handbook of Eschatology* (Oxford: 2007) 427–445.

Hadot P., *Philosophy as a Way of Life: Spiritual Exercises from Socrates to Foucault*, trans. A.I. Davidson (Cambridge, MA: 1995).

Haynes D.J., "Bakhtin and the Visual Arts", in Smith P. – Wilde C. (eds.), *A Companion to Art Theory* (Oxford: 2002) 292–302.

Kavanaugh L., "The Time of History/The History of Time", in idem (ed.), *Chrono-Topologies: Hybrid Spatialities and Multiple Temporalities* (Amsterdam – New York, NY: 2010) 91–124.

Koselleck R., "'Space of Experience' and 'Horizon of Expectation': Two Historical Categories", in idem, *Futures Past: On the Semantics of Historical Time*, trans. and with an introduction by K. Tribe (New York, NY: 2004 [1979]) 255–275.

Kunz E., *Protestantische Eschatologie: Von der Reformation bis zur Aufklärung.* Handbuch der Dogmengeschichte 4, fasc. 7c/1 (Freiburg – Basel – Vienna: 1980).

Le Goff J., *La naissance du purgatoire* (Paris: 1981).

Malý T. – Suchánek P., *Images of Purgatory: Studies in Religious Imagination and Innovations (The Czech Lands, 1600–1800)*, trans. S. Roberts (Rome: 2021).

Martin J.J., *A Beautiful Ending: The Apocalyptic Imagination and the Making of the Modern World* (New Haven, CT – London: 2022).

Nicolai B., "Westbau und Westportal des Berner Münsters", in Nicolai B. – Schweizer J. (eds.), *Das Berner Münster: Das erste Jahrhundert. Von der Grundsteinlegung bis zur Chorvollendung und Reformation (1421–1517/1528)* (Regensburg: 2019).

Novick P., *That Noble Dream: The "Objectivity Question" and the American Historical Profession* (Chicago, IL: 1988) 135–138.

Ott L. – Naab E., *Eschatologie in der Scholastik.* Handbuch der Dogmengeschichte 4, fasc. 7b (Freiburg – Basel – Vienna: 1990).

Pollard R.M. (ed.), *Imagining the Medieval Afterlife* (Cambridge: 2020).

Polti Antonino, *Della felicità suprema del cielo libri tre* (Perugia, Giovan Berardino Rastelli: 1575).

Proser A., "Telling Images: The Subject of Hell in Asian Art", in idem (ed.), *Comparative Hell: Arts of Asian Underworlds* (New York, NY: 2022).

Schäfer P., *Eschatologie: Trient und Gegenreformation.* Handbuch der Dogmengeschichte 4, fasc. 7c/2 (Freiburg – Basel – Vienna: 1984).

Sladeczek F.-J., *Erhart Küng: Bildhauer und Baumeister am Münster zu Bern (um 1420–1507). Untersuchungen zur Person, zum Werk und zum Wirkungskreis eines westfälischen Künstlers der Spätgotik* (Bern: 1990).

The Vulgate Bible: Douay-Rheims Translation, ed. E. Swift, 6 vols. (Cambridge, MA: 2010–2013).

Weiskott E., "Futures Past: Prophecy, Periodization, and Reinhart Koselleck", *New Literary History* 52.1 (2021) 169–188.

PART 1

Cosmology and Eschatology

∴

Depicting the Universal Conflagration: Time, Space, and Artifice in Peter Paul Rubens's *Fall of the Damned*

Christine Göttler

Abstract

This chapter offers a new interpretation of Rubens's most intriguing eschatological work, the large painting of the *Fall of the Damned* of about 1621, now in the Alte Pinakothek, Munich. While the seven-headed dragon and the mass of human bodies falling toward a bottomless hell refer to the final verses of the *Book of Revelation*, the fiery cataclysm engages with the vivid description of the elemental meltdown at the end of times described in the *Second Epistle of Peter*. It will be shown that *2 Peter* 3:10–13, a biblical source that has not previously been associated with Rubens's painting, acquired new topicality in the debates about the nature of the heavens that had become even more relevant with the astronomical discoveries of the 1610s. Focusing on the moment when time and space dissolve into eternity, Rubens created a powerful apocalyptic narrative that responded to the eschatological anxieties of his time and a general awareness that the world had grown old. Moreover, Rubens's eschatological painting shared in the sense, common in the early modern period, that cosmological and eschatological imaginaries of world transformation and historical space-time relations were closely interrelated. The heavenly phenomena that telescopes had now made visible to the human eye could be understood both as supernatural spectacles staged by God and as indications that the old Aristotelian world order could no longer be upheld.

Keywords

apocalypse – conflagration – fluid heavens – neo-stoicism – telescope

A dark mood pervades the account by Abraham Gölnitz of his two-year journey through France and the Netherlands from May 1624 to June 1626, published as

| DOI:10.1163/9789004688247_003

Ulysses Belgico-Gallicus in Leiden in 1631.[1] The Gdańsk-born geographer dedicated the book to Duke John Christian of Legnica-Brzeg (Silesia) and his two sons, who had sided with the largely Protestant Estates in the Bohemian revolt of 1618. The event marked the beginning of a long and devastating civil war that lasted over thirty years, was accompanied by famine and epidemics, and coincided with a particularly cold phase of the Little Ice Age. Gölnitz's visit in May 1624 to the house of Peter Paul Rubens, 'Europe's living miracle' as Gölnitz called him, seemed to have reinforced his sense that the end of the world was imminent. The artwork that impressed him most was a *Last Judgement* apparently assessed at the value of more than 5,000 florins. Gölnitz describes how the sight of bodies either delighting in heaven or being tormented in hell affected the minds of the viewers with a range of opposing emotions alternating between hope of salvation and fear of hell, giving them a foretaste of future rewards or punishments.[2] Rubens seems to have remembered the encounter, since in 1633 he obtained a copy of the *Ulysses Belgico-Gallicus* to present it to his eldest son, Albert, who was nineteen years old at the time.[3] The painting referred to by Gölnitz may have been the so-called *Small Last Judgement*, now in the Alte Pinakothek, Munich [Fig. 2.1],[4] or any other version of the subject

---

1   Gölnitz Abraham, *Ulysses Belgico-Gallicus* (Leiden, Officina Elzeviriana: 1631). For the eschatological atmosphere at the Silesian court of Duke John Christian, to which Gölnitz's travelogue seems to refer: Mauran P., "Itinéraires calvinistes dans l'Europe du début de la guerre de Trente Ans: Abraham Gölnitz en son temps", *Dix-septième siècle* 280 (2018) 533–550. It's a pleasure to thank the two peer reviewers for their helpful suggestions and Frank Fehrenbach, Fabio Frosini, and Aaron M. Hyman for reading and discussing various versions of this chapter. I gratefully acknowledge the insightful comments I received when presenting versions of this chapter during my stays as a senior fellow at the DFG-Centre for Advanced Studies "Imaginaria of Force", Universität Hamburg (October to December 2023) and as the Robert Janson-La Palme *76 Visiting Professor in the Department of Art and Archaeology, Princeton University, in Spring Semester 2024. I am especially grateful to my co-editor Wietse de Boer for his committed interest in my project and for generously sharing his expertise over the past few years.

2   Gölnitz, *Ulysses Belgico-Gallicus* 71–72.

3   Rubens acquired the copy of the *Ulysses Belgico-Gallicus* for his son Albert from Balthasar Moretus: Arents P., *De Bibliotheek van Pieter Pauwel Rubens: Een reconstructie*, ed. F. Baudouin – L. Baudouin – F. Cockx-Indestege J. De Die – M. de Schepper (Antwerp: 2001) 293–294, Q8.

4   Peter Paul Rubens, *The Small Last Judgement*, oil on panel, 184.5 × 120.4 cm, Munich, Alte Pinakothek, inv. no. 611. Freedberg D., *Rubens: The Life of Christ after the Passion*, Corpus Rubenianum Ludwig Burchard 7 (London: 1984) 213–218, no. 51; Renger K. – Denk C., *Flämische Malerei des Barock in der Alten Pinakothek* (Munich – Cologne: 2002) 324–327; Neumeister M., *Alte Pinakothek: Flämische Malerei* (Munich: 2009) 300–301. Interestingly, the painting was originally conceived as a *Fall of the Damned*, but through the addition of an arched top and a narrow plank along the left side turned into a *Last Judgement*.

FIGURE 2.1   Peter Paul Rubens, *The Small Last Judgement*, ca. 1621/22. Oil on oak panel,
184.5 × 120.4 cm. Munich, Alte Pinakothek, inv. no. 611
IMAGE © BAYERISCHE STAATSGEMÄLDESAMMLUNGEN
(PHOTO: SIBYLLE FORSTER)

that Rubens created after completion of the *Great Last Judgement* for the new Jesuit church in Neuburg, Bavaria [see Fig. 2.3]. Indeed, in April 1618 Rubens wrote to Sir Dudley Carleton, the English ambassador to the Netherlands, to offer him for 1,200 florins a smaller copy of it 'begun by one of my pupils', but which 'would be entirely retouched by my own hand, and by this means would pass as original'.[5] This is by far the most highly priced item on the list of paintings Rubens offered to Carleton in exchange for his antiquities.

Why were Rubens's eschatological paintings so highly sought after? This chapter seeks to answer this question by exploring Rubens's apocalyptic imagination in the so-called *Fall of the Damned* of about 1621, now also in Munich's Alte Pinakothek [Fig. 2.2].[6] With its dramatic sky exploding into fire, its infinite number of human figures pulled and pushed down by demons, its display of extreme expressions of horror and repulsion, of pain and distress, the *Fall of the Damned* is arguably Rubens's most disturbing, but also his most ambitious eschatological painting. Like the smaller versions of the *Last Judgement* paintings mentioned above, the *Fall of the Damned* was a more exploratory side product of the prestigious Bavarian commissions, which in addition to the *Great Last Judgement* also included a *Fall of the Rebel Angels* [see Fig. 2.4] and a *Woman of the Apocalypse* [see Fig. 2.5]. Executed by his own hand rather than with the help of his well-trained workshop in Antwerp, this large painting was most probably destined for one of Rubens's patrons or friends. Its striking rendering of the conflagration in the heavens and its exclusive focus on the ultimate eschatological fall of both the damned and the seven-headed dragon is unique and must have captured – and unsettled – the eyes of the viewers.

How did Rubens conceive of the universal end of all things, when time and space will dissolve into an eternity of either heaven or hell? And how did he collapse the eschatological future into present time? It will be shown

---

5   Peter Paul Rubens to Sir Dudley Carleton, Antwerp, 28 April 1618: Rubens P.P., *The Letters of Peter Paul Rubens*, trans. Magurn R. Saunders (Cambridge, MA: 1955) 61, Letter 28. The size of the painting is given as 13 × 9 feet. Schön J., *Die Ziffernrechnung oder Rechenkunst* (Bamberg: 1805) 318, converts the Antwerp foot to 28.55 cm, which makes a total size of 371 × 257 centimetres.

6   Peter Paul Rubens, *The Fall of the Damned*, oil on panel, 286 × 224 cm, Munich, Alte Pinakothek, inv. no. 320. Freedberg, *Rubens: The Life of Christ after the Passion* 219–232, no. 52; Roh F., "Rubens' Höllensturz", *Münchner Jahrbuch der bildenden Kunst* 10 (1916–1918) 189–197; Renger – Denk, *Flämische Malerei des Barock in der Alten Pinakothek* 330–333, no. 320 (with complete bibliography of older literature); Neumeister, *Alte Pinakothek: Flämische Malerei* 294–295.

FIGURE 2.2   Peter Paul Rubens, *The Fall of the Damned*, ca. 1621. Oil on oak panel, 286 × 224 cm. Munich, Alte Pinakothek, inv. no. 320

FIGURE 2.3   Peter Paul Rubens, *The Great Last Judgement*, ca. 1617. Oil on canvas, 608.5 × 463.5 cm. Munich,
Alte Pinakothek, inv. no. 890
IMAGE © BAYERISCHE STAATSGEMÄLDESAMMLUNGEN

FIGURE 2.4 Peter Paul Rubens, *The Fall of the Rebel Angels*, 1621/22, oil on canvas,
438 × 291.5 cm. Munich, Alte Pinakothek, inv. no. 306
IMAGE © BAYERISCHE STAATSGEMÄLDESAMMLUNGEN

FIGURE 2.5　Peter Paul Rubens, *The Woman of the Apocalypse*, ca. 1623–1625, oil on canvas,
554.5 × 370.5 cm. Munich, Alte Pinakothek, inv. no 891
IMAGE © BAYERISCHE STAATSGEMÄLDESAMMLUNGEN
(PHOTO: ANDREAS WERNER)

that Rubens's dramatic rendering of the final cosmic conflagration in the *Fall of the Damned* engages with the then increasingly accepted notion that the celestial space is mutable and thus not so different from the earthly space, a view that eventually became integrated into religious thought. Rubens's choice of the unusual subject was inspired by a period interest in Stoic notions of fire, as well as by attempts to reconcile Stoic cosmology, Christian eschatology, and new astronomical observations. In the following I approach Rubens's *Fall of the Damned* from three interrelated perspectives, each in a subsection of this chapter: I first reflect on the painting's likely function as a collection piece made for a stately home rather than a liturgical space which was the destination of most of Rubens's eschatological works. I then discuss the painting's central biblical sources that nourished Rubens's imagination, the vivid account of the end of times in the *Book of Revelation* and the imagery of the universal conflagration in the *Second Epistle of Peter*. In two final subsections, I relate Rubens's depiction of the apocalyptic fire both to his early exposure to Stoic ideas of the universal conflagration and to a rapidly growing interest in observing the celestial novelties through the telescope, which in turn had a powerful impact on the eschatological imagination. How did Rubens's *Fall of the Damned* shape the experience of time and space, earthly and heavenly, worldly and otherworldly, real and imaginary?

1   **A Painting for a Religious Expert and Connoisseur?**

A brief discussion of the monumental altarpieces Rubens created at about the same time will help us to better understand the uniqueness of his *Fall of the Damned*. The first of these commissions was the *Great Last Judgement*, produced for Wolfgang Wilhelm, Count of Palatine-Neuburg, for the high altar of the Court Church of Our Lady in Neuburg, which the ruler, newly converted to Catholicism, had given to the Jesuits [Fig. 2.3].[7] The altarpiece was installed as early as 1618, while Rubens's paintings for the side altars, an *Adoration of the Shepherds* and a *Descent of the Holy Spirit*, were put in place one year later. With

---

7   Peter Paul Rubens, *The Great Last Judgement*, oil on canvas, 608.5 × 463.5 cm, Munich, Alte Pinakothek, inv. no. 890. Freedberg, *Rubens: The Life of Christ after the Passion* 201–206, no. 49; Renger K., *Peter Paul Rubens: Altäre für Bayern* (Munich: 1990) 25–39, 55–56, 64–66, 81–85; Renger – Denk, *Flämische Malerei des Barock* 320–323; Neumeister, *Alte Pinakothek* 268–271; Maxwell S., "Artful Negotiator: Peter Paul Rubens' Intervention in the Cause of Catholic Bavaria", in Scholz Williams G. – Haude S. – Schneider C. (eds.), *Rethinking Europe: War and Peace in the Early Modern German Lands* (Leiden: 2019) 125–141, at 132–133; Smith J. Chipps, *Sensuous Worship: Jesuits and the Art of the Early Catholic Reformation in Germany* (Princeton, NJ: 2002) 144, 152–154.

its enormous size of more than six metres in height (without its undoubtedly also massive frame) the *Last Judgement* must have made a huge impact on an audience whose confessional orientations were less than stable. Rarely represented in liturgical spaces in that period, the subject gestured toward Michelangelo's (entirely different) elaboration on the theme in the Sistine Chapel, one of Catholicism's most sacred sites. But at Neuburg, the emphasis was on the intercessory power of the Virgin, the patroness of the church, and the rewards of the blessed who, helped by angels, slowly ascend to the empyrean, the luminous abode of God, while the damned are cast down into the jaws of hell. The new decoration celebrated Wolfgang Wilhelm's conversion to the Catholic faith as a result of his alliance with Duke Maximilian of Bavaria, whose sister Magdalene he had married in 1613. Rubens's paintings showcased the transformation of the Lutheran stronghold into an ally of the Catholic League on the verge of the century's most destructive war.[8]

The two other commissions engage with the most frequently illustrated visions of *Revelation* 12: the portentous encounter between the woman surrounded by the sun, the moon, and twelve stars, and the 'great red dragon' with 'seven heads' threatening her and the male child to whom she is about to give birth (*Revelation* 12:1–6); and the subsequent episode of the war that broke out in heaven as St. Michael fought the dragon and cast him and his allies out (*Revelation* 12:6–10).[9] Rubens's *Fall of the Rebel Angels* of 1621/22, also commissioned by Wolfgang Wilhelm and possibly destined for the altar of the old court chapel at his residence, is a virtuoso display of the artist's skills in rendering dynamic movement [Fig. 2.4].[10] The warrior angel's beautiful sinuous

8   Maxwell, "Artful Negotiator" 132–133.

9   Here and in the following I cite from *The Vulgate Bible: Douay-Rheims Translation*, ed. E. Swift, 6 vols. (Cambridge, MA: 2010–2013). Instead of *Apocalypse of St. John* (vol. 6, 1315–1405) I use the more common *Book of Revelation*.

10   Peter Paul Rubens, *The Fall of the Rebel Angels*, oil on canvas, 438 × 291.5 cm, Munich, Alte Pinakothek, inv. no. 306. Vlieghe H., *Rubens: Saints*, 2 vols., Corpus Rubenianum Ludwig Burchard 8 (Brussels: 1973) 2:126–129, no. 135; Renger, *Peter Paul Rubens: Altäre für Bayern* 46–55, 85; Renger – Denk, *Flämische Malerei des Barock* 312–315; Juntunen E. – Pawlak A., "'Bellissimo e difficilissimo' – Zur Ikonographie von Rubens' Engelsturz in der Alten Pinakothek in München", in Juntunen E. (ed.), *Rubens im Blick: Ausgewählte Werke unter Revision* (Stuttgart: 2007) 15–47; Neumeister, *Alte Pinakothek* 298–299. It is now assumed that the painting was made for the altar in the "Old Court Chapel" at the Neuburg residence, the chapel dedicated to Catholic worship before the "New Court Chapel", dedicated to Protestant worship, was built in 1543; the residence was linked to the Jesuit church by a passageway: Smith, *Sensuous Worship* 105; Volk-Knüttel B., "Überlegungen zum ursprünglichen Standort von Rubens' 'Engelsturz' für Neuburg: Mit einem Exkurs zu Constantino de' Servi", *Neuburger Kollektaneenblatt* (2007) 5–32.

pose is contrasted with the tangled downward spiral of the dragon and his evil allies, plummeting toward the earth in defeat. An angel holding a bundle of flames pushes down the dragon's grotesquely upward twisting tail, with which he had swept away 'the third part of the stars of heaven and cast them to the earth' (*Revelation* 12:4). The inverted and contorted poses of the two demons in the immediate foreground reverberate with the memory of Titian's depictions of the *Dannati*, the four transgressors (Tityus, Sisyphus, Tantalus, and Ixion), sentenced by Jupiter to eternal punishment in Hades.[11] Painted by Titian for Mary of Austria, the sister of the Holy Roman Emperor Charles V and herself the regent of the Netherlands, these powerful political allegories aimed against the enemies of Habsburg rule were originally displayed in the Great Room of her new castle at Binche near Brussels.[12]

Rubens's *Woman of the Apocalypse*, executed between 1623 and 1625 for Bishop Veit Adam von Gepeckh for the high altar of Freising Cathedral, staged the Virgin Mary as the primary patroness of the diocese and the protectress of Bavaria whose intercession was seen as the decisive factor in the victory of the Catholic troops at the Battle of the White Mountain in 1620; the painting thus consolidated confessional loyalties in the face of war [Fig. 2.5].[13] Moreover, Rubens depicted the Virgin standing on a solid moon (as described by Galileo), while trampling a snake, thus approximating her to the Immaculata and the Virgin of Victory who would crush Protestant 'heresy'.

Like the *Great Last Judgement* and the *Fall of the Rebel Angels*, Rubens's *Small Last Judgement* and the *Fall of the Damned* subsequently passed to the Picture Gallery of Elector Palatine Johann Wilhelm II (1658–1716) in Düsseldorf, where they stayed until 1806, when they were transferred, along with the other paintings of the collection, to Munich.[14] However, in contrast to Rubens's large altarpieces for Bavarian churches, commissioned at a time of the rising confessional

---

11   For Rubens's use of Hendrick Goltzius's *Four Disgracers*: Juntunen – Pawlak, "'Bellissimo e difficilissimo'" 30–31.

12   For an excellent study of Titian's canvases of the four *Furias* and their status as exemplary works in rendering horror: Falomir M., *Las Furias: Alegoría política y desafío artístico*, exh. cat., Museo Nacional del Prado, Madrid (Madrid: 2014).

13   Peter Paul Rubens, *The Woman of the Apocalypse*, oil on canvas, 554.5 × 370.5 cm, Munich, Alte Pinakothek, inv. no. 891. Renger, *Peter Paul Rubens: Altäre für Bayern* 68–80, 85–86; Renger – Denk, *Flämische Malerei des Barock* 316–319; Neumeister, *Alte Pinakothek* 301–302; Smith J. Chipps, "Rubens, Bishop Veit Adam von Gepeckh and the Freising High Altar, 1623–1625", in Duerloo L. – Smuts R.M. (eds.), *The Age of Rubens: Diplomacy, Dynastic Politics and the Visual Arts in Early Seventeenth-Century Europe* (Turnhout: 2016) 255–274.

14   Freedberg, *Rubens: The Life of Christ after the Passion* 22, 201 (*The Great Last Judgement*, 1691); 213 (*The Small Last Judgement*, by 1705), 219 (*The Fall of the Damned*, before 1716); Vlieghe, *Rubens: Saints* 2:126–129, no. 135 (*The Fall of the Rebel Angels*, 'very probably

polarization that resulted in the Thirty Years' War, the *Fall of the Damned* cannot be linked to a specific site of worship, and little is known of its early history. The first mention of Rubens's painting dates from the 1670s, when it came on the market in the Netherlands and caused an immediate sensation. Art dealers outbid each other to get their hands on it, until it was finally acquired by the Duke of Richelieu, the great-nephew of Cardinal Richelieu, who had inherited his artworks. Once displayed in his cabinet, Rubens's *Chûte des Réprouvez*, as it was called, 'astonished the whole of Paris, conveying yet another idea of his merit', as French critic Roger de Piles, Rubens's most trustworthy biographer, reported in a letter to Philip Rubens, the artist's nephew in Antwerp.[15] In the detailed ekphrasis of the *Dissertation sur les ouvrages des plus fameux peintres* of 1681, de Piles emphasizes the utmost difficulty of the subject due to the 'great number of figures' that could not be painted from nature but required a 'lively imagination' and a 'firm mind': 'The expressions need to be extremely lively and everything needs to appear in tumultuous movement and disorder arising from fear'.[16] De Piles's commentary, which he expanded from edition to edition of the *Dissertation*, made Rubens's *Fall of the Damned* one of the Flemish master's most admired artworks by about 1700, seen as marking a turning point in his handling of movement, colour, and chiaroscuro effects.

In the *Dissertation*, de Piles also gives us an indication of the early history of the painting. He notes that Rubens had made the 'Chûte des Réprouvez' for the 'bishop of Antwerp, his close friend', in other words, the recently deceased Ambrosius Capello, who served as Bishop of Antwerp from 1654 until his death in 1676.[17] Indeed, in his testament of 14 March 1674, Bishop Capello bequeathed all his paintings to the Dominican convent of St. Paul in Antwerp, where he had been a novice. He particularly mentions 'de groote schilderij van den *Engelenval* geschildert van Petro Paolo Rubbens', stipulating that the painting should not be sold for less than 'five or six thousand guilders' – a considerable

---

in or shortly after 1671'). The dates in brackets indicate when these works entered the Düsseldorf Picture Gallery.

15   Ruelens C., "La vie de Rubens par Roger de Piles", *Rubens-Bulletijn* 2 (1883) 157–211, at 170–171 (Roger de Piles to Philip Rubens, Paris, 26 February 1677): 'M^r le Duc de Richelieu a fait venir un tableau de la *Chute des Damnez de la main de nostre brave Rubens*, qui estonne tout Paris, et qui donne tout une autre idée encore de son mérite' (italics in original).

16   Piles Roger de, *Dissertation sur les ouvrages des plus fameux peintres* (Paris, Nicolas Langlois: 1681) 86–96, at 87–88: 'une imagination vive et nette, un esprit droit, juste, et bien rempli des regles de l'Art [...]. Que les expressions y doivent estre extrémement animées, et que tout y doit paroître dans un mouvement tumultueux, et dans un desordre, qui donne de l'effroy'.

17   Piles, *Dissertation* 25: 'la chûte des Réprouvez, pour l'Evesque d'Anvers son intime amy'.

sum which gives us a preview of the stir that the painting would cause when it came on the market.[18] Given these circumstances, it seems not unlikely that Rubens's 'groote schilderij', mentioned by Capello, is indeed identical with his 'Chûte des Réprouvez' for the 'bishop of Antwerp' in Richelieu's collection. But when exactly the *Fall of the Damned* came into the possession of Ambrosius Capello must remain speculative. Capello entered the Dominican monastery of St. Paul in Antwerp in 1612, when Michael Ophovius, Rubens's close friend, was its prior.[19] In 1621 (the assumed date of the painting's execution) Capello had just returned to the Spanish Netherlands from his studies in Salamanca to take on a teaching position at the Jesuit collegiate university in Douai. He was highly educated, widely travelled, well-connected with the intellectual elites both at home and abroad, and an avid collector of art. If he was indeed the painting's first owner, Capello would have displayed all the defining features of an expert connoisseur. Educated in the best theological tradition and deeply interested in the visual arts, he would have admired Rubens's skill to conjure the world's fiery end at a dark moment in history, when the hostilities between the Spanish and the Dutch had resumed with renewed vigour. He would also have recognized that the painting needed to be seen not only from a distance but also up close, revealing an almost microscopic view of the explosion that, according to Scripture, marks the end of time.

2   Depicting the World's Final Moments

The curious iconography of Rubens's *Fall of the Damned* still puzzles art historians today. It has been assumed that Rubens was referring primarily to Jesus's apocalyptic discourse on the casting of the wicked into the 'everlasting fire,

---

18   Theunissens L., "Testaments des premiers évêques d'Anvers", *Analectes pour servir à l'histoire ecclésiastique de la Belgique* 15 (1878) 83–139, at 119–136 ("Testament d'Ambroise Capello, septième évéque évêque d'Anvers, 16 mars 1674"), at 132: 'Item laete ende maecke aen het voorscreven convent der Predickheeren binnen dese stadt alle myne schilderyen, dewelcke naer myne aflyvicheyt bevonden sullen worden in mynen sterffhuyse, behalven nochtans degene, die ick by legaet oft donatie *inter vivos*, gelyck hier vooren noch geschreven is, wechgegeven oft gelegateert syn. En sullen nochtans de voorscreve paters Predickheeren de groote schilderye van den engelenval, geschildert van Petro Paulo Rubbens, niet minder mogen vercoopen als omtrent vyff a ses duysent guldens'. Freedberg, *Rubens: The Life of Christ after the Passion* 226, erroneously writes that the painting was bequeathed to the 'Dominican Fathers in Ghent'.

19   On Ambrosius Capello: Marinus M.J., *De contrareformatie te Antwerpen (1585–1676): Kerkelijk leven in een grootstad* (Brussels: 1995) 90–95; *Biographie Nationale de Belgique* 3 (1866) 293–95 (E.H.J. Reusens).

which was prepared for the devil and his angels' in *Matthew* 25:41 or that he combined this last text with *Revelation* 12:7–9, describing the 'great battle in heaven' between Michael and his angels and the dragon and his angels.[20]

In Rubens's painting, however, neither Christ judging the wicked nor the apostate angels as followers of Satan are depicted. Furthermore, neither of these two biblical passages elaborates on the all-consuming fire that is so prominent in Rubens's painting and can be regarded as its main protagonist. With its vivid imagery, language of colour, and emphasis on sensory perception, especially sight, the *Book of Revelation* was undoubtedly an important source.[21] But while the cosmogonic battle between the Archangel Michael and Satan in the form of a dragon (as described in *Revelation* 12:7–9) is indeed referred to in Rubens's complex painting, his central interest was in the final scenes of *Revelation* 20: John's vision of the world at the split second before its destruction, when 'fire [came down] from God out of heaven' devouring the seduced nations, and the devil 'was cast into the pool of fire and brimstone' (*Revelation* 20:9–10).

In the light-flooded opening at the top left appear the heavenly warriors led by the Archangel Michael; the fact that they are armed with shields and thunderbolts – rather than flaming swords – underlines that the central theme of the painting is a universal conflagration. Nude figures are tumbling down from a vertiginous height across a vast space that seems to rotate around itself. Their downward spiralling movement toward a bottomless fiery pit attests to their fallen sinful nature, their unaccountable number to the efficacy of Satan's deceptive schemes. Humans, demons, and beasts clump together in swirling clusters. The longer one looks, the more figures are revealed, emerging from and disappearing into the fiery explosion, engulfed in blazing flames to the left, thick clouds of smoke above, sulphuric fumes to the right. Bodies are shown in various motions and contortions, under rapidly changing lights and at varying distances from the viewer. At the very forefront, three corpulent figures rotate around each other in slow motion, their shimmering flesh tones testifying to Rubens's virtuoso handling of transparent skin. Rubens cited them

---

20   Freedberg, *Rubens: The Life of Christ after the Passion* 224; Neumeister, *Alte Pinakothek: Flämische Malerei* 294; Renger – Denk, *Flämische Malerei des Barock* 330.

21   Huber K., "Imagery in the Book of Revelation", in Koester C.R. (ed.), *The Oxford Handbook of the Book of Revelation* (Oxford: 2020), https://doi.org/10.1093/oxfordhb/9780190655433 .013.3 (accessed 12.04.2023). The language of colour is addressed by García Ureña L. "The Book of Revelation and Visual Culture", in Schröter J. – Nicklas T. – Puig i Tàrrech A. (eds.), *Dreams, Visions, Imaginations: Jewish, Christian and Gnostic Views of the World to Come* (Berlin – Boston, MA: 2021) 487–504. See also Blount B.K., *Revelation: A Commentary* (Louisville, KY: 2009).

from Mantegna's celebrated engraving *Bacchanal with the Crowing of Silenus*, a source he frequently used, but transposed them from their setting of pastoral poetry to that of a nightmarish eschatology.[22] While Mantegna's Silenus is being lifted and crowned to sing of the creation of the world, as told in Virgil's *Sixth Eclogue*, Rubens's unfortunate counterpart is being tormented by two devils. The lifelike appearance of the brightly illuminated figures, as if they had just been resurrected from death to eternal death, heightens the sense of immediacy and sets them apart from the much darker colour of the demons who drag them downwards by their hair, their death shrouds, or snakes.

The importance of the *Book of Revelation* is evident from the appearance of the seven-headed 'great dragon' on the lower right, close to the fiery pit at the bottom of the picture, its dark shape hardly discernible in the blaze of the burning heavens. With its seven heads and ten horns, the heads each crowned with a diadem, the 'great dragon' is the dominant opponent of God, identified with 'the old serpent, who is called the devil, and Satan, who seduceth the whole world' (*Revelation* 12:9).[23] It finds its evil double in the 'beast coming up out of the sea' (*Revelation* 13:1), which also displays seven heads and ten horns, however with diadems not upon its heads but upon its horns. Both the dragon and the beast draw on an older imaginary of the monstrous, exploited since the Middle Ages in illustrations of the Bible's most enigmatic book. Rubens shows the dragon turned upside down with its belly exposed, its seven heads no longer crowned, but growling and biting, and its tail comically drawn between its legs as if it were terrified by its precipitous fall. In John's visionary account, the dragon is thrown twice into the fiery abyss, first, in *Revelation* 12:9, together with its own follower angels (or fallen angels) in the 'great battle in heaven' against the archangel Michael, and then again, along with those seduced by him, in *Revelation* 20:9, after he had been released from the prison where he was kept for a thousand years, in the final battle preceding the Last Judgement that marks the end of human history. Rubens created a single, seemingly continuous space to accommodate these two falls from heaven that are situated at different moments in the eschatological future, and also to evoke the fall of the rebel angels at the beginning of time, not mentioned in the Scriptures. As a painter and commentator and in emulation of the visionary account, Rubens fully exploited the spectacular dimensions of the apocalyptic world with its

---

22   Andreas Mantegna, *Bacchanal with Silenus*, before 1475, engraving with drypoint, 30.5 × 43.8 cm, New York, The Metropolitan Museum of Art, inv. no. 29.44.15. Freedberg, *Rubens: The Life of Christ after the Passion* 225.

23   Villiers G.R., "Prime Evil and Its Many Faces in the Book of Revelation", *Neotestamentica* 34.1 (2000) 57–85, at 58.

FIGURE 2.6   Peter Paul Rubens, *The Fall of the Damned*. Detail of Fig. 2.2, showing the middle section of the 'pool of fire', painted on an added plank of wood

IMAGE © BAYERISCHE STAATSGEMÄLDESAMMLUNGEN (PHOTO: SIBYLLE FORSTER)

battles, beasts, and elemental commotions. The low horizon, formed by the rim of a bottomless crater, separates a flaming sky from an equally fiery earth.

As with some of his other works, Rubens came up with new ideas in the process of painting. At one point he added a plank about fifty centimetres wide to the bottom of the panel, thus expanding his composition to include the 'pool of fire and brimstone' into which the dragon is about to fall [Fig. 2.6].[24] Rubens's predella-like, horizontally oriented scene reinforces the spatial dimensions of the newly emerging hell, linking it directly to the space-time of the viewer. Two drawings, sketched on the two halves of an originally folded sheet of paper, now in the British Museum, document how Rubens developed the imagery of his apocalyptic hell from that of a hunting scene commissioned by Duke Maximilian of Bavaria for his residence at Schleissheim [Fig. 2.7].[25] Rubens drew on the most violent motifs of the deadly hunt to create an apocalyptic menagerie of the most ferocious predators, to which the many serpents slithering through the tangle of monstrous creatures, biting and constricting each other and the other beasts, added an extra dimension of horror.[26]

Rubens's painting – depicting the dragon thrown into the pool of fire and the fire devouring the countless number of those he had seduced – may thus be viewed as an imaginative visual ekphrasis of *Revelation*'s visionary description of the destruction of the cosmic order before it is recreated. However, *Revelation* 20:9, 'and there came down fire from God out of heaven and devoured them', does not fully explain the unusually vivid and dynamic

---

24   Technical analysis conducted at the Alte Pinakothek in 1993 confirmed that the added board was painted entirely by Rubens. Near the joint the primer was planed away, and the paint layer is therefore much brighter, as is clearly visible in the lion's paws: Poll-Frommel V. – Renger K. – Schmidt J., "Untersuchungen an Rubens-Bildern – Die Anstückungen der Holztafeln", *Jahresbericht: Bayerische Staatsgemäldesammlungen* (1993) 24–35, at 26–27.

25   Peter Paul Rubens, Studies for a *Lion Hunt* and of a large dragon and fighting animals and monsters, pen and brown ink, on a double sheet with a horizontal fold in the middle, 573 × 485 mm, recto, London, British Museum, Department of Prints and Drawings, inv. no. 1885-5-9-5. Freedberg, *Rubens: The Life of Christ after the Passion* 232–233, cat. 52a; Balis A., *Rubens: Hunting Scenes*, trans. P.S. Falla, Corpus Rubenianum Ludwig Burchard 18/2 (London: 1986) 130–132, cat. 6a; Rowlands J., *Rubens: Drawings and Sketches*, exh. cat., British Museum, London (London: 1977) 82–84, cat. 89; Seligman I., *Lines of Thought: Drawing from Michelangelo to Now*, exh. cat., touring exhibition (London: 2016) 99, cat. 57.

26   On the motifs cited from Rubens's hunting scenes: Balis, *Rubens: Hunting Scenes* 130–132, cat. 6a. On the horror associated with Laocoön's snakes: Loh M.H., "Outscreaming the Laocoön: Sensation, Special Affects, and the Moving Image", *Oxford Art Journal* 34.3 (2011) 393–414; Clifton J., "The Face of a Fiend: Convulsion, Inversion, and the Horror of the Disempowered Body", *Oxford Art Journal* 34.3 (2011) 373–392.

FIGURE 2.7 Peter Paul Rubens, Studies for a *Lion Hunt* and of a large dragon and fighting animals and
monsters. Pen and brown ink, on a double sheet with a horizontal fold in the middle,
57.3 × 48.5 cm, recto. London, British Museum, Department of Prints and Drawings,
inv. no. 1885-5-9-51

rendering of the world's fiery end. Rubens read, or, rather, reimagined, I would argue, John's vision through the lens of an equally powerful end-time prophecy, that of the fiery dissolution of the cosmos at the end of times, as described in the *Second Epistle of Peter* (2 *Peter* 3:10–13). The decisive lines are:

10   But the day of the Lord shall come as a thief, in which the heavens shall pass away with great violence and the elements shall be melted with heat and the earth and the works that are in it shall be burnt up.

11   Seeing then that all these things are to be dissolved, what manner of people ought you to be in holy conversation and godliness,

12   looking for and hasting unto the coming of the day of the Lord, by which the heavens, being on fire, shall be dissolved and the elements shall melt with the burning heat of fire?

13   But we look for new heavens and a new earth according to his promise, in which justice dwelleth.[27]

Adapting Stoic notions of the destruction of the earth by water and fire to Christian beliefs, the most probably second-century author, who authoritatively presents himself as the Apostle Peter, takes to task the 'scoffers', who doubt the coming of the parousia. He reminds them of the past Flood, in which 'the world that then was [...] perished', and of the impending fire, in which 'the heavens and the earth which are now' will pass away (2 *Peter* 3:6–7). This is indeed the only account in the Bible of a twofold cosmic destruction of the world, first by water in Noah's flood, and then by fire at the end of times.[28] While the fire of *Revelation* 20:9 is punitive and partial, the fire of 2 *Peter* 3:10–13 burns down the whole world, dissolving the elements (or *stoicheia*, as the author calls them) from which it was created.[29] The author's use

---

27   2 *Peter* 3:10–13: '10 Adveniet autem dies Domini ut fur, in qua caeli magno impetu transient, elementa vero calore solventur, terra autem et quae in ipsa sunt opera exurentur. 11 Cum haec igitur omnia dissolvenda sint, quales oportet esse vos in sanctis conversationibus et pietatibus, 12 expectantes et properantes in adventum diei Domini, per quam caeli ardentes solventur et elementa ignis ardore tabescent? 13 Novos vero caelos et novam terram secundum promissa ipsius expectamus, in quibus iustitia habitat'.

28   Adams, *The Stars Will Fall from Heaven: Cosmic Catastrophe in the New Testament and Its World* (London: 2007) 200.

29   Adams, *The Stars Will Fall from Heaven* 222–224. Adams convincingly argues that the *stoicheia* in 2 *Peter* 3:10 and 12 refer to the physical elements rather than the celestial bodies. See also Frey J., "Second Peter in New Perspective", in Frey J. – Dulk M. den – Watt J.G. van der (eds.), *2 Peter and the Apocalypse of Peter: Towards a New Perspective* (Leiden: 2019) 7–74, especially 30–38; Donelson L.R., *I & II Peter and Jude: A Commentary* (Louisville, KY: 2010) 276–279 (on 2 *Peter* 3:10–13); Horst P.W. van der, "'The Elements Will Be Dissolved with Fire': The Idea of Cosmic Conflagration in Hellenism, Ancient Judaism, and Early

FIGURE 2.8   Peter Paul Rubens, *The Fall of the Damned*. Detail of Fig. 2.2, showing Rubens's depiction of the
final conflagration where some of the areas are touched up with dots

of the term *rhoizēdòn* ('with a thunderous noise', translated as 'magno impetu' in the Vulgate) conveys the otherwise unimaginable explosion of a cosmos in flames.

Rubens combined the two end-time fires: the punitive fire that devours the nations deceived by the devil (as described by John), and the fire that sets the entire cosmos ablaze (as suggested by Peter). As in 2 *Peter*:10–13, Christ is conspicuously absent from Rubens's composition. In no other of his eschatological paintings did Rubens portray the flames engulfing the wicked with such intensity and detail [see Figs. 2.1, 2.3, 2.4, 2.5]. To accentuate the cosmic turmoil of a world in dissolution, he applied dots and spots of different colours throughout the composition: yellow and red around the seven-headed dragon to intensify the effect of the flickering flames, and yellowish-white in the area not yet caught by the fire next to the black smoke [Fig. 2.8]. His lavish use of reds, oranges, and yellows – the colours of heat and fire – underscores the elemental energy of the cosmic upheaval, creating the impression that the elemental collapse is taking place in the here and now.

3   **Mutable Heavens**

But why this interest in the supernatural *stoicheion* of fire and the elemental dissolution of the heavens? From the late sixteenth century onward, 2 *Peter* 3:10, 'the heavens shall pass away with great violence', was increasingly invoked in support of a mutable and generative starry sky, a view that was later confirmed by telescopic observation and that seriously undermined the prevailing Aristotelian theories of celestial perfection. One prominent figure who openly supported these ultimately Stoic ideas was the young Jesuit theologian Roberto Bellarmino (1542–1621). Lecturing on Thomas Aquinas's *Genesis* commentaries in his *Summa Theologica* at the Jesuit college in Louvain (1570–1576), Bellarmino referred to 2 *Peter* 3:10–13 to make a case for the corruptibility of the celestial heavens, a bold statement that he later modified and partially withdrew.[30] Bellarmino left it open whether the heavens will dissolve in a substantial sense – disappearing altogether – or in an accidental

Christianity", in idem (ed.), *Hellenism – Judaism – Christianity: Essays on Their Interaction* (Kampen: 1994) 227–251. On the Stoic understanding of the periodic cosmic conflagration as a 'creative' fire: White M.J., "Stoic Natural Philosophy (Physics and Cosmology)", in Inwood B. (ed.), *The Cambridge Companion to the Stoics* (Cambridge: 2006) 124–152, especially 125–127, 133–138.

30   Baldini U. – Coyne G.V. (eds.), *The Louvain Lectures (Lectiones Lovanienses) of Bellarmine and the Autograph Copy of His 1616 Declaration to Galileo* (Vatican City: 1984) 8–11 ('Whether by its nature the sky is corruptible'; 'Whether the sky may in fact corrupt').

sense – changing appearance, but continuing to exist. While St. Gregory and St. Jerome maintained that the heavens would change their appearance only, St. Basil and St. John Chrysostom had asserted that they would indeed cease to be. Bellarmino insisted that the views of the latter were supported by Scripture, even though they went against the Aristotelian doctrine of the incorruptibility of the heavens as defended by Thomas Aquinas and the scholastic tradition. Regarding the question 'Whether by its nature the sky is corruptible' he refers to the 'opinion held by most of the church fathers' that the physical heaven (*coelum*) consists either of various elements or just 'one of them, for instance, fire' and is therefore corruptible.[31] He goes on to point out that 'all of the Stoics held that the sky (*coelum*) was fire', as explained in Cicero's *De natura deorum* (On the nature of the Gods) and Macrobius's commentary on Cicero's *Somnium Scipionis* (Dream of Scipio).[32] Bellarmino further cites John Philoponus (ca. 490–570) and John of Damascus (ca. 675/676–ca. 749), who both concluded, contrary to Aristotle, that celestial matter is corruptible.[33] Bellarmino delivered his Louvain lectures before the appearance of an unusually bright new star in November 1572. Once this brilliant new phenomenon had been spotted in the starry sky above the moon, it further shattered the Aristotelian model of a universe composed of solid and impenetrable spheres, and shifted Jesuit opinion in favour of a homogeneous, permeable, and even corruptible heaven, although its possible corruptibility remained a matter of debate.[34]

---

31 Baldini – Coyne (eds.), *The Louvain Lectures* 8–9, 31, notes 15 and 16: 'Altera est fere omnium patrum, quod coelum sit corpus vel compositum ex elementis, vel sit unum ex elementis, v.g. ignis, ac proinde corruptibile'.

32 Ibidem: 'Schola stoicorum tota putat coelum esse igneum'. Bellarmine's references are to Cicero, *De natura deorum* 2, 15, where Cleanthes argues that the sun and 'the other heavenly bodies' are composed of fire, 'the glow of life and health [...] the universal preservative, giving nourishment, fostering growth, sustaining, bestowing sensation': Cicero, *De natura deorum*, trans. H. Rackham (Cambridge, MA – London: 1972) 160–161 (2, 15); and to Macrobius, *Commentarii in Somnium Scipionis* 1, 20, 7: Macrobius, *Commentary on the Dream of Scipio*, trans. W.H. Stahl (New York: 1952) 169 (1, 20, 7): 'There is another reason for calling it [the sun] the heart of the sky: the nature of fire is always involved in motion and perpetual agitation; the sun, moreover, as we have stated, has been regarded as the source of ethereal fire; therefore, the sun's function in the ether is the same as the heart's function in the animal'.

33 Baldini – Coyne (eds.), *The Louvain Lectures* 8–9. For the importance of John Philoponus and John of Damascus for the early-modern scholastic tradition: Grant E., "Were There Significant Differences between Medieval and Early Modern Scholastic Natural Philosophy? The Case for Cosmology", *Nous* 18 (1984) 5–14.

34 Lattis J.M., *Between Copernicus and Galileo: Christoph Clavius and the Collapse of Ptolemaic Cosmology* (Chicago, IL – London: 1994) 147–156.

Bellarmino's well-attended Louvain lectures were widely known through several transcripts and gained fresh relevance in the 1610s, when the newly invented telescope made it possible to glimpse the vastness of space that until then had been hidden from human eyes. Moreover, the publication of Galileo's *Sidereus nuncius* (Starry messenger, 1610) led to a plethora of tracts on the heavens and a rapid increase in telescopic observations. It was therefore no coincidence that, in August 1618, Federico Cesi, the founder of the Accademia dei Lincei in Rome, shared his own thoughts on the fluid and penetrable nature of the heavens with Bellarmino – by then a powerful cardinal – as documented in detail by Paolo Galluzzi.[35] In his brief reply of the same month, Bellarmino assured Cesi that he too knew that 'the heaven is not hard and impenetrable like iron, but soft and easily penetrable like air'.[36] However, whereas at Louvain Bellarmino had still defended the then rather unorthodox view that the stars and planets moved freely 'like fish in the water and birds in the air', he now doubted that it was possible to explain the movements of the planets and stars without seeing them as contained in spheres.[37] He thus partially returned to the Aristotelian model of spheres moved by the *primum mobile*, to which the heavenly bodies adhere. The exchange of letters between Cesi and Bellarmino took place just a few weeks before the appearance of the three comets that would result in the general acceptance, including by Jesuit writers, of a changeable supralunar world, continuous with the sublunar one. It conveys a sense of the deep uncertainties arising from the fact that the immutability and indestructibility of the cosmos were no longer guaranteed.

As Peter Barker and others have shown, the renewed interest in ancient Stoic physics, shared by Bellarmino, Galileo (as a young man), Rubens, and many of

---

35   The letter-treatise became known under the title *De caeli unitate et tenuitate, fusaque et pervia stellarum motibus natura ex Sacris Litteris* (On the unity and tenuousness of the heavens and on their diffused and penetrable nature [giving way] to the movement of the stars according to sacred scripture): Galluzzi P., *The Lynx and the Telescope: The Parallel Worlds of Cesi and Galileo*, trans. P. Mason (Leiden: 2017) 221–233. Both Cesi's letter-treatise (dated 14 August 1618) and Bellarmine's response (dated 25 August 1618) are published at the end of the Jesuit Christoph Scheiner's *Rosa Ursina sive Sol* (Bracciano, Andreas Phaeus: 1626–1630) 777–784, under the heading "De caelo liquido".

36   Scheiner Christophorus, *Rosa Ursina sive Sol* (Bracciano, Andreas Phaeus: 1626–1630) 784 (Roberto Bellarmino to Federico Cesi, 25 August 1618): '[...] coelum non esse durum, et impenetrabile instar ferri, sed molle et facillime penetrabile instar aëris: *haec enim omnia sciebam*' (italics in original).

37   Ibidem 784. For Bellarmino's use of the fish and birds simile: Baldini – Coyne (eds.), *The Louvain Lectures* 18–19: '[...] stellas non moveri ad motum coeli, sed motu proprio sicut aves per aerem, et pisces per aquam'.

their contemporaries, had a profound impact on the emerging sciences.[38] It is in this context that I would like to present the proposition put forward by the celebrated Flemish philosopher and philologist Justus Lipsius in his *Physiologia Stoicorum* (Physics of the Stoics) of 1604 concerning the kinds of fire involved in the process of dissolution and recreation of the heavens, which he described with reference to 2 *Peter* 3:10–13.[39] At the time of the publication of the highly influential treatise, Rubens was in the service of Vincenzo Gonzaga II, Duke of Mantua, who, however, allowed him to continue his studies of ancient and Italian art in Rome. Also in Rome was his older brother Philip, who had studied with Lipsius in Louvain and had become his favourite pupil; from 1605 until his return to Antwerp in the summer of 1607 he served as librarian and secretary to Cardinal Ascanio Colonna. The two brothers lived together and undoubtedly discussed Lipsius's recent works in their vibrant circle of friends, which included a prominent member of the Lincei, the German Paracelsian physician Johannes Faber, who treated Peter Paul Rubens for pleurisy and shared Cesi's and the academicians' interest in the exploration of the heavens.[40]

Fire plays a central role in Lipsius's *Physiologia Stoicorum*, published in a second edition in 1610. Lipsius's aim was twofold: to establish a general framework for understanding Stoic views of nature and to reconcile these with Christian thoughts about God's creation of the world. Fire is introduced in the

38   Barker P., "Stoic Contributions to Early Modern Science", in Osler M.J. (ed.), *Atoms, Pneuma, and Tranquillity: Epicurean and Stoic Themes in European Thought* (Cambridge: 1991) 135–154; idem, "Stoic Alternatives to Aristotelian Cosmology: Pena, Rothmann and Brahe", *Revue d'histoire des sciences* 61.2 (2008) 265–286; Grant, "Were There Significant Differences"; Joly B. – Moreau P.-F., "Stoic Physics in the 16th and 17th Centuries: A Hidden Presence", *Revue d'histoire des sciences* 61.2 (2008) 1–5; Reeves E., *Painting the Heavens: Art and Science in the Age of Galileo* (Princeton, NJ: 1997) 57–90.

39   Contributions to Lipsius's *Physiologia Stoicorum* include the chapters in Hirai H. – Papy J. (eds.), *Justus Lipsius and Natural Philosophy* (Louvain: 2011). See also Saunders J.L., *Justus Lipsius: The Philosophy of Renaissance Stoicism* (New York, NY: 1955) 117–217; Morford M., *Stoics and Neostoics: Rubens and the Circle of Lipsius* (Princeton, NJ: 1991) 169–171; Papy J., "Lipsius's (Neo-) Stoicism: Constancy between Christian Faith and Stoic Virtue", in Blom H.W. – Winkel L.C. (eds.), *Grotius and the Stoa* (Assen: 2004) 47–72; idem, "Justus Lipsius", in Zalta E.N. (ed.), *The Stanford Encyclopedia of Philosophy* (Spring 2019 edition), https://plato.stanford.edu/archives/spr2019/entries/justus-lipsius/ (accessed 20.07. 2022).

40   Philip Rubens returned to Antwerp in July 1607 to take care of his ailing mother: Paolini C., "L'ultima lettera di Justus Lipsius ad Ascanio Colonna: Philip Rubens, l'ambiente romano e l'ideale neo-stoico condiviso con il fratello Peter Paul", in Simonato L. (ed.), *Leggere il Barocco: Cortocircuiti scultorei tra Otto e Novecento* (Rome: 2018) 59–63; Baldriga I., *L'Occhio della lince: I primi lincei tra arte, scienza e collezionismo (1603–1630)* (Rome: 2002) 149–170; Galluzzi, *The Lynx and the Telescope* 221–222, 225, note 22.

treatise's first book, where Lipsius defines nature with reference to Diogenes Laertius and Cicero as a 'craftsmanlike', 'artistically working' fire, noting its similarities to a 'fiery breath'. Lipsius emphasizes the Stoic distinction between a corruptive and corruptible elemental fire and a creative and generative fire, identical with 'all the force and life of the world' and thus also standing for the Demiurge or God, the creator and governor of the world.[41] Christian and Stoic views of the cosmic conflagration or *ekpurôsis* are discussed in chapters 22 and 23 of the treatise's second book, dedicated to the four elements.[42] It is here that Lipsius invokes 2 *Peter* 3:10 to reflect on the nature of the divine fire involved in the destruction and the recreation of the world – the very subject of Rubens's painting. With reference to 2 *Peter* 3:7, 'the heavens and the earth which are now by the same [God's] word are kept in store, reserved unto fire against the day of judgement and perdition of the ungodly men', and 2 *Peter* 3:10, 'the heavens shall pass away with great violence and the elements shall be melted with heat and the earth and the works that are in it shall be burnt up', Lipsius points to similar aspects in the Stoic and Christian imagery of the world-conflagration, even though the Christians, in contrast to the Stoics, do not believe that it will keep recurring.[43] As Kuni Sakamoto has shown, in order to make the fundamentally different Stoic and Christian approaches appear more similar, Lipsius argues that the Stoics distinguished between two kinds of fire, a 'mixed' or material one that will destroy the old universe, purging it from evil, and a very 'pure' aethereal one (identical with God) that will give rise to the new one and give it form.[44] Rubens, with his deep interest in the pictorial representation

---

41   Lipsius Justus, *Physiologia Stoicorum* (Antwerp, Officina Plantiniana, Joannes Moretus: 1604) 12. See Laertius Diogenes, *Lives of Eminent Philosophers*, trans. R.D. Hicks, vol. 2: *Books 6–10* (Cambridge – London: 1970) 260–261: Zeno (7, 1, 156); Cicero, *De natura deorum* 176–179 (2, 22). For the importance of Lipsius's theories for Rubens's works: Esposito T., "Ignis artificiosus: Images of God and the Universe in Rubens's Depiction of Antique Shields", *Early Modern Low Countries* 2.2 (2018) 244–277.

42   Sakamoto K., "Eclecticism as Seneca's Heritage: Evil and the Cosmic Cycle in Justus Lipsius", in Hirai – Papy (eds.), *Justus Lipsius and Natural Philosophy* 97–106; Hirai H., "Seneca's *Naturales quaestiones* in Justus Lipsius' *Physiologia Stoicorum*: The World-Soul, Providence and Eschatology", in Beretta M. – Citti F. – Pasetti L. (eds.), *Seneca e le scienze naturali* (Florence: 2012) 117–140, at 131–132.

43   Lipsius, *Physiologia Stoicorum* 137. See Sakamoto, "Eclecticism as Seneca's Heritage" 105, note 45.

44   Lipsius, *Physiologia Stoicorum* 134: 'Sed quem hunc ignem? Aethereum et purum, observa. Mixtus est ille, qui vastabit; purus et a materia paullatim reducendus ille, qui gignet denuo et formabit'. See Joly B., "Le problème du feu", in Hirai – Papy (eds.), *Justus Lipsius and Natural Philosophy* 53–61; Sakamoto, "Eclecticism as Seneca's Heritage" 105. For the world-conflagration in Stoic philosophy: Long A.A., *From Epicurus to Epictetus: Studies in Hellenistic and Roman Philosophy* (Oxford: 2006) 256–282.

of elemental forces, must have been struck by Lipsius's comments on the universal conflagration; he must have sought to render in his painting the unsurpassed power of God's fire, both world-destroying and world-creating, and thus, of course, also draw attention to the potency of his own art.

4   Spectacles in the Starry Skies

By 1621, the Jesuits, too, would endorse the fluidity and mutability of the heavens. This change of opinion was prompted by three unusually bright comets appearing in quick succession in the night sky during the autumn of 1618, just a few months after the outbreak of the war. In the Netherlands, the historical coincidence of these two events raised fears of all kinds of calamities, as Tabitta van Nouhuys has documented with many examples.[45] But the comets of 1618 were also the first ones to be observed with the telescope. The Jesuits seized the opportunity to measure and compare their paths across the sky at their establishments in Italy, Germany, France, Spain, and the Spanish Netherlands. Once a celestial origin was attributed to them, the comets could be taken as evidence not only of the mutability, but also of the continuing generative power of the heavens. Or, as one Giovanni Battista Lauri of Perugia is reported to have said, the heavens were telling us with these brilliant fires that they had been wrongly accused of being barren, and that they could still give birth to even more beautiful stars than those created by God in primeval times.[46]

The renowned Flemish Jesuit theologian Cornelius a Lapide, in his hitherto unstudied exegetical commentary on 2 *Peter* 3:10–13, refers to this spectacular heavenly occurrence and its implications for religious thought.[47] Written

---

45   Nouhuys T. van, *The Age of Two-Faced Janus: The Comets of 1577 and 1618 and the Decline of the Aristotelian World View in the Netherlands* (Leiden: 1998) 542–555. See also Parker G., *Global Crisis: War, Climate Change and Catastrophe in the Seventeenth Century* (New Haven, CT: 2013) 11–13.

46   Scheiner, *Rosa Ursina sive Sol* 687 (book 4, part 2, chapter 25): '*Vereque ex inde intelleximus caelum hisce ignibus, per intervalla exorientibus, ostendere nobis duntaxat voluisse, se sterilitatis minime accusandum. Posse autem in dies stellas parere longe pulchriores*, quod in sui primordio pulcherrimas procreavit' (italics in original).

47   Lapide Cornelius a, "Commentaria in Secundam Sancti Petri Epistolam", in idem, *Commentaria in Acta Apostolorum, Epistolas Canonicas, et Apocalypsin* (Antwerp, Martin Nutius: 1627) 354–443, at 422–430. On a Lapide: Fischer B.D. – François W. – Gerace A. – Murray L., "The 'Golden Age' of Catholic Biblical Scholarship (1550–1650) and Its Relation to Biblical Humanism", in Lange van Ravenswaay J.M.J. – Selderhuis H.J. (eds.), *Renaissance und Bibelhumanismus* (Göttingen: 2020) 217–274, at 253–256; Gibert P., "The Catholic Counterpart

in Rome in the early 1620s, but not published until 1627, the volume, which also contains a Lapide's interpretation of the *Book of Revelation*, could not have been known to Rubens when he painted his *Fall of the Damned*. But even though Rubens and a Lapide most probably never met, their lives intersected in a number of ways. Rubens designed an unusually complex title page for the first of a Lapide's exegetical works, the *Commentaria in Pentateuchum Mosis* (Commentary on the Five Books of Moses), published in Antwerp in 1616, the year in which a Lapide had left Louvain to teach Hebrew and Scripture at the Collegio Romano.[48] A Lapide would have been introduced to the workings of the telescope at the Collegio Romano, most likely by its head mathematician Orazio Grassi, while Rubens may have attended one of the public viewings of the comets held at the Antwerp Jesuit college or gazed at the comets through the telescope belonging to his friend, the Portuguese merchant and banker Emmanuel Ximenes.[49] In the autumn of 1618, he had just completed the monumental canvases for the high altar of the Jesuit church in Antwerp. Both Rubens and a Lapide shared a strong interest in classical literature, the latest archaeological findings, and the emerging natural sciences. In his exegetical works a Lapide examined in detail not only Augustine and the Church Fathers, but also Lucretius, Virgil, Ovid, and Pliny as well as the most recent literature, including the positions of Protestant authors. Most of these books can also be found in Rubens's library.

Like his fellow Jesuits at this time, a Lapide opposed millenarianism, but he nonetheless saw the world as 'ageing' (*senescens*), exhorting his readers to stay alert since the end will be unexpected.[50] The trope of a world grown old also

---

and Response to the Protestant Orthodoxy" in Sæbø M. (ed.), *Hebrew Bible, Old Testament: The History of Its Interpretation*, vol. 2: *From the Renaissance to the Enlightenment* (Göttingen: 2008) 758–773, at 764–767; Murray L., "Jesuit Hebrew Studies after Trent: Cornelius a Lapide (1567–1637)", *Journal of Jesuit Studies* 4 (2017) 76–97; idem, *Jesuit Hebrew Studies after Trent: Franciscus Toletus and Cornelius a Lapide* (Göttingen: 2019) 105–154.

48 Lapide Cornelius a, *Commentaria in Pentateuchum Mosis* (Antwerp, Martin Nutius and Jan van Meurs: 1616). Logan A.-M. – Plomb M.C., *Peter Paul Rubens: The Drawings*, exh. cat., The Metropolitan Museum of Art, New York (New Haven, CT – London: 2004) 174–176, cat. 51.

49 Nouhuys, *The Age of Two Faced Janus* 252–253. The 1617 inventory of the household of Emmanuel Ximenes in Antwerp also lists a 'three-part tube made of leather for seeing far away': Göttler C. – Moran S.J., *Reading the Inventory: The Possessions of the Portuguese Merchant-Banker Emmanuel Ximenez (1564–1632) in Antwerp* (2014), http://ximenez.unibe .ch/inventory/reading/ (accessed 28.01. 2024).

50 On a Lapide's 'mitigated millenarianism' and his use of the trope of the decaying world: Armogathe J.-R., "Per annos mille: Cornelius a Lapide and the Interpretation of *Revelation* 20:2–8", in Kottman K.A. (ed.), *Catholic Millenarianism: From Savonarola to the Abbé Grégoire*, Millenarianism and Messianism in Early Modern European Culture 2 (Dordrecht:

sustains a Lapide's commentary on the *Second Epistle of Peter*. In his extensive interpretation of 2 *Peter* 3:10, 'the heavens shall pass away with great violence', a Lapide includes a remarkable personal insertion on the question of which of the heavens are to perish, the starry heavens ('caelos sidereos') – the supralunar region – or the airy heavens ('caelos aëreos') – the sublunar region, close to the earth.[51] While the first opinion (that the starry heavens will dissolve) contradicts the Aristotelian model of an immutable and indestructible supralunar world, the second one (that the airy heavens will dissolve) resolutely supports it. A Lapide himself takes what he calls the 'middle position', namely that Peter's 'caeli' include both the airy heaven and the aethereal heaven with the stars.[52] Like Bellarmino and others, a Lapide distinguishes between the airy heaven, the starry heaven, and the empyrean, each with its own specific physical nature.[53] The empyrean is made of incorruptible aether, so that the blessed can 'move naturally and walk and talk like us in this air'. The starry heaven is also composed of aether, but of a divisible, changeable kind like air; in it the planets move like fish in the water, as suggested by St. Basil and St. Ambrose.[54] In the supralunar sphere, a Lapide thus makes a distinction between two heavens, the heaven of the blessed, the empyrean, invisible to our eyes, eternal and unchangeable, and the visible heaven of the stars, corruptible and destined to be corrupted ('visibile, corruptibile, et corrumpendum'), like the men and women on earth for whom it was created.[55]

2001) 45–51, at 51. See also: Osculati R., "*Hic Romae*: Cornelio a Lapide commentatore dell'Apocalisse al Collegio Romano", in Rusconi R. (ed.), *Storia e figure dell'Apocalisse fra '500 e '600* (Rome: 1996) 301–330. On the anti-millenarian tendencies of the Jesuit interpretation of the *Book of Revelation*: Armogathe J.-R., "Interpretations of the Revelation of John: 1500–1800", in McGinn B. (ed.), *The Encyclopedia of Apocalypticism*, vol. 2: *Apocalypticism in Western History and Culture* (New York, NY: 1998) 185–203, at 189–191; McGinn B., "Wrestling with the Millennium: Early Modern Catholic Exegesis of Apocalypse 20", in Amanat A. – Bernhardsson M.T. (eds.), *Imagining the End: Visions of Apocalypse from the Ancient Middle East to Modern America* (London – New York, NY: 2002) 148–167, 363–371.

51   Lapide, "Commentaria in II Epistolam S. Petri" 423–424.

52   Ibidem 424: 'Mihi media sententia placet, scilicet per caelos hic intelligi tam sidereos quam aëros'.

53   For Bellarmine's distinction between the *caelum aëreum, sidereum*, and *empireum* that he made when teaching in Louvain from 1570 to 1576: Blackwell R.J., *Galileo, Bellarmine, and the Bible: Including a Translation of Foscarini's Letter on the Motion of the Earth* (Notre Dame, IN: 1991) 40–43; Randles W.G.L., *The Unmaking of the Medieval Christian Cosmos, 1500–1760: From Solid Heavens to Boundless Aether* (Aldershot: 1999) 44–46.

54   Lapide, "Commentaria in II Epistolam S. Petri" 423. On St. Basil's view of the heavens: Randles, *The Unmaking of the Medieval Cosmos* 3–4.

55   Lapide, "Commentaria in II Epistolam S. Petri" 423: '[…] distinxisse duplex caelum, unum nobis invisibile in quo habitant beati, quod ait esse aeternum et immutabile, alterum visibile et stellis distinctum, illudque esse corruptibile et corrumpendum, cum scilicet homines in terra esse desierint, quorum causa creatum est'.

Telescopic evidence is first invoked when a Lapide discusses the arguments of those who assume that Peter was referring to the starry heavens, which they understand as being of a fluid rather than a solid nature, 'like air or, rather, a kind of aether', thus being 'capable of change and corruption'.[56] Through their 'dioptre' (lens) mathematicians were able to see – and he himself had witnessed – the transitory spots or blemishes ('maculae') speckling the sun, moon, and stars.[57] As further proof that alterations occur in the sidereal region a Lapide mentions the gigantic, sword-shaped comet first seen on 18 November 1618, with its tip beneath Crater and its lower part extending toward the shoulder of Centaur, and then, on 30 November, with its tip pointing toward the heart of the Hydra and its lower part below the Hydra. Since no parallax could be measured, in other words, the celestial object appeared in the same position irrespective of the spot from which it was observed, the (Jesuit) mathematicians concluded that it must be at a great distance from the moon in the 'loftiest and vastest heavens'. But this meant that Aristotle had erred in believing that these worlds were eternal and incorruptible.[58] A Lapide's detailed description matches the second of the three comets, ironically the one that, according to Grassi, did 'from lack of brilliance [...] not greatly kindle men's minds'.[59]

A Lapide again refers to new sights in the sky when he elaborates on his own view, namely that according to 2 *Peter* 3:10 both the airy and the starry heavens will dissolve; here his aim is to point out the limits of Aristotelian

---

56 Lapide, "Commentaria in II Epistolam S. Petri" 423: 'Hos enim caelos censent [...] non esse solidos, sed fluidos instar aëris, ac proprie esse aetherem, qui mutationis et corruptionis sit capax: quia *omne alterabile est corruptibile*, ait Aristot[eles], liber I de Generat[ione]' (italics in original). In the first book of *De generatione et corruptione* Aristotle introduces the key terms of his physics: generation, corruption, alteration, and growth applying to all natural sublunary forms. For the debate over the supercelestial waters, once the fluid nature of the heavens was accepted: Randles, *The Unmaking of the Medieval Christian Cosmos* 97, 99.

57 Lapide, "Commentaria in II Epistolam S. Petri" 423: 'Sic enim mathematici in sole, luna et stellis per dioptram deprehenderunt, mihique ostenderunt maculas, non tantum stabiles, sed et mobiles euntes et redeuntes'.

58 Ibidem 423: 'Hunc, inquam, cometem iudicarunt mathematici insignes non fuisse in aëre, sed longe super aërem in ipsis caelis sidereis, imo super omnes caelos inferiores, idque demonstrarunt ex ingenti eius parallaxi, quae non nisi in caelis sublimibus et vastissimis fieri potuisse videtur: errasse ergo Aristotelem, qui censuit mundos esse aeternos et incorruptibiles'. A Lapide erroneously mentions an 'enormous', rather than a missing parallax.

59 [Grassi Orazio], "On the Three Comets of the Year 1618: An Astronomical Disputation Presented Publicly in the Collegio Romano of the Society of Jesus by One of the Fathers of that Same Society (Rome, Jacobus Mascardus: 1619)", in *The Controversy of the Comets of 1618: Galileo Galilei, Horatio Grassi, Mario Guiducci, Johann Kepler*, trans. S. Drake – C.D. O'Malley (Philadelphia, PA: 1960) 8. Grassi's anonymously published treatise was a Lapide's likely source. Grassi's authorship was, however, well known.

physics, which do not take into account God's absolute power to intervene in natural phenomena. At the world's final moment, a Lapide argues, the heavens, together with the sun, moon, and stars, will not return to the abyss from which they were formed, but will rise much more splendid than they were before to conform to the altered appearance of those resurrected to glory. A Lapide insists that this does not detract from Aristotle but rather adds to him: what Aristotle meant was that the starry heavens are by nature incorruptible, which is true. The Scriptures, conversely, are about God's purpose, which is to go beyond nature and to supernaturally reform and bless mankind, and for the sake of mankind the whole world and the heavens as well. However, the world cannot be reformed unless it is first melted and dissolved. A Lapide refers to the melting of gold, the most precious metal, to argue that Peter's repeated use of the verb 'dissolvere' does not mean to 'destroy' ('corrumpere'), but to 'melt' ('liquari'): 'Just as gold, when it is melted, does not spoil, but becomes more perfect, so also the heavens, although being incorruptible, are melted to become all the more solid'.[60]

In a convoluted (but not particularly uncommon) argument a Lapide reasons that the 'new phenomena' ('nova phaenomena') in the heavens were not natural alterations, but supernatural manifestations of God's universal power – now rendered visible to human eyes through the telescope – and that they thus fell outside Aristotle's natural philosophy. And a Lapide follows with a list of the new discoveries made primarily by Galileo that suggest the fluidity of the heavens: the spots on the sun and the planets recently observed through the 'optical tube'; the orbiting of Mercury, Venus, and Mars around the sun detected by the same tube (and in accordance with the Tychonic system); the four 'new stars' around Jupiter and the two around Saturn that had been sighted; and, finally, the *nova* of 1572 and the comets that appeared in the celestial region in 1618. This all means, a Lapide concludes, that the heavens are not completely unchangeable and incorruptible, but that God is establishing his power to alter and change them at his will and thus prepare them for their ultimate transformation.[61]

---

60   Lapide, "Commentaria in II Epistolam S. Petri" 426: 'Hac ratione nihil detrahitur, sed potius additur Aristoteli. Ille enim solum naturam spectavit, iuxta quam dixit caelos esse incorruptibiles, quod verum est. Sed S. Script. praeter naturam tradit Dei decretum, ac gratiam et gloriam, qua Deus supernaturaliter homines, et propter homines caelos, totumque orbem reformabit et beabit; reformari autem nequit, nisi quod prius periit, id est, dissolutum aut liquatum est [...] Denique liquari non est corrumpi; aurum enim liquando non corrumpitur, sed perficitur; sic caeli, licet incorruptibiles, liquabuntur, ut magis solidentur'.

61   Ibidem 426: 'Quae omnia significant caelos non omnino esse immutabiles et incorruptibiles, sed Deum ut suam in eis ostendat potentiam [...] pro libito illos alterare et immutare, ac disponere et praeparare ad ultimam plenamque immutationem'.

A Lapide's elaborate exegesis of 2 *Peter* 3:10 demonstrates how deeply the newly visible phenomena in the heavens affected the minds of the many who were then gazing at the stars.[62] To the learned churchman the view through the telescope revealed a very different truth from that seen by Galileo, the man who had actually made these new discoveries. If for Galileo the celestial novelties were proof of his Copernican convictions, for a Lapide they manifested God's supreme power on the most sublime stage of the universe. At about the same time that a Lapide's exegetical volume with the commentary on the *Second Epistle of Peter* appeared, the German Jesuit astronomer Christoph Scheiner, in his seminal work *Rosa Ursina Sol* (1626–1630), saw the telescope as the key to 'enter the hitherto inaccessible realm of the sun, and not only to see the buried treasures of celestial philosophy, but also to lift them up and bring the long hidden truth to the world'.[63]

In Scheiner's evocative language, the heavenly 'treasures', once 'unearthed' by means of the telescope, reveal knowledge about a distant world subjected to a different temporal order. Scheiner was one of the first in early modern Europe to observe that the sun, the most sublime body of the heavens, had blemishes, and thus the Aristotelian division between immutable celestial and changeable terrestrial matter could no longer be maintained. In the *Rosa Ursina Sol*, Scheiner lists several scriptural passages, including 2 *Peter* 3:10–13, that suggest a transient or fluid sky; he adds testimonies from church fathers, ancient philosophers, as well as more recent theologians (such as Bellarmino and Cornelius a Lapide), natural philosophers (such as Cesi), and astronomers (Johannes Kepler, Galileo, Tycho Brahe, and Christoph Rothmann, along with the Jesuits Johann Baptist Cysat and Orazio Grassi), which clearly speak for a fluid, fiery, or mixed heaven.[64] By the time the results of Scheiner's decades of research were published in the late 1620s, the Jesuits had finally adjusted their views to accept the fluid nature of the heavens as suggested by their observations of the comets. This was also true of a Lapide. But unlike Scheiner, a

---

62   On knowledge of the 'new phenomena' within anti-Copernican circles: Grant E., *Planets, Stars, and Orbs: The Medieval Cosmos, 1200–1687* (Cambridge: 1994) 351–361, 649.

63   Scheiner, *Rosa Ursina sive Sol* 606 (book 4, part 2, chapter 12): 'Nunc autem telioscopii invento et patefacto usu, fas est regiones illas aetherias, et aulas divinas propius accedere, ipsamque solis regiam, hucusque inaccessam intrare, et inde absconsos phylosophiae caelestis thesauros reclusos non tantum intueri, sed et auferre, orbique terreno toti latentem diu veritatem inferre'.

64   Scheiner, *Rosa Ursina sive Sol* 625–698 (book 4, part 2: "De caeli et syderum natura ignea"), and 699–770 (book 4, part 2: "De caeli liquida substantia, pro natura caeli liquida"), especially chapters 26 ("Auctoritates ex Sacra Scriptura" 699–730), 27 ("Auctoritates theologorum neotericorum, philosophorum et physiologorum" 731–746), 28 ("Antiquorum philosophorum auctoritates" 747–754), 29 ("Auctoritates astronomorum" 755–770).

Lapide used the telescope not as an instrument of astronomical observation, but of theological speculation. The 'truth' it revealed to him concerned the nature of the very place where, sometime in the future, God would begin his ultimate work of transforming the present world, in the process of which the heavens and all the elements would first melt away in a roaring conflagration to be formed anew in the most perfect way.

5   Conclusion: Rubens's Fire

In this chapter I have studied Rubens's eschatological imagination in the context of a broader preoccupation with the world's final moments at a time of cultural, religious, and political crisis, when various cosmological and confessional views were competing against each other. My focus was on the process of God's ultimate transformation of space, time, and matter at the very moment when the old world ceases to exist and the new one begins to emerge. I hope to have shown that, at the turn of the seventeenth century, the physical nature of the heavens as compared to that of the earth became a question of central importance, passionately debated by religious professionals, philosophers, astronomers, and artists alike, regardless of the world system to which they adhered. Was the supralunar world indeed perfect and unchanging, as Aristotle and Christian doctrine had taught for centuries until the recent past, or was it, like the mutable and corrupt terrestrial sphere, subject to an endless cycle of generation and decay? While the telescope finally "confirmed" the view that the substance of the starry sky was changeable, conjectures about its fluid and permeable nature had already been circulating for a long time, motivated either by a close reading of Scripture and the Greek fathers (as in the case of Bellarmino) or by the observation of comets that as products of the starry sky also proved its undiminished generative force. Using the example of Flemish philosopher Lipsius's Stoic elemental theory and of Flemish theologian a Lapide's exegesis of 2 *Peter* 3:10–13, I have argued that the physical nature of the heavens also affected the vision of the universal meltdown at the end of time, which will also sweep away all human works.

Given the circles in which Rubens moved, he must have been familiar with the debates synthesized by a Lapide and Scheiner in favour of a fluid nature of celestial matter and a Lapide's insistence that the original creation will not be totally destroyed, but recycled, refined, and perfected, even if he did not share these authors' anti-Copernican stance. Rubens was certainly aware of the long tradition that highlighted fire's ambivalent agency, described by Pliny in the *Natural History* as a 'vast and unruly element, and one which causes us to doubt whether it is more a destructive or a creative force'.[65] The prominence of 2 *Peter* 3:10 in the period literature on the substance of the heavens must have had a strong impact on Rubens's eschatological imagination, and may have prompted him to make this demiurgic elemental force, traditionally associated with the heavens (or a theft from the heavens), the primary focus of his most experimental eschatological painting. In so doing, he shifted the focus of attention from God (who is neither mentioned in 2 *Peter* 3:10 nor depicted in Rubens's painting) to the supernatural power of the element at God's command and made the heavens, the stage of God's cosmological spectacle, also a site for the display of his own art.

Like a Lapide, Rubens would have understood the elements or *stoicheia* of 2 *Peter* 3:10, with reference to Presocratic and Stoic theories, as the primary constituents that make up the living world.[66] Rubens would have related them to the colours, thought to have emerged from the elements when they separated from chaos, and he may well have known that Empedocles, in order to explain the creation of all things through the combination of the four elements by Love and Strife, referred to the example of painters who, by mixing a few colours, 'prepare forms resembling all things'.[67] The subject of Rubens's painting, however, is the dissolution, rather than the creation of 'all things', or, more precisely, the reversal of the creation in the final cataclysm, when the heavens, the earth, the elements and the works that are in it will melt and metamorphose at the frightening speed so compellingly described by a Lapide in his exegesis of 2 *Peter* 3:10.

Rubens envisioned the final conflagration as a massive explosion spreading across the sky, filling it with flames and smoke of all hues and shades. Rather than simply descending, as suggested in the *Book of Revelation*, the fiery mass leaps up in whirling motions, rotating with it a multitude of bodies, shown

---

65   Pliny the Elder, *Natural History*, vol. 10: *Books 36–37*, trans. D.E. Eichholz (Cambridge, MA: 1962) 158–159 (36.68).

66   Lapide, "Commentaria in II Epistolam S. Petri" 426. Mander Karel van, *Het Schilder-Boeck* (Haarlem, Paschier van Wesbusch: 1604; reprint, Utrecht: 1969), credits Empedocles for having been the first to introduce earth, water, air, and fire as the 'principal substances' ('hooftsstuffen') of which the material world was made ("Wtleggingh op den Metamorphosis Pub. Ovidii Nasonis", fol. 1 v).

67   On the close relationship between colours and elements, both of which were believed to appear at the very beginning of the creation: Mander, *Het Schilder-Boeck*, fol. 50 v ("Den grondt der edel vry schilder-const", chapter 13, stanza 4). On Galileo's use of Empedocles's comparison in his *Dialogo sopra i due massimi sistemi del mondo* (Dialogue concerning the two chief world systems) of 1632 (acquired by Rubens shortly after its publication): Kelly P., "A Patchwork of Passages: On the Nature of Imitation in Galileo's Alphabet and Painting Metaphors", *Ciceroniana On Line* 4.1 (2020) 185–204, at 199–200.

as if emerging from the chaos into which the world seems to be returning. A Lapide emphasizes that the works that 'shall be burnt up' refer both to the works of nature and those of art, and there is little doubt that Rubens would have thought of the fate of his own works of art, too. There is something deeply disturbing about the clouds of smoke and fumes that, upon closer inspection, reveal themselves to be densely intertwined figures, as if the formative power usually associated with these airy apparitions has gone awry. On the verge of its dissolution, the burning cosmos seems to reveal an uncanny vitality, producing figures and forms that disappear before they become clearly visible. Rubens made full use of the bozzata technique, generally reserved for the so-called 'dead colouring layer', the first layer of painting consisting of the design accentuated with paler, 'cadaverous' colors.[68] Blurring the boundaries between form-dissolving and form-generating processes Rubens aligned his painterly art with fire's dual powers to both create and destroy, in other words to display its creative power through the work of destruction. Rubens was certainly aware of the difficulty involved in rendering the visionary accounts of St. John and St. Peter about the earth's final moments and made use of all possible graphic means to provoke horror and fear in the viewer and at the same time to inspire admiration for his skill in staging a powerful biblical ekphrasis with pigments and paints.

De Piles, in his detailed commentary on the painting in his *Dissertation* of 1681, distinguished between two modes of reception: that of the 'ignorant' ('ignorans'), who, after looking at the painting for a while, avert their eyes because they cannot bear its terrible effect, and that of the 'most learned connoisseurs' ('les plus savans Connoisseurs'), who quickly convert the terror ('terreur') caused by the sight into 'admiration' for the art.[69] Indeed, it remains a challenge to look at the painting for any length of time, and it will come as no surprise that Rubens did not pursue the subject further. In its ambiguous appeal, however, the *Fall of the Damned* remains an important document of a dark imagination of an exhausted world that will one day dissolve into the elements, particles, or atoms, of which it was once made.

---

68   Hout N. van, *Rubens Unveiled: Notes on the Master's Painting Technique* (Antwerp: 2012) 62–64.
69   Piles, *Dissertation* 88–89.

Bibliography

Adams E., *The Stars Will Fall from Heaven: Cosmic Catastrophe in the New Testament and Its World* (London: 2007).

Arents P., *De Bibliotheek van Pieter Pauwel Rubens: Een reconstructie*, ed. F. Baudouin – L. Baudouin – E. Cockx-Indestege – J. De Bie – M. de Schepper (Antwerp: 2001).

Armogathe J.-R., "Interpretations of the Revelation of John: 1500–1800", in McGinn B. (ed.), *The Encyclopedia of Apocalypticism*, vol. 2: *Apocalypticism in Western History and Culture* (New York, NY: 1998) 185–203.

Armogathe J.-R., "Per annos mille: Cornelius a Lapide and the Interpretation of *Revelation 20:2–8*", in Kottman K.A. (ed.), *Catholic Millenarianism: From Savonarola to the Abbé Grégoire*, Millenarianism and Messianism in Early Modern European Culture 2 (Dordrecht: 2001) 45–51.

Baldini U. – Coyne G.V. (eds.), *The Louvain Lectures (Lectiones Lovanienses) of Bellarmine and the Autograph Copy of His 1616 Declaration to Galileo* (Vatican City: 1984).

Baldriga I., *L'Occhio della lince: I primi lincei tra arte, scienza e collezionismo (1603–1630)* (Rome: 2002).

Balis A., *Rubens: Hunting Scenes*, trans. P.S. Falla, Corpus Rubenianum Ludwig Burchard 18/2 (London: 1986).

Barker P., "Stoic Contributions to Early Modern Science", in Osler M.J. (ed.), *Atoms, Pneuma, and Tranquillity: Epicurean and Stoic Themes in European Thought* (Cambridge: 1991) 135–154.

Barker P., "Stoic Alternatives to Aristotelian Cosmology: Pena, Rothmann and Brahe", *Revue d'histoire des sciences* 61.2 (2008) 265–286.

Blackwell R.J., *Galileo, Bellarmine, and the Bible: Including a Translation of Foscarini's Letter on the Motion of the Earth* (Notre Dame, IN: 1991).

Blount B.K., *Revelation: A Commentary* (Louisville, KY: 2009).

Cicero, *De natura deorum*, trans. H. Rackham (Cambridge, MA – London: 1972).

Clifton J., "The Face of a Fiend: Convulsion, Inversion, and the Horror of the Disempowered Body", *Oxford Art Journal* 34.3 (2011) 373–392.

Donelson L.R., *I & II Peter and Jude: A Commentary* (Louisville, KY: 2010).

Esposito T., "*Ignis artificiosus*: Images of God and the Universe in Rubens's Depiction of Antique Shields", *Early Modern Low Countries* 2 (2018) 244–277.

Falomir M., *Las Furias: Alegoría política y desafío artístico*, exh. cat., Museo Nacional del Prado, Madrid (Madrid: 2014).

Fischer B.D. – François W. – Gerace A. – Murray L., "The 'Golden Age' of Catholic Biblical Scholarship (1550–1650) and Its Relation to Biblical Humanism", in Lange van Ravenswaay J.M.J. – Selderhuis H.J. (eds.), *Renaissance und Bibelhumanismus* (Göttingen: 2020) 217–274.

Freedberg D., *Rubens: The Life of Christ after the Passion*, Corpus Rubenianum Ludwig Burchard 7 (London: 1984).

Frey J., "Second Peter in New Perspective", in Frey J. – Dulk M. den – Watt J.G. van der (eds.), *2 Peter and the Apocalypse of Peter: Towards a New Perspective* (Leiden: 2019) 7–74.

Galilei Galileo, *Dialogue Concerning the Two Chief World Systems: Ptolemaic and Copernican*, trans. and with rev. notes by S. Drake (New York, NY: 2001).

Galluzzi P., *The Lynx and the Telescope: The Parallel Worlds of Cesi and Galileo*, trans. P. Mason (Leiden: 2017).

García Ureña L., "The Book of Revelation and Visual Culture", in Schröter J. – Nicklas T. – Puig i Tàrrech A. (eds.), *Dreams, Visions, Imaginations: Jewish, Christian and Gnostic Views of the World to Come* (Berlin – Boston, MA: 2021) 487–504.

Gibert P., "The Catholic Counterpart and Response to the Protestant Orthodoxy", in Sæbø M. (ed.), *Hebrew Bible, Old Testament: The History of Its Interpretation*, vol. 2: *From the Renaissance to the Enlightenment* (Göttingen: 2008).

Gölnitz Abraham, *Ulysses Belgico-Gallicus* (Leiden, Officina Elzeviriana: 1631).

Göttler C. – Moran S.J., *Reading the Inventory: The Possessions of the Portuguese Merchant-Banker Emmanuel Ximenez (1564–1632) in Antwerp* (2014), http://ximenez .unibe.ch (accessed 28.01.2024).

Grant E., "Were There Significant Differences between Medieval and Early Modern Scholastic Natural Philosophy? The Case for Cosmology", *Nous* 18 (1984) 5–14.

Grant E., *Planets, Stars, and Orbs: The Medieval Cosmos, 1200–1687* (Cambridge: 1994).

[Grassi Orazio], "On the Three Comets of the Year 1618: An Astronomical Disputation Presented Publicly in the Collegio Romano of the Society of Jesus by One of the Fathers of that Same Society (Rome, Jacobus Mascardus, 1619)", in *The Controversy of the Comets of 1618: Galileo Galilei, Horatio Grassi, Mario Guiducci, Johann Kepler*, trans. S. Drake – C.D. O'Malley (Philadelphia, PA: 1960).

Hirai H., "Seneca's *Naturales quaestiones* in Justus Lipsius' *Physiologia Stoicorum*: The World-Soul, Providence and Eschatology", in Beretta M. – Citti F. – Pasetti L. (eds.), *Seneca e le scienze naturali* (Florence: 2012) 117–140.

Hirai H. – Papy J. (eds.), *Justus Lipsius and Natural Philosophy* (Brussels: 2011).

Horst P.W. van der, "'The Elements Will Be Dissolved with Fire': The Idea of Cosmic Conflagration in Hellenism, Ancient Judaism, and Early Christianity", in idem (ed.), *Hellenism – Judaism – Christianity: Essays on Their Interaction* (Kampen: 1994) 227–251.

Hout N. van, *Rubens Unveiled: Notes on the Master's Painting Technique* (Antwerp: 2012).

Huber K., "Imagery in the Book of Revelation", in Koester C.R. (ed.), *The Oxford Handbook of the Book of Revelation* (Oxford: 2020), https://doi.org/10.1093/oxfordhb /9780190655433.013.3 (accessed 12.04.2023).

Joly B., "Le problème du feu", in Hirai H. – Papy J. (eds.), *Justus Lipsius and Natural Philosophy* (Brussels: 2011) 53–61.

Joly B. – Moreau P.-F., "Stoic Physics in the 16th and 17th Centuries: A Hidden Presence", *Revue d'histoire des sciences* 61.2 (2008) 1–5.

Juntunen E. – Pawlak A., "'Bellissimo e difficilissimo' – Zur Ikonographie von Rubens' Engelsturz in der Alten Pinakothek in München", in Juntunen E. (ed.), *Rubens im Blick: Ausgewählte Werke unter Revision* (Stuttgart: 2007) 15–47.

Kelly P., "A Patchwork of Passages: On the Nature of Imitation in Galileo's Alphabet and Painting Metaphors", *Ciceroniana On Line* 4.1 (2020) 185–204.

Laertius Diogenes, *Lives of Eminent Philosophers*, trans. R.D. Hicks, vol. 2: *Books 6–10* (Cambridge – London: 1970).

Lapide Cornelius a, *Commentaria in Pentateuchum Mosis* (Antwerp, Martin Nutius and Jan van Meurs: 1616).

Lapide Cornelius a, "Commentaria in Secundam Sancti Petri Epistolam", in idem, *Commentaria in Acta Apostolorum, Epistolas Canonicas, et Apocalypsin* (Antwerp, Martin Nutius: 1627) 354–443.

Lattis J.M., *Between Copernicus and Galileo: Christoph Clavius and the Collapse of Ptolemaic Cosmology* (Chicago, IL – London: 1994).

Lipsius Justus, *Physiologia Stoicorum* (Antwerp, Officina Plantiniana, Joannes Moretus: 1604).

Logan A.-M. – Plomb M.C., *Peter Paul Rubens: The Drawings*, exh. cat., The Metropolitan Museum of Art, New York (New Haven, CT – London: 2004).

Loh M.H., "Outscreaming the Laocoön: Sensation, Special Affects, and the Moving Image", *Oxford Art Journal* 34.3 (2011) 393–414.

Long A.A., *From Epicurus to Epictetus: Studies in Hellenistic and Roman Philosophy* (Oxford: 2006).

Macrobius, *Commentary on the Dream of Scipio*, trans. W.H. Stahl (New York, NY: 1952).

Mander Karel van, *Het Schilder-Boeck* (Haarlem, Paschier van Wesbusch: 1604; reprint, Utrecht: 1969).

Marinus M.J., *De contrareformatie te Antwerpen (1585–1676): Kerkelijk leven in een grootstad* (Brussels: 1995).

Mauran P., "Itinéraires calvinistes dans l'Europe du début de la guerre de Trente Ans: Abraham Gölnitz en son temps", *Dix-septième siècle* 280 (2018) 533–550.

Maxwell S., "Artful Negotiator: Peter Paul Rubens' Intervention in the Cause of Catholic Bavaria", in Scholz Williams G. – Haude S. – Schneider C. (eds.), *Rethinking Europe: War and Peace in the Early Modern German Lands* (Leiden: 2019) 125–141.

McGinn B., "Wrestling with the Millennium: Early Modern Catholic Exegesis of Apocalypse 20", in Amanat A. – Bernhardsson M.T. (eds.), *Imagining the End: Visions of Apocalypse from the Ancient Middle East to Modern America* (London – New York, NY: 2002) 148–167, 363–371.

Morford M., *Stoics and Neostoics: Rubens and the Circle of Lipsius* (Princeton, NJ: 1991).

Murray L., "Jesuit Hebrew Studies after Trent: Cornelius a Lapide (1567–1637)", *Journal of Jesuit Studies* 4 (2017) 76–97.

Murray L., *Jesuit Hebrew Studies after Trent: Franciscus Toletus and Cornelius a Lapide* (Göttingen: 2019) 105–154.

Neumeister M., *Alte Pinakothek: Flämische Malerei* (Munich: 2009).

Nouhuys T. van, *The Age of Two-Faced Janus: The Comets of 1577 and 1618 and the Decline of the Aristotelian World View in the Netherlands* (Leiden: 1998).

Osculati R., "*Hic Romae*: Cornelio a Lapide commentatore dell'Apocalisse al Collegio Romano", in Rusconi R. (ed.), *Storia e figure dell'Apocalisse fra '500 e '600* (Rome: 1996) 301–330.

Paolini C., "L'ultima lettera di Justus Lipsius ad Ascanio Colonna: Philip Rubens, l'ambiente romano e l'ideale neo-stoico condiviso con il fratello Peter Paul", in Simonato L. (ed.), *Leggere il Barocco: Cortocircuiti scultorei tra Otto e Novecento* (Rome: 2018) 59–63.

Papy J., "Lipsius's (Neo-) Stoicism: Constancy between Christian Faith and Stoic Virtue", in Blom H.W. – Winkel L.C. (eds.), *Grotius and the Stoa* (Assen: 2004) 47–72.

Papy J., "Justus Lipsius", in Zalta E.N. (ed.), *The Stanford Encyclopedia of Philosophy* (Spring 2019 edition), https://plato.stanford.edu/archives/spr2019/entries/justus-lipsius/ (accessed 20.07. 2022).

Parker G., *Global Crisis: War, Climate Change and Catastrophe in the Seventeenth Century* (New Haven, CT: 2013).

Piles Roger de, *Dissertation sur les ouvrages des plus fameux peintres* (Paris, Nicolas Langlois: 1681).

Poll-Frommel V. – Renger K. – Schmidt J., "Untersuchungen and Rubens-Bildern – Die Anstückungen der Holztafeln", *Jahresbericht: Bayerische Staatsgemäldesammlungen* (1993) 24–35.

Randles W.G.L., *The Unmaking of the Medieval Christian Cosmos, 1500–1760: From Solid Heavens to Boundless Æther* (Aldershot: 1999).

Reeves E., *Painting the Heavens: Art and Science in the Age of Galileo* (Princeton, NJ: 1997).

Renger K., *Peter Paul Rubens: Altäre für Bayern* (Munich: 1990).

Renger K. – Denk C., *Flämische Malerei des Barock in der Alten Pinakothek* (Munich – Cologne: 2002).

Roh F., "Rubens' Höllensturz", *Münchner Jahrbuch der bildenden Kunst* 10 (1916–1918) 189–197.

Rowlands J., *Rubens: Drawings and Sketches*, exh. cat., British Museum, London (London: 1977).

Rubens P.P., *The Letters of Peter Paul Rubens*, trans. Magurn R. Saunders (Cambridge, MA: 1955).

Ruelens C., "La vie de Rubens par Roger de Piles", *Rubens-Bulletijn* 2 (1883) 157–211.

Sakamoto K., "Eclecticism as Seneca's Heritage: Evil and the Cosmic Cycle in Justus Lipsius", in Hirai H. – Papy J. (eds.), *Justus Lipsius and Natural Philosophy* (Brussels: 2011) 97–106.

Saunders J.L., *Justus Lipsius: The Philosophy of Renaissance Stoicism* (New York, NY: 1955).

Scheiner Christophorus, *Rosa Ursina sive Sol* (Bracciano, Andreas Phaeus: 1626–1630).

Seligman I., *Lines of Thought: Drawing from Michelangelo to Now*, exh. cat., touring exhibition (London: 2016).

Smith J. Chipps, *Sensuous Worship: Jesuits and the Art of the Early Catholic Reformation in Germany* (Princeton, NJ: 2002).

Smith J. Chipps, "Rubens, Bishop Veit Adam von Gepeckh, and the Freising High Altar, 1623–1625", in Duerloo L. – Smuts R.M. (eds.), *The Age of Rubens: Diplomacy, Dynastic Politics and the Visual Arts in Early Seventeenth-Century Europe* (Turnhout: 2016) 261–274.

Theunissens L., "Testaments des premiers évêques d'Anvers", *Analectes pour servir à l'histoire ecclésiastique de la Belgique* 15 (1878) 83–139.

Villiers G.R., "Prime Evil and Its Many Faces in the Book of Revelation", *Neotestamentica* 34.1 (2000) 57–85.

Vlieghe H., *Rubens: Saints*, 2 vols., Corpus Rubenianum Ludwig Burchard 8 (Brussels: 1973).

Volk-Knüttel B., "Überlegungen zum ursprünglichen Standort von Rubens' 'Engelsturz' für Neuburg: Mit einem Exkurs zu Constantino de' Servi", *Neuburger Kollektaneenblatt* (2007) 5–32.

White M.J., "Stoic Natural Philosophy (Physics and Cosmology)", in Inwood B. (ed.), *The Cambridge Companion to the Stoics* (Cambridge: 2006) 124–152.

CHAPTER 3

A Castle in the Air? Space, Time, and Sensation in Gabriel de Henao's *Empyreologia*

Wietse de Boer

Abstract

This chapter explores a theological defence and re-proposition of medieval Christian cosmology in the age of scientific revolution. In his massive work entitled *Empyreologia* (1652), the Spanish Jesuit Gabriel de Henao offered a 'Christian philosophy' of the highest heaven. It was a culmination of decades of neo-scholastic engagement with cosmology and astronomy. Henao, however, remained largely oblivious to the findings of the new science (and the challenge of the Protestant Reformation). Instead, he sketched a mostly traditional moral-theological universe whose spatio-temporal configuration served as the fitting environment in which the blessed were destined to dwell in glory. Most distinctive was the Jesuit's insistence on the corporeal nature of both the place and the existence of the resurrected: the latter reaped their eternal reward especially in the form of bodily movement and sensation. This assumption raised numerous questions: how far could the blessed see or hear? Could they touch Christ and the Virgin Mary? Was there communication between heaven and hell, heaven and earth? These were not idle questions: the make-up of heaven mattered well beyond the realm of theological inquiry. The Jesuit, in fact, addressed his book not only to theologians and philosophers, but also to mystical thinkers and preachers. The chapter concludes by examining the moral underpinnings of Henao's spiritual construct, its role in offering an orthodox template for spiritual, ritual, literary, and artistic representations, and its relevance for thriving practices of meditation and mysticism.

Keywords

empyrean – sensation – cosmology – resurrection – chronotope – Gabriel de Henao

In 1652, the Spanish Jesuit Gabriel de Henao published a massive work, completed five years earlier, entitled *Empyreologia*.[1] It was, as the rest of the title explained, a 'Christian philosophy' of the empyrean, the ultimate heavenly sphere, the abode of God, the saints, and the blessed.[2] Henao (1612–1704), born in Valladolid, was a long-time philosophy and theology professor at Oviedo, Valladolid, and finally Salamanca. Known as one of the most learned men of his time, he was widely consulted on all matters theological: it was said that his written responses, if collected, would have filled eight or nine large tomes.[3] The *Empyreologia* certainly shows off his learning: in two hefty folio volumes, Henao offered a systematic treatment of the nature, substance, and properties of the empyrean heaven. The first analysed the material and spiritual nature of the empyrean, properties such as movement (or lack thereof), light, and incorruptibility, qualities including the size and external shape of the empyrean, and the presence of colours, sounds, and smells. The second volume, introduced by an overview of the empyrean's influences on other heavenly bodies, focused especially on its residents, in order: God, Christ, the Virgin Mary, the angels, and the blessed both before and after the general resurrection. Henao further discussed questions about other 'bodies' in the empyrean (the Eucharist, the cross and other instruments of the passion, the bodies of angels, and saints'

---

1   Henao Gabriel de, *Empyreologia, seu Philosophia Christiana de Empyreo Coelo*, 2 vols. (Lyon, sumptibus Philippi Borde, Laurentii Arnaud, et Claudii Rigaud: 1652). The publication was approved by the Castilian province of the Society of Jesus on 25 May 1647, and by the doctors of the Sorbonne, the substitute vicar-general of Lyon, and the royal procurator on 31 January and 1 February 1652. The reasons for the delay – to which Henao refers in the book's dedication ('cum editio longius protenta sit quam sperabamus', ibidem, fol. a [4] r) – are unclear. Note: I am most grateful for the insightful comments on a draft of my chapter offered by this volume's co-editor, Christine Göttler, as well as those of two anonymous peer reviewers.

2   On the history of the empyrean, see Gilson É., "À la recherche de l'Empyrée", *Revue des études italiennes* 11 (1965) 147–161; Nardi B., "La dottrina dell'Empireo nella sua genesi storica e nel pensiero dantesco", in idem, *Saggi di filosofia dantesca* (2nd ed., Florence: 1967) 167–214; Maurach G., *Coelum empyreum: Versuch einer Begriffsgeschichte*, Texte und Abhandlungen zur Geschichte der Exacten Wissenschaften (Wiesbaden: 1968); Lindemann B.W., *Bilder vom Himmel: Studien zur Deckenmalerei des 17. und 18. Jahrhunderts* (Worms am Rhein: 1994) 28–39; Lerner M.-P., *Le monde des sphères*, 2 vols. (Paris: 1996–1997) 1:215–220; and Grant E., *Planets, Stars, Orbs: The Medieval Cosmos, 1200–1687* (Cambridge: 2009) 371–389.

3   Bernard P., "Henao (Gabriel de)", *Dictionnaire de théologie catholique*, vol. 6/2 (Paris: 1925), 2147–2148. Bernard emphasizes Henao's role in the debates and controversies regarding the *scientia media*. In the later 1650s, in fact, his treatise *Scientia media historice propugnata* (Lyon: 1655) was reviewed by the Roman Inquisition (Archivio del Dicastero per la Dottrina della Fede, Rome, U.V. U.V. 46, fasc. 21; Iansenismus 03 F 1 e 1 (1556–1558), fols. 428–528). This did not keep him from publishing additional works on the issue in 1674 and 1685. To my knowledge, little else is known about Henao's biography, milieu, and career.

clothes) before embarking on a discussion of the 'external and internal material actions of the inhabitants of the empyrean'. Actually, this long section of
the work was largely focused on the 'external actions', that is, the movements
of glorified bodies and, especially, the functioning of their corporeal senses.

Not long after the book's publication, Henao's sensory heaven fell prey to
venomous anti-Jesuit or more broadly anti-Catholic ridicule, which was echoed well into the nineteenth century.[4] Serious scholarship largely ignored
it until quite recently, but even now the *Empyreologia* lacks an attentive
study. This is somewhat surprising, because the last few decades have seen
an upsurge of interest in the contributions of the Jesuits – from Christopher
Clavius to Athanasius Kircher and beyond – to early modern cosmology and
astronomy.[5] As will become clear in what follows, an explanation for this
lacuna may nevertheless be suggested. This chapter by no means fills the gap,
as it is narrowly tailored to address the theme of the present volume. That is, it
sets out to reconstruct the temporal and spatial coordinates which Henao posited or assumed as he sought to make sense of the ultimate heavenly sphere.
The Spanish Jesuit did not examine this configuration as such or methodically.
Yet not only did his discussions of the empyrean and the blessed regularly reference questions of space and time, but he considered the very architecture
of the *Domus Dei* to be expressly designed to enable its inhabitants' peren-
nial existence. Of course, this idea was hardly original per se. As Jeffrey Burton
Russell has observed, speaking of ancient Jewish and early Christian traditions,
'[t]he role of space and time in the concept of heaven is related to the presence
of bodies there, which requires that it be in some sense a place'.[6] This was also
the premise of medieval scholastics. But Henao developed it painstakingly into
an all-encompassing construct within which actions – of the blessed, angels,
as well as Christ – could unfold and be rendered comprehensible. Even so,
the main expressions of empyrean existence made it radically different from

---

4 See, for example, *La morale pratique des Jésuites representée en plusieurs histoires arrivées
   dans toutes les parties du monde* (Cologne, Gervinus Quentel: 1669) 271–275; Bayle Pierre,
   "Loyola, Ignace de", *Dictionaire historique et critique* (5th ed., Amsterdam etc., P. Brunel et al.:
   1740) 3: 146–147 n. v; D'Israeli Isaac, *Curiosities of Literature*, vol. 1 (London: s.a.) 368; *All the
   Year Round*, Third Series, vol. 2 (London: 1889) 180.

5 Introductions to the large and growing bibliography include Feingold M. (ed.), *Jesuit Science
   and the Republic of Letters* (Cambridge, MA – London: 2003); Wootton D., "Jesuits and
   the New Astronomy", in idem, *Galileo: Watcher of the Skies* (New Haven, CT: 2010) 111–124;
   Rabin S.J., "Early Modern Jesuit Science: A Historiographical Essay", *Journal of Jesuit Studies* 1
   (2014) 88–104; Carolino L.M., "Astronomy, Cosmology and Jesuit Discipline, 1540–1758", in
   Županov I.G. (ed.), *The Oxford Handbook of the Jesuits* (Oxford – New York, NY: 2019) 670–707.

6 Russell J.B., *A History of Heaven: The Singing Silence* (Princeton, NJ: 1997) 15.

the here-and-now of earthly experience. The corporeal activities in which the blessed could indulge were essentially two: movement and sensation.

Henao's endeavour, as one scholar has noted, represented the last gasp of a long theological and natural-philosophical tradition that described the empyrean as a distinct place within the cosmos. The term *empyreum coelum* – chosen to highlight its luminosity – originated in early-Christian neo-Platonism and was already ingrained in tradition when neo-scholastic theologians sought to give it a more precise definition.[7] The *Glossa ordinaria* described it as the 'intellectual' heaven intended as the angels' dwelling place on the first day of Creation. By 1241, however, the theologian William of Auvergne defined it as 'the *corporeal* place for the angels and the souls of the saints'.[8] Three years later, the Parisian theology faculty affirmed this view, emphasizing the corporeality of both the *locus* and its inhabitants.[9] If this axiom still undergirded Henao's *Empyreologia*, the same was largely true for two other Jesuit works published almost contemporaneously: Nicolas Caussin's *Domus Dei* (1650) and Giovanni Battista Riccioli's *Almagestum Novum* (1651).[10] These texts capped a period of renewed interest in the theme among Jesuit scholars, including leading

---

7   Maurach, *Coelum empyreum* devotes most of its pages to the reconstruction of this ancient and early-medieval tradition.

8   Lerner, *Le monde des sphères* 1:216–217. The cited phrase (with emphasis added) was part of William of Auvergne's condemnation of the idea that the saints dwelt in the waters above the firmament. Cf. also Grant, *Planets* 372–374.

9   Armogathe J.R., *La nature du monde: Science nouvelle et exégèse au XVIIe siècle* (Paris: 2007) 218 n. 6 (based on Denifle H., *Chartularium universitatis parisiensis* [Paris: 1889] 1:171): 'firmiter [...] credimus, quod idem locus corporalis, scilicet coelum empireum, angelorum et animarum sanctarum erit et corporum glorificatorum'.

10   Randles W.G.L., *The Unmaking of the Medieval Christian Cosmos, 1500–1760: From Solid Heavens to Boundless Æther* (Aldershot, Hants. – Brookville, VT: 1999) 144–150. On Henao, see brief remarks in Baroja J.C., *Las formas complejas de la vida religiosa (Religión, Sociedad y carácter en la España de los siglos XVI y XVII)* (Madrid: 1978) 124–127; Hart C. – Stevenson K.G., *Heaven and the Flesh: Imagery of Desire from the Renaissance to the Rococo* (Cambridge: 1995) 114; Hecht C., *Die Glorie: Begriff, Thema, Bildelement in der europäischen Sakralkunst vom Mittelalter bis zum Ausgang der Barock* (Regensburg: 2003) 41; Armogathe, *La nature du monde* 220–222. On Riccioli, see Graney C.M., *Setting Aside All Authority: Giovanni Battista Riccioli and the Science against Copernicus in the Age of Galileo* (Notre Dame, IN: 2015) and Dinis A., *A Jesuit against Galileo? The Strange Case of Giovanni Battista Riccioli's Cosmology* (Braga: 2017). The bibliography on Caussin is largely confined to his moral-theological and rhetorical works: see among other titles, Kapp V., "Skandalöse Orthodoxie bei Nicolas Caussin", in Titzmann M. – Laufhütte H. (eds.), *Heterodoxie in der Frühen Neuzeit* (Tübingen: 2006) 191–200; Conte S. (ed.), *Nicolas Caussin: Rhétorique et spiritualité à l'époque de Louis XIII. Actes du colloque de Troyes (16–17 septembre 2004)* (Berlin: 2007); Piqué B., "Pascal, Caussin et l'astronomie moralisée: Note sur une citation dans les *Pensées*", *Dix-septième siècle* 290.1 (2021) 117–123.

figures like Francisco Suárez (1548–1617), Roberto Bellarmino (1542–1621), and Leonardus Lessius (1554–1623). This engagement, as has been suggested, responded both to the new astronomy and to early Lutheran reconsiderations of the empyrean.[11]

Verification of this hypothesis, which largely goes beyond the scope of this contribution, should be attentive to the differences among these theologians. Of the three Jesuits whose work appeared around the mid-seventeenth century, Riccioli, an astronomer himself, sought to rethink the properties of the empyrean in light of the new science, among other things by refuting Johannes Kepler's work. Caussin occasionally referred to astronomical discoveries but largely retained the established theological conception of heaven. Henao's book was clearly the most traditional. Its author blithely ignored contemporary advances in astronomy and, despite naming Martin Luther among heretical interpreters, focused on reviving the Aristotelian-scholastic interpretation of the empyrean that had dominated late-medieval cosmology. Central to this construct were the sensory faculties attributed to the blessed. The interest of the *Empyreologia* thus does not lie in its originality, nor in the way in which it responded to competing astronomical interpretations. Instead, Henao summed up, probed, and elaborated in encyclopaedic detail a centuries-old moral-theological – rather than natural-philosophical – understanding of the Christian universe at the very point when it had become increasingly precarious.

1   The Chronotope of the Empyrean

To analyse Henao's universe, Mikhail Bakhtin's concept of the chronotope may prove useful. With this idea, freely borrowed from Albert Einstein's notion of the space-time continuum, Bakhtin sought to draw attention to the 'intrinsic connectedness of temporal and spatial relationships that are artistically expressed in literature'. This fusion, in which time 'thickens' and space 'becomes charged and responsive to the movements of time, plot and history', was determinative both for genre distinctions and for 'the image of man in

---

11   Mehl L., "La fiction théologique du ciel empyrée, de Luther à Descartes", *Revue des sciences religieuses* 92.2 (2017) 193–210. Mehl's article, however intriguing, does not document these presumed influences on Jesuit ideas about the empyrean, including those of Henao, who is mentioned repeatedly. Nor is it developed in Mehl's impressive book, *Descartes et la fabrique du monde: Le problème cosmologique de Copernic à Descartes* (Paris: 2019). The influence of the new science is discussed, however, in Carolino, "Astronomy, Cosmology, and Jesuit Discipline", which rightly insists on the diversity of opinion among Jesuit scholars.

literature'.[12] To apply this concept to paradise is at first sight counter-intuitive, since the hereafter assumes the cessation or collapsing of time. But Bakhtin himself countenanced this idea. Any vision of an ideal world, he suggested, tends to distance it in space and time from the present one (for instance, in a Golden Age), yet privileging 'a superstructure for reality (the present) along a vertical axis of upper and lower' over one that 'move[s] forward along the horizontal axis of time'. This also applies to the afterlife, where the 'extratemporal and eternal quality is perceived as something simultaneous with a given moment in the present; it is something contemporaneous'.[13] Hence Dante's vision in the *Commedia*: here the poet presented a world, consisting of the circles of hell, purgatory, and heaven stacked on top of each other, 'that has its life and movement tensely strung along a vertical axis'. Dante's project, then, was 'to synchronise diachrony'.[14]

Bakhtin confined his discussion of the chronotope to literature, but left open the possibility that it might be applied to 'other areas of culture'.[15] These no doubt include religious forms of engagement with the hereafter, including those found in theological speculation, spiritual exercises, meditations, visions, rituals, and artistic representations. In exploring these imaginary worlds, it behoves us to distinguish two elements: on the one hand, the ways in which intellectuals, poets, and artists imagined the otherworldly space-time configuration, and its connection to the 'actions' of its inhabitants; on the other, the experiential engagement which the devout developed with these elements – their "consumption", as it were – which was embedded in a spatial and temporal setting of its own. This essay focuses mostly on the former aspect: Henao himself defined his work explicitly as an intellectual endeavour, the foundation of proper devotional engagement. In one of a number of methodological prefaces, he defined the utility of his work as serving the 'intellect' rather than the 'will'. The will referred to the moral edification that would result from the contemplation of the empyrean. Henao certainly wished for his soul,

---

12   Bakhtin M.M., "Forms of Time and of the Chronotope in the Novel", in idem, *The Dialogic Imagination*, ed. M. Holquist, trans. C. Emerson – M. Holquist (Austin, TX: 1981) 84–258, at 84–85.

13   Ibidem 148. This aspect of Bakhtin's interpretation is developed, not altogether convincingly, with reference to late-medieval eschatology, by Schmolinsky S., "The Production of Future: Chronotope and Agency in the Middle Ages", in *Space/Time Practices and the Production of Space and Time*, issue 145 of *Historical Social Research / Historische Sozialforschung* 38.3 (2013) 93–104.

14   Bakhtin, "Forms of Time" 157; one suspects that his notion of a 'vertical axis of upper and lower' in fact originated in his reading of Dante.

15   Ibidem 84.

'purified of worldly affects and free from mundane concerns, to aspire only to the celestial, eternal, and divine'.[16] Yet his book was not focused on moral goals (*ad mores*): he preferred to 'leav[e] this Sparta to others'. His was the work of a theological specialist, an 'empyreologist' (*empyreologus*).[17] Just as 'astrology' was the science of stars, empyreology was the science of heaven, understood as the 'see of the blessed'.[18] At the end of this chapter we will return to the possible connections between Henao's theological speculations and the devotional purposes they were meant to serve.

2   Sensation and the Cosmological Tradition

If Henao's cosmology was deeply rooted in medieval Christian eschatology, so was his emphasis on sensation. In fact, his work was the culmination, and quite possibly the last significant expression, of a long tradition that associated the theology of paradise with speculations about the reconstitution of the bodily senses.[19] Precisely on this point, the Jesuit Caussin, in his already mentioned

---

16   Henao, *Empyreologia* 1:2b: 'Et a me quidem optandum fuisset atque enitendum, ut [...] animus a terrenis affectibus depuratus et mundialibus curis liber nihil nisi caeleste, aeternum, ac divinum anhelaret'.

17   Ibidem: 'aliis hanc Spartam relinquo'.

18   Ibidem 1:1a: 'Empyreologiam voco, non secus ac scientia et sermo de astris dicitur astrologia. Nomen *empyreum* prolatum sine adminiculo substantivi significat ex communi usu caelum, quod est beatorum sedes' (italics in original).

19   This aspect remains neglected in the rich scholarship on the history of heaven and the afterlife. See, for instance, McDannell C. – Lang B., *Heaven: A History* (New Haven, CT – London: 1988); Russell, *A History of Heaven*; Delumeau J., *Histoire du paradis*, 3 vols. (Paris: 1992–2000); Emerson J.S. – Feiss H. (eds.), *Imagining Heaven in the Middle Ages: A Book of Essays* (New York, NY: 2000), where Emerson's chapter focuses on the senses in visionary experience; McGrath A., *A Brief History of Heaven* (Malden, MA: 2003); Muessig C. – Putter A. (eds.), *Envisaging Heaven in the Middle Ages* (London – New York, NY: 2007); and Gill M.J., *Angels and the Order of Heaven in Medieval and Renaissance Italy* (New York, NY: 2014). The same is true for studies of bodily resurrection, including Heinzmann R., *Die Unsterblichkeit der Seele und die Auferstehung des Leibes: Eine problemgeschichtliche Untersuchung der frühscholastischen Sentenzen- und Summenliteratur von Anselm von Laon bis Wilhelm von Auxerre* (Munster: 1965); Weber H.J., *Die Lehre von der Auferstehung der Toten in den Haupttraktaten der scholastischen Theologie von Alexander von Hales zu Duns Skotus* (Freiburg – Basel – Vienna: 1973), esp. 168–172; Bynum C.W., *The Resurrection of the Body in Western Christianity, 200–1336* (New York, NY: 1995) and Lambert E., *Singing the Resurrection: Body, Community and Belief in Reformation Europe* (New York, NY: 2018). Compare also works on the beatific vision, such as Boersma H., *Seeing God: The Beatific Tradition in Christian Thought* (Grand Rapids, MI: 2018), and on the senses in medieval

Domus Dei, parted ways with Henao: for Caussin, perception in heaven was purely intellectual. It was 'misguided to think that no soul can exist except by seeing, hearing, or smelling through the corporeal senses'.[20] For his part, Giovanni Battista Riccioli, in his *Almagestum Novum*, confirmed the existence of the empyrean as a distinct *locus*, but largely avoided discussion of the sensation of the blessed dwelling there.[21]

Henao's older view of the embodied nature of sensation in paradise was grounded in two principles of scholastic theology. The first was the resurrection of the body, the notion that human souls would be reincarnated following the Last Judgement. Particularly, the blessed would see their bodies reconstituted "in glory", that is, cleansed of the stains of original sin and in a state of perfection. Of necessity, this was also true of the organs of sense perception. The

---

religion, including Macdonald R. – Murphy E.K.M. – Swann E.L. (eds.), *Sensing the Sacred in Medieval and Early Modern Culture* (London – New York, NY: 2018). For art-historical studies, see Hecht, *Die Glorie*; Lindemann, *Bilder vom Himmel*; Pereda F., "*Pictura est Lingua Angelorum*: Fray Juan Ricci, una teoría teológica del arte", in Marías F. – Pereda F. (eds.), *Fray Juan Ricci: Tratado de la Pintura Sabia*, 2 vols. (Toledo: 2002) 1:43–87; and Cousinié F., *Gloriae: Figurabilité du divin, esthétique de la lumière et dématérialisation de l'œuvre d'art à l'âge baroque* (Rennes: 2018). Long ago, Alberto Tenenti, in his *Il senso della morte e l'amore della vita* (Turin: 1957), showed how fifteenth-century Italian churchmen and humanists embraced the notion of corporeal sensation in paradise, but its origins certainly go further back. A study focused on the Spanish Baroque, Martínez Arancón A., *Geografía de la eternidad* (Madrid: 1987), has the merit of discussing, largely on the basis of devotional literature, both the spatial aspects of heaven (ibidem 146–176) and the sensory pleasures of the blessed (ibidem 249–263), along with the corresponding features of hell.

20   Caussin Nicholas, *Domus Dei, in qua de mirabilibus coeli totaque astrologia et vita coelesti luculenter et copiose disseritur* (Paris, sumptibus Ioannis du Bray: 1650) 130: 'Insipidum est cogitare nullam esse animam nisi per corporeos sensus videat, aut audiat, aut odoretur, aut gustet [...]'. This point about Caussin was made earlier by Randles, *The Unmaking of the Medieval Christian Cosmos* 146 (whose assertion that this demonstrates 'how much the French classical mind was diverging from the Baroque spirit of southern Catholic Europe' may be questioned).

21   Randles, *The Unmaking of the Medieval Christian Cosmos* 149. The source is Riccioli Giovanni Battista, *Almagestum novum. Pars Posterior Tomi Primi* (Bologna, ex typographia haeredis Victorii Benatii: 1651) lib. IX, sec. I, cap. I, 204–209 (Randles's reference to page 224 appears to be erroneous). Riccioli here defends the notion of the empyrean as a distinct place, which he calls 'spiritual' because of its subtleness (*ob subtilitatem*) and because it is 'invisible to us' (ibidem 206). But he accepts the presence of the bodies of the blessed and acknowledges the occurrence of speech and vision (ibidem 209). Speech is possible, despite the thinness of the air, because the internal organs no longer have to process food and excrement, nor handle respiration. Vision is necessary for the same reason the empyrean has colours: the visual experience of the blessed needs to be superior to human perception on earth.

second, related principle was the dual, human-divine nature of Christ. It was his humanity, revived when he rose from the dead and ascended to heaven, which necessitated that bodily sensation be restored to the blessed, whose features mirrored those of Christ. These principles were embedded within a unified, but hierarchically stratified cosmology that assumed a universe at once physical, spiritual, and moral. This last aspect, the conception of a universe organized to reflect moral doctrines – starting with a hell located at the centre of the earth, and a heaven at the outermost edge of the cosmos –, had obvious implications for the actions (and thus, the sensations) which post-Judgement humans could expect to undertake. This was as true for the damned in hell as for the blessed in heaven. Accordingly, not only did sensation include corporeal acts of perception, but the pain or pleasure these offered represented the just reward for sin or virtue.

In paradoxical contrast to Henao's adherence to this tradition – in a compendium that went out of its way to trace the key authorities, biblical, patristic, and scholastic – stood his proud claim of innovation. To this the Jesuit dedicated a special preface 'on the novelty of empyreology' (*de novitate empyreologiae*). And he explained: 'While I follow in the footsteps of many, none has expressly discussed and gathered in one work all that pertains to the empyrean'.[22] To modern readers the remark may seem puzzling. On the one hand, the word 'novelty' had long had negative connotations – a prejudice clearly shared by Henao.[23] On the other hand, Henao's book ignored the astronomical revolution that, by the mid-seventeenth century, was obviously well-established in scientific circles and had begun to inform theological debates as well. To be sure, Henao distinguished his book from astronomy ('astrology') from the start, defining it as a work of 'Christian philosophy', which was a sibling of 'natural philosophy'.[24] Even so, he followed the opinion of his fellow Jesuits Pedro Fonseca (1528–1599) and Bartolomeo Amico (1562–1649) that it would be absurd 'to exclude the empyrean from the purview of physics'.[25]

---

22   Henao, *Empyreologia* 1:6b: 'Multorum vestigiis insisto, nullius tamen qui ex professo discusserit, collegeritque in unum corpus pertinentia ad empyreum'.
23   See, e.g., his dismissive remarks about *neoterici* (modern writers), ibidem 1:178a–b: 'Hinc non arridet mihi quidam neothericus definiens unionem physicam quatenus sit *vinculum quo aliud perficitur* [...]. Alius neothericus, ut subterfugeret postremam hanc obiectionem, dixit [...]'.
24   Ibidem 1:1a–b.
25   Ibidem 1:2a: 'Sed P. Petrus Fonseca lib. 5 Metaphysicae cap. 4, q. 2, sect. 7, v. *licet quoque*, significat, emphyreum [sic] non sine absurdo excludendum a consideratione physica. Quare ad eam spectat per sapientissimum virum; cui adhesit P. Bartholomaeus Amicus tract. 8 Physicorum q. 11, dub. 4, art. et conclusione 3. In eadem ego sum existimatione'.

This statement, however, did not signal an openness to the discoveries of the new science. Parts of the *Empyreologia* may suggest an effort to push back against the work of physicists.[26] As for astronomy, Henao's work seems to reflect an anti-Copernican consensus among the Jesuits, reached around mid-century, following several decades of engagement with the new science.[27] Whatever the cause or context, Henao's work evidently assumed without question the pre-Copernican hierarchical cosmos. Of this the empyrean was the incorruptible, immobile, and (to mortals) invisible summit. These last two qualities had already led Thomas Aquinas to state that the empyrean could not be studied by reason: for that to be possible, motion and vision were prerequisites.[28] Henao himself explained in some detail why the empyrean was invisible from earth.[29] The contrast with Galileo's non-hierarchical, continuous, and irregular universe could not be greater. The Jesuit's emphasis on the presence of *sensibilia* (colours, sounds, smells) and the ability of the blessed to perceive them only reinforces the disconnect. Galileo himself had famously noted the non-sensory drift of the new science by observing that 'philosophy is written in this great book that stands continuously opened before our eyes – that is to say, the universe –, but it cannot be understood if we do not first learn the language and the characters in which it is written. The language is mathematical, and characters are triangles, circles and other geometrical figures'. Human knowledge of the natural world ('corpi esterni') was thus built, as Galileo concluded towards the end of the book, on 'figures, numbers, and movements, but not smell, nor tastes, nor sounds, which I do not believe are anything more than names outside the living animal'.[30] Galileo's point on the senses constituted a deliberate dismissal of scholastic-Aristotelian cosmology. Elsewhere, his disdain for this tradition is palpable: in the *Dialogue Concerning the Two Chief World Systems* (1632), the tangible qualities Aristotle had attributed to

---

26   Thus Maurach, *Coelum empyreum* 3 (who refers to Book I [surely Part I], *Exercitio* 7), although this point is yet to be demonstrated more fully.

27   See Finocchiaro M.A., *Retrying Galileo, 1633–1922* (Berkeley, CA: 2005) 80–83; Carolino, "Astronomy, Cosmology" 480.

28   Thomas Aquinas, *Sent.* II, d. 2, q. 2, art. 1.

29   Henao, *Empyreologia* 1:223–226.

30   Galilei Galileo, *Il saggiatore*, ed. and comm. O. Bonomi – M. Helbing (Rome: 2005) 120: 'La filosofia è scritta in questo grandissimo libro che continuamente ci sta aperto dinanzi a gli occhi (io dico l'universo), ma non si può intendere se prima non s'impara a intender la lingua, e conoscer i caratteri, ne' quali è scritto. Egli è scritto in lingua matematica, e i caratteri son triangoli, cerchi, ed altre figure geometriche [...]'; and ibidem 287: 'e stimo bene che, tolti via gli orecchi le lingue e i nasi, restino bene le figure i numeri e i moti, ma non già gli odori nè i sapori nè i suoni, li quali fuor dell'animal vivente non credo che sieno altro che nomi [...]'.

heaven – particularly, its density and hardness – led the character Sagredo to observe: 'What excellent stuff, the sky, for anyone who could get hold of it for building a palace'. This had complex implications for a sphere which was also transparent, discussion of which was quickly shut down by Sagredo's interlocutor, Salviati: 'But let us forsake these palaces, or more appropriately these castles in the air [...]'.[31] Galileo used a common phrase to express his ironic dismissal.[32] Yet, as we shall see, it captures quite accurately, if unintentionally, Henao's traditionalist understanding of the empyrean – an understanding that for him and his intended audience surely did not imply an absurdity.

More broadly, Galileo's approach to understanding the cosmos mathematically, outside and beyond human sensation – excluding only vision, traditionally viewed as the noblest sense and obviously the one needed for astronomical observations – serves to reinforce the idiosyncratic nature of Henao's project. With its emphasis on the sensory experiences of the elect, to whom the resurrection of the body restored the full faculties of perception of 'living animals' (to use Galileo's term), the Jesuit's project was geared to the devotional engagement with the cosmos, in the afterlife as much as in the here and now. The contrast was certainly not limited to these two thinkers. As Michael Sauter has argued, the groundwork for the early-modern astronomical revolution was laid by the reception of Euclidian geometry during the later Middle Ages. Over time, the resulting mathematical conception of space, which came to be seen as both idealized and homogeneous, was to provoke a revolution in the understanding of heaven and earth.[33] To the extent that this entailed a humanization of space, as Sauter has claimed, in the sense that humans put themselves in the command centre of observation, analysis, and control, it is clear that this phenomenon was radically different from the anthropocentrism of medieval cosmology, inherent in the bodily properties of the glorified, and still evident

---

31   Galilei Galileo, *Dialogue Concerning the Two Chief World Systems*, trans. S. Drake, intro. A. Einstein (Berkeley, CA – Los Angeles, CA: 1967) 69. The same passage is cited in Randles, *The Unmaking of the Medieval Christian Cosmos* 22; also note, in the same context, the ironic points about touch. For the Italian, see Galilei, *Dialogo sopra i due massimi sistemi del mondo, Tolemaico e Copernicano*, ed. and comm. O. Bonomi – M. Helbing (Padua: 1998) 1:74–75: 'SAGR.: Che bella materia sarebbe quella del cielo per fabbricar palazzi, chi ne potesse avere, così dura et tanto trasparente! [...] SALV.: [...] Ma lasciamo star questi palazzi o per dir meglio castelli in aria, e non impediamo signor Simplicio'.

32   On this expression, see Zagoury D., "Vasari's Castle in the Air", *Journal of the Warburg and Courtauld Institutes* 81 (2018) 249–267.

33   Sauter M.J., *The Spatial Reformation: Euclid between Man, Cosmos, and God* (Philadelphia, PA: 2019).

in early-modern Catholic eschatology and the contemplative, devotional, artistic, and literary conceits or practices derived from it.

The remarkable durability of Aristotelian-scholastic cosmology in the age of scientific revolution is worth noting. Until recent decades, in fact, historians commonly assumed perspectives that diminished the significance of views like Henao's, which represent a wide array of early modern forms of religious speculation and experience. On the one hand, historians of science tended to privilege the innovative, seemingly forward-looking developments that sustained a narrative of progress. On the other hand, historians of philosophy and cosmology measured neo-scholastic cosmology with the yardstick of modern astronomy and hence considered it either for its engagement with the new science or as a survival. Since Amos Funkenstein's pathbreaking *Theology and the Scientific Imagination* (1986), such narratives have gradually given way, if not to the kind of fusion of religious and scientific thought posited by Funkenstein, to more complex understandings of their connections and interactions.[34] Hence the discovery of the persistence and adaptability of scholastic natural philosophy in early modern scientific projects.[35] What remains largely overlooked are the numerous forms and expressions of theological speculation, like Henao's, which not only refused accommodation with the new science, but whose lessons were primarily meant, not to contribute to natural philosophy, but to instruct the contemplative imagination.

3   Space, Distance, and Function

Pace Galileo, then, Gabriel de Henao continued in the footsteps of many Catholics who for centuries had described the empyrean as a house, city, palace, or theatre. It may come naturally to assume that the learned Jesuit here thought

---

34   See, e.g., Feldhay R., "Religion", in Park K. – Daston L. (eds.), *Early Modern Science*, The Cambridge History of Science 3 (Cambridge: 2006) 727–755; Grant, *Planets, Stars*; idem, "The Partial Transformation of Medieval Cosmology by the Jesuits in the Sixteenth and Seventeenth Centuries", in Feingold (ed.), *Jesuit Science* 127–156; and Lerner, *Le monde des sphères*.

35   See, for example, Leijenhorst C., "Jesuit Concepts of *spatium imaginarium* and Thomas Hobbes's Doctrine of Space", *Early Science and Medicine* 1.3 (1996) 355–380; Smith J.E.H., "Spirit as Intermediary in Post-Cartesian Natural Philosophy", in Göttler C. – Neuber W. (eds.), *Spirits Unseen: The Representation of Subtle Bodies in Early-Modern European Culture*, Intersections 9 (Leiden – Boston, MA: 2007) 269–291; Dupré S., "The Return of the Species: Jesuit Responses to Kepler's New Theory of Images", in De Boer W. – Göttler C. (eds.), *Religion and the Senses in Early Modern Europe*, Intersections 26 (Leiden – Boston, MA: 2013) 473–488.

metaphorically. That was the way in which one of his readers, the Neapolitan Theatine Giovan Battista Giustiniani, appeared to consider his own 'observations' of the empyrean.[36] But Henao explicitly rejected such an interpretation, stressing repeatedly that the empyrean was a true corporeal space – a *locus* where heavenly beings actually resided. Thus he forcefully criticized Cardinal Cajetan's understanding of the presence of angels in heaven as 'metaphorical', taking care to note that other Thomists, such as the Dominican Domingo Bañez (1528–1604) and the Mercedarian Francisco Zumel (ca. 1540–1607), agreed with him on this point.[37] In a parallelism we see repeated across the *Empyreologia*, Henao observed something similar in hell: demons existed there '*per praesentiam realem*', not '*metaphoricam*': hence biblical references to hell as a place were to be understood literally.[38]

Whence this insistence? For Henao, the corporeal nature of the empyrean derived directly from its main purpose and rationale. Early in volume 2, dedicated to the relationship between the empyrean and its inhabitants, he cited the late-medieval preacher Vincent Ferrer – who in turn had quoted Thomas Aquinas – to articulate the core principle to which we have already referred: 'The empyrean has been ordered mainly to be the dwelling of the blessed, and more for the sake of men, whose bodies will be glorified and will need a place (*locus*), than for angels, who do not need a place'.[39]

---

36   De Boer W., "A Neapolitan Heaven: The Moral Universe of G.B. Giustiniani", in De Boer – Göttler (eds.), *Religion and the Senses* 363–392.

37   Henao, *Empyreologia* 2:115b: 'non ideo dicendum est cum Caietano, metaphoricam tantum ibi praesentiam eis competere'. Lerner, *Le monde des sphères* 1:377 n. 88 notes that Cajetan considered the existence of the empyrean biblically unfounded, thus parting ways both with Aquinas, of whose work he was a leading interpreter, and with most of his own contemporaries. On Francisco Suárez's views of Cajetan, see Lindemann, *Bilder vom Himmel* 31–39.

38   Henao, *Empyreologia* 2:116b: 'Existentia daemonum in orco per praesentiam realem offert non contemnendum argumentum. Si respondeatur, esse etiam metaphoricam, quatenus daemones sint in poena, ad quam orcus est deputatus. Contra. [...] Praeterquam quod sacrae Scripturae verba de existentia daemonum, et animarum damnatarum in inferno tanquam in loco intelligenda sunt ad litteram, ex regula S. Augustini; siquidem nec absurditas, nec impossibilitas ulla nos cogat confugere ad alias acceptiones metaphoricas'.

39   Henao, *Empyreologia* 2:32a: '*Empyreum principaliter ordinatum, ut sit habitatio beatorum, et hoc magis propter homines, quorum corpora glorificabuntur, quibus locus debetur, quam propter angelos, qui loco non indigent*' (italics in original). Henao referred to Vincent Ferrer's Sermo 4 in Dominica 1 Adventus, which in turn quoted Thomas's *Sententiae* II, d. 2, q. 2, a. 1: see Ferrarius Vincentius, *Opera omnia* [...] *studio ac diligentia fratrum praedicatorum regii Valentini conventus*, Tomus primus (Valencia, typis Iacobi de Bordazar et Artazù: 1693) 21a.

Thus, for Henao, the conception of heaven as a corporeal place was essential for a proper understanding of its true nature. Hence the attention he devoted in his first volume, book IV, to the physical properties of the empyrean – its size, mass, and distance from the earth. In this section Henao drew on multiple authorities, particularly Jesuits, who used biblical exegesis to answer such questions about the cosmos – a premise, of course, which had been strongly contested by Galileo. For our purposes the issue of distance is most relevant, as it had implications for human interactions with heaven. In fact, Henao here spoke of 'the distance between the empyrean and us'. It was a question that had a long speculative tradition behind it. Henao followed his fellow-Jesuit Petrus Thyraeus (1546–1601) in estimating the distance 'between us and the tenth heaven' to be 75,577,155 miles; others, he acknowledged, had suggested greater or shorter distances. And while 'the astronomers' believed spaces beyond the tenth heaven to be outside human understanding, he nevertheless relied on Alfonso Salmerón and others to suggest that the empyrean was farther removed from the firmament (i.e., the tenth heaven) than the latter from earth.[40] The point was clear if paradoxical: these authors sought to quantify the immeasurable, or even unknowable, distance separating humans from the empyrean. Other sources cited by Henao used travel time for this calculation: according to Barthélemy de Chasseneuz (1480–1541), a lead object dropped from the empyrean would take five hundred years to reach earth. Conversely, in Cornelius a Lapide's view, a person ascending from earth needed to travel eight hundred days at a speed of one hundred miles per day to reach the concave surface of the empyrean.[41] Even so, 'the eyes of the blessed shall see the

---

40 Henao, *Empyreologia* 1:300a: 'Ex distantia inter nos et empyreum concipicit [sic] Thyraeus supra huius magnitudinem numerans inter nos et vel caelum decimum milliaria 75577155. Alii plura, alii pauciora computant. Et quidem quamvis astronomis decimae spherae distantiam designantibus adhibeatur fides, superat humani ingenii industriam ulteriora spatia dimetiri. Nihilominus Salmeron tomo 11, tract. 36. pag. 372, inquit, Empyreum fortasse plus distare a firmamento, quam hoc a terra'. Cf. Thyraeus Petrus, *Opera de variis apparitionibus Dei et Christi angelorumque* [...] (Cologne, ex officina Cholin. sumptibus Petri Cholini: 1611) 176 and Salmerón Alfonso, *Commentarii in Evangelicam Historiam et in Acta Apostolorum*, t. 11, *Qui de resurrectione et ascensione Domini inscribitur* (Cologne, apud Antonium Hierat et Ioannem Gymnicum: 1614) 295 ('ut homo integrum iter emetiens vix octo millibus annorum ad firmamentum valeat pertingere, nedum ad empyreum, quod fortasse plus distat a firmamento: idcirco infinita opus fuit virtute, ut in momento perveniret ad empyreum').

41 Henao, *Empyreologia* 1:300a: 'Cassanaeus 12. parte Cathalogi gloriae mundi consideratione 2. memoriae prodit dictum a nonnullis, *quod si massa plumbea a caelo empyreo descenderet, via* [sic, for vix] *in quingentis annis ad terram veniret.* [...] Maius quid tradit Cornelius in cap. 1 Gen., v. 16 et in 3 Baruch, v. 25, necnon in 11 Mathaei, v. 12. Nimirum si quis per octo mille annos ascendens e terra pertransiret quotidie centum milliaria, vix

earth from afar' (*Isaiah* 33:17). Henao borrowed this biblical reference from his fellow-Jesuit Jacob Tierens (Tirinus), who had commented: 'They see the earth and all earthly things from afar, that is, from a distance in the empyrean heaven, and they shall look down upon everything as if it were a single point of dirt and nothingness'.[42] Distance was thus directly connected to visual perception and communication between the two worlds: the Tierens quote complemented Henao's earlier point that the empyrean was invisible from earth. Distance also had implications for other forms of human engagement. Cornelius a Lapide, in his hypothetical scenario of a human 'ascending' to the empyrean heaven, made this explicit: 'Since this was impossible to man, God granted that we may strive to reach it not with the feet of our body, but with the affects of our mind'.[43] He referred, of course, to devotional practice – a topic to which we shall return.

As for Henao, corporeality was important not only to establish the relations between heaven and earth, but also to distinguish the empyrean from the void that existed beyond it. In his second volume, he spent copious ink to settle a curious question which had already worried other Jesuits, including Suárez, Lessius, Martín de Roa (1559–1637), and Caussin.[44] Did Christ, the blessed, and the angels reside in heaven, on top of it (technically, 'on the convex surface of the empyrean'), or even beyond? Several authoritative sources seemed to support these last two options, but Henao rejected them resolutely. Consider, for instance, St. Paul's reference to the 'high priest over the house of God' (*Hebrews* 10:21), which Henao read as a reference to Christ, and contrast it with Christ's assurance that '[i]n my Father's house there are many mansions' (*John* 14:2).[45] The first verse might suggest that Christ dwelt on top of the empyrean, the second, that the blessed resided within it.[46]

---

perventurum ad concavam empyrei superficiem'. For Henao's sources, see Chasseneuz Barthélemy de, *Catalogus gloriae mundi* (Venice, apud haeredes Vincentii Valgrisii: 1576) 238; Lapide Cornelius a, *Commentaria in Pentateuchum Mosis* (Antwerp, apud Martinum Nutium: 1623) 51 (comment on *Genesis* 1:16); idem, *Commentaria in Ieremiam prophetam, Threnos et Baruch* (Antwerp, apud Martinum Nutium: 1621) 373 (on *Baruch* 3:25); idem, *Commentarius in quatuor Evangelia* (Antwerp, apud Martinum Nutium: 1639) 246 (on *Matthew* 11:12).

42   Henao, *Empyreologia* 1:300a. Tirinus Jacobus, *In Sacram Scripturam Commentarius* (Antwerp, apud Petrum Bellerum: 1645) 1:616.

43   Lapide, *Commentarius in quatuor Evangelia* 246: 'Et quia hoc erat homini impossibile, Deus concessit, ut ad illud non pedibus corporis, sed affectibus mentis contenderemus'.

44   Randles, *The Unmaking of the Medieval Christian Cosmos* 138–139, 144, and 145; on Suárez, see Lindemann, *Bilder vom Himmel* 31–39.

45   Henao, *Empyreologia* 2:30b.

46   Randles, *The Unmaking of the Medieval Christian Cosmos* 145–146 indicates that Caussin also discussed this problem, and came to a similar conclusion as Henao.

Before we discuss how the Spanish Jesuit resolved the issue, it is worth asking what prompted his anxious speculation. The reason was, essentially, a concern about hierarchy. This is evident in his remark that God was 'by nature more sublime than the entire orb [of heaven], and exists outside it', as Cyril of Alexandria had said, and yet was 'at the same time intimately present within that heaven'.[47] As for the blessed, Henao spent some time answering the objection that their nobility should place them above the empyrean: how could its roof be higher than the glorified? The Jesuit's response was in line with his description of the empyrean's general rationale. The blessed resided in the empyrean, because it was deliberately designed to serve as their abode: this arrangement derived 'from the right disposition and constitution of the universe'.[48] The placement of the glorified did not signify the superiority of the empyrean's roof over their heads, but was motivated 'by the fact that the status of bodies within it is more fitting for their preservation and for their external functions'.[49] This last point is crucial: the blessed needed the *space* that was the empyrean for their bodies to be reconstituted and function. Elsewhere, Henao explained this idea in a passage that is worth analysing in some detail.

The starting point was that it was 'not believable' that God would have created 'such a beautiful domicile and palace as the empyrean' if he intended his 'celestial courtiers' to live 'on its rooftiles'. Henao here obviously slips into metaphor, yet it remains important to remember his earlier insistence that the *place* he described was altogether real, that is, corporeal, as was the existence of its inhabitants. Hence he asked what prince would relegate his palace servants to such quarters. Perhaps even more important was the implication that, in this scenario, earth itself would offer better prospects than heaven: its 'mountains, valleys, springs, rivers, gardens, flowers, and the manifold beauty of things would delight all senses'. This bounty was evidently lacking if one went above and beyond the empyrean: 'What, in fact, gives bodily pleasure in that vast and horrid imaginary space?' (Henao here used the Aristotelian-scholastic term *spatium imaginarium* to describe the infinite void that could be thought

---

47   Henao, *Empyreologia* 2:33b: 'et ita quidem asseritur, ut etsi Deus *naturali proprietate toto orbe sublimior sit, et extra illum existat,* iuxta S. Cyrillum Alexandrinum lib. de recta fide ad Theodosium, tamen simul etiam sit intime praesens ipsi coelo intrinsecus' (italics in original).

48   Ibidem 37a: 'ex recta universi dispositione seu constitutione'.

49   Ibidem: 'ex eo quod status corporum infra ipsam aptior est horum conservationi et functionibus externis'.

to exist beyond the boundaries of the empyrean.)[50] 'For there all light, charm (*amoenitas*), and beauty would be absent'.[51]

In short, the basic question concerning the abode of the blessed returned to the already mentioned premise: that space needed to be a real place with the amenities capable of delivering the pleasures its inhabitants deserved. This, in turn, required the operation of the bodily senses, Henao went on to say: 'imaginary spaces outside the empyrean are not fit for the actions of the glorified bodies, namely seeing, hearing, smelling, breathing, and exhaling, for in a vacuum all these things cannot naturally exist'. Of course, this natural order could be overruled by means of miracles. But that was an undesirable escape hatch, based on an old principle of scholastic theology, akin to Ockham's razor: it would mean that 'miracles are needlessly multiplied and the laws of nature infringed'. It was simply not credible that God would have created 'a theatre for glorified humans in a space so abhorrent to nature as to be incapable of sustaining their bodies and external functions'.[52] In other words, the spatial design of paradise was congruent with the corporeal operations of its inhabitants, especially those of the bodily senses. These operations did not necessarily include locomotion. While some theologians (he admitted) had made the same argument as for the senses, Henao argued that the blessed had the gift of supernatural agility: this would allow them to move beyond the empyrean without resorting to miracles.[53]

---

50   Leijenhorst, "Jesuit Concepts of *spatium imaginarium*"; in greater detail, Grant E., *Much Ado about Nothing: Theories of Space and Vacuum from the Middle Ages to the Scientific Revolution* (Cambridge: 1981) 116–181.

51   Henao, *Empyreologia* 2:34a: 'Stabiliter quinto, quia incredibile videtur, Deum condidisse tam pulchrum domicilium et palatium, quam est empyreum, ut non intra ipsum, sed quasi supra tegulas habitent coelestes aulici. Quis credat, principem, relicta amplissimae et ornatissimae domus regiae habitatione, suos supra tectum transferre palatinos, ibique eis mansiones designare? Certe melior videtur fore beatorum sors, si concederetur commorari in terra, ubi, ut ponderat Lessius, montes et valles, fontes et flumina, horti et flores, et multiplex rerum pulchritudo sensus omnes oblectaret. Quid enim erit voluptatis corporeae in vasto illo et horrido spatio imaginario? Cum in ipso neque lux neque amoenitas neque pulchritudo ulla erit'.

52   Ibidem: 'Et confirmatur, quia spatia imaginaria extra empyreum non sunt commoda actionibus glorificatorum corporum, videndi scilicet, audiendi, olfaciendi, loquendi, respirandi, et expirandi; nam in vacuo haec omnia fieri naturaliter nequeunt; sine necessitate autem multiplicantur miracula et totius naturae infringuntur leges. Est etiam miraculosa conservatio corporum extra summum coelum, si considerentur penes naturalia. Ergo credibile non est constitutum a Deo theatrum hominum glorificatorum in spatio, quod adeo horretur a natura, utpote ineptum conservationi corporum et externis eorum functionibus'.

53   Ibidem 2:34a–b.

4 The State of Fluidity

A further step in understanding Henao's conception of space involves its consistency, for this determined its suitability as a 'medium' for the actions of its inhabitants. On this point Henao joined a few neo-scholastics in rejecting the Aristotelian argument that the empyrean's interior was solid.[54] Certainly, he believed – as did Lessius, Adam Tanner (1572–1632), Roa, and Raffaele Aversa (1589–1657) – that its bottom, or 'concave surface', was solid. God's house, the second book of *Chronicles* had noted, was 'firm', even 'most firm' (2 *Paralipomenon* 6:39 and 6:33); and the book of *Revelation* (21:12) claimed it had 'a great, tall wall'. The rationale was the following: if the visible *machina* that served as humans' earthly dwelling had a 'solid, firm, and stable pavement', the invisible world constructed as the abode of the immortals was bound to have one as well.[55] Henao further accepted (as did the authors previously cited) that the empyrean's 'convex surface' was also solid. If it thus made sense that this heaven was bounded by a hard shell, and if its concave surface was solid, there was no good reason why its convex counterpart should not be so as well. Moreover, the 'supreme domicile' deserved to be adorned with a roof. But its interior was fluid. Henao did not accept all arguments in favour of this position, such as Tanner's. For him, the decisive reason was again connected with the empyrean's purpose: since God meant it to serve as 'perpetual and stable domicile' in which the blessed, having achieved the 'immortality of their bodies, would dwell corporeally', it would need to be 'suitable for habitation'.[56] In this regard, liquidity – referring here to a fluid, non-solid substance – was superior to 'marble or crystal'.[57] In addition, permeability was another necessary condition for the blessed to be able (again, without recourse to a miraculous intervention) to penetrate the empyrean and move around within it. Likewise, speech was impossible unless the empyrean's inner substance was 'breathable' (*spirabilis*), just as hearing and olfaction required that it be 'divisible' (*scindibilis*) and liquid. This did not mean that solid surfaces or objects were lacking within the liquid that made up most of the empyrean's interior: thus it included a 'solid' surface which, 'like a theatre stage or mountain top', served as the floor

---

54 Randles, *The Unmaking of the Medieval Christian Cosmos* 146–147 dismisses Henao's thinking by observing that, on this point, he merely followed Lessius.

55 Henao, *Empyreologia* 1:307a.

56 Ibidem 308b: 'quia cum empyreum conditum sit a Deo, ut in ipso tanquam in perpetuo et stabili domicilio degant corporaliter beati immortalitatem corporum consequuti, oportuit construi habitationi commodum'.

57 Ibidem: 'Sed nisi liquidum ponatur, non erit commodum magis quam marmor aut crystallus'.

on which the blessed would stand as they adored Christ as their prince; and it also featured thrones on which Christ and his Mother would be seated at that time. Such features were not strictly necessary for these functions to occur, 'but they contribute to the greater beauty of the celestial palace and the display of greater majesty'.[58] Henao went on to answer several objections, but time and again he defended his position based on the need for the empyrean to serve its purpose as the proper abode of the blessed, whose 'actions' (including speech, hearing, and olfaction) should occur 'conveniently' and if possible without miraculous shortcuts.[59]

5   Space, Time, Perception

Henao thus created a framework and stage for the actions of the blessed well before analysing the working of the senses at the end of volume 2. To this we now turn. An important qualification is in order here. Henao's discussion excluded two of the canonical five senses: 'the actions of the glorified bodies', he pointed out in an already quoted remark, included 'seeing, hearing, smelling, breathing, and exhaling'. Conspicuously absent are taste and touch. Henao explained this exclusion towards the end of his book, in introducing the chapter on taste: taste and touch did not require an 'external medium' to operate. Taste was internal to the body, and touch was, literally, immediate. Strictly speaking, then, these senses fell outside the purview of his study, which was focused on the senses in the empyrean only to the extent that the latter induced these actions 'as a corporeal medium'.[60] (For the sake of completeness, he included chapters on taste and touch anyway, but kept them brief.) This conception of heaven was, in fact, the premise of his entire discussion of sensation. Prefacing his discussion of vision, Henao reminded his readers that, precisely because the empyrean was itself a 'corporeal space', it led directly (*immediate*) to the external actions of the senses, albeit mediated by internal mechanisms.[61] This was of course consistent with his entire conception of the empyrean.

---

58   Ibidem 309a: 'Praeter pavimentum theatri erunt solidi aliqui throni pro Christo saltem et eius sanctissima genitrice [...]. Neque hi throni aut illud pavimentum necessaria erunt, ut beati pedibus insistant [...]: sed conducent ad maiorem pulchritudinem regiae caelestis et ad ostentationem maioris maiestatis'.

59   Ibidem 309a–310b.

60   Ibidem 2:283a: 'Ad eius actus non opus est medio externo, uti neque ad actus tactus. Ideoque tractatio de gustu non pertinet ex iure stricto ad nos, qui eatenus agimus de actibus externis incolarum empyrei, quatenus hoc ut medium corporeum conducit ad illos'.

61   Ibidem 216: 'De externis [actionibus], inquam, ad quas immediate conducit empyreum, qua est locus corporeus, non sic, sed mediate ad internas materiales, ideoque de illis potiori iure et prius est agendum'.

Thus Henao's discussion of space and distance is largely confined to vision, hearing, and smell. He introduced vision by examining its objects throughout the empyrean. These began with Christ – the most perfect object of perception – followed by the Virgin Mary, then the angels, and so on down the hierarchy, including the four elements. The Jesuit's extensive discussion of one specific question may be useful to gauge his understanding of vision: could the glorified in heaven see the damned suffering in hell?[62] The question had a long history. Henao began by citing Peter Auriol (ca. 1280–1322), who had answered in the affirmative. Yet, he did not want to take Auriol's word for it. A review of multiple prior authorities (including biblical verses and church fathers such as Augustine) seemed to confirm this kind of vision, but not that it was corporeal, as Auriol had assumed. Augustine spoke of intellectual vision, and others appeared to do so as well. Mental, spiritual, or intellectual vision did not pose difficulties or questions concerning the space and distance to be traversed. Henao allowed that this type of vision was possible, but he was not satisfied with this explanation. He laid out several reasons as to why the corporeal vision of hell should also be possible for the blessed in paradise. First, the blessed could view the damned by supernatural means – for instance, 'with their bodies elevated to produce species in their glorified eyes', or 'with divinely infused species'.[63] Second, several authorities attested that Christ was capable of seeing the damned in hell. It made sense, then, that the blessed were, too. For other reasons, as well, the spectacle of the damned in agony should be a pleasurable experience for the blessed (*'beatis erit delectabile'*), corporeally as much as spiritually.[64] Third, some authorities, albeit not all, allowed that the blessed could move 'naturally' from the empyrean into hell and observe the damned at close range. Thus, St. Antoninus, in his *Summa*, had denied the possibility of long-distance vision, but noted that the blessed 'will be able *ad placitum* to descend corporeally from heaven'. John Major, in his commentary on Thomas's *Summa*, had apparently allowed both options, given that the senses of the blessed were 'well disposed' and that 'they can move and transform themselves at will, either in steps or instantaneously'.[65] And Henao spent

---

62   The entire discussion can be found ibidem 265a–270b.

63   Ibidem 266b: 'Et censeo primo, a quovis beato ex sua sede empyrea videri posse supernaturaliter orci incolas, vel elevatis horum corporibus ad producendas species in glorificatis oculis, vel infusis speciebus divinitus, vel supplente Deo concursum obiectivum, praestandum alias ab obiectis'. See on the species in meditative practice, Dupré, "The Return of the Species".

64   Henao, *Empyreologia* 2:266b: '[...] et aliunde beatis erit delectabile intueri corporaliter damnatorum poenas, haud secus, ac est delectabile intueri mentaliter'.

65   Ibidem: 'Ita S. Antoninus 3. p. summae tit. 30. c. et §4, *videbunt* (inquit) *beati et oculo corporali poenam damnatorum non quidem in coelo existentes propter nimiam distantiam, sed*

several more pages discussing the possibilities and obstacles for natural vision to be capable of reaching from heaven into hell.

It was thus critical for Henao that this kind of visual perception – one that crossed cosmic boundaries – be corporeal. It confirmed the close link and consonance between the cosmos as a corporeal space and the resurrection of human bodies after the Last Judgement, even if it posed difficult questions as to how perception worked in the otherworldly environment. Was long-range vision possible there? Did the blessed have locomotion that allowed them to leave the empyrean and cross into hell? Regardless of the answers, Henao's questions underscore his adherence to the moral foundation of medieval cosmology: sensory experience in the afterlife served the purposes of punishment and recompense. Hence the stark rationale for the blessed's ability to see the suffering in hell: it intensified their exclusive enjoyment of the empyrean delights and thus enhanced their reward.

Henao similarly examined speech and hearing as embodied phenomena, excluding internal or spiritual discourse from his discussion. Speaking, song, and hearing were possible because the empyrean's interior was a 'fitting medium'. The ability of the blessed to engage in all three was (as with vision) connected to the properties of Christ: the gospels testified that Christ's glorified body spoke even before his ascension. And afterwards, he was able to address Saul, on his way to Damascus, with corporeal speech (*Acts* 9); here Henao assumed that Christ spoke from heaven, not allowing the possibility that he was in two places at once. In other words, his bodily produced words travelled from heaven to earth. During the Last Judgement, moreover, Christ rendered his final verdicts in corporeal speech, necessitating that the souls could hear him.[66]

But Henao also offered more mundane reasons for why it made sense for the blessed to have embodied speech and hearing. The first argument was physical. The glorified bodies had movement; hence, so did their tongues (which were in fact 'flexible') as they articulated sounds and modulated their speech with letters and syllables. The second was social. The blessed formed 'a human society and polity', which required communication by means of sounds signifying and expressing 'interior concepts'. The third argument was a tautology we have already encountered. Since speech was a form of perfection that distinguishes

---

poterunt ad placitum corporaliter de coelo descendere' (italics in original). 'Indicat Maior in 4. distinct. 50. quaest. 1. vers. *Ad secundam dubitationem*, dicens, beatos posse videre poenas damnatorum, quia habebunt oculos corporis et mentis optime dispositos; et *possunt movere vel mutare se quolibet successive vel instantanee*' (italics in original).

66   Ibidem 273a.

humans from wild animals, it was inconceivable that it would not return, or be without even greater excellence, in the blessed's permanent abode. The fourth offered a similar comparison. Just as the Church Militant praised God both orally and mentally, so too would the Church Triumphant.[67] And so forth.

Henao here did not dwell explicitly on the spatial aspects of speech and hearing: for instance, he did not ask how sound travels. He simply assumed that speech occurred within the spatial structure and the fluid medium that constituted the interior of the empyrean. How else could one imagine it as the essential form of communication in a 'human society and polity', except as occurring within a palace, castle, or city – to use Henao's own architectural terminology? Nor did he ask whether human speech was capable of travelling to hell or elsewhere, though the example of Christ speaking to Saul suggested that it could. Instead, his discussion was focused on two different problems. One was social, the other moral. What language did the blessed speak? Did heavenly song and music raise moral concerns, perhaps even associations with pagan and Muslim dreams and practices?

In discussing smell, however, Henao spoke more explicitly about the mechanism and extent of its diffusion.[68] First he established the considerable theological consensus that the bodies of the blessed exuded the sweetest odors. If mortal bodies smelled, why not immortal ones as well? Obviously, eschatological distinctions applied: Henao spent a paragraph detailing the stench of hell, including its spatial reach. Vincent Ferrer, in a sermon on the General Resurrection delivered at Caen (Normandy), had explained that the damned were so fetid that, if one of their bodies were placed in Caen, its smell would carry all the way to Paris. The point was that the empyrean would, in perfect contrast, abound in the purest smells, yet without evaporation or exhalation from the body, as several authorities had pointed out (for, among other reasons, the body no longer needed to cool off). The empyrean's fluid nature allowed odours to spread as easily as they did on earth and through air. They moved thanks to the same medium as did sound. If there were smells, there was olfaction, which occurred either directly (*immediate*) or mediated by species. Hence the empyrean was not itself odoriferous; it was merely a vehicle of smell. Finally, Henao took care to note, almost in passing, that there was no 'indecency or inappropriateness' in this olfactory paradise. It was an isolated moral reference in Henao's self-styled "scientific" work, a point to which we shall return.

---

67   Ibidem 273b.
68   Ibidem 281a–282b.

6   Temporality

In sum, this sensory paradise rested not only on a corporeal concept of the hereafter, but also on a spatial construct that permitted the movement and actions of bodies and sensory species. What about time?

The *Empyreologia* engaged with temporality on multiple levels. First, Henao considered the empyrean's place within the history of the universe, particularly its creation. He took issue with theologians, like Agostino Steuco (1496/7–1549) and Claude de Sainctes (1525–91), who assumed its existence before the creation of the physical world. De Sainctes had described the empyrean as 'uncreated light springing forth from eternity [*a diurnitate*], the source and glory of our beatitude'.[69] Henao rejected this viewpoint, especially because nothing besides God was uncreated and eternal. In fact, God created the empyrean after the visible world, which according to Genesis had occurred at the beginning of time – 'In principio creavit Deus caelum et terram' (*Genesis* 1:1) – before he did anything else.[70] Even the creation of light (*Genesis* 1:3: 'Fiat lux') did not refer to the empyrean, Henao noted elsewhere: the latter realm had had its own light, different from the sun, moon, and stars, from the time of its own creation.[71]

The Jesuit also dealt repeatedly with questions connected to the unfolding story of human history and redemption. Had Christ left the empyrean occasionally before the Last Judgement? Had he, as reported by some, secretly ascended to heaven and there constructed the 'city of the blessed' as a twelve-year-old? Henao rejected this view.[72] Had he gone there after his resurrection, but still before his 'solemn' ascension? Again, the answer was negative, at least as far as Christ's humanity was concerned. It was unknown (as Henao agreed with Aquinas) where he dwelt in that 'intermediate time', when not appearing to Mary, his disciples, or others, but the Jesuit found the conjecture that he was in the earthly paradise plausible.[73] In contrast, he peremptorily declared as 'Catholic truth' that no one – either in soul or in body and soul – had preceded Christ as the 'first inhabitant of the empyrean'. This was implied, as the Jesuit

---

69   Ibidem 1:51: according to De Sainctes, 'Quid vero sit (empyreum caelum) secundum scripturas et creaturarum ordinem atque contemplationem, probabilius respondetur, non statuendum esse aliquod corpus, aut aliquem locum corporeum, aut aliquid denique creatum, sed lucem increatam a diurnitate emicantem, beatitudinis nostrae et gloriae fontem [...]'.

70   Ibidem 52.

71   Ibidem 222.

72   Ibidem 2:47.

73   Ibidem 52.

Juan Maldonado (1533–1583) had noted, in the scriptural statement that he would prepare his Father's house for his followers (*John* 14:2–3).[74] Henao asked similar, and equally complicated, questions about the Virgin Mary, her soul and her body. When did her soul begin enjoying the beatific vision and arrive in heaven? Amidst contrasting opinions, Henao followed Suárez in thinking that it was right after her death, for her soul, being immaculate, required neither judgement nor purgation. Was her body already there? Henao answered in the affirmative, not only based on authoritative sources, but also due to an exemption the Mother of God deserved from general biblical pronouncements regarding death and resurrection.[75] And the Jesuit proceeded to ask whether similar exemptions existed for other human souls and bodies.[76] This time the answer was yes for souls, but no for bodies. Biblical, patristic, and subsequent theological tradition, Henao noted, had abundantly demonstrated the existence of souls in the empyrean before the general resurrection of bodies.[77] His focus was on a less-explored issue: to demonstrate, that is, in what celestial place they were beatified.[78] He distinguished eight 'classes' of theologians whose opinions varied on this point. Some allowed the presence of the blessed in heaven or 'high spheres', but not in the empyrean. They did not, or not always, enjoy the beatific vision. Others thought that a stay in purgatory was unavoidable, even without suffering pain. Yet others believed that the saints even had to pass through hell. A further group denied altogether that they had access to heaven and the beatific vision before the Last Judgement. Why did this chronology matter? Henao did not ask this question expressly, but it is not hard to guess that he sought to establish the presence in heaven of the Virgin and the other saints – body and/or soul – at the current time. This had obvious implications for devotional practice in the here-and-now.

As for the empyrean itself, Henao was firm that the ultimate heavenly sphere was immobile, hence unchanging with the passage of time. In making this case, he referred once more to the necessary connection between the order of the empyrean and the condition of its inhabitants: 'The status of the blessed is devoid of all change. Hence it is necessary that their domicile resemble the condition of the beatific state in its immobility'. Here he cited Durandus, who had posited the similarity between places (*locos*) and the beings who found themselves in them (*locatos*). Second, as the 'special house of God' the empyrean

---

74   Ibidem 52–53.
75   Ibidem 67–77.
76   Ibidem 133.
77   Ibidem 134–145.
78   Ibidem 134.

should conform to his immanent state of rest rather than the transience of motion. Third, Henao relied once more on the argument of perfection. Since for a body to be released from motion constituted perfection, it was necessary for the empyrean – as a most excellent body naturally and properly located in the 'supreme place' – to be 'altogether free of local motion'. A fourth argument rested on the fundamental distinction between the empyrean and the rest of the universe, including the sidereal spheres. The latter came to a standstill during the Last Judgement, 'as generation and corruption, which are now served by motion, will then be lacking'. If that was the case, it applied all the more to the empyrean, which did 'not serve generation and corruption of sublunar things' in the first place: 'or at least it is not ordained towards this end'.[79]

Nevertheless, Henao's empyrean was by no means static. In fact, the very notion of 'external actions' – of bodily movement and the operations of the senses – suggested temporality. Henao did not make this observation explicitly, but it is implied in questions such as the following. If Christ was the highest object of vision, does this mean that the blessed watched him continuously, or not? Could they take their eyes off him, if only briefly? What happened if they moved somewhere else, even to hell?[80] Likewise, did the blessed hear continuously? And if the use of the tongue in speech and song assumed temporal progression, did the heavenly choirs ever have a break?[81]

While pedestrian questions like these could be seen to stem from the idle curiosity of mortals incapable of grasping the inscrutable condition of the hereafter, Henao treated the subject of temporality also at a more fundamental level. Speaking of the highest object of corporeal vision – Christ's humanity – he argued that its 'ultimate perfection' consisted in its 'exercise', as was also the case for the 'actions of the other external forces'. In other words, a faculty was not fulfilled unless it was deployed in action. Second, when glorified vision was 'complete' (*integer*) and 'fulfilled' (*perfectus*), it must necessarily have its 'functions' and 'pleasures'. Indeed, he noted, the empyrean contained 'objects on

---

79   Ibidem 1:243b: 'Prima, beatorum status est liber ab omni mutatione. Ergo oportet ut eorum domicilium sapiat status beatifici conditionem in immobilitate. [...] Secunda, empyreum est speciale Dei domicilium. Ergo magis assimilabitur Deo in actu secundo immanente quietis, quam in transeunte motus. [...] Tertia, corpus aliquod motu absolvi, est magna perfectio. Ergo cum empyreum sit corpus adeo excellens occupetque supremum locum in mundo, tanquam sibi naturalem et proprium, erit omnino liberum a motu locali. Quarta, in die extremi iudicii cessabit motus caeli syderei, quia tunc deficiet omnis generatio et corruptio, quibus nunc deservit motus ille. Sed empyreum non deservit generationi et corruptioni rerum sublunarium, aut saltem hunc in finem non est conditum. Ergo semper immotum stat'.

80   Ibidem 2:247b–251a.

81   Ibidem 279b–280b.

which [glorified vision] can focus conveniently and with delight'. What point would there be for such objects to exist, as Augustine had suggested, unless they served the corporeal eyes? Moreover, the empyrean's interior, where the blessed resided, had the requisite properties – lucidity and transparency – for this visual perception to be possible.[82] This environment also allowed for the mutual observation of the glorified, without which 'the heavenly court would be a republic of the blind'. That position – held by Henao's fellow Jesuit Juan de Salas (1553–1612) – was clearly unthinkable for Henao: 'What is the value of having one's visual faculty unimpaired if it is never exercised in the see of the blessed?' A third argument was that humans were glorified not only in the soul but also in the body and the senses. The glorification of the latter consisted especially in the 'most pure and chaste pleasures' that would result from 'the decent and seemly exercise of the senses'. Fourth, it was only fair that the senses, 'which in this life are the soul's associates in facing the passions and are the instrument of virtue and merit, in the other life join the soul in its glory and pleasures, and are not cheated out of their reward and remuneration'. For this to be the case, though, it was 'necessary that the senses not remain entirely idle, but rather engage in the most joyous and decent operations'.[83] Fifth, since God punished the senses of the damned harshly, he should all the more reward those of the blessed. And finally, Henao endorsed Thomas's point that without sensation the blessed would be in a dreamlike state rather than awake following the resurrection of the body.

Thus, even after the cessation of time, Henao envisioned the blessed to be perennially engaged in bodily and sensory operations, conceived as *interactions*

---

82 Ibidem 244a: '[...] oportet eius potentiae [*scil.* visus] usum generatim stabilire rationibus, quae etiam deservient ad externarum aliarum potentiarum actus comprobandos. Prima itaque ratio sit, exercitium visus glorificati est eius ultima perfectio, ad quam suapte natura ordinatur: ergo visui glorificato denegandum non est. Secunda, visus glorificatus integer erit et perfectus: ergo habebit in empyreo suas functiones et oblectamenta; nam nec deerunt obiecta, circa quae convenienter et delectabiliter versari possit. [...]'.

83 Ibidem 244b: '[...] P. Salas tom. 1. in I.2 tract. 1, disp. et sect. 14 n. 110 ait, nihil cogere ad affirmandum mutuum conspectum glorificatorum hominum, si extituri essent supra empyrei convexam superficiem. Sed me cogit ea ratio; quod alioqui curia coelestis esset quasi caecorum respublica. Quid enim interesset habere illaesam facultatem visivam, si eam nunquam exercerent in beatis sedibus? [...] Tertia ratio, [...] corporis autem et sensuum glorificatio eo praecipue dirigi videtur, ut ex decenti honestoque sensuum exercitio sequantur purissimae castissimaeque oblectationes. Quarta, par est, ut sensus, qui in hac vita societatem cum animo in passionibus et tribulationibus subeunt, et qui instrumentum sunt virtutis ac meriti, consortes sint animi quoad gloriam et oblectationes in altera vita, praemioque suo et remuneratione non fraudentur. Ad id autem opus est, ne sensus maneant omnino otiosi, sed ut potius prodeant in operationes iucundissimas ac decentissimas'.

with the bodies, objects, and spatial environment of the empyrean, hell, and the other spaces of a post-Judgement cosmos. The idea of actions unfolding in a dimension of suspended time, of movement in an immobile place, was a conundrum the learned Jesuit chose not to disentangle.

7   A Christian Sparta: Meditation, Prefiguration, and the Moral Universe

From an empirical perspective Henao's highest heaven no doubt deserves Galileo's ironic qualification of a castle in the air. In fact, the Jesuit's empyreology proposed something quite close to it, although his venture obviously differed drastically in intent and context. Henao's hereafter was effectively designed to serve the purposes of a narrative imagination: it offered both a rationalization and a template for the exploration of an idealized heavenly space and the things that happened there in concrete, embodied ways. Henao did not dwell on the uses his readers or the devout could make of his construct. As noted earlier, his was largely an intellectual project. But he recognized that the contemplation of the empyrean had an essential moral and spiritual objective. This was of course related to the rationale underlying its design (and that of the entire otherworldly universe): its chronotope made sense only as a framework for the ultimate moral drama and in the function of its role as a system of punishment and reward. It thus mirrored, at least obliquely, the conditions of this-worldly human existence. In his book the Jesuit referred only occasionally to this vital premise. Nevertheless, the speculative universe he constructed was meant to engage the devotional imagination of his contemporaries. The subtitle of his work described it as 'most necessary for philosophers, scholastic and mystical theologians, biblical scholars, and preachers of God's Word'. Writing at a time of thriving practices of meditation and mysticism, Henao no doubt aimed to set a standard of orthodoxy for spiritual, literary, and artistic forms of representation prone to sliding into the realm of uncontrolled speculation or sensuality. It is no surprise that he dedicated the first volume to his friend Sancho de Dóriga y Valdés, Inquisitor of Granada, who had read the book in draft form, and the second to the well-connected humanist and bibliophile Lorenzo Ramírez de Prado (1583–1658), who among other significant offices was a familiar of the Holy Office and signed off as approver on many print publications.[84]

---

84   Ibidem 1:dedication, and 2:dedication. On Dóriga y Valdés, see the entry in Suárez C., *Escritores y artistas asturianos: indice bio-bibliografico*, 7 vols. (Madrid: 1936–1959), https:// españolito.es/index.php/encyclopedia/doriga-y-valdes-sancho/ (accessed 14.05.2024).

Nor is it hard to envision spiritual uses of Henao's work, in which the movements and sensations of the blessed modelled participatory experiences rooted in some form of bodily or imaginative sensory engagement. Direct evidence of this is offered by a set of lectures, based on Henao's book, and delivered in Naples just two years after its publication by the Theatine Giovan Battista Giustiniani.[85] Here Giustiniani referred twice to artistic and ritual representations of paradise. The first was a critical assessment of the famous Florentine garden of Pratolino, designed (according to Francesco de' Vieri) to evoke the joys of paradise. It was, as recent scholarship on Renaissance gardens has abundantly shown, only one example of many.[86] Giustiniani's second reference was even more telling: it spoke of coeval Neapolitan celebrations of the Blessed Gaetano da Thiene, co-founder of the Theatine order, which had turned the city itself into the scene of a ritual prefiguration of paradise. Images of Gaetano, the Virgin and Child, and other saints, mechanical contraptions suggesting the heavenly spheres, music, flowers, and lights – all provided the faithful processing through the city with the sensory stimuli that might conjure up the experience, however temporary, of joining the blessed in heaven. The focus here was on vision, hearing, and smell. These were, as we have seen, the senses which Henao's analysis had privileged because they involved mediated perception, largely bypassing those based on immediate transmission, touch and taste. Giustiniani, too, downplayed the latter, but he did so especially on moral grounds: they were too strongly associated with the sins of the flesh.

These Neapolitan celebrations were hardly alone in their anticipatory and participatory evocation of the empyrean. Multi-media representations in streets, squares, and churches, drawing on a long history in late-medieval religion, became quintessential components of Baroque religiosity, and they were replete with references to the heavenly *patria*.[87] Henao's book, and Giustiniani's reading of it, offer an illuminating example of how theological speculation on the chronotope of paradise could help project heavenly scenes

On Ramírez de Prado, see Solís de los Santos J., "Ramírez de Prado, Lorenzo", in *Diccionario biográfico español*, https://dbe.rah.es/biografias/34250/lorenzo-ramirez-de-prado (accessed 24.04.2024); Entrambasaguas J. de, *Una familia de ingenios: Los Ramírez de Prado* (Madrid: 1943) 241–257; Mañas Núñez M., "Aproximación al Pentecontarchos de Lorenzo Ramírez de Prado: Gramática, retórica y filosofía", *Studia Philologica Valentina* 10.7 (2007) 379–409.

85   See De Boer, "A Neapolitan Heaven".

86   Fagiolo M., *Lo specchio del paradiso: il giardino e il sacro dall'Antico all'Ottocento* (Cinisello Balsamo: 1998).

87   For some examples, see Davidson C. (ed.), *The Iconography of Heaven* (Kalamazoo, MI: 1994); Filippi D.V., "Sonic Afterworld: Mapping the Soundscape of Heaven and Hell in Early Modern Cities", in Gibson K. – Biddle I. (eds.), *Cultural Histories of Noise, Sound and Listening in Europe, 1300–1918* (New York, NY: 2016) 186–204.

onto the ritual spaces and times of earthly communities, competing with other such configurations (like those of a Golden Age or Land of Cockaigne) created by gardens and public festivities. Likewise, they suggest how neo-scholastic theories of sense perception may have informed the ways in which artistic and ritual communication was conceived, understood, and promoted. These practices also raise vital questions about the meditative exercises of this period.[88] To what extent did they reflect the spatio-temporal configuration of heaven which a learned theologian like Henao made into a pillar of his *Empyreologia*? Did their narratives reflect the sensory operations he deduced from the nature of resurrected bodies and their heavenly abode? To what extent were these operations mirrored in the experiences of the practitioners of contemplation? Henao clearly assumed such connections, as references to Teresa of Avila and Marina de Escobar suggest; and he undoubtedly intended to offer an authoritative roadmap.[89] But it remains for future scholarship to determine the relationship between learned speculation about heaven's chronotope and the lived experiences of mystics.

Bibliography

Armogathe J.R., *La nature du monde: Science nouvelle et exégèse au XVIIe siècle* (Paris: 2007).

Bakhtin M.M., "Forms of Time and of the Chronotope in the Novel", in idem, *The Dialogic Imagination*, ed. M. Holquist, trans. C. Emerson – M. Holquist (Austin, TX: 1981) 84–258.

Baroja J.C., *Las formas complejas de la vida religiosa (Religión, Sociedad y carácter en la España de los siglos XVI y XVII)* (Madrid: 1978).

Bernard P., "Henao (Gabriel de)", *Dictionnaire de théologie catholique*, vol. 6/2 (Paris: 1925), 2147–2148.

Boersma H., *Seeing God: The Beatific Tradition in Christian Thought* (Grand Rapids, MI: 2018).

Bynum C.W., *The Resurrection of the Body in Western Christianity, 200–1336* (New York, NY: 1995).

Carolino L.M., "Astronomy, Cosmology and Jesuit Discipline, 1540–1758", in Županov I.G. (ed.), *The Oxford Handbook of the Jesuits* (Oxford – New York, NY: 2019) 670–707.

---

88   For an example, see chapter 8 in this volume.
89   Henao, *Empyreologia* 1:45 (where Henao refers both to Teresa of Avila and Marina de Escobar, and the *Vida* of the latter written by the Jesuit Luis de la Puente).

Caussin Nicholas, *Domus Dei, in qua de mirabilibus coeli totaque astrologia et vita coelesti luculenter et copiose disseritur* (Paris, sumptibus Ioannis du Bray: 1650).

Chasseneuz Barthélemy de, *Catalogus gloriae mundi* (Venice, apud haeredes Vincentii Valgrisii: 1576).

Conte S. (ed.), *Nicolas Caussin: Rhétorique et spiritualité à l'époque de Louis XIII. Actes du colloque de Troyes (16–17 septembre 2004)* (Berlin: 2007).

Cousinié F., *Gloriae: Figurabilité du divin, esthétique de la lumière et dématérialisation de l'œuvre d'art à l'âge baroque* (Rennes: 2018).

Davidson C. (ed.), *The Iconography of Heaven* (Kalamazoo, MI: 1994).

De Boer W., "A Neapolitan Heaven: The Moral Universe of G.B. Giustiniani", in De Boer W. – Göttler C. (eds.), *Religion and the Senses in Early Modern Europe*, Intersections 26 (Leiden – Boston, MA: 2013) 363–392.

Delumeau J., *Histoire du paradis*, 3 vols. (Paris: 1992–2000).

Dinis A., *A Jesuit against Galileo? The Strange Case of Giovanni Battista Riccioli's Cosmology* (Braga: 2017).

Dupré S., "The Return of the Species: Jesuit Responses to Kepler's New Theory of Images", in De Boer W. – Göttler C. (eds.), *Religion and the Senses in Early Modern Europe* (Leiden – Boston, MA: 2013) 473–488.

Emerson J.S. – Feiss H. (eds.), *Imagining Heaven in the Middle Ages: A Book of Essays* (New York, NY: 2000).

Entrambasaguas J. de, *Una familia de ingenios: los Ramírez de Prado* (Madrid: 1943) 241–257.

Fagiolo M., *Lo specchio del paradiso: il giardino e il sacro dall'Antico all'Ottocento* (Cinisello Balsamo: 1998).

Feingold M. (ed.), *Jesuit Science and the Republic of Letters* (Cambridge, MA – London: 2003).

Feldhay R., "Religion", in Park K. – Daston L. (eds.), *Early Modern Science*, The Cambridge History of Science 3 (Cambridge: 2006) 727–755.

Filippi D.V., "Sonic Afterworld: Mapping the Soundscape of Heaven and Hell in Early Modern Cities", in Gibson K. – Biddle I. (eds.), *Cultural Histories of Noise, Sound and Listening in Europe, 1300–1918* (New York, NY: 2016) 186–204.

Finocchiaro M.A., *Retrying Galileo, 1633–1922* (Berkeley, CA: 2005).

Galilei Galileo, *Dialogue Concerning the Two Chief World Systems*, trans. S. Drake, intro. A. Einstein (Berkeley, CA – Los Angeles, CA: 1967).

Galilei Galileo, *Dialogo sopra i due massimi sistemi del mondo, Tolemaico e Copernicano*, critical ed. and comm. by O. Bonomi – M. Helbing (Padua: 1998).

Galilei Galileo, *Il saggiatore*, ed. and comm. O. Bonomi – M. Helbing (Rome: 2005).

Gill M.J., *Angels and the Order of Heaven in Medieval and Renaissance Italy* (New York, NY: 2014).

Gilson É., "À la recherche de l'Empyrée", *Revue des études italiennes* 11 (1965) 147–161.

Graney C.M., *Setting Aside All Authority: Giovanni Battista Riccioli and the Science against Copernicus in the Age of Galileo* (Notre Dame, IN: 2015).

Grant E., *Much Ado about Nothing: Theories of Space and Vacuum from the Middle Ages to the Scientific Revolution* (Cambridge: 1981).

Grant E., "The Partial Transformation of Medieval Cosmology by the Jesuits in the Sixteenth and Seventeenth Centuries", in Feingold, M. (ed.), *Jesuit Science and the Republic of Letters* (Cambridge, MA – London: 2003) 127–156.

Grant E., *Planets, Stars, Orbs: The Medieval Cosmos, 1200–1687* (Cambridge: 2009).

Hart C. – Stevenson K.G., *Heaven and the Flesh: Imagery of Desire from the Renaissance to the Rococo* (Cambridge: 1995).

Hecht C., *Die Glorie: Begriff, Thema, Bildelement in der europäischen Sakralkunst vom Mittelalter bis zum Ausgang der Barock* (Regensburg: 2003).

Heinzmann R., *Die Unsterblichkeit der Seele und die Auferstehung des Leibes: Eine problemgeschichtliche Untersuchung der frühscholastischen Sentenzen- und Summenliteratur von Anselm von Laon bis Wilhelm von Auxerre* (Munster: 1965).

Henao Gabriel de, *Empyreologia, seu Philosophia Christiana de Empyreo Coelo*, 2 vols. (Lyon, sumptibus Philippi Borde, Laurentii Arnaud, et Claudii Rigaud: 1652).

Kapp V., "Skandalöse Orthodoxie bei Nicolas Caussin", in Titzmann M. – Laufhütte H. (eds.), *Heterodoxie in der Frühen Neuzeit* (Tübingen: 2006) 191–200.

Lambert E., *Singing the Resurrection: Body, Community and Belief in Reformation Europe* (New York, NY: 2018).

Lapide Cornelius a, *Commentaria in Ieremiam prophetam, Threnos et Baruch* (Antwerp, apud Martinum Nutium: 1621).

Lapide Cornelius a, *Commentaria in Pentateuchum Mosis* (Antwerp, apud Martinum Nutium: 1623).

Lapide Cornelius a, *Commentarius in quatuor Evangelia* (Antwerp, apud Martinum Nutium: 1639).

Leijenhorst C., "Jesuit Concepts of *spatium imaginarium* and Thomas Hobbes's Doctrine of Space", *Early Science and Medicine* 1.3 (1996) 355–380.

Lerner M.-P., *Le monde des sphères*, 2 vols. (Paris: 1996–1997).

Lindemann B.W., *Bilder vom Himmel: Studien zur Deckenmalerei des 17. und 18. Jahrhunderts* (Worms am Rhein: 1994) 28–39.

Macdonald R. – Murphy E.K.M. – Swann E.L. (eds.), *Sensing the Sacred in Medieval and Early Modern Culture* (London – New York, NY: 2018).

Mañas Núñez M., "Aproximación al Pentecontarchos de Lorenzo Ramírez de Prado: Gramática, retórica y filosofia", *Studia Philologica Valentina* 10.7 (2007) 379–409.

Martínez Arancón A., *Geografía de la eternidad* (Madrid: 1987).

Maurach G., *Coelum empyreum: Versuch einer Begriffsgeschichte*, Texte und Abhandlungen zur Geschichte der Exacten Wissenschaften (Wiesbaden: 1968).

McDannell C. – Lang B., *Heaven: A History* (New Haven, CT – London: 1988).

McGrath A., *A Brief History of Heaven* (Malden, MA: 2003).

Mehl L., "La fiction théologique du ciel empyrée, de Luther à Descartes", *Revue des sciences religieuses* 92.2 (2017) 193–210.

Mehl L., *Descartes et la fabrique du monde: Le problème cosmologique de Copernic à Descartes* (Paris: 2019).

La morale pratique des Jésuites representée en plusieurs histoires arrivées dans toutes les parties du monde (Cologne, Gervinus Quentel: 1669).

Muessig C. – Putter A. (eds.), *Envisaging Heaven in the Middle Ages* (London – New York, NY: 2007).

Nardi B., "La dottrina dell'Empireo nella sua genesi storica e nel pensiero dantesco", in idem, *Saggi di filosofia dantesca* (2nd ed., Florence: 1967) 167–214.

Pereda F., "*Pictura est Lingua Angelorum*: Fray Juan Ricci, una teoría teológica del arte", in Marías F. – Pereda F. (eds.), *Fray Juan Ricci: Tratado de la Pintura Sabia*, 2 vols. (Toledo: 2002), vol. 1, 43–87.

Piqué B., "Pascal, Caussin et l'astronomie moralisée: Note sur une citation dans les *Pensées*", *Dix-septième siècle* 290.1 (2021) 117–123.

Rabin S.J., "Early Modern Jesuit Science: A Historiographical Essay", *Journal of Jesuit Studies* 1 (2014) 88–104.

Randles W.G.L., *The Unmaking of the Medieval Christian Cosmos, 1500–1760: From Solid Heavens to Boundless Æther* (Aldershot, Hants. – Brookville, VT: 1999).

Riccioli Giovanni Battista, *Almagestum novum. Pars posterior tomi primi* (Bologna, ex typographia haeredis Victorii Benatii: 1651).

Russell J.B., *A History of Heaven: The Singing Silence* (Princeton, NJ: 1997).

Salmerón Alfonso, *Commentarii in Evangelicam Historiam et in Acta Apostolorum*, t. 11, *Qui de resurrectione et ascensione Domini inscribitur* (Cologne, apud Antonium Hierat et Ioannem Gymnicum: 1614).

Sauter M.J., *The Spatial Reformation: Euclid between Man, Cosmos, and God* (Philadelphia, PA: 2019).

Schmolinsky S., "The Production of Future: Chronotope and Agency in the Middle Ages", in *Space/Time Practices and the Production of Space and Time*, issue 145 of *Historical Social Research / Historische Sozialforschung* 38.3 (2013) 93–104.

Smith J.E.H., "Spirit as Intermediary in Post-Cartesian Natural Philosophy", in Göttler C. – Neuber W. (eds.), *Spirits Unseen: The Representation of Subtle Bodies in Early-Modern European Culture*, Intersections 9 (Leiden – Boston: 2007) 269–291.

Tenenti A., *Il senso della morte e l'amore della vita* (Turin: 1957).

Thyraeus Petrus, *Opera de variis apparitionibus Dei et Christi angelorumque* [...] (Cologne, ex officina Cholin. sumptibus Petri Cholini: 1611).

Tirinus Jacobus, *In Sacram Scripturam Commentarius* (Antwerp, apud Petrum Bellerum: 1645).

Weber H.J., *Die Lehre von der Auferstehung der Toten in den Haupttraktaten der scholastischen Theologie von Alexander von Hales zu Duns Skotus* (Freiburg – Basel – Vienna: 1973).

Wootton D., "Jesuits and the New Astronomy", in idem, *Galileo: Watcher of the Skies* (New Haven, CT: 2010) 111–124.

Zagoury D., "Vasari's Castle in the Air", *Journal of the Warburg and Courtauld Institutes* 81 (2018) 249–267.

CHAPTER 4

Kepler's *Somnium* as Purgatorial Journey

Aviva Rothman

Abstract

In place of the motionless earth at the centre of the hierarchically ordered Ptolemaic system, the Copernican system posited a moving, de-centred earth in a vastly larger (some argued infinite) cosmos. This raised questions both about the old hierarchy and traditional Christian conceptions of heaven and hell, and about the earth's uniqueness and the privileged status of its inhabitants. In answer to these questions, Johannes Kepler, like some of his contemporaries, reimagined Eden as an epistemological state, rather than simply a physical space. Kepler used his *Somnium* to posit the moon as a metaphorical purgatory, knowledge of which enabled astronomers to reach divine truth on and about the earth. Kepler likewise argued that it was not stability or centrality of position but rather reasoned, moving perspective that signalled the privileged status of the earth, and enabled its inhabitants to recognize their divine likeness.

Keywords

Kepler – *Somnium* – purgatory – cosmology – heliocentrism

In his 1615 letter *On the Pythagorean and Copernican Opinion about the Mobility of the Earth, and the Stability of the Sun*, Carmelite Father Paolo Antonio Foscarini considered, as just one of the many challenges to traditional theology posed by the heliocentric system, the respective places of heaven and hell.[1] Theologians always placed hell in the centre of the world, Foscarini noted, and its very name, *inferno*, indicated the necessity of this placement: for what was lowest, in a spherical system, if not the very centre? But, Foscarini argued – giving voice to the anti-Copernican opponents of the new system – 'if the earth moved around the sun, it would necessarily follow that hell, together with the earth, was in heaven, and revolved with the earth around the sun in

---

1   Many thanks to Wietse de Boer and Christine Göttler for organizing this project and for their helpful advice and suggestions, as well as to the other participants and contributors. All translations are by the author, unless stated otherwise.

the third heaven – and nothing could be more monstrous and absurd than this'.[2] Later in the letter, Foscarini – himself a supporter of the Copernican approach – supplied a potential answer to this argument, one that relied on "low" and "high" as relative to the cosmos as a whole, with the earth still at the centre relative to the larger whole.[3]

This argument, among the others offered by Foscarini to support heliocentrism, did not sway the authorities who placed his letter on the Index of Prohibited Books, alongside Copernicus's 1543 *On the Revolutions*, in 1616.[4] But it did indicate that cosmological and eschatological questions often went hand in hand in the seventeenth century, an age where 'new philosophy calls all in doubt'.[5] Jesuit Giovanni Battista Riccioli – a supporter of the Tychonic world system – likewise considered the place of hell in the Copernican world system in one of the 126 arguments for or against the motion of the earth in his 1651 *New Almagest*, though he didn't deem it one of the more serious arguments.[6] While some worried about the place of hell and heaven in a world where the earth was in motion, others simply explored the contours of those realms and ours alongside each other. Thus Galileo both revealed new features of the moon, the sun, and the stars, and also mapped the landscape of Dante's hell and charted its dimensions.[7] John Donne imagined St. Ignatius of Loyola in hell but then ejected him and sent him instead to the moon, as missionary-colonizer.[8] And in *Paradise Lost* Milton described Satan's shield as a moon just like the one Galileo had revealed, 'whose orb, through optic glass the Tuscan artist views [...] rivers or mountains in her spotty globe'.[9] These cosmological and

---

2   Foscarini Paolo Antonio, *Lettera sopra l'opinione de' pittagorici, e del Copernico, della mobilità della terra e stabilità del sole* (Naples, Lazaro Scoriggio: 1615) 17: 'se la Terra si movesse attorno il Sole, bisognarebbe seguirne, che l'Inferno insieme con la Terra fussero nel Cielo, e girasse l'Inferno ancor esso con la Terra intorno il Sole nel terzo Cielo: del che non' puo esser cosa piu monstruosa, e absorda'.

3   For another discussion of the relationship between the new cosmology and the respective places of heaven and hell, see Danielson D., *Paradise Lost and the Cosmological Revolution* (Cambridge: 2014).

4   See Finocchiaro M., *The Galileo Affair: A Documentary History* (Berkeley, CA: 1989) 148–149.

5   Donne John, *An Anatomy of the World: The First Anniversary* (London, Samuel Macham: 1611), line 205.

6   Riccioli Giovanni Battista, *Almagestum Novum* (Bologna, Victor Benatius: 1651).

7   See Peterson M., *Galileo's Muse: Renaissance Mathematics and the Arts* (Cambridge, MA: 2011) and Bredekamp H., *Galileo's Thinking Hand: Mannerism, Anti-Mannerism and the Virtue of Drawing in the Foundation of Early Modern Science* (Berlin – Boston, MA: 2019).

8   Donne John, *Ignatius His Conclave or His Inthronisation in a Late Election in Hell* (London, N.O. for Richard Moore: 1611).

9   Milton John, *Paradise Lost: A Poem Written in Ten Books* (London, Peter Parker: 1667), book 1, lines 287–291. For Satan's shield in Milton's *Paradise Lost*, see chapter 6 in this volume.

eschatological linkages, whether serious or playful, cosmographic or poetic, were inspired not only by the theological questions that Foscarini and others had raised, but also by the nautical discoveries of the previous two centuries and the telescopic discoveries of this one. If 'the sun is lost, and th'earth';[10] if the earth was but one small planet among many, and the cosmos infinitely larger than had previously been supposed; if there were lands, peoples, and planets previously unknown; what, then, did all this mean for Christ's privileged message, and for the central importance of humans in the larger cosmos? How might salvation be understood, in this newly imagined terrain?

This chapter will consider the ways in which Johannes Kepler approached some of these questions and linked the cosmological and the eschatological via a fictional journey to the moon in his dream-narrative *The Somnium* (The dream).[11] Written around 1608 but published posthumously, the *Somnium* describes a dream in which a young Icelandic boy learns from his witch-mother about a daemon who has visited a place called Levania (our own moon) [Fig. 4.1]. Summoned by the mother, the daemon recounts what it is like on the moon, what kinds of inhabitants occupy it, and what the earth looks like from the perspective of those inhabitants. As Kepler himself noted in the footnotes to the text, the purpose of the story was to argue for the Copernican world system via a shift in perspective that would help readers challenge what they had previously supposed.[12] As I will argue in this chapter, Kepler used the text to likewise articulate an eschatological vision of sorts, wherein the moon functioned as a metaphorical purgatory, knowledge of which enabled humans to reach divine truth on and about the earth. That state of truth was itself imagined as a kind of paradise, albeit an epistemological rather than a physical one, much like the knowledge-based paradise imagined by other seventeenth-century philosophers of nature, as will be discussed later in this chapter. Further, for Kepler that truth highlighted the significant place of the earth in the cosmos, still of central importance even though it was no longer at the physical centre of things. Kepler's moon, as seen through the *Somnium*, was both of and not of this world: the latter because of its physical position in the heavens and its purgatorial ability to cleanse our problematic preconceptions, and the former because what it actually revealed was that some heavenly

---

10   Donne, *Anatomy of the World* 207.

11   See Rosen E., *Kepler's Somnium: The Dream, or Posthumous Work on Lunar Astronomy* (New York, NY: 1967) for commentary.

12   See Rothman A., *The Pursuit of Harmony: Kepler on Cosmos, Confession, and Community* (Chicago, IL: 2017) 261–265. See also Chen-Morris R., *Measuring Shadows: Kepler's Optics of Invisibility* (University Park, PA: 2016) 172–185.

FIGURE 4.1   Frontispiece of Johannes Kepler, *Somnium, seu opus posthumum de astronomia lunari* (Frankfurt, Saganus Silesiorum: 1634)
PUBLIC DOMAIN

objects were just like the earth, and that reaching paradise required us to go, purified, back home.

1   Kepler's *Somnium* as a Purgatorial Text

While a student at Tübingen University, Kepler composed a short disputation that considered how celestial phenomena would appear to an observer on the moon. He revived the idea in 1608 when he drafted the *Somnium*, structured as a story within a story, which begins with Kepler dreaming of a mother and son – the latter named Duracotus – who enlist a daemon to help them travel to the moon. In later years, Kepler wrote lengthy numbered explanatory notes that he appended to the text to clarify his arguments, and the book was not published until 1634, four years after his death.

The linkage between the journey of the *Somnium* and the purgatorial journey is one that Kepler himself signalled at the very start of the text. Early on in the story, Duracotus tells the reader that as a child his mother would frequently take him to visit Iceland's Mount Hekla. He likewise notes that his mother's death has recently freed him to tell his tale, as in life she had worried greatly about how the story would be received, impressing upon him that 'the arts are loathed by many vicious people who malign what their dull minds fail to understand, and make laws harmful to mankind. Condemned by these laws, not a few persons have perished in the chasms of Hekla'.[13] Why the repeated references to this mountain at the very start of a story of a journey to the moon?

Learned readers would have recognized Mount Hekla, a volcano often referred to even in the sixteenth and seventeenth centuries as the 'Gateway to Hell'. It was a known landmark prominently depicted on early modern maps: so iconic, in fact, that it is visible even on the opening map of the world in Mercator's *Atlas*. Later in the *Atlas*, it appears on the map of Iceland itself, with the label 'mons perpetuo ardens' ('the perpetually burning mountain').[14] Ortelius's map of Iceland similarly marks Hekla as a mountain that 'perpetually condemned to storms and snow, vomits stones with a terrible noise' [Figs. 4.2 and 4.3].[15] The noise from Hekla was thought to come not just from stones, but from 'the howling and screaming of souls', as the description in later editions of Mercator's *Atlas* explained.[16] While it was included in mathematical cartographic renderings of this world, Hekla thus clearly also signified something otherworldly.[17]

---

13   Kepler Johannes, *Somnium, seu opus posthumum de astronomia lunari* (Frankfurt, Saganus Silesiorum: 1634) 1: 'Multos esse perniciosos osores artium, qui quod prae hebetudine mentis non capiunt, id calumnientur; legesque figant iniuriosas humano generi; quibus sane legibus non pauci damnati, Heclae voraginibus fuerint absorpti'.

14   Mercator Gerardus, *Atlas sive cosmographicae meditationes de fabrica mundi et fabricati figura* (Duisburg, Albert Buys: 1595).

15   Ortelius Abraham, *Theatrum Orbis Terrarum* (Antwerp, Plantin Press: 1595): 'perpetuis damnata estib[us] et nivib[us] horrendo boatu lapides evomit'.

16   Mercator Gerardus, *Atlas, de novo plurimis in locis emendatus, multisque novis tabulis auctus* (Amsterdam, Henricus Hondius: 1628): 'animarum [...] eiulatum et quiritationem'.

17   See Poole K., *Supernatural Environments in Shakespeare's England: Spaces of Demonism, Divinity, and Drama* (Cambridge: 2011) 113–121.

FIGURE 4.2   Gerardus Mercator, Map of Iceland with Mount Hekla. From: *Atlas sive cosmographicae meditationes de fabrica mundi et fabricati figura* (Amsterdam, Jodocus Hondius: 1619)
PUBLIC DOMAIN

FIGURE 4.3   Abraham Ortelius, Map of Iceland with Mount Hekla. From: *Theatrum orbis terrarum* (Antwerp, Plantin Press: 1595)
PUBLIC DOMAIN

Kepler explained in the footnotes to the *Somnium* why he chose Iceland as the setting for his story. As he wrote, 'in this remote island I perceived a place where I might fall asleep and dream'.[18] The kind of dream he had in mind had its roots in ancient literature, in Plutarch, whose *Face of the Moon*, explained Kepler, 'ventures out into the American ocean and describes to us such an arrangement of islands as a modern geographer would probably apply to [...] regions situated around Iceland'; and in Lucian, whose *True Story* has him sailing, in Kepler's words, 'out past the Pillars of Hercules into the ocean', where he, 'carried aloft with his ship by whirlwinds, is transported to the moon'.[19] Kepler added that what further prompted this particular story, linking Iceland, Hekla, and the moon, was this accident:

> At that time there was for sale in Prague Lucian's book about the trip to the moon [...] bound with it were the stories of St. Brendan and St. Patrick's Purgatory in the earth beneath Mount Hekla, the Icelandic volcano. Moreover, since Plutarch, in accordance with the belief of pagan theology, located the purgatory of souls on the moon, I decided that when I set out from the moon I would prefer to take off from Iceland.[20]

We have, then, a weaving together of multiple eschatological references. St. Patrick's Purgatory is situated, according to Kepler, beneath Mount Hekla, in Iceland, where our story begins. (Though the Purgatory of St. Patrick had been traditionally located in Ireland, Kepler here merged it with the idea of Mount Hekla as the entrance to Purgatory, based in part on the work of sixteenth-century writer and cartographer Olaus Magnus, whom Kepler mentioned by name in his notes to the *Somnium*.) Lucian travels past the Pillars of Hercules and ends up on the moon, but also – before the journey has ended – in both Tartarus and the Elysian Fields. Plutarch sets out from Iceland to the moon, which, it turns out, is the setting for reward and punishment, as one

---

18   Kepler, *Somnium* 29: 'in hac vero remota insula locum ego mihi dispexi dormiendi et somniandi'.

19   Ibidem 30: '[...] in Oceanum Americanum exspaciatur, describitque nobis situm talem insularum, quem geographus aliquis modernus [...] regionibus circum Islandiam sitis probabiliter applicaverit [...] ultra columnas Herculis in oceanum [...] rapiturque ventorum turbinibus cum ipsa navi sublimis, et Lunae invehitur'.

20   Ibidem: 'Id temporis Pragae venalis esset libellus Luciani de navigatione in lunam [...] iunctis narrationibus S. Brandani et de Purgatorio Patriciano in subterraneis Islandici montis Heclae ignivomi; cum etiam Plutarchus ex sententia theologiae gentilium, purgatorium animarum statueret in luna, placuit mihi, profecturo in lunam, potissimum ex Islandia solvere'.

of Plutarch's characters reveals.[21] Kepler's references to Hekla, to St. Patrick's Purgatory, to Lucian, and to Plutarch, all in the course of a journey to the moon, are a gesture to this larger backdrop.[22]

At the same time, Kepler would have been very familiar with the moon's symbolic resonances, and the fact that these were often quite ambiguous. While Hell was clearly earthly and corrupt, and heaven celestial and pure, the moon occupied a sort of in-between. It could sometimes signify the Church, or Christendom as a whole, or the mortal side of Christ's nature. It could as easily signify that which could not be perfected (as in Pope Gregory the Great's linkage of the moon with 'all fallen, mutable, and earthly things'), as that which, while corrupted, could.[23] Thus in the twelfth-century writings of Alexander Neckam, lunar spots were the physical sign of original sin, which would ultimately be cleansed such that in the end of times 'both the material Moon and holy church will be spotless before the Lamb'.[24]

The story of Kepler's *Somnium* rises from Hekla (the entrance to hell, or to purgatory) to the moon and then descends back again to earth.[25] Of course, in the story itself, only the daemon itself has actually experienced the journey to the moon, which is recounted for both the protagonist and the reader. In that recounting, the daemon explains that that journey, when experienced by humans, is one of intense, purgatorial suffering. Limbs must be untangled so that 'the body is not torn top from bottom'; it is 'intensely cold and impossible to breathe'; upon landing humans experience a sensation of 'unspeakable weariness in all their limbs, from which they only recover much later so

---

21   Plutarch, *Moralia*. trans. H. Cherniss and W.C. Helmbold, vol. 12 (Cambridge, MA: 1957) 209–211: 'Just as our earth contains gulfs that are deep and extensive, one here pouring in towards us through the Pillars of Herakles and outside the Caspian and the Red Sea with its gulfs, so those features are depths and hollows of the Moon. The largest of them is called "Hecate's Recess", where the souls suffer and exact penalties for whatever they have endured or committed after having already become spirits; and the two long ones are called "the Gates" for through them pass the souls now to the side of the Moon that faces heaven and now back to the side that faces earth. The side of the Moon toward heaven is named "Elysian plain", the hither side, "House of counter-terrestrial Persephone"'.

22   On the *Somnium* and its relationship to these texts, see Chen-Morris R., "Shadows of Instruction: Optics and Classical Authorities in Kepler's *Somnium*", *Journal of the History of Ideas* 66.2 (2005) 223–243.

23   See Montgomery S., *The Moon in Western Imagination* (Tucson, AR: 1999) 50–52.

24   Ibidem 69.

25   See also Reiss T., *The Discourse of Modernism* (Ithaca, NY: 1982) 157, who writes of the associations of 'a "rising from the underworld" (Hekla, writes Kepler) with a resurrection; the ambiguity of an ascent from one purgatory to what might well prove another (the moon)'.

that they can walk'.[26] Upon making the journey, however, those humans learn much about this new world and their own, as do Kepler and the reader, courtesy of the daemon. What, then, do we learn on this journey to this place of in-betweens?

2 The Lessons of the *Somnium*

In the story, the daemon tells Duracotus about one central feature of Levania: 'its science of astronomy is completely different' from the astronomy developed here on earth, for 'although the appearance of the fixed stars is the same for Levania as it is for us, it observes the motions and sizes of the planets differently than we do here'.[27] Inhabitants of Levania, or Lunarians – giant, hellish, serpentlike creatures[28] – divide their world into two hemispheres, based on whether or not 'Volva' (our earth) is visible; the Subvolvan region is always able to view Volva, while the Privolvan region can never view it. The Lunarians have certain beliefs about both their own world and their Volva, established by observation and common sense. For one, 'to its inhabitants, while the stars hasten along, Levania seems to stand unmoved, no less than our earth does to us humans'.[29] Further, while Volva does appear immobile in the sense that it remains in one spot in the heavens, it is not motionless to the inhabitants of Levania: 'it rotates [...] in its place, and displays a remarkable variety of spots, with the spots crossing continuously from east to west'.[30] This is, in fact, how the Subvolvans measure time: 'one such rotation, wherein the same spots return, is considered one hour of time by the Subvolvans'.[31]

---

26   Kepler, *Somnium* 6–7: '[...] ne corpus a podice, caput a corpore gestetur [...] ingens frigus, et prohibita respiratio [...] ineffabili membrorum omnium lassitudine, a qua sero admodum se recipiunt, ut ambulent'.

27   Ibidem 8: 'alia sit totius apud ipsos astronomiae ratio [...] etsi siderum fixorum aspectus tota Levania habet nobiscum eosdem, motus tamen planetarum et quantitates, ab iis, quas nos hic videmus, observant diversissimas'.

28   See Nicolson M., "Kepler, the *Somnium*, and John Donne", *Journal of the History of Ideas* 1.3 (1940) 259–280 at 279: 'Visitors to Kepler's moon, in short, would have found themselves in just such a world as was experienced by the wandering fallen angels in Milton's hell'.

29   Kepler, *Somnium* 9: '[...] suis incolis immota stare videtur, currentibus astris, quam terra nostra nobis hominibus'.

30   Ibidem 19: '[...] intra tamen locum suum [...] gyratur, et admirabilem macularum varietatem successive explicat, assidue ab ortu in occasum translatis maculis'.

31   Ibidem: '[u]na igitur talis revolutio, quando eaedem maculae redeunt, Subvolvanis habetur pro una hora temporali'.

Though Kepler simply narrated this story in the text itself, in the footnotes – composed in later years – he explained its significance. In one of the first notes, he wrote: 'The goal of my *Somnium* is to construct an argument for the motion of the earth, or rather, to offer a counter-argument to the universal opposition of humankind from the example of the moon'.[32] The crux of that argument is as follows:

> what are for us the most important features of the whole world – the twelve celestial signs, the solstices, the equinoxes, the tropical years, the sidereal years, the equator, the colures, the tropics, arctic circles, and celestial poles – are all tied to the very narrow globe of the earth, and exist in the imagination of earthly inhabitants alone. Thus if we transfer the imagination to another sphere, everything needs to be conceived differently.[33]

That is, our astronomy and all the preconceptions on which it depends are all relative to our specific celestial position, but if we were positioned elsewhere, we would see things very differently.

This is specifically relevant when it comes to the question of the mobility of the earth. We perceive the earth to be immobile; we perceive our balls to stand immobile with us, or to fall in the direction we send them; we perceive the moon to move around us. Yet, 'the Lunarians, too, think that their lunar surface, and the ball of Volva suspended on high above it, stand still in their place, while we know for certain that the moon is one of the movable stars'.[34] The lesson, for Kepler, is clear: if we consider things from the perspective of the Lunarians, we can recognize that common sense perceptions don't always reveal the truth of the matter. As he wrote, 'everyone screams that the motion of the stars around the earth and the immobility of the earth are apparent to the eyes. I retort that to the eyes of the Lunarians the rotation of our earth, their Volva, is apparent,

---

32   Ibidem 31: 'Somnii mei scopus sit, argumentum pro motu terrae, seu solutionem potius objectionum ab universali contradictione gentis humanae desumptarum, moliri exemplo lunae'.

33   Ibidem 48: '[...] quae nobis sunt inter totius mundi praecipua; duodecim signa coelestia, solstitia, aequinoctia, annos tropicos, siderios, aequatorem, coluros, tropicos, polares, polos mundi; omnia restringi ad angustissimum globum telluris solaque terricolarum imaginatione constare: ut si ad alium globum transferamus imaginationem, omnia mutata concipere necesse sit'.

34   Ibidem 56: '[...] et Lunares putant lunarem suam planitiem et Volvae pilam in sublimi suspensam super ea, stare loco; cum certo sciamus, lunam esse unum ex mobilibus sideribus'.

as is the immobility of their moon'.[35] If we respond that they are wrong, the response applies equally to ourselves: 'If they were to argue that the lunatic senses of my Lunarian people are deceived, I retort, with equal right, that the terrestrial senses of the inhabitants of earth lack reason'.[36] This turning of the tables, and all that it reveals, is 'the more secret goal of this fable'.[37] Lucian's other lunar voyage, the *Icaromennipus*, used the moon as a lens through which to reveal lessons about life on earth that went beyond the physical; from the moon, his hero reveals, 'the life of man in its entirety disclosed itself to me, and not only the nations and cities but the people themselves as clear as could be'.[38] Kepler's lunar voyage leaves the reader with a different kind of truth, physical and astronomical: the truth of heliocentric theory.

Yet this truth went beyond the physical too. For the heliocentric theory was more to Kepler than just an astronomical theory, or even than just a physical one (though he was one of the first to combine the two). It had central theological implications as well. As Kepler explained in his other work, he believed that the sphere was the most perfect of figures, and that it represented the Trinity, in which 'there are three parts, the centre, the surface, and the intermediate space, so that with one denied, the rest collapse, and they are distinct among themselves, so that one is not the other'.[39] The spherical cosmos pointed directly to the Trinity as well, because of 'the beautiful harmony of things at rest: of the sun, the fixed stars, and the intermediate area, with God the Father, and the Son, and the Holy Spirit'.[40] In other words, the two immobile points of reference at the centre and the periphery (the sun and the fixed stars), along with the space through which the movable planets traversed, had a built-in similitude to the divine. That the central point representing God the Father was the sun, and not the earth, was clear to Kepler not only for

35 Ibidem 60: 'Clamant omnes, oculis expositos esse motus siderum circa terram, terrae quietem: regero ego, oculis lunarium expositam esse gyrationem nostrae terrae, suae Volvae, quietem vero suae lunae'.

36 Ibidem: 'Si dixerint, decipi lunarium meorum populorum sensus lunaticos: pari ego iure regero, decipi Terricolarum sensus terrestres ratione cassos'.

37 Ibidem: '[...] occultiorem illum scopum huius fabulae'.

38 Quoted in Montgomery, *The Moon in Western Imagination* 38.

39 Kepler Johannes, *Epitome astronomiae Copernicanae* (Linz, Johannes Plancus: 1618) 48–49: '[...] tria sunt, centrum, superficies, et aequalitas intervalli; quorum uno negato caetera corruunt, suntque distincta inter se, ut unum non sit alterum'.

40 Kepler Johannes, *Prodromus dissertationum cosmographicarum, continens mysterium cosmographicum* (Tubingen, Georgius Gruppenbachius: 1596) 6: '[...] illa pulchra quiescentium harmonia, Solis, fixarum et intermedia, cum Deo Patre, et Filio et Sancto Spiritu'.

astronomical and physical reasons, but also for theological ones. The sun, he argued, was 'the principal body of the whole world'.[41] He explained:

> The perfection of the world consists in light, heat, motion, and harmony of motions [...]. As pertains to light, the sun itself is not only the most beautiful and is even, as it were, the eye of the world, but it also illuminates, paints, and adorns the bodies of the rest of the world as a source of light or a very bright torch. [...] With respect to heat, the sun is the hearth of the world. [...] With respect to motion, the sun is the first cause of the motions of the planets and the first motor of the universe, by the very reason of its body. [...] Finally, with respect to the harmony of motions, the sun occupies that place in which alone the motions of the planets acquire the appearance of quantities moderated harmonically.[42]

To Kepler, only heliocentrism represented the true Trinitarian structure of the cosmos, and it was only by reference to the central sun that the harmonies with which God had archetypally arranged that cosmos could be appreciated.

The earth, however, also held a crucial place. It was no accident, Kepler argued, that the earth was positioned exactly in the middle of the primary cosmic bodies, with Mars, Jupiter, and Saturn above it, and Venus, Mercury, and the sun below. In this sense, the earth truly was the centre of all things, and it needed to be so, for

> we on Earth can scarcely see Mercury, the last of the primary planets, on account of the nearby and excessive brightness of the sun. How much less will Mercury be visible on Jupiter or Saturn! Thus it seems that this sphere was allotted to man with this ultimate plan: that he be able to contemplate all the planets.[43]

---

41   Kepler Johannes, *Epitomes astronomiae Copernicanae, Liber quartus* (Lenz, Johannes Plancus: 1620) 439: 'totius mundi corpus praecipuum'.

42   Ibidem 439–441: 'Mundi perfectio consistit in luce, calore, motu, et harmonia motuum [...]. Nam quod lucem attinet, ea cum sol ipse pulcherrimus est, et quidam veluti oculus mundi, tum vero mundi reliqui corpora ipse ut fons lucis aut clarissima fax, illuminat, pingit, exornat [...]. Quoad calorem, sol focus mundi est. [...] Quo ad motum, sol est prima causa motus planetarum universi, primusque motor, etiam ratione sui corporis [...]. Denique quoad harmoniam motuum, sol illum locum obtinet, in quo solo planetarum motus faciunt apparentiam quantitatum harmonice contemperatarum'.

43   Kepler Johannes, *Dissertatio cum Nuncio Sidereo* (Prague, Daniel Sedasanus: 1610) 32: '[...] nos in tellure Mercurium, planetarum primariorum ultimum, vix visu apprehendimus, propter propinquam et nimiam solis claritatem. Quanto minus in Iove vel Saturno,

More important even than its central position, the earth needed to be *mobile*. For Kepler, the sun, representing God the Father, deserved its position of absolute centrality. Such a position would not be appropriate for humans, nor would it help them fulfil their task of appreciating the wonders of God's creation. As Kepler explained:

> The sun is in the centre of the world and is the heart of the world: it is the source of light and heat, and the origin of life and heavenly motion. But it seems that man should unperturbedly stay away from that royal throne. Heaven is for the Lord of Heaven, the Sun of justice, while the earth he gave to the children of men. For although God has no body and needs no dwelling place, nevertheless more of the power that governs the world is in the sun (or as it says everywhere in Scripture, in the heavens) than in the other spheres. Therefore, man should recognize his poverty and the riches of God due to this difference in dwelling place. He should recognize that he is not the source and origin of the world's adornment, but that he depends on its source and true origin. Add this as well, which I said in the *Optics*: For the sake of the contemplation toward which man was made and equipped with eyes, man could not have stayed at rest in the centre. Rather, he needed to circle around on the annual voyage of this earth for the purpose of observation. This is no different from how surveyors of inaccessible things exchange station for station in order to acquire from the distances of the stations a proper foundation for triangulating measurement.[44]

This, in Kepler's view, is the answer to the problem heliocentrism posed for man's place in the universe, a question he phrases as follows:

Mercurius conspicuus erit? Summo itaque consilio hic globus homini videtur attributus, ut omnes planetas contemplari posset'.

44   Ibidem 31: 'Sol quidem in centro mundi est, cor mundi est, fons lucis est, fons caloris, origo vitae motusque mundani est. At videtur homo aequo animo illo throno regio abstinere debere. Caelum caeli Domino, soli iustitiae, terram autem dedit filiis hominum. Nam etsi Deus corpus non habet nec habitaculo indiget, in sole tamen (ut passim per scripturam in caelo) plus exerit virtutis, qua mundus gubernatur, quam in globis caeteris. Agnoscat igitur homo ipsius etiam habitaculi sui distinctione suam indigentiam, Dei abundantiam; agnoscat se non esse fontem et originem ornatus mundani, sed a fonte et ab origine vera dependere. Adde et hoc, quod in Opticis dixi; contemplationis causa, ad quam homo factus, oculisque ornatus et instructus est, non potuisse hominem in centro quiescere; sed oportere, ut navigio hoc telluris, annuo motu circumspacietur, lustrandi causa: non secus atque mensores rerum inaccessarum, stationem statione permutant, ut triangulo mensorio iustam basin ex stationum intervallis concilient'.

If there are globes in the heaven similar to our earth, are we then in com-
petition with them over which of us possesses the better part of the universe? [...] How, then, are all things created on account of man? How are
we the masters of God's work?[45]

His answer, here, is that we are still the masters of God's work, for we are in the
prime position to observe it, understand it, and worship its Creator.

Still further, motion in this heliocentric world, of both the earth and the
other planets around a central sun, is theologically important because of
what that motion produces: the harmonies. The elliptical paths of the planets
produce extreme speeds that generate polyphonic cosmic harmonies, which
archetypally originate in and imitate God the Divine Harmonist:

The motions of the heavens are nothing but a certain perpetual concord
(rational, not audible) through dissonant tunings [...] tending toward
fixed and prescribed resolutions specific to these six terms (just as with
voices), and marking and distinguishing with those notes the immensity
of time.[46]

True astronomy reveals this, and earthly polyphonic music imitates this;
through both, humans can 'taste, to an extent, the pleasure of God the Creator
in his works, by the most agreeable sense of pleasure he feels from this imitator
of God, Music'.[47] Astronomers on a moving earth can use their mobile position to understand these harmonies, while at the same time a moving earth
itself participates in generating these divine songs, since it too, according to
heliocentric theory, has been granted a voice. In its song, a mournful prayer of
mi fa mi, it expresses the famine and misery present for so long and the longing
for a redemptive end to that suffering.[48]

---

45   Ibidem 29: 'Si sunt in caelo globi, similes nostrae telluris, anne igitur cum illis in certamen
      venimus utri meliore mundi plaga teneant? [...] Quomodo igitur omnia propter homi-
      nem? Quomodo nos domini operum Dei?'.

46   Kepler Johannes, *Harmonices Mundi* (Linz, Johannes Plancus: 1619) 212: 'Nihil igitur
      aliud sunt motus coelorum, quam perennis quidam concentus (rationalis non vocalis)
      per dissonantes tensiones [...] tendens in certas et praescriptas clausulas, singulas
      sex terminorum (veluti vocum) iisque notis immensitatem temporis insigniens et
      distinguens'.

47   Ibidem: '[...] suavissimo sensu voluptatis, ex hac Dei imitatrice musica perceptae,
      quadamtenus degustare'.

48   See Pesic P., *Music and the Making of Modern Science* (Cambridge, MA: 2014) 73–88.

3   From Purgatory to Paradise

Kepler positioned the world of the *Somnium* as a purgatory of sorts, one particularly suited to reveal important cosmological and theological truths. Crucially, he did so at a time when purgatory itself was going through a process of reimagination. Purgatory, from at least the twelfth century, was conceived both as a physical space and as an intermediate state for sinners on their way to paradise. Whether located in the centre of the earth near hell, on the moon, or, in Dante's telling, on a tall mountain directly opposite Jerusalem on the globe, the labours of purgatory prepared the soul so that it could reach paradise pure. Protestant reformers famously attacked and ultimately dissolved the place of purgation. Long before Kircher used his magic lantern to imagine and project images of purgatorial fire,[49] Luther had decried purgatory as 'the greatest falsehood'[50] and Tyndale had labelled it a 'poet's fable'.[51] They and others who attacked purgatory objected in particular to its lack of scriptural foundation, its association with the pope, and its linkage to potential clerical abuses.[52] Yet not all Protestants objected to the notion of purgation itself; instead, those who believed that labour pertained to salvation stressed that this was only before death, and required earthly labour. For these figures, justification by faith did not mean that grace could not be squandered; in the words of seventeenth-century Quaker William Gibson, 'sloth, negligence, and unwatchfulness' might lead to the loss of salvation, while diligent earthly labour helped to guarantee it.[53]

If purgatory moved to the realm of the living, it was in good company. Paradise, too, went through its own reimagining, and could sometimes take on a decidedly terrestrial cast. In the past, too, there were those who placed Eden on earth, and there were debates about whether this meant that it was located in *part* of the earth or that the whole earth was once Edenic.[54] These debates took on new life in early modernity, alongside the intense focus of reformers on

---

49   See Buonanno R., *The Stars of Galileo Galilei and the Universal Knowledge of Athanasius Kircher* (Cham: 2014) 71–74.

50   Luther Martin, *Luther's Works*, ed. J. Pelikan – H.T. Lehmann, vol. 4 (Berkeley, CA: 1955) 315.

51   Greenblatt S., *Hamlet in Purgatory* (Princeton, NJ: 2002) 3.

52   See, for example, Marshall P., *Beliefs and the Dead in Reformation England* (Oxford: 2002) and Koslofsky C., *The Reformation of the Dead: Death and Ritual in Early Modern Germany, 1450–1700* (New York, NY: 2000).

53   Picciotto J., "Progress and the Space of Prehistory", *Thresholds* 25 (2002) 18.

54   See Duncan J., "Paradise as the Whole Earth", *Journal of the History of Ideas* 30.2 (1969) 171–186.

the scriptural story of Genesis and the relationship between the early knowl-edge of Adam, the tree of knowledge, and the fall of man. Protestants, in particular those devoted to the study of nature, came to argue, in good Augus-tinian tradition, that the prelapsarian earth was characterized by a perfection lost in the face of original sin; the expulsion from Eden, in this sense, was not a move from one place to another, but rather a transformation of one place *into* another.[55]

This way of thinking recast not just the idea of original nature, but also the idea of the original Adamic knowledge. Adam famously named all the animals in Eden because of his clear grasp of nature and its underlying truths, and it was that linkage between nature, human knowledge, and truth that had been severed with the Fall. As Peter Harrison has argued, all this paved the way for a belief that a new kind of science, one that was able to reach through all the confusion and reveal the nature of things, might repair the effects of original sin and allow man to regain what Adam once had.[56] Science, then, was the path to paradise.[57] Thomas Sprat of the Royal Society wrote, of Adam naming the creatures in Eden, that 'this had bin the only Religio, if men had continued innocent in Paradise';[58] Hooke likewise wondered, as he peered through his microscope, whether 'Adam might from some such contemplation give names to all creatures?'[59]

The problem, after Eden had been lost, was that the senses often deceived, and truth was elusive. Science, however, and the instruments that it con-structed, might fill the breach. As Hooke explained in the *Micrographia*, 'by the addition of such *artificial Instruments* and *methods*, there may be, in some manner, a reparation made for the mischiefs, and imperfection, mankind has drawn upon it self [...] whereby every man, both from a deriv'd corruption, innate and born with him, and from his breeding and converse with men, Is very subject to slip into all sorts of errors'.[60] The true knowledge offered by the experimental philosophy, in Hooke's view, would yield a new paradise that learned from the mistakes of the old, such that while 'at first mankind *fell* by *tasting* of the forbidden Tree of Knowledge, so we, their Posterity, may be in part *restor'd* by the same way [...] by *tasting* too those fruits of Natural

---

55   Ibidem.

56   Harrison P., *The Fall of Nature and the Foundations of Science* (Cambridge: 2009).

57   Picciotto J., "Reforming the Garden: The Experimentalist Eden and 'Paradise Lost'", *English Literary History* 72.1 (2005) 23–78.

58   Ibidem 25.

59   Ibidem 27.

60   Hooke Robert, *Micrographia* (London, J.M., and J. Allestry: 1665) i.

knowledge, that were never yet forbidden'.[61] Tycho Brahe likewise organized the grounds of his astronomical observatory at Uraniborg, particularly the botanical gardens that surrounded it, to represent an Eden resurrected by the pursuit of natural knowledge.[62]

The spokesman extraordinaire for the attempt to use knowledge of nature to rebuild Paradise on earth was Francis Bacon. The goal of Bacon's new method of science, outlined in his *Great Instauration*, was to investigate whether 'commerce between the mind of man and the nature of things [...] might by any means be restored to its perfect and original condition'.[63] He believed that the eschatological prophecy of *Daniel* 12:4 signalled both that science would lead to a paradise at the end of days, and also that that time was nigh: for when 'many go to and fro', i.e. when voyages of discovery and exploration become a signature of the times, and 'knowledge will be increased', through the discovery of natural causes, then Daniel's prophecy would be fulfilled. That fulfilment would bring man back to the Eden where it all began: 'For man by the fall fell at the same time from his state of innocence and from his dominion over creation. Both of these losses however can even in this life be in some part repaired; the former by religion and faith, the latter by arts and sciences'.[64] Bacon placed this passage from the *Book of Daniel* on the frontispiece of his *Great Instauration*, beneath the image of a ship sailing through the Pillars of Hercules, those boundaries of the ancient world beyond which one could, and should, sail no further [Fig. 4.4]. Odysseus, in Dante's *Inferno*, tried to sail past those pillars, and his hubris cost him dearly. For Bacon, however, the Pillars have already been breached; the ship does not venture past them, but returns home, sailing back through them after a successful journey beyond their limits. That return is, Bacon suggests, to a world transformed, and a paradise regained. In that paradisical world, the very plan of Creation was once again legible to humans – a plan that, in Kepler's words from *The Harmony of the World*, 'God stood ready for six thousand years for someone to contemplate'.[65]

---

61   Ibidem vii–viii.

62   See Christianson J.R, *On Tycho's Island: Tycho Brahe, Science and Culture in the Sixteenth Century* (Cambridge: 2003) 109–110.

63   Bacon Francis, *The Philosophical Works of Francis Bacon*, vol. 4, ed. James Spedding (London, Longman and Co.: 1861) 7. See also Iliffe R., "The Masculine Birth of Time: Temporal Frameworks of Early Modern Natural Philosophy", *The British Journal for the History of Science* 33.4 (2000) 427–453.

64   Bacon, *The Philosophical Works* 247–248.

65   Kepler, *Harmonices Mundi* 179: '[...] Deus ipse per annorum sena millia contemplatorem praestolatus est'.

FIGURE 4.4 Francis Bacon, Frontispiece of *Instauratio magna* (London, Joannes Billius: 1620)

4   Conclusion

Most people, Kepler believed, did not recognize the motion of the earth and the centrality of the sun because of the limitations of their senses and the misuse of their reason. His lunar journey in the *Somnium* attempts to remedy that, offering his readers a different perspective from which to view their surroundings and a reasoned argument for the motion of the earth and the central immobility of the sun. After the journey, he hoped, they would be convinced of the truths of heliocentrism. And as we saw earlier, those truths were astronomical, physical, and theological; they represented the Trinity, reaffirmed man's centrality, and demonstrated that it was only on a moving body positioned among the various planets that humans could appreciate and truly know the works of Creation. It is in this sense that I argue for the journey itself, from Hekla to the moon, as an epistemological kind of purgatorial labour. Kepler frames that journey not merely in broadly eschatological terms, but in specifically purgatorial ones, from the setting of the story to the suffering of the journey that the daemon describes. Further, in the course of that journey, truth is gradually revealed; the return to earth is then a return to a paradise wherein God might be fully and freely worshipped as Kepler believed that he should. Though for Kepler himself the specifics of that worship were largely Lutheran, his conception of theological truth transcended the specifics of confession; 'Christ the Lord who spoke this word', he wrote, '[…] neither was nor is Lutheran, nor Calvinist, nor Papist'.[66] Kepler's reimagining of purgatory, while linked to that of other Protestant natural philosophers, was intended for everyone.

In another, earlier dream, Cicero's dream of Scipio, the dreamer looks down on earth 'from on high, in a certain bright and clear place, full of stars'.[67] Only there is he able to fully appreciate the cosmic harmonies, elaborated in Macrobius's later commentary on that dream. Kepler, likewise, took his dreamer to the moon, but taught him there that the harmonies could, in fact, be appreciated on earth – but only if it moved. In that case, the earth itself participated in generating those harmonies. According to Joseph Glanvill,

---

66   Kepler Johannes, *Glaubensbekenntnis* (Strasbourg, s.n.: 1623) 26: 'Christus der Herr, welcher diese Wort aussgesprochen […] Lutherisch noch Calvinisch, noch Papistisch gewest, noch ist'.

67   Cicero M.T., "Somnium Scipionis", in idem, *The De senectute, De amicitia, Paradoxa, and Somnium Scipionis of Cicero and the Life of Atticus*, ed. Charles Anthon (New York, NY: 1867) 94: 'de excelso, et pleno stellarum, illustri et claro quodam loco'.

Adam's knowledge was so pure that 'he had as clear a perception of the earth's motion as we think we have of its quiescence'.[68] Kepler's reader is a new Adam, with Adam's awareness of an earth singing its song as it marked its circuit around the sun. Dante's Odysseus travelled through the Pillars of Hercules on the way to purgatory, but his journey ended in hell. Bacon's ship travelled through the Pillars of Hercules and journeyed to an earthly paradise.[69] The reader of Kepler's dream, by contrast, bypasses the Pillars and travels directly to purgatory via the moon; returning, he has reached a worldly paradise like Bacon's. There, much like Dante's traveller, he can finally see the sun. For this is a paradise where the light of heliocentrism shines clearly and wherein nature '[…] has whispered to the Human mind about herself, and about what she is like in her innermost bosom'.[70]

Bibliography

Bassler O.B., "Theology and the Modern Age: Blumenberg's Reaction to a Baconian Frontispiece", *New German Critique* 84 (2001) 163–192.

Bredekamp H., *Galileo's Thinking Hand: Mannerism, Anti-Mannerism and the Virtue of Drawing in the Foundation of Early Modern Science* (Berlin – Boston, MA: 2019).

Buonanno R., *The Stars of Galileo Galilei and the Universal Knowledge of Athanasius Kircher* (Cham: 2014).

Chen-Morris R., "Shadows of Instruction: Optics and Classical Authorities in Kepler's *Somnium*", *Journal of the History of Ideas* 66.2 (2005) 223–243.

Chen-Morris, R., *Measuring Shadows: Kepler's Optics of Invisibility* (University Park, PA: 2016).

Christianson J.R., *On Tycho's Island: Tycho Brahe, Science and Culture in the Sixteenth Century* (Cambridge: 2003).

Cicero M.T., "Somnium Scipionis", in idem, *The De Senectute, De Amicitia, Paradoxa, and Somnium Scipionis of Cicero and the Life of Atticus*, ed. C. Anthon (New York, NY: 1867).

Danielson D., *Paradise Lost and the Cosmological Revolution* (Cambridge: 2014).

---

68   Glanvill Joseph, *The Vanity of Dogmatizing* (London, E.C. for Henry Eversden: 1661). Quoted in Picciotto, "Reforming the Garden" 27.

69   See also Bassler O.B., "Theology and the Modern Age: Blumenberg's Reaction to a Baconian Frontispiece", *New German Critique* 84 (2001) 163–192.

70   Kepler, *Harmonices Mundi* 208: '[…] sese ipsam, qualis existat penitissimo sinu, menti humanae […] insusurravit'.

Donne John, *An Anatomy of the World* (London, Samuel Macham: 1611).

Donne John, *Ignatius His Conclave or His Inthronisation in a Late Election in Hell* (London, N.O. for Richard Moore: 1611).

Duncan J., "Paradise as the Whole Earth", *Journal of the History of Ideas* 30.2 (1969) 171–186.

Finocchiaro M., *The Galileo Affair: A Documentary History* (Berkeley, CA: 1989).

Foscarini Paolo Antonio, *Lettera sopra l'opinione de' pittagorici, e del Copernico, della mobilità della terra e stabilità del sole* (Naples, Lazaro Scoriggio: 1615).

Glanvill John, *The Vanity of Dogmatizing* (London, E.C. for Henry Eversden: 1661).

Greenblatt S., *Hamlet in Purgatory* (Princeton, NJ: 2002).

Harrison P., *The Fall of Nature and the Foundations of Science* (Cambridge: 2009).

Hooke Robert, *Micrographia* (London, J.M., and J. Allestry: 1665).

Iliffe R., "The Masculine Birth of Time: Temporal Frameworks of Early Modern Natural Philosophy", *The British Journal for the History of Science* 33.4 (2000) 427–453.

Kepler Johannes, *Prodromus dissertationum cosmographicarum, continens mysterium cosmographicum* (Tubingen, Georgius Gruppenbachius: 1596).

Kepler Johannes, *Dissertatio cum Nuncio Sidereo* (Prague, Daniel Sedasanus: 1610).

Kepler Johannes, *Epitome astronomiae Copernicanae* (Linz, Johannes Plancus: 1618).

Kepler Johannes, *Harmonices Mundi* (Linz, Johannes Plancus: 1619).

Kepler Johannes, *Epitome astronomiae Copernicanae, Liber Quartus* (Linz, Johannes Plancus, 1620).

Kepler Johannes, *Glaubensbekenntnis* (Strasbourg, s.n.: 1623).

Koslofsky C., *The Reformation of the Dead: Death and Ritual in Early Modern Germany, 1450–1700* (New York, NY: 2000).

Luther Martin, *Luther's Works*, vol. 4., ed. J. Pelikan – H.T. Lehmann (Berkeley, CA: 1955).

Marshall P., *Beliefs and the Dead in Reformation England* (Oxford: 2002).

Mercator Gerardus, *Atlas sive cosmographicae meditationes de fabrica mundi et fabricati figura* (Duisburg, Albert Buys: 1595).

Mercator Gerardus, *Atlas, de novo plurimis in locis emendatus, multisque novis tabulis auctus* (Amsterdam, Henricus Hondius, 1628).

Milton John, *Paradise Lost: A Poem Written in Ten Books* (London, Peter Parker: 1667).

Montgomery S., *The Moon in Western Imagination* (Tucson, AR: 1999).

Nicolson M., "Kepler, the Somnium, and John Donne", *Journal of the History of Ideas* 1.3 (1940) 259–280.

Ortelius Abraham, *Theatrum Orbis Terrarum* (Antwerp, Plantin Press: 1595).

Pesic P., *Music and the Making of Modern Science* (Cambridge, MA: 2014).

Peterson M., *Galileo's Muse: Renaissance Mathematics and the Arts* (Cambridge, MA: 2011).

Picciotto J., "Progress and the Space of Prehistory", *Thresholds* 25 (2002) 14–19.

Picciotto J., "Reforming the Garden: The Experimentalist Eden and 'Paradise Lost'", *English Literary History* 72.1 (2005) 23–78.

Plutarch, *Moralia*, trans. H. Cherniss – W.C. Helmbold, vol. 12 (Cambridge, MA: 1957).

Reiss T., *The Discourse of Modernism* (Ithaca, NY: 1982).

Riccioli Giovanni Battista, *Almagestum Novum* (Bologna, Victor Benatius: 1651).

Rosen E., *Kepler's Somnium: The Dream, or Posthumous Work on Lunar Astronomy* (New York, NY: 1967).

Rothman A., *The Pursuit of Harmony: Kepler on Cosmos, Confession, and Community* (Chicago, IL: 2017).

PART 2

Underlands and Netherworlds

∵

CHAPTER 5

The Birth of Hell: An Angel, His Fall, and His Reign among Us

Matteo Al Kalak

Abstract

This chapter analyses the birth of hell with special attention to early modern Italy (sixteenth to eighteenth centuries), understood as a special laboratory for the Catholicism born from the Council of Trent. In particular, representations of the origin of the *locus inferni* in poetry and art will be examined. After a summary of the theological background, the chapter offers a path through the works of some literary figures who addressed the origin of hell in their works; subsequently, it shows the pictorial and sculptural production that confronted the theme. In all cases, the cosmic struggle that led to the birth of the physical and subterranean hell is emphasized, and, in addition to the figure of Lucifer, the role of the archangel Michael as the personification of the powers of good stands out.

Keywords

hell – Lucifer – St. Michael – Italy – Catholicism

From the Middle Ages onwards, the need to depict the afterlife and identify its structure was one of the most fundamental concerns for Western Christianity. As has been amply demonstrated, delineating the geography of the world beyond, determining its location in time and space, and establishing an internal order within the various regions of the afterlife made it possible, first and foremost, to redefine power relations among people: the earthly and heavenly realms mirrored each other, and the order given to the afterworld was intended to teach people how to behave in order to obtain the rewards (or avoid the punishments) of eternity, as well as to instruct them about the means to obtain these rewards (primarily obedience to the Church). In this context, a special mention must go to the "construction" of hell, a place whose appearance, like that of purgatory, became increasingly well-defined.[1] In the centuries that marked the transition to the modern age, theologians, philosophers, artists, and scholars intensified their efforts to outline the contours and forms of the land of eternal damnation, sometimes introducing significant innovations. Within the Catholic sphere, two main avenues were explored: on the one hand, the physicality of hell – in other words its real existence in space – was reaffirmed; on the other, a moral reading of the dark realm was promoted, focusing on the sin of its lord, Satan, and its inhabitants. Such aspects coalesced with a certain degree of clarity in the accounts of the origins of hell, which began to proliferate in the decades following the rift between Catholics and Protestants.

The present chapter aims to shed light on this theme, dividing the discussion into two parts: the first will summarize the long debate on the genesis of hell and the nature of Satan's sin, culminating in the work of the Jesuit theologian Francisco Suárez, who, a few decades after the Council of Trent, incorporated the medieval tradition into the culture of the Counter-Reformation under a new guise. The second will examine popular interpretations of these beliefs through poetic texts and artistic depictions that portrayed the birth of the kingdom of evil. As mentioned, the period under consideration lies between the sixteenth and eighteenth centuries, which witnessed confessional clashes and a need to redefine the content of faith, including with regard to the structure of the afterlife (one of the burning issues of religious controversy at the time). The chosen context is Italy, which, due to the presence of the centre of the Catholic faith, served as a laboratory for the whole of Roman Catholic Christianity.

1   The Great Battle

To understand beliefs about the birth of hell between the Middle Ages and the modern age, the starting point is certainly the cosmic battle described in the *Book of Revelation*, chapter 12. Before the kingdom of evil was formed, two angels had faced each other: Michael, the warrior saint who led the forces of good, and Lucifer, a being possessed with a rare beauty who rebelled against his creator. The scene was described in a highly evocative passage, which many

---

1 On purgatory, I refer to Le Goff J., *The Birth of Purgatory* (Chicago, IL: 1984 [1981]). On hell, in addition to the references in the following notes, I cite only a few recent texts: Minois G., *Histoire des enfers* (Paris: 1991); Vorgrimler H., *Geschichte der Hölle* (Munich: 1993); Ehrman B.D., *Heaven and Hell: A History of the Afterlife* (New York, NY: 2020).

scholars have commented on over the centuries.[2] The author of the sacred text, identified as John the Apostle, reports a vision of a 'great sign' appearing in the sky: a woman clothed with the sun above the moon and crowned with twelve stars. She is evidently pregnant and crying out from the pain of labour. Suddenly, the horizon is torn apart by a red dragon with seven heads and ten horns, capable of hurling a third of the stars of the firmament down to earth with a flick of its tail. The dragon and the woman confront each other: the serpent tries to devour the male child she has just given birth to. The child – for whom a messianic destiny is foretold – is, however, carried off to the throne of God, while the woman flees into the desert to a shelter prepared for her. It is at this point that a clash begins in which Michael and his angels are pitted against the dragon, who is in turn assisted by other angels loyal to him. The defenders of the child delivered by the woman prevail, and the dragon – 'that old serpent, who is called the devil and Satan' – is cast down to earth together with his followers. Heaven is thus liberated and filled with a song of joy to celebrate Christ's victory. The dragon finally attempts to take revenge, pursuing the woman, who, protected by God and the earth itself, manages to save herself. The serpent rages against the woman's children who, *Revelation* explains, are Jesus's disciples. Eight chapters later, the dragon returns, again characterized as 'that old serpent, who is called the devil and Satan': it is chained in an abyss by an angel for a thousand years, after which it is released for the last battle before the end of time.[3] Finally, it is cast into the 'pool burning with fire and brimstone', where it will be subjected to eternal torment.

These few details indicate that the meaning of the episode should not be sought in an explanation of hell's origins or the devil's power, but rather in the overall framework of the last book of the Bible, which, in its own language, retells the story of Jesus and humanity during the great persecutions against the first Christian communities. It is nonetheless easy to understand why the vision of the battle between Michael and the apocalyptic monster was interpreted by various authors as a cosmogony, leading back to the beginnings of the history of salvation and, as it were, to the origins of hell.[4] Three elements contributed to this interpretation: first, the defensive feat of Michael, a sort of alter ego of Lucifer; second, the ancient serpent-dragon Satan, an

---

2   *Revelation* 12:1–18, from which the following information and quotations are taken.
3   *Revelation* 20:1–15.
4   An interpretation of the text as referring to Satan's rebellion, rather than to the Church's state of persecution, is already present in the work of some Fathers, such as Oecumenius; see Monaci Castagno A., "I commenti di Ecumenio e di Andrea di Cesarea: Due letture divergenti dell'Apocalisse", *Memorie dell'Accademia delle Scienze di Torino* 5.5 (1981) 304–426.

amalgamation of the tempter of Genesis, who introduced sin into the world, with the tales of ancient mythology; and third, the underworld, understood as the outcome of the clash between good and evil, closely associated with the depths of the earth.

Proceeding in order, we must first consider Michael. Worship of the archangel – the defender of the gates of paradise and hero of heaven – dates back a long way in Western Christianity. His figure appears five times in Scripture, always associated with the heavenly armies: Michael is their leader, and the etymology of his name (Mi-ka-El = who is like God?) reaffirms God's supremacy over his enemies.[5]

The aforementioned passage from *Revelation* states that it was Michael who opposed the subversive plan of the dragon, the second actor in the scene. The latter, the text states, is the devil. Indeed, it has been ascertained that the description of the war in heaven hinges on the codification of the figure of Satan, developed in the evolution from late Judaism to the beginnings of the Christian religion. The origins of the Christian devil and his fall from heaven can be traced back to apocryphal apocalyptic literature. A first group of texts, referring to the figure of the patriarch Enoch, is heavily influenced by the myths of Babylonian culture. Between 210 and 60 BC, these writings trace the origin of evil, describing a revolt by the angels under the leadership of Semihazaz. The rebels included Azazel, Belial, Mastem, Satanael, and Sammael: these angels copulated with women, begetting the giants who plagued the earth. To punish them, God instructed four good angels, including Michael, to drive the giants into the abyss. According to other texts, such as the *Book of Jubilees* (135–105 BC), the rebellion was led by Mastema (a name based on the root *stm* – to hate – akin to *stn* – to oppose, obstruct, accuse – from which Satan derives): Mastema-Satan is the tempter. Other apocrypha of the same era link Satan to the serpent of Genesis: Satan instructs the serpent to make himself the bearer of his will and to lead mankind into error. His hatred for the inhabitants of the earth stemmed from his refusal to worship God's creatures: Michael was therefore forced to banish him. Many of these ideas then spilled over into the culture of the Essenes – close to the context in which Jesus lived – which

---

5 Mara M.G., "Michele Arcangelo", in *Bibliotheca Sanctorum* (Rome: 1967) 9:410–446. For an analysis of the topos of the cosmic battle between good and evil, also visible in the struggle between Michael and Satan, see Forsyth N., *The Old Enemy: Satan and the Combat Myth* (Princeton, NJ: 1987) 105–211 (and 252–257 for the interpretation of the figure of Satan in *Revelation* chapters 12 and 20).

had reinterpreted the eastern myths, attributing a decisive role to Satan as the embodiment of evil.[6]

Given that these were the foundations for the figures of the angel and the dragon, it is hardly surprising that the devil's rebellion – whether or not related to the passage from *Revelation* – was linked, from the Middle Ages onwards, to the birth of hell. Two elements help to fuel this image: the fall of the rebel and the place far from heaven to which he is hurled. The notion of a fall seems to be well established since the first centuries of the Christian era. Fathers such as Gregory the Great (ca. 540–604), who played a key role in shaping medieval demonology, write of a fall dating back to the beginning of the world, when humankind had not yet been created.[7] This fall necessarily implies a landing point: while during the first millennium there was a degree of inconsistency regarding the prison into which Lucifer and the demons were flung – on earth, underground, or in the air close to the earth's surface –, the subterranean realm was gradually identified as the chosen, or predominant, place where Satan and his followers are imprisoned. In any case, the earth and its surroundings (aerial or subterranean) are the realm of the evil one, and the torment to which he is subjected is real and perceptible (mostly through the medium of fire). The basic ingredients of hell are therefore already in place, even if the idea of hell in relation to the fall of Satan is, in the first millennium, still shifting and under construction.

This portrayal poses a question that is not easy to answer and is, in many respects, disruptive: why was Satan hurled to the earth and why did Archangel Michael, on divine orders, cast him out of heaven? What motivated him to turn against God? And, above all, how is it possible that the intelligence of the Creator, who knows everything before it happens, could have permitted such a subversion of the cosmic order?[8] While the birth of hell – or the condition of hellish torment – was a response to the need to restore a balance between good and evil, it also raised many questions, and many others remained unresolved.

---

6 On the genesis of the figure of the devil, the essential aspects are summarized here: Minois G., *Le diable* (Paris: 1998); Mangenot E. – Ortolan T., "Démon", in *Dictionnaire de théologie catholique* (Paris: 1908), vol. 4.1, 321–407, particularly 322–339; Russell J.B., *The Devil: Perceptions of Evil from Antiquity to Primitive Christianity* (Ithaca, NY – London: 1977) 107–155.

7 Russell J.B., *Lucifer: The Devil in the Middle Ages* (Ithaca, NY – London: 1984) 94.

8 The above questions are also interwoven with discussions on the nature of angels. On this subject, with reference to monotheistic religions, see Hamidović D., *L'insoutenable divinité des anges: Essai historique* (Paris: 2018).

2   Lucifer's Sin

The certainty that the devil had fallen from his state of grace and had been physically banished to a place called hell (or, at the very least, to the earthly regions) by the armies of Archangel Michael was accompanied, for many centuries, by an intense debate on the nature of Satan's sin. The question was by no means secondary, for while it shed light on the very origin of evil, it also justified the characteristics and configuration of hell in its material dimension. As will be further discussed, the place of punishment reflected its genesis, recalling its salient features by analogy or opposition.

For many of the early Fathers, who partly echoed concepts from Jewish mysticism, Satan's fall was the result of his jealousy towards man, just as the disgrace of the rebel angels was due to concupiscence and the desire to copulate with women. However, Satan's creatural side continued to question the relationship between good and evil and God's responsibility for the devil's action (free? permitted? preordained?).[9] In the second century, Irenaeus confirmed the nature of the devil as an angel created by God, presenting his guilt as an act of apostasy: from this characteristic, the saint from Lyons inferred Satan's limited power and his essential subordination to divine authority, contrary to any dualistic deviation.[10] Over the course of two centuries, an interpretation of Satan's sin as a sin of pride, committed before the creation of mankind (which became the prevailing conception), gained ground. St. Jerome in particular reinforces this reading and relates it, among other passages, to the excerpt from the *Apocalypse* described at the beginning.

> The devil, who was mighty and fell, did not die. For angels' dignity cannot suffer death, but only the fall [...]. Read John's Apocalypse: when the dragon fell from heaven, he took with him a third of the stars.[11]

With sometimes significant variations, medieval writers revived this tradition, especially the depiction of the devil as an angel who fell as a result of pride. Even Thomas Aquinas did not deviate from this interpretation.[12] Specifically,

---

9   See Russell J.B., *Satan: The Early Christian Tradition* (Ithaca, NY – London: 1981) 30–50.

10   Ibidem 80–88.

11   St. Jerome, *De Psalmo LXXXI*, in *Patrologia latina*, vol. 26, 1128–1129: 'Diabolus vero qui princeps fuit et cecidit, non mortuus est. Neque enim potest angelica dignitas mortem recipere, sed tantum ruinam [...] Legite Apocalypsim Joannis: Draco quando de coelo cecidit, tertiam partem stellarum secum duxit'. See also Mangenot – Ortolan, "Démon" 366.

12   Below, I have drawn on the summary by Russell, *Lucifer* 193–207; Mangenot – Ortolan, "Démon" 395–397.

God had offered the devil the supernatural grace that would make him entirely happy, but he had refused it. According to Aquinas, Satan wanted to be like God, that is, he decided that he was free to determine his own salvation, independently of God's supernatural gift. He did not, therefore, desire to equal God, since he knew it was impossible to become like him by elevating his nature: instead, he wished to resemble him, not through divine concession, but through his own direct action ('propria virtute et non virtute Dei'). Thomas also believed that Satan had sinned through pride and, as many authors had argued before him (Cassian, Gregory the Great, Rupert of Deutz), the battle described in the twelfth chapter of *Revelation* reproduced what had happened an instant after the creation of the angels, when the devil and his acolytes had been thwarted by Michael. Following the fall, the demons dwelt in hell, where they tormented the damned, but since God wanted to make use of them, some of them were relocated to the dark ether.

It is reasonable to ask what part of this debate reached the modern age when Western Christendom was faced with the rift between Catholics and Protestants. A large part of the Reformation agreed on the existence of hell: Luther, Melanchthon, Zwingli, and Calvin had no doubts about the presence of a place intended for reprobates; however, in some of the more radical fringes of the Protestant world (e.g., the Anabaptists), doctrines emerged that essentially questioned the place of eternal punishment. What should be noted is that, in the Protestant sphere, the entire structure of the afterlife underwent significant transformations and, with the abolition of purgatory (a "timed" hell), man's otherworldly fate was dramatically polarized between salvation and damnation.[13] This is not the place to elaborate further on the reformers' ideas and views concerning the devil's action in the life of man, but suffice it to say that these changes had inevitable repercussions in the Catholic sphere. For theologians and preachers loyal to Rome, the underworld and the account of its birth as the result of a clash between the forces of good and evil remained relevant, as did its interpretation within a strictly tripartite framework (place of bliss – place of damnation – place of purgation).

Efforts to reread the medieval tradition in the light of the new demands of the Tridentine Church – emphasizing hell's physicality and adapting its appearance to the spirituality of the Counter-Reformation – emerged on several occasions. The most authoritative and, in many respects, the most comprehensive treatise on this subject was *De angelis* by the Jesuit Francisco Suárez (1548–1617), which gave a detailed description of Lucifer as a rebel angel, his damnation,

---

13   There is a summary in Vorgrimler, *Geschichte* (2nd ed., 1994) 234–240.

and his host of followers. The work, published posthumously in 1620, was rightly considered 'the most complete overview of angelology and demonology in the modern age' and successfully mediated between the Thomist and Scotist positions, reaffirming Christ's lordship over angelic creatures.[14] Two whole books, the seventh and eighth, focused on the evil angels, their fall, and the opposition unleashed against God and his faithful.[15] Suárez first sought to shed light on the many legendary or fanciful aspects surrounding the battle waged in the mists of time: the existence of evil angels was in keeping with the Christian faith, but there had never been any earthly angels from which the giants had been born. It was heresy to believe that angels were evil by nature: in truth, their sin stemmed from an act of will, manifested in pride understood as an unruly love of oneself and one's own excellence. Since Satan's guilt was not a mere desire, but was oriented towards an actual realization, it could not coincide with the goal of equalling God – a desire in itself impossible to achieve. According to Suárez, who followed certain theological hypotheses of his time, Lucifer desired the hypostatic union of the Logos with his angelic nature, assuming that God himself had revealed the mystery of Jesus's incarnation to the angels. Satan did not therefore wish to make himself like God, but rather aimed to unite his nature with the divine, thereby acquiring superiority, which is the root of the sin of pride. In the Spanish theologian's vision, there was no way Satan could have believed he could emancipate himself from God, since he knew full well that his created nature made him infinitely inferior to his creator. Before he brought about his own ruin and fell, he was a seraph, that is, he belonged to the highest hierarchy, but he was not superior to the other seraphim, so Michael, for example, could consider himself his equal. Lucifer had induced many other angels to follow in his footsteps: again, their sin had consisted in believing that their leader was entitled to hypostatic union with the Word. Although Satan's sin had preceded that of his disciples, they had all been cast down together. Their transgression, however close in time, could only have occurred after their creation: probably as early as the first day, while God was forming heaven and earth, Satan and his angels were driven out. None of them had repented within the time they had been given to do so: they were therefore doomed to eternal damnation.

---

14   Lavatori R., *Gli angeli: Storia e pensiero* (Turin: 1991) 177–180, quote at 177.
15   Mangenot – Ortolan, "Démon" 398–400. References are to Suárez Francisco, *Pars secunda Summae Theologiae de Deo rerum omnium creatore in tres praecipuos tractatus distributa, quorum primus De Angelis* (Lyon, sumptibus Iacobi Cardon et Petri Cavellat: 1620). For an overview of Suárez's ideas, see Salas V.M. – Fastiggi R.L. (eds.), *A Companion to Francisco Suárez* (Leiden – Boston, MA: 2015).

Suárez's text thus set out, and partly revised, many of the ideas developed in previous eras, transferring them into the new language of Tridentine Catholicism. With regard to the birth of hell, there are various shared elements between Thomas Aquinas's teachings and sixteenth-century doctrines: Lucifer had been created free and had sinned after his creation (the debate on the intervening time interval was unresolved); the angels who had followed him had become demons and had been cast down. Lucifer's guilt lay in his pride: for the Thomist tradition, his refusal to submit to God and desire to resemble him, not through divine grace, but through his own virtue ('propria virtute'); for Suárez, his desire to unite himself hypostatically with God. According to Thomas, Lucifer was the greatest of angels, while for Suárez he was a seraph like many others: in both cases, he had persuaded other angels to follow him, although they were outnumbered by those who remained faithful to God.

Their fall had given rise to hell – a subterranean, physical place ('locum corporeum') lacking any further description – where the rebels spent their existence: some devils, according to Thomas, remained in the air to tempt men until the final judgement. Lucifer, on the other hand, was waiting chained in his kingdom for the day when, at the end of time, he would launch his last attack: probably – Suárez commented, recalling the text of *Revelation* – the devil was 'locked up and sealed [and] he was not allowed to leave there until the last times of the tribulation imposed by the Antichrist'.[16]

To all intents and purposes, the lengthy discussions on the birth of hell, as well as the explanations of its real and perceptible existence, became part of the framework of Tridentine Catholicism along with the well-defined personality of its ruler. In the following pages, an attempt will be made to analyse how theological considerations were filtered into the collective imagination of the modern age, particularly through literary and artistic works: even more than theologians' discussions, it was iconographic and narrative models that influenced popular conceptions and cemented the idea of a physical hell, created in the mists of time following a battle between opposing forces that were personified and active in the world.

To this end, two specific periods will be considered. The initial focus will be on the decades following the Council of Trent, at a time when theology was arriving at systematizations such as those of Suárez: from the 1560s onwards, the theme of the war in heaven became increasingly popular and, in many

---

16   Suárez, *Pars secunda* 724 (vol. 8, ch. 17, no. 10): 'clausum et signatum' and 'non esse permittendum inde exire usque ad ultima tempora tribulationis Antichristi'. For Suárez's interpretation of *Revelation*, evoked by the reference to the Antichrist, see Armogathe J.-R., *L'Anticristo nell'età moderna: Esegesi e politica* (Florence: 2004) 46–50.

respects, defined the salient features of the narrative about hell in the modern age until at least the Baroque period (mid-seventeenth century). This discussion will be followed by an examination of the visual transpositions of the subject throughout the entire modern era, with the aim of identifying continuity and discontinuity in the representations that guided the devotion of the faithful.

3   A Clash in Verse: Poetry and the Birth of Hell

As discussed above, for centuries theology had proceeded to rework the biblical tradition, seeking to understand where the underworld originated, who exactly the devil was, what brought about his fall, and who and what he became the leader of. We have considered the biblical foundations and interpretations behind the account of the birth of hell. In order to examine how all this spilled over and interacted with the imagery of Counter-Reformation Italy, we must look at other sources, predating the work of Suárez, which, in the literary sphere, demonstrated a remarkable attention to this subject. It is almost superfluous to recall how Lucifer's fall was a relatively popular theme throughout the modern age – for instance in Sannazaro's *De partu Virginis* – and, to broaden our gaze to Europe, how its popularity peaked in, among other works, Milton's *Paradise Lost*.[17] With regard to Italy and the extensive body of texts on the subject, a useful starting point is offered by the poem composed by Antonino Alfano in 1568, and dedicated, as the title states, to the *Battaglia celeste tra Michele e Lucifero* (Celestial battle between Michael and Lucifer).[18] Little is known about its author, except that he died in Palermo ten years after publishing his work (16 August 1578).[19] Nevertheless, this slim booklet was the progenitor of an obscure tradition concerning the epic fall of the rebel angel. Alfano's writing had originated in the context of the Accademia degli Accesi in Palermo, commissioned by Viceroy Francesco Ferdinando d'Avalos in late

---

17   See chapter 6 in this volume.

18   Alfano A., *La battaglia celeste tra Michele e Lucifero, di Antonino Alfano gentil'huomo palermitano* (Palermo, Mayda: 1568).

19   Asor Rosa A., "Alfano, Antonio", in *Dizionario Biografico degli Italiani*, vol. 2 (Rome: 1960), https://www.treccani.it/enciclopedia/antonio-alfano_(Dizionario-Biografico) (accessed 11.07.2023). On Alfano's work see Bagni I., *La battaglia celeste tra Michele e Lucifero* (Ph.D. dissertation, University of Pisa: 2013), with a critical edition of the work; and Borsetto L., *Andar per l'aria: Temi, miti, generi nel Rinascimento e oltre* (Ravenna: 2009) 47–68, in particular 49–54.

sixteenth-century Sicily.[20] Alfano was most likely inspired by the Siege of Malta, during which, in 1565, Catholic forces had resisted and overcome the Ottoman threat, foreshadowing the final defeat at Lepanto. Rather than speaking of 'poets' dreams and fables' as in the chivalric poems, it was fitting to celebrate the first great clash – the 'first, true, and heavenly battle' – that preceded everything else.[21]

Many of the elements mentioned above return in the various cantos in an original synthesis that in fact deviated from strict doctrinal definitions. Alfano's account immediately introduced Lucifer's sin: pride, of course, but with traits only partly similar to those envisaged by theology. The connection between Satan's pride and Christ's incarnation is present in the *Battaglia celeste*: instead of the desire for hypostatic union with God (reserved for the Son), there is, however, seething anger, hatred, and pride directed at the mystery of the incarnation. Satan shows an irrepressible aversion to the human nature that Christ assumed: hence the violent attack on the heavenly plans and the struggle to subvert the design of the eternal Father. Lucifer's deranged intention was to eliminate the Son of God, i.e. to subvert the Creator's plan, and to remain the only being equal to God in heaven.[22]

Theological tradition was therefore tamed in favour of the more easily understood sin of pride: Satan wants to be like God, and Christ is the obstacle in his path. In the second canto, Lucifer utters very clear words in this regard: 'I will set my throne upon the stars / and I will be equal to the infinite power / of the Most High'.[23] To be like God – a theme reminiscent of the temptation of the first man, as well as Satan's rebellion (*Genesis* 3:4–5) – was thus the goal of Lucifer who, as a consequence, could not accept the humiliation of worshipping 'such an ignoble semblance' as the humanity assumed by Jesus. Based on these premises, Lucifer convinces other creatures to rebel: Alfano accepts the tradition, which cannot be traced to the biblical text, whereby some of the angels side against God and some remain neutral, supporting neither the Creator nor Satan: the former are assigned to hell; the latter to the realm of air.[24] Following a consultation between Lucifer and his acolytes, the poem

---

20   Girardi R., "Figure e misure del petrarchismo siciliano: l'esperienza degli Accesi", *Filologia e critica* 13 (1988) 27–78.

21   Alfano, *La battaglia*, fol. Aii v: 'sogni e favole de i poeti' and 'prima, vera et celeste battaglia'.

22   Ibidem, fol. 23 r.

23   Ibidem, fol. 25 v: 'Porrò il mio trono sugli astri/ e sarò uguale alla forza infinita/ dell'Eccelso'; ibidem for the following quotation: 'un'apparenza così vile'.

24   Ibidem, fol. 26 r: 'un'apparenza così vile'. The neutral angels, present in various medieval traditions and in Fathers such as Origen, are also mentioned by Dante (*Inferno* III, 38–39).

dwells on the battle and ends with the scene in which Satan, defeated, runs to prepare hell for his troops:

> Here now heaven is shaking off
> The new monsters, expelling them from its eternal bosom.
> First to leave the high spheres is the serpent
> Who swiftly flees to create hell.[25]

The rebels, transformed into monsters, and the serpent – that is, Lucifer presented as the tempter from *Genesis* – are cast out of heaven: Satan slides down to earth and creates hell by himself. In Alfano's vision, the prince of darkness is also the architect of his kingdom, or at least the figure who organizes its space in order to house his hosts. The short poem opens with the lights of the empyrean and ends with the cruel reality of the underworld, in which Lucifer, angry and proud, takes refuge like a wounded animal.

There is therefore little doubt that the idea of the genesis of hell as a result of Lucifer's fall and of the epic battle that saw him pitted against Archangel Michael was by this time part of the popular imagination (in Alfano's case, an expression of high culture). The subject, which is present in many works inspired by Scripture and sacred content, received a certain amount of attention in Italy between the sixteenth and seventeenth centuries, as demonstrated by other texts that focused on it after the *Battaglia celeste*.

Moving further north, we can examine, for example, the works of the Friulian humanist Erasmo di Valvasone (1528–1593).[26] The owner of a small fiefdom on the borders of the Venetian Republic, he came into contact with literary circles in the capital. Having authored an early vernacularization of Statius (*La Thebaide* [Venice, Franceschi: 1570]), he explored the sacred theme and in 1590 published the three cantos of the *Angeleida* (Venice, Somasco: 1590).[27] The episode of the war in heaven was addressed in this work: ample space was given to Lucifer's sin and, in the last of the three cantos, to the foundation of hell. Using

---

25   Alfano, *La battaglia*, fol. 59 v: 'Ecco ora il Cielo che si scuote di dosso/ I nuovi mostri, cacciandoli dal suo seno eterno./ Per primo, toccò al serpente che dalle alte sfere/ Fugge veloce a fabbricare l'inferno'.

26   Favaro M., "Valvasone, Erasmo di", in *Dizionario biografico degli Italiani*, vol. 98 (Rome: 2020), https://www.treccani.it/enciclopedia/erasmo-di-valvasone_(Dizionario-Biografico) (accessed 11.07.2023).

27   Valvasone Erasmo di, *Angeleida del sig. Erasmo di Valvasone. Al serenissimo principe Pasqual Cicogna et alla illustrissima Sig. di Venetia* (Venice, Somasco: 1590). On the work, see now the edition by Luciana Borsetto (Alessandria: 2005).

the free will with which God had endowed him,[28] Satan had, according to tradition, succumbed to pride.[29] On the nature and content of this sin, similar arguments emerge to those seen in Alfano, albeit with a significant variation: 'the most beloved, strongest' angel had turned his gaze 'to his beauty', soon feeling overcome with pride.[30] The *propria virtute* of theology – Lucifer trusting in himself and not in God's grace – crosses over into exaggerated vanity and a blind assertion of supremacy, as Satan himself cries out to his followers at the end of the first canto in order to incite them to war: 'There is none greater than I: let all honour me'.[31] As a result of this rebellion, the most beautiful of angels, humiliated by Michael, sinks into the 'eternal prison' that lies 'in the abyss'.[32] In a reversal in which high and low are inverted, Lucifer therefore ends up being crushed by the weight of the realm into which he has fallen: he was superior to all, the poet writes, and now the realm of evil bears down on him with its oppressive weight.[33]

The verses on the birth of hell, in relation to its lord, are of great interest. The dark realm would not have been necessary, because everything, in the beginning, was created pure and innocent.[34] However, the 'infernal cavern' had been necessitated by Satan's sin. After the battle was lost, the earth had opened wide to receive the rebel angel into its bowels and to immediately confine him: '[...] the frightened earth opened up for him / with a wide chasm / and he fell to the centre: / the earth then pulled itself together and enclosed him inside'.[35]

As in Alfano's octaves, it is Lucifer who hurls himself down and seeks refuge far from heaven. The chasm that opens is the reaction through which the earth, horrified by the rebel angel, lets him plunge down. After falling into the abyss, Satan looks around to survey the endless prison to which he is condemned. Both he and his acolytes lament their lost homeland with a mixture of regret and anger.[36]

---

28   See Valvasone, *Angeleida* I, 50; fol. 9 r (I use the numbering of the cantos and octaves given in the printed text; the pagination follows).

29   Ibidem I, 23, fol. 4 v.

30   Ibidem I, 26, fol. 5 r: 'il più amato, il più forte'; 'alla sua bellezza'.

31   Ibidem I, 123, fol. 21 v: 'Non vi è nessuno più grande di me: tutti mi onorino'.

32   Ibidem I, 1, fol. 1 r: 'carcere eterno'; 'nell'abisso'.

33   Ibidem I, 23, fol. 4 v: 'Era superiore: ora tutto il peso/ del regno che ha costruito gli grava addosso' ('He was superior: now the whole weight/ of the kingdom he built rests on him').

34   Ibidem I, 21, fol. 4 v. The following quotation is also taken from here.

35   Ibidem II, 131, fol. 45 r: '[...] si aprì per lui/ con un ampio baratro la terra impaurita/ ed egli cadde fino al centro:/ la terra si si tornò poi a unire e lo chiuse dentro'.

36   Ibidem III, 1, fol. 45 v; III, 7, fol. 46 v.

The hellish cavern is described as having the most typical traits of the literary and figurative tradition: airless, filthy, gloomy, and lit only by fire that burns without extinguishing, yet surrounded by icy walls.[37] Satan is effectively 'the unhappy king' of this dwelling, who, removed from the empyrean, turns his thoughts 'to founding a new kingdom': his crown is made of darkness and he pronounces his decrees from seven hideous mouths.[38] The infernal space is organized by Lucifer who allocates assignments and duties, ultimately unleashing the hosts of evil to tempt and disrupt humanity.

To round off this brief overview, it is worth mentioning a few versions which, in the same decades as Alfano and Valvasone, appeared to gain ground, testifying to a constantly changing landscape. They are presented in a little book – *Il caso di Lucifero in ottava rima* (The case of Lucifer in octave rhyme) by Amico Agnifilo (1555–1601) – published in L'Aquila in 1582.[39] A descendant of the cardinal of the same name who had governed the Abruzzi diocese in the fifteenth century, Agnifilo authored several poems on sacred subjects.[40] His work on the fall of Satan consisted of a single 124-octave canto recounting the events that unfolded at the dawn of creation. Lucifer's sin and the nature of the rebel angel were described in a similar manner to what we have seen: having possessed great valour and beauty, Satan had now become the most hideous of demons.[41] His sin was to overturn God's will – 'the eternal fate' – in order to proclaim himself king of the universe. This behaviour is proof of the madness into which the devil fell in order to 'give himself the name of almighty'.

It is interesting to note how Agnifilo adopts an argument from theology, namely the impossibility of the creature equalling the Creator. Yet, Lucifer continues in his purpose, blinded by his yearning for power: what is the use, he asks himself, of being superior to all in light and glory if one cannot be like God?[42] The paradoxical essence of the heavenly rebellion emerges in *Il caso di Lucifero*: it is divine power that has given Satan so much strength and has certainly already prophesied his rebellion. However, desire drives the angel to turn against his maker: while realizing that he wants too much, at the same time Satan is unable to restrain himself, driven by the grandeur of his nature.[43]

37   Ibidem III, 2; fol. 45 v.
38   Ibidem III, 8; fol. 46 v: 'l'infelice re'; 'a fondare un nuovo regno'.
39   Agnifilo Amico, *Il caso di Lucifero in ottava rima, del signor Amico Cardinali Aquilano abbate di S. Giovanni di Collimento* (L'Aquila, Dagano: 1582).
40   Dragonetti A., *Le vite degli illustri Aquilani* (Aquila: 1847) 30–31.
41   Agnifilo, *Il caso* 10, from which the following quotations are also taken: 'l'eterno fato' and 'attribuirsi il nome di onnipotente'.
42   Ibidem 11.
43   Ibidem 12.

Although the rebel's ambition is described as an impulse that is both irresistible and insane at the same time, this delusion is accompanied by the illusion of impunity: being pure spirit ('my limbs are impassive and divine'), Satan believes that he will never be able to suffer the pain inflicted by fire and ice which, as it turns out, await him.[44] The act of revolt is marked by the transformation of Lucifer and his followers who, in a flash, become hideous, dark beings.[45] Yet the protagonist of the entire poem is not Lucifer, but God himself. He is the driving force behind all the action; he is the one who shows his indignant and enraged countenance in response to the devil's pride. Whereas in the other poems God seems to rise above the disputants, here he is an avenger of the revolt, and Michael is presented as an instrument of his fury: 'He will be punished for it [...]. His guilt is too grave and enormous'.[46] Indeed, it is precisely the curse which, over many octaves, the Creator hurls at Lucifer and his followers that has led to a different interpretation of the genesis of hell. While in Alfano and Valvasone it is Satan's fall that provokes the earth's reaction, in which a deep chasm opens up, in Agnifilo God's prescience has already shaped the place to which Satan is destined. In his invective against the rebels, God commands his hosts to confine Lucifer to the centre of the universe, in eternal darkness.[47] Divine justice has already prepared a place with chains 'of ice and fire', in which the two elements – without cancelling each other out – inflict their torment on Lucifer, making his immortality the worst of punishments.[48] Finally, God himself vetoes any possible repentance of Satan and the other rebels, lest they arouse his forgiveness: 'Foolish sin / shall not be followed by repentance, lest mercy / move my eternal goodness'.[49] Agnifilo's work portrays a warlike and wrathful deity who, certain of his victory, opens the prison prepared for the rebels at the outbreak of war. The moment a heavenly voice speaks out against the devil, hell opens up and Lucifer, stricken with sorrow, goes so far as to wish he had always been buried under the ground: 'With that horrible cry / hell opened up and the earth shook'.[50]

Lucifer is defeated and, chained by Michael, confined to hell.[51] Plunging into it, he curses himself and the day he was created and, in order not to see

---

44   Ibidem 12: 'le mie membra sono impassibili e divine'.
45   Ibidem 14.
46   Ibidem 16: 'Pena ne avrà [...]. La sua colpa è troppo è grave ed enorme'.
47   Ibidem 19.
48   See ibidem 20–21: 'di ghiaccio e di fuoco'.
49   Ibidem 21: 'Al folle peccato/ non segua il pentimento, affinché la pietà/ non muova la mia bontà eterna'.
50   Ibidem 25: 'A quel grido orribile/ si aprì l'inferno e tremò la terra'.
51   Cf. ibidem 28–29.

God, sinks into the earthly cavity: 'My desire is to descend into hell'.[52] The battle ends with an exorcism-like scene in which Michael annihilates his enemy
by invoking divine authority and banishing the outcast to the 'dark centre':
Lucifer, like a wounded bear, weeps and shakes his head, staring at the abyss
that has opened up and where 'he must be stuck forever'.[53]

Agnifilo therefore introduces a variant in the debate about the genesis of
hell: it did not arise from Satan's fall, but was prepared by divine omniscience:
'Gehenna is [...] / prepared by God, black and deep'.[54] The chasm in which the
rebel angel is locked for eternity is therefore not the result of his banishment
from heaven, but a place that God created at the centre of the universe and
which, with Satan's sin, reveals its existence.

The events surrounding the genesis of the underworld continued to reverberate in the various corners of Italy throughout the modern age. Moving to a
later date, similar motifs are found in the *Caduta di Lucifero* (Fall of Lucifer) by
Giovanni Battista Composto (1613).[55] Three cantos recall the fall of heaven's
most resplendent seraph 'from bright Olympus to the dark abysses'.[56] Having
learnt that the Son of God would clothe himself in human flesh, Lucifer, contemplating his own angelic beauty, succumbs to pride and refuses to worship
the man-Christ: if the weak creature (man) is allowed to associate himself
with the divine nature, why should this not also be granted to an angel?[57]
In the second book, the archangels, led by Michael, express their outrage at
the deranged affront, until, in the following book, the battle rages: Lucifer is
cast out and the earth opens up to enclose him in its belly: 'the deep caverns
opened the abysses'.[58]

Confirming characteristics that were now well defined, these motifs return
three decades later in the *Rappresentazione della vittoria*, a verse work by
Florentine academic Francesco Chelli that describes Saint Michael's victory.[59]
This poem, for which stage directions are given at the beginning (including
the melody to be used), is divided into four parts: first Michael, Gabriel, and

52   Ibidem 30: 'Il mio desiderio è scendere nell'inferno'.
53   Ibidem 31–33: 'centro oscuro' and 'deve stare fisso in eterno'.
54   Cf. ibidem 37: 'La Geena è [...]/ preparata da Dio, nera e profonda'.
55   Composto Giovan Battista, *La caduta di Lucifero di Giovan Battista Composto academico
      Otioso detto il Fisso* (Naples, Carlino: 1613). On Composto, see Palmisciano V., "Per una bio-
      grafia di Giovan Battista Composto", *Archivio Storico per la Province Napoletane* 137 (2019)
      427–432 (limited to biographical information).
56   Composto, *La caduta* 2: 'dall'Olimpo luminoso ai bui abissi'.
57   Ibidem 13–15.
58   Ibidem 46: 'le profonde caverne aprirono gli abissi'.
59   Chelli Francesco, *La rappresentatione della vittoria che hebbe in cielo s. Michele archangelo
      nella battaglia contro a Lucifero e suoi seguaci, di Francesco Chelli fiorentino* (Siena, Loggia
      del Papa: 1640).

Raphael prepare for battle after discussing the irrationality of Satan's sin. His rebellion is motivated, once again, by his desire not to bow before the Son of God incarnate in wretched human nature: the most beautiful of angels claims to be similar to God and to surpass, with his strength, the Logos made man.[60] In the second and third parts – highlighting a distinctly pedagogical and moral purpose – the deadly sins and the virtues that oppose them discuss what is happening and, at the opening of the last scene (part four), Michael and Lucifer face each other in the final confrontation that ends with Satan's expulsion to a dark hell full of torment and pain.

These cases, which date back to the most expansive phase of the Counter-Reformation, show that the fundamental characteristics of the birth of hell, its physicality, and its moral significance were by then well established. Hell is the result of a sin of pride and is therefore shaped like a cavity: a consequence of Lucifer's desire to exalt himself, it must necessarily be a cavern, the quintessential "lowest" place (hence the etymology of the word 'inferno', which comes from the Latin term 'infernus', meaning 'of the lower regions'). Everything is reversed: he who was meant to rise becomes the lowest; the most beautiful becomes the ugliest; he who was destined for light is plunged into darkness, and so on. On the nature of this pride, writers' inventiveness seems to distance itself from the doctrinal discussion, of which it nevertheless retains one element: the fall of Satan relates to the incarnation of Christ. Not, however, in the terms in which Suárez framed it (envy of the hypostatic union of the Word with the Father), but because of Satan's unwillingness to worship the Son, since the latter assumed the wretched human nature. Lucifer's pride is also expressed in wanting to be like God or superior to the Son. This rebellion is joined by various angels persuaded by Satan (the minority of the angelic hosts): the result is a clash between good and evil that ends with the victory of the leader Michael, whose personhood varies in its degree of autonomy from God's wrath. Lucifer and his followers are plunged into an underground chasm which, in many accounts, the devil himself moulds into his own kingdom.

4   Dancing Angels, Monstrous Demons, and Chasms of Fire: Artistic
       Representation

To appeal to the senses, an important contribution also came from the visual arts, which seized every opportunity to take inspiration from the epic struggle between the angelic hosts. The fall of Lucifer, understood as the origin of hell

---

60   Ibidem, fol. B3 v.

and the opposition between good and evil, was a theme explored by numerous artists, usually in connection with the figure of Michael. Indeed, the birth of the kingdom of evil often provided a simple backdrop for the glorious figure of the archangel, portrayed at the moment of victory over the enemy: nascent hell, as will be further discussed, is mostly denoted by plays of light, dark backdrops, and fissures in the ground, although there are some notable exceptions.

Representations of the cosmic battle, the fall of the rebel angels, and the otherworldly hollows were a motif that had frequently appeared in art, featuring in numerous works. Below we examine a number of works intended for worship (private or public) that focused on the theme. The chosen cases are just a small selection within a dense, very vibrant framework: some of them will be discussed more for their value as models or for the originality with which they interpreted the infernal subject; others will be mentioned more quickly to show the continuity and discontinuity of certain iconographic elements. In all these cases, we can easily discern a fundamental confirmation of the interpretation of Satan's sin as an act of pride, punished by the power of God, and of the birth of hell – physical, subterranean, and fiery – as a consequence of this rebellion.

First of all, it should be noted how, in the early sixteenth century, at the height of the Protestant Reformation, Lucifer's expulsion by Archangel Michael was a very popular theme in Italy due to its obvious parallels with the ongoing anti-heretical offensive. In 1518, Leo X – the pope who first addressed the Lutheran emergency – and his cousin Lorenzo II de' Medici, Duke of Urbino, sent King Francis I of France a painting from Raphael's workshop (now in the Louvre and known as *Le Grand saint Michel*), which soon became a point of reference [Fig. 5.1].[61] Documented in Fontainebleau around 1537, *Le Grand saint Michel* was constantly associated with the power of French monarchs, who were celebrated as defenders of the faith and the Church. Without dwelling on the work's evident political function, the depiction of the defeated Lucifer is of particular interest. The devil is crushed beneath the graceful feet of Michael, 'un danseur céleste' ('a heavenly dancer') as Sylvie Béguin described him. The hell to which Lucifer is assigned is barely sketched out: the earth surrounds the rebel's body, forming a kind of cavern; smoke and flames – an allusion to the infernal underworld – come out of its fissures, which seem to open as he falls. In addition to the usual bestial features – dark wings and a dragon's tail, horns,

---

61   See the entry by Béguin S., "Raphaël, un nouveau regard", in Béguin S. – Pierrette J.-R. – Viatte F. (eds.), *Raphaël dans les collections françaises*, exh. cat., Galeries nationales du Grand Palais (Paris: 1983) 53–146, at 90–92. Cf. also *Raphaël: Les dernières années* (Paris: 2012) 129–134. For an entry on the work and an up-to-date bibliography, see further https://collections.louvre.fr/en/ark:/53355/cl010060771 (accessed 10.07.2023).

FIGURE 5.1   Raphael, *Le Grand Saint Michel*, 1518. Oil transferred from wood to
canvas, 268 × 160 cm. Paris, Musée du Louvre, inv. no. 610
IMAGE © RMN-GRAND PALAIS (MUSÉE DU LOUVRE),
THIERRY OLLIVIER

and gnashing teeth – Satan clutches a two-pronged grappling hook in his hand, with which he will drag souls into his kingdom. A hell that is merely alluded to, which in other paintings of the same period (such as Marco d'Oggiono's *Tre arcangeli* – Three archangels, painted around 1516) is revealed more explicitly as a precipice [Fig. 5.2].[62] *Le Grand saint Michel* had a considerable influence, both through the sketch of the painting – sent to the Ferrarese court in September 1518 – and through the circulation of engravings and the testimony of various artists who probably visited Raphael's workshop before the painting left for France.[63]

A far more complex scene was presented a few years later by Domenico Beccafumi (ca. 1486–1551) in two paintings depicting the expulsion of the rebel angels. This case is particularly interesting because there are two versions of the work, both commissioned from the artist by the Carmelites of Siena. Around 1524, Beccafumi created a first panel, which was never completed: after his death, it was moved to the Ospedale di Santa Maria della Scala, finally ending up in the Pinacoteca Nazionale in Siena, where it is currently kept [Fig. 5.3]. Neither the reasons why the painter did not finish the painting, nor why the Carmelites requested a second version have been ascertained. Evidently inspired by the passage from *Revelation* on the war in heaven, the altarpiece interpreted the theme with innovative designs which, according to Vasari's account, featured a 'pioggia d'ignudi molto bella' ('a very beautiful rain of nude figures'), i.e. the bodies of Lucifer's followers falling to the ground under the blows of the hosts led by Michael, with inspiration from Michelangelo.[64] Compared to the famous Sistine nudes, Beccafumi's nudes are slender and elongated and manifest shame, in keeping with the sinfulness that they are intended to represent. Above, heroic, luminous angels fight beneath the open arms of God the Father who, shown in faded colours, watches discreetly. In the part below, dedicated to the rebels, the opening of the infernal abyss is alluded to by the contrast between light and darkness, and by flames and lapilli; but it is also signified by the fall of Lucifer, depicted as a hydra, into a lake of fire

---

62   As the title suggests, the work depicts three angels, with Michael in the centre driving a monstrous Lucifer into a cavity that has opened up in the ground. On the painter, I refer only to the overview in Serafini A., "Marco da Oggiono", in *Dizionario Biografico degli Italiani*, vol. 69 (Rome: 2007), https://www.treccani.it/enciclopedia/marco-da-oggiono_%28Dizionario-Biografico%29/ (accessed 10.07.2023).

63   According to Tom Henry and Paul Joannides, both Battista Dossi and Perin del Vaga may have seen the painting in Raphael's workshop (*Raphaël: Les dernières années* 132).

64   Angelini A., "Domenico Beccafumi, 1519–1527", in Barocchi P. – Sricchia Santoro F. (eds.), *Domenico Beccafumi e il suo tempo*, exh. cat., Pinacoteca Nazionale, Siena (Milan: 1990) 127–155, at 152–153 (from which the quotations from Vasari are also taken).

FIGURE 5.2 Marco d'Oggiono, *Altarpiece of the Three Archangels*, ca. 1516. Oil on wood,
          255 × 190 cm. Milan, Pinacoteca di Brera, inv. no. 447
          IMAGE © PINACOTECA DI BRERA

FIGURE 5.3 Domenico Beccafumi, *The Fall of the Rebel Angels*, ca. 1524. Oil on wood,
347 × 227 cm. Siena, Pinacoteca Nazionale

surrounded by mountains (perhaps a quotation from *Revelation* 20:10). The scene, as Vasari put it, is 'confusa' ('confused'), and Beccafumi demonstrates an original approach in which the figures lack a true centre of gravity: the relationship between the cursed angels and the depths of the earth does not, however, seem to be in question, as indicated by one of the supine figures in the foreground whose head seems almost to be sucked towards the hollows of the underworld.

While in Beccamfumi's first attempt the individual motifs are embedded in a chaotic narrative, they emerge more legibly in the second version of the work, dated 1528, kept in the church of San Niccolò del Carmine in Siena, for which the 1524 altarpiece was also intended [Fig. 5.4].[65] Here, the upper section of the painting depicts God seated on a throne, surrounded by the angelic hosts arranged in two tiers: below him, in the centre of the composition, is Michael brandishing his sword and driving Satan towards the centre of the earth (this is how Vasari, who saw the work in 1535 together with Baldassarre Peruzzi, interpreted the scene). Hell is once again strongly associated with the earth and the idea of a fiery cavity: Beccafumi devises a solution in which the underworld consists of two caverns where architectural elements (an arch and vaults) are used to make the ravines less wild and more like a forge than a chasm. Within them, fire is generated by sudden explosions. However, we can discern a second, invisible but intuitable, level: Lucifer, in the form of a dragon, is thrust by Michael's foot towards a hole from which a very strong fiery glow emanates, and the bodies of the rebels emerge into view from underground (some half visible, some only with their heads, some sitting on the edge of a cavity). One could therefore say that, conceptually, the second version of Beccafumi's *San Michele* organizes the narrative into four levels, ordered from top to bottom: the empyrean where God sits with an imperturbable air; the confines of heaven guarded by a fierce Michael who touches the earth with his feet; the ground towards which the rebels are driven; the depths of the earth placed outside the scene and evidenced by the play of light.

Such comprehensive iconography depicting the fall of the rebel angels is unusual. Nevertheless, it is the first sign of a trend to clearly define hell's material contours and its moral function discussed above. It is therefore no wonder that, in the same decades in which poetry was exploring the birth of hell, the latter was also making an increasingly tangible appearance in painting. A striking example in this respect is *La battaglia tra gli angeli fedeli e gli angeli ribelli* (The battle between faithful angels and rebel angels), painted in the late

65   Guiducci A.M., "Domenico Beccafumi: 1528–1537", in Barocchi – Sricchia Santoro, *Domenico Beccafumi* 168–170.

FIGURE 5.4 Domenico Beccafumi, *The Fall of the Rebel Angels*, ca. 1528. Oil on wood,
347 × 225 cm. Siena, Church of San Niccolò al Carmine

1570s by Giorgio Vasari, probably with the assistance of Jacopo Zucchi, for the Chapel of St. Michael in the Vatican commissioned by Pope Pius V [Fig. 5.5]. The iconography of this important space in the papal palaces leaves no room for doubt: seven angels in warrior pose (including Michael driving out Lucifer) pierce the demons (seven, like the deadly sins) with their weapons, while above heaven appears to have been freed of the rebels. The evil beings are plummeting to the ground where the land is engulfed in high flames and hazy smoke, amidst ruined buildings.[66]

Highly conspicuous flames, covering almost half of the painted surface, also characterize the expulsion of the rebel angels Federico Zuccari frescoed around 1599/1600 on the wall of one of the nave chapels of a church renowned for its symbolic and exemplary value: that of the Gesù in Rome.[67] Michael and his angels hurl the monstrous, writhing bodies of the demons into a fiery chasm, in which the rebels are torn apart, while – in the fresco on the opposite wall – other angels free the souls in purgatory.[68]

The theme was very popular in Roman circles and, after Pius V, another pope – Paul V Borghese – commissioned Andrea Commodi to paint a fresco depicting the fall of the rebel angels for the Quirinale (around 1612). The work was never realized, but the surviving sketch reveals, alongside the iconography centred on the figure of Michael, the development of a representation of the piled-up, disordered bodies of the rebels, for whom the earth opened up a ravine – also alluded to in Commodi's sketch – identified with hell.[69]

Two decades later, around 1635/1636, a painting that had an enormous impact on the Counter-Reformation imagination of the theme was produced: Guido Reni's Saint Michael, again in Rome, in Santa Maria della Concezione [Fig. 5.6].[70] The painting presents elements similar to Raphael's model,

---

66   Aurigemma M.G., "Torre Pia in Vaticano: Architettura, decorazione, committenza, tras-
      formazioni di tre cappelle vasariane", *Römisches Jahrbuch der Bibliotheca Hertziana* 39
      (2009/2010) 65–164, in particular 105–108, where it is mentioned that Michelangelo orig-
      inally also intended to depict the fall in the Sistine Chapel.

67   See Bailey G.A., *Between Renaissance and Baroque: Jesuit Art in Rome, 1565–1610* (Toronto:
      2003), with a discussion of Zuccari's work in the Church of the Gesù (with previous
      bibliography).

68   Acidini Luchinat C., *Taddeo e Federico Zuccari, fratelli pittori del Cinquecento* (Milan –
      Rome: 1999) 2:181–191, in particular 182.

69   Pierguidi S., "Da Michelangelo a Andrea Commodi: Storia di un programma iconografico
      mai realizzato", *Studi romani* 51 (2003) 272–279; Papi G. – Petrioli Tofani A. (eds.), *Andrea
      Commodi: Dall'attrazione per Michelangelo all'ansia del nuovo* (Florence: 2012).

70   Pepper D.S., *Guido Reni: A Complete Catalogue of His Works with an Introductory Text*
      (Oxford: 1984), 272, no. 154, which mentions several copies of the work.

FIGURE 5.5   Giorgio Vasari, Chapel of St. Michael with the vault fresco depicting the *Fall of Lucifer and the Rebel Angels*, ca. 1571. Vatican City, Vatican Palace

FIGURE 5.6
Guido Reni, *St. Michael*,
1635/36. Oil on canvas,
293 × 202 cm. Rome,
Church of Santa Maria
della Concezione
dei Cappucini
IMAGE © FOTOTECA
FEDERICO ZERI,
BOLOGNA

portraying the devil crushed to the ground by the mighty figure of the archangel. The moment captured by the painter is that of the clash, or rather of
its epilogue: we can foresee the fate that will befall the rebel from the crevice
that appears in the ground, unleashing the flash of lightning (a fissure that
explicitly became a chasm in later paintings, from Guercino's *San Michele* of
1644 – emancipated from Reni's model that the painter may have known – to
Francesco Cozza's version, dating from the sixth decade of the seventeenth
century).[71] One detail is particularly noteworthy: in Reni's painting, Michael
holds in his hand a chain which, recalling the twentieth chapter of *Revelation*,

71   For Guercino's painting in the church of San Niccolò in Fabriano, see Mahon D. (ed.),
      Giovanni Francesco Barbieri: Il Guercino, 1591–1666 (Bologna: 1991) 262–263. For Cozza's
      painting: Castellani P. (ed.), *Tra cielo e abisso: Scoperta e restauro del San Michele arcan-
      gelo in lotta col demonio di Francesco Cozza* (Rome: 2013).

will be used to annihilate his adversary. However, it also marks the essential nature of hell, a prison and site of eternal incarceration from which there is no escape. The iron cord is found, with a variant, in the bronze group by Bolognese sculptor Alessandro Algardi who, mindful of Reni's iconography, portrays Lucifer already chained by his left forearm and driven to the ground, whose infernal depths cannot however be glimpsed [Fig. 5.7].[72]

The same context for which Algardi's sculptural group was intended – the monastery of San Michele in Bosco in Bologna – is the setting for another interpretation of the fall of Satan offered by the painter Domenico Maria Canuti in 1659.[73] The artist courageously chose to paint his fresco in a particularly prominent and visible position on the church's triumphal arch. At the top, the figure of the archangel, bearing a shield and spear, is shown crushing the head of the falling Lucifer with one foot. Dense black smoke, an allusion to the infernal haze, rises from the lower extremities towards which many rebel angels slide, displaying monstrous and bestial features. Some of these are only partly visible because they have already been swallowed up in the earthly cavities. A scroll, held by one of the rebels with a despairing demeanour, recalls the nature of Satan's sin, quoting the prophet Isaiah (14:14): 'Sarò simile all'Altissimo' ('I will be like the Most High'). Pride has been overcome, and hell, with its darkness, is the place where it will be eternally punished. The choice of such a location, framing the presbytery, can certainly be ascribed to the fact that the place is named after Archangel Michael. One cannot, however, fail to recognize the visual combination of the scene of the fall and the tabernacle below, which appears to somehow refer to the connection between Lucifer's sin and the envy aroused by Christ's incarnation by virtue of his hypostatic union with the Father.

The theme of the fall returns in the works of another outstanding artist, Luca Giordano, who interpreted it in multiple ways. For the most part, they confirm the content already outlined, albeit according to new stylistic and compositional models. One original element is worthy of note, namely the presence of the throne of Lucifer (with reference to *Isaiah* 14, also quoted

---

72   The statue (*San Michele abbatte Lucifero* – St. Michael strikes down Lucifer) was commissioned for the monastery of Monte Oliveto and later arrived in Bologna. According to new archival investigations, the work was finished prior to May 1652: Fagiani M., "Il *San Michele che sconfigge il demonio* di Alessandro Algardi", *Prospettiva* 173 (2019) 71–75. It is currently kept in the Civic Museums of Bologna; see *Introduzione al Museo civico medievale, Palazzo Ghisilardi-Fava* (Bologna: 1987) 85–86.

73   For Canuti, the subject of several recent papers, I simply refer to the general catalogue: Stagni S., *Domenico Maria Canuti, pittore (1626–1684): Catalogo generale* (Rimini: 1988) 42–43, 138.

FIGURE 5.7   Alessandro Algardi, *St. Michael Overcoming the Devil*, before 1652. Bronze.
Bologna, Museo Civico Medievale
IMAGE © FOTOTECA FEDERICO ZERI, BOLOGNA

in Canuti's fresco)[74] in the 1657 altarpiece for the Church of the Ascension
in Chiaia (in Naples) and in the later altarpiece for the Minoritenkirche in

---

74   'How art thou fallen from heaven, O Lucifer, who didst rise in the morning? [...] And thou
      saidst in thy heart: I will ascend into heaven, I will exalt my throne above the stars of
      God [...] I will ascend above the height of the clouds, I will be like the most High. But yet
      thou shalt be brought down to hell, into the depth of the pit'.

Vienna. Particularly in the first, the painter offers an exegesis of Satan's sin: while brandishing the sword of fire, Michael (accompanied by the inscription 'Quis ut Deus') points to the seat on which God the Father is seated. A little further down, a similar throne stands empty in the sky: the base bears the inscription 'Sarò simile all'Altissimo' ('I will be like the Most High'). Lucifer, in the guise of a warrior, has just been thrown out of this throne: Michael crushes him with his foot, while the demons are also cast down.[75] Hell is not visible in the depiction: no glow can be seen coming from underground, unlike the strong chiaroscuro effect, reminiscent of fire, in the painting for the Minoritenkirche and in a third version now in Berlin.[76]

As mentioned in connection to Algardi, sculpture also sought to represent the birth of hell. Looking ahead to the eighteenth century, an extraordinarily evocative example is offered by a work that is in many respects unique, namely *La caduta degli angeli ribelli* (The fall of the rebel angels) by Francesco Bertos, dating to the 1730s [Fig. 5.8]. It should be noted that, in contrast to the above cases, this composition was not intended for a place of worship, but for a private residence: with the advent of the Enlightenment, the spectacular and majestic birth of hell seems to have become a *divertissement* for scholarly circles, although popular devotion had by no means abandoned it. Long attributed to Agostino Fasolato, the group features around sixty figures carved from a single block of stone.[77] A stack of piled-up bodies, falling ruinously, is topped by Michael drawing his customary sword of fire. The archangel scatters his enemies by holding up his shield on which the words 'Quis ut Deus' recall divine superiority. Satan holds a two-pronged grappling hook in his hands, a symbol, as in Raphael, of his tempting nature. The sculpture is understood to have been commissioned by Marcantonio Trento, a member of the Knights of Malta, who, according to some interpretations, envisaged it as an allegory of triumph over evil embodied by heretics and infidels. The extravagance of this pyramidal composition attracted numerous visitors to Palazzo Papafava in Padua, where the statue was housed. It was visited by the theologian Antonio

---

75   On Chiaia's painting, Ferrari O. – Scavizzi G., *Luca Giordano: L'opera completa* (Naples: 2000) 1:258, cat. A 49a.

76   For the two paintings in Vienna and Berlin, see *Luca Giordano, 1634–1705* (Naples: 2001) 146–149; Ferrari – Scavizzi, *Luca Giordano* 1:282, cat. A 195.

77   See Semenzato C., *La Caduta degli angeli di Agostino Fasolato* (Padua: 1972); Avery C., *The Triumph of Motion: Francesco Bertos (1678–1741) and the Art of Sculpture. Catalogue Raisonné* (Turin: 2008) 93–94: both attribute the sculpture to Fasolato. For the attribution to Bertos: De Vincenti M. – Guerriero S., *La Caduta degli angeli ribelli* (Rome: 2021).

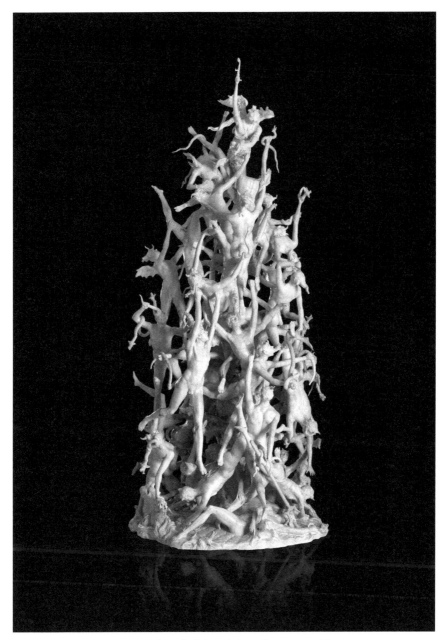

FIGURE 5.8   Francesco Bertos, *The Fall of the Rebel Angels*, 1730s. Marble, 168 × 80 × 81 cm.
Vicenza, Gallerie d'Italia
IMAGE © ARCHIVIO PATRIMONIO ARTISTICO INTESA SANPAOLO

Rosmini, who did not particularly appreciate its style,[78] and by the great novelist Herman Melville, who saw in it the heroic flair of Satan.[79]

The virtuoso technical quality of the composition and the choice of the unusual subject matter of the *Fall of the Angels* for a sculptural work are all the more significant when considered in relation to Bertos's biography: suspicious of the artist's astonishing skill, the Inquisition summoned him to examine the contribution that the devil himself had supposedly made to the creation of his works, revealing how the artist's adopted language deviated from traditional models or, if nothing else, perplexed the judges of faith.[80] Only focusing on the connection between Lucifer's rebellion and the birth of hell, there is no doubt that Bertos also embraced the idea that the earth opened up to receive and confine the rebels. Specifically, the sculptor fashioned a monstrous mouth which, according to an ancient figurative tradition, represents the entrance to the infernal cavern. A chasm is therefore ready for the mass of bodies – which take on the features of demons as they fall – towards which some of them are already sliding. The ground is shaken and disturbed, teeming with reptiles and monsters, and Lucifer's two-pronged grappling hook points towards it, foretelling how he will drag the souls of the damned there.

It is evident how each of the examples referred to is situated within a specific context which, in addition to the theological datum (and sometimes even more than this), calls into question other elements ranging from artistic debate to patronage, from the political aims of the individual works to the contexts in which and for which they were produced. Nevertheless, these cases offer an insight into characteristics and shifts regarding the origins of hell and the relationship between its creation and Satan's sin.

5   Conclusions

Considering all these examples, various recurring elements emerge, caught in a state of constant tension between doctrinal formulation and communicative needs. Compared to theology, imagery – both poetic and artistic – applies certain simplifications, aimed on the one hand at moralizing the process of creating hell, and on the other at materializing it. In all portrayals, the genesis of hell

---

78   Rizzioli E.G., "Antonio Rosmini e *La Caduta degli angeli fulminati da Michele* di Agostino Fasolato: Alcune considerazioni su una visita in Casa Papafava", *Atti e Memorie dell'Accademia Galileiana di Scienze, Lettere e Arti* 118 (2005–2006) 121–180.

79   Planiscig L., "Fasolato's Satan and Melville", *Art News* 50 (1952) 21.

80   For the Inquisition's intervention against Bertos: Avery, *The Triumph* 37, 78–86.

is linked to sin: although with different explanations and variations, hell is always presented as the fruit of the sin of pride committed by Lucifer. It originates as a consequence of this act of rebellion and, in the narratives in which it appears to already exist, it is preordained by God – omniscient and prescient – to punish the angels who will rise against him. Precisely because it derives from pride (which, according to some, is engendered by a desire to be equal to God, and, according to others, by opposing the incarnation of Jesus), hell is a low place, relegated to the abyss. The parallel endeavour, as mentioned, is to make its existence concrete: the element in which it is rooted is the earth. Hell resides in its depths, lies underground, and is generated, in most cases, from a fissure in the ground. What can be glimpsed are mostly the flames and glow of fire, which contrast with the other distinguishing element: darkness. It is difficult, in non-literary representations, to render the presence of the frost which, with fire, torments Satan and his followers, without one element negating the other. All sources, however, portray a state of despair and anger into which the rebel angels fall, aware of the terrible punishment that awaits them, but unable to repent.

In a play of contrasts, Lucifer is lord of this subterranean place, which he usually commands and governs: his destiny, however, is to remain imprisoned here, as shown by the chain which, in many cases, Michael wields against him. His sceptre, reminiscent of the trident of ancient gods, is a grappling hook. Emphasized more in iconography than in literary accounts, this tool embodies the role of mankind's tempter assumed by Satan immediately after his fall as a response to the banishment inflicted on him by God.

This representation is supported in particular by two passages of Scripture that are invoked: the apocalyptic battle and the prophecy of Isaiah, which recalls Lucifer's ruinous defeat. By contrast, the Gospel passage from *Luke*, in which Jesus compares Satan and his followers to a falling thunderbolt, appears to remain in the background (*Luke* 10:18). Finally, literary texts and visual arts made frequent reference to the tensions running through society: the mighty figure of the tempter, struck down and humiliated by Michael, the warrior of God, became an image that reflected the many infidelities to the religion governed by the Catholic Church: Satan's rebellion was that of the Turk who suffered rightful punishment between Malta and Lepanto; or, indeed, the heresy against which Peter's successors fought gloriously.

While theology pursued its course and revived the medieval tradition, inserting it into the new framework of Tridentine Catholicism, artists and poets contributed to enriching the collective imagination with colours and figures. Hell, born in the mists of time, was a living and present reality, and, beneath the feet of men of the modern age, a world of ice and fire, in which the prince of darkness exercised his dominion, was still seething.

Bibliography

Acidini Luchinat C., *Taddeo e Federico Zuccari, fratelli pittori del Cinquecento* (Milan – Rome: 1999).

Angelini A., "Domenico Beccafumi, 1519–1527", in Barocchi P. – Sricchia Santoro F. (eds.), *Domenico Beccafumi e il suo tempo*, exh. cat., Pinacoteca Nazionale, Siena (Milan: 1990) 127–155.

Armogathe J.-R., *L'Anticristo nell'età moderna: Esegesi e politica* (Florence: 2004).

Avery C., *The Triumph of Motion: Francesco Bertos (1678–1741) and the Art of Sculpture. Catalogue Raisonné* (Turin: 2008).

Bailey G.A., *Between Renaissance and Baroque: Jesuit Art in Rome, 1565–1610* (Toronto: 2003).

Béguin S., "Raphaël, un nouveau regard", in Béguin S. – Pierrette J.-R. – Viatte F. (eds.), *Raphaël dans les collections françaises*, exh. cat., Galeries nationales du Grand Palais (Paris: 1983) 53–146.

Borsetto L., *Andar per l'aria: Temi, miti, generi nel Rinascimento e oltre* (Ravenna: 2009).

De Vincenti M. – Guerriero S., *La Caduta degli angeli ribelli* (Rome: 2021).

Ehrman B.D., *Heaven and Hell: A History of the Afterlife* (New York, NY: 2020).

Erasmo di Valvasone, *Angeleida*, ed. L. Borsetto (Alessandria: 2005).

Ferrari O. – Scavizzi G., *Luca Giordano: L'opera completa* (Naples: 2000).

Forsyth N., *The Old Enemy: Satan and the Combat Myth* (Princeton, NJ: 1987).

Hamidović D., *L'insoutenable divinité des anges: Essai historique* (Paris: 2018).

Lavatori R., *Gli angeli: Storia e pensiero* (Turin: 1991).

Le Goff J., *The Birth of Purgatory* (Chicago, IL: 1984 [1981]).

Mahon D. (ed.), *Giovanni Francesco Barbieri: Il Guercino, 1591–1666* (Bologna: 1991).

Mangenot E. – Ortolan T., "Démon", in *Dictionnaire de théologie catholique* (Paris 1908), vol. 4.1, 321–407.

Minois G., *Histoire des enfers* (Paris: 1991).

Minois G., *Le diable* (Paris: 1998).

Papi G. – Petrioli Tofani A. (eds.), *Andrea Commodi: Dall'attrazione per Michelangelo all'ansia del nuovo* (Florence: 2012).

Pepper D.S., *Guido Reni: A Complete Catalogue of His Works with an Introductory Text* (Oxford: 1984).

Russell J.B., *The Devil: Perceptions of Evil from Antiquity to Primitive Christianity* (Ithaca, NY – London: 1977).

Russell J.B., *Satan: The Early Christian Tradition* (Ithaca, NY – London: 1981).

Russell J.B., *Lucifer: The Devil in the Middle Ages* (Ithaca, NY – London: 1984).

Semenzato C., *La Caduta degli angeli di Agostino Fasolato* (Padua: 1972).

Stagni S., *Domenico Maria Canuti, pittore (1626–1684): Catalogo generale* (Rimini: 1988).

Vorgrimler H., *Geschichte der Hölle* (Munich: 1993).

CHAPTER 6

'Oh How Unlike the Place from Whence They Fell!' John Milton's Primordial Hell in *Paradise Lost*

Antoinina Bevan Zlatar

Abstract

John Milton's biblical epic *Paradise Lost* (1674) famously begins in hell. Unlike Virgil's Hades or Dante's Inferno, which are situated at the centre of the earth, Milton locates his infernal realm in outer chaos, arguing that hell was perhaps created before the earth and certainly before the earth was corrupted by the Fall of mankind. It is only in Book x after Adam and Eve have eaten the apple that Sin and Death build a bridge connecting hell to earth. These spatial and temporal specifications have implications for the kind of hell we encounter.

This chapter argues that Milton is exceptional in evoking a primordial hell, the place prepared for Satan and the rebel angels rather than the hell destined for the wicked after the Last Judgement. It is a place reserved for the mighty, embodied fallen angels who, far from the sadistic demons of the homiletic visual tradition, have not yet lost all their original beauty and angelic features. After exploring the biblical and patristic sources that Milton drew on for his infernal narrative and commented on in his *De Doctrina Christiana*, I analyze the experience of this unique hellscape. These sophisticated infernal inhabitants are still capable of suffering the torment of exile from the beatific vision of God – *poena damni* – as well as everlasting pain – *poena sensus*. If this hellscape is rendered in painful detail, Milton is reluctant to dwell on human punishment after death. Indeed, the Archangel Michael's prophesy to Adam ends by focusing not on divine retribution but on grace and eternal bliss.

Keywords

John Milton – *Paradise Lost* – Milton's *De Doctrina Christiana* – primordial hell – fallen angels – human punishment

1   Space and Time

John Milton's biblical epic *Paradise Lost: A Poem in Twelve Books* (1674) begins
its action in hell and remains there for the whole of Book I and two thirds of
Book II. After relocating to heaven in Book III, the rest of the poem will take
place in Eden with a flashback to the War in Heaven and a flashforward to
the postlapsarian future. Milton thus makes hell the setting for some 2,000
lines of blank verse – a fifth of the poem's 10,000 lines. For many readers it is
the first two books that make the epic worth reading. Indeed, for many today
these may be the only two books they read. As the poem's reception history
attests, the main source of attraction is not hell per se but the character of its
chief inhabitant – Satan.[1] For the Romantic poets Blake and Shelley and their
modern heirs, Satan is the revolutionary hero of Liberty who waged war on a
tyrannical God; Satan's incarceration in hell is yet more proof of God's des-
potic sadism. In the twentieth and twenty-first centuries, post Freud, the focus
has tended to be on Satan's state of mind, his inner torments, 'the hell within
him' (IV.20), a state that he conceals from his fellow rebels but confesses to as
soon as he escapes the fire and arrives on earth. Thus, in 1954, J.B. Broadbent
argued that the physical scenery of the rebel angels' abode is subsidiary to
the evocation of their 'inner hell'. Indeed, he hears a strain in the verse when
the physical horrors are described as though Milton 'is irritated at having to
support the more sophisticated and Christian notion of an inner hell with the
classico-medieval flames and sulphur [...] if there is a fault in Milton's Hell it
is the unnecessary flames and smoke, which tend to obliterate the emotional
torture'.[2] Broadbent's article provoked ripostes from Ernest Schanzer and
Merritt Y. Hughes who, with different inflections, argued for a greater interplay between the physical and the psychological torment.[3] More recently, Neil
Forsyth has proposed that Satan's realization once on earth that 'Which way
I flie is Hell; my self am Hell' (IV.75) is a mark of a new post-Reformation sub-
jectivity akin to that of two fictional students of Wittenberg, Marlowe's Faustus
and Shakespeare's Hamlet; for Forsyth it is this psychological depth that makes
Satan so appealing.[4]

---

1   See Leonard J., *Faithful Labourers: A Reception History of Paradise Lost, 1667–1970*, 2 vols.
    (Oxford: 2013) for a detailed overview of the critical reception of the poem. It seems signifi-
    cant that while there is a lengthy chapter on 'Satan' in vol. II, Leonard records little interest
    in hell per se; there is no entry for hell in the index.
2   Broadbent J.B., "Milton's Hell", *A Journal of English Literary History* 21.3 (1954) 170–171.
3   Schanzer E., "Milton's Hell Revisited", *University of Toronto Quarterly* 24.2 (1955) 136–145, and
    Hughes M.Y., "Myself am Hell", *Modern Philology* 54.2 (1956) 80–94.
4   Forsyth N., *The Satanic Epic* (Princeton, NJ: 2003) 148–152.

A tendency to avert the gaze from hell as a place of physical punishment in order to focus on the psychological turmoil of Satan, betrays, I suggest, a certain unease that the great John Milton continued to believe in a hell where the sinner would suffer both *poena damni*, the spiritual pain caused by the loss of the beatific vision of God, and *poena sensus*, the pain inflicted on the body.[5] Surely, by the time *Paradise Lost* was published in the late seventeenth century belief in hell and its punishments was in decline?[6] Historians propose different reasons for hell's demise. Philip Almond charts a shift from the physical to the spiritual pain of the damned analogous to the changes in the penal system documented by Foucault, a move from torture of the body to punishment of the soul for reformist rather than retributive ends. Almond concludes 'Thus, under the pressure of a changing European sensibility to punishments inflicted on the body, the prisoners of hell were there to be incarcerated no longer *for* punishment but *as* punishment'.[7] In *After Lives*, a lucid guide to heaven, hell, and purgatory from the ancient Egyptians to yesterday, John Casey suggests that it is 'outrage at the cruelty of the traditional doctrine that will eventually drive hell from center stage in the Christian consciousness to the wings, or even into oblivion'. Casey cites a treatise contemporary with Milton's poem, the Baptist divine Samuel Richardson's *A Discourse of the Torments of Hell* (1658). Richardson detected serious empirical problems with traditional aspects of hell, but what was opprobrious was the idea of eternal punishment itself. The torments of hell could not be attributed to a merciful God.[8]

In what follows I will argue that Milton's hell – its location, geography, and climate – is a primordial hell, a place prepared for the mighty fallen angels who have not yet lost all their beauty, and whose suffering is inextricably physical and psychological as befits Milton's monist philosophy of matter. It is not the place destined for wicked human beings and reprobate angels after the Last

---

5   For this patristic distinction and its adoption by both Protestants and Catholics in early modern Europe and beyond, see Patrides C.A., "Renaissance and Modern Views on Hell", *The Harvard Theological Review* 57.3 (1964) 217–236.

6   See Walker D.P., *The Decline of Hell: Seventeenth-Century Discussions of Eternal Torment* (London: 1964).

7   Almond P.C., *Heaven and Hell in Enlightenment England* (Cambridge: 2008) 100; and idem, *Afterlife: A History of Life after Death* (London: 2016) 131–151.

8   Casey J., *After Lives: A Guide to Heaven, Hell, and Purgatory* (Oxford: 2009) 193–222, here 216. Other histories of hell and the afterlife include: Minois G., *L'Histoire des enfers* (Paris: 1991); Camporesi P., *The Fear of Hell: Images of Damnation and Salvation in Early Modern Europe* (Cambridge: 1991) and Hamm J. – Robert J. (eds.), *Unterwelten: Modelle und Transformationen* (Würzburg: 2014).

Judgement, about which Milton remains consistently vague.[9] Indeed, unlike Virgil's Hades, unlike Dante's Inferno, Milton locates hell not at the centre of the earth but far beneath it in chaos. He explains his rationale for this in the Argument that prefaces Book I: 'not in the centre (for [...] earth may be supposed as yet not made, certainly not yet accursed) but in a place of utter darkness, fitliest called chaos'. Given the Bible's notorious silence regarding the generation of the angels, the timing of their creation had been a matter of debate among the church fathers. If Origen, Gregory, Chrysostom, Ambrose, and Jerome thought that the creation of the angels preceded the creation of the visible world, Augustine, Peter Lombard, and Aquinas posited that the angels were created on the first day of Creation (implicit in the 'heavens' of *Genesis* 1:1). As for the time of the angelic Fall, that too was contested. Origen proposed that it occurred before the creation of the world, the position tentatively entertained by Milton here. Augustine grappled with this question repeatedly and ultimately posited that the angels fell at the moment of their creation on the first day of Creation, a position adopted by Aquinas.[10]

Concern with the order in which divine history occurs is an abiding feature of *Paradise Lost*, but, according to the conventions of his chosen genre – epic – Milton starts his story *in medias res* in hell rather than when Satan first sins in heaven. We must wait for the Archangel Raphael's account of the War in Heaven in Books V and VI for Satan's backstory. Nevertheless, as Alistair Fowler has shown, a chronology of events can be reconstructed if we assume that Milton's 'day' is a biblical day consisting of an evening followed by a morning. Following Augustine, Satan (then called Lucifer) falls through pride, but it is the exultation of the Son of God that is the catalyst for his rebellion (v.600–672) and marks the first day in the story. The War in Heaven occurs on days 2 to 4. Expelled from heaven, the rebels fall for nine days (days 4 to 13) and lie 'rolling in the fiery gulf' for a further nine days (days 13 to 22). Satan awakes and rouses his troops on day 22, and then travels through chaos to earth arriving in Eden on day 24. Meanwhile, God the Father and the Son create the world on days 14 to 19. The Archangel Raphael lunches and converses with Adam and Eve on

---

9   For a rich introduction to the history of the 'Last Things' and the impact of the Reformation on its material culture, see Göttler C., *Last Things: Art and the Religious Imagination in the Age of Reform* (Turnhout: 2010).

10 Milton implicitly adopts Origen's position in *De Doctrina Christiana*, ed. J.K. Hale – J.D. Cullington, The Complete Works of John Milton 8 (Oxford: 2012) 299 (Book I.7). For an overview of the patristic debate, see Raymond J., *Milton's Angels: The Early-Modern Imagination* (Oxford: 2013) 65–67, 73–77; Jones D.A., *Angels: A Very Short Introduction* (Oxford: 2011) 100–102, and Wiebe G.D., *Fallen Angels in the Theology of Saint Augustine* (Oxford: 2021) 53–95.

day 24. At noon on day 32, Adam and Eve fall and, before sunset on the same day, the Son passes judgement on them. The following morning, the Archangel Michael reveals the biblical future to Adam while Eve dreams, and at noon the man and the woman are expelled from Eden. Auspiciously, this is the 33rd day, comfortingly proleptic of the death and resurrection of Christ aged 33.[11]

Yet, from the perspective of hell in the opening two books of the poem, the Fall of Adam and Eve in Book IX is still in the future and must not appear pre-destined. Milton is an advocate of free will and strives to make his characters appear to choose their own destiny. Thus, while Sin and Death have entered the cosmos and are introduced as two 'formidable shape[s]' (II.649) sitting inside hell's 'thrice threefold [...] gates' (II.645), their status as allegories, as insubstantial, shadowy ideas, is repeatedly foregrounded. As yet there is no connection between hell and our universe; it is only after the Fall of the human pair that Sin and her son Death will construct 'a bridge / Of length prodigious' joining hell to 'the wall / Immovable of this now fenceless world' (X.301–303). Moreover, during the dialogue in heaven in Book III,[12] God the Father and the Son will make a series of distinctions between the Fall of the angels and the Fall of man, distinctions with clear eschatological consequences.

The Father will seek to explain to the Son that, despite his omniscience, despite predestination, he is not the author of sin.[13] No, he created angels and human beings 'Sufficient to have stood, though free to fall. / Such I created all the ethereal powers / And spirits, both them who stood and them who failed; / Freely they stood who stood, and fell who fell' (III.99–102). Trespassers are 'authors to themselves in all' (III.122). He then makes a distinction between the sin of the fallen angels and the sin of man:

> The first sort by their own suggestion fell,
> Self-tempted, self-depraved: man falls deceived
> By the other first: man therefore shall find grace,
> The other none. (III.129–132)

The divine duo prophesy that man will die for his disobedience, that the Son will become man and suffer death to satisfy the Father's justice, that he will

---

11   Fowler A., "Introduction", in Milton John, *Paradise Lost*, ed. A. Fowler (rev. 2nd ed. Harlow: 2007 [1968]) 29–33.

12   For a discussion of the controversies surrounding the 'dialogue in heaven', see Bevan Zlatar A., "God Talk: Seeing and Hearing the Dialogue in Heaven in *Paradise Lost*", *Milton Studies* 63 (2021) 211–241.

13   For an overview of the doctrine of predestination and its potential to drive a wedge between ethics and eschatology, see Almond, *Afterlife* 121–126.

rise again 'to redeem what hellish hate, / So easily destroyed' (III.300–301). At the end of the dialogue, the Father tells the Son of the Last Things:

> forthwith from all winds
> The living, and forthwith the cited dead
> Of all past ages to the general doom
> Shall hasten, such a peal shall rouse their sleep.
> Then all thy saints assembled, thou shalt judge
> Bad men and angels, they arraigned shall sink
> Beneath thy sentence; hell, her numbers full,
> Thenceforth shall be for ever shut. (III.326–333)

At the end of the poem, the Father sends the Archangel Michael to banish the human pair from Eden, but instructs him first to console Adam by revealing 'what shall come in future days' (XI.114). 'Days' is a relative term. Michael's revelation, over a thousand lines of poetry, spans the whole of biblical history and beyond to the end of time:

> so shall the world go on,
> To good malignant, to bad men benign,
> Under her own weight groaning, till the day
> Appear of respiration to the just,
> And vengeance to the wicked, at return
> Of him so lately promised to thy aid,
> The woman's seed, obscurely then foretold,
> Now amplier known thy saviour and thy Lord,
> Last in the clouds from heaven to be revealed
> In glory of the Father, to dissolve
> Satan with his perverted world, then raise
> From the conflagrant mass, purged and refined,
> New heavens, new earth, ages of endless date
> Founded in righteousness and peace and love,
> To bring forth fruits, joy and eternal bliss. (XII.537–551)

The Last Judgement is prophesied to occur at some unspecified time in the future, but Michael pays the punishment of the wicked scant attention, focusing instead on the Saviour. God the Father had prophesied that after the Last Judgement 'hell, her numbers full, / Thenceforth shall be for ever shut' (III.332–333), but here Michael seems to be proffering an alternative fate for Satan and sinners. The Saviour will come 'to dissolve / Satan with his perverted

JOHN MILTON'S PRIMORDIAL HELL IN *PARADISE LOST*

world', but whether this involves a return to primal matter or annihilation he fails to specify. Instead, he quickly moves on to happier tidings, to how the Saviour will raise 'New heavens, new earth' purged by a conflagration, and will usher in 'eternal bliss'. It is this promise of grace and everlasting bliss that allows Adam and Eve to leave Eden not in desperation but consoled.

These distinctions have implications for the hell we are to encounter. Milton's poem is not concerned with the hell of homiletic literature and the sculptures and paintings of the Last Judgement which evolved in the expectation 'that the faithful would [...] be frightened into Heaven'.[14] Milton's hell is not the hell of Dante or Giotto; it is not the hell of the Limbourg brothers in the *Très Riches Heures du Duc de Berry*, ca. 1415 [Fig. 6.1]. Milton's Satan is not the monstrous infernal king who ingests and excretes the human damned into a bed of fire, and his followers are not the sadistic demons who fan the flames with giant bellows or mete out punishments on men and women that accord with the sin committed. In Milton's hell there are no instruments of torture, no knives or iron tongs or red-hot pokers to torment the murderer or the glutton or the fornicator. Miltonists who remark on the absence of sadistic devils in this hell or wonder whether the fallen angels look like the grotesque demons of the medieval tradition do not seem to have made this distinction.[15] Such sins will come as a consequence of the Fall of Adam and Eve, and while sinful behaviour will abound in Michael's revelation to Adam, how such sins are to be punished by a good God is never specified. As we shall see, Milton's *De Doctrina Christiana* remains equally vague regarding the nature of the punishment in store for reprobate human beings. I would like to suggest that, if Milton's Satan and his rebel angels are unlike the inhabitants of the Limbourg brothers' hell, they are far closer to the angelic beings in their illumination *The Fall of Lucifer and the Rebel Angels* [Fig. 6.2]. Unlike other such depictions which focus on the angels' metamorphosis into demons as they fall, the Limbourg rebels are beautiful golden-winged, blue-robed beings amazed as their fair heads hit the smouldering soil of hell.[16] Their celestial origins rather than their demonic future are signalled by their vacant seats in the heavenly court above.

---

14   Patrides, "Renaissance and Modern Views on Hell" 218.

15   The absence of sadistic torture is noted by Frye R.M., *Milton's Imagery and the Visual Arts: Iconographic Tradition in the Epic Poems* (Princeton, NJ: 1978) 90–91. Dobranski S., *Milton's Visual Imagination* (Cambridge: 2015) 115, muses: 'Perhaps just as Medusa was made hideous so that glimpsing her face would turn men to stone, the fallen angels in their changed appearance have also become monstrous'.

16   For an introduction to the Limbourg brothers, the art of limning, and their artistic milieu, see Dückers R. – Roelofs P. (eds.), *The Limbourg Brothers: Reflections on the Origins and the Legacy of Three Illuminators from Nijmegen* (Leiden: 2009); and Husband T.B., *The Art of*

FIGURE 6.1   The Limbourg Brothers, *Hell*, ca. 1416. Manuscript illumination, 29 × 21 cm. From:
Les Très Riches Heures du duc de Berry, Ms. 65, fol. 108 r. Musée Condé, France
IMAGE © CLICHÉ IRHT-CNRS

FIGURE 6.2 The Limbourg Brothers, *The Fall of the Rebel Angels*, ca. 1416. Manuscript illumination, 29 × 21 cm. From: *Les Très Riches Heures du duc de Berry*, Ms. 65, fol. 64 v. Musée Condé, France

IMAGE © CLICHÉ IRHT-CNRS

Milton was a monist who believed that all creation was *ex Deo* and therefore good. In *Milton among the Philosophers*, Stephen Fallon explains monism
thus: 'Instead of being trapped in an ontologically alien body, the soul is one
with the body. Spirit and matter become for Milton two modes of the same
substance: spirit is rarefied matter, and matter is dense spirit. All things, from
insensate objects through souls, are manifestations of this one substance'.[17]
Given that God creates everything from this same dynamic substance, the difference between spirit and matter is one of degree not kind. The Archangel
Raphael who is sent to educate Adam and Eve spells out this continuum:

> O Adam, one almighty is, from whom
> All things proceed, and up to him return,
> If not depraved from good, created all
> Such to perfection, one first matter all,
> Indued with various forms, various degrees
> Of substance, and in things that live, of life;
> But more refined, more spirituous, and pure,
> As nearer to him placed or nearer tending
> Each in their several active spheres assigned,
> Till body up to spirit work, in bounds
> Proportioned to each kind. (v.469–479)

This philosophy of matter has implications for Milton's angels who, placed
closest to God at the top of the scale of being, are created far more 'refined,
more spirituous, more pure' than human beings, but still substantial enough
to partake of human food. The Archangel Raphael famously sits down to eat
with gusto the 'dulcet creams' (v.347) that Eve has prepared for him. When
Satan and his rebels disobey God, however, they become less refined, less
spirituous, less pure, more material and thus heavier – 'gross by sinning grown'
(vi.661), and, crucially, susceptible to corporeal pain. At the beginning of the
poem, the fallen angels are darker, heavier versions of their former selves but

---

Illumination: The Limbourg Brothers and the Belles Heures of Jean de France, Duc de Berry
(New York: 2008) 296 and 299. Husband argues that the Limbourg brothers' *Fall of the
Rebel Angels* is informed by the iconography of an angelic Fall by a follower of Simone
Martini (ca. 1340–1342) in the Musée du Louvre (inv. no. DL 1967-1-a). The Louvre panel
is different in one key respect, however: the angels are shown metamorphosing into inky
black bestial demons, a visual trope that will be explored in later representations of the
angelic Fall.

17   Fallon S., *Milton among the Philosophers: Poetry and Materialism in Seventeenth-Century
England* (Ithaca, NY: 2007) 80.

still recognizably angels – ruined, faded, yes, but not bestially monstrous. They will fall deeper into materiality as the narrative unfolds, reaching their nadir in Book X when Satan returns to hell to announce the Fall of man. Expecting a hero's welcome, he boasts how he seduced Adam and Eve with nothing less than an apple and got away with nothing more than the threat of a bruised head. In punishment for his inability to understand God's metaphors, he and his supporters will be metamorphosed into 'monstrous serpents' (x.514) and made to eat fruit that turns to bitter ash in their mouths, a 'humbling' meted out once a year.[18]

2 Milton's Sources for Hell

In *The Devil: A Mask without a Face*, Luther Link argues that representing the devil graphically in sculpture or paint posed huge challenges because the devil was a composite cemented out of different biblical episodes with different narrative origins. These differences are betrayed in his multiple names: *Satan* the Hebrew for 'adversary'; *Lucifer* meaning 'bringing light', Jerome's Latin translation of the Hebrew 'helel' or the Greek 'eosphoros'; and the *devil* derived from Greek 'diabolos' meaning an obstructive 'opponent' and latinized as 'diabolus'. According to Link 'The Devil, whether tormenting Job or egging on Pilate or tempting Jesus or ruling Hell, is discontinuous in his various roles. He has no history [...]. He is not a person. He may have many masks, but his essence is a mask without a face'.[19] In *Paradise Lost*, Milton gives Satan a history and a face, he makes him into the adversary of Christ of the *Book of Revelation* who falls like the Lucifer of *Isaiah* 14:12 and becomes the serpent of *Genesis* 3. Of course, Milton was not the first to do so. It was in response to the pagan critic Celsus and his critique of Christianity as borrowed myth, that the Greek theologian and biblical scholar Origen (ca. 185–ca. 254) wove together key biblical proof texts to construct the fullest account of the devil as an envious member of a heavenly court. 'No one can know the origin of evil, who has not grasped the truth about the so-called Devil and his angels, and who he was before he became a Devil and how he became a Devil'.[20] Augustine (354–430), the much more influential Latin church father, would then disseminate this story in

---

18   Milton's narrator compares this 'fruitage fair' to 'Sodom's apples'. See Edwards K., *Milton and the Natural World: Science and Poetry in Paradise Lost* (Cambridge: 1999) 148–149.

19   Link L., *The Devil: A Mask without a Face* (London: 1995) 19–27, here 15.

20   Origen, *Contra Celsum*, trans. H. Chadwick (Cambridge: 1953), Book IV, chapter 65.

The City of God.[21] Indeed, William Poole has proposed that it was the tripartite thematic structure of the second, twelve-book half of *The City of God* that gave Milton the cue for his tripartite structure of angelic Fall, human Fall, and biblical history from Cain and Abel to the end of time.[22]

What of hell the place of the damned? Neil Forsyth points out that while it is an essential feature of the Christian cosmos, there is little evidence for it in Jewish literature. *Sheol,* the Old Testament abode of the dead, or *Gehenna,* where the bodies of criminals were thrown into fires that burned perpetually, was 'little more than a spooky burial ground or vague place of the dead'. It was in the Septuagint, the Greek version of the Old Testament, that *Sheol* was translated as 'Hades', the underworld of the classical tradition and best rendered in Book VI of Virgil's *Aeneid.*[23] It is in the New Testament that we find references to a place of punishment where there is fire that is never quenched, brimstone, darkness, a place of weeping and gnashing of teeth, references that would be linked to apparently similar references in the Old Testament. Over time, the clergy and the laity, heretics and their opponents, writers and graphic artists would construct an infernal realm peopled by bad human beings and their demonic tormenters, one that often incorporated the worst of terrestrial life: contemporary instruments of torture, natural disasters, urban overcrowding, and pollution.[24]

Milton's biblical epic is deeply invested in describing an extraterrestrial infernal place according to what Milton understood to be the preeminent source of truth about God and his creatures – the Bible – but in ways that ring

---

21 Forsyth, *The Satanic Epic* 24–76, especially 43–45. For a more detailed discussion of the history of Satan the apocalyptic enemy of Christ and the role played by Origen and Augustine in constructing it, see Forsyth N., *The Old Enemy: Satan and the Combat Myth* (Princeton, NJ: 1987).

22 Poole W., *Milton and the Making of 'Paradise Lost'* (Cambridge, MA: 2017) 163.

23 Forsyth, *The Satanic Epic* 201. For *Sheol* in the Book of Job and a discussion of the absence of belief in reward and punishment in the hereafter in early Judaism, see Casey J., *After Lives* 53–64. For a thought-provoking discussion of translations of Virgil's 'Hades' as 'hell' versus 'underworld', the latter as a marker of a modern will to separate the classical place from the more abstract Christian concept of a state of being, see Tudeau-Clayton M., "'Underwor(l)ds', l'ancien et le nouveau: De Virgile à Ben Jonson", in Laroque F. – Lessay F. (eds.), *Esthétiques de la nouveauté à la Renaissance* (Paris: 2001) 59–76.

24 Almond, *Heaven and Hell,* 81–100, particularly 83 and 84, argues that the torments of hell as described in the early modern homiletic literature were magnifications of the pains of actual illnesses and disease as well as the sufferings inflicted on criminals in actual prisons. Link, *The Devil* 136, draws attention to the instruments of torture depicted in Last Judgement hellscapes: 'Few people realize that the tortures in Hell are mostly accurate representations of contemporary practice. This explains why the punishments and suffering seem real even if the devils do not'.

true in aesthetic terms. Milton takes the scant biblical evidence for the Fall of Satan and his bad angels and the minimal biblical details regarding the place prepared for their punishment and brings before our eyes and ears a hells-cape peopled with emphatically embodied and psychologically convincing fallen angels, a dramatic scene that spans 2,000 lines of his poem. The genre he chooses is classical epic, and his chief fallen angel is depicted as a colossal winged classical warrior. But time and again Milton asserts that it is the Bible that is the true and original account, that classical tales may contain aspects of the truth, but are posterior, secondary 'fables'. If the sights in Virgil's Hades are terrifying, those in this hell are worse.[25] As we shall see, Milton makes the reader acutely aware of the challenges posed by this audacious task of visualizing and dramatizing his meagre sources without falsifying them.

Milton's biblicism is nowhere more apparent than in his *De Doctrina Christiana*, his systematic theology in Latin, serendipitously rediscovered in manuscript in 1823. It is a theological commonplace book where biblical places from both Testaments are collated under headings, a genre that flourished after the Reformation, its most famous example being Calvin's *Institutes*. Milton's models were William Ames's *Medulla* (1623) and the *Compendium theologiae* (1626) by the Basel theologian Johannes Wolleb. Roughly half of the total text of *De Doctrina Christiana* is made up of biblical quotations, and Milton's Bible of choice was the Latin Junius-Tremellius-Beza Bible, especially the versions of 1598 for the New Testament, and 1624 for the Old Testament. There is internal evidence that it was a work in progress, that it became more heterodox over time, and that Milton had intended to publish it.[26] Chapter 30 of Book I, 'On Holy Scripture', is where he advocates *sola scriptura* – 'And so the rule and canon of faith is scripture alone' (1.30.807) – and, less conventionally, where he delineates the concept of 'a twofold scripture: the external scripture of the written word, and the internal one of the holy spirit, which he, as a result of God's promise, has etched [exaro: to write on tablets] on believers' hearts' (1.30.811). This internal scripture guides Milton through what he acknowledged to be corruptions in the biblical text, but it is also what gives him license to make terse biblical proof texts into divinely inspired epic narrative.

It is routinely observed that *De Doctrina Christiana* says little about Satan or hell in its pages, but two chapters in particular show Milton mining the Bible

---

25   See *Paradise Lost* I.197 and II.626, discussed below.
26   See Hale J.K. – Cullington J.D., "Introduction", in Milton, *De Doctrina Christiana* xix–lxiv. For a lucid assessment of its theology, see Hale J.K., *Milton's Scriptural Theology: Confronting 'De Doctrina Christiana'* (Leeds: 2019). For its generic context and relevance for *Paradise Lost*, see Poole, *The Making of Milton's 'Paradise Lost'* 89–104.

to substantiate or speculate about theological positions highly pertinent to my reading of the hell of *Paradise Lost*. Chapter 9 of Book 1 'On the Special Governance of Angels' provides us with Milton's biblical proofs for the existence of 'evil' angels, their choice to revolt from God, the chronology of their Fall, and the punishments meted out:

> But angels are good or evil, Luke 9:26 and 8:2, for it is agreed that very many of them revolted from God of their own accord before the fall of man: John 8:44: [...] *the father of falsehood*; 2 Peter 2:4 [*God*] *did not spare the angels who sinned*; Jude 6: *the angels who did not maintain their original state*, [...]. (*De Doctrina Christiana*, I.9.347)

> The evil angels have been reserved for punishment: [...] 2 Peter 2:4: *he thrust them down into hell and delivered them to chains of darkness, reserving them for damnation*; [...] Matthew 25:41: [...] *into* [*that*] *eternal fire which has been prepared for the devil and his angels*; Rev. 20:10: *they will be tortured* [...] *until the ages of ages*. (*De Doctrina Christiana*, I.9.353)[27]

After conceding that 'sometimes they are able to wander over the whole earth, the air, and even heaven to carry out God's judgements', he concludes 'Yet their proper place is the Abyss [Abyssus], whence one may not leave without permission' which he corroborates with 'Matt. 12:43: *he walks through dry places seeking rest*' and 'Rev. 20:3: *he hurled him into the Abyss and closed it up*' (I.9.353). He is insistent that their powers are limited to what God permits or commands: 'Nor can they do the least thing without God's command' (I.9.353). Ultimately, all is aggravated by their despair of salvation:

> Their knowledge is indeed great, but such as tortures rather than consoles them, so that they utterly despair of their salvation [...] Jas 2:19: *the demons believe and are terrified*, for they are being reserved for punishment, as above. (*De Doctrina Christiana*, I.9.353)

Of particular pertinence to the *dramatis personae* of *Paradise Lost*, we are also told that 'evil' angels 'keep their ranks': Beelzebub is their 'prince' but '[t]heir supreme leader is the author of all evil-doing and hinderer of [all] good' (I.9.355) – Satan.

---

27   All citations are from *De Doctrina Christiana*, a parallel text edition translated by J.K. Hale – J.D. Cullington.

It is not until Chapter 33 of Book I, 'On complete Glorification, including Christ's Second Coming and the Resurrection of the Dead and the Conflagration of This World', that Milton painstakingly reconstructs the chronology of the Last Judgement using *Revelation* 20 and *Matthew* 25 as proof texts. Satan and the evil angels will be judged first followed by human beings. Satan, he states categorically, will be 'condemned to everlasting punishment. Revelation 20:7–9' (1.33.887). But he is more tentative with regard to wicked human beings:

> The second death, the punishment of the damned, seems [videtur esse posita] to consist in the loss of the supreme good, that is, of divine grace and protection and the beatific vision – which [loss] is commonly termed the punishment of deprivation [*damnum*] – and in eternal torment, which is termed the punishment of sense. (1.33.891)

Having introduced the idea of *poena damni* and *poena sensus*, he concedes that the severity and duration of these punishments is variously described, and that punishments vary in proportion to the sins committed. Finally, he turns to nomenclature. 'The place of punishment is called **Hell**' ('Locus poenae **Infernus** vocatur'): '*Topheth*' of *Isaiah* 30:33; '*the Gehenna of fire*' of *Matthew* 5:22; '*the furnace of fire*' of *Matthew* 13:42; and '*the lake of fire*' of *Revelation* 20:15 (1.33.893). And then, right at the end of the section on the damned, he speculates about the actual location of the infernal realm:

> Hell's location seems [videtur esse] to be outside this world [...] Nor are there reasons lacking: if the hell of the damned is indeed the same as that which had been prepared for the devil and his angels, as said above in Matt. 25:41, and [if] the apostasy of the devil took place before the fall of man, it is unlikely that hell should be prepared within the world, and in the bowels of an earth not yet cursed. (1.33.893)

He cites Chrysostom and Luther as authorities,[28] and, with the irreverent humour that occasionally surfaces in the treatise, he asks 'If the whole world will eventually be burnt up [...] what will happen to hell if it is situated in the centre of the earth? [...] it would be a really splendid finish for the damned!' (1.33.893).

---

28 See Kelley M. (ed.), *Complete Prose Works of John Milton*, vol. 6 (New Haven, CT: 1973) 630, n. 32, who cites Chrysostom, 'Hom. In cap. Matt, xxv', but finds no evidence for Milton's statement regarding Luther.

What is striking here is Milton's tentativeness with regard to several eschatological commonplaces. If the rebel angels are condemned to everlasting punishment, he is less certain about the fate of reprobate human beings at doomsday. There is a hesitancy in 'It *seems* to consist in [...] the punishment of deprivation and [...] the punishment of sense' (my emphasis). Additionally, the penalty is not fixed but calibrated according to the sin committed. As for the location of hell, Milton speculates. 'It *seems* to be outside this world' (my emphasis), a position substantiated by a series of ifs – *if* hell is the same as that place prepared for the fallen angels, *if* they fell before the Fall of mankind. *De Doctrina Christiana* is often speculative. It is less a credo than a reasoned discussion of possibilities, a work in progress. As a poet rather than an amateur theologian, Milton will have to make choices, but his epic will often allow for multiple options or points of view.

3   Experiencing Hell

> The infernal serpent; he it was, whose guile
> Stirred up with envy and revenge, deceived
> The mother of mankind, what time his pride
> Had cast him out from heaven, with all his host
> Of rebel angels, by whose aid aspiring
> To set himself in glory above his peers,
> He trusted to have equalled the most high,
> If he opposed; and with ambitious aim
> Against the throne and monarchy of God
> Raised impious war in heaven and battle proud
> With vain attempt. Him the almighty power [44]
> Hurled headlong flaming from the ethereal sky
> With hideous ruin and combustion down
> To bottomless perdition, there to dwell
> In adamantine chains and penal fire,
> Who durst defy the omnipotent to arms.
> Nine times the space that measures day and night
> To mortal men, he with his horrid crew
> Lay vanquished, rolling in the fiery gulf
> Confounded though immortal: but his doom
> Reserved him to more wrath; for now the thought
> Both of lost happiness and lasting pain
> Torments him; round he throws his baleful eyes
> That witnessed huge affliction and dismay

Mixed with obdurate pride and steadfast hate:
At once as far as angels' ken he views
The dismal situation waste and wilde,
A dungeon horrible, on all sides round
As one great furnace flamed, yet from those flames
No light, but rather darkness visible
Served only to discover sights of woe,
Regions of sorrow, doleful shades, where peace
And rest can never dwell, hope never comes
That comes to all; but torture without end
Still urges, and a fiery deluge, fed
With ever-burning sulphur unconsumed:
Such place eternal justice had prepared
For those rebellious, here their prison ordained
In utter darkness, and their portion set
As far removed from God and light of heaven
As from the center thrice to the utmost pole.
Oh how unlike the place from whence they fell! (1.34–75)

Like all epics, *Paradise Lost* begins with an invocation to a muse and a question. But here the muse is ultimately the Holy Spirit and the question is momentous: what or who caused the first man and woman to fall, and, implicitly, what or who is responsible for evil? The answer: 'The infernal serpent' (1.34). The narrator, his prayer for inspiration granted, tells us in brief the whole story of the proud angel who 'Raised impious war in heaven' but lost, and how God hurled him headlong down to hell. The grammar of lines 44 to 49 famously imitates the action of falling itself while the aspirate consonants of 'Him [...] / Hurled headlong [...] / hideous' make us hear the fall as a cosmic rush of air. 'Bottomless perdition', reminiscent of the 'bottomless pit' of *Revelation* 9:1–2, introduces a yoking of the concrete 'bottomless' and the abstract 'perdition', the first of many oxymora in this *topographia*. The narrator then allows us to see the fallen angels 'rowling in the fiery gulf / Confounded though immortal' and, with 'now' instigating a change to the dramatic present, we are made privy to Satan's tormenting thoughts 'of happiness lost and lasting pain' and zoom in on his eyes. In a fine discussion of Milton's hellfire, John Steadman observed that 'Satan's first dramatic action [...] is an act of vision [...] and what he beholds is a torture-chamber'.[29] Satan's first act in the poem is indeed to look – 'Round he throws his baleful eyes' – but what he sees is more complex than

---

29   Steadman J., *Milton's Biblical and Classical Imagery* (Pittsburgh, PA: 1984) 130.

Steadman implies. 'Witnessed' can mean 'observe' but it can also mean 'evince' or 'show'. Are those eyes observing the hellscape in front of him? Or are they bearing witness to Satan's physical and psychological affliction, and betraying his signature emotions – pride and hate? Perhaps he only looks outward when 'At once as far as angels' ken he views'.[30] What does he see? It quickly becomes apparent that *topographia*, the description of the hellscape, merges with *psychographia*, a description of Satan's state of mind. If 'chains', 'penal fire', 'a dungeon horrible' seem concrete, and the simile borrowed from *Matthew* 13:42 'as one great furnace flamed' only slightly less so, 'dismal situation', 'sights of woe', 'regions of sorrow', and 'doleful shades' remain abstract projections of Satan's mental suffering. The seemingly finite space of a 'Dungeon' or a 'great furnace' is simultaneously a vast wild space of varied 'sights', 'regions', and 'shades'.

Yet, Satan's view is not just a projection of his state of mind. He also sees and feels the fire as an instrument of endless physical pain or *poena sensus*: 'but torture without end / Still urges, and a fiery deluge, fed / With ever-burning sulphur unconsum'd'. The fire begins as soon as Satan is hurled out of heaven, he is described as 'flaming [...] / With hideous ruin and combustion down' like a comet. He and his 'horrid crew' land in a huge expanse of liquid fire, 'a fiery gulf', and roll there for nine days. They are said to be 'confounded', a strong adjective connoting mental confusion or perplexity. Later they will be described as 'entranced' (1.301), and in a state of 'astonishment' (1.317), a word derived from *ex tonere*, the physical-psychological effect of their nine-day fall and the shock of landing in a lake of fire. Still prostrate on the burning lake, Satan will turn to his partner in crime, later known as Beelzebub, and deliver a speech of proud defiance, a valiant attempt at a dualist separation of body and mind. But the narrator is quick to undermine this specious division: 'So spake the apostate angel, though in pain, / Vaunting aloud, but rackt with deep despair' (1.125–126). Soon Satan will leave the lake for 'dry land', but the land is made of fire, too – 'If it were Land that ever burned / With solid, as the lake with liquid fire' (1.228–9). As the narrator intimates with ironic metonymy, all contact with this burning soil is extremely painful: 'Such resting found the sole / Of unblest feet' (1.238–239).

Milton's fire burns but does it illuminate? '[Y]et from those flames / No light, but rather darkness visible'. Much ink has been spilled over the paradoxical 'darkness visible'. The scriptural source was the description of the land of the dead in *Job* 10:22, 'the light was as darkness', and it had provoked speculation

---

30   Forsyth, *The Satanic Epic* 77–78.

amongst the church fathers.[31] Basil had distinguished between fire that burns and fire that provides joyous light; if mankind could not separate these two qualities, God could. Here, though, Milton grants the flames enough light to reveal the dismal geography and its tortures. As so often in *Paradise Lost*, Satan's perspective merges imperceptibly with the view and voice of the narrator: 'where peace / And rest can never dwell, hope never comes / That comes to all'. This last subclause indicates a return to the moralizing voice of the human narrator who will conclude with

> Such place eternal justice had prepared
> For those rebellious, here their prison ordained
> In utter darkness, and their portion set
> As far removed from God and light of heaven
> As from the centre thrice to the utmost pole.
> Oh how unlike the place from whence they fell! (1.70–75)

The light or lack thereof is now 'utter darkness', indicative of hell's location 'As far removed from God and light of heaven / As from the centre thrice to the utmost pole'. Miltonists disagree about whether the narrator is providing an exact, measurable location for hell relative to earth and heaven.[32] I think we are left with a semblance of precision that dissipates under scrutiny. More important than the precise geometrical distance is the theological message that infernal darkness represents the loss of the light of heaven and the beatific vision of God, that the darkness of hell is both physical and psychological, *poena sensus* and *poena damni*. Oh how unlike the place from whence they fell!

4   Looking at Satan

My close reading of the poem's first sight of hell has drawn attention to Milton's complex visualization of a place unseen, a place created out of sparse biblical intimations. By means of a divinely inspired narrator whose view blends with that of Satan, Milton strives to render the geographical, meteorological horror of this space and its effects on its chief inhabitant. But what does Satan look

---

31   Steadman, *Milton's Biblical and Classical Imagery* 122–127, cites the commentaries of Basil, Gregory the Great, Aquinas, and Bonaventure. For early modern commentaries, see Almond, *Heaven and Hell* 87–90.

32   See Wright B.A., "Masson's Diagram of Milton's Spaces", *The Review of English Studies* 21.81 (1945) 42–44.

like? This is no cosmetic question: appearance is an ontological issue indicating how far these fallen angels still resemble their former selves, how far they have fallen down the scale of being into greater materiality.[33] If Satan's first action in the poem is an act of vision, his first words register the shock of the changed appearance of his partner, Beelzebub:

> If thou beest he; but oh how fallen! how changed
> From him, who in the happy realms of light
> Clothed with transcendent brightness didst outshine
> Myriads though bright. (1.84–87)

Echoing *Isaiah* 14:12 'How art thou fallen from heaven, O Lucifer, son of the morning! how art thou cut down to the ground, which didst weaken the nations!', Satan even questions Beelzebub's identity. But the nature of the change remains unspecified; it seems to have occasioned a loss of divine light, a darkening. Satan will admit that he too has 'changed in outward lustre' (1.97). Much later on earth, Ithuriel and Zephon will fail to recognize Satan. 'Know ye not me?' (IV.828) he asks, to which Zephon replies 'thou resemblest now / Thy sin and place of doom obscure and foul' (IV.839–840).

For more detail we must wait for the narrator's description. Yet, the difficulty involved in depicting this supernatural protagonist is great, a difficulty conveyed in the narrator's use of what is the most distinctive rhetorical figure of Books I and II – the epic simile. Milton's similes draw attention to the gap between the *icon* and the subject or give the reader a choice between a series of *icons*, as though no one *icon* is capable of rendering the whole truth. The first epic simile in the poem is the so-called Leviathan simile:

> Thus Satan talking to his neerest mate
> With head uplift above the wave, and eyes
> That sparkling blazed, his other parts besides
> Prone on the flood, extended long and large
> Lay floating many a rood in bulk as huge
> As whom the fables name of monstrous size,
> Titanian, or Earth-born, that warred on Jove,
> Briarios or Typhon, whom the den
> By ancient Tarsus held, or that sea-beast
> Leviathan, which God of all his works
> Created hugest that swim the ocean stream:

---

33   Dobranski, *Milton's Visual Imagination* 108–134 makes this case by focusing not on Satan but on his crew of fallen angels.

> Him haply slumbring on the Norway foam
> The pilot of some small night-foundered skiff,
> Deeming some island, oft, as seamen tell,
> With fixèd anchor in his scaly rind
> Moors by his side under the lee, while night
> Invests the sea, and wishèd morn delays:
> So stretcht out huge in length the arch-fiend lay
> Chained on the burning lake, nor ever thence
> Had risen or heaved his head, but that the will
> And high permission of all-ruling heaven
> Left him at large to his own dark designs. (1.192–213)

We begin with his eyes 'that sparkling blazed' and then quickly move on to his body: '[H]is other parts besides / Prone on the flood extended long and large / Lay floating many a rood' (1.194–196). We must be content with the highly unspecific 'other parts' and a shift in emphasis to dimension. Extended – a long word – introduces the alliteration of 'long and large / Lay floating', the sense of Satan's length reinforced through the enjambment. As for 'rood', this was a unit of measurement for land equal to 40 square rods or a quarter of an acre.[34] But our narrator is careful to remain suggestively imprecise: Satan lay 'many' a rood long. It is now that he resorts to a chain of *icons* linked by 'or'. Satan is *like* the Titans and Giants of Hesiod's *Theogony*, 'whom the Fables name of monstrous size', or, more authoritatively, he is *like* the biblical Leviathan 'which God of all his works / Created hugest that swim th' ocean stream'. The narrator strives to convey the 'bulk' and size, the fabulous enormity and materiality of this fallen angel, and, through a final twist in the simile's long tail, evokes Satan's deceptiveness via the old trope of the whale that mariners mistake for an island.[35]

If this long and famous concatenation of *icons* leaves us with a sense of bestiality, I suggest that this beastliness is proleptic: the giants of classical myth, the Leviathan of Job are only in the postlapsarian future. Here in Book I, Satan has changed in appearance but he is not the monster of the hell of the medieval and early modern pictorial tradition of the Last Judgement. He has not yet developed the animal traits borrowed, as Luther Link has argued, from the pagan iconography of Pan – horns, goat's ears, hoofs and a tail, or the shaggy

---

34   *Oxford English Dictionary* 7.a.

35   For a fuller account of this simile and Milton's strategies of visualization, see Bevan Zlatar A., "'In the Image of Their Glorious Maker': Looking at Representation and Similitudes in *Paradise Lost*", in Bevan Zlatar A. – Timofeeva O. (eds.), *What Is an Image in Medieval and Early Modern England?*, Swiss Papers in English Language and Literature 34 (Tübingen: 2017).

hair, open mouth with prominent teeth and tongue of the Egyptian dwarf
god Bes.[36] He has angels' wings and though infinitely larger than the heroes
of the classical tradition, he is clearly imagined as a classical warrior in the
next simile:

> He scarce had ceased when the superior fiend
> Was moving toward the shore; his ponderous shield
> Ethereal temper, massy, large and round,
> Behind him cast; the broad circumference
> Hung on his shoulders like the moon, whose orb
> Through optic glass the Tuscan artist views
> At evening from the top of Fesole [sic],
> Or in Valdarno, to descry new lands,
> Rivers or mountains in her spotty globe.
> His spear, to equal which the tallest pine
> Hewn on Norwegian hills, to be the mast
> Of some great admiral, were but a wand,
> He walkt with to support uneasie steps
> Over the burning marle, not like those steps
> On heaven's azure, and the torrid clime
> Smote on him sore besides, vaulted with fire. (1.283–298)

An epic trope since Homer's *Iliad*, the narrator now describes the protagonist's armour. It is of 'ethereal temper' as befits an angel but is 'ponderous'
and 'behind him cast' as we expect of a fallen angel in retreat from the divine
thunder and lightning. The shield is *like* the moon which contributes to the
sense of Satan's being of cosmic proportions and dwelling in the dark. But the
narrator specifies 'like the moon, whose orb / Through optic glass the Tuscan
artist views'. This is the orb seen by Galileo through his telescope, an instrument that changed the way mankind viewed the heavens and corroborated
the Copernican heliocentric model. Here, Galileo's telescope serves further
to magnify this shield suggesting that it is a 'globe', a whole world that Satan
is carrying on his shoulders. The most telling detail, however, is the adjective
'spotty'. 'Spotty' refers to the 'imperfections' that the telescope controversially
revealed in a sphere hitherto deemed perfect, but 'spotty' also refers to the
macula of sin that Satan has brought into the cosmos.[37] The narrator next
focuses on Satan's great spear and again insists on its enormity: the tallest tree

---

36   Link, *The Devil* 35–75.
37   Nicolson M., "Milton and the Telescope", *ELH* 2.1 (1935) 1–32. For Milton and Galileo,
       see Arthos J., *Milton and the Italian Cities* (London: 1968); Cesare M.A., *Milton in Italy:*

hewn for the tallest battleship is but a fairy's 'wand' compared to this. And, bathetically, Satan now uses it as a walking-stick to steady his faltering steps.[38]

Later, we are given another description of Satan standing in front of the host of rebel angels, a description that includes a close-up of his face, a *prosopographia*:

> he above the rest
> In shape and gesture proudly eminent
> Stood like a tower; his form had yet not lost
> All her original brightness, nor appeared
> Less than archangel ruined, and the excess
> Of glory obscured: as when the sun new ris'n
> Looks through the horizontal misty air
> Shorn of his beams, or from behind the moon
> In dim eclips disastrous twilight sheds
> On half the nations, and with fear of change
> Perplexes monarchs. Darkened so, yet shone
> Above them all the archangel: but his face
> Deep scars of thunder had intrenched, and care
> Sat on his faded cheek, but under brows
> Of dauntless courage, and considerate pride
> Waiting revenge: cruel his eye, but cast
> Signs of remorse and passion to behold
> The fellows of his crime, the followers rather
> (Far other once beheld in bliss) condemned
> For ever now to have thir lot in pain,
> Millions of spirits for his fault amerced
> Of heaven, and from eternal splendours flung
> For his revolt, yet faithfull how they stood,
> Their glory withered. (1.589–612)

Once again the narrator resorts to meteorological or astrological similes, straining to convey the changes wrought on his visage, the former divine light now obscured like the sun through morning mist or, more sinisterly, like the

---

Contexts, Images, Contradictions (New York, NY: 1991) and Reeves E., *Painting the Heavens: Art and Science in the Age of Galileo* (Princeton, NJ: 1999).

38   For another reading of this simile, see Dobranski, *Milton's Visual Imagination* 90–107. For the use of optical, telescopic, and mirroring devices in the material culture of the Last Things in the Counter-Reformation, see Göttler, *Last Things* 5–10, 16–22, 220–223, 268–272.

sun eclipsed by the moon. But what is striking is the emphasis on Satan's being a recognizable if lesser version of his former self, 'nor appeared / Less than archangel ruined', his cheek 'faded' like a withered flower. Nor is he incapable of 'remorse' for his fellow angels, or oblivious of what they have lost: 'for his fault amerced / Of heaven, and from eternal splendors flung, / For his revolt'. It is crucial that we do not imagine Satan here as a fallen angel in the process of metamorphosing into bestiality, a physical degeneracy indicative of total spiritual decay. He must appear as a faded version of his dazzling heavenly self, capable of revenge but also of remorse, a tragic figure who suffers *poena damni* but cannot repent.

5   Exploring Hellscape

In Book 11, we are granted a more expansive view of hell and a more detailed account of the experiences of its inhabitants. Once Satan has left on his mission to explore God's latest creation – earth – we see how the other fallen angels 'entertain / The irksome hours' (11.526–527) until his return. What becomes immediately apparent is that these are highly sophisticated fallen angels. They are clearly in terrible pain but suppress it stoically: some attempt to assuage it by engaging in competitive sports or military drill or hurling 'with vast Typhoean rage' (11.539) rocks and hills; others 'more mild' sing narcissistically but with angelic harmony of 'Their own heroic deeds' (11.549); others retire to a hill to debate 'Providence, foreknowledge, will, and fate' (11.559), but, comments the narrator, to their 'false philosophy' they 'found no end, in wandering mazes lost' (11.561). Yet others go off 'On bold adventure to discover / That dismal world, if any clime perhaps / Might yield them easier habitation' (11.571–573). Here they encounter the four rivers of hell borrowed from Virgil's *Aeneid* Book VI – 'Abhorrèd Styx', 'Sad Acheron', 'Cocytus [...] of lamentation loud', and 'fierce Phlegeton', and far off 'Lethë the river of oblivion' (11.577–584). And beyond the rivers they perceive that 'a frozen continent / Lies dark and wild, beat with perpetual storms / Of whirlwind and dire hail' (11.587–589). Now it is cold that 'performs the effect of fire', and the contrast between the pain of fire and the pain of ice extends the horrors of their *poena sensus*. And now Milton introduces monstrous forms:

> Thither by harpy-footed Furies haled,
> At certain revolutions all the damned
> Are brought: and feel by turns the bitter change
> Of fierce extremes, extremes by change more fierce,

> From beds of raging fire to starve in ice
> Their soft ethereal warmth, and there to pine
> Immovable, infixed, and frozen round,
> Periods of time, thence hurried back to fire. (11.596–603).[39]

In vain the fallen angels struggle to attain one drop from the river of forgetfulness but 'Medusa with Gorgonian terror' (11.611) bars the way. It is then that we witness 'their lamentable lot':

> In confused march forlorn, the adventrous bands
> With shuddring horror pale, and eyes aghast
> Viewed first their lamentable lot, and found
> No rest: through many a dark and dreary vale
> They passed, and many a region dolorous,
> O'er many a frozen, many a fiery alp,
> Rocks, caves, lakes, fens, bogs, dens, and shades of death,
> A universe of death, which God by curse
> Created evil, for evil only good,
> Where all life dies, death lives, and nature breeds,
> Perverse, all monstrous, all prodigious things,
> Abominable, inutterable, and worse
> Then fables yet have feigned, or fear conceived,
> Gorgons and Hydras, and Chimeras dire. (11.615–628)

Once again, the grammar mimics the sense of the endlessness of this hellscape by being one long fourteen-line sentence. The landscape, far from offering rest is inhospitable at every turn, the impediments rendered in the heavily stressed metrical feet of 'Rocks, caves, lakes, fens, bogs, dens, and shades of death'. As the sentence nears its end, the narrator's voice dominates, but rather than attempt to describe this 'universe of death [...] / Where all life dies, death lives, and nature breeds, / Perverse, all monstrous, all prodigious things', he invites us to imagine all the terrifying creatures of classical literature – Gorgons and Hydras and Chimeras – but insists that the perversions of Hell are far worse than mere fables. That the experience of hell was worse than the worst of terrestrial horrors was a homiletic commonplace;[40] here Milton complicates this

---

39   Duncan J.E., 'Milton's Four-in-One Hell', *Huntington Library Quarterly* (1957) 128, reads 'all the damned' as a reference to the punishment of the wicked 'apparently thousands of years in the future'.

40   See Almond, *Heaven and Hell* 83–85, 88–89, 93.

idea by asserting the truth of his biblically inspired infernal realm compared to the feigned fables of the classical tradition.

Milton's hell is carefully located in space and somewhat more tentatively in time. He situates it in outer chaos rather than at the centre of the earth, arguing that it was perhaps created before the earth and certainly before the earth was corrupted by the Fall of Adam and Eve. It is a place prepared for the mighty fallen angels who are darker, tortured versions of their former selves, yet still far closer to the beautiful angels depicted by the Limbourg brothers [Fig. 6.2] than to the bestialized, sadistic demons in their version of hell [Fig. 6.1]. This should not surprise us. Milton's hell is a primordial hell rather than the place destined for the punishment of wicked human beings after the Second Coming and the Last Judgement. Indeed, Milton seems reluctant to dwell on the punishment allotted to reprobate human beings. Instead, from Book IV until the end of the poem the focus is on the human couple's blissful life in the garden, their Fall into sin and their agony at disappointing their maker. But, unlike the fallen angels who were 'self-tempted, self-depraved' and will not ask for forgiveness, Adam and Eve repent and find grace. In Eden the emphasis is on divine mercy towards mankind, not on punishment. Thus, when the Son of God sentences Adam and Eve, far from inflicting or being associated with immediate punishment, he prophesies his First Coming and the Redemption, and then tenderly clothes the man and the woman in their nakedness. Meanwhile, God the Father delegates: on the 33rd day he gives the Archangel Michael the task of telling Adam how diabolical human beings will be to one another east of Eden, and how, through a Saviour, he and Eve will at the end of time attain eternal bliss.

Bibliography

Primary Sources

The Bible (King James Version).

Milton John, *De Doctrina Christiana*, ed. J.K. Hale and J.D. Cullington, The Complete Works of John Milton, vol. 8 (Oxford: 2012).

Milton John, *De Doctrina Christiana*, ed. M. Kelley, The Complete Prose Works of John Milton, vol. 6 (New Haven, CT: 1973).

Milton John, *Paradise Lost*, ed. A. Fowler (rev. 2nd ed. Harlow: 2007 [1968]).

Origen, *Contra Celsum*, trans. H. Chadwick (Cambridge: 1953).

Secondary Sources

Almond P.C., *Heaven and Hell in Enlightenment England* (Cambridge: 2008).

Almond P.C., *Afterlife: A History of Life after Death* (London: 2016).

Arthos J., *Milton and the Italian Cities* (London: 1968).

Bevan Zlatar A., "'In the Image of Their Glorious Maker': Looking at Representation and Similitudes in *Paradise Lost*", in Bevan Zlatar A. – Timofeeva O. (eds.), *What Is an Image in Medieval and Early Modern England?*, Swiss Papers in English Language and Literature 34 (Tübingen: 2017).

Bevan Zlatar A., "God Talk: Seeing and Hearing the Dialogue in Heaven in *Paradise Lost*", *Milton Studies* 63 (2021) 211–241.

Broadbent J.B., "Milton's Hell", *A Journal of English Literary History* 21.3 (1954) 161–192.

Camporesi P., *The Fear of Hell: Images of Damnation and Salvation in Early Modern Europe* (Cambridge: 1991).

Casey J., *After Lives: A Guide to Heaven, Hell, and Purgatory* (Oxford: 2009).

Cesare M.A., *Milton in Italy: Contexts, Images, Contradictions* (New York, NY: 1991).

Dobranski S., *Milton's Visual Imagination* (Cambridge: 2015).

Dückers R. – Roelofs P. (eds.), *The Limbourg Brothers: Reflections on the Origins and the Legacy of Three Illuminators from Nijmegen* (Leiden: 2009).

Duncan J.E., "Milton's Four-in-One Hell", *Huntington Library Quarterly* 20.2 (1957) 127–136.

Edwards K., *Milton and the Natural World: Science and Poetry in* Paradise Lost (Cambridge: 1999).

Fallon S., *Milton among the Philosophers* (Ithaca, NY: 2007).

Forsyth N., *The Old Enemy: Satan and the Combat* Myth (Princeton, NJ: 1987).

Forsyth N., *The Satanic Epic* (Princeton, NJ: 2003).

Frye R.M., *Milton's Imagery and the Visual Arts: Iconographic Tradition and the Epic Poems* (Princeton, NJ: 1978).

Göttler C., *Last Things: Art and the Religious Imagination in the Age of Reform* (Turnhout: 2010).

Hale J.K., *Milton's Scriptural Theology: Confronting* De Doctrina Christiana (Amsterdam: 2019).

Hamm J. – Robert J. (eds.), *Unterwelten: Modelle und Transformationen* (Würzburg: 2014).

Hughes M.Y., "Myself am Hell", *Modern Philology* 54.2 (1956) 80–94.

Husband T.B., *The Art of Illumination: The Limbourg Brothers and the Belles Heures of Jean de France, Duc de Berry* (New York, NY: 2008).

Jones D.A., *Angels: A Very Short Introduction* (Oxford: 2011).

Leonard J., *Faithful Labourers: A Reception History of Paradise Lost, 1667–1970* (Oxford: 2013).

Link L., *The Devil: A Mask without a Face* (London: 1995).

Minois G., *L'Histoire des enfers* (Paris: 1991).

Nicolson M., "Milton and the Telescope", *ELH* 2.1 (1935) 1–32.

Patrides C.A., "Renaissance and Modern Views on Hell", *The Harvard Theological Review* 57.3 (1964) 217–236.

Poole W., *Milton and the Making of* Paradise Lost (Cambridge, MA: 2017).

Raymond J., *Milton's Angels: The Early-Modern Imagination* (Oxford: 2013).

Reeves E., *Painting the Heavens: Art and Science in the Age of Galileo* (Princeton, NJ: 1999).

Schanzer E., "Milton's Hell Revisited", *University of Toronto Quarterly* 24.2 (1955) 136–145.

Steadman J., *Milton's Biblical and Classical Imagery* (Pittsburgh, PA: 1984).

Tudeau-Clayton M., "'Underwor(l)ds', l'ancien et le nouveau: De Virgile à Ben Jonson", in Laroque F. – Lessay F. (eds.), *Esthétiques de la Nouveauté à la Renaissance* (Paris: 2001) 59–76.

Wiebe G.D., *Fallen Angels in the Theology of Saint Augustine* (Oxford: 2021).

Wright B.A., "Masson's Diagram of Milton's Spaces", *The Review of English Studies* 21.81 (1945) 42–44.

CHAPTER 7

God's Underlands: Athanasius Kircher's Epic Journey in the *Mundus Subterraneus*

Monica Azzolini

Abstract

The famous Jesuit polymath, Athanasius Kircher, memorably stated that his remarkable two-volume scientific account of the underground, the *Mundus subterraneus* (1664) was born out of his fear of dying after crossing the Strait of Messina during the earthquake of 1638. Even assuming that this was true, this essay argues that a series of concurring elements enriched Kircher's reflections on both the afterlife and what lies within the bowels of the earth. One of these factors was the growing contemporary interest in the material remains of early Christianity preserved in the Roman catacombs; a second was the mounting influence of Virgil's *Aeneid* and its representation of the underworld within the humanistic and artistic circles of early modern Rome. By focusing on key passages from Kircher's letter of dedication to Alexander VII, the importance of the rediscovery of the catacombs, the relevance of the verses from Virgil's *Aeneid* that recount Aeneas's encounter with his father Anchises in the nether regions, and the significance of Jan Brueghel the Elder and Jan Brueghel the Younger's hellish landscapes, this essay paints a rich picture of Kircher's roman environment, where reflections about the afterlife often accompanied an interest in the excavation and extraction of both relics and natural objects and a keen appreciation for vivid depictions of hell and purgatory. These elements point to the convergence of eschatological, scientific, and mythopoetic themes that help us identify Kircher's work as a superb example of the unique synthesis of theology and natural philosophy, cosmology and eschatology that characterizes Baroque science.

Keywords

Athanasius Kircher – Virgil's reception – Roman catacombs – excavation – underworld

• • •

> and now, already well within that gate,
> across the circles – and alone – descends
> the one who will unlock this realm for us.
>
>   DANTE, *Inferno*, VIII, 128–130[1]

∴

We rarely look down and when we do, the earth's surface meets the eye. Even in broad daylight, darkness and impenetrability block our view and we cannot look any further, we cannot go any deeper. The dearth of sensorial experience impedes knowledge and leaves us in the realm of the imagination. Looking down has never been simple, and this lack of understanding, coupled with darkness, has made the underground a site of fear, uncertainty, secrecy, and even sinfulness.[2] Possibly, no early modern author was more captivated by the metaphor of light and darkness than the venerable Father Athanasius Kircher, the most productive Jesuit author of the seventeenth century, eccentric polymath, *Germanus incredibilis*, and indefatigable author of encyclopaedic works.[3] From his esoteric treatment of optics and perspective in his *Ars*

---

1   'e già di qua da lei discende l'erta, / passando per li cerchi sanza scorta, / tal che per lui ne fia la terra aperta'. Alighieri Dante, *La Divina Commedia*, ed. U. Bosco – G. Reggio (Florence: 1979), *Inferno*, VIII, vv. 128–130. I started working on Kircher's *Mundus subterraneus* during my visit to the Firestone Library at Princeton in the summer of 2019. I am incredibly grateful to the Princeton University Library for their financial support, and to their staff for their unwavering assistance during my visit. Additionally, I would like to extend my gratitude to Tony Grafton for his constant encouragement and support as I approached the rather daunting figure of Athanasius Kircher, *Germanus incredibilis*, voracious reader, and true polymath of the early modern period. My thanks go to Luca Ciancio for the precious references to relevant primary sources he so generously shared with me. I also want to thank Christine Göttler and Wietse de Boer for inviting me to participate in this wonderful project and for providing insightful suggestions on various versions of this essay.

2   On the impenetrability of the earth to sight and its place in various cultural and historical contexts, see the stimulating reflections in Kroonenberg S., *Why Hell Stinks of Sulfur: Mythology and Geology of the Underworld*, trans. A. Brown (London: 2013) 7–8; Macfarlane R., *Underland: A Deep Time Journey* (New York, NY – London: 2020), ch. 1. See also Mattes J., "Mapping the Invisible: Knowledge, Credibility and Visions of the Earth in Early Modern Cave Maps", *The British Journal for the History of Science* 55 (2022) 53–80.

3   The best biography of Athanasius Kircher remains John Edward Fletcher's monumental *A Study of the Life and Works of Athanasius Kircher, 'Germanus Incredibilis': With a Selection of His Unpublished Correspondence and an Annotated Translation of His Autobiography*, ed. E. Fletcher (Leiden – Boston, MA: 2011).

magna lucis et umbrae (1646) with its wonderfully suggestive frontispiece (on which more later), to his joint exploration of the celestial and the underground realms in his *Itinerarium extaticum quo mundi opificium* [...] *nova hypothesi exponitur ad veritatem* (1656) and its companion volume, the *Iter extaticum secundum, qui et mundi subterranei prodromus dicitur* (1657), Kircher demonstrated his propensity for exploring in equal measure both the light and the darkness of God's creation. The triumph of these efforts is most certainly his monumental *Mundus subterraneus* (1664), a work that resituated knowledge of what lies under the surface of the earth at the centre of seventeenth-century theological and scientific investigations.[4] In writing this enormous work in two volumes Kircher had a wealth of literary, historical, and scientific sources at his disposal. In addition, he also drew heavily on personal experience and the experience of his correspondents.

Before exploring some of the sources and models that may have inspired this unique work, however, it is essential to remember that the *Mundus subterraneus*, like other works of natural philosophy penned by Kircher, fulfilled one of the aims outlined in the Jesuit order's mission, namely expanding the knowledge of God's creation. The first rule of the professor of philosophy as stated in the *Ratio Studiorum* summarized this goal admirably by declaring that

> since the humanities or natural sciences prepare the intellectual powers for theology and assist in the perfect understanding and practical application of religious truth and by virtue of their content contribute to the attainment of this goal, the teacher whose heart is set on advancing the honour and glory of God should teach these secular subjects in a spirit which will prepare his students, and especially his Jesuit students, for the study of theology.[5]

It is neither surprising nor regrettable, therefore, that Kircher's scientific works were pervaded with religious imagery and are imaginative themselves. More surprising, instead, is that he devoted so many pages to the study of a natural realm, that of *fossilia*, that had been largely neglected by Aristotle and had little fortune among classical and medieval commentators, who (except for

---

4   Kircher Athanasius, *Itinerarium exstaticum quo mundi opificium id est coelestis expansi, siderumque tam errantium, quam fixorum natura, vires, proprietates* [...] *nova hypothesi exponitur ad veritatem* (Rome, Vitale Mascardi: 1656); idem, *Iter extaticum secundum qui et mundi subterranei prodromus dicitur* (Rome, Vitale Mascardi: 1657).

5   Farrell A.P., s.J., *The Jesuit Ratio Studiorum of 1599* (Washington, DC: 1970) 40. For the original Latin of the 1616 edition, www.uni-mannheim.de/mateo/camenaref/societasjesu.html#sj3 (accessed 02.02.2024).

Theophrastus and Albertus Magnus) only added marginally to what Aristotle had said in the *Meteorology*.[6] There is little doubt that the *Mundus subterraneus* represents the most comprehensive natural-philosophical summa of the knowledge of what lies beneath the earth's surface written in early modern times. Even when the content is not particularly innovative – although it often is – the way the material was pulled together, ordered, and illustrated makes it a magnificent example of Baroque science.

In this essay, I will first address some of Kircher's reasons for turning his attention to the underground, and then, in the second part of the essay, I will look at the influential classical models that he chose for recounting his imaginative journey into darkness and the underworld. As my analysis aims to demonstrate, the Roman humanistic context in which Kircher operated and the renewed interest in excavating the classical and religious past of the Eternal City provided powerful stimuli for Kircher. In Kircher's mind, I argue, a journey through the Roman catacombs or a journey through natural underground channels could equally spur meaningful reflection on salvation and the Last Things. For this reason, Kircher's work seamlessly weaves together naturalistic, religious, and eschatological themes to provide a masterly celebration of God's invisible creation.

1   **Journeying through Light and Darkness: Looking under the Surface**

The theme of light and darkness (or *lux et umbrae*) was not just linked to Kircher's *Ars magna lucis et umbrae* (1646), dedicated to the physical, astronomical, astrological, and metaphysical properties of light (a text which also discussed the power of the sun above and below the earth's surface); it was also subtly connected to Kircher's other major work, the *Mundus subterraneus*, which he dedicated to Pope Alexander VII (vol. 1) and Holy Roman Emperor Leopold I (vol. 2).[7] On the elaborate frontispiece of the *Ars magna lucis et umbrae*, Kircher had already hinted at the theme of darkness under the surface of the earth. The anthropomorphic Sun-Mercury on the left of the image (tattooed with astrological symbols and holding a caduceus with the signs of the planets) radiates his light onto a burning mirror held by the feminine figure

---

6   Magnus A., *Opera omnia*, ed. A. Borgnet (Paris: 1890), vol. 5 (*Mineralium Libri V*) 1–116; Theophrastus, *De lapidibus*, ed. and trans. D.E. Eichholz (Oxford: 1965).

7   Kircher Athanasius, *Ars magna lucis et umbrae* (Rome, Lodovico Grignani for Hermann Scheus: 1646); idem, *Mundus subterraneus in XII libros digestus* (Amsterdam, Johannes Janssonius van Waesberge: 1664).

of the Moon on the opposite side, and to another mirror hidden in an underground cave placed in the lower right corner [Fig. 7.1]. Casting light on what lies under the surface, therefore, was a theme that had been dear to Kircher for some time. The study of light, however, was not purely scientific and experimental. Rather, as Koen Vermeir has convincingly argued in relation to the *Ars magna*, it carried deep theological and eschatological meaning. In the *Ars magna*, for instance, pious souls travel in straight lines of light to ascend to God. The scientific study of light thus assumes eschatological meaning through the use of anagogical imagery. In other words, scientific concepts and phenomena act as anagogical metaphors to suggest to the reader the soul's elevation towards God.[8] Within this framework, meditating on natural phenomena is seen as a means of elevation towards the Creator. For this reason, as Vermeir stresses, in Kircher's work science and technology are never separate from metaphysics and theology, but they serve as a means to gain deeper knowledge of God in preparation for life after death.[9] Thus, studying Kircher's scientific works without being attentive to their theological and spiritual meanings and without grasping the meditative and transcendental functions of their imagery and images risks missing a crucial element of his work.[10]

Take the *Itinerarium extaticum*. As Jacqueline Glomski has argued in a short article, Kircher's *Itinerarium extaticum* and, by extension, its companion volume, the *Iter extaticum secundum*, were works of cosmic fiction that displayed all the features of Baroque literature: a florid and evocative style, a blurred perception of reality, an appeal to the senses, along 'with reminiscences of the Counter-Reformation mystical tradition (including the Ignatian *Exercitia spiritualia*, and apocalyptic and Solomonic writings)'.[11] The protagonists of both journeys are the human Theodidactus and the angel accompanying him on his journeys, Cosmiel. In the first dialogue of the *Itinerarium extaticum* Cosmiel guides Theodidactus from planet to planet and to the

---

8   Vermeir K., "Athanasius Kircher's Magical Instruments: An Essay on 'Science', 'Religion' and Applied Metaphysics", *Studies in History and Philosophy of Science* 38 (2007) 363–400, at 380.

9   Ibidem 379–380, 387–390. On the use of optical devices for devotional practices in the sixteenth and seventeenth centuries, see Göttler C., *Last Things: Art and Religious Imagination in the Age of Reform* (Turnhout: 2010).

10 Vermeir highlights this principle in his discussion of Kircher's experiments in the *Ars magna* by encouraging us 'to read his instruments in a religious and metaphysical way as "visualizations of the invisible"' ("Athanasius Kircher's Magical Instruments" 391).

11 Glomski J., "Religion, the Cosmos, and Counter-Reformation Latin: Athanasius Kircher's *Itinerarium extaticum* (1656)", in Steiner-Weber A. – Enenkel K.A.E. (eds.), *Acta Conventus Neo-Latini Monasteriensis. Proceedings of the Fifteenth International Congress of Neo-Latin Studies* (*Münster: 2012*) (Leiden: 2015) 227–236, at 227.

FIGURE 7.1   Frontispiece of Athanasius Kircher, *Ars magna lucis et umbrae in decem libros digesta* (Rome, Sumptibus Hermanni Scheus: 1646)

fixed stars to explore their properties and configurations, while the second, entitled *De providentia Dei in mundi opificio elucescente* (On the providence of God shining forth in the workmanship of the world), is more technical, explaining the functioning of the cosmos and dispelling some Aristotelian misconceptions that Theodidactus still held in favour of the new astronomy of Tycho Brahe.[12] The stated aim, however, is to illustrate God's providential plan through his works. Casting light – indicated by the term *elucescente* in the title – is precisely what Cosmiel does as God's servant and messenger. As a fictional contrivance to transition from the first to the second journey, more-over, Kircher introduces the figure of Hydriel (another angel), who, seeing Theodidactus asleep in a garden, introduces him to the theme of water, includ-ing underground water. This new fictional character fulfils also the function of moving the narrative from above to underground. Thus, upon returning, Cosmiel explains to Theodidactus the technical structure of the underground, and then, in the last dialogue, accompanies him on a journey below ground. The subtitle of the *Iter extaticum secundum* reveals Kircher's intentions: to lay bare (*exponitur ad veritatem*) the structure of the terrestrial globe together with what is hidden in it and the deepest secrets of nature through the veil of fiction (*per ficti raptus integumentum*).[13]

As scholars have noted, the second journey is shorter than the first as Kircher makes it explicit that he is working through the material for a longer work by using the phrase 'prelude to the underground world' (*Mundi subterranei pro-dromus*) in the subtitle. And indeed, the larger book appeared, in the remark-able format of two hefty volumes full of information about the structure of the earth and its secrets: his *Mundus subterraneus*. While in the aftermath of Galileo's trial astronomy would have appeared too risky a subject for Kircher to pursue, geo-cosmology may have seemed a safer and more suitable subject by which to propose new neo-Aristotelian theories about the earth. According to the goals outlined in the *Ratio Studiorum*, moreover, this type of inquiry was intended to tackle theological subjects.

However, this may not have been the only reason why Kircher decided to turn inward and downward. There were additional reasons why an exploration of the underworld was both timely and topical. First, Kircher tells his reader

---

12   For brief summaries of these works and links to digital editions, see the NOSCEMUS database entries, https://wiki.uibk.ac.at/noscemus/Itinerarium_exstaticum; https://wiki .uibk.ac.at/noscemus/Iter_extaticum_II (accessed 02.02.2024).

13   Kircher, *Iter extaticum secundum*, titlepage: 'Terrestris globi structura, una cum abditis in ea constitutis arcanioris naturae reconditoriis, per ficti raptus integumentum exponitur ad veritatem'.

that his interest in the earth's physiology grew out of a personal experience that brought him close to death and fostered sustained meditations on the afterlife. As he was travelling around the Mediterranean, first to Malta and then to Sicily, he was caught in the middle of renewed seismic activity in the region. This placed him in close contact with the mighty forces of nature that governed the underworld and prompted some reflections on his own mortality. As he tells us in the opening pages of the *Mundus subterraneus*, while crossing the Strait of Messina by boat on 24 March 1638 with some companions, he witnessed the eruptions of Stromboli and Etna and the earthquake that accompanied them. He was so close to dying that he promised that, should he survive, he would write a work about the earth's interior.[14] Second, in the sixteenth century there had been a growing interest in the Roman and Christian archaeology of the area in and around Rome. This interest, coupled with excavations related to material extraction for building, meant there were ample opportunities to see 'earth workers' digging in and around Rome.[15]

As numerous historians have emphasized, starting from the mid-1500s, Rome became the focus of unprecedented, large-scale investigations of the material and archival remains of early Christianity.[16] This process, it has been highlighted, was steered from above, from the top of the Church hierarchy, and was advanced by Counter-Reformation initiatives that included Cesare Baronio's new martyrology of 1586 and the posthumous appearance

---

14 Kircher, *Mundus*, vol. 1, Praefatio, fols. ** 1 r–** 3 r. See also Fletcher, *A Study of the Life and Works of Athanasius Kircher* 37. Of course, this explanation could be also read as a literary device.

15 On the term 'earth workers', and their visibility/invisibility in eighteenth-century sources, see Barnett L., "Showing and Hiding: The Flickering Visibility of Earth Workers in the Archives of Earth Science", *History of Science* 58 (2020) 245–274. For an art-historical study that takes a 'bottom-up' approach and follows ancient artworks from the moment of their excavation to their circulation across Italy and beyond, see Furlotti B., *Antiquities in Motion: From Excavation Sites to Renaissance Collections* (Los Angeles, CA: 2019).

16 The literature on this topic is extensive and cannot be summarized fully here. For recent, state-of-the-art accounts and provocative arguments, see Schwab M.E. – Grafton A., *The Art of Discovery: Digging into the Past in Renaissance Europe* (Princeton, NJ: 2022), and Lewis N.D., *The Early Modern Invention of Late Antique Rome* (Cambridge: 2020); see also Ditchfield S., "Reading Rome as a Sacred Landscape, c. 1586–1635", in Coster W. – Spicer A. (eds.), *Sacred Space in Early Modern Europe* (Cambridge: 2005) 167–192. For an elegant and informative history of catacomb archaeology that sums up some of the essential scholarship, see also Hirschfeld A.K., "An Overview of the Intellectual History of Catacomb Archaeology", in Brink L., O.P. – Green D. (eds.), *Commemorating the Dead: Texts and Artifacts in Context. Studies of Roman, Jewish and Christian Burials* (Berlin – New York, NY: 2008) 11–38.

of Antonio Bosio's *Roma sotterranea* (1635).[17] In fifty years, Simon Ditchfield has suggested, Rome rose from its ashes to become 'a shining beacon of the Counter-Reformation'.[18] Part of this process, as Bosio's work suggests, involved recovering the material evidence of the city's early Christian past. It is not by chance that Antonio Tempesta's famous map of Rome of 1593, the ideal guide for any wealthy pilgrim, was dedicated to Giacomo Bosio, Antonio's uncle. As Ditchfield highlights, the map gave prominence to the new orders – the Oratorians and the Jesuits – and their homes, the church of Santa Maria in Vallicella and the Jesuit church of the Gesù. These two orders were heavily involved in the market of early Christian relics.[19]

The historical depth of this Christian tradition materialized in the form of buildings and objects reclaimed from the mixture of soil and debris that stood between the feet of early modern Romans and the Christian catacombs of Santa Priscilla that were "rediscovered" in 1578.[20] The discovery of this subterranean city filled Romans with awe and wonder. The fact that these were the tombs of early Christians infused the discovery with eschatological meaning. While the legend recounts that some Roman labourers found these catacombs while digging for *pozzolana* – a natural silicious or silicious-aluminous material known since ancient times for its ability to react with water to form a very hard and waterproof compound – the truth was probably more prosaic. The presence of catacombs in and around Rome was well known from historical sources, but the city had never seen so much engineering work as in the time of the Counter-Reformation. The recovery of early Christianity soon involved going underground and exploring darkness to reimagine a pristine Christian time on which the Church of the Counter-Reformation could remodel itself. As Bosio explored the topography of Rome equipped with patristic texts, papal documents, and saints' *vitae* to reconstruct an earlier, more authentic Christian topography, Kircher did the same more imaginatively, piecing together antiquarian and scientific information about the space under the surface of the earth. Whereas Bosio's work, *Roma sotterranea*, saw the 'priority of

---

17   Ditchfield, "Reading Rome" 167.
18   Ibidem 168.
19   Ibidem 169–170.
20   This was indeed a rediscovery, but the scale of extraction changed substantially. For earlier uses of the Roman catacombs see Oryshkevich I., *The History of the Roman Catacombs from the Age of Constantine to the Renaissance* (Ph.D. dissertation, Columbia University: 2003); for a famous case where those who met underground came to the attention of the ecclesiastical authorities for plotting the pope's murder, D'Elia A., *A Sudden Terror: The Plot to Murder the Pope* (Cambridge, MA: 2009). On the event, which included the erudite humanist Pomponio Leto, see also Schwab – Grafton, *Digging into the Past* 16–17.

text over trowel', Kircher's *Mundus subterraneus* tried to bridge theology and science, theory and experience in two very different volumes; while Bosio's work emphasized the incompleteness of his information and the martyrdom of early Christians, Kircher's imaginative journey supplied a partly fictional, partly eschatological, and partly experiential view of the earth from within.[21]

As Kircher stated in the dedication letter to Pope Alexander VII appended to the first volume of the *Mundus subterraneus*, in entering the nether regions of the earth he would encounter the souls of those who await salvation. He declared, 'I am making my way to the lower parts of the earth. There, I will also find a part of your Apostolic Kingdom, where happy souls, as if in exile, await your keys, with which you will open the treasure of the Church for them and supply them with the means to travel to their home more swiftly'.[22] As the material remains of martyrdom were supposed to lead the faithful to meditate on the greatness of God, so Kircher's journey into the bowels of the earth ought to cast light onto the secret marvels of nature created by the same God. The sacred space that was associated with the souls of those who had sinned – which, despite being unnamed, seemingly corresponds to the place of purgatory – was also a sacred space filled with wondrous nature to be explored.

Kircher scholars who have written on the *Mundus subterraneus* may not have fully appreciated the significance of contemporary attempts to explore the underground around Rome and Latium (and elsewhere in Italy) for Kircher's own explorations of nature below the ground. One of the reasons may be due to Kircher himself: as noted, the German Jesuit prefaced his work with the account of his life-changing experience at sea during the dreadful earthquake of 1638 and explicitly credited this event as the source of his commitment to explore the underworld. This genealogy story, however, seems to obfuscate the fertile stimuli that were coming from Rome itself, both from archaeological excavation and from specific themes and representations of the underworld. This argument is reinforced by the fact that Kircher and Bosio shared the same patronage network around Cardinal Barberini.[23] Another reason may be that

---

21   On Bosio's predominantly textual approach, see Ditchfield S., "Text before Trowel: Antonio Bosio's *Roma sotterranea* revisited", *Studies in Church History* 33 (1997) 343–360; and Ditchfield, "Reading Rome" 178–189.

22   Kircher, *Mundus*, vol. 1, "Dedicatio", fol. * 3 v: 'Ego vero interea in inferiores partes terrae iter adorno: illic etiam apostolici tui regni partem aliquam reperturus in loco, ubi felices animae velut in exilio claves tuas expectant, quibus Ecclesiae thesauros eis aperias, et tanquam viaticum ad patriam citius adeundam suppedites'.

23   Cardinal Francesco Barberini (1597–1679) and Giovan Battista Pamphilj (1574–1655) were long-time friends belonging to the same circle. See Merola A., "Francesco Barberini", *Dizionario Biografico degli Italiani* 6, 1964, https://www.treccani.it/enciclopedia/francesco-barberini_%28Dizionario-Biografico%29/ (accessed 02.02.2024). See also Russell S.,

current ways of conceptualizing the history of science, the history of religion, and the history of archaeology tend to conceal the existing connections among these cultural enterprises in the early modern period, imposing anachronistic divisions and applying presentist interpretations to material that was conceived and consumed within a different and more cross-disciplinary intellectual framework.[24] The recovery of the tombs of early Christians, at the crossroads between religion and archaeology, intersects with the vision of the souls' salvation as they travel towards God. Descending alive into the region of the dead only to rise again to the surface of a renewed Christianity would have had deep eschatological meaning for early modern Romans.

Given the conspicuous absence of purgatory in the Holy Scripture, moreover, its existence, as historians have highlighted, became a cornerstone of the Reformation and Counter-Reformation debate.[25] Historians have maintained that the sixteenth century was arguably the Golden Age of Catholic writing about purgatory.[26] The Council of Trent reaffirmed that 'the suffrages of the faithful' helped those souls that were in purgatory, and the Jesuits wrote extensively about purgatory, more than any other order. At least according to one historian, 'the doctrine of purgatory clearly fitted well into their appeal to a mitigated and less strenuous teaching on the Beyond, and substantially widened the scope of methods by which salvation might be attained'.[27] In

---

"Antiquarianism and the Villa Pamphilj on the Janiculum Hill in Rome", *Papers of the British School at Rome* 82 (2014) 237–264, at 240.

24   For examples of how some of these areas intersected in the early modern period, see Grafton A., "Humanism and Science in Renaissance Prague: Kepler in Context", in idem, *Defenders of the Text: The Traditions of Scholarship in an Age of Science, 1450–1800* (Cambridge, MA: 1991) 178–203; Buchwald J.Z. – Feingold M., *Newton and the Origin of Civilization* (Princeton, NJ: 2013). For examples related to medicine, see Siraisi N.G., "History, Antiquarianism, and Medicine: The Case of Girolamo Mercuriale", *Journal of the History of Ideas* 64 (2003) 231–251; idem, *History, Medicine and the Traditions of Renaissance Learning* (Ann Arbor, MI: 2007). For the adoption of similar methods among humanists, philosophers, and natural historians, see Blair A., "Humanist Methods in Natural Philosophy: The Commonplace Book", *Journal of the History of Ideas* 53 (1992) 541–551; idem, *Too Much to Know: Managing Scholarly Information before the Modern Age* (New Haven, CT: 2010); Krämer F., "Ulisse Aldrovandi's *Pandechion Epistemicon* and the Use of Paper Technology in Renaissance Natural History", *Early Science and Medicine* 19 (2014) 398–423; idem, "Ein papiernes Archiv für alles jemals Geschriebene. Ulisse Aldrovandis *Pandechion epistemonicon* und die Naturgeschichte der Renaissance", *NTM. Zeitschrift für Geschichte der Wissenschaften, Technik und Medizin* 21.1 (2013) 11–36. For a broader analysis of the later period, see Daston L. – Most G.W., "History of Science and History of Philologies", *Isis* 106 (2015) 378–390, at 382–383.

25   Marshall P., *Beliefs and the Dead in Reformation England* (Oxford: 2002), esp. chs. 2 and 3.

26   Sullivan H., *Grotesque Purgatory: A Study of Cervantes's Don Quixote, Part II* (University Park, PA: 1996) 79.

27   Ibidem 79–80.

Kircher's case, I would argue, one method to obtain salvation was to meditate on and admire the extraordinary world contained in the bowels of the earth.

While exploring natural caves and visiting the Roman catacombs are now seen as distinct enterprises, Kircher may have thought differently. In the first volume of the *Mundus subterraneus*, he dedicates a chapter to the numerous caves, gaps, and underground paths within the earth (Caput XX: *De antris, hiatibus, et innumeris terrae meatibus*). Here he connects the Roman catacombs, 'with which *Roma subterranea* deals abundantly', with other imaginative underground spaces like hell, purgatory, and limbo, but also with the oracle of Delphi, the caves of the giants in Palestine and Sicily (*humanae cryptae*), and those of the sibyls and the muses in the Agro Cumano near Naples (this syncretism is very typical of Kircher, of course). Following the humanist Jacques Gaffarel, he then seamlessly moves from the theoretical to the technical, making a distinction between natural and artificial caves and describing their salubrity or lack thereof. He thus provides examples of both natural and artificial caves. Among the natural caves, he mentions Mount Sorano near Grosseto (which he had personally visited) and the Aeolian Islands on the coast of Sicily; among the artificial caves, he lists the Neapolitan underground pathways near Posillipus and those of Syracuse.[28] All these spaces, at least in Kircher's eyes, possess the same ontological status.

There is no doubt, furthermore, that the *Mundus subterraneus* reveals some continuity with Kircher's other fully topographical work dedicated to Rome and its surroundings, his *Latium*, which appeared in 1669. As Harry B. Evans has argued convincingly, Kircher's interest in the topography of Italy, Tuscany and Latium in particular, had led him to write another account of a "journey", *Iter Etruscum*.[29] In Kircher's own words, the work had been a long-term undertaking requiring considerable investment of time and money, a book 'in which Etruscan civilisation is described from Noah's offspring to the present day, its political status is set forth, and marvellous things of nature are explained

---

28   Kircher, *Mundus* 1:118. Here Kircher cites as his source a work by the French scholar and priest Jacques Gaffarel (1601–1681) entitled *Mundus subterraneus*, but a work by that title does not seem to have been published. Gaffarel published, however, a short synopsis in French, *Le monde sousterrein ou description historique et philosophique* (Paris, C. Du Mesnil: 1654), which divides the caves into divine, human-made, animal-made, natural, and artificial. It is possibly to this work that Kircher refers in the *Mundus subterraneus*. I thank Luca Ciancio for pointing me to this work. Gaffarel is also the author of the influential *Curiositez inouyes sur la sculpture talismanique des Persans, horoscope des patriarches et lecture des estoilles* (Paris, H. Du Mesnil: 1629). Ch. 5 of this text discusses natural and artificial stones and talismans. On this neglected author, see Hirai H. (ed.), *Jacques Gaffarel between Magic and Science* (Pisa – Rome: 2014).

29   Evans H.B., *Exploring the Kingdom of Saturn: Kircher's Latium and Its Legacy* (Ann Arbor, MI: 2012) 2–6.

which I observed in its mountains, cities, territories, rivers, lakes, and its many hot springs [...]'.[30] Kircher had travelled personally to various sites and had planned to have the work lavishly illustrated; he mentioned these early explorations (including, as we have seen, his visit to Mount Sorano) in the *Mundus subterraneus*. His investigations of the area near Viterbo allowed him to encounter people who were living underground, 'in a manner like that of the troglodytes of Malta'; this underground settlement was under the jurisdiction of Prince Camillo Pamphilj. Kircher emphasized how he had employed a local guide and had seen these places with his own eyes, but also that numerous other sources pointed to similar habitations elsewhere, as recounted in the Jesuits' annual letters: in parts of India common people lived in subterranean passages, and so did people in parts of Africa and near the Caspian Sea. He then remarked, 'I will say nothing here about the underground crypts in Rome, where so many martyrs and popes hid during the time of the persecution; the reader may consult *Roma subterranea* about them'.[31] The fact that these explorations were carried out on the Pamphilj's estate was not inconsequential, moreover. As Charles Dempsey has highlighted, the Barberini and Pamphilj circles shared 'common antiquarian interests', and the Pamphilj invested significant economic resources in fashioning a genealogy that reached back to Numa Pompilius, who succeeded Aeneas as founder of Rome. Anchoring their genealogy in a remote past of historical significance was functional in claiming the heightened prominence of their family in sixteenth-century Rome. As Susan Russell and Ingrid Rowland have documented amply, one of the ways in which this was achieved was through the patronage of artists, humanists, and antiquarians and the commissioning of works focused on the archaeology of early Christianity and Aeneas's legend (on which more in the concluding section of this essay).[32]

As Massimiliano Ghilardi has convincingly argued, moreover, earlier scholarship had maintained that the "birth" of early Christian archaeology was

---

30 This is how Kircher described the work to his long-time patron and dedicatee, Duke August of Brunswick-Lüneburg. I cite from Evans's translation, *Exploring the Kingdom* 3.

31 Kircher, *Mundus* 2.99: 'Non dicam hic de subterraneis Romae urbis cryptis, ubi tot sancti martyres una cum pontificibus sanctis persecutionis tempore delituerunt, de quibus lector *Romam subterraneam* consulat'. I quote from Evans's translation again, *Exploring the Kingdom* 4. Evans incorrectly attributes the work to Paolo Aringhi. However, Aringhi, an Oratorian, had only taken Bosio's work and expanded it. He published it with the title *Roma subterranea novissima* in 1651, but Bosio's work had already appeared (posthumously) in Italian in 1632. Bosio had been working on his *Roma subterranea* since the early 1590s.

32 Russell, "Antiquarianism and the Villa Pamphilj"; Rowland I., "Vergil and the Pamphili Family in Piazza Navona, Rome", in Farrel J. – Putnam M.C.J. (eds.), *A Companion to Vergil's Aeneid and Its Tradition* (Oxford: 2010) 253–269.

largely, or even exclusively, associated with Filippo Neri and the Oratorians. In part, Ghilardi maintains, this was due to Antonio Muratori's incorrect association of Bosio with the Oratorians (possibly because Paolo Aringhi, who published an augmented edition of Bosio's work, was indeed an Oratorian). Muratori's influential account grew into the legend that saw Bosio and Neri excavate together. As Ghilardi amply documents, however, the Oratorians were not the first to develop an interest in early Christian material remains. Indeed, the Jesuits, under whose guidance Bosio had studied, were already working on early Christian relics before the crucial date of 31 May 1578, when allegedly some *cavatori di pozzolana* had accidentally rediscovered the sacred burial site of St. Priscilla (now called 'di Anonimo di via Anapo' as the identification has been challenged multiple times).[33] It is difficult to believe that Father Kircher, who at some point fashioned himself as a new Hermes Trismegistus, would have not been extremely fascinated by the discovery by members of the German College of the Jesuits of the catacombs of St. Hermes on the old *Salaria* road in November of 1576. Access to what Ghilardi calls 'a goldmine of saints' required an extremely long wooden ladder. The extraction of relics from this site, moreover, was so intense that it caught the eyes of the Church hierarchy: Ghilardi quotes a document reporting the 1628 interrogation of three Jesuits who described the long and dangerous ladder leading down to the tunnel, the indefatigable work of the *fossori* (the workmen), and the criteria these Jesuits applied to intentionally select only the relics of martyrs. The three Jesuits availed themselves of the advice of other church figures who belonged to a selected group of experts and who were Bosio's friends. A detailed report on how to operate these extractions, entitled *Pratica per estrarre li corpi de' Santi Martiri da sagri cimiteri di Roma* (How to extract the bodies of martyred saints from the Roman catacombs) was issued under the Pontificate of Alexander VII, in the years around 1662–1667, around the time Kircher published his *Mundus subterraneus*. Ghilardi notes, moreover, that this was not the only site over which the Jesuits had control for the extraction and translation of relics. Some of these relics, perhaps unsurprisingly, fed a veritable market aimed at boosting the cult of Christian saints both in Europe and beyond.[34] The picture that emerges from these documents is clearly one of low- and high-level practitioners working together, and of churchmen deeply invested in exploring the underground and recovering early Christian objects in order

---

33   Ghilardi M., "Miniere di santità. La riscoperta delle catacombe romane: oratoriani o
      gesuiti?", in Dompnier B. – Nanni S. (eds.), *La mémoire des saints originels entre XVIᵉ et
      XVIIIᵉ siècle* (Rome: 2019) 377–514.
34   Ibidem 384–394.

to foster the cult of early saints in the growing economy of salvation of which purgatory was an important part.

Kircher's sustained interest in caves and catacombs is attested also by his correspondence: in the third edition of the *Mundus subterraneus* he included, as he often did in parts of his works, a letter-report from the Italian traveller to the East, Cornelio Magno (1638–1692), detailing his exploration of the grottos of Antiparos.[35] To highlight that Kircher himself was no armchair naturalist or antiquarian, however, one has just to remember how, in a separate work entitled the *Historia Eustachio-Mariana* (1665), he claimed to have identified the ruins of an early Christian church on the top of a mountain near Tivoli; Kircher had subsequently made this place, La Mentorella, his own special place of devotion. Openly comparing himself with a farmer clearing thorns, ploughing fields, and digging stones out of the ground, Kircher emphatically recounted how, guided by the works of ancient writers, he had climbed a rough terrain, to reach

> a lonely, fearsome area, surrounded by a crown of huge, rocky cliffs. It was truly a place filled with dread, since the stony peaks of the mountains seemed to strike the sky with their height, and the precipices of the overhanging cliffs that ended in dizzying and fearful chasms seemed to suggest the underworld.[36]

The comparison Kircher made with the fearsome realm of the underworld is significant. In this period, finding God in frightful, liminal places almost became Kircher's signature. As Evans highlights, there is something of this account that reminds us of Kircher's equally wondrous description of exploring Vesuvius.[37]

---

35   The three-page section on caves in vol. 1 (ch. 20), was expanded to twelve pages when Kircher added Magno's letter. See Kempe S. – Naumann G. – Dunsch B., "Athanasius Kircher's Chapter XX 'About Caves, Fractures and the Innumerable Passages of the Earth' and the Grotto of Antiparos from 'Mundus Subterraneus', 1678, translated from Latin", in Filippi M. – Bosák P. (eds.), *Proceedings of the 16th International Congress of Speleology, Czech Republic, Brno, July 21–28, 2013* (Prague: 2013) 1:59–64 (with German translation of Kircher's passage). On Magno, see the brief note by Almagià R., "Magni, Cornelio", in *Enciclopedia Italiana* (Rome: 1934), https://www.treccani.it/enciclopedia /cornelio-magni_%28Enciclopedia-Italiana%29/(accessed 02.02.2024).

36   The translation, this time from the *Historia Eustachio-Mariana*, comes once again from Evans, *Exploring the Kingdom* 7.

37   Ibidem 8.

Of course, some of Kircher's journey was imaginative. According to him, an inscription identified the location as the very place where St. Eustachius underwent conversion to Christianity in the fourth century CE, and Constantine, the first emperor to embrace Christianity, founded the church. In practice, Maren Elisabeth Schwab and Anthony Grafton argue, such an inscription may never have existed – there is no evidence that connects it with Constantine. This fact, however, does not invalidate the assertion that Kircher was not only an avid reader, but also an eager explorer.[38] If mines were 'trading zones', to use Pamela Long's apt expression, so were catacombs. Where antiquarian interests mixed with theological and eschatological ones to result in reflections on the death and future salvation of early martyrs, there was sometimes space not only for an economy of relics, but also for scientific observation.[39] Roman engineering and hydraulics, after all, were being rediscovered and valued among artisans and architects around the same time, as the Eternal City was being revamped to accommodate the growing need of water (both potable and not) among the populace and the upper classes.[40]

Despite being advertised in other publications, Kircher's *Iter Etruscum* never saw the light of day. The book was "killed" by Jesuit censorship. As Evans and others have highlighted, this was not the first or last time Kircher had succumbed to internal Jesuit control. His slim but extremely interesting *Diatribe de prodigiosis crucibus* (Discourse on prodigious crosses, 1661) nearly suffered the same fate.[41] As a theologian and a natural philosopher, Kircher had been

---

38   The story has been recounted most recently in Schwab – Grafton, *The Art of Discovery* 2–5. See also Evans, *Exploring the Kingdom* 6–9. Cf. Tschudi V.P., *Baroque Antiquity: Archaeological Imagination in Early Modern Rome* (Cambridge – New York, NY: 2017), ch. 5 (focusing on Kircher), who argues that 'Athanasius the antiquarian relied minimally on the investigation of ruins and instead on ideals of erudition, the hunt for patrons, and the propagation of faith', at 177. I resist the interpretation that the bookish mode of investigation excludes the experiential one.

39   On the significance of mining as a place for the development of practical and experimental epistemologies, see Long P.O., *Openness, Secrecy and Authorship: Technical Arts and the Culture of Knowledge from Antiquity to the Renaissance* (Baltimore, MD – London: 2003), ch. 6, and Morel T., *Underground Mathematics: Craft Culture and Knowledge Production in Early Modern Europe* (Cambridge: 2022).

40   Long P.O., *Engineering the Eternal City: Infrastructure, Topography, and the Culture of Knowledge in Late Sixteenth-Century Rome* (Chicago, IL: 2018). For a fascinating account of how Roman engineering knowledge and techniques were embodied in everyday artisanal practices in the sixteenth and seventeenth centuries, see also Mukerji C., *Impossible Engineering: Technology and Territoriality on the Canal du Midi* (Princeton, NJ – Oxford: 2009).

41   On this intriguing text, see now Tutino S., "The Mystery of Mount Vesuvius's Crosses: Belief, Credulity, and Credibility in Post-Reformation Catholicism", *Journal of the History of Ideas* 83 (2022) 207–227.

asked to express his opinion on a perplexing phenomenon that happened in Naples after an eruption in 1660: black and red crosses had started appearing on linen across the city, and the population had tended to interpret these as bad omens. As Stefania Tutino has detailed in a recent article, such phenomena required careful management on the part of the state and church authorities, who could not neglect to assuage people's fear.[42] Kircher's work had tried to fully naturalize the phenomenon as caused by the various metals that had been spewed into the air by the mighty volcano. His fellow Jesuit censors, however, were not entirely pleased with the Jesuit's excessive insistence on the natural character of the phenomenon. They thus suggested changes that Kircher mostly implemented and allowed the text to appear with the Jesuit general's permission.[43]

Despite being the target of censorship, the indefatigable Kircher was not deterred from continuing his work on chorography, or indeed exploring the underground. After publishing the slim *Historia Eustachio-Mariana*, the German polymath worked steadily on the *Mundus subterraneus*, which appeared in 1665, and his *Latium*, which was finally published in 1671. Indeed, Kircher makes his ambition clear early on, defining the work contained in the *Mundus subterraneus* as new knowledge or *organum* that reveals truthfully the workings of God. The term *organum* here has the double meaning of knowledge and instrument, but is also a clear reference to Aristotle's *Organum*.[44] The subterranean realm is both harmonious and ordered according to God's providence. Kircher introduces his journey to Pope Alexander VII, the dedicatee, endowing the *Summum Sacerdotem* with the gift of light and casting him as a second radiant manifestation of God's power, both a guide and a source of light. In the dedication, Kircher presents himself as a man in need of a guide to enlighten his path as he starts his journey in the nether regions of the earth. In order to 'enter the underworld, which is hidden from us and leading to a more shrouded world', Kircher pleads emphatically, 'may I be permitted to enter my foot fearlessly; for the introductions which I consider [writing], I must trust your propitious work, by whose light I may describe this darkness clearly, lest the darkness tramples upon me wandering and toiling in the labyrinth of the lower world'.[45] Kircher thus casts his journey under Alexander VII's guiding

---

42   Ibidem.

43   Ibidem 220–221.

44   Kircher, *Mundus*, vol. 1, "Praefatio", fol. ** 1 r: 'Organum hoc, optimo jure hujus operis argumentum, quod Mundi Subterranei nomine inscripsimus, dici potest'.

45   Ibidem, "Dedicatio", fol. * 3 v: 'Ego vero interea in inferiores partes terrae iter adorno [...]. Ut autem in subterranea disclusi a nobis et reconditioris mundi adita, mihi pedem intrepide liceat introferre; ad introductiones, quas meditor, propitio tuo fidere mihi est opus: ad

light in overt Virgilian and Dantesque undertones. As I shall illustrate in the second section of this essay, this Virgilian echo is not limited to this early passage in the dedication. Rather, it is central to the way in which Kircher frames the whole enterprise, construing his own persona as a new Aeneas.

2   The Eschatological Imagination: Kircher as the New Aeneas

There is little doubt that living in Rome formed Kircher's appreciation not only for early Christian catacombs but also for the figure of Virgil and his hero, Aeneas. As Paula Findlen has argued, like Aeneas Kircher had been forced to flee his homeland. His arrival in Rome, moreover, was almost providential, as he had been heading to Vienna to take up the post of court mathematician when, thanks to the influence of the French savant Nicolas-Claude Fabri de Peiresc and Cardinal Francesco Barberini, he was invited to Rome to take over Christoph Scheiner's post as professor of mathematics at the Collegio Romano.[46]

Kircher was bound to have read Virgil abundantly as a Jesuit student: a staple of humanist education, Virgil had become a favourite author within the new religious order.[47] The *Ratio Studiorum* of 1599 consolidated a programme of studies that was put in place much earlier (it took fourteen years of work for the *Ratio Studiorum* to reach its full formulation). After having laid the basis of grammar, students proceeded to learn eloquence by studying the works of Cicero, Sallust, Livy, and by reading Virgil's *Aeneid* (with the notable exception of the salacious Book IV) and some Horace. Virgil returned to the classroom in the higher grammar classes, where the students studied Virgil's *Eclogues*, but also Book IV of the *Georgics*, and Books V and VII of the *Aeneid*.[48] The Roman poet was championed as the best model for epic poetry; in Kircher's time, as his order achieved the peak of its success, Virgil was even considered by some

---

cuius lucem possim tenebras illas describere luculenter, ne tenebrae conculcent me in labyrintho inferioris mundi errantem et laborantem [...]'.

46   Findlen P., *Possessing Nature: Museums, Collecting and Scientific Culture in Early Modern Italy* (Berkeley, CA: 1996) 334–335; on Peiresc's friendship with Cardinal Barberini, see Sarasohn L.T., "Nicolas-Claude Fabri de Peiresc and the Patronage of the New Science in the Seventeenth Century", *Isis* 84 (1993) 70–90.

47   Kallendorf C., *In Praise of Aeneas: Virgil and Epideictic Rhetoric in the Early Renaissance* (Hanover, NH: 1989); Haskell Y., "Practicing What They Preach? Vergil and the Jesuits", in Farrel – Putnam (eds.), *A Companion to Vergil's Aeneid* 203–216.

48   Farrell, *The Jesuit* Ratio Studiorum 79–80, 84–94. For the original Latin of the 1616 edition, www.uni-mannheim.de/mateo/camenaref/societasjesu.html#sj3 (accessed 02.02.2024).

'the leader of the Muses', to be imitated, and, ideally, surpassed.[49] As Yasmin Haskell has observed, at times the Jesuits remodelled their favourite author creatively, as in the case of the Jesuit Antonio Possevino, who criticized him harshly, but equally often took from him what was useful and appropriate and left aside what was not.[50]

The choice of Virgil, moreover, may have been reinforced by a solid and venerable localized humanistic culture revolving around the papal court that modelled itself after Virgil's style and themes. In a recent study, Geoffrey Glodzik has argued very convincingly how 'in Rome, Vergil's adopted city, this passion [for his work] was pursued with particular fervour, purposefully placing the poet at the centre of the city's narrative in the early Cinquecento'.[51] As Glodzik highlights, Virgil's language, genres, and themes were functional in articulating a vision of Rome's providential destiny as the city of God. He concludes that 'Vergilianism, based upon an application of Vergil particular to Rome, became the language of the prevailing discourse of papal Rome'.[52] For early sixteenth-century Roman humanists, therefore, Virgil's authority provided a way to anchor papal authority and dignity in the distant past and create an ideal line of descent for the Eternal City. As we have seen, this anchoring Rome in the past, which served to make it the centre of Christianity in the Counter-Reformation, was later reinforced by the rediscovery of another phase of this teleological history, early Christianity and its martyrs.

As historians of Virgil's reception have emphasized, different environments allowed for different interpretative frameworks to develop around Virgil's work, and this, in turn, provides historians with privileged points of access into the Renaissance world of learning and the works of the authors who readapted Virgil to their ends.[53] By the time of the Counter-Reformation, even Greek and Roman gods were put at the service of a providential Christian narrative of salvation. Virgil's fourth eclogue was read as an account of the birth of a miraculous

---

49   Haskell, "Vergil and the Jesuits" 205.

50   Ibidem.

51   Glodzik J.A., *The Reception of Vergil in Renaissance Rome* (Leiden – Boston, MA: 2023) 1.

52   Ibidem.

53   Ibidem 3. Glodzik develops this argument by building on the reception studies of Hardie, Kallendorf, and L.B.T. Houghton. For analogous considerations, embedded in specific local contexts or related to specific Virgilian texts, see Hardie P., *The Last Trojan Hero: A Cultural History of Virgil's Aeneid* (London – New York, NY: 2014); Kallendorf C., *Virgil and the Myth of Venice* (Oxford: 1999); idem, *The Protean Virgil* (Oxford: 2015); Houghton L.B.T. – Sgarbi M. (eds.), *Virgil and Renaissance Culture* (Tempe, AZ: 2018). Cf. Wilson-Okamura D.S., *Virgil in the Renaissance* (Cambridge: 2010), who has a tendency to universalize Virgil across Europe and is less attentive to space and place.

child and proof that Virgil had anticipated the birth of Jesus, and Virgil's Latin work provided the essential element of continuity between the founding of Rome and the rebirth of the Eternal City in the sixteenth century.[54] The attractiveness of the Virgilian model for a journey in the underworld may have been enhanced by contemporary artistic trends. As Christine Göttler has richly documented, at the end of the sixteenth century the ability of Flemish painters like Jan Brueghel the Elder to paint airy, fiery, or ethereal substances was particularly appreciated by Roman patrons; this in turn motivated Brueghel's sons to further develop these curious iconographies. Göttler convincingly argues that the 'poetic hells' Brueghel the Elder depicted in the period from about 1594 to 1608 were 'most likely motivated by some of Jan's early patrons in Rome'; and we know that he had frequented the catacombs, as he had scribbled his name and the year 1593 on the wall of the St. Domitilla catacomb that had been discovered the same year by Antonio Bosio.[55] Already by the mid-sixteenth century, nocturnal, hellish landscapes had become so popular that they began to be mass-produced and often signed with Bosch's name (Bosch having been the one who inspired the genre).[56] The lustrous, small-format copper plates of Jan Brueghel the Elder catered to this taste and were often seen in direct relation to the works of Bosch. Collectively, these painted hells are indicative of a strong fascination with the underworld within the elite Roman circles Kircher frequented. Significantly for my argument, moreover, Jan Brueghel the Elder expanded on Bosch's choice of religious imageries of purgatory and hell to include mythological, historical, and allegorical themes, including the scene of Aeneas's descent into the underworld. Book VI, as historians have highlighted, was often chosen for its exemplary Christian values and as representative of hell's landscape. Caves, tunnels, the shimmering of light on metallic surfaces, the rendering of smoke and flames that were the subject of these paintings were also natural elements that concerned Kircher.[57] That the Virgilian theme was so popular is demonstrated by the existence of three versions of *Aeneas*

---

54   Rowland, "Vergil and the Pamphili Family" 257–258.
55   Göttler C., "Fire, Smoke and Vapour: Jan Brueghel's 'Poetic Hells'", in Göttler C. – Neuber W. (eds.), *Spirits Unseen: The Representation of Subtle Bodies in Early Modern European Culture* (Leiden – Boston, MA: 2007) 19–46, at 25; see also idem, *Last Things* 335–373, at 343.
56   Göttler, "Fire, Smoke and Vapour" 26; idem, *Last Things* 345.
57   Kallendorf C., "From Virgil to Vida: The *Poeta Theologus* in Italian Renaissance Commentary", *Journal of the History of Ideas* 56 (1995) 41–62; Göttler, "Fire, Smoke and Vapour" 33–34; idem, *Last Things* 335–376; Honig E., *Jan Brueghel and the Senses of Scale* (University Park, PA: 2016) 89–91.

FIGURE 7.2   Jan Brueghel the Elder, *Aeneas and the Cumaean Sibyl in the Underworld*,
ca. 1600–1625. Oil on copper, 26.8 × 35.3 cm. Copenhagen, Thorvaldsens Museum,
inv. no. B44
IMAGE © THORVALDSENS MUSEUM

with the Cumaean Sibyl in the Underworld, one of the key scenes of Book VI
[Figs. 7.2, 7.3].

In fashioning his exploration of the underworld as an epic journey, Kircher
thus followed in the steps of earlier humanists and contemporary artists: he
simply added another example of the ingenious reworkings of Virgil's *Aeneid*
in Western culture. Of the many "Virgils" of the Renaissance, however, Kircher
chose that of the *Aeneid*, Book VI as it was functional to his own literary purposes for the *Mundus subterraneus*: the book recounted Aeneas's journey to
the underworld, provided a brief overview of God's cosmos, and played frequently with the theme of light and darkness. Kircher, as the New Aeneas, was
ready to cast light on the creation of God below the earth's surface as well as
its relationship with the celestial realm. As mentioned, the urge to reflect on
life after death and explore the nature of the nether regions may have emerged
from personal experience, but soon afterwards Kircher went well beyond it to
investigate 'the greatness and richness of the whole of nature and the greatest

FIGURE 7.3 Jan Brueghel the Younger, *Aeneas and the Cumaean Sibyl in the Underworld*,
1630s. Oil on copper, 26.7 × 35.9 cm. New York, The Metropolitan Museum of Art,
inv. no. 1991.444
IMAGE © THE METROPOLITAN MUSEUM OF ART

variety of things' and reveal the 'causes of secret virtues through keen investigation based on the marriage of art and nature necessary to human life with
the working of experiments as well as the application of reason and new methods of investigation'.[58]

Kircher did not hide his debt towards Virgil in the *Mundus subterraneus*.
Rather, he made it explicit from the very start. The titlepage of the first volume
features a *cartouche* that echoes very closely some key verses from Book VI of
the *Aeneid*: 'Spiritus intus alit totamque infusa per artus / mens agitat molem
et magno se corpore miscet' (*Aeneid* VI, 726–727) [Figs. 7.4, 7.5].[59] Book VI

---

58 Kircher, *Mundus*, titlepage: 'Universae denique Naturae maiestas et divitiae summa rerum
    varietate exponuntur. Abditorum effectuum causae acri indagine inquisitae demonstran-
    tur; cognitae per Artis et Naturae coniugium ad humanae vitae necessarium usum experi-
    mentorum apparatu, necnon novo modo et ratione applicantur'.

59 The phrase 'Intus alit' also appears on the frontispiece of *De igne subterrraneo physica
    prolusio* ([s.n.], [s.l.]: 1641), a short work by the Florentine court physician Giovanni Nardi.
    Nardi's image of the earth, with its lands, seas, and volcanoes, is very reminiscent of
    Kircher's famous 'Systema Ideale Pyropylaciorum'. I owe this reference to Luca Ciancio,

FIGURE 7.4 Frontispiece of Athanasius Kircher, *Mundus subterraneus in XII libros digestus* (Amsterdam, Johannes Janssonius van Waesberge: 1664)
IMAGE COURTESY OF THE HISTORY OF SCIENCE COLLECTIONS, UNIVERSITY OF OKLAHOMA LIBRARIES

FIGURE 7.5   Frontispiece of Kircher, *Mundus subterraneus*. Detail of Fig. 7.4, showing the
             Cartouche with verses from *Aeneid*, VI, 726–727: 'Spiritus intus alit totamque
             infusa per artus / mens agitat molem et magno se corpore miscet'

represents a crucial juncture in Virgil's epic poem: this is the moment when
Aeneas concludes his troubled journey and finally settles in Latium. Crucially,
it is a moment that preludes Aeneas's rebirth as the founder of Rome. The
Virgilian verses are part of a larger "cosmological" section of the epic poem
that takes place in the nether regions of the earth. Book VI recounts how the
Trojan hero arrived on the shores of Italy with his fleet and dropped off anchor
near present-day Naples. Following his late father's recommendation, he travelled to the Temple of Apollo, where he met the sibyl, a priestess, and prayed to
Apollo for the chance of settling in Latium. Aeneas had one additional wish: he
asked the sibyl if he could travel to Dis – the underworld – to meet his father's
spirit one last time. To be allowed to travel, the sibyl responded, Aeneas had to
accomplish a task: he needed to receive a sign that he was ready for such a journey; he needed to travel to a forest and find a golden bough. If the bough broke
off the tree easily, Aeneas was ready to travel (*Aeneid* VI, 95–150). Predictably,
Aeneas returned with the bough and the sibyl took him to the gate of Dis.

   Aeneas's journey here deepens, both metaphorically and physically, as
Charon ferries him across the river Styx into the underworld. After some wandering, the Trojan hero reaches the Blessed Groves, where good souls wander in their journey towards the Fields of Gladness. Here he meets his father
Anchises who explains to him the meaning of his long journey and the future

who is exploring Galileo's interest in Nardi's work. On Nardi, see Andretta E., "Nardi,
Giovanni", *Dizionario Biografico degli Italiani* 77 (2012), https://www.treccani.it/enciclo
pedia/giovanni-nardi_(Dizionario-Biografico)/ (accessed 16.05.2024).

that awaits him and his progeny as founders of a new dynasty, the Romans. Having met Anchises, Aeneas attempts three times to embrace him, and three times he fails as his father's image vanishes in his arms (*Aeneid* VI, 700–705). At this point, noticing a crowd of people on the shore of a river, Aeneas asks the name of the river and why these people are there. Anchises replies that these are the souls of people who drink the waters of Lethe, the river of oblivion, before returning to inhabit other bodies. Thus, in this last meeting, Anchises does much more than illustrate the meaning of Aeneas's past and future: he also explains to his son how the universe works, and how the souls of people are reborn (*Aeneid* VI, 710–751). In Anchises words,

> First, you must grasp that the heaven and earth and the sea's liquid
>   flatness,
> Also the gleaming sphere of the moon, constellations, the huge sun
> Feed on internal Energy. *Mind, which suffuses these cosmic*
> *Limbs, pervades the vast body and keeps the mass vital.* This mixture
> Generates life within humans and beasts, flying creatures, and also
> Monsters Ocean spawns below marbled plains on its surface.
> Fire endows them with force, and the source of the seeds for that fire
> Is, though it's slowed and restricted by noxious bodies, the heavens.
>   (*Aeneid* VI 724–731)[60]

In Virgil's cosmogony, everything in nature is infused with one great spirit, which resides temporarily in the body, to be released and purified upon death to re-enter into another. Why did Kircher choose these specific Virgilian verses 'Spiritus intus alit totamque infusa per artus / mens agitat molem et magno se corpore miscet' (*Aeneid* VI, 726–727) as the opening of his work? Kircher here continues a long tradition of adaptation and recontextualization of this famous passage. This tradition is so rich and complex that historian of philosophy Brunello Lotti has dedicated an entire book to its reception in medieval and early modern times. As Lotti explains, vv. 724–727, and especially vv. 726–727, are often cited on their own, without any specific reference to the doctrine of metempsychosis there expressed – the already mentioned souls of people who drink the waters of Lethe, the river of oblivion, before returning to inhabit other bodies – which was clearly unacceptable to Christian doctrine.[61] We can presume that even for somebody like Kircher, who – as Ingrid Rowland

---

60   Virgil, *Aeneid*, trans. F. Ahl (Oxford: 2007) 151–152 (emphasis mine).
61   Lotti B., *"Spiritus intus alit …" La ricezione di un luogo filosofico virgiliano nel pensiero moderno* (Florence: 2021) 9.

quipped – could express 'radical opinions about the cosmos and religion beneath the nose of the Roman Inquisition', supporting the theory of reincarnation would have been a troublesome move.[62] For Kircher, however, those verses had other meanings related more to the structure of God's cosmos than to the issue of metempsychosis. Their function here is rather to underscore how God's spirit permeates everything in nature, not just above the earth's surface, but also below. As Lotti stresses, the success of these verses resides in their malleability to interpretation: while hinting at the relationship between the World Spirit (*anima mundi*) and matter, they are not otherwise particularly specific.[63] The fact that they belonged to the book where more than elsewhere Aeneas is identified as the first Roman, moreover, clearly responded to contemporary concerns.

Kircher returns to the same Virgilian verses cited on the frontispiece in chapter IV of the second volume of the *Mundus subterraneus*, in a section dedicated to the Sun. As Ingrid Rowland has highlighted, the passage has the double function of reminding the reader that Virgil's 'naturally Christian soul' had grasped how God had imparted the breath of life to matter in the act of Creation' and how the physical structure of the universe points the way to Christian revelation.[64] As both Rowland and Lotti point out, moreover, the verses carry a third meaning, which is given by the place in which these verses are inserted. The chapter in which Virgil's lines appear is an ode to the power of the sun, its working, its virtues, its properties, and its influence on the sublunary world. In Kircher's words, God – the world's most wise architect – created the sun, 'the trusted prince of the world, the origin and source of all heat and light, of life, source of the lower world, true and natural elemental fire' from the primordial chaotic mass of the Universe, whose nature and substance Kircher had already described abundantly in his *Itinerarium extaticum*.[65] For Kircher the sun is a kind of mind (*mens*), a spirit that guides nature, a governing body, a vicar of the true divinity, which shines its light on the sacraments of God's occult wisdom; it makes them manifest by rescuing them from chaos and the dark abyss, so that from that *visible* and material divinity (the Sun), the *invisible* majesty of God beyond this world might be made known to mortals. It is the sun, with its mighty mass, that makes the whole world fecund with its

62   Rowland, "Vergil and the Pamphili Family" 267.
63   Lotti, *"Spiritus intus alit"* 10–12.
64   Rowland, "Vergil and the Pamphili Family" 267.
65   Kircher, *Mundus* 2:57–58.

motion, pregnant with his power: 'By its work, it invokes nothing more in the nature of things than divine providence'.[66]

Importantly, this passage of the *Mundus subterraneus* has more affinity with Anchises's speech than the rest of the work, where Kircher progressively moves away from the celestial spheres and cosmological explanations to explore the structure of the earth. Much like Virgil, as a prelude to his travel underground Kircher tries to explain how the cosmos works, but he does so by drawing from the latest scientific knowledge available to early moderns. The visible, material manifestation of God, the sun, will illuminate everything that lies unseen within the earth. Moreover, while at a cursory reading Kircher's description of the sun may appear to be set firmly within the Aristotelian-Ptolemaic system, its centrality as a giver of life and driver of transformation embodies the Jesuit's sympathies for Tycho Brahe's theory. In line with fellow Jesuit Christoph Scheiner's mature theories about the sunspots (*umbrae*) in the *Rosa Ursina* (1660), Kircher postulated that the sun's spots were the result of the fluid nature of the sun's surface,[67] which caused its surface to look like the sea ruffled by the wind [Fig. 7.6].[68]

As classicists and historians have pointed out, Virgil's display of cosmological knowledge is not unique, or indeed, surprising. Poets in antiquity were expected to show a mastery of cosmology, comprising astronomy, philosophy, and the poetry of the universe.[69] Virgil revisits this tradition both in the *Georgics* (2 and 3) and in the *Aeneid*, partly inspired by the earlier example of Lucretius. Far from being a simple display of erudition, however, these elements – "history" and "science" – intentionally create a double bind between this life and the afterlife, between individual lives and world history. As Philip Hardie beautifully put it, the *Aeneid* exemplifies Virgil's attempt to create 'general

---

66   Ibidem 58: 'Quo quidem opere in rerum natura divinam providentiam nihil magis indigitat'. It is significant that *indigito* literally means to call upon, invoke a deity.

67   Ibidem 59: 'Haec autem umbrarum lucularumque phaenomena, nulla ratione, extra discum solarem, sed ex ipsa corporis superficie quasi ebullire, hisce rationibus comprobatur'. On the heated debate about the nature of sunspots that ensued between Galileo and Scheiner, see Ingaliso L., '"*Mater una vera, veritas una phaenomeni est*': La *Theorica Solis* nella *Rosa Ursina* di Christoph Scheiner", *Galilaeana* 10 (2013) 25–39, as well as Giudice F., "Galileo's Cosmological View from the Sidereus Nuncius to Letters on Sunspots", *Galilaeana* 11 (2014) 49–64.

68   Kircher, *Mundus* 2:58: '[...] subinde totam solaris hemisphaerii apparentis superficiem hererogeneam ex umbris et luculis conflatam, eundemque Solem tanquam mare fluctibus aspertum, et fluctuantibus undique undis crispum, neque id eodem modo, sed tempore diverso, diversas versare vicies [...]'. Cf. Scheiner Christoph, *Rosa Ursina* (Bracciano, apud Andream Phaeum Typographum Ducalem: 1626–1630) 346.

69   Hardie P., *Virgil's Aeneid: Cosmos and Imperium* (Oxford: 1986).

FIGURE 7.6 Frontispiece of Christoph Scheiner, *Rosa Ursina sive Sol ex admirando facularum et macularum suarum phoenomeno varius* (Bracciano, Apud Andream Phaeum Typographum Ducalem: 1626–1630). Detail showing the ruffled nature of the sun's surface and the sunspots. Zurich, ETH-Bibliothek, Rar 10152
PUBLIC DOMAIN

correspondences between events in the natural *cosmos* and events in the human, historical world'.[70] In particular, cosmological themes appear in two passages, the *Song* of the epic bard Iopas at the end of the first book (740–746), and the first part of the *Speech of Anchises* in the sixth (724–751), in which, in Hardie's words, 'cosmology leads into eschatology'.[71] Much in the same way, I contend, Kircher's *Mundus subterraneus* contains elements that bind the underworld and its workings with the history of humankind and of Christianity. Allegory proper, once again in Hardie's words, 'dispenses with the restrictions of time and space; it involves the simultaneous presentation of two orders of reality [...] one of a particular and one of a general nature'.[72] As we explore

---

70   Ibidem 63.
71   Ibidem 51.
72   Ibidem 66.

the underworld described by Kircher in his *Mundus subterraneus*, those two planes constantly overlap and alternate, and, in the process, we discover God's invisible creation and the power of God himself. God's workings, however, are hidden in darkness, and it is Kircher's journey of exploration that will reveal them to the Christian reader.

While Kircher casts his journey in eschatological terms, there is also a very concrete aspect to this account: these travels, based on his readings of natural philosophy but also on personal experience, ought to take the reader into the depths of earthly, "technical", and scientific knowledge and beyond, to illuminate their understanding of the power of Creation. In moving from the epic genre to prose, natural philosophy expands as epic disappears, and eschatology thus leads to cosmology and geology.

3   Conclusions

Scholars who have paid attention to Kircher's *Latium* have at best recorded his naturalistic interests, registering them as odd idiosyncrasies in a context devoted to classical and religious antiquarianism.[73] Describing the content of *Latium*, Victor Tschudi said:

> The parts are divided into chapters that deal not only with the geography of the locations but equally with topographical, historical, biographical and archaeological details connected with them. Kircher even writes on topics such as hydraulics and botany. For example, in his text on Tivoli, he recounts first the history and origin of the town; then the variety of villas, ancient and new, as well as other structures; and finally the "works of nature" that could be seen in the territory.[74]

The inclusion of 'works of nature', however, is surprising only if we focus on disciplinary boundaries and assume that our own interests in investigating Kircher correspond to his in writing *Latium*. Such a division, I argue, cannot be maintained for at least two reasons: first, a rich body of scholarship has successfully put different areas of Kircher's interests in dialogue; second, this seems to miss the larger intellectual framework in which Kircher's enterprise and aims are to be situated. As a polymath at the service of an intellectual

---

73   Exemplary of the first mode is Evans, *Exploring the Kingdom*; of the second, in parts, Tschudi, *Baroque Antiquity*.
74   Tschudi, *Baroque Antiquity* 175.

enterprise of the Counter-Reformation and as a member of one of the most militant and engaged orders of the early modern period, his main aim was to advance 'the honour and glory of God' by finding God's power and greatness in all of nature. As Tschudi sums it up elsewhere in his important study, Kircher aimed to make God's governance 'manifest on all levels of existence, of which he found evidence in the grandest scheme and the tiniest pattern in nature'.[75] But God's natural realm and that of those men who chose to follow his guidance were never too far apart: early relics and figured stones equally functioned for Kircher as powerful testimonies of the power of the Creator. They were evidence of his presence and immanence in the world. Meditating on this realm of light and darkness – the underworld – was also a way to accompany the soul towards its final destination.

In this essay I have tried to demonstrate how Kircher's *Mundus subterraneus* fitted into a longer series of projects that saw the German Jesuit explore the wonders of nature and art both above and below ground. The real and imaginary journeys he embarked on from the late 1630s to the 1660s laid the foundations for his eschatological journey in the *Mundus subterraneus* and were deeply connected with it: the study of the workings of the cosmos and of the underworld was instrumental in elevating the human spirit towards its Creator and meditating upon the Last Things.

When Kircher ventured underground, he was well-equipped with useful classical and literary models to frame his journey. The Jesuits' investment in early Christian Rome and the trafficking of relics from the Roman catacombs certainly created a powerful stimulus to look into the dark recesses of the earth; the omnipresence of the Virgilian narrative, which clearly permeated the mind of every young Jesuit, and the lively interest in artistic representations of the "invisible", of darkness, and of Aeneas's journey, in particular, provided the best literary and artistic model for his own journey. Secular antiquities, sacred relics, and natural specimens invisible to the naked eye were made visible through his indefatigable work. So was the faithful's path from death to rebirth and salvation modelled on the journey of Aeneas. For Kircher, the different objects of his study of the underworld fulfilled one simple function: to demonstrate God's might and presence and allow his readers to reflect on the Last Things. As Schwab and Grafton have argued, 'Kircher showed no sense of strain or conflict when he applied the most-up-to-date methods of antiquarian research to Christian material'.[76] By the same token, the reader's admiration for the marvels of the earth's interior could function as a means of meditation on death

---

75   Ibidem.
76   Schwab – Grafton, *The Art of Discovery* 19.

and salvation, purgatory and hell. Signs of God's presence could only be read by somebody who possessed Kircher's erudition and was plugged into the rich culture of the Roman curia. Kircher's reading of the Book of Nature was not going to be impeded by the physical limitations of sight. Where human sight stopped, the light of God would lead and illuminate the path to salvation.

Bibliography

Alighieri Dante, *La Divina Commedia*, ed. U. Bosco – G. Reggio (Florence: 1979).

Almagià R., "Magni, Cornelio", in *Enciclopedia Italiana* (Rome: 1934), https://www.trec cani.it/enciclopedia/cornelio-magni_%28Enciclopedia-Italiana%29/ (accessed 02.02.2024).

Andretta E., "Nardi, Giovanni", *Dizionario Biografico degli Italiani* 77 (2012), https://www.treccani.it/enciclopedia/giovanni-nardi_(Dizionario-Biografico)/ (accessed 16.05.2024).

Barnett L., "Showing and Hiding: The Flickering Visibility of Earth Workers in the Archives of Earth Science", *History of Science* 58 (2020) 245–274.

Blair A., "Humanist Methods in Natural Philosophy: The Commonplace Book", *Journal of the History of Ideas* 53 (1992) 541–551.

Blair A., *Too Much to Know: Managing Scholarly Information before the Modern Age* (New Haven, CT: 2010).

Buchwald J.Z. – Feingold M., *Newton and the Origin of Civilization* (Princeton, NJ: 2013).

Daston L. – Most G.W., "History of Science and History of Philologies", *Isis* 106 (2015) 378–390.

D'Elia A., *A Sudden Terror: The Plot to Murder the Pope* (Cambridge, MA: 2009).

Ditchfield S., "Text before Trowel: Antonio Bosio's *Roma sotterranea* Revisited", *Studies in Church History* 33 (1997) 343–360.

Ditchfield S., "Reading Rome as a Sacred Landscape, c. 1586–1635", in Coster W. – Spicer A. (eds.), *Sacred Space in Early Modern Europe* (Cambridge: 2005) 167–192.

Evans H.B., *Exploring the Kingdom of Saturn: Kircher's Latium and Its Legacy* (Ann Arbor, MI: 2012).

Farrell A.P., s.j., *The Jesuit Ratio Studiorum of 1599* (Washington, DC: 1970).

Findlen P., *Possessing Nature: Museums, Collecting and Scientific Culture in Early Modern Italy* (Berkeley, CA: 1996).

Fletcher J. E., *A Study of the Life and Works of Athanasius Kircher, 'Germanus Incredibilis': With a Selection of His Unpublished Correspondence and an Annotated Translation of His Autobiography*, ed. E. Fletcher (Leiden – Boston, MA: 2011).

Furlotti B., *Antiquities in Motion: From Excavation Sites to Renaissance Collections* (Los Angeles, CA: 2019).

Gaffarel Jacques, *Curiositez inouyes sur la sculpture talismanique des Persans, horoscope des patriarches et lecture des estoilles* (Paris, H. Du Mesnil: 1629).

Gaffarel Jacques, *Le monde sousterrein ou description historique et philosophique* (Paris, C. Du Mesnil: 1654).

Ghilardi M., "Miniere di santità. La riscoperta delle catacombe romane: oratoriani o gesuiti?", in Dompnier B. – Nanni S. (eds.), *La mémoire des saints originels entre XVIe et XVIIIe siècle* (Rome: 2019) 377–514.

Giudice F., "Galileo's Cosmological View from the Sidereus Nuncius to Letters on Sunspots", *Galilaeana* 11 (2014) 49–64.

Glodzik J.A., *The Reception of Vergil in Renaissance Rome* (Leiden – Boston, MA: 2023).

Glomski J., "Religion, the Cosmos, and Counter-Reformation Latin: Athanasius Kircher's *Itinerarium extaticum* (1656)", in Steiner-Weber A. – Enenkel K.A.E. (eds.), *Acta Conventus Neo-Latini Monasteriensis. Proceedings of the Fifteenth International Congress of Neo-Latin Studies (Münster: 2012)* (Leiden: 2015) 227–236.

Göttler C., "Fire, Smoke and Vapour: Jan Brueghel's 'Poetic Hells'", in Göttler C. – Neuber W. (eds.), *Spirits Unseen: The Representation of Subtle Bodies in Early Modern European Culture* (Leiden – Boston, MA: 2007) 19–46.

Göttler C., *Last Things: Art and Religious Imagination in the Age of Reform* (Turnhout: 2010).

Grafton A., "Humanism and Science in Renaissance Prague: Kepler in Context", in idem, *Defenders of the Text: The Traditions of Scholarship in an Age of Science, 1450–1800* (Cambridge, MA: 1991) 178–203.

Hardie P., *Virgil's Aeneid: Cosmos and Imperium* (Oxford: 1986).

Hardie P., *The Last Trojan Hero: A Cultural History of Virgil's Aeneid* (London – New York, NY: 2014).

Haskell Y., "Practicing What They Preach? Vergil and the Jesuits", in Farrel J. – Putnam M.C.J. (eds.), *A Companion to Vergil's Aeneid and Its Tradition* (Chichester: 2010) 203–216.

Hirai H. (ed.), *Jacques Gaffarel between Magic and Science* (Pisa – Rome: 2014).

Hirschfeld A.K., "An Overview of the Intellectual History of Catacomb Archaeology", in Brink L., O.P. – Green D. (eds.), *Commemorating the Dead: Texts and Artifacts in Context. Studies of Roman, Jewish and Christian Burials* (Berlin – New York, NY: 2008) 11–38.

Honig E.A., *Jan Brueghel and the Senses of Scale* (University Park, PA: 2016).

Houghton L.B.T. – Sgarbi M. (eds.), *Virgil and Renaissance Culture* (Tempe, AZ: 2018).

Ingaliso L., "'Mater una vera, veritas una phaenomeni est': La *Theorica Solis* nella *Rosa Ursina* di Christoph Scheiner", *Galilaeana* 10 (2013) 25–39.

Kallendorf C., *In Praise of Aeneas: Virgil and Epideictic Rhetoric in the Early Renaissance* (Hanover, NH: 1989).

Kallendorf C., "From Virgil to Vida: The *Poeta Theologus* in Italian Renaissance Commentary", *Journal of the History of Ideas* 56 (1995) 41–62.

Kallendorf C., *Virgil and the Myth of Venice* (Oxford: 1999).

Kallendorf C., *The Protean Virgil* (Oxford: 2015).

Kempe S. – Naumann G. – Dunsch B., "Athanasius Kircher's Chapter xx 'About Caves, Fractures and the Innumerable Passages of the Earth' and the Grotto of Antiparos from 'Mundus Subterraneus', 1678, translated from Latin", in Filippi M. – Bosák P. (eds.), *Proceedings of the 16th International Congress of Speleology, Czech Republic, Brno, July 21–28, 2013* (Prague: 2013), vol. 1, 59–64.

Kircher Athanasius, *Ars magna lucis et umbrae* (Rome, Lodovico Grignani for Hermann Scheus: 1646).

Kircher Athanasius, *Itinerarium exstaticum quo mundi opificium id est coelestis expansi, siderumque tam errantium, quam fixorum natura, vires, proprietates […] nova hypothesi exponitur ad veritatem* (Rome, Vitale Mascardi: 1656–1657).

Kircher Athanasius, *Iter extaticum secundum qui et mundi subterranei prodromus dicitur* (Rome, Vitale Mascardi: 1657).

Kircher Athanasius, *Mundus subterraneus in XII libros digestus* (Amsterdam, Johannes Janssonius van Waesberge: 1664).

Krämer F., "Ein papiernes Archiv für alles jemals Geschriebene: Ulisse Aldrovandis *Pandechion epistemonicon* und die Naturgeschichte der Renaissance", *NTM. Zeitschrift für Geschichte der Wissenschaften, Technik und Medizin* 21.1 (2013) 11–36.

Krämer F., "Ulisse Aldrovandi's *Pandechion Epistemicon* and the Use of Paper Technology in Renaissance Natural History", *Early Science and Medicine* 19 (2014) 398–423.

Kroonenberg S., *Why Hell Stinks of Sulfur: Mythology and Geology of the Underworld*, trans. A. Brown (London: 2013).

Lewis N.D., *The Early Modern Invention of Late Antique Rome* (Cambridge: 2020).

Long P.O., *Openness, Secrecy and Authorship: Technical Arts and the Culture of Knowledge from Antiquity to the Renaissance* (Baltimore, MD – London: 2003).

Long P.O., *Engineering the Eternal City: Infrastructure, Topography, and the Culture of Knowledge in Late Sixteenth-Century Rome* (Chicago, IL: 2018).

Lotti B., *"Spiritus intus alit …" La ricezione di un luogo filosofico virgiliano nel pensiero moderno* (Florence: 2021).

Macfarlane R., *Underland: A Deep Time Journey* (New York, NY – London: 2020).

Magnus A., *Opera omnia*, ed. A. Borgnet (Paris: 1890), vol. 5 (*Mineralium Libri V*) 1–116.

Marshall P., *Beliefs and the Dead in Reformation England* (Oxford: 2002).

Mattes J., "Mapping the Invisible: Knowledge, Credibility and Visions of the Earth in Early Modern Cave Maps", *The British Journal for the History of Science* 55 (2022) 53–80.

Merola A., "Francesco Barberini", *Dizionario Biografico degli Italiani* 6, 1964, https://www.treccani.it/enciclopedia/francesco-barberini_%28Dizionario-Biografico%29/ (accessed 02.02.2024).

Morel T., *Underground Mathematics: Craft Culture and Knowledge Production in Early Modern Europe* (Cambridge: 2022).

Mukerji C., *Impossible Engineering: Technology and Territoriality on the Canal du Midi* (Princeton, NJ – Oxford: 2009).

Oryshkevich I., *The History of the Roman Catacombs from the Age of Constantine to the Renaissance* (Ph.D. dissertation, Columbia University: 2003).

Rowland I., "Vergil and the Pamphili Family in Piazza Navona, Rome", in Farrel J. – Putnam M.C.J. (eds.), *A Companion to Vergil's Aeneid and Its Tradition* (Oxford: 2010) 253–269.

Russell S., "Antiquarianism and the Villa Pamphilj on the Janiculum Hill in Rome", *Papers of the British School at Rome* 82 (2014) 237–264.

Sarasohn L.T., "Nicolas-Claude Fabri de Peiresc and the Patronage of the New Science in the Seventeenth Century", *Isis* 84 (1993) 70–90.

Scheiner Christoph, *Rosa Ursina* (Bracciano, apud Andream Phaeum Typographum Ducalem: 1626–1630).

Schwab M.E. – Grafton A., *The Art of Discovery: Digging into the Past in Renaissance Europe* (Princeton, NJ: 2022).

Siraisi N.G., "History, Antiquarianism, and Medicine: The Case of Girolamo Mercuriale", *Journal of the History of Ideas* 64 (2003) 231–251.

Siraisi N.G., *History, Medicine and the Traditions of Renaissance Learning* (Ann Arbor, MI: 2007).

Sullivan H., *Grotesque Purgatory: A Study of Cervantes's Don Quixote, Part II* (University Park, PA: 1996).

Theophrastus, *De lapidibus*, ed. and trans. D.E. Eichholz (Oxford: 1965).

Tschudi V.P., *Baroque Antiquity: Archaeological Imagination in Early Modern Rome* (Cambridge – New York, NY: 2017).

Tutino S., "The Mystery of Mount Vesuvius's Crosses: Belief, Credulity, and Credibility in Post-Reformation Catholicism", *Journal of the History of Ideas* 83 (2022) 207–227.

Vermeir K., "Athanasius Kircher's Magical Instruments: An Essay on 'Science', 'Religion' and Applied Metaphysics", *Studies in History and Philosophy of Science* 38 (2007) 363–400.

Virgil, *Aeneid*, trans. F. Ahl (Oxford: 2007).

Wilson-Okamura D.S., *Virgil in the Renaissance* (Cambridge: 2010).

PART 3

Visions of Heaven and Hell

∵

Ecstatic Visions: The Eschatological Imagination of Spanish Mystic Juana de la Cruz (d. 1534)

Minou Schraven

Abstract

Heir to the inner spirituality promoted by Cardinal Cisneros, the mystic Juana de la Cruz (Juana Vásquez Gutiérrez, 1481–1534) is best known for her weekly visionary sermons delivered in the convent of S. María de la Cruz in Cubas near Madrid. Transcribed by her fellow nuns, these visions offer a unique conceptualization of the celestial realm. Besides familiar eschatological concepts, such as the Tree of Life, the Narrow Gate, and the New Jerusalem, we encounter inventions that are specific of Juana's imagination, among them the Castle of Blood, the Hospitals of Mercy, and the staircases of coral and pearls connecting purgatory and heaven. Another characteristic is the abundance of celestial pageants, in which Christ acts as both stage-director and protagonist. Involving the entire celestial community of saints, angels and blessed souls in a continuous reliving of His life, the pageants serve as didactic instruments both for the celestial community and for the audiences of Juana's sermons. Besides unpacking the elements of time and space, this chapter contextualizes Juana's celestial imagination within the rich religious festival culture of early modern Castile, in particularly its Corpus Christi processions and the religious plays staged in churches and convents, particularly those in Cubas.

Keywords

early modern Castile – Juana de la Cruz – eschatological imagination – Spanish mysticism – religious festival culture

For thirteen years, the Spanish mystic Juana de la Cruz (1481–1534) had a weekly appointment with Christ in heaven. Surrounded by her fellow nuns of the Franciscan convent S. María de la Cruz in Cubas (present-day Cubas de la Sagra), Juana would go in ecstacy and visit the celestial realm. Occasionally, high-placed visitors would come to the monastery to witness these raptures, among them a young Charles v and the archbishop of Toledo, Cardinal Francisco Ximines de Cisneros (1436–1517): testimonies of the great authority attributed to this *santa viva*. While her body lay motionless on the floor of her cell, a low-register voice, supposedly that of Christ, recounted Juana's experiences and teachings she received up in heaven: collected as *El Libro de Conhorte* (Book of consolation), 72 of these sermons have come to us.[1]

Based on these sermons and other sources written in the convent of Cubas shortly after her death, this chapter will explore how Juana de la Cruz envisioned and navigated the time and space of the celestial realm.[2] In Juana's time, it was generally believed that souls were judged twice: once immediately after death (the immediate or particular judgement) and at the end of earthly time (the Final or Last Judgement).[3] According to the Scriptures, this Last Judgement involves the second coming of the Messiah, that is Christ. He will assign each soul, both of the living and the dead, to either paradise or hell. At that point, humanity and the earth as we know it will cease to exist, and both heaven and earth will be made anew.[4] In expectation of that event, the heaven that Juana visits while in rapture is inhabited by Christ, the Virgin Mary, the angels, saints, and those blessed souls who have already been admitted to the celestial realm, either immediately after their death, or after having atoned for their sins in purgatory. Besides familiar eschatological concepts, such as the Tree of Life, the Narrow Gate, and the New Jerusalem, there are inventions

---

1 *El Libro del Conhorte* survives in two manuscripts: Madrid, Real Biblioteca de El Escorial, ms. J-II-18 and Archivio Apostolico Vaticano, Congregazione dei Riti, ms. 3074. The sermons were published only in recent times: García Andrés I., *El Conhorte: Sermones de una Mujer. La Santa Juana (1481–1534)*, 2 vols. (Madrid: 1999), unfortunately, not available digitally. Six of these sermons have now been translated into English: *Mother Juana de la Cruz, 1481–1534: Visionary Sermons*, ed. Boon J.A. – Surtz R.E., The Other Voice in Early Modern Europe: The Toronto Series 47 (Toronto: 2014).

2 This chapter focuses on the sermons of Juana de la Cruz. I will discuss the cult of Juana's miracle-working prayer beads as it developed in the century following her death, in my forthcoming monograph *Blessed and Indulgenced Objects in Early Modern Catholic Worlds*. On these beads: Owens S.E., "El legado del rosario milagroso en los escritos de viage de sor Ana de Christo hacia Filipinas", *Boletín de monumentos historicos, tercera epoca* 30 (2014) 22–35.

3 Issued by Pope Benedict XII in 1336, the bull *Benedictus Deus* established the doctrine of the particular judgement, meaning that the souls, once separated from their bodies, receive their reward or punishment immediately after death: Bates S., "Preparations for a Christian Death: The Later Middle Ages", in Booth P. – Tingle E. (eds.), *A Companion to Death, Burial and Remembrance in Late Medieval and Early Modern Europe* (Leiden – Boston, MA: 2020) 72–105.

4 Tingle E., "Changing Western European Visions of Christian Afterlives, 1350–1700: Heaven, Hell, and Purgatory", in Booth – Tingle (eds.), *A Companion to Death, Burial and Remembrance* 33–71.

that are specific to Juana's imagination, among them the Castle of Blood, the Hospitals of Mercy, and the staircases of coral and pearls connecting purgatory and heaven.[5] But Juana's conception of the afterlife truly stands out for the many pageants, or *figuras* as Juana calls them. With Christ acting as a stage director, these pageants involve the entire celestial community in a continuous reliving and celebrating of Christ's life and the Passion. Besides looking into their role as didactic instruments, this chapter examines their relation to representations of heaven in the religious festival culture of Juana's time, in particularly Corpus Christi processions and religious plays staged in convents, such as that of Cubas. A final point of interest will be how Juana's visionary imagination may be connected to the material culture of devotion as it existed in the convent of Cubas.

1   Juana de la Cruz in Her Time

Born in 1481 as Juana Vásquez y Gutiérrez in a family of modest origins, Juana lived through tumultuous times: she was eleven years old when the last Muslim stronghold fell into Christian hands. With the victory of Granada, Ferdinand of Aragon and Isabella of Castile brought their project of Reconquista to its fulfillment. The Catholic Monarchs charged the Archbishop of Toledo, Cardinal Francisco Cisneros, with a programme of religious reform for their realm, in which any other religion other than Catholicism was to be eradicated. Jewish and Muslim citizens were forced into either conversion or exile, and mass conversions were the order of the day. Meanwhile, the printing press of the newly opened theological university in Alcalá de Henares (the current Complutense University of Madrid) poured out translations of spiritual and theological works that until then had not been accessible in Spain, among them mystical texts of Catherine of Siena (1347–1380) and Angela of Foligno (1248–1309).[6] In the circles of Cisneros, there was also vivid interest in contemporary Italian mystics, such as *santa viva* Lucia Brocadelli of Narni (1476–1544).[7] From this

5   Luengo Balbás M., *Juana de la Cruz: Vida y obra de una visionaria del siglo XVI* (Ph.D. dissertation, Universidad Complutense de Madrid: 2016).

6   Acosta-García P., "Women Prophets for a New World: Angela of Foligno, Living Saints, and the Religious Reform Movement in Cardinal Cisneros' Castile", in Morrás M. – Sanmartín Bastida R. – Kim Y. (eds.), *Gender and Exemplarity in Medieval and Early Modern Spain* (Leiden – Boston, MA: 2020) 136–162.

7   Herzig T., *Savonarola's Women: Visions and Reform in Renaissance Italy* (Chicago, IL: 2008), about *sante vive* Lucia Brocadelli and Colomba da Rieti (1471–1501).

fertile soil emerged a generation of Spanish mystics, starting with Juana de la Cruz and María de Santo Domíngo (ca. 1485–ca. 1524).[8]

Like Juana, María was renowned for her mystical visions and prophecies delivered while in a state of rapture. And like Juana, this *santa viva* could count on the protection of powerful patrons, among them King Ferdinand II of Aragon (1452–1516) and Cardinal Cisneros. Thanks to their support, María was acquitted when she had to stand trial on charges of feigned sanctity and lascivious behaviour between 1508 and 1510.[9] She could finally take on the position of prioress of the Dominican convent built for her in her hometown Aldeanuova, a position she would hold until her death.[10]

These were the very years in which all female convents and *beateríos* (tertiary houses for religious women) in the realm were turned into enclosed convents under the direction of an abbess.[11] In 1509, Juana de la Cruz would become the first abbess of the Clarissan convent in Cubas that she had joined at the end of the fifteenth century.[12]

In the year before, Juana had started to go regularly into ecstasy. While her body lay motionless on the ground for hours on end, she would give testimony of her experiences in heaven in dynamic and vivid prose, transferring teachings she received in heaven from no other than Christ himself. Transcribed by a fellow nun, aptly called María Evangelista, 72 of these sermons were collected in *El Libro de Conhorte*. The compilation loosely follows the structure of the

---

8   Surtz R.E., *Writing Women in Late Medieval and Early Modern Spain: The Mothers of Teresa of Avila* (Philadelphia, PA: 1995); Herzig T., "Female Mysticism, Heterodoxy, and Reform", in Mixson J.D. – Roest B. (eds.), *A Companion to Observant Reform in the Late Middle Ages and Beyond* (Leiden – Boston, MA: 2015) 255–282.

9   Bilinkoff J., "A Spanish Prophetess and Her Patrons: The Case of Maria de Santo Domingo", *The Sixteenth Century Journal* 23.1 (1992) 21–34. María claimed that Lucia da Narni appeared to her in visions. In 1502, Dominican preacher and reformer Antonio de la Peña (d. 1512) had published a pamphlet in Seville about the stigmata of Lucia Brocadelli (Herzig, *Savonarola's Women* 96). De la Peña defended María de San Domingo during her trials.

10   In 1518, two of María's visions were transcribed and published as the *Libro de Oración*, while other visions have been published in recent years: Giles M.E., *The Book of Prayer of Sor María of Santo Domíngo: A Study and Translation* (Albany, NY: 1990); Sanmartín Bastida R. – Luengo Balbás M., *Las Revelaciones de María de Santo Domíngo, 1480/86–1524* (London: 2014).

11   There is no standard definition of the position of *beata* in early modern Spain: in essence, they were lay women living a religious life in service of God, either alone or in a community, often adhering to a tertiary order: Braguier L., *Servantes de Dieu: Les 'beatas' de la Couronne de Castile 1450–1600* (Rennes: 2019).

12   Acosta-García P., "Radical Succession. Hagiography, Reform and Franciscan Identity in the Convent of the Abbess Juana de la Cruz (1481–1534)", *Religions* 12 (2021) 1–23.

liturgical year, supposedly that of 1509, from the Incarnation (Sermon 1) and Nativity (Sermon 2) to the events of the Holy Week (Sermons 16–19), followed by sermons about the lives of saints and episodes in the Scriptures, not unlike medieval sermon compilations.[13] Strikingly, these sermons were enriched with a wealth of details not mentioned in the canonical texts. In Sermon 50 (Nativity of the Virgin), Mary dances nude to prove her virtue towards God; and there is the retelling of *Genesis* 3, in which the blame for the Fall of Man is put on the serpent rather than on Eve (Sermon 72: Creation of Adam). Both sermons have been analysed from the perspective of gender studies.[14]

Within the vast tradition of conventual accounts of spiritual journeys, Juana's sermons are truly exceptional. Whereas in María's texts, Christ is presented as speaking in the first person, those of Juana are in dialogue form, making her an active participant and interlocutor in the events she describes. Given that women were banned from preaching from the pulpit, as they still are, the only option open to them was to preach while in a state of rapture.[15] For Juana and María, their ecstatic mysticism authorized their teachings, including expansions and alterations of canonical texts. But it did not preclude them from running into difficulties, as the Inquisition trials of María de San Domingo demonstrate. So, as a matter of caution, Juana insisted that she shared her teachings at the explicit request of her guardian angel (or of God, or the Virgin Mary), not of her own will. She also pinned part of the blame on her fellow sisters in the convent, who always wanted to learn more about the revelations:

> You are never satiated by what I have told you, and you always desire to learn more about the things that God has willingly disclosed to me. And likewise, my guardian angel has implored me, and his Divine Majesty has given me consent to disclose them [...]. And that is why I have told you the secret things that have been revealed to me, or part of them.[16]

---

13   Acosta-García P., *Liturgy and Revelation in the Book of the Conhorte by the Abbess Juana de la Cruz 1481–1534* (Leiden – Boston, MA: forthcoming).

14   Surtz, *Writing Women in Late Medieval and Early Modern Spain* 104–126; Boon J.A., "At the Limits of (Trans)Gender: Jesus, Mary and the Angels in the Visionary Sermons of Juana de la Cruz (1481–1534)", *Journal of Medieval and Early Modern Studies* 48.2 (2018) 261–300.

15   Roest B., "Female Preaching in the Late Medieval Franciscan Tradition", *Franciscan Studies* 62 (2004) 119–154.

16   *Vida y fin*, fols. 75 v–76 r, as cited in Luengo Balbas, *Juana de la Cruz* 205: 'Pues aun no estáys contenta con quanto os he dicho, que todavía queréys saver más de las cosas que Dios es servido de me mostrar. Y ansímesmo me a dicho mi sancto ángel e su Divina Magestad contento os las diga [...]. Y en esta causa os he dicho las cosas secretas que

Recently, research into the performative character of these events has proposed that we consider them as co-creations involving both the visionary and her fellow nuns. As indispensable bystanders, they not only took care of Juana's physical well-being while she was in rapture, but they also encouraged her, asked for clarifications, and served as witnesses to these extraordinary events.[17] Having a mystic within the enclosed convent walls was an asset for the community. Fostering and disseminating these performances was therefore a viable strategy for attracting fame and patronage.[18] Rather than ascribing El Conhorte to a single author, it is therefore preferred to suppose a wider, collective authorship. The same applies to Juana's biography Vida y fin (Life and death) produced within the convent of Cubas. As it contains an account of her funeral and the ensuing cult at her tomb, it was presumably written in the years following Juana's death.[19] Whereas the visions and teachings in El Conhorte take place in heaven, those in the Vida y fin are mostly situated in purgatory, reflecting Juana's preoccupation with saving souls from purgatory in the last decades of her life.

2   The Celestial World of Juana de la Cruz

Apart from its overall festive character, a characteristic element of the sermons in El Conhorte is the surprisingly human and jovial nature of Christ. We encounter him while having a fit of temper (Sermon 1: the Incarnation), playing card games, throwing dice (Sermon 4: Epiphany), and playing the guitar and tambourine (Sermon 44: the expulsion of the merchants from the Temple): evidence, as Jessica Boon has argued, of the 'eternal dual nature of Christ'.[20]

In many sermons, Christ takes charge as stage director, instructing his friends ('mis amigos') on how to organize the pageants and lay out the scenes.[21]

me an sido mostradas, o parte dellas'. The manuscript Vida y fin de la bienaventurada virgen sancta Juana de la Cruz is in the Real Biblioteca de El Escorial, K-III-13 and has been digitized in the Catálogo de Santas Vivas (1400–1550), a project of the Complutense University of Madrid: http://catalogodesantasvivas.visionarias.es/ (accessed 13.05.2024).

17   Luengo Balbas, Juana de la Cruz 199, 204–208.
18   For a similar case of collective authorship in a convent in Milan, see Cappuccilli E., "In the Steps of Birgitta of Sweden: The Reluctant Authority of Paola Antonia Negri (1508–1555)", Renaissance Studies 35 (2021) 582–599.
19   Acosta-García, "Radical Succession".
20   Boon J.A., "Christ in Heavenly Play: Christology through Mary's Eyes in the Sermons of Juana de la Cruz (1481–1534)", Archiv für Reformationsgeschichte 102.1 (2011) 243–266.
21   Sermon 24 (Ascension of Our Lord), García Andrés, El Conhorte 812,: 'Ahora, mis amigos, pues vosotros me hacéis una fiesta de la mi gloriosa y maravillosa Ascensión'; and

According to Juana, the purpose of these *figuras* was to recreate events of Christ's life as they happened on earth 'as a remembrance of all things Our Lord spoke, suffered, and accomplished there':

> In heaven, they stage pageants and remembrances of this world and of all the people that inhabit it, and of the precious seed and words that he himself sowed among them, and of all the mysteries that took place here on earth; because, once having left our world, he [Our Lord] Himself got permission from His Father to stage pageants and memories and remembrances of everything that he discussed, suffered and accomplished here [on earth].[22]

Yet, while the overall atmosphere in Juana's heaven is that of a joyous and abundant court pageant, the sacrificial nature of Christ is always present, as the tribulations of the Passion need to be suffered over and again. Among the many banquets staged in heaven is the one in Sermon 4 (the Epiphany), where the tables are set with precious cups and vessels. Promising to satiate and restore his 'amigos' invited to the feast, Christ opens his side wound, from which flows a rivulet of clear and sweet-smelling water. While pouring this in the chalices and cups, still more liquids and foods appear from the wounds of his left hand and feet.[23] Then he flies up over the tables:

> And then he flew up, and laid himself on the banquet tables. And from all the wounds and marks on his abused body came forth many kinds of freshly baked bread and pastries, sweet and savory. And he said to his

---

Sermon 16 (Palm Sunday), García Andrés, *El Conhorte* 583, as cited in Luengo Balbás, *Juana de la Cruz* 235: 'queiero y es mi voluntad, que me hagan hoy fiesta aquellos que en la tierra me quisieron ensalzar por rey y yo no lo quise consentir'.

22   Sermon 12 (Parable of the Sower), García Andrés, *El Conhorte* 512, as cited in Luengo Balbás, *Juana de la Cruz* 236: 'Hacen en el reino de los cielos figuras y memoria del campo de esto mundo y de todas las gentes que están en él, y de la preciosa simiente y palabras que él mismo sembró sobre él, y de todos los misterios que acá en la tierra le acontecieron; por cuanto Él mismo pidió licencia al Padre celestial, cuando de este mundo subió, para hacer figuras y memoria y remembranzas de todo cuanto acá habló y padeció y obró'.

23   Sermon 4 (Epiphany), García Andrés, *El Conhorte* 342–343, as cited in Luengo Balbás, *Juana de la Cruz* 123: 'Ahora, mis amigos, yo os hartaré y os recrearé, que escrito es que "en mí son hallados pastos, y holganza, y deleite y abastiamento". Y diciendo estas palabras, a deshora le abrió la llaga de su sagrado costado y le manaba de él un caño de agua muy clara y olorosa; y, por semejante, caía en todos los cálices y tazas, y aguaba el vino y templábalo. Y de las mano siniestra le manaba otro licor muy precioso y oloroso, y de las llagas de los pies le salían muchedumbre de manjares'.

guests kindly and lovingly: 'Take this, my friends, and eat and indulge yourselves with these sweet pastries and food coming forth of my own body'.[24]

With these instances of Christ gently offering himself as food, Juana stands in the tradition of female mystics of the later Middle Ages, who perceived the body of Christ as a nurturing mother, his wounds and blood as precious nourishments.[25] In her sermons, Juana indeed insists on the importance of meditating continuously on the Passion of Our Lord, vital for the salvation of our souls:

> And the pageants [in heaven] that are sometimes made about the Passion and the great joy that is derived from them, demonstrate to us sinners that we must take delight and consolation in meditating about the Passion of Our Lord Jesus Christ, and that we must weep and shed tears in continuation, and that should be our food.[26]

This insistence on meditating on the Passion ties in with ordonnances such as those issued in Seville in 1487 that all inhabitants, including the recently converted Jews and Muslims, should have a devotional image of the Passion in their homes:

> Because it is reasonable that the homes of faithful Christians be provided with and protected by the memory of the Passion or Our Redeemer

---

24 Ibidem: 'Y luego voló en alto, y púsose sobre las mesas. Y a deshora salieron de todas las llagas y azotes que padeció en su sagrado cuerpo, muchedumbre de panes y roscas muy recientes y dulces y sabrosas. Y hablábalos Él muy amorosa y benignamente diciendo: "Tomad, mis amigos, y comed y embriagaos de las dulcedumbres y manjares de mí mismo"'. The passage continues with citations of *John* 6:51 ('I am the living bread which came down from heaven'), and 15:5 ('I am the vine, you are the branches'): 'Que escrito es de mí, que soy pan vivo y vino muy dulce y manjar muy sabroso de los que me saben gustar. Y también es escrito que "Yo soy pan vivo que descendí del cielo" y "Yo soy verdadera vid y vosotros los sarmientos"'.

25 Bynum C.W., *Jesus as Mother: Studies in the Spirituality of the High Middle Ages* (Berkeley, CA: 1982); Giles R.D., "'Mira mis llagas': Heridas divinas en las obras de Brígida de Suecia y Teresa de Jesús", *Ehumanista. Journal of Iberian Studies* 32 (2016) 34–49.

26 Sermon 9 (Septuagesima Sunday), García Andrés, *El Conhorte* 462, as cited in Luengo Balbás, *Juana de la Cruz* 164: 'Y en las figuras que algunas veces hacen de la Pasión y se deleitan mucho en ellas, nos dan a entender a nosotros pecadores, que nos debemos de deleitar y recibir consolación de pensar en la Pasión de Nuestro Señor Jesuchristo, y debemos continuamente llorar y derramar lágrimas por ella, y que éste debería ser nuestro manjar'.

Jesus Christ and his Holy Mother, we wish and command that every true Christian have in his home some painted image of the cross on which Our Lord Jesus Christ suffered, and some painted images of Our Lady or of the male or female saints that they may move and inspire those who live there to acts of devotion.[27]

In Sermon 9 on Septuagesima Sunday (the ninth Sunday before Easter, when masses start to be celebrated in a sombre and penitential character), the blessed souls in Juana's heaven beg a reluctant Christ to commemorate the Passion with them. They recall that on that particular Sunday, all altars on earth are covered in mourning cloth and priests wear dark liturgical vestments. As Maria Luengo Balbás has shown, this passage becomes an instruction on how to meditate on the Passion and its images, so central in the devotion of mystics like Juana:

When we ponder over your most holy face and it reminds us of how it was crowned with thorns, and when we look at your precious facial traits beaten and spat upon, at your cherished, torn beard, and at your beautiful neck tied with a thick and cruel rope, and gaze at your most holy body so mercilessly tormented and wounded, and at your delicate hands and feet perforated and driven through with nails, and at your pious heart pierced so coldheartedly, our spirits and hearts are crushed to the breaking point with agony, and our only desire is to weep for you until the end of times.[28]

---

27   Fray Hernando de Talavera, *Católica Impugnacion* (Seville: 1478), as cited by Pereda F., *Images of Discord: Poetics and Politics of the Sacred Image in Fifteenth-Century Spain* (Turnhout: 2018) 15 (trans. C. López-Morillas): 'Iten, porque es cosa razonable que las casas de los fieles cristianos sean munidas y guardadas de la memoria de la pasión de nuestro Redentor Jesucristo y de su bendita Madre, queremos y ordenamos que cada fiel cristiano tenga en la casa de su morada alguna imagen pintada de la cruz, en que nuestro Señor Jesucristo padeció, y algunas imágines pintadas de nuestra Señora o de algunos santos o santas, que provoquen y despierten a los que allí moran a haber devoción'. This pamphlet circulated widely until the Inquisitions placed it on the Index. See also Robinson C., *Imagining the Passion in a Multiconfessional Castile: The Virgin, Christ, Devotion and Images in the Fourteenth and Fifteenth Centuries* (University Park, PA: 2013).

28   Sermon 9 (Septuagesima Sunday), García Andrés, *El Conhorte* 450, as cited in Luengo Balbás, *Juana de la Cruz* 167: 'Que cuando miramos la tu muy santa cabeza y se nos acuerda cómo fue coronada de espinas, y tu preciosa faz abofeteada y escupida, y tus preciosas barbas mesadas, y tu hermoso cuello atado con soga muy gruesa y cruel, y tu santísimo cuerpo tan cruelmente atormentado y llagado, y tus delicadas manos y pies horadados y enclavados, y tu muy piadoso corazón partido con tan gran crueldad, nuestros espíritus y

The blessed souls then go about in procession carrying a banner depicting Christ on a throne, surrounded by angels. But all of a sudden, the overall festive mood of this *figura* changes as the image of Christ transforms into a naked, contorted body with blood issuing from its wounds, as it did during the Crucifixion. The bleeding image orders the terrified blessed souls to call out at the top of their voices to those on earth 'worthy of hearing the message of redemption, so that they will drop dead of fear'.[29] Meanwhile, the trappings and draperies of the throne morph into mirrors depicting people on earth lining up to take confession. The stems with flowers that the angels were carrying transform into menacing axes. Only after those on earth have properly confessed, the celestial scene returns to its original festive state.[30] The *figura* hammers home one of Juana's recurring admonitions: not all souls will be saved.

3   A Celestial Space in Constant Flux

At no point does Juana give a detailed or coherent description of what heaven looks like. Her audience, and that includes us, needs to piece together her celestial conception from disparate and at times outright contradictory fragments scattered across the sermons and her biography *Vida y fin*. María Luengo Balbás has underlined the repetitive, ill-defined, and generic character of Juana's descriptions of heaven and its affinities with late medieval descriptions of ideal cities.[31] There is indeed a striking parallel with the eschatological poem *De Jerusalem Caelesti* of Franciscan friar Giacomino da Verona, dated to ca. 1275. In it, Giacomino extolls the magnificence of the buildings, the luminosity of the marbles, and the amenity of its rivers and vegetation, which together form the perfect backdrop against which angels and saints worship God / Christ in perpetuity.[32] Likewise, in Juana's heaven, the magnificent

---

ánimas desfallecen y se traspasan de dolor, y deseamos nunca hacer otra cosa sino llorar por ti siempre'.

29   Sermon 9 (Septuagesima Sunday), García Andrés, *El Conhorte* 455, as cited in Luengo Balbás, *Juana de la Cruz* 167: 'Deshora fue la imagen mudada y desnuda, y apareció toda llagada y corriendo sangre como cuando el Señor estaba puesto en la cruz, y empezó a dar grandes voces que sonovan hasta la tierra, que si las personas fueran dignas – dijo el Señor – las oyeran y cayeran muertas de miedo'.

30   Sermon 9 (Septuagesima Sunday), García Andrés, *El Conhorte* 462, as cited in Luengo Balbás, *Juana de la Cruz* 168.

31   Luengo Balbás, *Juana de la Cruz* 221–229.

32   Contini G.F., "Giacomino da Verona", in idem, *Letteratura italiana delle origini* (Florence: 1991) 134–138. The full title of this poem is De Jerusalem Caelesti et de pulcritudine eius et beatitudine et gaudia sanctorum, with De Babilonia civitate infernali as its counterpart.

buildings and walkways shine brighter than gold, and at the centre of each church stands the ornate throne of a saint, who is constantly being venerated.

> I witnessed that magnificent feasts were being organized all across heaven, and I saw how in every street and district there was a temple complex consisting of very large and grand structures and turrets and walkways that were shining more than gold or precious stones; and in each church one of the glorious saints was exalted, seated on a very high and decorated throne, and all around them many tributes and sacrifices were being performed.[33]

The rather generic character of Juana's celestial space is due to the fact that everything is in constant flux: elements solidify for the occasion of pageants in order to dissolve immediately afterwards, as was the case in the Septuagesima sermon. We learn more about this fluid state in Sermon 24 (the Ascension), when Christ asks the blessed souls to arrange for a pageant in his honour:

> And then, says Our Lord, those blessed souls quickly came over, bringing along spacious halls and rooms, adorned walls and hangings. Because God desires it and it is his wish, all things [in heaven] are movable and can be transferred from one location to the other and placed wherever one chooses.[34]

At times, we assist at the creation of entirely new spaces, such as the wide streets ('muy grandes calles') opening up in honour of the Virgin and St. Joseph in the sermon about the Flight into Egypt. The new avenues are decorated with

---

See also Lilley, K.D., "Cities of God? Medieval Urban Forms and Their Christian Symbolism", *Transactions of the Institute of British Geographers* 29.3 (2004) 296–313.

33   Sermon 2 (The Nativity), García Andrés, *El Conhorte* 277, as cited in Luengo Balbás, *Juana de la Cruz* 222: 'Oyó como hacían muy grandes fiestas por todas las partes del Cielo y vio como en cada calle y en cada cantón estaba hecho un templo, lleno de edificios y torres y adarves muy altos y grandes y rasplandecientes más que de oro y de piedras preciosas, y en cada uno de aquellos templos estaba ensalzado uno de los gloriosos santos, y puesto en un trono muy alto y adornado, y allí alrededor le hacian muy grandes honras y sacrificios'.

34   Sermon 24 (Ascension of Our Lord), García Andrés, *El Conhorte* 812, as cited in Luengo Balbás, *Juana de la Cruz* 235: 'Y luego fueron, dijo el Señor, aquellos bienaventurados, con grande prisa y traían salas y cámaras muy grandes, y rocas adornadas y entoldadas. Esto, porque cuanto Dios quiere y es su voluntad, todas las cosas son movibles y se pueden traer a una parte y a otra, y ponerse adonde quieseren'.

gold tapestries and precious stones; the walls of its large arches covered with sweet-smelling flowers and roses; the pavement with gems.[35]

Elsewhere, Juana states that heaven is organized in three hierarchical layers, not unlike the late medieval paintings of heaven by Fra Angelico or Tommaso Botticini. In the lowest region of Juana's heaven, the blessed souls dwell at different heights based on their merit; on the second level reside the saints and the nine choirs of the angels, while the topmost part is inhabited by Christ.[36] Juana's conception may also be linked to festival *apparati* of this period, such as the stage sets designed for the coronation banquet of Fernando de Antequera in Saragossa in 1414. On this occasion, a pageant about the Coronation of the Virgin was performed, involving a representation of heaven consisting of three wheels, with human figures dressed as angels sitting on them. When the new King of Aragon made his entrance, these angels burst into song and played their instruments.[37]

In yet another sermon, Juana tells about the throne of Our Lord on top of a 'hovering, self-driven cloud', 'brighter than the sun and bigger than the entire world', so that He is able to enjoy all the festivities and celebrations that are staged in heaven.[38]

When he is not in the mood to travel, Christ invites the saints over to his castle, which is located in the highest regions of heaven: 'Come to my castle and royal dwellings, Peter, as I do not wish to descend to yours for now; once

---

35   Sermon 6 (Flight into Egypt), García Andrés, *El Conhorte* 394, as cited in Luengo Balbás, *Juana de la Cruz* 228: 'A deshora, empezaron todos a hacer muy grandes calles emparamentadas, y todas de paramentos de oro y de piedras preciosas, las cuales calles había en ella muchas leguas y pasos, y todas ellas eran hechas a manera de portales muy largos, y las paredas de ellos erano todas de flores y rosas muy olorosas y finas y hermosas, enseridas y tendidas a manera de paredes muy altas y grandes. Y por todos aquellos [...] caminos y calles había muchedumbre de joyas y riquezas y tezoros, todos echados por el suelo, y árboles y yerbas con diversidad de flores y frutas y olores y sabores'.

36   Sermon 12 (Parable about the Sower), García Andrés, *El Conhorte* 513, as cited in Luengo Balbás, *Juana de la Cruz* 223: 'Por cuanto en el reino de los cielos, hay algunos que están más altos, y otros más bajos, según que cada uno tuvo los merecimientos'. Compare Tommaso Botticini, *Assumption of the Virgin*, ca. 1475. Tempera on wood, 228 × 377 cm. London, National Gallery, inv. no. NG1126.

37   Surtz R.E., "Music and Spectacle", in Knighton T. (ed.), *Companion to Music in the Age of the Catholic Monarchs* (Leiden – Boston, MA: 2016) 145–172.

38   Sermon 54 (Admonitions to us sinners), García Andrés, *El Conhorte* 1201, as cited in Luengo Balbás, *Juana de la Cruz* 224: 'Appareciò allí [...] una nube muy blanca y hermosa y resplandeciente más que el sol y más grande que todo el mundo, en la cual nube estaba hecho y adornado el tálamo y trono del Señor [...] y ella misma se andaba por el cielo, sin que ningún ángel ni santo la llevase ni trajese'.

you have reached my realms, I will prepare a feast for you'.[39] The castle is close to that of his mother, the Virgin Mary, that Christ visits quite often. The structure is made of the purest crystal, and free from any blemish or imperfection, in order to underline Mary's virginity and overall importance in the hierarchy of heaven.[40]

The castle of Christ is an invention of Juana. It is also called the 'Castle of Blood': each time Christ petitions God his father for mercy for the sinners on earth and souls still in purgatory, angels take blood from His wounds to this very castle.[41]

> That castle, so large, bright and marvelous, says Our Lord Jesus Christ, is called the Castle of Blood, since each time that He receives His most holy wounds in order to ask his father [remission] for the sinners on earth and for the souls in purgatory, and when some most glorious blood issues from them, the holy angels retrieve it with cloths more delicate than silk and brighter than gold, and they deposit them in chalices, platters and vessels of silver and precious stones; with solemn songs and reverence they bring them up to that wonderful castle, and they lay out the precious cloths over the walkways and battlements and deadlights and poles.[42]

Omnipresent in this castle and across sermons of *El Conhorte* (see the sermon on Septuagesima Sunday), Christ's salvific blood was central to late-medieval devotional practices that were so important for the *sante vive*.[43] At this point, Christ tells Juana that there are infinite indulgences to be gained from the

---

39   Sermon 11 (Feast of the Chair of St. Peter), García Andrés, *El Conhorte* 488, as cited in Luengo Balbás, *Juana de la Cruz* 225: 'Anda, Pedro, vete tú a mi alcázar y moradas reales, que yo no quiero descender por ahora a las tuyas; que acá arriba, en mis alturas, te haré la fiesta'.

40   Sermon 70 (the Conception of the Virgin); García Andrés, *El Conhorte* 1426–1428, as cited in Luengo Balbás, *Juana de la Cruz* 226.

41   Ibidem.

42   Sermon 33 (Nativity of John the Baptist), García Andrés, *El Conhorte* 953, as cited in Luengo Balbás, 174: 'El cual castello, tan grande y resplandeciente y maravilloso, dijo nuestro Señor Jesuchristo, se llama castillo sanguíneo, por cuanto cada vez que recienta sus sacratíssimas llagas para demandar misericordia al Padre para los pecadores de la tierra y para las ánimas del purgatorio y le sale alguna gloriosísima sangre de ellas, la cogen los santos ángeles en unos como pañecitos más delgados que de sirgo y más resplandecientes que de oro, y los ponen en cálices y platos y vasos de plata y piedras preciosas, y lo llevan con grandes cánticos y reverencias a aquel alcázar tan maravilloso, y tienden los preciosos pañuelos encima de los adarves y almenas y ventanas y árboles'.

43   Bynum C.W., *Wonderful Blood: Theology and Practice in Late Medieval Northern Germany and Beyond* (New York, NY: 2011).

devout contemplation of this castle, and that many blessed souls come to this area. So, even though they have already gained their place in heaven, these souls still do benefit from indulgences, either for themselves of for those still in purgatory or on earth. Christ is also adamant that the doors of this castle may not be opened until the day of the Last Judgement.[44]

4   Juana's *Figuras* and Corpus Christi Processions

Before considering the way that Juana conceived of purgatory and hell, we should look further into possible sources of inspiration for these celestial pageants. Besides the stage sets for pageants performed at banquets, there are also those staged during Corpus Christi processions. Established by papal bull in 1264, the liturgical solemnity centring on the real presence of Christ in the Eucharist was celebrated on the first Thursday after Trinity Sunday, or sixty days after Easter.[45] With the institution of a solemn procession for Corpus Christi, Pope John XXII established in 1317 a tradition that would become a high point for Catholic communities across the world. By the late fifteenth century, Corpus Christi processions in Spain included representatives of secular and religious governing bodies and institutions, and ever larger numbers of carnivalesque figures, masked actors, and moving carts with theatrical representations, musicians, and dancers. As Teofilo Ruiz has put it, viewers and participants were thus offered 'a gradual ascent, from the carnal and banal through the serious themes of sacred history, to the contemplation of the Body of Christ'.[46]

From Valencia to Toledo, and from Catalayud (near Saragossa) to Madrid, Corpus Christi processions included floats with representations of the Last Judgement, the Harrowing of Hell, the martyrdom of saints and the Descent from the Cross. To single out just one of them, the procession in late

---

44   Sermon 33 (Nativity of John the Baptist), García Andrés, *El Conhorte* 953: 'Cuando algunas ánimas han de salir del purgatorio [...], y las lleavan al cielo por las hacer muy grande gracia y merced y por darles muy grande indulgentia, las llevan para que vean y acaten aquel precioso castello. Porque cualquiera que le acata y mira con amor y compasión de su pasión, gana infinitos millares de indulgencias para quien las quieren dar, por lo cual los bienaventurados van muchas veces a le mirar y acatar. Y este castillo, dijo el Señor, nunca las puertas de él se han da abrir hasta el día del juicio final'.

45   Rubin M., *Corpus Christi: The Eucharist in Late Medieval Culture* (Cambridge – New York, NY: 1991).

46   Ruiz T.F., "From Carnival to Corpus Christi", in idem, *A King Travels: Festive Traditions in Late Medieval and Early Modern Spain* (Princeton, NJ: 2012) 246–292.

fifteenth-century Barcelona included 161 ranks of participants and 22 floats with representations of sacred history, all paid for by the Cathedral. The first of them represented the Creation of the world, while the second float featured hell, Lucifer, four devils, and the *tarasca*: the fire-spitting dragon conquered by St. Michael, one of the beloved staples of Corpus Christi processions in Spain.[47] The twenty floats that followed were alternated with entertaining carnivalesque representations, such as battles between angels and twenty-four devils, and a fight with swords between the good angels, led by St. Michael, and the fallen angels. The apostles and evangelists introduced the focal point of the procession: the elaborate reliquary, or *custodia*, with the consecrated Host, the Corpus Christi.

The vivid battle scenes between angels and demons throughout *El Conhorte* must owe a great deal to these theatrical elements of Corpus Christi processions. There is also a parallel with the way that Christ shows his wounds during banquets in *El Conhorte*: in the *Auto de la Pasión* (Pageant of the Passion) for the Corpus Christi procession in Toledo, Christ instructs the souls in limbo to look upon the wounds on his hands and feet, inviting them to follow him.[48]

Plays of local Corpus Christi processions were reposed every year, and elements of them would be incorporated in the event of royal entries or other important events.[49] On top of that, there was also a rich tradition of Nativity and Assumption plays in churches across Spain. The text of the Assumption play staged in the Cathedral of Valencia in 1420 suggests that there was a stage set representing the canopy of heaven, with both horizontal and vertical axes and a device ('araceli') moving actors impersonating Christ, the Virgin, and the angels up and down its various levels.[50]

Religious theatre was also performed in convents: in the 1450s a *Representación del Nacimiento de Nuestro Señor* was written for the nuns of the Real Monastero de la Consolación in Calabanzanos, in the province of Palencia.[51] The third scene of this play contains a 'momeria a lo divino' (pantomime with

47   Ibidem 266–267.
48   Surtz, *Music and Spectacle* 148, citing from Torroja Menéndez C. – Rivas Palá M., *Teatro en Toledo en el siglo XV: Auto de la Pasión de Alonso de Campo* (Madrid: 1977) 181. Director of the Cathedral choir, Alonso de Campo was in charge of the Corpus Christi processions in Toledo from 1481 until his death in 1499.
49   Surtz, *Music and Spectacle* 144–148.
50   Stern C., "The Medieval Theatre between Scriptura and Theatrica", in Gies D.T. (ed.), *The Cambridge History of Spanish Literature* (Cambridge – New York, NY: 2008) 123.
51   The author of the play, Gómez Manrique (1412–1490), was the son of Leonor of Castille (1390–1470), patron of this Clarissan convent and its prioress since 1468. In that year, she was succeeded by her daughter, María.

a religious subject-matter) in which Virgin Mary has a foreshadowing of the Passion, during which the instruments of the Passion are presented to her. This theme, so dear to Franciscan devotion, is also present in *El Conhorte* in Sermon 2 (the Nativity), where Mary, just after giving birth, has a premonition of the way her Son will die on the Cross.[52]

There was a vivid tradition of staging religious plays in Juana's monastery of S. María de la Cruz in Cubas, as is demonstrated in the *Libro de la Casa*. This manuscript, a collection of writings produced at the convent, starts with two *autos* (religious plays) written for the Feast of the Assumption, on August 15.[53] The second of these plays, 'performed in the afternoon', starts with a dialogue between God the Father and Lucifer that quickly turns into a fierce dispute over the Immaculate Conception, rigorously defended by the Franciscan order.[54] Following from the stage directions, all lights were extinguished during the fight between God and Lucifer and their angelic squadrons, so that the battle is rather heard than seen. Only once the fallen angels have been defeated and cursed three times by God the Father, the light returns. Now the angels are seen kneeling down for the Virgin, who ascends to heaven accompanied by the song *O gloriosa domina*. The Virgin promises to be a good advocate, and God hands over the staff of judgement ('la vara de mi justicia') to St. Michael, and the festive finale consists in a communal singing of the *Laudate Dominum*. Like the Nativity play in Calabanzanos, this *auto* of the Assumption is again presented in eschatological terms, underlining the Virgin's intercession for souls in their quest for salvation. The inclusion of yet another battle between good and bad angels shows the preference for these themes in the enclosed convent community. Unfortunately, there is only scant evidence for the staging of these plays and who could attend them. Perhaps it is indicative that the first Assumption play is said to be performed 'in the *casa de la labor* (work house) on the day of the burial of Our Lady', and that it ends with 'a procession of the Apostles carrying the bier with Our Lady on their shoulders *to the lower choir*' (emphasis mine).[55] The lower choir would be the part of the convent church that was open to visitors from outside the convent. Elsewhere in the *Libro de la Casa*, it

52   Stern, "The Medieval Theatre".

53   *Libro de la Casa*, Biblioteca Nacional de España, ms. 9661, http://bdh.bne.es/bnesearch /detalle/bdh0000072668 (accessed 21.06.2023).

54   Ibidem, fol. 4 r: 'Este auto es el que se haze el día de la asumpción de Nuestra Señora en la tarde. Gánase mucho haziéndola' (This play is performed on the Feast of the Assumption of Our Lady in the afternoon. Many indulgences are gained by doing this).

55   Ibidem, fol. 2 r: 'Este auto es el que hazen en la casa de la labor el día de la sepoltura de Nuestra Señora'. Ibidem, fol. 3 v.: 'Va la procession al Coro basso y llevan los apóstoles a Nuestra Señora en hombros, y de las andas va S. Juan con la palma y S. Pedro y el Angel'.

is said that the Assumption play, staged 'in the refectory', pleased Christ very much; as he had stated in Sermon 57 (the Assumption) that all those involved in the Assumption play, including those building the stage, could count on many graces.[56]

5   Purgatory and the Hospitals of Mercy

In the biography *Vida y fin*, Juana and her guardian angel visit the New Jerusalem, said to be located at the outskirts of heaven.[57] In Juana's conception, this place contains all churches that exist on earth, albeit far more beautiful and adorned with precious stones. In these churches hermits, friars, and deacons are engaged in continuous prayers and masses, just as they were while living on earth. Angels and virgins assist them, to make up for 'eventual blemishes' on the souls of these clerics. All across this New Jerusalem, large numbers of penitent souls are seen moving forward on their knees, while beating their chests and issuing laments. At the margins of this New Jerusalem, angels run 'Hospitales de la misericordia' (Hospitals of Mercy) for the souls who have just been liberated from purgatory. In these hospitals the souls can rest for a few days, while angels tend to their horridly smelling wounds inflicted on them by the devils while they were in purgatory.[58] Besides new vestments, the souls receive instructions about the prayers, songs, and dances that they will be performing from now on in heaven. Just before being escorted to heaven, the souls receive their very last indulgence granted to them by God.[59]

Ibidem, fol. 40 r mentions the *Auto* of the Assumption performed on this location: 'en el auto que se haze esto mismo día en la casa de la labor; concedió el Señor muchas gracias'.

56   Ibidem, fol. 40 r: 'Y en el que hazen el día de la Sancta Asumpción, en el refitorio, concedió el Señor grandes gracias, y dixo el mismo Señor, en un sermón que hizo en el santo *Conorte* de la sancta asumpción, que gustaba se hiziesse, y dio la industria para ello. Y no tan solamente concedió el Señor gracias en el auto, sino también a quien dixere que se haga y ayudare a poner el tablado'.

57   *Vida y fin*, chapter 12, as cited in Luengo Balbás, *Juana de la Cruz* 428–442; see also http://catalogodesantasvivas.visionarias.es/ (accessed 13.05.2024).

58   About the fight between angels and devils over souls, see Brilliant V., "Envisaging the Particular Judgment in Late-Medieval Italy", *Speculum* 84.2 (2009) 314–346.

59   *Vida y fin*, fol. 64 v, as cited in Luengo Balbás, *Juana de la Cruz* 231: 'Llaman los sanctos ángeles los hospitales de la misericordia, porque allí meten a rezar las ánimas, quando algunas fiestas las sacan de Purgatorio y para las limpiar de sus males odores y curarles las llagas que los demonios les an hecho. Allí las apiadan de todas las maneras de piedades [...] e las visten y adornan. Y las enseñan los sanctos ángeles cómo an de adorar al Señor y a todos sus misterios, e cómo an de hazer todas las çeremonias y cuentas que los

Close to these celestial Hospitals of Mercy, in a big open natural space abounding in abundant vegetation, flowers, and fresh water, stands the Tree of Life. Great numbers of souls are resting comfortably in its shadow, its branches carrying deliciously smelling flowers and the sweetest of fruits. Beautifully crafted golden vessels with the finest bread and other delicious food hang on its branches, to signify that all good comes from the wood of the cross, so closely connected to the Tree of Life in Franciscan devotion.[60] The brooks and rivulets that spring forth from the tree's trunk and its roots complete this idyllic scene, one of the very few in Juana's eschatological conception of heaven.

God had chosen this tree as the site of his throne, upon which is seated the Holy Spirit, appearing like a splendid seraph surrounded by multitudes of angels.[61] Near the tree, there is an image of the Crucifixion, and close by images of the Virgin Mary, St. John, and two of the Marys standing at the foot of the cross, at times seemingly in motion, 'como si estuviesen vivas' (as if they were alive), changing their poses and gestures.[62] From the description, it is not clear whether this is a painted image or a sculpture. Around it, there is a constant coming and going of blessed souls doing penitence and asking for intercession. They are harassed by particularly nasty and menacing demons, whom angels have to ward off in fierce combat.[63] Not all petitions for intercession are granted, however. In that case, the Christ figure on the cross takes on a dramatic and contorted expression. Blood is issuing from deep wounds, while the head of Christ is moving in great agony from side to side, 'as if wishing to cover his ears'. There is a connection with Sermon 9 (Septuagesima Sunday), where the banner with the image of Christ suddenly changes into a Man of Sorrows.

The presence of these images, so central in early modern devotion, begs the question to what extent the visions of Juana de la Cruz were inspired by devotional images within convents.[64] The *Libro de la Casa* contains extensive lists of miracle-working images within the convent of Cubas, which, when prayed

çelestiales bienabenturados van e hazen en honrra e alabanza de Dios, e a tañer y cantar con que loen su criador de allí'.

60   Salonius P., "The Tree of Life in Medieval Iconography", in Estes D. (ed.), *The Tree of Life: Themes in Biblical Narrative* (Leiden – Boston, MA: 2020) 280–343, esp. 316–320.

61   *Vida y fin*, fol. 65 v., as cited by Luengo Balbás, *Juana de la Cruz* 231.

62   *Vida y fin*, fol. 65 v, as cited in Luengo Balbás, *Juana de la Cruz* 229–234: 'A e se mudan a tiempos e vezes de diversidad de maneras, e todas muy devotas'.

63   Ibidem: 'Viendo los demonios el gran thesoro e bienabenturanza que las ánimas resçiven en aquel lugar, pésales mucho, quiriéndola quitar y estorvar por todas las maneras que ellos pudiesen. Y atrévense, con gran ossadía y rabia que tienen'.

64   See Sanmartín Bastida R., "En torno al arte y las visionarias", *Medievalia* 18.2 (2015) 357–367, for a discussion of image-induced visions of *sante vive* María de Ajofrín (ca. 1455–1489) and María Vela y Cueto (1561–1617).

to, yielded indulgences, specifying the numbers of souls that could be saved from purgatory. The most important of these miracle-working images was an old wooden sculpture of Our Lady and the Child standing on an altar in the choir. The nuns of S. Maria de la Cruz were very devoted to it; they carried it in procession on Apparition Day, the day the community commemorated the apparition of the Virgin to a young girl named Inez in 1449 at the location of their very church. In Juana's time, the community had the statue restored, replacing the head and changing her gesture. Some of the nuns liked the changes to the sculpture, others did not. Sensing the commotion, Juana asked for permission to have the sculpture for two days on an altar in her cell. While praying to it, she had two visions. On the first night, the Virgin appeared to her, stating that she wanted the image to be duly consecrated 'as is fit for images that are venerated on church altars'. The second night, Juana had a vision of Christ, seated on a magnificent throne and dressed as a bishop to say Mass, with multitudes of angels and saints around him. Christ blessed the sculpture of his mother with most devout and reverential words, while the angels and saints sang sweet songs.[65] And Christ made sure that the devils witnessed this consecration, scaring them 'by showing the very virtue that God instils in his Holy Church and the images that are venerated there'.[66]

6   Connecting Heaven, Hell, and Purgatory

In Sermon 9 (Septuagesima Sunday), we learn that the voices of the blessed souls may be heard on earth. But to enter heaven is another matter, for, as announced in the Gospels, the gate to heaven is 'a narrow one' (*Matthew* 7:13–14). In Sermon 54 (Admonitions for us sinners), Juana describes indeed a narrow gate, decorated with precious stones and radiating with bright and coloured light, 'like the rays of the morning sun'.[67] Many souls, dressed humbly, present themselves at this gate for their salvation. But as they undress, their bodies show

---

65   Libru de la Casa, fol. 44 r–48 r· "Revelación que esta imagen de la Virgen hizo a Juana". I will return to this sculpture and its miracle-working properties in my forthcoming monograph *Blessed and Indulgenced Objects in Early Modern Catholic Worlds*.

66   Ibidem, fol. 46 r.

67   Sermon 54 (Admonitions for us sinners), García Andrés, *El Conhorte* 1184, as cited in Luengo Balbás, *Juana de la Cruz* 238: 'En medio de la claridad [del cielo], apareció una puerta muy chiquita y angosta, mas era toda muy rica y llena de piedras preciosas, y salían de ella unos rayos muy claros y pintados. Y los unos eran blancos y otros colorados y otros verdes y otros amarillos y otros de muchos y diversos colores, los cuáles rayos erano como del sol cuando sale. A significación que dentro de aquella puerta estaba el sol de justicia'.

festering contusions and deep wounds, representing their many sins. Only
when they have properly atoned, the narrow gate becomes wide, allowing the
souls to pass through without difficulty.[68] At this point, the angels and blessed
souls welcome them to heaven, and give them new vestments. Meanwhile,
Christ keeps waiting at the narrow gate, always anxious to welcome newly
repented souls.

Most souls must atone for their sins in purgatory before they can be admitted to heaven. In Sermon 58 (The Feast of St. Francis), purgatory and heaven
are connected by means of two monumental staircases: one red as coral, signifying Christ's Passion, and the other white as pearls, signifying the virginity of
Our Lady. The steps of the staircases are wide enough to contain thousands of
souls. Holding hands, Christ and St. Francis descend the staircase together on
their way to liberate souls from purgatory. Meanwhile, multitudes of angels
stand on guard on the staircases, preventing souls from ascending to heaven,
for not all souls will be saved.[69]

Like heaven, hell, and purgatory remain in Juana's conception at best
ill-defined spaces. She envisages hell as a prison, where the damned souls are
condemned to eternal punishments for the sins they committed during their
lifetimes. Punishments in purgatory are no less cruel, but at least there is the
absolute assurance that one will be saved. As in Dante's *Inferno*, there exists a
correlation between the punishments and the sins committed: souls guilty of
superbia are tied with their heads to their feet; those who were greedy are now
either naked or clad in old, stinking garments with holes, while flames and
worms eat their way through their bodies.[70]

While Juana frequently travels to heaven and purgatory, she never ventures
in person into hell. Remarkably, in *El Conhorte* we learn about hell from the

---

68   Ibidem, 1186: 'cuando empezaban a entrar o cuando habían metido el medio cuerpo,
      hacíaseles la puerta tan ancha y holgada, que cabían y entraban muy holgadamente y
      sin ningún trabajo nu pelligro. Y no solamente, digo el Señor, que cabía uno a uno, mas
      cupieran muchos juntos si quisieran entrar'.

69   Sermon 58 (St Francis), García Andrés, *El Conhorte* 1248, as cited in Luengo Balbás, *Juana
      de la Cruz* 240: 'En este mismo día, es abierto el cielo, y a deshora son aparecidas dos
      escaleras, la una colorada como de rubíes y corales, y la otra blanca como de perlas. Las
      cuales escaleras son tan largas que llegan desde el cielo hasta el purgatorio, y tan anchas
      que caben por ellas infinitos millares de ánimas. Y la escalera colorada significaba la su
      pasión y la escalera blanca significa la virginidad y pureza y méritos de Nuestra Señora
      la Virgen María. Y que ambas escaleras están llenas y cercadas de ángeles. Y desciende él
      mismo por ellas trayendo de la mano a San Francisco y van entrambos al purgatorio'.

70   *Vida y fin*, fol. 108 r: 'Y como los demonios les demandavan los peccados que hizieron, y las
      penas que les davan por ellas a las ánimas que havían peccado'.

figuras created in heaven for the instruction of the blessed souls about rewards and punishments in the afterlife.[71] In Sermon 14 (Temptation in the desert), Christ asks the angels to create a meadow and divide it into two parts. One side is to be filled with flowers and vegetation, 'todo muy deleitoso'; the other is covered in precious tapestries and textiles, painted with marvellous colours, 'like the sun rays of the early morning, some of them greenish, some of them colored, and others like a prism'.[72] These tapestries depict hell with its furnaces and fires containing the souls of the damned, eaten by demons looking like disfigured dogs and wolves. Juana makes a comparison with tapestries of the 'grandes señores' in their aristocratic mansions, although those in heaven are (of course) much more beautiful.[73]

But hell is also present in the convent of Cubas itself. Juana instils fear within her fellow nuns as she recounts her visions of devils assaulting their very own convent. They fill it from floor to ceiling, as crawling poisonous vermin and reptiles, ferocious dogs, wolves, bulls and lions, and ravens, vultures, and bats. The areas most affected are the confessional and the kitchen, the area that centres on the fulfilment of the basic need of nourishment, the rejection of which is so central in the self-fashioning of *sante vive*.[74]

---

71   Sermon 63 (Sts Simon and Jude), García Andrés, *El Conhorte* 1310, as cited in Luengo Balbás, *Juana de la Cruz* 247: 'Una figura muy dolorosa y espantable a los de su santo reino para que ellos viesen con cuánta razón y justicia condana él a los malos y pecadores, la qual figura fue hecha en esta manera: que a deshora, aparecieron muchedumbre de pueblos, así de mujeres como de hombres. Y que a donde aparecieron tambien [...] muchas cárceles y prisiones y muchas forcas y muchas maneras de armas y de tormentos muy crueles'.

72   Sermon 14 (Temptation in the desert), García Andrés, *El Conhorte* 555, as cited in Luengo Balbás, *Juana de la Cruz* 248: 'Y en otra parte del mismo desierto pusieron unos como paramentos muy ricos y pintados, come de rayos de sol cuando sale por la mañana, que tiene unos rayos como verdes, y otros como colorados y otros como de otras colores y pinturas'.

73   Ibidem: 'Y en aquellos tan ricos paramentos, dijo el Señor y Redentor nuestro Jesucristo, estaba pintado el infierno y los hornos y los fuegos y ánimas que en él hay, y los demonios, así como canes y lobos muy disformes, que se comían las tristes ánimas. Y por semejante, estaban allí pintadas todas las penas que hay en el infierno, así como acá en tierra tienen los grandes señores en los paños y adornamentos de sus palacios y cámaras historias; salvo que, lo de allá, es todo muy claro y hermoso y resplandeciente'.

74   *Vida y fin*, fol. 79 v, as cited in Luengo Balbás, *Juana de la Cruz* 207: 'E veyenlas en muchos géneros de figuras, el suelo del monasterio estar lleno dellos a manera de animalías rastables come culebras, lagartas e salamanquesas, e de otras muchas manera de sabandixas ponzoñosas. Ansímiso veya dellos como canes, lobos, toros y leones, e osos, e todo género de bestias bravas e de carga. Veyalos en el ayre a manera de cuerbos, e buytres, y murciégalos, y de otras figuras muy temerosas y feas'.

7   Eternal and Cyclical Time in the Afterlife

Time in the afterlife is an eternal time: once a soul is in hell, its punishments will last forever. And the same goes for a soul admitted to heaven. But because of the obligation to keep the memory of Christ's sacrifice alive, the episodes of his life are relived over and over. As we have seen in Sermon 9 (Septuagesima Sunday), the blessed souls pleaded with Christ to relive the Passion with them. The *Vida y fin* explains that souls are obliged to do this as the prudent vassals that they are, redeemed by the precious blood of their Lord:

> Given that God is eternity without end, he wishes that all his mysteries are celebrated, exalted, contemplated, and lamented in continuation; and it is only just that he demands this from his prudent vassals, who have been redeemed by his precious blood.[75]

Since time is relived time and again, Christ occasionally returns to his infancy. In Sermon 6 (the Flight into Egypt), he is crying like a hungry baby for the breast of his mother:

> As he felt compassion for his sweet mother, he got hold of her virgin breasts and started to suckle as if he wanted to drink, calling for her with a tender and delicate voice, as a hungry infant, sighing: 'mama, mama, mama'. And with this lament, the Saviour returned to his glorious mother.[76]

When Christ is a small boy, he wants the blessed souls to become children as well, so that they can play together.[77] And just as Christ has to relive the Passion over and over again, the same goes for the martyrs. In Sermon 64 (All

---

75   Ibidem., fol. 63 r, as cited in Luengo Balbás, *Juana de la Cruz* 21: 'Que assí como Dios es eterno e sin fin, así quiere que todos sus misterios sean sin fin eternalmente çelebrados, engrandeçidos e contemplados e llorados, según la justa raçón lo requiere lo hagan sus basallos cautivos e remididos por su preçioso sangre'.

76   Sermon 6 (Flight into Egypt), García Andrés, *El Conhorte* 386, as cited in Luengo Balbás, *Juana de la Cruz* 131: 'Hubó compasión de su dulce madre, y empezóle a asir de sus virginales tetas y a sacárselas como que quería mamar, y empezó a llamarla con una voz muy tierna y compasión viva, así como niño necesitado, diciéndole con gemido "mamá, mamá, mamá." Y así con este llanto, tornó el mismo Salvador a su gloriosa madre'.

77   Sermon 4 (Epiphany), García Andrés, *El Conhorte* 333, as cited in Luengo Balbás, *Juana de la Cruz* 267: 'No quiero yo, ahora, hombre ni mujeres grandes, sino niños y niñas chiquitos para con que yo juegue, pues estoy hecho niño'.

Saints), Christ tells Juana how all angels and martyrs had gathered in a lush meadow. Then Christ appeared along with his mother, St. John the Baptist, and all those who would be resurrected on the Day of the Last Judgement.[78] A magnificent banner of gold and velvet, decorated with pearls and precious stones, was high up in the air, attached with ropes to the Palace of the Holy Trinity. Upon the sounds of trumpets, all saints gathered in the meadow. At that same moment, the angels were transformed into soldiers armed with swords, lances, and other ferocious weapons. The angels, '*pretending* to be bold and brave', launch the attack and start to massacre the saints with blades, so much 'that *it looked as* if they gutted and beheaded all of them' (emphasis mine). Even if the angels were just pretending to be fierce executioners, by now the meadow is drenched by rivers of blood, in which animals are splashing around with gusto. Then God appears, asking the saints in a loving voice what terrible fate has happened to them, and restores them to their blissful state.[79]

How does all this relate to the Last Judgement, when the world and heaven as we know it will be destroyed? In Sermon 24 (the Ascension), Christ asks his friends to prepare a meadow for him, where all souls of times past, present, and future will be gathered, in the expectation that one day all thrones in his heavenly realm will be filled with blessed souls.

> As token of gratification and consolation, I beg you to create for me a wide, luscious meadow that offers space for all baptised souls that I have created [so far] and will create [in the future]; for those who are already in hell, and the ones that will be condemned to go there; and also for those who live [presently] on the earth, and those who are already established and enthroned in my Holy Reign [...]. For I tell you that I am not satisfied nor am I fulfilled, unless all thrones present in my kingdom will be filled with souls that I have created and that I will create in the future, for I am the true and omniscient God and the vastest ocean and deepest abyss of all unknowable wisdom without compare, and I know very well who will need to saved and who deserves damnation.[80]

---

78   Sermon 64 (All Saints), García Andrés, *El Conhorte* 386, as cited in Luengo Balbás, *Juana de la Cruz* 131.

79   Ibidem.

80   García Andrés, *El Conhorte* 812, as cited in Luengo Balbás, *Juana de la Cruz* 235: 'Yo os ruego que me hagáis un placer y consolación de hacerme un grande y deleitoso campo en donde quepan todos los bautizados que yo crié, y tengo de criar; así los que están en el infierno, come los que han de ir allá; y así los que están en la tierra como los que están ya acá en esto mi santo reino colocados y ensalzados [...]. Porque os digo y os certifigo que no tengo gozo lleno ni cumplido hasta que todas estas sillas que están en mi santo

These words of Christ, identifying himself as the 'true and omniscient God, the vastest ocean and deepest abyss of wisdom without compare', recall the third vision of the Italian mystic Angela da Foligno, whose writings had such a profound effect on Juana de la Cruz and her circles. In the vision, Angela recounts that she was once standing in church when she had a life-changing insight, by which God revealed her his infinite omnipotence:

> And at that point, the eyes of my soul were opened, and I witnessed the fullness and expansion of God that comprised the entire world, that is, what is on this side of the sea, and on the other, what is inside the sea and in the depths and in everything that I saw I could perceive nothing if not the omnipotence of God, in an ineffable manner that is impossible to express or tell.[81]

Juana's Sermon 20 asserts that the celebrations and pageants in heaven will continue until the Last Judgement, when the world and heaven will be made anew. The celebrations and pageants of Juana's eschatological imagination, grounded in a cyclical notion of time, will then come to an end. As John of Patmos had envisioned in his *Revelations*, the New Jerusalem will then descend on the new earth. In this city, there will be no temples (unlike Juana's New Jerusalem), as God and the Lamb will be venerated everywhere.

In conclusion, we can say that the celestial imagination of Juana de la Cruz is a most complex construction that challenges time and space as we know it. A close reading of the sermons suggests how deeply a visionary as Juana was connected to the religious and material culture of her time: her texts contain echoes of visions of earlier mystics, such as Angela da Foligno, while the extraordinary pageants staged in Juana's celestial world are embedded in the

---

reino sean lleanas de ánimas que yo crié y tengo de criar, porqué yo soy Dios verdadero y sapientisimo, y piélago y abismo de toda la ciencia incomprensible y sin comparación, sé muy bien todos los que se han da salvar y los que se han de condenar'.

81   *Libro de la bienaventurada sancta Angela de Fulgino en el qual se nos muestra la verdadera carrera para seguir las pisadas de nuestro redemptor y maestro Jesu Christo* (Toledo, sucesor de Pedro Hagenbach por mandado de fray Francisco Ximenez: 1510), fol. xx v: 'Y luego al punto me fueron abiertos los ojos de mi anima, y vi una plenitud y henchimiento de Dios, la qual comprendia a todo el mundo, conviene a saber, allende la mar, y aquende la mar y esa mar y abismos, y todas las cosas en la quales no veia otra cosa sino sola la potencia divinal, por una manera ineffabile que ni se puede dezir ni contar'. The Latin version had been published in 1505: *Liber qui dicitur Angela de Fulginio: in quo ostenditur nobis vera via qua possumus sequi vestigia nostri redemptoris* (Toledo, sucesor de Pedro Hagenbach iussu Francisci Ximenez archiepiscopi: 1505), and also circulated in manuscript form.

rich religious festival culture alive in both convents and Corpus Christi processions in early modern Spain.

Bibliography

Acosta-García P., "Women Prophets for a New World: Angela of Foligno, Living Saints, and the Religious Reform Movement in Cardinal Cisneros' Castile", in Morrás M. – Sanmartín Bastida R. – Kim Y. (eds.), *Gender and Exemplarity in Medieval and Early Modern Spain* (Leiden – Boston, MA: 2020) 136–162.

Acosta-García P., "Radical Succession: Hagiography, Reform and Franciscan Identity in the Convent of the Abbess Juana de la Cruz (1481–1534)", *Religions* 12 (2021) 1–23.

Bates S., "Preparations for a Christian Death: The Later Middle Ages", in Booth P. – Tingle E. (eds.), *A Companion to Death, Burial and Remembrance in Late Medieval and Early Modern Europe* (Leiden – Boston, MA: 2020) 72–105.

Bilinkoff J., "A Spanish Prophetess and Her Patrons: The Case of Maria de Santo Domingo", *The Sixteenth Century Journal* 23.1 (1992) 21–34.

Boon J.A., "Christ in Heavenly Play: Christology through Mary's Eyes in the Sermons of Juana de la Cruz (1481–1534)", *Archiv für Reformationsgeschichte* 102.1 (2011) 243–266.

Boon J.A., "At the Limits of (Trans)Gender: Jesus, Mary and the Angels in the Visionary Sermons of Juana de la Cruz (1481–1534)", *Journal of Medieval and Early Modern Studies* 48.2 (2018) 261–300.

Boon J.A. – Surtz R.E. (eds.), *Mother Juana de la Cruz: Visionary Sermons* (Toronto: 2014).

Braguier L., *Servantes de Dieu: Les 'beatas' de la Couronne de Castile 1450–1600* (Rennes: 2019).

Brilliant V., "Envisaging the Particular Judgment in Late-Medieval Italy", *Speculum* 84.2 (2009) 314–346.

Bynum C.W., *Jesus as Mother: Studies in the Spirituality of the High Middle Ages* (Berkeley, CA: 1982).

Bynum C.W., *Wonderful Blood: Theology and Practice in Late Medieval Northern Germany and Beyond* (New York, NY: 2011).

Cappuccilli E., "In the Steps of Birgitta of Sweden: The Reluctant Authority of Paola Antonia Negri (1508–1555)", *Renaissance Studies* 35 (2021) 582–599.

García Andrés I., *El Conhorte: Sermones de una Mujer. La Santa Juana (1481–1534)*, 2 vols. (Madrid: 1999).

Giles M.E., *The Book of Prayer of Sor María of Santo Domíngo: A Study and Translation* (Albany, NY: 1990).

Giles R.D., "'Mira mis llagas': Heridas divinas en las obras de Brígida de Suecia y Teresa de Jesús", *Ehumanista. Journal of Iberian Studies* 32 (2016) 34–49.

Hernández R., *Immaculate Conceptions: The Power of Religious Imagination in Early Modern Spain* (Toronto: 2019).

Herzig T., *Savonarola's Women: Visions and Reform in Renaissance Italy* (Chicago, IL: 2008).

Herzig T., "Female Mysticism, Heterodoxy, and Reform", in Mixson J.D. – Roest B. (eds.), *A Companion to Observant Reform in the Late Middle Ages and Beyond* (Leiden – Boston, MA: 2015) 255–282.

Kopania K., "Animated Sculptures of the Crucified Christ: Origins, Development and Impact", *Material Religion* 14.4 (2018) 545–558.

Lilley K.D., "Cities of God? Medieval Urban Forms and Their Christian Symbolism", *Transactions of the Institute of British Geographers* 29.3 (2004) 296–313.

Luengo Balbás M., *Juana de la Cruz: Vida y obra de una visionaria del siglo XVI* (Ph.D. dissertation, Universidad Complutense de Madrid: 2016).

Owens S.E., "El legado del rosario milagroso en los escritos de viage de sor Ana de Christo hacia Filipinas", *Boletín de monumentos historicos, tercera epoca* 30 (2014) 22–35.

Pereda F., *Images of Discord: Poetics and Politics of the Sacred Image in Fifteenth-Century Spain* (Turnhout: 2018).

Poutrin I., *Le voile et la plume: Autobiographie et sainteté féminine dans l'Espagne moderne* (Madrid: 1995).

Robinson C., *Imagining the Passion in a Multiconfessional Castile: The Virgin, Christ, Devotion and Images in the Fourteenth and Fifteenth Centuries* (University Park, PA: 2013).

Roest B., "Female Preaching in the Late Medieval Franciscan Tradition", *Franciscan Studies* 62 (2004) 119–154.

Rubin M., *Corpus Christi: The Eucharist in Late Medieval Culture* (Cambridge – New York, NY: 1991).

Ruiz T.F., "From Carnival to Corpus Christi", in idem, *A King Travels: Festive Traditions in Late Medieval and Early Modern Spain* (Princeton, NJ: 2012).

Salonius P., "The Tree of Life in Medieval Iconography", in Estes D. (ed.), *The Tree of Life: Themes in Biblical Narrative* (Leiden – Boston, MA: 2020) 280–343.

Sanmartín Bastida R., "En torno al arte y las visionarias", *Medievalia* 18.2 (2015) 357–367.

Sanmartín Bastida R. – Luengo Balbás M., *Las Revelaciones de María de Santo Domíngo, 1480/86–1524* (London: 2014).

Stern C., "The Medieval Theatre between Scriptura and Theatrica", in Gies D.T. (ed.), *The Cambridge History of Spanish Literature* (Cambridge – New York, NY: 2008).

Surtz R.E., *Writing Women in Late Medieval and Early Modern Spain: The Mothers of Teresa of Avila* (Philadelphia, PA: 1995).

Surtz R.E., "Music and Spectacle", in Knighton T. (ed.), *Companion to Music in the Age of the Catholic Monarchs* (Leiden – Boston, MA: 2016) 145–172.

Tingle E., "Changing Western European Visions of Christian Afterlives, 1350–1700. Heaven Hell, and Purgatory", in Booth P. – Tingle E. (eds.), *A Companion to Death, Burial and Remembrance in Late Medieval and Early Modern Europe* (Leiden – Boston, MA: 2020) 33–71.

Torroja Menéndez C. – Rivas Palá M., *Teatro en Toledo en el siglo XV: Auto de la Pasión de Alonso de Campo* (Madrid: 1977).

CHAPTER 9

Describing the Inconceivable in Eighteenth-Century Methodist and Quaker Visions of the Afterlife

Martha McGill and Luke Holloway

Abstract

Although the Bible warns that the nature of the afterlife is beyond human conception, believers have persistently made attempts to envisage and describe otherworldly realms. This chapter explores accounts of journeys to heaven and hell that were written or collected by Quakers and Methodists in eighteenth-century England and America. Both denominations encouraged adherents to look inwards to detect the signs of grace, but visionaries devoted relatively little space to the emotional impact of their experiences. Their accounts are more revealing when it comes to the transfiguration of bodies in otherworldly realms: the chapter considers the separation of body and soul, the appearances of deceased family and friends, and the mystical qualities of celestial attire. Visionaries typically portrayed people in the afterlife as simultaneously familiar and unfamiliar. They employed similar strategies when describing environmental features such as buildings, gardens, and lakes. By discussing sublime landscapes in relation to their earthly counterparts, visionaries provided scaffolding for the imaginative labour of envisaging the afterlife. Although Quaker and Methodist theologians reiterated the scriptural cautions against speculation about the afterlife, the preservation and circulation of these visionary accounts indicates that wider spiritual communities viewed heaven and hell as valid objects of religious reflection.

Keywords

afterlife – Methodists – Quakers – visions – heaven

While life after death is a fundamental Christian tenet, the Bible offers limited insight into the nature of the afterlife.[1] Heaven is joyful and hell terrible,

---

1   We are grateful for the helpful comments of this chapter's anonymous peer reviewers.

but the specifics remain beyond mortal ken: 'Eye hath not seen, nor ear heard, neither have entered into the heart of man, the things which God hath prepared for them that love him'.[2] This scriptural caution did not preclude historical endeavours to envisage the contours of otherworldly realms. Medieval and early modern Christians speculated on the nature of the afterlife in sermons, theological tracts, literary works, and artworks. Some individuals went further still, reporting visionary journeys to heaven, hell, or purgatory. Visions of the afterlife were a popular genre in the Middle Ages, but became more contested following the Reformation.[3] Protestant clerics persisted in sermonizing and theorizing about the nature of the afterlife, even as they criticized Catholics for venturing beyond the bounds of Scripture.[4] Visionary experiences nevertheless fell under greater scrutiny, with Protestant theologians typically suggesting that miracles had been confined to the early centuries of Christianity.[5] In England in 1562, the draper Ellis Hall was pilloried and imprisoned for 'seducinge the people by publyshynge ffallce Revelations' about a journey to heaven and hell.[6]

However, Protestant culture was fractured, and different individuals or groups took different positions on when legitimate supernatural belief veered into superstition. This chapter focuses on experiences written or collected by eighteenth-century Quakers and Methodists in England and America. Although leading Quaker and Methodist theologians reiterated traditional cautions against speculating too far on the nature of the afterlife, clerics and laypeople of both denominations scrutinized dreams and visions, considering them potential avenues of communication between humans and the

---

2 1 *Corinthians* 2:9, King James Version (KJV).

3 See Zaleski C., *Otherworld Journeys: Accounts of Near-Death Experience in Medieval and Modern Times* (New York, NY – Oxford: 1987); Gardiner E. (ed.), *Visions of Heaven and Hell before Dante* (New York, NY: 1989); Muessig C. – Putter A. (eds.), *Envisaging Heaven in the Middle Ages* (New York, NY: 2006); Adams G.W., *Visions in Late Medieval England: Lay Spirituality and Sacred Glimpses of the Hidden Worlds of Faith* (Leiden – Boston, MA: 2007) 17–54; Pollard R.M. (ed.), *Imagining the Medieval Afterlife* (Cambridge – New York, NY: 2020).

4 Marshall P., *Beliefs and the Dead in Reformation England* (Oxford – New York, NY: 2002) 188–194.

5 See Walker D.P., "The Cessation of Miracles", in Merkel I. – Debus A.G. (eds.), *Hermeticism and the Renaissance: Intellectual History and the Occult in Early Modern Europe* (Washington, DC – London: 1988) 111–124; Walsham A., "Miracles in Post-Reformation England", in Cooper K. – Gregory J. (eds.), *Signs, Wonders, Miracles: Representations of Divine Power in the Life of the Church*, Studies in Church History 41 (Woodbridge: 2005) 273–306; Soergel P.M., *Miracles and the Protestant Imagination: The Evangelical Wonder Book in Reformation Germany* (Oxford – New York, NY: 2012).

6 Quoted in Marshall P., "Judgement and Repentance in Tudor Manchester: The Celestial Journey of Ellis Hall", in his *Invisible Worlds: Death, Religion and the Supernatural in England, 1500–1700* (London: 2017) 51–58, at 51.

divine.[7] The rich literature on Quaker and Methodist dreams and visions has tended to mention otherworldly journeys only in passing, and most dedicated studies have focused on evangelical narratives in the American context. Douglas L. Winiarski provides a detailed exploration of an evangelist's account of heaven from the winter of 1741–1742, arguing that visionary encounters from the Great Awakening sat uncomfortably with the Calvinist theology already established in New England, while Erik R. Seeman highlights how dreams and visions allowed the bereaved to continue relationships with loved ones in heaven.[8] This chapter uses accounts produced on both sides of the Atlantic, and concerned with hell as well as heaven, to offer an alternative view of how eighteenth-century religious communities speculated about the afterlife. Despite conceding that aspects of the afterlife were indescribable, visionaries offered detailed accounts that reimagined physical and affective states, as well as spatial and temporal dimensions. Philip Almond's valuable *Heaven and Hell in Enlightenment England* reflects on the cultural significance of the afterlife by tracing the fluxes of theological debate.[9] However, our body of sources demonstrates how laypeople might sidestep religious leaders' instruction, with visionaries developing vivid depictions of the afterlife that made imaginable the supposedly inconceivable.

1   Source Material

Quakerism was founded by the English dissenter George Fox during the civil war period (1642–1651), and despite persecution by the authorities, the

---

7 See Kirschner A., "'Tending to Edify, Astonish, and Instruct': Published Narratives of Spiritual Dreams and Visions in the Early Republic", *Early American Studies* 1.1 (2003) 198–229; Taves A., *Fits, Trances, and Visions: Experiencing Religion and Explaining Experience from Wesley to James* (Princeton, NJ – Oxford: 2000); Sobel M., *Teach Me Dreams: The Search for Self in the Revolutionary Era* (Princeton, NJ – Oxford: 2002); Gerona C., *Night Journeys: The Power of Dreams in Transatlantic Quaker Culture* (Charlottesville, VA: 2004); Juster S., *Doomsayers: Anglo-American Prophecy in the Age of Revolution* (Philadelphia, PA: 2006); Mack P., "The Unbounded Self: Dreaming and Identity in the British Enlightenment", in Plane A.M. – Tuttle L. – Wallace A.F.C. (eds.), *Dreams, Dreamers, and Visions: The Early Modern Atlantic World* (Philadelphia, PA: 2013) 216–224; Plane A.M., *Dreams and the Invisible World in Colonial New England: Indians, Colonists, and the Seventeenth Century* (Philadelphia, PA: 2014).

8 Winiarski D.L., "Souls Filled with Ravishing Transport: Heavenly Visions and the Radical Awakening in New England", *William and Mary Quarterly* 61.1 (2004) 3–46; Seeman E.R., *Speaking with the Dead in Early America* (Philadelphia, PA: 2019) 73–103. See also Gerona, *Night Journeys* 9, 25, 163–164.

9 Almond P.C., *Heaven and Hell in Enlightenment England* (Cambridge – New York, NY: 1994). Almond's more recent book, *Afterlife: A History of Life After Death* (Ithaca, NY – London: 2016) is more sweeping in scope.

movement rapidly drew thousands of adherents. Quaker theology departed from Calvinism by stressing humankind's free will and asserting the possibility of salvation for all. Quakers also believed that there was a divine spark within every individual, and they allowed anyone who was moved by the Holy Spirit to speak at meetings.[10] Non-adherents criticized Quakerism as enthusiastical, pointing to Quakers' sometimes rapturous experiences of divine presence. Owen Davies writes that by the 1720s, 'the Quakers had distanced themselves from the miraculous spiritual milieu their founder had promoted'.[11] Methodism filled the gap left by this retreat. Spearheaded by the theologian John Wesley, it developed from the 1730s as part of a broader movement of religious revivalism in England and America. Methodism also allowed for free will and universal salvation. It promoted a highly emotional form of spirituality, commonly characterized as 'heart religion'.[12]

Neither denomination had an established orthodoxy on the nature of the afterlife. Early generations of Quaker theologians seldom speculated on the topic. Robert Barclay's *Apology for the True Christian Divinity* (Latin edition 1676; English edition 1678), the 'first widely read systematic theology of Friends', criticized opponents of the Quakers for 'maliciously' claiming that 'we deny any heaven or hell, but that, which is within us'.[13] However, Barclay had little to say about the actual nature of the afterlife. He warned against 'high and curious speculations of religion' and rebuked those who 'seek to terrifie themselves from sin, by multiplying thoughts of death, hell and judgment, and by presenting to their imaginations the happyness and joyes of heaven'. Only God's Spirit could empower a human to overcome sin, so these imaginative forays had no more value than Adam's fig leaves.[14] John Wesley reflected more fully on the topic, discussing the nature of heaven and hell in sermons and published commentaries. He also advocated for the controversial doctrine of an intermediate state. The Westminster Confession professed that dead souls went directly to heaven or hell, underlining that '[b]eside these two places

10   For an introduction, see Allen R.C. – Moore R., with contributors, *The Quakers, 1656–1723: The Evolution of an Alternative Community* (University Park, PA: 2018).

11   Davies O., "Wesley's Invisible World: Witchcraft and the Temperature of Preternatural Belief", in Webster R. (ed.), *Perfecting Perfection: Essays in Honor of Henry D. Rack* (Eugene, OR: 2015) 147–172, at 149.

12   Mack P., *Heart Religion in the British Enlightenment: Gender and Emotion in Early Methodism* (Cambridge – New York, NY: 2011). See also Coffey J. (ed.), *Heart Religion: Evangelical Piety in England and Ireland, 1690–1850* (Oxford – New York, NY: 2016).

13   Dandelion P., *An Introduction to Quakerism* (Cambridge – New York, NY: 2007) 54; Barclay Robert, *An Apology for the True Christian Divinity* ([Aberdeen?]: 1678) 411.

14   Barclay, *An Apology for the True Christian Divinity* 11:10, 259–260.

for souls separated from their bodies, the Scripture acknowledgeth none'.[15] Wesley – alongside a number of Anglicans – suggested instead that dead souls travelled to heaven or hell only at the Last Judgement. In the meantime, the damned suffered torments in the realm of Hades, while the righteous reposed in Abraham's Bosom.[16] Still, Wesley professed himself unsure of the precise nature of the intermediate state: 'who can define or describe the place of spirits?' He similarly warned against 'play of the imagination' when it came to the nature of hell, considering the subject too 'awful', and reiterating a traditional Protestant exhortation: 'Let us keep to the written word'.[17] In his commentary on the Book of Revelation he likewise stressed that 'we must be content to know only, what is expressly revealed in this Book'.[18]

These cautions notwithstanding, Quakers and Methodists alike recorded dreams and visionary experiences about the afterlife. The following analysis draws primarily on source material preserved in the John Rylands Research Institute and Library, Manchester, and the Society of Friends Library in London – respectively, England's main Methodist and Quaker archival repositories.[19] Seven detailed descriptions of dreams or visions about visits to the afterlife, plus one account of a deceased woman appearing in a dream to discuss the afterlife, are held in Mary Bosanquet Fletcher's collection of Methodist manuscripts in the John Rylands Research Institute and Library. The collection covers the late eighteenth and early nineteenth centuries, and of the sources used here, those that are dated come from the second half of the eighteenth century. The visionaries are not all identifiable, but they include four women and one man. Most are from England, though there is some

---

15   "The Westminster Confession of Faith, 1646", in Tudur Jones R. – Long A. – Moore R. (eds.), *Protestant Nonconformist Texts, Vol. 1: 1550 to 1700* (Aldershot: 2007) 165–189, sec. XXXII.1, at 189.

16   See Marino B.R., *Through a Glass Darkly: The Eschatological Vision of John Wesley* (Ph.D. dissertation, Drew University: 1994) 129–161, 184–216. On the broader debate see Marshall, *Beliefs and the Dead* 188–231; Almond, *Heaven and Hell* 38–80; Prichard R.W., *The Nature of Salvation: Theological Consensus in the Episcopal Church, 1801–73* (Urbana, IL: 1997), 141–144; Spellman W.M., "Almost Final Things: Jeremy Taylor and the Dilemma of the Anglican View of the Dead Awaiting Resurrection", *Anglican and Episcopal History* 63.1 (1994) 35–50.

17   Wesley John, "Of Hell", Sermon LXXVIII in *Sermons on Several Occasions: By the Rev. John Wesley*, ed. T. Jackson, vol. 2 (London: 1825) 261–271, at 267.

18   Idem, "Human Life a Dream", Sermon CXXV in *Sermons on Several Occasions*, vol. 2, 713–720, at 716; idem, *Explanatory Notes Upon the New Testament* (London: 1755), commentary on *Revelation* 4:2, 688.

19   See the tables below for full details. Another Methodist account is extracted in Norris C.M., *Thomas Wride and Wesley's Methodist Connexion* (Abingdon – New York: 2020) 183–184.

American material transcribed by English authors. Some accounts were later published, but only one has been subject to detailed scholarly analysis.[20] John Wesley's *Arminian Magazine* published further visions of hell and the Last Judgement; most are significantly less detailed, but this chapter does draw on some accounts of hell.[21] In most cases the visionaries made explicit reference to heaven or hell. Even where they mentioned only 'a glorious place' or similar, there is no evidence that they shared Wesley's vision of an intermediate state distinct from heaven or hell. The vexed debates about the intermediate state were largely confined to theologians; Methodist laypeople, like those of other Protestant denominations, typically defaulted to the post-Reformation orthodoxy that framed heaven and hell as the only possible destinations for the dead.

The five manuscripts in the Society of Friends Library date from around the same period and were produced in England. Three describe the experiences of women and two the experiences of men. Aspects of the texts might reflect distinct religious traditions, as in the case of the Quaker woman who emphasized the plain clothes and furnishings used in heaven, but in general the Quaker accounts are closely aligned with those of the Methodists.[22] Indeed, one of the Quaker visionaries relayed their account to a Methodist preacher, knowing him to be a 'serious and religious man', and mentioned seeing a Methodist woman in heaven.[23] Most or all of the thirteen manuscripts are copies, and all likely passed between different parties. Both denominations had a rich culture of manuscript exchange, with written records of spiritual trials, conversion experiences, and divine blessings buttressing their projects of community-building.[24] At least one of the accounts was also publicly

---

20   Cope R. – Kime B. (eds.), "'The Vision': A Dream Account Collected and Preserved by Mary Bosanquet Fletcher", *Wesley and Methodist Studies* 8.1 (2016) 52–66.

21   "A Strange Account", *Arminian Magazine* 7 (March 1784) 160–162; Townroe Richard, "The Experience of Mr. Richard Townroe", *Arminian Magazine* 16 (July 1793) 381–385; Elliott Richard, "A Short Account of Mr. Richard Elliott, Preacher of the Gospel", *Arminian Magazine* 19 (December 1796) 571–577; Pipe John Sanders, "The Experience of Mr. Pipe", *Arminian Magazine* 20 (August 1797) 365–370. For discussion of the visionary material in the *Arminian Magazine*, see Iwig-O'Byrne L., *How Methodists Were Made: The* Arminian Magazine *and Spiritual Transformation in the Transatlantic World, 1778–1803* (Ph.D. dissertation, University of Texas: 2008) 82–91.

22   On the Quaker woman see below, at 263.

23   Temp MSS 58/5/25, fols. 1 r, 2 r.

24   See Winckles A.O., "'Pray for the Unworthy Scribbler': The Textual Cultures of Early Methodist Women", in King R.S. (ed.), *After Print: Eighteenth-Century Manuscript Cultures* (Charlottesville, VA: 2020) 27–51; Rosen R.M., "Copying Hannah Griffitts: Poetic

preached.[25] Even when their dates and authors cannot be confirmed, these accounts illustrate that adherents of both denominations considered detailed descriptions of the afterlife to be worth preserving and circulating.

The visionaries were likely aware of theological cautions about the difficulties of envisaging the afterlife. Assertions that elements of heaven or hell were beyond conception or description recur across the accounts. Nevertheless, their otherworldly excursions are reported in some detail. Most took place in dreams, but this does not mean that they were considered mere fantasy. In an account set down in 1789 and preserved in the Methodist archival collection, the visionary Elizabeth Haden underlined that during her journey to the afterlife, she was 'not [...] in a dream or asleep any more than I am now'.[26] In general, though, the distinction between experiences that took place while awake and while asleep was not as important as we might imagine.[27] For Methodists and Quakers alike, dreams could be divine messages. In a dream from 1760, described in a letter in 1787 and preserved in the Methodist collection, an unknown Philadelphian visionary wrote: 'I awoke with such a powerfull impression on my mind, that I cannot but think this was a vision, rather than a common Dream'.[28] Quakers were typically more cautious than Methodists in their appraisals of apparently supernatural experiences, and more inclined to censor dream accounts. However, they still allowed that dreams might be divinely inspired.[29] Both denominations typically taught that people should not speculate about the origin of their religious dreams, but instead use them as guides for how to live. If they advanced the dreamer's spiritual journey, they were probably supernatural in nature.[30] In recording and communicating their experiences, the visionaries invested both dreams and waking visions of the afterlife with spiritual import.

2   Affective Experience of the Afterlife

In recent years, the study of Christianity has been revitalized by scholars from two comparatively modern fields: the history of the body and the history of

---

Circulation and the Quaker Community of Scribes", in Tarter M.L. – Gill C. (eds.), *New Critical Studies on Early Quaker Women, 1650–1800* (Oxford – New York, NY: 2018) 167–185.

25   MAM Fl 6/6/26a.

26   MAM Fl 33/2/9 4.

27   See Rivière J., *Dreams in Early Modern England: 'Visions of the Night'* (Abingdon – New York, NY: 2017) 89–132.

28   MAM Fl 33/5/10, fol. 2 v.

29   Mack, "The Unbounded Self" 217–218, 220–221; Gerona, *Night Journeys* 28–29, 24.

30   Mack, "The Unbounded Self" 217.

emotions. Work in these areas has revealed the significance of physical and emotional experiences for early modern Protestants and Catholics alike.[31] At the same time, the physical and affective dimensions of religion were culturally conditioned, with variation over time and between different denominations. Protestant culture broadly understood conversion to be a process of inner transformation, with God's grace reworking patterns of thinking and feeling.

But orthodox contemporaries typically derided the physical manifestations of grace that earned seventeenth-century Quakers their epithet, while they criticized eighteenth-century revivalist groups as enthusiastical in their passionate or visionary experiences of the divine. Responsive to broader social pressures, eighteenth-century Quaker leaders generally taught that the godly should forbear human passions and cultivate the peace of assurance.[32] Methodist spirituality, by contrast, was associated with intense emotional fluctuation. However, both movements were explicit about the importance of the body and emotions in religious practice, with adherents expected to look inwards to detect signs of God's grace.[33]

Since heaven and hell were defined as places of (respectively) joy and misery, we might expect emotions to loom large in Quaker and Methodist accounts of the afterlife. Certainly, visionaries made some use of this framework of analysis, delineating heaven and hell through the emotions of their inhabitants. An account of the celestial journey of a man called Josiah Firth (d. Yorkshire, 1758?), communicated to the Methodist preacher John Nelson in Derbyshire in 1760, described how Firth passed through the gates of heaven and saw that all of the souls within 'appeared most glorious and happy'.[34] The anonymous author from Philadelphia met with their deceased mother, who informed them that 'the Tongue of men or angels can not discribe the inexpressable happiness of the blessed *above*'.[35] The visionaries who visited heaven seldom shared the unbounded joy of the angels and dead souls therein,

---

31   See Lindman J.M. – Tarter M.L. (eds.), *A Centre of Wonders: The Body in Early America* (Ithaca, NY – London: 2001); Lindman J.M., *Bodies of Belief: Baptist Community in Early America* (Philadelphia, PA: 2008); Karant-Nunn S.C., *The Reformation of Feeling: Shaping the Religious Emotions in Early Modern Germany* (Oxford – New York, NY: 2010); Ryrie A., *Being Protestant in Reformation Britain* (Oxford – New York, NY: 2013); McNamara R.F., "The Emotional Body in Religious Belief and Practice", in Lynch A. – Bromhall S. (eds.), *The Routledge History of Emotions in Europe, 1100–1700* (Abingdon – New York, NY: 2020) 105–118; Fischer E. – Tippelskirch X. von (eds.), *Bodies in Early Modern Religious Dissent: Naked, Veiled, Vilified, Worshiped* (Abingdon – New York, NY: 2021).

32   Eustace N., *Passion Is the Gale: Emotion, Power, and the Coming of the American Revolution* (Chapel Hill, NC: 2008) 98–101.

33   Mack, *Heart Religion*.

34   Temp MSS 58/5/25, fol. 2 r.

35   MAM Fl 33/1/13, fol. 6 r; MAM Fl 33/5/10, fol. 2 r.

but the sight of heaven did induce positive feelings. In an experience from 1772, a Yorkshire Methodist apparently called Elisaz Hunt noted of her entrance to heaven that 'I seemd all peace'.[36] A Quaker woman's dream from 1762, widely circulated and tentatively attributed to Esther Rutter, refers to emotional states particularly frequently.[37] Rutter (presuming her authorship) saw 'Composure and Sweetness', as well as 'pleasure', in the faces of those in heaven. She also witnessed 'very Sorrowful' souls being ushered to hell. Hell made Rutter feel 'Horror', 'Sorrow', and 'great Bitterness of Spirit'; it was only after waking that her 'much disturbed Mind was favoured with a Calm'.[38] For the most part, though, emotional responses to the afterlife were noted only briefly, especially in manuscript accounts and (an overlapping category) those concerned primarily with heaven rather than hell.[39]

Focusing on Anglo-American prophecy in the late eighteenth and early nineteenth centuries, Susan Juster writes that women's visions especially emphasized bodily sensation. Their descriptions of the horrors of the apocalypse were 'palpable', and they had deeply empathetic, often physical responses to Christ's suffering.[40] In comparison, our body of source material makes only brief mention of internal experiences. As Phyllis Mack explores, eighteenth-century Quakers and Methodists were relatively uninterested in the specific messages of dreams; far more significant were 'the emotions generated by the dream'.[41] The accounts we are concerned with contain little in the way of religious polemic, nor did they follow the common seventeenth-century practice of framing visionary experience as a caution for unbelievers. Several instead conclude with a statement about how the experience influenced the religious development of the visionary. In an account published in the *Arminian Magazine* in 1796, the Methodist preacher Richard Elliott described a dream about hell with the note that 'the impressions it made on my mind were both deep and lasting'.[42] In general, though, visionaries devoted significantly more space to describing the afterlife than to analysing their emotions, bodily sensations, or other personal reactions. The warnings of Barclay and Wesley

---

36   MAM Fl 33/1/13, fol. 9 v.
37   On authorship of this MS see below, at 270, note e.
38   MS Vol. S 480, 123–127. See the discussions in Eustace, *Passion is the Gale* 100–101, and Gerona, *Night Journeys* 160–164.
39   A particularly emotional printed account is Townroe, "The Experience of Mr. Richard Townroe".
40   Juster, *Doomsayers* 119.
41   Mack, "The Unbounded Self" 208.
42   Elliott, "A Short Account of Mr. Richard Elliott" 574.

notwithstanding, the project of envisaging the afterlife became itself a form of devotional practice.

3 Transfigured Bodies

The status of the soul after death was traditionally a fraught theological topic. Following the twelfth-century 'birth of purgatory', Catholic theologians were tasked with explaining how an immaterial soul could suffer the torments of purgatorial flames. The range of answers included the idea that a soul might have some measure of substance.[43] Protestant culture did not have to contend with purgatory, but as souls were not reunited with their bodies until the Last Judgement, there remained thorny questions about what form they took in the interim. This was another topic on which Quaker and Methodist theologians discouraged unnecessary speculation.[44] Writing in 1684, the Quaker evangelist Stephen Crisp listed 'the state of the soul after the death of the body' as one of various 'subtle and abstruse questions' suggested by Satan to 'amuse the minds of the simple, and to cause the weak in the faith to err'.[45] John Wesley wrote that 'the Inhabitants of [heaven] have spiritual Bodies: Yet these spiritual Bodies are also real Bodies [...] [they] take up a finite and a determinate Space'.[46] These bodies were 'purer than the unspotted Firmament, brighter than the Lustre of the Stars', and 'Endued with Vigour, Strength, and Activity, such as we cannot now conceive'.[47] When it came to the bodies of those in the intermediate state, though, Wesley was uncertain: 'We cannot tell, indeed, how we shall then exist or what kind of organs we shall have: the soul will not be encumbered with flesh and blood; but probably it will have some sort of ethereal vehicle, even before God clothes us "with our nobler house of empyrean light"'.[48]

---

43   See Mowbray D., *Pain and Suffering in Medieval Theology: Academic Debates at the University of Paris in the Thirteenth Century* (Woodbridge: 2009) 104–130.

44   Early generations of Quaker theologians did engage in extensive and fraught debates about the nature of Christ's body. See Pennington M., *Quakers, Christ, and the Enlightenment* (Oxford: 2021), esp. 135–159.

45   Crisp Stephen, *A Faithful Warning and Exhortation to Friends to Beware of Seducing Spirits* (London: 1684) 13.

46   Wesley, *Explanatory Notes Upon the New Testament*, commentary on *Revelation* 21:15, at 752.

47   Ibidem, commentary on *Philippians* 3:21, at 532; commentary on 1 *Corinthians* 15:43, at 462.

48   Idem, *The Letters of the Rev. John Wesley, A.M.*, ed. J. Telford, vol. 6 (London: 1931), letter to Mary Bishop April 17 1776, at 214.

In describing visits to the afterlife, visionaries had to dip their toes into these troubled theological waters. In 2 *Corinthians* 12, Paul records a visionary journey to the third heaven, a realm of paradise in early Christianity. He notes that his visit took place 'whether in the body, I cannot tell: God knoweth'.[49] But the visionaries generally departed from this scriptural precedent, portraying themselves as clearly separated from their earthly bodies. Commonly, visionaries were in a state of bodily ill-health or weakness immediately prior to the vision. The journey to the afterlife came as a release for the soul, while the body remained in a deathlike state. Another anonymous account preserved in the Methodist collections is labelled 'The Dream of the Crowns', because the visionary in heaven looked down on saints on earth – that is, those who were faithful to Christ – who wore crowns of varying levels of brightness. The visionary prefaced their experience with the explanation that 'I dreamed I was sitting in a Chair, and was going to die, every vein and nerve, seemed to give up their life to Him, who gave it'. Jesus then appeared, and 'my spirit instantly left the body'.[50] The Methodist Mary Matthews (ca. 1713–1788) from Madeley, Shropshire, described a vision that occurred when she was 'old and feeble'. She declared that 'I lost all sence of outward things and found my self as stript of this old clay body'.[51] The idea that the body was a clay prison for the soul was a familiar Christian trope, but various scholars have argued that there was a change in emphasis in the eighteenth century. Earlier generations had typically understood the human body as a porous construction, readily penetrated – and potentially engulfed – by the Holy Spirit. In the eighteenth century, changes in medical theory and practice pre-empted a cultural shift towards envisaging the body instead as a hermetically sealed, self-regulating entity. Against this backdrop, visionaries placed less stress on how the Holy Spirit could illuminate the soul within the body, focusing instead on escaping corporeal boundaries.[52]

The early modern body was responsible for relaying information about the external environment to the soul, with the senses serving as 'the links between the inner and the outer worlds'.[53] But humans also possessed spiritual senses.

---

49   KJV.

50   MAM Fl 33/5/6, fol. 1 r.

51   MAM Fl 33/3/11, fol. 2 r.

52   Mack P., "Religious Dissenters in Enlightenment England", *History Workshop Journal* 49 (1999) 1–23; Juster, *Doomsayers* 96–133; Lindman, *Bodies of Belief* 63–64. For broader discussions of the eighteenth-century shift from porous to bounded bodies, see especially Taylor C., *A Secular Age* (Cambridge, MA: 2007) 35–41, 300–302.

53   De Boer W. – Göttler C., "Introduction: The Sacred and the Senses in an Age of Reform", in idem (eds.), *Religion and the Senses in Early Modern Europe* (Leiden – Boston, MA: 2013) 1–13, at 2–3.

In a discussion of early modern Protestant conversion narratives, Abigail Shinn underlines how the soul could – in the absence of the body – become a 'locus for sensory perception'.[54] Barclay urged his readers to become acquainted with the 'Heavenly voice in thy heart', after which they would be reborn able to 'see, feel, tast[e], handle, and smell the things of the Spirit'.[55] Spiritual senses were more widely discussed in the context of the eighteenth-century evangelical movement. In a bid to avoid accusations of enthusiasm, revivalist leaders commonly taught that visions were experienced internally with the 'eye of Faith', rather than through the bodily senses.[56] The theory of spiritual senses allowed the soul to experience the afterlife fully prior to reunion with the body at the Last Judgement. Wesley suggested that the 'lower' senses of touch, smell, and taste ended with death. However, sight and hearing existed 'in a far greater degree, in a more eminent manner than now', with the soul becoming 'all eye, all ear, all sense, in a manner we cannot yet conceive'.[57] While visionaries did not suggest that the mechanics of seeing or hearing had fundamentally changed, they did describe deeply affecting visual and auditory experiences: glory that beamed excessively brightly and voices of surpassing sweetness were typical examples.[58]

When it came to form and movement, there was scope to explore more fully the ways in which a disembodied soul was unlike a fleshy body. Several visionaries stressed that their new forms were light, fast-moving, and insubstantial. Mary Matthews wrote that 'I appeard to my self so light I could have gone ten thousand mile in a moment'.[59] At the same time, envisaging a form without the solidity of flesh was challenging, and visionaries sometimes ascribed a degree of materiality to their souls. One male visionary whose account was preserved in the Methodist collection described being confined to his bed with pleurisy. When an angel appeared and invited him on a journey, he replied 'how can you ask me? do you not see how ill I am? scarce able to stir, or move in my Bed'. He then found himself leaving the body and passing 'like a Vapor, or smoak [...] thro' the wall or Cieling!' However, he retained enough physicality that

54 Shinn A., "The Senses and the Seventeenth-Century English Conversion Narrative", in Macdonald R. – Murphy E.K.M. – Swann E.L. (eds.), *Sensing the Sacred in Medieval and Early Modern Culture* (Abingdon – New York, NY: 2018) 99–116, at 104.

55 Barclay, *An Apology for the True Christian Divinity* 2:16, 40.

56 See Juster, *Doomsayers* 115–116; Taves, *Fits, Trances, and Visions* 47–75; Schmidt L.E., *Holy Fairs: Scotland and the Making of American Revivalism*, 2nd ed. (Grand Rapids, MI: 2001) 145–153, esp. 148.

57 Wesley, "The Good Steward", Sermon LI in *Sermons on Several Occasions*, vol. 1, 636–648, at 641.

58 See below, at 260–261.

59 MAM Fl 33/3/11, fol. 2 v.

his guide later 'seizd' him by the hand and "dragg'd" him'.[60] The Bristol Quaker Joseph Fry (1728–1787), who experienced an elaborate celestial journey in 1776, noted that those on the road to heaven did not feel the cold, nor any gravitational pull towards earth. A 'bulky' friend of his who needed a staff to walk found himself newly nimble, and promptly hurled the staff away. But their journey was still marked by seemingly physical challenges. Moving in a party of people, they arrived at a set of steep stone steps. The men gave their hands to the women, and they proceeded 'with great care'. A heavenly guide later gave his hand to each traveller in turn.[61] Here we see how the supposedly nimble disembodied soul might teeter in the manner of a fleshy body, while the social obligations conferred by sexed bodies reasserted themselves.

Another anonymous account in the Methodist collection similarly explored the physicality of the soul in heaven. The account was penned by an individual who used the celestial journey to explore the paradise reserved for 'the Indian Nations' (the indigenous peoples of America), who 'knew nothing of their fallen state, nor of their Redeemer'.[62] The author described the beginning of their vision as follows: 'a weakness seized my whole Frame as if I was going to Expire I strove to stir but could not Instantly my spirit seemed to leave my Body'. A guardian angel conducted the visionary to heaven, where the pair 'glided along without the labour of moving our Feet'. However, the visionary soon felt a 'want of Rest'. The angel led them to a shady bower where they sat down for a time, until the angel declared 'do not suppose you are come here to be Idle'.[63] In this case, the visionary's disembodied spirit seemed subject to a distinctly physical weariness. For all that they emphasized the separation of body and soul, many visionaries continued to envisage bodily constraints or a sense of solidity in the afterlife, exemplifying the difficulties of depicting a mode of being beyond human experience.

Christ, angels, and dead souls were at a greater step of remove from earthly life. Descriptions of Christ and angels emphasized their transcendental qualities, but also tended to be formulaic, focusing overwhelmingly on radiance. The Yorkshire Methodist Elizabeth Dickinson (1773–1793) found that 'The Glory that beamed from [Christ] was so great, she could not bear to behold it', while the Liverpool Quaker Ann Kenyon had a vision of angels with faces

60   MAM Fl 33/5/8, fols. 1 v, 2 r.

61   Temp MSS 302/1/5, fols. 1 r–1 v, 5 v, 6 v.

62   The Quaker William Penn had a similar theory about divisions in the afterlife. See Endy M.B., "William Penn's Contributions to Early Quaker Thought", in Angell S.W. – Dandelion P. (eds.), *Early Quakers and Their Theological Thought 1647–1723* (Cambridge – New York, NY: 2015) 239–255, at 248–252.

63   MAM Fl 33/5/12, fol. 1 r.

as bright 'as the Sun shining in it's [sic] full Strength'.[64] Usually angels took male forms, though Kenyon did see a female angel, which convinced her that women might permissibly preach.[65] Several visionaries also noted the beauty of heavenly voices; Dickinson heard a song by the 'blessed company before the Throne' that was 'so divine and heavenly; language fails to paint either the sweetness, or harmony of their voices'.[66] Devils featured less frequently than angels, but their separation from mortals might similarly be conveyed through references to inhuman bodies: the printed account of a 1783 vision by John Taylor of Bewdley, Worcestershire (b. ca. 1760), recalls how devils appeared 'like bears, lions, and other wild beasts'.[67] Kenyon's female angel excepted, visionaries generally stuck to culturally established modes of conveying the nature of Christ, angels, and devils.

Seventeenth- and eighteenth-century theologians were divided over the question of whether dead souls would look as they had on earth.[68] Colleen McDannell and Bernhard Lang argue that while Renaissance depictions of heaven foregrounded sensual pleasure, seventeenth-century Protestants and Catholics favoured a 'theocentric' model whereby the joy of heaven stemmed solely from the divine presence.[69] In the mid eighteenth century, the visionary writings of Emmanuel Swedenborg birthed a 'modern' conception of heaven in which love for humans took precedence over love for God.[70] The Methodist and Quaker accounts do not go that far; heaven continued to be first and foremost about divine worship. However, it was common for visionaries to describe joyous meetings with family members or friends. These individuals were usually transformed, but not beyond the point of being recognizable. Again, brightness was a common theme. Elisaz Hunt saw her sister, who 'appeard very bright', as well as the Methodists Paul Greenwood (d. 1767) and the aforementioned John Nelson (d. 1774). The face of the former was 'like a beam of the sun'.[71] Similarly, the visionary who had the 'Dream of the Crowns' described seeing the minister William Brammah (d. 1780), who 'shone with

---

64   MAM Fl 6/6/26a, fol. 1 r; MS Vol. S 480 137.
65   MS Vol. S 480 137–138.
66   MAM Fl 6/6/26a, fol. 1 v.
67   "A Strange Account" 162.
68   Almond, *Heaven and Hell* 100–105.
69   McDannell C. – Lang B., *Heaven: A History*, 2nd ed. (New Haven, CT – London: 2001) 145–180.
70   Ibidem 181–227.
71   MAM Fl 33/1/13, fol. 9 v. Nelson was still alive at the time of the vision (he recorded an account of it, though omitting his own presence – see table below), so the sighting of him may have been meant as prophecy.

such lustre, that my eyes could scarce behold him'.[72] Dead souls might be pure to different degrees; Hunt wrote that 'some appeard much brighter then others'.[73] The more marked contrast was with wicked souls, who were associated with darkness and hellfire. Esther Rutter described a procession of sinners who smelled strongly of brimstone. She noted that 'there appeared a Blackness in every Face'. More nightmarish was a 'very fine Person' who, on closer inspection, had flames emanating from her eyelids.[74]

Visionaries sought to portray dead souls as simultaneously familiar and fundamentally transformed. Mary Matthews described meeting a much-loved minister who had 'such a resemblence of his former self th[a]t I shd have known him among a thousand'. He smiled and reached out a hand to her, but his body 'was not like flesh and blood'. Matthews wrote: 'I dont know how to discribe it it was all Light and white, I never seen any thing like it to discribe it by but it was very beautifull'.[75] Some adopted an idea propounded by the Lutheran theologian Jakob Böhme, who was influential especially among early generations of Quakers.[76] Böhme suggested that 'the paradisiacal man is clear like transparent glass, and [...] fully penetrated by the light of the divine sun'.[77] The anonymous visionary who wrote of the afterlife of the 'Indian Nations' described meeting former acquaintances who took human shapes, but had bodies 'Clear as the most fine Glass and without the sound of Voice'.[78] John Taylor likewise saw in heaven 'transparent persons, very beautiful and glorious'.[79] Most strikingly, Esther Rutter witnessed lustrous people with sweet, composed countenances whom she initially imagined were Quakers meeting together. On closer inspection, she realized one respect in which the figures were wholly unfamiliar: 'I [...] looked to see if I could distinguish Men from Women but could not'.[80] Portrayals of dead souls mirrored portrayals of angels in that the soul's purity was expressed by its outer form, but they also offered more experimental reconceptualizations of the human body: skin became

---

72   MAM Fl 33/5/6, fol. 1 v.

73   MAM Fl 33/1/13, fol. 9 v.

74   MS Vol. S 480 124, 125.

75   MAM Fl 33/3/11, fol. 2 v.

76   See Spencer C.D., "James Nayler and Jacob Boehme's *The Way to Christ*", in Kershner J.R. (ed.), *Quakers and Mysticism: Comparative and Syncretic Approaches to Spirituality* (Cham: 2019) 43–62.

77   Böhme Jakob, *The Signature of All Things: With Other Writings*, ed. C. Bax, trans. John Ellistone (London – New York, NY: 1912) ch. 11:51, 141.

78   MAM Fl 33/5/12, fol. 1 r.

79   "A Strange Account" 162.

80   MS Vol. S 480 123.

glasslike, blood and bones and sinews morphed into outpourings of light, and sexed features melted away.

In the sensuous heaven that was popular during the Renaissance, nudity was not uncommon.[81] With the shift to a theocentric heaven, modesty prevailed. All the same, visionaries made it clear that clothing in the afterlife was unlike clothing on earth. Generally, angels and dead souls in heaven wore shirts or robes 'white as snow', with girdles, and bare feet.[82] The anonymous man with pleurisy described in detail the clothing of the angel who guided him to heaven:

> he was cloath'd in a dazzling, white Linnen or Cambrick Robe, with a girdle of a beautiful, twill'd, holland tape was bound, about his breast, and tied before in a Beau knot. Another girt his waist in the same manner, and he had over his tight Bodic'd Coat, a looser Garment, the Delicacy of the Workmanship caught my Attention, such Cloth – such fine thread – such exquisite wrought button holes, I cd not conceive.[83]

The 'exquisite wrought button holes' are a wonderful example of how earthly things were embellished to convey the nature of heaven.

Other visionaries again relied heavily on the imagery of effulgence. Josiah Firth dreamt that he travelled through a field full of noxious weeds before coming to a high wall. There was a hole in the wall, so small that he was obliged to strip before passing through. He then found himself 'immediately clothed, but his garments were so bright and glorious that he was almost afraid to look at them'.[84] Ann Kenyon similarly saw angels dressed in white robes that were 'Glittering exceedingly as if they were set with precious Stones'.[85] But Quakerism taught that clothing ought to be simple, and Esther Rutter was more critical of ostentatious garb. She described how 'a number of Persons Richly dressed passed by, they smelled so strong of Brimstone that I was almost Suffocated'. Later she saw a figure in hell 'grandly Dressed and Powdered'. The saints, in contrast, wore plain robes.[86] Clothing reflected the state of the soul – and seemingly influenced it. Joseph Fry reported that his clothes were set alight by angels while he was on the road to heaven. The clothing flared

---

81   See McDannell – Lang, *Heaven* 111–144, esp. 122–123, 125, 137–140, 143.
82   'White as snow' from MAM Fl 33/1/13, fol. 2 v.
83   MAM Fl 33/5/8, fol. 1 v.
84   Temp MSS 58/5/25, fol. 1 v.
85   MS Vol. S 480 137.
86   Ibidem 124, 125, 123.

into nothing without his coming to harm, and he was freshly clad in a white linen vest and a 'robe with a golden girdle'. After donning this outfit, he became 'very pleasant and nimble'.[87] *Vestis virum facit*, or 'clothes make the man', was a maxim recorded by Desiderius Erasmus in the early sixteenth century, but here the clothing seemed to have a power beyond the proverbial.[88]

In their portrayals of physical and affective states in the afterlife, Methodist and Quaker visionaries defied cautions about the impossibility of conceptualizing heaven and hell. Reinvented humans were simultaneously familiar and unfamiliar. The soul left the casing of the body and gained new powers of movement, yet retained some of the qualities of flesh. The forms of dead souls remained human-like, but might be transparent or transfigured by light. Clothing took on a mystical quality, translating and potentially transforming the soul it swaddled. The emotional experience of heaven or hell was relatively understated. Some visionaries did outline their emotional reactions, and the emotional after-effects of the experience took on especial significance in both Quaker and Methodist cultures. However, the richness of these accounts lies primarily in their imaginative explorations of transformed bodies and environments. Although Quakers and Methodists are rightly associated with an inward-looking form of religious practice, transcendental spiritual experiences could also revolve around beautifully fashioned buttonholes.

4   The Environment of Heaven and Hell

When it came to envisaging the scenery of heaven and hell, Scripture offered some hints: *Revelation* 21 and 22 describe heaven as a city full of light, and hell as a 'lake of fire'. But theologians struggled to determine how literally to read Revelation's often cryptic pronouncements. The Quaker founder George Fox considered the heavenly city a metaphor for a community of believers: 'all who are within the light of Christ [...] are members of this city'.[89] John Wesley did not go this far, but in his commentary on Revelation he urged the need for 'a deep Reverence' and 'spiritual Wisdom' when interpreting statements about heaven, 'that we may neither understand them too literally and grossly, nor go too far from the natural Force of the Words'. He suggested that the city was 'an Abode distinct from its Inhabitants; and proportioned to them

---

87   Temp MSS 302/1/5, fols. 5 r–5 v.

88   Erasmus Desiderius, *Adages* III.i.60, reproduced in Barker W. (ed.), *The Adages of Erasmus* (Toronto: 2001) 240.

89   Fox George, *The Journal of George Fox*, ed. J.L. Nickalls (Cambridge – New York, NY: 1952) 575.

who take up a finite and a determinate Space'. However, 'The Gold, the Pearls, the precious Stones, the Walls, Foundations, Gates, are undoubtedly figurative Expressions'.[90] Some visionaries may have intended their descriptions of elaborate gardens or glittering cities to be read allegorically: dreams that functioned as social commentary were a tradition in Quakerism especially.[91] Whether they desired their accounts to be read literally or figuratively, the visionaries implied that reflecting on transcendental environments was a valid means of spiritual progression.

The geographical features typically described by the visionaries – buildings, cities, gardens, pathways, ravines – could be found on earth. At the same time, visionaries portrayed disorienting infusions of sublime lighting, cities with inhumanly perfect walls, and dreamlike time-warps. Hell was associated with darkness, pits, fire, storms, and the anguished screams of the damned. Elements of the natural world were subject to nightmarish transformations; Richard Elliott described a 'boundless region of burning sand, agitated with eternal storms'.[92] In general, though, the more elaborate descriptions were reserved for heaven. In line with earlier depictions, heaven was typically framed as either Revelation's city of light or a garden mirroring the earthly paradise of Eden.[93] It was associated with beauty, joyful music, elevation, and the light that emanated from the divine presence. Joseph Fry described a building 'of white transparent marble [...] admitting light every way, without any appearance of windows'.[94] Ann Kenyon explained that 'I beheld a Glorious City whose walls exceeded the polished Gold, the Gates thereof appeared to be precious Pearls; it had no need of the Sun to enlighten it, for the Lamb dwelt therein, who was the Light thereof'.[95] Some visionaries endeavoured to convey the extraordinary qualities of this light. The visionary who wrote of the afterlife of the 'Indian Nations' said of the Christian heaven: 'The Light was White like that of silver, exceeding clear, but not dazzling'.[96] The Methodist man with pleurisy explained that 'The air had a sweet clear Light infinitely surpassing that of the Sun, moon, or Stars – But yet of a mildness transportingly clear'.[97]

As well as being beautiful, heaven was extremely regular and orderly – a stark contrast with the dirty and chaotic urban centres of eighteenth-century

---

90   Wesley, *Explanatory Notes Upon the New Testament*, commentary on *Revelation* 21:15, 752.
91   See Gerona, *Night Journeys* 3–8.
92   Elliott, "A Short Account of Mr. Richard Elliott" 573; recalls *Revelation* 20:14.
93   McGrath A.E., *A Brief History of Heaven* (Malden, MA: 2003) 11–12, 18–19.
94   Temp MSS 302/1/5, fol. 3 v.
95   MS Vol. S 480 139.
96   MAM Fl 33/5/12, fol. 1 r.
97   MAM Fl 33/5/8, fol. 2 r.

England.[98] The man with pleurisy found that 'the whole city was all of one, undivided piece of stone, spoken at once into Being, order, and beauty, by the great Creator of all things'.[99] The visionary who described the heaven of the 'Indian Nations' wrote of the Christian heaven: 'I could not pretend to describe the beauty and Order of this place it so far transcends all human Ideas'. The lands set aside for indigenous Americans were similarly beautiful, but 'seem'd to want pruning and dressing'; it was only the Christian paradise that reached transcendent levels of order.[100] While some visionaries spoke of golden gates and jewelled walls, others found heavenly perfection in austerity. Esther Rutter described a white, bright house 'like the reflection of the Sun'. Even furniture was dispensed with; Rutter was perplexed to see people apparently seated, but without any obvious supports. Meanwhile, a room on the road to hell 'appeared grandly wainscoted and beautifully Painted with different Colours'.[101]

The Quaker Joseph Fry's journey to heaven was in the tradition of John Bunyan's 1678 allegory *The Pilgrim's Progress*: Fry passed through various settings that reflected and critiqued human folly. He came to first 'a large gothic building, a little like a cathedral, very heavy, and almost darkened with abundance of carved ornaments, the shape and distinction of which were very much defaced, by the repetition of white wash, upon them, to keep them clean'. The place had 'vast extensive rooms, as large as Westminster-hall'. He wondered if he had come to the house of God, but soon determined he had not, noting 'the slovenly way they had taken of cleaning the inside, by such quantities of white-wash'.[102] Like Rutter, Fry disparaged human notions of grandeur. He was similarly dismissive of 'a large pleasure-garden belonging to the society of this spacious edifice; decorated at vast expense, with grottoes and artificial flowers of an enormous size; but nothing either natural or beautiful among them'. Later on his road to heaven, though, he passed through 'a most beautiful garden, in which were trees and flowers, surprizingly magnificent, inexpressibly various, and altogether beyond what I could have had any conception of in nature'. Fry found himself 'as much convinced that every production in this garden was the immediate work of Infinite Wisdom; as I had been before, that the paltry pleasure-garden [...] was planned and executed by mere human contrivance'.[103] By discussing sublime landscapes in relation

---

98   On the parallels between hell and eighteenth-century urban environments, see Almond, *Heaven and Hell* 81–82.
99   MAM Fl 33/5/8, fol. 2 v.
100   MAM Fl 33/5/12, fol. 1 r.
101   MS Vol. S 480 123–124.
102   Temp MSS 302/1/5, fols. 1 v–2 r.
103   Ibidem, fols. 2 r–2 v.

to earth-like counterparts, visionaries provided scaffolding for the imaginative labour of envisaging the afterlife.

Finally, time might work differently in the afterlife. Analysing medieval visions of heaven and hell, Eileen Gardiner highlights the recurring sense that 'the visionary has entered a time warp'.[104] In the accounts considered here, there is some suggestion that visionaries' understanding of time might be distorted. John Taylor reported that he seemed to be in hell for five or six years; in fact, his vision lasted less than two days.[105] Heaven, meanwhile, was a place where present and future might conflate – thus Elisaz Hunt saw both deceased and living acquaintances in heaven.[106] The passage of time might also be measured by different metrics. The visionary who wrote of the heaven prepared for the 'Indian Nations' found that angels had their own version of human timespans: when they referenced periods of weeks or months, they were careful to explain that they meant angels' weeks and angels' months.[107] In general, however, the dimension of time remains little explored in the accounts. This perhaps indicates the purpose of the texts: the visionaries sought not to conceptualize every aspect of the afterlife, but rather to construct scenes of supernatural glory and terror that might serve as devotional aids.

5   Conclusion

Methodist and Quaker visions offer fascinating insight into how and why laypeople envisaged the afterlife. While the nature of heaven and hell was theoretically beyond human conception, visionaries offered richly detailed reflections on the ways in which people and environments might be transfigured. Bodies became newly light, nimble, or even transparent; faces glowed with divine illumination or burned with hellfire. Clothing expressed and perhaps influenced the state of the soul. Buildings, gardens, and lakes were infused with either heavenly resplendence or hellish decay. However, the afterlife retained familiar elements. Bodies were typically identifiable and continued to have physical limitations. Clothing took recognizable forms, even featuring worldly accessories like buttonholes (albeit exquisite ones). Earthly landscapes were upgraded

---

104   Gardiner E., "Sensory Experience in Visions of Heaven and Hell", paper delivered at International Medieval Congress, University of Leeds (2018), https://www.academia.edu /37218953/Sensory_Experience_in_Visions_of_Heaven_and_Hell (accessed 23.01.2023) 17.

105   "A Strange Account" 162.

106   See above, n. 71.

107   MAM Fl 33/5/12, fols. 1 v–2 r.

rather than reconstrued. Thus, the visionaries sought to render the afterlife imaginable and comprehensible. They did not attempt to address every possible theological conundrum, but rather to paint vivid scenes that might inspire spiritual progression. Quaker and Methodist theologians cautioned against speculating on divine mysteries, instead urging followers to focus their devotional practice on the internal operations of the Spirit. Nevertheless, the preservation and circulation of visionary accounts suggests that wider spiritual communities considered heaven and hell to be valid objects of religious reflection. Despite (or because of) its enigmas, the afterlife persistently exerted a powerful hold over early modern Christian imaginations.

Manuscripts in the John Rylands Research Institute and Library, Manchester

Shelfmark	Visionary	Transcriber / copyist	Date / place of vision	Date / place of original MS	Date / place of copy	Extent	Content
MAM Fl 6/6/26a[a]	Elizabeth Dickinson (1773–1793)	Elizabeth Ritchie (1754–1835)	27 Aug. 1792, Yorkshire	13 Sep. 1793, Otley	N/A	ca. 1250 words	Visit to heaven and hell
MAM Fl 33/1/13[b]	Inhabitant of Bethlehem, Pennsylvania (child of Mary Atwood)	Sarah 'Sally' Lawrence (1759–1800)	Sep. 1760, Bethlehem, Pennsylvania	Sent Sep. 1787 from Philadelphia	18th c., Leytonstone?	ca. 900 words	Visionary is visited by the spirit of their deceased mother, who talks about heaven
MAM Fl 33/1/13[c]	Elisaz Hunt[d]	Sarah 'Sally' Lawrence (1759–1800)	5 Sep. 1772, Hanging Heaton?[e]	18th c.	18th c., Leytonstone?	ca. 900 words	Visit to heaven and hell

---

a   Extracts are published in Lloyd G., "Repression and Resistance: Wesleyan Female Public Ministry in the Gener- After 1791", *Proceedings of the Wesley Historical Society* 55 (2005) 101–114, at 108–109. A full version is given at "Descri of GB 133 MAM/FL/6/6/26A", *Archives Hub*, https://archiveshub.jisc.ac.uk/data/gb133-mam/fl/mam/fl/6/6 (accessed 25.01.2022).

b   There is a published version at "An Account of a Dream, Written by an Inhabitant of Bethlehem, in Pensylv *Methodist Magazine* 35 (October 1812) 761–763.

c   There is a brief summary of the account in Nelson John, "The Remains of John Nelson: Fragment Third", *Arm Magazine* 9 (May 1786) 256–257.

d   This seems to be the name given; Elisas and Elisar are also possible readings. The Nelson account above give first initial as S.

e   Place as given in Nelson, "The Remains of John Nelson".

Manuscripts in the John Rylands Research Institute and Library, Manchester (*cont.*)

Shelfmark	Visionary	Transcriber / copyist	Date / place of vision	Date / place of original MS	Date / place of copy	Extent	Content
MAM Fl 33/3/11	Mary Mat[t]hews (ca. 1713–1788)	Mary Bosanquet Fletcher (1739–1815)	18th c., Madeley	18th c.	Leytonstone?	ca. 1150 words	Visit to 'a glorious place' where Jesus presided on a throne[f]
MAM Fl 33/3/12	Mary Mat[t]hews (ca. 1713–1788)	Mary Bosanquet Fletcher (1739–1815)	18th c., Madeley	18th c.	Leytonstone?	ca. 650 words	Rough/ shorter version of MAM Fl 33/3/11
MAM Fl 33/2/9	Elizabeth Haden	?	18th c., England[g]	10 Feb. 1789, London	?	ca. 2900 words	Visit to a realm peopled with angels
MAM Fl 33/5/6	?	?	18th c., Yorkshire or Lincolnshire?[h]	?	?	ca. 450 words	Visit to heaven. 'Dream of the Crowns'
MAM Fl 33/5/8	Unknown male	?	18th c.?	18th c.?	?	ca. 950 words	Visit to heaven
MAM Fl 33/5/10	Inhabitant of Bethlehem, Pennsylvania	?	Sep. 1760, Bethlehem, Pennsylvania	Sent Sep. 1787 from Philadelphia	?	ca. 1000 words	Another version of MAM FL 33/1/13, with some differences
MAM Fl 33/5/12[i]	?	?	18th c., America?	18th c., America?	?	ca. 1550 words	Visit to paradise

f Quotation at fol. 2 v.
g Haden was born in New England but returned to England aged 5.
h Based on the preaching circuits of two ministers named in the account, William Brammah and John Shaw.
i The published version is Cope – Kime (eds.), "'The Vision'".

Manuscripts in the Library of the Society of Friends, London

Shelfmark	Visionary	Transcriber / copyist	Date / place of vision	Date / place of original MS	Date / place of copy	Extent	Content
Temp MSS 58/5/25	Josiah Firth (d. 1758?)[a]	John Nelson (ca. 1707–1774), George Harrison (1747–1827)	1750s?, Yorkshire?	Told in 1760, Derbyshire	22 Jan. 1833, Darlington	ca. 1350 words	Visit to heaven and hell
Temp MSS 302/1/5	Joseph Fry (1728–1787)[b]	?	26 Dec. 1776, Bristol	18th c., Bristol?	?	ca. 3000 words	Visit to paradise ('that ultimate, permanent rest, that is prepared for the people of God')[c]
MS Vol. S 480, pp. 123–7[d]	Esther Rutter?[e]	Richard Pike of Lurgan, Ireland (1748–1810)	30 Oct. 1762	18th c.	Lurgan	ca. 1450 words	Visit to heaven and hell
MS Vol. S 480, pp. 137–9	Ann Kenyon	Richard Pike of Lurgan, Ireland (1748–1810)	18th c., Liverpool	18th c.	Lurgan	ca. 650 words	Vision of angels
MS Vol. S 480, pp. 139–40	Ann Kenyon	Richard Pike of Lurgan, Ireland (1748–1810)	18th c., Liverpool	18th c.	Lurgan	ca. 300 words	Visit to 'the Blessed Regions above'[f]

a A Josiah Firth was buried in Rotherham, Yorkshire, in 1758. "England, Yorkshire, Bishop's Transcripts, 1547–1957", viewed on *FamilySearch*, https://www.familysearch.org/ark:/61903/1:1:68ZD-WJJT (accessed 25.01.2022).

b There is another version, from a MS transcribed by Joseph Fry's grandson Richard Fry in 1832, at *The Journal of the Friends Historical Society* 17.2 (1920) 49–58. See this text for identification of the author and notes on other versions.

c Quotation at fol. 6 v.

d There are published versions at "Anecdotes of Thomas Scattergood and His Times", *The British Friend* 12 (December 1850) 293–294, and "A Remarkable Dream of Mrs M*****", *The Intellectual Repository and New Jerusalem Magazine* 60 (November 1839) 651–654. See Eustace, *Passion of the Gale*, 100–101 and 517 n. 81 for more versions.

e A note at the end of the MS states 'It is supposed to be Esther Rutter of Bristol that had this dream'. The version in "Anecdotes of Thomas Scattergood and His Times" gives the author as Hester Moxie, and states that the dream is also erroneously attributed to Catharine Phillips. Gerona notes that Esther Moxham (born Esther Rutter in Bristol, 1730), Esther Moxson, Hester Moxie, Mary Peasley, and Catherine Phillips were all given as candidates, and suggests that Hester Moxie and Esther Moxson may have had similar dreams, making the account a 'collective' creation (Gerona, *Night Journeys* 163–164).

f Quotation at 139.

Bibliography

Printed Primary Sources

"A Remarkable Dream of Mrs M*****", *The Intellectual Repository and New Jerusalem Magazine* 60 (November 1839) 651–654.

"A Strange Account", *Arminian Magazine* 7 (March 1784) 160–162.

"An Account of a Dream, Written by an Inhabitant of Bethlehem, in Pensylvania", *Methodist Magazine* 35 (October 1812) 761–763.

"Anecdotes of Thomas Scattergood and His Times", *The British Friend* 12 (December 1850) 293–294.

Barclay Robert, *An Apology for the True Christian Divinity* ([Aberdeen?]: 1678).

Böhme Jakob, *The Signature of All Things: With Other Writings*, ed. C. Bax, trans. John Ellistone (London – New York, NY: 1912).

Cope R. – Kime B. (eds.), "'The Vision': A Dream Account Collected and Preserved by Mary Bosanquet Fletcher", *Wesley and Methodist Studies* 8.1 (2016) 52–66.

Crisp Stephen, *A Faithful Warning and Exhortation to Friends to Beware of Seducing Spirits* (London: 1684).

Elliott Richard, "A Short Account of Mr. Richard Elliott, Preacher of the Gospel", *Arminian Magazine* 19 (December 1796) 571–577.

Erasmus Desiderius, *The Adages of Erasmus*, ed. W. Barker (Toronto: 2001).

Fox George, *The Journal of George Fox*, ed. J.L. Nickalls (Cambridge – New York, NY: 1952).

Fry Joseph, "A Vision", *The Journal of the Friends Historical Society* 17.2 (1920) 49–58.

Gardiner E. (ed.), *Visions of Heaven and Hell before Dante* (New York, NY: 1989).

Nelson John, "The Remains of John Nelson: Fragment Third", *Arminian Magazine* 9 (May 1786) 256–257.

Pipe John Sanders, "The Experience of Mr. Pipe", *Arminian Magazine* 20 (August 1797) 365–370.

Pollard R.M. (ed.), *Imagining the Medieval Afterlife* (Cambridge – New York, NY: 2020).

Townroe Richard, "The Experience of Mr. Richard Townroe", *Arminian Magazine* 16 (July 1793) 381–385.

Wesley John, *Explanatory Notes Upon the New Testament* (London: 1755).

Wesley John, *The Letters of the Rev John Wesley, A.M.*, ed. J. Telford, 8 vols. (London: 1931).

Wesley John, *Sermons on Several Occasions: By the Rev. John Wesley*, ed. T. Jackson, 2 vols. (London: 1825).

"The Westminster Confession of Faith, 1646", in Tudur Jones R. – Long A. – Moore R. (eds.) *Protestant Nonconformist Texts, Vol. 1: 1550 to 1700* (Aldershot: 2007) 165–189.

Databases

Archives Hub (Jisc) https://archiveshub.jisc.ac.uk.

British Periodicals (ProQuest: 2022) https://www.proquest.com/britishperiodicals.

FamilySearch (The Church of Jesus Christ of Latter-day Saints: 2022) https://www
.familysearch.org.

Secondary Sources

Adams G.W., *Visions in Late Medieval England: Lay Spirituality and Sacred Glimpses of the Hidden Worlds of Faith* (Leiden – Boston, MA: 2007).

Allen R.C. – Moore R., with contributors, *The Quakers, 1656–1723: The Evolution of an Alternative Community* (University Park, PA: 2018).

Almond P.C., *Heaven and Hell in Enlightenment England* (Cambridge – New York, NY: 1994).

Almond P.C., *Afterlife: A History of Life after Death* (Ithaca, NY – London: 2016).

Bouldin E., *Women Prophets and Radical Protestantism in the British Atlantic World, 1640–1730* (Cambridge – New York, NY: 2015).

Brekus C.A., *Strangers and Pilgrims: Female Preaching in America, 1740–1845* (Chapel Hill, NC: 1998).

Coffey J. (ed.), *Heart Religion: Evangelical Piety in England and Ireland, 1690–1850* (Oxford – New York, NY: 2016).

Dandelion P., *An Introduction to Quakerism* (Cambridge – New York, NY: 2007).

Davies O., "Methodism, the Clergy, and the Popular Belief in Witchcraft and Magic", *History* 82.226 (2002) 252–265.

Davies O., "Wesley's Invisible World: Witchcraft and the Temperature of Preternatural Belief", in Webster R. (ed.), *Perfecting Perfection: Essays in Honor of Henry D. Rack* (Eugene, OR: 2015) 147–172.

De Boer W. – Göttler C. (eds.), *Religion and the Senses in Early Modern Europe* (Leiden – Boston, MA: 2013).

Endy M.B., "William Penn's Contributions to Early Quaker Thought", in Angell S.W. – Dandelion P. (eds.), *Early Quakers and Their Theological Thought 1647–1723* (Cambridge – New York, NY: 2015) 239–255.

Eustace N., *Passion Is the Gale: Emotion, Power, and the Coming of the American Revolution* (Chapel Hill, NC: 2008).

Fischer E. – Tippelskirch X. von (eds.), *Bodies in Early Modern Religious Dissent: Naked, Veiled, Vilified, Worshiped* (Abingdon – New York, NY: 2021).

Gardiner E., "Sensory Experience in Visions of Heaven and Hell", paper delivered at International Medieval Congress, University of Leeds (2018), https://www.academia
.edu/37218953/Sensory_Experience_in_Visions_of_Heaven_and_Hell.

Gerona C., *Night Journeys: The Power of Dreams in Transatlantic Quaker Culture* (Charlottesville, VA: 2004).

Hardtke T. – Schmiedel U. – Tan T. (eds.), *Religious Experience Revisited: Expressing the Inexpressible?* (Leiden – Boston, MA: 2016).

Iwig-O'Byrne L., *How Methodists Were Made: The* Arminian Magazine *and Spiritual Transformation in the Transatlantic World, 1778–1803* (Ph.D. dissertation, University of Texas: 2008).

Juster S., "Mystical Pregnancy and Holy Bleeding: Visionary Experience in Early Modern Britain and America", *William and Mary Quarterly* 57.2 (April 2000) 249–288.

Juster S., *Doomsayers: Anglo-American Prophecy in the Age of Revolution* (Philadelphia, PA: 2006).

Karant-Nunn S.C., *The Reformation of Feeling: Shaping the Religious Emotions in Early Modern Germany* (Oxford – New York, NY: 2010).

Kirschner A., "'Tending to Edify, Astonish, and Instruct': Published Narratives of Spiritual Dreams and Visions in the Early Republic", *Early American Studies* 1.1 (2003) 198–229.

Lindman J.M., *Bodies of Belief: Baptist Community in Early America* (Philadelphia, PA: 2008).

Lindman J.M. – Tarter M.L. (eds.), *A Centre of Wonders: The Body in Early America* (Ithaca, NY – London: 2001).

Lloyd G., "Repression and Resistance: Wesleyan Female Public Ministry in the Generation after 1791", *Proceedings of the Wesley Historical Society* 55 (2005) 101–114.

Mack P., "Religious Dissenters in Enlightenment England", *History Workshop Journal* 49 (1999) 1–23.

Mack P., *Heart Religion in the British Enlightenment: Gender and Emotion in Early Methodism* (Cambridge – New York, NY: 2011).

Mack P., "The Unbounded Self: Dreaming and Identity in the British Enlightenment", in Plane A.M. – Tuttle L. – Wallace A.F.C. (eds.), *Dreams, Dreamers, and Visions: The Early Modern Atlantic World* (Philadelphia, PA: 2013) 216–224.

Marino B.R., *Through a Glass Darkly: The Eschatological Vision of John Wesley* (Ph.D. dissertation, Drew University: 1994).

Marshall P., *Beliefs and the Dead in Reformation England* (Oxford – New York, NY: 2002).

Marshall P., *Invisible Worlds: Death, Religion and the Supernatural in England, 1500–1700* (London: 2017).

McDannell C. – Lang B., *Heaven: A History*, 2nd ed. (New Haven, CT – London: 2001).

McGinn B., *Visions of the End: Apocalyptic Traditions in the Middle Ages* (New York, NY: 1979).

McGrath A.E., *A Brief History of Heaven* (Malden, MA: 2003).

McNamara R.F., "The Emotional Body in Religious Belief and Practice", in Lynch A. – Bromhall S. (eds.), *The Routledge History of Emotions in Europe, 1100–1700* (Abingdon – New York, NY: 2020) 105–118.

Mowbray D., *Pain and Suffering in Medieval Theology: Academic Debates at the University of Paris in the Thirteenth Century* (Woodbridge: 2009).

Muessig C. – Putter A. (eds.), *Envisaging Heaven in the Middle Ages* (New York: 2006).

Norris C.M., *Thomas Wride and Wesley's Methodist Connexion* (Abingdon – New York, NY: 2020).

Pennington M., *Quakers, Christ, and the Enlightenment* (Oxford: 2021).

Plane A.M., *Dreams and the Invisible World in Colonial New England: Indians, Colonists, and the Seventeenth Century* (Philadelphia, PA: 2014).

Prichard R.W., *The Nature of Salvation: Theological Consensus in the Episcopal Church, 1801–73* (Urbana, IL: 1997).

Pullin N., *Female Friends and the Making of Transatlantic Quakerism, 1650–1750* (Cambridge – New York, NY: 2018).

Rivière J., *Dreams in Early Modern England: 'Visions of the Night'* (Abingdon – New York, NY: 2017).

Rosen R.M., "Copying Hannah Griffitts: Poetic Circulation and the Quaker Community of Scribes", in Tarter M.L. – Gill C. (eds.), *New Critical Studies on Early Quaker Women, 1650–1800* (Oxford – New York, NY: 2018) 167–185.

Ryrie A., "Sleeping, Walking and Dreaming in Protestant Piety", in Martin J. – Ryrie A. (eds.), *Private and Domestic Devotion in Early Modern Britain* (Farnham: 2012) 73–92.

Ryrie A., *Being Protestant in Reformation Britain* (Oxford – New York: 2013).

Schmidt L.E., *Holy Fairs: Scotland and the Making of American Revivalism*, 2nd ed. (Grand Rapids, MI: 2001).

Seeman E.R., *Speaking with the Dead in Early America* (Philadelphia, PA: 2019).

Shinn A., "The Senses and the Seventeenth-Century English Conversion Narrative", in Macdonald R. – Murphy E.K.M. – Swann E.L. (eds.), *Sensing the Sacred in Medieval and Early Modern Culture* (Abingdon – New York, NY: 2018) 99–116.

Sobel M., *Teach Me Dreams: The Search for Self in the Revolutionary Era* (Princeton, NJ – Oxford: 2002).

Soergel P.M., *Miracles and the Protestant Imagination: The Evangelical Wonder Book in Reformation Germany* (Oxford – New York, NY: 2012).

Spellman W.M., "Almost Final Things: Jeremy Taylor and the Dilemma of the Anglican View of the Dead Awaiting Resurrection", *Anglican and Episcopal History* 63.1 (1994) 35–50.

Spencer C.D., "James Nayler and Jacob Boehme's *The Way to Christ*", in Kershner J.R. (ed.), *Quakers and Mysticism: Comparative and Syncretic Approaches to Spirituality* (Cham: 2019) 43–61.

Tarter M.L., "Written from the Body of Sisterhood: Quaker Women's Prophesying and the Creation of a New Word", in Tarter M.L. – Gill C. (eds.), *New Critical Studies in Early Quaker Women, 1650–1800* (Oxford – New York, NY: 2018) 69–88.

Taves A., *Fits, Trances, and Visions: Experiencing Religion and Explaining Experience from Wesley to James* (Princeton, NJ – Oxford: 2000).

Taylor C., *A Secular Age* (Cambridge, MA: 2007).

Walker D.P., "The Cessation of Miracles", in Merkel I. – Debus A.G. (eds.), *Hermeticism and the Renaissance: Intellectual History and the Occult in Early Modern Europe* (Washington, DC – London: 1988) 111–124.

Walsham A., "Miracles in Post-Reformation England", in Cooper K. – Gregory J. (eds.), *Signs, Wonders, Miracles: Representations of Divine Power in the Life of the Church*, Studies in Church History 41 (Woodbridge: 2005) 273–306.

Webster R., "Seeing Salvation: The Place of Dreams and Visions in John Wesley's *Arminian Magazine*", in Cooper K. – Gregory J. (eds.), *Signs, Wonders, Miracles Representations of Divine Power in the Life of the Church*, Studies in Church History 41 (Woodbridge: 2005) 376–388.

Webster R., *Methodism and the Miraculous: John Wesley's Idea of the Supernatural and the Identification of Methodists in the Eighteenth-Century* (Lexington, KY: 2013).

Wigger J.H., *Taking Heaven by Storm: Methodism and the Rise of Popular Christianity in America* (Oxford – New York, NY: 1998).

Winckles A.O., "'Pray for the Unworthy Scribbler': The Textual Cultures of Early Methodist Women", in King R.S. (ed.), *After Print: Eighteenth-Century Manuscript Cultures* (Charlottesville, VA: 2020) 27–51.

Winiarski D.L., "Souls Filled with Ravishing Transport: Heavenly Visions and the Radical Awakening in New England", *William and Mary Quarterly* 61.1 (2004) 3–46.

Zaleski C., *Otherworld Journeys: Accounts of Near-Death Experience in Medieval and Modern Times* (New York, NY – Oxford: 1987).

CHAPTER 10

From the Isle of Patmos to the Territory of the Plumed Serpent: Eschatological Imaginations Sparked by the Virgin of Guadalupe in Colonial New Spain

Raphaèle Preisinger

Abstract

The earliest printed account of the apparition legend revolving around the Virgin of Guadalupe, published by Miguel Sánchez in 1648, describes the miraculous impression of the Virgin's image on the cloak of an indigenous Mexican as the fulfilment of the eschatological expectations aroused by the vision of St. John on the Isle of Patmos. Adopting an understanding of Holy Scripture informed by medieval typology, Sánchez construes the vision of the Apocalyptic woman in chapter 12 of the *Book of Revelation* as an annunciation of the Virgin of Guadalupe in Mexico. By locating the fulfilment of eschatological prophecies in colonial New Spain, Sánchez evidenced a millenarist outlook. Examining the way in which the otherworldly materialized in the Virgin of Guadalupe, this essay argues that the vision of the end times sparked by this Christian icon was one in which different cultural traditions were inextricably intermeshed and traditional eschatological expectations drastically reconfigured.

Keywords

Virgin of Guadalupe – Miguel Sánchez – New Spain – *criollo* patriotism – Nahua worldview

Millenarianism, the belief that Christ's Second Coming was imminent, was widespread in the Roman Catholic Church at the onset of European expansion into the "New World". In fact, this apocalyptic, prophetic mystical outlook, which originated in the Franciscan reform movements of the Middle Ages, constituted one of the cornerstones of the intellectual foundation upon which Spain's overseas empire was built. Many missionaries believed that the Son of

God would only return after all humans had been exposed to his teachings, and this conviction underpinned the tremendous zeal with which friars set out on hazardous missionary journeys across oceans and continents. The millenarian mindset, which was particularly widespread among the Franciscans, was thus fundamental to the spirit of the colonial enterprise in the Americas, and it can be detected in the paintings, architecture, and writings that emerged from the Spanish viceroyalties.[1]

The Spanish conquerors were certain that they had been chosen by divine providence to evangelize the "New World Gentiles". But roughly a century and a quarter after the conquest of Aztec Tenochtitlan, a slightly different providential scheme emerged, which secured Mexico the most preeminent role. As the creole population of Mexico developed a deep attachment to their *patria*, Mexico, the history of salvation began to be reinterpreted. In the new narrative the Spaniards were relegated to the second row, while Mexico was transformed into a new Holy Land and its population became the new Chosen People. At the centre of this conceptualization was the 1531 appearance, at Tepeyac on the outskirts of the city of Mexico, of what would be the Americas' most prominent Christian cult image: the Virgin of Guadalupe [Fig. 10.1]. The event was understood in eschatological terms as foreshadowing Christ's final return, and this gave the former Aztec capital a crucial role in the leadup to the parousia. But even more importantly, the conquest of the New World could now be understood as an act of God's will that aimed at enabling the Virgin's enduring manifestation in Mexico.

This new interpretation of the history of salvation lies at the heart of the exegesis applied to the Virgin of Guadalupe in the earliest printed account of the Virgin's miraculous impression on a native Mexican's cloak.[2] Written by the creole preacher Miguel Sánchez and published in 1648, the *Imagen de la Virgen María, Madre de Dios de Guadalupe* recounts the indigenous neophyte Juan

---

1 On the decisive role of millenarianism for the colonization of the "New World" see Phelan J.L. *The Millenial Kingdom of the Franciscans in the New World* (Berkeley, CA: 1970), and Prosperi A., *America e apocalisse e altri saggi* (Pisa – Rome: 1999).

2 Little is known about Miguel Sánchez's life. He was held in esteem by the viceroys and archbishops of New Spain, and he occupied the positions of vicar of the sanctuary of the Virgin of the Remedies and consecutively those of chaplain of the nuns of San Jerónimo and of the Real Hospital de los Indios. He also tried, unsuccessfully, to obtain the position of chair of theology of the Real y Pontificia Universidad de México. On Sánchez's biography, see Wobeser G. von, *Orígenes del culto a nuestra señora de Guadalupe, 1521–1688* (Mexico City: 2020) 165–166. Thanks to his *Imagen de la Virgen María, Madre de Dios de Guadalupe*, Sánchez is considered the first in a series of four seventeenth-century creole authors who strove to establish this miraculous image's historicity, an undertaking for which they became known as the "four evangelists" of the Virgin of Guadalupe.

FIGURE 10.1   *Our Lady of Guadalupe*, before 1556. Oil and tempera on cloth, 175 × 109 cm.
Mexico City, Basílica of Our Lady of Guadalupe
PHOTO BY THE AUTHOR

Diego's four visionary encounters with Mary. In the first of these encounters, the Virgin asks him to inform the bishop of her wish for a sanctuary to be built in her honour on the spot at which they meet. Despite two more encounters with the Virgin, Juan Diego fails to convince the bishop of the verity of his account. During the final vision, Mary instructs Juan Diego to pick flowers in a location where nothing ever grows, which then provides him with evidence of his supernatural experience for the incredulous bishop. As Juan Diego opens his mantle to present the flowers to the bishop as tangible "proof" of his encounters with the Virgin, the bishop perceives lush forests and flourishing gardens. The flowers then fall to the ground, revealing an image of the Virgin on the cloth.[3]

Sánchez's *Imagen de la Virgen María, Madre de Dios de Guadalupe* draws from an understanding of Holy Scripture informed by medieval typology. He construes the episode of St. John's vision of the Apocalypse described in Chapter 12 of the *Book of Revelation*, in which a 'woman clothed with the sun, the moon under her feet, wearing a crown of twelve stars' appears in the heavens (*Revelation* 12:1), as an "Annunciation" that foretells the apparition of the Virgin in New Spain in 1531. He describes the Virgin's appearance in New Spain as her descent with the wings of the Mexican eagle into the territory of the plumed serpent, Quetzalcóatl, presenting the image venerated in Tepeyac as the fulfilment of the eschatological expectations aroused by the vision of St. John on the Isle of Patmos. It is the eschatological role ascribed to the Virgin of Guadalupe in this book that transforms Mexico into the staging ground for the apocalyptic events prophesized in Scripture, and lets the Tepeyac icon acquire the status of a "materialized mariophany". Such an interpretation of eschatological time and space aligns with Franciscan ideas stemming from the Spiritual branch of the order, which were profoundly shaped by the teachings of Joachim of Fiore and interpreted current events and figures in eschatological terms.[4]

The *criollo* author goes on to characterize the image of the Virgin venerated in Tepeyac as the most distinguished of all miracle-working images of her

3 Sánchez Miguel, *Imagen de la Virgen María, Madre de Dios de Guadalupe* (Mexico City, Imprenta de la Viuda de Bernardo Calderon: 1648). Sánchez's book was published with the financial support of the archbishopric of Mexico. It is dedicated to the treasurer of the Cathedral of Mexico, Pedro de Barrientos Lomelín. On the circumstances of the book's publication, see Wobeser, *Orígenes del culto a nuestra señora* 166–168.

4 Benz E., *Ecclesia spiritualis. Kirchenidee und Geschichtstheologie der franziskanischen Reformation* (Stuttgart: 1934). The seventeenth-century writings of the Franciscan friar and Peruvian creole Gonzalo Tenorio show just how important Joachim of Fiore's ideas were still in that century. Tenorio viewed himself as a spokesman of the creole population. The millennial light in which he cast the New World sanctified the lands of American-born Spaniards. On Tenorio, see Phelan, *The Millenial Kingdom of the Franciscans* 122–125.

because of the circumstances of its emergence. Sánchez ascribes the miraculous impression of the Virgin's image on the cloak of Juan Diego to the flowers bestowed on the protagonist by no one lesser than the Virgin herself. It
is the singularity of this process, of an image's materialization brought about
by flowers, that allows for Sánchez's lyrical equation of the Mexican icon to
the flowering rod of Aaron. Sánchez even characterizes all of the miracles performed through miracle-working images of the Virgin throughout history as
prefigurations of the Virgin of Guadalupe's apparition in Tepeyac. By extension, the location of that apparition, Tepeyac, becomes a Mexican Mount Zion,
the site of 'a New Jerusalem, a city of peace, descended from heaven and conquered with heaven's approval, a city with angelical sons and citizens at all
levels of hierarchy'.[5]

The inclusion of iconographical elements associated with the woman mentioned in *Revelations* facilitated an interpretation of the Virgin of Guadalupe as
signalling to mankind a new age in human history. But this is not unique; visual
representations of the Virgin Mary with the attributes of the *mulier amicta sole*
were widespread at the time of the image's creation. Iconography alone certainly does not explain how Sánchez could conceive of this particular image of
the Virgin as a materialized mariophany marking a turning point in the history
of salvation – as will be shown, answers need to be sought elsewhere.[6]

Sánchez's 1648 treatise came to determine how the Virgin of Guadalupe
was perceived. As his narrative was disseminated the Virgin of Guadalupe
was gradually elevated to the rank of the primary Virgin Mary in New Spain,
superseding the Virgin of the Remedies, who still held that position for most of
the seventeenth century.[7] As the starting point of a campaign to promote the
cult of an authentically American and specifically Mexican Virgin, Sánchez's
Imagen de la Virgen María, Madre de Dios de Guadalupe came to epitomize

---

5   Sánchez, *Imagen de la Virgen María*, fol. 17 r: 'una nueva Ciudad de Gerusalen, Ciudad de
    paz, Baxada del cielo, y con su favor conquistada, Con Hijos, y ciudadanos Angeles en todas
    hierarchias'. Unless otherwise specified, all translations are mine. On these particular aspects
    of Sánchez's interpretation of the Virgin of Guadalupe, see Wobeser G. von, *Orígenes del culto
    a nuestra señora de Guadalupe, 1521–1688* (Mexico City: 2020) 180–182.

6   On the iconography of the Virgin of Guadalupe, see Preisinger R., "(Re)framing the Virgin of
    Guadalupe: The Concurrence of Early Modern Prints and Colonial Devotions in Creating the
    Virgin", in Madar H. (ed.), *Prints as Agents of Global Exchange, 1500–1800* (Amsterdam: 2021)
    181–213.

7   The Virgin of the Remedies was a small saddle virgin that was initially principally venerated
    by the indigenous population. Since 1574, her cult was promoted by Mexico's city council. On
    the competing cults of the Virgin of Guadalupe and the Virgin of the Remedies in the seven-
    teenth century, see Peterson J.F., *Visualizing Guadalupe: From Black Madonna to Queen of the
    Americas* (Austin, TX: 2014) 232.

a patriotic *criollo* fervour that would ultimately fuel the campaign for and achievement of Mexico's independence from Spain in the early nineteenth century. The proximity of the Virgin of Guadalupe's shrines to a centuries-old pre-Columbian site of religious worship ensured that she would be intrinsically associated with the local environment.[8]

Historical research on the Virgin of Guadalupe is abundant, and she is among the most-studied Christian religious phenomena and sacred artifacts.[9] Sánchez's treatise has also become famous for the exegetical intricacies in which he enwraps the miraculous image, borrowing from medieval typology and Joachimite millenarianism to ascribe a providential status to the conquest of Mexico and the establishment of New Spain.[10] But the ontological framing of the Virgin's apparition has not yet been analysed in depth, and it both presents striking inconsistencies with contemporary Christian tradition and resonates with Nahua conceptions and narratives.

My claim in this chapter is that the Virgin of Guadalupe's ontological status as a sacred Catholic icon in Sánchez's *Imagen de la Virgen María, Madre de Dios de Guadalupe* is as much a product of indigenous epistemologies as it is of Counter-Reformation spirituality. In fact, Sánchez struggles to assimilate, through a Catholic theological lens, an indigenous set of beliefs about this icon that was current among certain groups of devotees by the end of the sixteenth century. Though it is certainly true that Sánchez drew heavily on St. Augustine,[11] my findings of repeated incongruencies between his work and previously established Catholic traditions confirm the assessment of

---

8   On the ceremonial site located on the hill of Tepeyácac, known later as Tepeyac, before the arrival of the Spaniards, see Wobeser, *Orígenes del culto a nuestra señora* 17–24.

9   Among the best-known monographs, are Lafaye J., *Quetzalcóatl et Guadalupe: La formation de la conscience nationale au Mexique (1531–1813)* (Paris: 1974); O'Gorman E., *Destierro de Sombras: Luz en el origen de la imagen y culto de nuestra Señora de Guadalupe del Tepeyac* (Mexico City: 1986); Noguez X., *Documentos guadalupanos: Un estudio sobre las fuentes de información tempranas en torno a las mariofanías en el Tepeyac* (Toluca – Mexico City: 1993); Poole S., *Our Lady of Guadalupe: The Origins and Sources of a Mexican National Symbol, 1531–1797* (Tucson, AZ: 1995); Brading D.A., *Mexican Phoenix: Our Lady of Guadalupe: Image and Tradition across Five Centuries* (Cambridge: 2001). The most recent contribution, which focuses on the sixteenth- and seventeenth-century history of devotion to the Virgin of Guadalupe, is Wobeser, *Orígenes del culto a nuestra señora*.

10   The text's eschatological interpretation is omnipresent in the vast literature on the Tepeyac icon. Its significance for the development of a Mexican *criollo* consciousness has been discussed by Lafaye, *Quetzalcóatl et Guadalupe* 320–335 and La Maza F. de, *El guadalupanismo mexicano* (Mexico City: 1953).

11   This aspect is analysed in detail by Matovina T., "Guadalupe at Calvary: Patristic Theology in Miguel Sánchez's *Imagen de la Virgen María* (1648)", *Theological Studies* 64 (2003) 795–811.

scholars who primarily credit Sánchez with "translating" an earlier account, itself situated at the crossroads of indigenous and Christian belief systems.[12] Juxtaposing key elements of Sánchez's narrative with the so-called *Nican Mopohua* (Here it is told), a Nahuatl text that has been identified as the basis of the *criollo* author's mediating efforts, reveals important borrowings from the latter. They include the eschatological framework intricately woven around the Virgin by Sánchez. His casting of the image as a durably materialized mariophany, as well as his typological interpretation of the Virgin's appearance in New Spain – around which the entire apocalyptic interpretation of both the icon and the Spanish conquest of Mexico revolve – in fact drew upon a local tradition in which the appearance of the Virgin in Tepeyac was already understood as a pivotal event in human history. Indigenous notions of sacrality and of cosmology thus inspired the conception of eschatological time and space in Sánchez's much-acclaimed account, and they underpin the providential status attributed to Mexico in this foundational text for New Spanish *criollo* patriotism.

To prove my point, I will first analyse the conceptual shift from a miracleproducing image to an image itself miraculously produced in the history of the veneration of the Virgin of Guadalupe, focusing on the ontological status ascribed to this icon in what is perhaps the earliest extant reproduction of the painting. I will then analyse the ways in which the image's apparition is described by Sánchez and point out key elements that seem irreconcilable with Christian tradition. Bringing these elements into conversation with the relevant passages in the *Nican Mopohua* – a Nahuatl account of the Virgin's miraculous apparition published as part of Luis Lasso de la Vega's *Huei Tlamahuizoltica* (The great happening) in 1649, but written earlier than Sánchez's *Imagen de la Virgen Maria, Madre de Dios de Guadalupe* – undergirds the claim that Sánchez was adapting an indigenous set of beliefs for a Christian audience throughout his book. Finally, Nahua notions of presence and representation are proposed as possible sources of inspiration for the peculiar ontological status ascribed to the Virgin of Guadalupe in the Tepeyac icon's painted "copy" and in Sánchez's account, and the possibility is explored that the eschatological framework devised by Sánchez is based upon a world-changing perspective already present in the *Nican Mopohua*.

---

12   On the controversial claims for literary precedents of Nahuatl texts and oral traditions underlying Sánchez's miracle account, see below, at 290–291.

1   **From Miracles Performed by the Virgin to the Miracle of Her Appearance**

The image of the Virgin of Guadalupe has been venerated on the hill of Tepeyac near Mexico City since at least 1556, when a heated conflict around the devotion it inspired broke out between the Franciscan provincial Francisco de Bustamante and the archbishop of New Spain, Alonso de Montúfar. By that year, the painting had acquired a robust reputation for working miracles and attracted many devotees, many of whom, at this early stage of Guadalupan veneration, seem to have been Amerindians.[13]

A reference to the miraculous origin of the image itself that predates Sánchez's *Imagen de la Virgen Maria, Madre de Dios de Guadalupe* is found in what is possibly the earliest extant copy of the painting, dated 1606 and signed by the Spanish-born artist Baltasar de Echave Orio [Fig. 10.2].[14] The way in which the Tepeyac icon is presented in this painting clearly reveals the intent to characterize the image as acheiropoietic, i.e. of divine origin and "not made by human hands", by visually referencing the famous veil of Veronica on which Christ's face was miraculously imprinted. Both corners of the depicted fabric bearing the image of the Virgin appear to be snatched up in the upper part of the painting, while laterally, the loose cloth noticeably buckles, pulled by gravity towards the ground. This mode of representation approximates the Virgin of Guadalupe to images in which Saint Veronica holds the *sudarium* of Christ in front of her body.

But parallels with this Vera Icon tradition extend even beyond the representation of the material support of the image. It has been argued that pictures of Veronica presenting the holy relic to the beholder allude to a "twofold

---

13   On this early stage of Guadalupan devotion, see Wobeser, *Orígenes del culto a nuestra señora* 77–83.

14   The dating and attribution of this painting is controversial because the forgery of signatures and assignment to earlier masters was a consistent feature of the 19th-century art market in Mexico. However, as Clara Bargellini points out, the painting is probably identical with a 'portrait and copy' of the original Tepeyac icon painted by Baltasar de Echave Orio and described in 1697 by Agustín de Vetancurt as being in the Church of San Francisco in Mexico City. On this painting, see Bargellini C., "The Colors of the Virgin of Guadalupe", in Wolf G. – Connors J. (eds.), *Colors Between Two Worlds: The Florentine Codex of Bernardino de Sahagún* (Florence: 2011) 3–25, 10–12. As explained by Peterson, *Visualizing Guadalupe* 163, by 1606, Echave Orio had already executed many commissions for the Church in New Spain. Sixteen of Echave Orio's paintings were slated for the retable of Santiago Tlatelolco. This is worth mentioning because this Franciscan monastery school is closely associated with the apparition legend of the Tepeyac icon as the site of Juan Diego's instruction.

FIGURE 10.2   Baltasar de Echave Orio, *The Virgin of Guadalupe*, 1606. Oil on canvas,
170 × 111 cm. Mexico City, Private collection
IMAGE: ARCA, ARTE COLONIAL, HTTPS://ARCAVI.UNIANDES.EDU.CO
/ARTWORKS/2549

FIGURE 10.3
Meister E.S., *St. Veronica with
the Sudarium*, 2nd third of
the 15th century. Engraving,
9.4 × 6.2 cm. Vienna, Albertina,
inv. no. DG1926/774
IMAGE © ALBERTINA, VIENNA

reality" by showing Christ's face as if it were actually floating in front of the
loosely falling textile, detached from its creases [Fig. 10.3].[15] While the legend
of the holy image miraculously transmitted to the saint's veil makes it a contact
relic, resulting from the impression of Christ's blood- and sweat-covered face
on the cloth,[16] such pictorial renderings also allude to a perfect mode of vision
unhindered by the limitations of physical sight. In this second version of the
Tepeyac painting, both a depiction and a copy of it, the image of the Virgin
encircled by a solar mandorla appears similarly "detached" from its material

---

15   Belting H., *Likeness and Presence: A History of the Image before the Era of Art* (Chicago, IL:
      1994) 428; on the 'trompe-l'oeil effect', as Victor Stoichita calls it, in images of the Veronica
      in Spanish art, see Stoichita V.I., *Visionary Experience in the Golden Age of Spanish Art*
      (London: 1995) 63–66.
16   On the different versions of the legend recounting the creation of the Roman *vera icon*
      see Wolf G., *Schleier und Spiegel: Traditionen des Christusbildes und die Bildkonzepte der
      Renaissance* (Munich: 2002) 45–51.

support, as can be seen at the very top and in the lower part of the painting, where the cloth folds touching the ground, while the image does not.[17]

The characterization of the Virgin of Guadalupe as an acheiropoietic image in this painted rendition of the Tepeyac icon is remarkable, as traditionally, miraculous Marian images were understood to be portraits, authenticated by their old age and the holiness of their painter, St. Luke. In Western Christianity, images believed to be *non manufactum* were almost exclusively highly vener-ated images of Christ, who was himself described by patristic doctrine as the perfect image of God, and they included the Vera Icon and the Turin shroud. These images were first and foremost understood to be contact relics that proved the historical existence of Christ.[18]

Paradoxically, this is precisely where the parallels between acheiropoietic images of Christ and the Tepeyac icon break down: an image of the Virgin adorned with the symbols of the woman "seen" by St. John on Patmos cannot possibly be understood as referring to Mary's earthly existence. Also, despite the fact that many images of Veronica's veil in which the cloth is presented frontally to the viewer depict the image of Christ's face as though floating, on a plane closer to the viewer than its material support, the points of reference for the respective extraordinary modes of seeing to which these images allude necessarily differ. While the depictions of the *sudarium* of Christ signal an unimpeded gaze into God's own face as the fulfilment of all human aspira-tional sight, i.e. the restoration of perfect vision in the afterlife, the Virgin's floating representation in the painting of the Tepeyac icon points to visionary experience, a momentary glimpse into a mode of seeing that transcends the physical. The chiaroscuro effects used on the Virgin support this interpreta-tion, as visionary experience is often represented and alluded to by dazzling light. The left half of the Virgin's body is highlighted by a light source of unde-terminable origin, one which leaves certain areas – such as the upper part of her sleeves and her right cheek – markedly in shadow. The contours of her form are further encircled by a bright light, an effect that is almost entirely

---

17   This artwork is kept in a private collection in Mexico City and is extremely difficult to access. Peterson, *Visualizing Guadalupe* 159, describes the image as 'hovering apart from the laws of gravity'. The image caption of fig. 6.1 (160) suggests that she was able to see it.

18   On this fundamental distinction between cult images of Christ and the Virgin see Belting, *Likeness and Presence* 47–77. On the introduction of the legend of St. Luke in the West, which came to dominate the discourse with respect to Marian images, see Bacci M., *Il pennello dell'Evangelista: Storia delle immagini sacre attribuite a san Luca* (Pisa: 1998).

absent in the original cult image [Fig. 10.1]. In combining acheiropoietic elements with visionary associations, the painting attributed to Echave Orio conveys an interpretation of how the image appeared that is extraordinary in that
it grants the Virgin of Guadalupe a unique status in the history of venerated
Christian images.

2   Contradictory Rationales for the Image's Appearance

In Sánchez's 1648 account of the Virgin's miraculous apparition, the visionary and acheiropoietic status of the Tepeyac icon are also inextricably intermeshed. Before analysing precisely how, according to Sánchez, the venerated
image came to be, I would like to briefly point out both the inherent contradiction within and the novelty of such a double status. While Veronica's veil and
the Turin shroud were understood to be the result of a moment of physical
contact miraculously and durably recorded in cloth, visionary experiences of
the sacred are generally associated with fleeting sight, offering but a momentary glimpse of a world beyond our existence. Material records of God's earthly
manifestation on the one hand, and transient experiences of otherworldly
vision on the other, in fact constitute opposite poles of the spectrum of visual
experience. Indeed, no other Christian icon seems to be positioned in quite
the same way at this seemingly paradoxical intersection of different modes of
seeing. Even though the later Middle Ages gave rise to increasing occurrences
of materialization of the divine, the status of the Tepeyac icon, simultaneously
created via contact with the sacred and standing as the durable record on cloth
of a visionary encounter with the divine, is unique.[19]

In Sánchez's account, the flowers miraculously bestowed on Juan Diego
play a crucial role in explaining the image's creation.[20] To appreciate their full
meaning, it is necessary to examine his last encounter with the Virgin. In this
episode, on the Virgin's instruction, Juan Diego gathers the flowers on the hill
where he had first met her. The flowers, themselves considered to be the result
of a miraculous intervention by the Virgin, are said to be of all different kinds
when they first appear, although they are recurringly described solely as 'roses'

---

19   On the materialization of the divine in late medieval piety, see Bynum C.W., *Christian
      Materiality: An Essay on Religion in Late Medieval Europe* (New York, NY: 2011).

20   On the role of the flowers in this account and later references to it, see Bargellini, "The
      Colors of the Virgin of Guadalupe" 16–22.

in Sánchez's narrative.[21] The author metaphorically refers to them as 'a heavenly spring, an orchard from Paradise'. Once Juan Diego has brought the flowers to the Virgin, she takes them in her hands so that their miraculous potency will reappear before giving them back to Juan Diego.[22] This motif is of particular importance, as it transforms the flowers themselves into contact relics – albeit of a Marian apparition. Although the combination of visionary associations and the status of a touch relic is a trait shared by the rosary – which, according to Alanus de Rupe, was received by St. Dominic during a visionary encounter with the Virgin[23] – what is unique and novel in the legend of the Virgin of Guadalupe is the transformative or generative potency of the flowers after they are handed back to Juan Diego.

According to Sánchez's account, the flowers become the object of a vexing experience of sight even before Juan Diego is received in audience by bishop Zumárraga. As the bishop's assistants, triggered by curiosity, try to grasp some of the roses gathered in Juan Diego's folded mantle, these turn out to be signs instead of objects, as they appear to be 'painted, engraved or woven motifs' on the cloth. Bewildered by the flowers' transmuting properties, the assistants allow Juan Diego access to the bishop, to whom the former recounts his conversations with the Virgin and her gift of the roses as proof of the veracity of his words. As Juan Diego opens his mantle, the bishop perceives lush forests and flourishing meadows – 'a sacred forest, a miraculous spring season, an "abbreviated" orchard of roses, lilies, carnations, broom, jasmines, and violets' – visionary extrapolations derived from the perception of the flowers

---

21   In the *Nican Mopohua*, by contrast, the flowers are repeatedly described as 'various precious flowers, like the ones of Castile'. For the purposes of this chapter, I have used the transcription of the *Nican Mopohua* and its translation into Spanish published in Léon-Portilla M., *Tonantzin Guadalupe: Pensamiento náhuatl y mensaje cristiano en el "Nican Mopohua"* (Mexico City: 2000) 91–159.

22   Sánchez, *Imagen de la Virgen María*, fols. 27 r–27 v: 'Cortolas todas, y recogiendo aquella Primavera del cielo, y atesorando aquel Berjel del Parayso, en su tosca, pobre, y humilde Manta, limpia si con la blancura en su color narivo, bolviendo las dos puntas y estremos de lo baxo al pecho con las dos manos y braços, enlaçandolos del proprio ñudo pendiente de su cuello, (que es el comun estilo, y traxe de los Indios) baxó de aquel Sagrado monte, á la presencia de MARIA Virgen, à cuyos ojos, y obediencia puso rosas, y Flores cortadas por su mandato. La Santisima Madre, coxiendolas es sus manos para que segunda vez renaciessen Milagros, recobrasen Fragrancias, se virificassen en Olores, y refrescassen en rozios, se las restituye'. On the flower-motif in Sánchez's account, see also Bargellini C., "The Virgin of Guadalupe: A Painting of New Spain", https://ism.yale.edu/sites/default/files/files/The%20Virgin%20of%20Guadalupe.pdf (accessed 03.08.2022).

23   On the rosary, see Winston-Allen A., *Stories of the Rose: The Making of the Rosary in the Middle Ages* (University Park, PA: 1997) 72.

that echo and amplify the description of Juan Diego's collecting of them. Then the flowers fall, 'leaving painted [on the mantle] the Virgin Mary, the Mother of God, in her Holy Image' that is now venerated in her sanctuary.[24] The sensual dimension of the revelation materialized in the Guadalupe icon crystallizes in the flowers provided by the Virgin. This motif would have left any contemporary reader acquainted with earlier traditions around holy images puzzled, as this is the only known case in which flowers are involved in the miraculous production of an image.

If we pay close attention, it seems that in Sánchez's book the Tepeyac icon holds a status somewhere between original and copy. On the one hand, upon seeing the image of Mary imprinted on cloth, Juan Diego was converted into the 'retouched portrait' of his namesake, the evangelist John, as he 'saw copied the image of Mary, that the other saw in the original in heaven'.[25] Here, the Virgin of Guadalupe is ascribed the status of a copy. On the other hand, Mary, in all her images, and in that of the Virgin of Guadalupe in particular, is herself 'the most perfect image, and copied from the original of God'. In this passage Sánchez adapts the notion that the Virgin Mary was the most faithful image of God in this world, an idea taken from the eighth- or ninth-century author Ambrosius Autpertus that Sánchez erroneously attributes to St. Augustine, to include material images of Mary. Sánchez even stresses the particular aptness of this ontological interpretation for the Tepeyac icon.[26] If, by analogy, the image venerated in Mexico becomes 'the most perfect image of God' – a description typically applied to Christ, the "incarnated Word" – then the icon itself also becomes an original.[27] Sánchez's reasoning here is unique compared

---

24 Sánchez, *Imagen de la Virgen María*, fols. 29 r–30 v: 'Ellos no sin admiracion quando las vieron, porque el tiempo de suyo la pedia, y atendieno á lo Fresco, Florido, y Hermoso, codiciosamente cada uno quiso quitar alguna de las Flores, y aviendo porfiado tres vezes, no pudieron, juzgando, y pareciendoles q[ue] en la candida manta estavan Pintadas, Gravadas, ó Texidas'; 'Descubrió la limpia manta para presentar el regalo del cielo al venturoso Obispo: este anciosso á recibirle, vido en aquella manta, una Santa Floresta, una Primavera Milagrosa, un Berjel abreviado de Rosas, Açucenas, Claveles, Lirios, Reramas, Iazmines, y Violetas, y que todas cayendo de la manta dexaron Pintada en ella à MARIA Virgen Madre de Dios, en su Santa Imagen q[ue] oy se conserva, guarda, y Venera en su Santuario de Guadalupe de Mexico'.

25 Ibidem, fol. 31 r: 'Siento, que en la ocasion Iuan el Consagrado Principe, del Iuan Evangelista en Pathmos ya retocado Retrato, pues à visto copiada la Imagen de MARIA, que el otro vido en el Original del cielo [...]'.

26 On Sánchez's incorrect attribution of this insight to St. Augustine, see Matovina, "Guadalupe at Calvary" 802–803.

27 Sánchez, *Imagen de la Virgen María*, fol. 5 r: 'que siendo MARIA Virgen la Imagen mas perfecta, y copiada del Original de Dios, privilegio que lleva siempre consigo en todas sus Imagines, y siendo la suya en nuestro Mexicano Guadalupe, tan milagrosa en las

to previous understandings of miraculous images, and the singularity of the status he ascribes to the Tepeyac icon suggests that he drew his inspiration from sources at least partially inspired by a different set of traditions.

3   Indigenous Forerunners to Sanchez's Account?

Contextualization of both the painting attributed to Echave Orio and Sánchez's text requires examining early indicators for the existence of an apparitionist tradition surrounding the Virgin of Guadalupe.[28] There has been much debate about when the legend of the Virgin of Guadalupe's miraculous origins, which has made her one of the most sacred images of Christianity, first developed. The controversy revolves around whether the so-called *Nican Mopohua* was written before and served as the basis for Sánchez's 1648 *Imagen de la Virgen María, Madre de Dios de Guadalupe*. While one group of scholars ascribes the invention of the miracle account to Sánchez, another attributes the narrative to Antonio Valeriano, an indigenous erudite who worked under the famous Franciscan friar and missionary Bernardino de Sahagún. This latter group claims authorship of the *Nican Mopohua* for Valeriano, stating that Lasso de la Vega should only be credited with compiling and editing his text.[29] In her

---

circunstancias, y tan primera en esta tierra, previno, dispuso, y obró su Dibujo primoroso en esta su tierra Mexico, conquistada á tan gloriosos fines, ganada para que apareciese Imagen tan de Dios'. On the "imago Dei" and its paradigmatic role in Christianity, see Angenendt A., *Geschichte der Religiosität im Mittelalter* (Darmstadt: 2000) 252–254.

28   A brief textual allusion to the Virgin of Guadalupe's appearance is made by Juan Suárez de Peralta in his *Tratado del descubrimiento de las Indias*, finished in 1589. He tells of a miracle-working image of the Virgin that appeared between cliffs. The Tepeyac icon seems to be linked to a Marian apparition in this account, but unfortunately the author gives no information on the circumstances surrounding this occurrence, nor on any visionary elements linked to it. Suárez de Peralta Juan, *Tratado del descubrimiento de las Indias* (Mexico City: 1990) 232. On this text and other indicators, such as the mention of several elements of the apparitionist tradition by the Poor Clare nun Ana de Cristo who travelled through Tepeyac in 1620, or the earliest datable textual mention of a divine origin of the image in an anonymous poem in 1634, see Wobeser, *Orígenes del culto a nuestra señora* 132–140. The motif of an image miraculously "discovered" between cliffs is reminiscent of the legend of the Extremenean Virgin of Guadalupe in Spain, a medieval black Madonna that lent the Mexican cult image its name. The Spanish sculpted icon is said to have "reappeared" in a cave-like sarcophagus in the mountains near Cáceres after having been hidden for safekeeping in the decade following the Muslim invasion of Andalucía. The Spanish Virgin of Guadalupe's legend is recounted in Peterson, *Visualizing Guadalupe* 21–22.

29   On this debate, see Wobeser, *Orígenes del culto a nuestra señora* 141–143. Von Wobeser counts Jacques Lafaye, David Brading, James Lockhart, Stafford Poole and Lisa Sousa

recent reassessment of the historical evidence, Gisela von Wobeser argues in favour of an earlier date for the *Nican Mopohua*, listing the following four points in support: Sánchez's admonition to the reader in his introduction, in which he mentions having used indigenous sources as the base for his narrative; the style of the *Nican Mopohua*, which she ascribes to indigenous authorship; early modern editorial practices permitting the publication of texts written by others under one's own name; and finally Luis Becerra Tanco's 1666 mention of a distinct indigenous origin for the apparition account and his statement that Sánchez's text followed a tradition derived from the '[old] projects of the Colegio de Santa Cruz [Tlatelolco]'. Von Wobeser confirms that the *Nican Mopohua* was indeed authored by the native humanist Antonio Valeriano and endorses a late sixteenth- or early seventeenth-century date for its composition. It furthermore seems to have been based on an even earlier oral tradition.[30]

As explained above, the ascription of an acheiropoietic status to the image and its simultaneous acquisition of visionary associations are reflected both in the painting attributed to Echave Orio and in Sánchez's account. It is likely that the legend of the image's miraculous apparition originally circulated only among a relatively small group of predominantly indigenous Guadalupe devotees and only became widely known after the publication of the printed miracle accounts written by Sánchez and Lasso de la Vega. This would explain why the image's miraculous creation is not included among the miracles associated with the Virgin in the second-oldest pictorial reference to the Tepeyac painting, the engraved "book of miracles" by Samuel Stradanus, an Antwerp artist who had immigrated to New Spain by 1604. This engraving was executed sometime between 1613 and 1622 to raise the alms necessary for the erection of a new sanctuary to house the Virgin of Guadalupe [Fig. 10.4]. As its purpose was to generate funds, this print was most likely directed primarily at the wealthy Spanish elite of Mexico, who might not have accepted a legend claiming the Virgin had appeared to a humble native "seer" and identifying the material

---

among those believing in the primacy of Sánchez's account, while she lists Edmudo O'Gorman, Ernesto de la Torre Villar, Miguel Léon-Portilla, Rodriguez Martínez Baracs and Francisco Miranda among those holding the opposite view. Noguez, *Documentos guadalupanos* 110–111, argues that Sánchez based his treatise on the Nahuatl *Nican Mopohua*, the *Nican Motecpana* (loosely, Here it is put in order) and their translation by Fernando de Alva Ixtlilxóchitl, as well as oral reports. On further sources used by Sánchez, see Wobeser, *Orígenes del culto a nuestra señora* 169–170.

30   Wobeser, *Orígenes del culto a nuestra señora* 141–151.

FIGURE 10.4   Samuel Stradanus, *Indulgence for Donation of Alms toward the Building of a Church Dedicated to the Virgin of Guadalupe*. Modern facsimile impression of the original engraving of ca. 1613–1615, 33 × 21.3 cm. New York, The Metropolitan Museum of Art, inv. no. 48.70
IMAGE © THE METROPOLITAN MUSEUM OF ART. PUBLIC DOMAIN

support of the image as an indigenous garment without the theological mediation later provided by Sánchez.[31]

4   The Virgin of Guadalupe – an Ixiptla of the Holy Mother?

The narrative of the *Nican Mopohua* is practically identical to Sánchez's account as described above, with a few interesting differences in terms of how the story is presented. In the Nahuatl account there is no explicit mention of Paradise when Juan Diego collects the flowers, nor of a miraculous potency being transmitted to them by the Virgin's touch, though the act of handing the flowers to the Virgin and of her then putting them back into Juan Diego's *tilma* is stressed. Once the assistants in the bishop's palace try to take hold of the flowers, the three-dimensional objects disappear before their eyes and the blooms now appear as if they were 'a painting or an embroidery, or something sewn' on the *tilma*. Here no moment of heavenly rapture precedes the discovery of the Virgin's image. However, as in Sanchez's text, the image of the Virgin is described as something that the flowers have somehow "left behind" as they fell. Of particular interest is the term used to describe that image as it appears, which is an especially reverential and affectionate form of the Nahuatl word *ixiptla, itlaçoixiptlatzin*.[32]

As explained by Serge Gruzinski, early in the history of Christian evangelization in New Spain the term *ixiptla* was applied by Franciscan missionaries to images of Christ and the saints. This limited the term's scope, in a Christian context, to just one type of materialization. But the Nahuatl term *ixiptla* is of course rooted in pre-conquest Mesoamerican conceptions of the world, and it denotes the perceivable, epiphanic presence of sacred power (within a vessel or form), the container of that sacred power, and/or the actualization of a force infused in an object. The term has typically been used to designate the presence of a deity in a human god-impersonator, furnished with a deity's attributes, or that deity's presence in an object. In order to become a deity's *ixiptla*, a god-impersonator underwent a process of ritual transformation into the supernatural entity; objects, in turn, were ritually created to become imbued with a deity's sacred powers.[33]

---

31   On the Stradanus print, see Peterson, *Visualizing Guadalupe* 138–158, who dates it to ca. 1613–1615, and Wobeser, *Orígenes del culto a nuestra señora* 100–103 and 129, who points out that all the miracles presented by this engraving occur among Spaniards.

32   Léon-Portilla, *Tonantzin Guadalupe* 124–150; the term *itlaçoixiptlatzin* appears on page 150. I thank Emilie Carreón Blaine for her kind help with the Nahuatl text.

33   On the term and concept of *ixiptla*, the foundational text is Hvidtfeldt A., *Teotl and *Ixiptlatli: Some Central Conceptions in Ancient Mexican Religion* (Copenhagen: 1958).

More recently, scholarly attention has shifted to the word *teixiptla* to stress the relationship between the impersonator and the embodied entity. Molly Bassett points out that the term *teixiptla* was not only used in the religious sphere. However, 'in contrast to other types of representatives and representations, such as a military delegate or a painted portrait, the *teixiplta* of a *teotl* [a god] complicates the Peircean isolation of the index and icon from the prototype by paradoxically both representing and presenting the deity'.[34] With regard to a figure like the Virgin Mary, this notion of both presenting and re-presenting is certainly fundamental.

The opening paragraph of the *Nican Mopohua* states that the Virgin first 'showed herself' to 'a little man' named Juan Diego, and that later her precious image 'appeared' before the recently elected bishop, Juan de Zumárraga.[35] In an indigenous context, both deities appearing in a vision and objects representing a god could be categorized as *ixiptla*.[36] Does this term, then, help us understand the capacity of the flowers to transmit sacred presence, and to create a visual representation of the Virgin on a piece of cloth? In the Guadalupe legend, the physical contact between the Virgin and the flowers seems to be crucial, as it is a detail stressed by both the *Nican Mopohua* and Sánchez's account. What is more, this detail, if meaningless, wouldn't be mentioned, as it is quite unnecessary for the evolution of the story's narration. Sánchez

Another key survey is Bassett M.H., *The Fate of Earthly Things: Aztec Gods and God-Bodies* (Austin, TX: 2015). See also Gruzinski S., *La guerre des images de Christophe Colomb à "Blade Runner" (1492–2019)* (Paris: 1990) 86–88; and Carreón Blaine E., "Un giro alrededor del ixiplta", in Baéz Rubí L. – Carreón Blaine E. (eds.), *Los estatutos de la imagen, creación-manifestación-percepción* (Mexico City: 2014) 247–274, who discusses how the term has been used in scholarship to date, stressing that a simple translation as "image or representation" is incorrect, as this would falsely limit its meaning. Gruzinski, *La guerre des images* 198 suggests considering this term in relation to the veneration of the Virgin of Guadalupe and the exegesis applied to it, but does not substantiate the relevance of this concept in Sánchez's or Lasso de la Vega's narratives beyond pointing to Sánchez's assertion of the Virgin's presence in the Tepeyac icon. Báez Rubí L., "*Wanderstrassen*: Traveling Images – Moving Ideas Between Continents", in Alloa E. – Cappelletto C. (eds.), *Dynamis of the Image: Moving Images in a Global World* (Berlin – Boston, MA: 2020) 79–102, engages in an analysis of this term's hermeneutic usefulness in relation to the Virgin of Guadalupe, centring her discussion on the 1666 deposition prepared by Luis Becerra Tanco, and thus on the reception of both the *Nican Mopohua* and Sanchez's *Imagen de la Madre de Dios*, in the second half of the seventeenth century. Her timeframe and questions thus clearly differ from those considered here.

34   Bassett, *The Fate of Earthly Things* 135. As pointed out in ibidem 134, the nonspecific object prefix *te-* means "someone's".

35   Léon-Portilla, *Tonantzin Guadalupe* 93.

36   On the semantic breadth of the term, see Gruzinski, *La guerre des images* 86.

is also very clear in stating that the physical act of the Virgin touching the flowers transfers to them a miraculous potency, and it seems to be the source of the flowers' vibrant qualities as he describes them. But what of the *Nican Mopohua*? In Nahua thought, plants associated with particular deities were believed to hold their sacred powers.[37] Is the link established in the account between the Virgin and the flowers, which she brings forth, combined with the notion of the ritual transformation of objects and persons into sacred entities, and the enduring power of such transformative processes, as contained in the term *(te)ixiptla*, enough to explain how the flowers could transmute and leave behind a material manifestation of Mary?

This is evidently the terrain upon which Christian and pre-Columbian notions of sacrality and materiality converge. That transformative processes could result in sacred presence was fundamental to the Catholic worldview, and centrally manifested in the transubstantiation of the host. Despite the wealth of theological writings on images that asserted a fundamental divide between the representation and the represented object of devotion – the heavenly prototype –, in pious practice, the divine could also be perceived as present in anthropomorphic forms, foremost but not exclusively in acheiropoietic images such as the *Vera icon*.[38] However, when a miraculous image was considered "not made by human hands", it was certainly never believed to have been brought forth by a transformative process triggered by an object – here a plant – that had been previously touched by an epiphanic apparition of a sacred figure. At best, an acheiropoieton could reproduce itself in another medium – effectively in a kind of printing process – by leaving a "copy" of itself behind. This was allegedly the case of the *mandylion* of Edessa, where the face of Christ was believed to have reproduced itself in a brick in Hierapolis under which it was concealed.[39]

---

37 On the relationship between deities and plants, see Lopez Austin A., *Cuerpo humano e ideologia: Las concepciones de los antiguos nahuas*, vol. 1 (Mexico City: 1980) 396–403.

38 While the decree on images adopted at the 25th session of the Council of Trent in 1563 essentially repeated the decisions on images of the Second Council of Nicaea, stating that the veneration of an image attains to the saintly subject it represents, pious practice ascribed sacred presence to venerated icons in the West since at least the High Middle Ages. Among the vast literature on the subject, see in particular De Boer W., *Art in Dispute: Catholic Debates at the Time of Trent with an Edition and Translation of Key Documents* (Leiden: 2022) and Belting, *Likeness and Presence*.

39 The so-called *keramion*, which is also part of the legend surrounding the mandylion, was believed to have been brought forth, as in a copying process, through the immurement with the mandylion. See Wolf, *Schleier und Spiegel* 23.

The notion that the flowers themselves 'left a trace' in both the *Nican Mopohua* and Sánchez's account is important for understanding the ideas undergirding the logic of the narrative.[40] Though the precedent of Christian touch relics would certainly explain the transmission of sacred potency, what remains here is not a visually similar copy of that which the support had touched (i.e. the flowers). Instead a visual transformation occurs, and the idea of a particle "remaining" is reminiscent of the notion of the *(te)ixiptla* as a detached part of the prototype, of the *(te)ixiptla*'s participation in the *teotl*'s 'distributed person'. An image of the Virgin such as the Tepeyac icon depicts Mary with characteristic and easily identifiable attributes, and this resonates with the fact that a *teotl*'s *ixiptla* was required to be recognizable.[41] Thus, it seems that Nahua notions of presence and representation as epitomized by the *ixiptla* were constitutive in bringing about the interpretation of the Virgin of Guadalupe as a durably materialized mariophany.

The dependence of the *Nican Mopohua* on both medieval Spanish apparition accounts of sacred Christian icons and pre-Columbian conceptions of sacrality has been noted by several scholars.[42] For example, among the central motifs inspired by the apparition legend of the medieval Black Madonna in the monastery of Santa Maria Guadalupe in Spain is the visionary encounter of a humble "seer" with the Virgin, who asks him to act on her behalf to erect a sanctuary in her honour at a designated site.[43] Other elements were undoubtedly borrowed from Nahua worldview, like the reference to the archetypical disfrasism (combining two complementary concepts or metaphors to express an idea) of the beginning of the world and of humankind, i.e. of history, which is used here to signal an occurrence of fundamental importance to the world. The author of the *Nican Mopohua* situates the miracle account in the early

---

40   Léon-Portilla, *Tonantzin Guadalupe* 150: 'Auh in yuh hualtepeuh / in ixquich nepapan Caxtillan xochitl, / niman oncan momachioti, / neztiquiz in itlaçoixiptlatzin / iz çenquizca ichpochtli Santa María'; Sánchez, *Imagen de la Virgen María*, fol. 30 r: 'y que todas [the flowers] cayendo de la manta dexaron Pintada en ella à Maria Virgen Madre de Dios, en su Santa Imagen'. Luis Becerra Tanco's translation of the term used in the *Nican Mopohua* to describe the manifestation, *Omamachiotinextiquiz*, as 'salió a verse figurada o impressa' ('she came out to become a figure or be imprinted'), retains, in the term "impressa", the idea of a "trace remaining". For Luis Becerra Tanco's translation and explanation of the Nahuatl term, see Báez Rubi, *"Wanderstrassen"* 87.

41   On the *(te)ixiplta*, see Bassett, *The Fate of Earthly Things* 136–138.

42   See for example Nebel R., *Santa María Tonantzin Virgen de Guadalupe: Religiöse Kontinuität und Transformation in Mexiko* (Immensee: 1992); and Wobeser, *Orígenes del culto a nuestra señora*.

43   For a brief comparative overview of key elements from both Guadalupe traditions, see Nebel, *Santa María Tonantzin* 165–170.

morning, 'when it was still dark night', to then describe the Virgin's apparitions as starting 'as it began to dawn'.[44] Another Nahua disfrasism is central to the underlying significance of the flower motif in the apparition legend, that of *In Xóchitl in Cuícatl* (Flower and song). At the beginning of the narrative the sweet song of birds is mentioned; considered in conjunction with the motif of the flowers which Juan Diego is summoned to pick, it signals revelation. This disfrasism stands for truth and beauty, with the birds a metaphor for mediation between the earthly and heavenly realms, while the flowers point to the fulfil- ment of the "truth" of the Guadalupe event as announced by the birdsong.[45]

Perhaps most important of all is the way in which the Nahuatl text presents the flowers discovered by Juan Diego on the little hill that the Virgin asks him to ascend. The *Nican Mopohua* simply describes Juan Diego's astonishment, stating that 'he was much amazed by how many flowers were spread out before him, which held open their corollas, various precious flowers, like the ones of Castile', and adds that 'the flowers were very fragrant, they were like precious pearls, filled with the dew of the night'. This description, and the way in which Juan Diego recounts what he saw to the bishop in the text, coincide with the indigenous belief in *Xochitlalpan*, the 'blooming land', or *Tonacatlalpan*, the 'land of our subsistence', both metaphorical designations for the *Tlalocan*, where the god of rain resided.[46] Sánchez's equation of Tepeyac, the site of the flower's appearance, with the Garden of Eden is conspicuously reminiscent of this Nahua "Paradise", where the richest flora and a fertile garden were found, and to where those who died from drowning, lightning, lepra, gout, syphilis or dropsy were destined.[47]

The interpretation of the Virgin of Guadalupe as a durably materialized mariophany in the *Nican Mopohua* thus builds upon Nahua notions of pres- ence and representation as epitomized by the *ixiptla*, on the one hand. On the other hand, it is embedded within a wider colonial context also informed by Nahua traditions in which the Virgin's appearance becomes a pivotal event in world history. Even the location to which the Virgin leads Juan Diego to pick

44   Léon-Portilla, *Tonantzin Guadalupe* 94–98; Nebel, *Santa María Tonantzin* 191–192 (refer ence is to 137, verse 6 and 7).

45   Léon-Portilla, *Tonantzin Guadalupe* 94 and 134ff.; Nebel, *Santa María Tonantzin* 192–195 (reference is essentially to 137 verse 8 and to the pages following 144, verses 126ff.).

46   On this connotation of the flowers, see Léon-Portilla, *Tonantzin Guadalupe* 52–53, who explains that meditating on the beauty of the flowers was a recurring theme in the old chants of the Nahuas.

47   On the *Tlalocan*, see Ibarra García L., *Das Weltbild der Azteken: Entstehung und Begrün- dung* (Berlin: 2016) 61.

flowers is presented as a threshold between this world and a paradisiacal indigenous setting.

5   Sánchez's Translation of Nahua Concepts into the Language of Eschatology and Christian Mysticism

Most of the aforementioned elements connected to the Nahua cultural sphere in the *Nican Mopohua* resonate with motifs in Sánchez's account that are rather foreign to Christian traditions. These demonstrate that the *criollo* author was no more than a "translator" of this erudite Nahuatl text, itself situated at the intersection of European and Mesoamerican conceptions of the world. Sánchez should certainly be credited with having further Christianized the native account of the apparition of the Virgin for a creole audience, but not with having invented the account and its complex system of symbols altogether. That his aim was to mediate between Spanish, or more broadly European, and Nahua concepts and worldviews becomes evident in the typological parallel he establishes between the "eagle man" Juan Diego and Saint John the Evangelist. According to the *Nican Mopohua*, Juan Diego originates from Cuautitlán, literally the 'place of the eagle', calling up the indigenous symbolic connection between the eagle and the sun, and by extension the chosen "People of the Sun", the Aztecs.[48] Sánchez evokes the eagle as the centuries-old Christian symbol for Saint John, the apocalyptical "viewer" on Patmos.

By placing the miracle account within an eschatological framework, Sánchez expands upon the world-changing perspective already present in the *Nican Mopohua*, as expressed via indigenous concepts such as the night/dawn-disfrasism mentioned above, and brings it to a *criollo* audience. As pointed out by Richard Nebel, the meaning of this world changing perspective lies in an analogy with the myth of the creation of the "fifth Sun".[49] The pre-Columbian Nahua of Central Mexico had a notion of time quite unlike the Christian linear conception. For them world time was a cycle of ages, each brought to an end by a cataclysmic event; these endings, however, precipitated new beginnings.

---

48   Léon-Portilla, *Tonantzin Guadalupe* 94. As explained by Nebel, *Santa María Tonantzin* 191, tradition has it that Juan Diego held the name Cuauhtlatoatzin, 'he who speaks like an eagle', before his baptism. This name indicates one's belonging to the Aztec order of the "eagle men", or, alternatively, one's ability to explain the wisdom of the god (of the sun), whose symbol is an eagle.

49   Nebel, *Santa María Tonantzin* 192–193. He claims that on a more metaphorical level, the allusion could also be understood to refer to the beginning of a new world and society under the colonial order.

According to their beliefs, the current, fifth, Sun, which had been preceded by four earlier worlds or Suns, would ultimately be destroyed by an earthquake.[50] Jacques Lafaye asserted that Aztec eschatological imagination, with its expectation that the god Quetzalcóatl would return, converged with the millenarianism of the Catholic evangelizers in a 'mystique nationale créole' (national creole mysticism) and that at an early stage this took concrete form in the Virgin of Guadalupe.[51] The Aztecs believed that Quetzalcóatl, who had created humanity in the current fifth age, would return from his exile and restore his reign, laying the foundations of a golden age under a new Sun. The initial identification by the indigenous of this returning sovereign, come to reappropriate his dominion, with Hernán Cortés, is among the most widely known *topoi* related to the conquest of Mexico, though the Aztecs quickly abandoned this view upon recognizing the Spaniards' human traits. Because Lafaye dismissed as conjectural the idea that the *Nican Mopohua*, published as part of Lasso de la Vega's *Huei Tlamahuizoltica*, was the literary precedent for Sánchez's *Imagen de la Virgen María, Madre de Dios de Guadalupe*, his account of the elements of Aztec and Christian "eschatological" expectations he saw converging in the Virgin of Guadalupe remained very vague.[52] More concretely, his failure to recognize that Sánchez based his narrative on the much older *Nican Mopohua* meant Lafaye was unable to see how the former inspired Sánchez's version.

Sánchez's efforts to reconcile Nahua traditions with Christian concepts are apparent throughout his book. In the passages describing the miraculous creation of the Guadalupe icon, the language he uses to recount the discovery of the Virgin's miraculous impression on the cloth of Juan Diego's *tilma* is decidedly that of Christian mysticism. The bishop's rapture, induced by the flowers, is missing in the *Nican Mopohua*'s explanation of how the image appeared, and should certainly be interpreted as an allusion to visionary experience. This interpretation is well in tune with the engraving reproduced in both Sánchez's and De la Vega's printed accounts, in which the bishop is the only person depicted as directly gazing at the Virgin's image [Fig. 10.5] – he is granted a

---

50   On the worldview of the Aztecs, see Ibarra García, *Das Weltbild der Azteken*. According to Wobeser, *Orígenes del culto a nuestra señora* 158, an eschatological perspective connected to the worldview of the Nahuas is also present in the allusion to questions relating to the origin and end of humanity on earth. These are expressed in the *Nican Mopohua* via the close relationship of the Virgin of Guadalupe with *Ipalnemohuani*, the 'giver of life'. On the Virgin's connection to *Ipalnemohuani*, see Léon-Portilla, *Tonantzin Guadalupe* 58–60.

51   Lafaye, *Quetzalcóatl et Guadalupe*, here esp. 9.

52   Ibidem 320–335.

FIGURE 10.5   Unknown artist, *The Apparition of the Image of Our Lady of Guadalupe of Mexico*. Engraving, 16 × 11.2 cm. From: Lasso de la Vega Luis, *Huei tlamahuiçoltica* (Mexico, Imprenta de Iuan Ruyz: 1649). Imprint owned by the John Carter Brown Library, Providence, RI, inv. no. BA649.L347h
IMAGE COURTESY OF THE JOHN CARTER BROWN LIBRARY AT BROWN UNIVERSITY

divinely privileged experience of sight.[53] Once the Virgin has appeared on Juan Diego's mantle, Sánchez's employment of mystical terminology increases; for instance, he describes the crowd gathered around the image as 'fallen in ecstasy admiring it, suspended in admiration, captivated in soft elevation, in tender elevations, by affection, in contemplative fascination'.[54]

But Sánchez's quotation of 2 *Corinthians* 3:18 in this context, 'Nos autem revelata facie gloriam Domini speculantes, in ea[n]dem imaginem transformamur a claritate in claritatem, tamquam a Domini spiritu' (But we all, with open face beholding as in a glass the glory of the Lord, are changed into the same image from glory to glory, even as by the Spirit of the Lord), reveals just how inappropriate the conceptual framework of Christian mysticism is for the processes at work in the miraculous impression of the Virgin's image on Juan Diego's *tilma*, at least as they are described by Sánchez himself.[55] This framework cannot have provided the original foundation upon which the miracle account was based. The passage from Corinthians points to the anthropological assumptions at the core of Christian contemplative theory: mankind, 'created in the image of God' (*Genesis* 1:26–27), was believed to have lost its original similitude to the Creator. It could only be regained by following the path set out by Christ, himself the perfect image of God. A conception of vision in which the contemplative soul was progressively led from the world without to the world within complemented this anthropological matrix.[56] The ultimate goal was mystical union with the divine, conceived as the unimpeded gaze into God's face.[57] The quotation from Corinthians could have been appropriately

---

53   The engraving is included between fols. 30 and 31 in the printed version of Sánchez's account used here, held by the Universidad Complutense de Madrid: Sánchez Miguel, *Imagen de la Virgen María*; it is also included in the used copy of Lasso de la Vega's *Huei tlamahuiçoltica*, held by the John Carter Brown Library (BA649.L347h [last printed page before the *Nican Mopohua* begins]): Lasso de la Vega Luis, *Huei tlamahuiçoltica omonexiti in ilhuicac tlatóca Çihuapilli Santa Maria Totlaçònantzin Guadalupe in nican huei altepenahuac Mexico itocayocan tepeyacac* (Mexico: Imprenta de Iuan Ruyz, 1649).

54   Sánchez, *Imagen de la Virgen María*, fol. 30 v: 'Descubierta la Imagen, Arrodillandose todos y quedaron en extasis admirados; en admiraciones suspensos, en suspensiones elevados, en elevaciones enternecidos, en ternuras arrobados, en arrobos contemplativos, en contemplaciones endulçados'.

55   Ibidem, fol. 30 v. The English citation from 2 *Corinthians* is taken from the King James Version of the Bible.

56   Augustine's threefold categorization of vision, leading from the outer world to the inner world, determined this conception of vision and knowledge. Augustine, "De genesi ad litteram libri duodecim", in Migne J.-P. (ed.), *Sancti Aurelii Augustini Hipponensis Episcopi Opera Omnia* (Paris: 1845) 245–486, book 12.

57   Angenendt, *Geschichte der Religiosität im Mittelalter* 252–257.

applied to a representation of Veronica's veil, but associating it with the *tilma* painting seems unfitting, as the image revealed is that of the Virgin and not of her Son. The unusual assignment of the status of "a perfect image of God" to the Teyepac icon, a material image showing the Virgin, doesn't let this association appear any less surprising.

Sánchez's contention that all those present at the event desired to be 'transformed into that image'[58] is yet another attempt to integrate the Guadalupe icon into the mentioned traditional Christian framework. It points to the author's struggle to make sense of the miracle story by juxtaposing the event with another miraculous instance of image-making, which is, however, not mentioned here. Indeed, the exegesis applied to the stigmatization of St. Francis was precisely that of a progressive, transformative restoration of the "imago Dei" brought about by following in the footsteps of Christ: it was believed that after Francis had internally conformed himself to Christ, the appearance of the Son of God 'sub specie Seraph' on Mount Alverna perfected this metamorphosis by bestowing on him the signs of Christ crucified, thereby outwardly completing his transformation.[59]

6   Conclusion

In exploring the striking synthesis of traditions in both the *Nican Mopohua* and Sánchez's *Imagen de la Virgen María, Madre de Dios de Guadalupe*, this chapter has aimed to show that elements generally taken for granted or unquestioned in Sánchez's canonical account of the Virgin of Guadalupe's appearance are in fact translations of Nahua conceptions of the sacred into Christian terms. Her unique status as a permanent mariophany – a notion that, attached to an image, did not previously exist in the Christian tradition – must have been inspired by Nahua notions of presence and representation. The integration of such a status into Catholic frameworks of the divine made it possible to ascribe to the image an eschatological role that was equally novel within the tradition

---

58   Sánchez, *Imagen de la Virgen María*, fol. 30 v: 'Todos nosotros, indignamente merecendores de aver visto la revelacion de MARIA, à luzes claras en aquesta su Imagen, nos hallamos tan movidos del espiritu de Dios, tan alumbrados de su claridad, tan encendidos de sus fervores, que à vivas ansias, eficazes desseos, coridales impulsos, queremos transformarnos en aquesta su Imagen'.

59   On the stigmatization of St. Francis as a process relating to renewal of the *imago Dei* see Preisinger R., *Lignum vitae: Zum Verhältnis materieller Bilder und mentaler Bildpraxis im Mittelalter* (Paderborn: 2014) 101–105; on the encounter of St. Francis with Christ 'sub specie Seraph', ibidem 220.

FIGURE 10.6   Gregorio José de Lara, *Vision of St. John on Patmos*
Tenochtitlan, eighteenth century. Oil on canvas,
120 × 112 cm. Oaxaca, Templo de Coixtlahuaca
IMAGE: PESSCA (PROJECT ON THE ENGRAVED
SOURCES OF SPANISH COLONIAL ART),
HTTPS://COLONIALART.ORG/ARTWORKS/3602B

of Catholic icons. The lasting popularity of Sánchez's exegesis of the *Book of Revelation* is demonstrated by a painting by Gregorio José de Lara showing St. John's Vision on Patmos Tenochtitlan [Fig. 10.6]. In this eighteenth-century rendering of the famous episode of Revelation in which the woman of the Apocalypse appears in the sky, the biblical seer is seen prognosticating the apparition of the Virgin of Guadalupe in Mexico.[60]

Both time and space of the eschatological imaginations unfurled in Sánchez's *Imagen de la Virgen María, Madre de Dios de Guadalupe*, which revolve around the apparition of the Virgin of Guadalupe, were an expression of Mexican creole patriotism deeply marked by millenarian expectations. Sánchez ends the

---

60   On this painting, see Cuadriello J., "Visiones en Patmos Tenochtitlan: La mujer águila", *Artes de México* 29 (1999) 10–23.

treatise with an exhortation to 'his readers and all the peoples of New Spain to take their place at Tepeyac', reaffirming the providential role he assigns to Mexico in the history of salvation. In the context of an 'ongoing cosmic battle [...] in which the Antichrist arises as a wild beast out of the water, supersedes the powers of the dragon, and seduces the whole world with his might', Sánchez, through the mediation of St. Augustine, offers the image of the Virgin of Guadalupe to St. John, with the words (a variation and elaboration on *John* 19:27): 'John, beloved disciple of Christ, behold your mother; behold her image of Guadalupe; [...] behold the honour of the city of Mexico; behold the glory of all the faithful inhabitants in this New World'.[61] At this final point, the hints that Sánchez makes throughout his book that we must recentre notions of Christian eschatology both in geographical and temporal terms crystallize into a clear assertion: Mexico, through the miraculous Virgin of Guadalupe, has become the staging ground for the imminent Last Things.

Bibliography

Angenendt A., *Geschichte der Religiosität im Mittelalter* (Darmstadt: 2000).

Augustine, "De genesi ad litteram libri duodecim", in Migne J.-P. (ed.), *Sancti Aurelii Augustini Hipponensis Episcopi Opera Omnia* (Paris: 1845) 245–486.

Bacci M., *Il pennello dell'Evangelista: Storia delle immagini sacre attribuite a san Luca* (Pisa: 1998).

Báez Rubi L., "*Wanderstrassen*: Traveling Images – Moving Ideas Between Continents", in Alloa E. – Cappelletto C. (eds.), *Dynamis of the Image: Moving Images in a Global World* (Berlin – Boston: 2020) 79–102.

Bargellini C., "The Colors of the Virgin of Guadalupe", in Wolf G. – Connors J. (eds.), *Colors Between Two Worlds: The Florentine Codex of Bernardino de Sahagún* (Florence: 2011) 3–25.

Bargellini C., "The Virgin of Guadalupe: A Painting of New Spain", https://ism.yale .edu/sites/default/files/files/The%20Virgin%20of%20Guadalupe.pdf (accessed 03.08.2022).

Bassett M.H., *The Fate of Earthly Things: Aztec Gods and God-Bodies* (Austin, TX: 2015).

---

61 Sánchez, *Imagen de la Virgen María*, fol. 96 r: 'Iuan querido discipulo de Christo; ves aqui á tu Madre; ves aqui á su Imagen de Guadalupe; [...] ves aqui à la honra de la Cuidad de Mexico; ves aqui à la gloria de todos los moradores fieles en aquel nuevo mundo'; see also ibidem, fol. 90 v–91 r and 94 v–95 r. The first two quotes are from Matovina, "Guadalupe at Calvary" 806.

Belting H., *Likeness and Presence: A History of the Image before the Era of Art* (Chicago, IL: 1994).

Benz E., *Ecclesia spiritualis: Kirchenidee und Geschichtstheologie der franziskanischen Reformation* (Stuttgart: 1934).

Brading D.A., *Mexican Phoenix: Our Lady of Guadalupe. Image and Tradition across Five Centuries* (Cambridge: 2001).

Bynum C.W., *Christian Materiality: An Essay on Religion in Late Medieval Europe* (New York: 2011).

Carreón Blaine E., "Un giro alrededor del ixiplta", in Baéz Rubí L. – Carreón Blaine E. (eds.), *Los estatutos de la imagen, creación-manifestación-percepción* (Mexico City: 2014) 247–274.

Cuadriello J., "Visiones en Patmos Tenochtitlan: La mujer águila", *Artes de México* 29 (1999) 10–23.

De Boer W., *Art in Dispute: Catholic Debates at the Time of Trent with an Edition and Translation of Key Documents* (Leiden: 2022).

Gruzinski S., *La guerre des images de Christophe Colomb à "Blade Runner" (1492–2019)* (Paris: 1990).

Hvidtfeldt A., *Teotl and *Ixiptlatli: Some Central Conceptions in Ancient Mexican Religion* (Copenhagen: 1958).

Ibarra García L., *Das Weltbild der Azteken: Entstehung und Begründung* (Berlin: 2016).

Lafaye J., *Quetzalcóatl et Guadalupe: La formation de la conscience nationale au Mexique (1531–1813)* (Paris: 1974).

La Maza F. de, *El guadalupanismo mexicano* (Mexico City: 1953).

Lasso de la Vega Luis, *Huei tlamahuiçoltica omonexiti in ilhuicac tlatóca Çihuapilli Santa Maria Totlaçònantzin Guadalupe in nican huei altepenahuac Mexico itocayocan tepeyacac.* (Mexico, Imprenta de Iuan Ruyz: 1649).

Léon-Portilla M., *Tonantzin Guadalupe: Pensamiento náhuatl y mensaje cristiano en el "Nican Mopohua"* (Mexico City: 2000).

Lopez Austin A., *Cuerpo humano e ideologia: Las concepciones de los antiguos nahuas*, vol. 1 (Mexico City: 1980).

Matovina T., "Guadalupe at Calvary: Patristic Theology in Miguel Sánchez's *Imagen de la Virgen María* (1648)", *Theological Studies* 64 (2003) 795–811.

Nebel R., *Santa María Tonantzin Virgen de Guadalupe: Religiöse Kontinuität und Transformation in Mexiko* (Immensee: 1992).

Noguez X., *Documentos guadalupanos: Un estudio sobre las fuentes de información tempranas en torno a las mariofanías en el Tepeyac* (Toluca – Mexico City: 1993).

O'Gorman E., *Destierro de Sombras: Luz en el origen de la imagen y culto de nuestra Señora de Guadalupe del Tepeyac* (Mexico City: 1986).

Peterson J.F., *Visualizing Guadalupe: From Black Madonna to Queen of the Americas* (Austin, TX: 2014).

Phelan J.L., *The Millenial Kingdom of the Franciscans in the New World* (Berkeley, CA: 1970).

Poole S., *Our Lady of Guadalupe: The Origins and Sources of a Mexican National Symbol, 1531–1797* (Tucson, AZ: 1995).

Preisinger R., *Lignum vitae: Zum Verhältnis materieller Bilder und mentaler Bildpraxis im Mittelalter* (Paderborn: 2014).

Preisinger R., "(Re)framing the Virgin of Guadalupe: The Concurrence of Early Modern Prints and Colonial Devotions in Creating the Virgin", in Madar H. (ed.), *Prints as Agents of Global Exchange, 1500–1800* (Amsterdam: 2021) 181–213.

Prosperi A., *America e apocalisse e altri saggi* (Pisa – Rome: 1999).

Sánchez Miguel, *Imagen de la Virgen María, Madre de Dios de Guadalupe* (Mexico City, Imprenta de la Viuda de Bernardo Calderon: 1648).

Stoichita V.I., *Visionary Experience in the Golden Age of Spanish Art* (London: 1995).

Suárez de Peralta Juan, *Tratado del descubrimiento de las Indias* (Mexico City: 1990).

Winston-Allen A., *Stories of the Rose: The Making of the Rosary in the Middle Ages* (University Park, PA: 1997).

Wobeser G. von, *Orígenes del culto a nuestra señora de Guadalupe, 1521–1688* (Mexico City: 2020).

Wolf G., *Schleier und Spiegel: Traditionen des Christusbildes und die Bildkonzepte der Renaissance* (Munich: 2002).

PART 4

Spiritual Reckoning and Refuge

∴

CHAPTER 11

Pondering Mary: Michelangelo's Farewell to Dante

Jane Tylus

Abstract

The late medieval and early modern period witnessed in Catholic contexts an extension or 'prolungamento' of goodbyes. Michelangelo's own inability to finish, and hence say goodbye to many of his works, both manifests this sense of *prolungamento* and introduces a disquieting new element that challenges the nature of human work as a means toward salvation. This is especially clear when we consider two aspects of Michelangelo's career. One is his representation of Mary, the mediator who typically intervenes to assure the worth of one's work. The other is his relationship to the poet he most admired, Dante, whose *Commedia* is very much a finished text that expresses hope in its own afterlife thanks in no small part to Mary's presence in its final canto. In furnishing a reading of the (unfinished) Medici chapel as well as a handful of Michelangelo's lyric poems for Vittoria Colonna, this essay situates the two Florentines, and two versions of Mary, within the framework of the changing spatial and temporal dynamics of the farewell at a time of religious turmoil.

Keywords

Michelangelo – Dante – Colonna – Reformation – lyric

What was Mary to Michelangelo? This essay will attempt to give a necessarily partial answer to a question that at first glance may seem to fit only tangentially with the concerns of this volume.[1] Yet the role that Mary played in Michelangelo's lifetime – and still today – as a consoling presence to whom Catholics pray 'now, and at the hour of [their] death', argues for her critical connections with the afterlife. As the only human without sin, Mary embodied, in the word's most literal sense, the capacity of the flesh to contain the

---

1   My thanks to the editors of the volume along with the two anonymous readers who gave extremely helpful advice and suggested further readings. I am also grateful for the comments of the many colleagues who participated in the online discussion of this paper in March, 2022.

divine. The increasing insistence throughout the Middle Ages on her bodily assumption into heaven created a reassuring continuity between humans on earth and the one human to retain her body in paradise up until the time of the resurrection of the blessed. The thirteenth-century narrative of her dormition from the *Legenda Aurea* expresses the hope not only of the apostles who sat at her bedside as she died, but of every Christian facing death. While those apostles claimed to have found consolation in Mary's presence after the ascension of Christ – 'Looking at you was as though we were seeing our Lord and Master, and we were consoled' – their 'only comfort' at the prospect of her imminent death 'is that we hope to have you as our mediatrix with God'.[2] Such a connection solidified Catholicism's insistence on tying the living to the dead, the earthly world to the heavenly one. Or as Brian Daley has noted, 'What was important was the news that one of our own kind – the source of the Saviour's humanity – already shared, after death, in the glorious life of the risen Christ, and that Christ had appointed her as our patron to help us navigate the same journey'.[3]

Yet as the following remarks will suggest, such consolation as offered by Mary's consoling presence is far from evident in the work of Michelangelo. Both his artistic work and his poems are conspicuously lacking in references to a Mary who might serve as an advocate or guide, and whose humanity might in turn redeem and validate Michelangelo's own, tortured humanness. This is a distinctive change from the Florentine whose poetic works Michelangelo prized above any others, Dante. At the close of the *Commedia*, Dante has Bernard of Clairvaux address Mary as she who 'gave to human nature so much nobility that its Creator did not disdain his being made its created'.[4] Mary's 'ennobling' of the human condition enables in turn Dante's search for Mary's assurance that his work would be recognized as an authentic representation of his journey to the afterlife and hence a validation of his fruitful time on earth.

But less than two centuries after Dante ended his masterpiece with a Marian invocation, Europe was witness to a radical questioning and recontextualization of this narrative about Mary's role at thresholds – those of

---

2 Voragine Jacobus de, *The Golden Legend*, trans. W.G. Ryan, 2 vols. (Princeton, NJ: 1993) 2:90.

3 Daley B.E., "At the Hour of Our Death: Mary's Dormition and Christian Dying in Late Patristic and Early Byzantine Literature", *Dumbarton Oaks Papers* 55 (2001) 71–89. As Daley notes, the story of Mary's dormition and assumption first emerged in the sixth century in the Eastern Orthodox church. See his edited collection, Daley B.E. (ed.), *On the Dormition of Mary: Early Patristic Homilies* (Crestwood, NY: 1998).

4 Dante, *Paradiso* 33:4–6: 'tu sè colei che l'umana natura / nobilitasti sí, che 'l suo fattore / non disdegnò di farsi sua fattura'. All citations are from Alighieri Dante, *The Divine Comedy of Dante Alighieri: Paradiso*, trans. A. Mandelbaum (Berkeley, CA: 1984), unless otherwise noted.

other humans as well as her own. Doubts about Mary's efficacy and that of the hundreds of saints who surround her in the empyrean translated into doubts about the value of human actions on earth.[5] If Dante's invocation of Mary is an attempt to valorize his poem, Michelangelo's respective silence with regard to Mary's mediating role is a noteworthy shift in the early modern landscape. Questioning – or more accurately, simply disregarding – Mary's efficacy becomes a means of questioning the efficacy of his own works and their ability to assure for him a place in heaven. As we turn to Michelangelo's poetry along with his artistic renderings of Christ's mother, especially in the unfinished Medici chapel in the New Sacristy of San Lorenzo, we will find a very different conception of the mediating status of artistic work, as well as of a Mary burdened by her humanity and that of her son. And such a burden could only produce in Michelangelo the sentiment of remorse that he vividly expresses in a late sonnet about his famous fellow Florentine: 'If only I were he!'.[6] It is to that precursor and his medieval moment that I'll turn first, in order to better understand why Michelangelo longed to have been Dante Alighieri.

As Jacobus de Voragine was composing his *Legenda Aurea*, Jacopo Turriti was at work on his mosaics of Mary's dormition in Santa Maria Maggiore, and Cimabue would soon begin his cycle of paintings on Mary's death and assumption in Assisi. They were not alone in this comparatively new attentiveness in Western Europe to the story of Mary's final days. The mid-thirteenth century also saw the development of the *stil nuovo* – poetry dedicated to an earthly beloved that in no small part takes its cue from the traditions of Marian devotion and the new emphasis on Mary's divine humanity.[7] Moreover, these poems were increasingly in the new vernaculars of late medieval Europe. Hence the troubadours of southern France, the court poets of Sicily, and the communal poets of Tuscany began their poetic revolution, introducing new languages

---

5   See, for just one example, the work of Rubin M., *Emotion and Devotion: The Meaning of Mary in Medieval Religious Cultures* (Budapest: 2009), particularly 25: 'Mary's place in late medieval culture became varied and ubiquitous [; by 1500] it also became increasingly vexed, tendentious, and disturbing'; and idem., *Mother of God: A History of the Virgin Mary* (New Haven, CT: 2009).

6   Sonnet 248, from Buonarroti Michelangelo, *The Poetry of Michelangelo: An Annotated Translation*, ed. and trans. J.M. Saslow (New Haven, CT: 1991) 421: 'Fuss'io pur lui!'. All further references to the Italian and English translation will be from this text unless otherwise indicated.

7   In a recent review of David Rothenberg's *The Flower of Paradise: Marian Devotion and Secular Song in Medieval and Renaissance Music*, in *Journal of the American Musicological Society* 65 (2012) 602, Elizabeth Eva Leach suggests that Rothenberg's 'binary' between secular and sacred is not as fruitful as recognizing the 'continuum of possibilities for the expression of desire'.

and new things – a 'newness never conceived before',[8] as Dante boldly put it in his *canzone, Amor, tu vedi ben*.

That Mary was a crucial aspect of that boldness is clear from the end of the *Convivio*, an extended set of commentaries Dante wrote on his own *canzoni* in the early 1300s. At the close of the fourth *trattato*, in what would be the final pages of this incomplete work, Dante had this to say about the best way to end a poem. The 'fabbricatore' or builder of a poem should use the close of his work to render it as noble and as beautiful as possible so that it might part from him even more celebrated and precious (*Convivio* IV.30).[9] Dante is following sound rhetorical principles that go back to Cicero, Seneca, and others, who urged that an orator's arguments should always finish with what is strongest, so they would remain in the ears of their audience. When Petrarch sent Boccaccio his translation into Latin of the final tale from the *Decameron*, he would use the word *validiora* – forceful – to characterize the way that a work should end (*fine operis*).[10] But while such an appeal might seem fairly routine, what is striking about Dante's phrasing is that his neologism *nobilitare* returns only once again in his writing: in the passage quoted above from Canto 33 of *Paradiso* referring to Mary as 'the one who gave to human nature so much nobility' ('nobilitasti sí'). It is only fitting that Dante invokes her at the close of the *Commedia*, as he seeks to dignify his poem by praising, and praying to, the mother of God.

But Dante also seeks his own salvation through such a project, and hence needs to retain what he has seen so that he can tell others and exercise a work of charity back on earth. Such becomes Bernard's final request for his charge: 'This too, O Queen, who can do what you would, I ask of you: that after such a vision, his sentiments be preserved intact'.[11] This act of strengthening poem and poet alike enables Dante to leave a single 'favilla' or spark to future

---

8   Alighieri Dante, *Rime*, ed. M. Barbi (Bologna: 1972) 100: 'la novità […] che non fu mai pensata in alcun tempo'.

9   Alighieri Dante, *Convivio*, ed. G. Inglese (Milan: 1999) 337: 'ciascuno buono fabricatore, ne la fine del suo lavoro, quello nobilitare e abbellire dee in quanto puote, acciò che più celebre e più prezioso da lui si parta'.

10   Petrarca Francesco, *Res seniles*, ed. S. Rizzo (Florence: 2017) 446, *Sen.* 17.3.10.

11   Dante, *Paradiso* 33:34–36: 'Ancor ti priego, regina, che puoi / ciò che tu vuoli, che conservi sani, / dopo tanto veder, li affetti suoi'; translation from Mandelbaum slightly emended. As Enrico Malato annotates the line, the request is that Dante 'will be able to recount […] such an extraordinary experience'; Alighieri Dante, *La Divina Commedia*, ed. E. Malato (Rome: 2018) 991, note. For a recent extended commentary on the canto, see Casadei A., *Dante: Inno alla Vergine, Paradiso canto XXXIII* (Milan: 2021).

readers.[12] Mary is not only Dante's 'way' to God – she authorized Beatrice's departure from Paradise to instruct Virgil to find the errant pilgrim – but Dante's means to *remembering* that way, and to making it available to us as readers so it might aid in our salvation, and his own.

Dante's closing canto did not go unremarked by his successors. Half a century later, Petrarch invoked Mary at the end of his most ambitious work in the vernacular, his *rime sparse*. As seen in his comment to Boccaccio, Petrarch too believed in endings characterized by strength and persuasiveness. Hence his prayer in his closing *canzone* to Mary – albeit one offered directly by himself, not by Bernard.[13] After praising the 'Vergine bella' for twelve stanzas, he turns at the end of the poem, and thus of the *Canzoniere* itself, with these lines:

> The day draws near and cannot be far, time so runs and flies, single sole Virgin; and now conscience, now death pierces my heart: commend me to your Son, true man and true God, that He may receive my last breath in peace.[14]

Written after 1369, and thus just a few years before his death, the poem shows Petrarch taking what Luca Marcozzi has called 'definitive control of what had to that point been an "open text"', as his *ultimo spirto* or final breath becomes the last word produced by that breath.[15] Yet these last words are addressed not to the poem, as would be the case in a typical congedo or final stanza, but the Vergine: as though she *were* the *canzone*, the messenger who speaks for the poet and goes off to find the right reader. In this case that reader is Mary's own son, whom Mary ideally will urge to welcome Petrarch's soul in peace, the same 'pace' that ends, in a more defiant way, Petrarch's famous *canzone* 128

---

12 Dante, *Paradiso* 33:71–72: 'ch'una favilla sol de la tua gloria / possa lasciare a la futura gente'.

13 On Petrarch's indebtedness to the final canto of the *Commedia*, see Martinez R., "Places and Times of the Liturgy from Dante to Petrarch", in Barański Z.G. – Cachey, Jr. T.J. (eds.), *Petrarch and Dante: Anti-Dantism, Metaphysics, Tradition* (Notre Dame, IN: 2009) 320–370, especially 348–350.

14 Italian text and English translation from Durling R., *Petrarch's Lyric Poems: The Rime Sparse and Other Lyrics* (Cambridge, MA: 1976) 582–583: 'Il dì s'appressa, et non pote esser lunge, / sì corre il tempo et vola, / Vergine unica et sola, / e 'l cor or conscienzia or morte punge: / raccomandami al tuo Figliuol, verace / omo et verace Dio, / ch'accolga 'l mio spirto ultimo in pace'.

15 Marcozzi L., "Making the *Rerum vulgarium fragmenta*", in Ascoli A. – Falkeid U. (eds.), *The Cambridge Companion to Petrarch* (Cambridge: 2015) 59.

dedicated to 'Italia mia'.[16] But this is not worldly peace Petrarch seeks, and he is no longer sending his poem to the lords of his broken country. Now it is the end of the night, with day pressing to arrive, and it won't be long before dawn and the swift death that awaits him. Mary is the one with whom the poet talks, and through her, Jesus the reader on whom Petrarch will bet. He makes that bet, moreover, based on this prayer that emerges from the secular, tainted, life project that is his *Canzoniere* – and the prayer that in this admittedly idealized reading may finally allow him to believe that he had some redemption through his art. No mere *canzone* sent out or 'avanzata' to an audience who may or may not appreciate it,[17] the final words to Mary are the capstone of the lifelong process that has now become a book, embodied by this loving mother who crashed through the divide between human and divine to retain her body in paradise and dignify the human race. Thus do we see the unfolding of a gene-alogy of *nobilitare* that uses Mary, 'one of our own', to bestow dignity upon the poem's creator as well as his creation.[18]

This is the genealogy that will come to haunt Michelangelo and more gen-erally, early modern Europe. The Reformation would take a different stance toward the status of human works and Mary's role in confirming the dignity of the human. If Petrarch and Dante represented a faith in the ability of their last words to move the noble lady who will in turn move her son, Martin Luther articulates endings in a very different way. This is clear from Luther's reflec-tions on the death of his thirteen-year-old daughter. As Craig Koslofsky writes, 'After her death the prayers of her parents for her salvation ceased. Magdalena was now beyond intercession. [...] "Separation" is the term Luther later used to describe her death – as when he says, "the separation troubles me beyond measure. It's strange to know that she is surely at peace and that she is well off there, and yet to grieve so much!"'.[19]

---

16   The poet's pause before the final 'stanza' of a lyric poem offers a potential for what Judith
       Peraino has called an 'imagined moment of imminent subjectivity' as the poet stands on
       a threshold to bid goodbye to his creation; see Peraino J., *Giving Voice to Love: Song and
       Self-Expression from the Troubadours to Guillaume de Machaut* (Oxford: 2011) 100.
17   See Dante's *Donne che avete intelletto*, line 48, in which he anticipates the moment of
       sending out his *canzone*: 'quand'io t'avró avanzata'; Alighieri Dante, *Rime Giovanili e della
       Vita Nuova*, ed. T. Barolini (Milan: 2009) 320.
18   See Cherchi P., *Verso la chiusura: Saggio sul Canzoniere di Petrarca* (Bologna: 2008) 174: 'La
       preghiera alla Vergine è già un canto "umanistico" alla *dignitas hominis*, e il motivo della
       terrestrità e della maternità e della corporeità che la pervade ne offre una conferma' ('The
       prayer to the Virgin is already a "humanistic" poem to human dignity, and the motif of
       earthliness, maternity, and corporeality that pervades it confirms this').
19   Koslofsky C., *The Reformation of the Dead: Death and Ritual in Early Modern Germany,
       1450–1700* (New York, NY: 2000), quoted on 153.

Koslofsky argues that Luther shocked his congregation in 1522 in Wittenberg 'with a relentless emphasis on the isolation of death'. Or as Luther put it in his sermon, 'The summons of death comes to us all, and no one can die for another. Everyone must fight his own battle with death by himself, alone. We can shout into each other's ears, but everyone must himself be prepared for the time of death: I will not be with you then, nor you with me'.[20] One might envision the crowded bedside scenes of the paintings of Mary's death by Duccio or Cimabue, in contrast to what Koslofsky characterizes as 'the permanent physical separation of the dead from the world of the living' as Protestant reformers forbade intercessions for the living by Mary and the saints, as well as the living's intercessions for the dead.[21] For Luther, Catholicism is about never saying goodbye. Rather, it embraces the indefinite extension of the living into the realm of the dead, as though its works, paltry summations of human life, were worthy – dignified – of being counted. If Mary was the *mediatrix* between heaven and earth; if purgatory embodied the refusal to say goodbye, the Reformation's abandonment of purgatory argues for the finality of life at the minute a body breathes its last – until the Last Judgement.

To this extent, Michelangelo presents an interesting case of an artist troubled by the prospect of complete separation at death from both the living and one's own works. Surely the saddest of Michelangelo's poems is a late sonnet that can be read as a congedo to his career, starkly different from Petrarch's *canzone* to the Virgin. Conceptualizing his life as about to end, the elderly Michelangelo, likely in his mid-late seventies, opens sonnet 285 with the unambiguous declaration that his journey is over and that he has already arrived at his final resting place: 'The voyage of my life at last has reached, across a stormy sea, in a fragile boat, the common port all must pass through, to give an accounting for every evil and pious deed'.[22] This accounting necessarily demands admitting that he 'recognize how laden with error was the affectionate fantasy that made art an idol and sovereign to me'[23] – an art that can no longer quiet or console him, let alone ensure his entrance into heaven. Thus he ends, bitterly: 'Neither painting

---

20 Ibidem 3, from a sermon of 9 March 1522 (translation Koslofsky's).

21 Ibidem 2. See Carlos Eire's succinct comment: 'Suddenly, death and the afterlife stopped being a communal experience. Barred from aiding the poor souls in purgatory [...] Protestants now faced the divine tribunal and their eternal destiny *alone*, at the end of *this* life'; *A Very Brief History of Eternity* (Princeton, NJ: 2009) 152.

22 Buonarroti, *The Poetry of Michelangelo* 476: 'Giunto è già 'l corso della vita mia, / con tempestoso mar, per fragil barca, / al comun porto, ov' a render si varca / conto e ragion d'ogni opera trista e pia'.

23 Ibidem: 'Onde l'affettuosa fantasia / che l'arte mi fece idol e monarca / conosco or ben com'era d'error carca'.

nor sculpture will be able any longer to calm my soul, now turned toward that divine love that opened his arms on the cross to take us in'.[24] The *volta* or turn that is typically enacted in the congedo to the poem itself – or in the final canto of *Paradiso* and the last stanza of Petrarch's final *canzone* to Mary – is here a volta toward a silent Christ. Michelangelo does not invoke Mary, just the nameless 'amor divino' that expresses itself on the cross through disembodied arms.[25]

Such sentiments regarding the insufficiency of human effort, far from limited to a single poem, in fact mark Michelangelo's career, at least its last three decades when the artist turned increasingly to poetry as a form of expression.[26] For sonnet 285 was hardly the first time that Michelangelo acknowledges the error with which he has been so burdened. Some twenty years earlier, in sonnet 159, with its telling first line – 'In order, lofty lady, to be less unworthy'[27] – Michelangelo likewise reflects on the heaviness of a belief held in error. As in the later poem that takes stock of an entire career, this misguided belief about the dignity of one's life arose in relationship to the meaning of Michelangelo's 'frail and fleeting work'.[28] Strikingly, those frail works are here posited in relationship to a figure of real force. This is not the suffering Christ on a cross, but a powerful female figure, an *alta signora* who one might think was Mary were it not for the fact that the autograph version of the sonnet was included in a letter to Vittoria Colonna in which Michelangelo 'alludes to unspecified gifts from the Marchesa'.[29] Or to quote the two *terzine*:

> And now I see clearly (*veggio ben*) what a mistake it was to think that the divine grace that rains down from you could be equaled by my frail, fragile work; // So do my wit, my art, my memory fail me, for a mortal being

---

24   Ibidem: 'Né pinger né scolpir fie più che quieti / l'anima, volta a quell'amor divino / c'aperse, a prender noi, 'n croce le braccia'.

25   For consideration of the several draft versions of the sonnet, see Wallace W., "'Certain of Death': Michelangelo's Late Life and Art", *Renaissance Quarterly* 28 (2015) 1–32, especially 16–19, noting that as Michelangelo revised the poem for possible publication, he moved from outright despair to a 'hope for salvation' given his address to Christ's 'open arms' (19).

26   Also see sonnet 160, where Michelangelo asks how the debtor can ever feel 'libero e sciolto' from his debt; Buonarroti, *The Poetry of Michelangelo* 316. The question of indebtedness continued to obsess him throughout his career, as seen in one of the last sonnets, 299, which ends with "l debito pagar non è presente' (the repayment of a debt is not a gift); ibidem 496.

27   Ibidem 314: 'Per esser manco, alta signora, indegno'.

28   Ibidem: 'l'opra mia caduca e frale'.

29   Ibidem 314–315, and there note Saslow's comment regarding the 'draft letter', 'which parallels the theme of the poem'.

can never – not even with a thousand attempts – repay a heavenly gift with something merely his own (159).[30]

On the one hand, 'veggio ben' – I [now] see clearly – looks back to Petrarch's first sonnet, in which he says at the same point in the poem (line 9), 'Ma ben veggio or' (But now I clearly see).[31] Petrarch likewise saw his error, for which he feels a remorse that will be echoed in the *canzone* to Mary. On the other hand, Michelangelo's wording anticipates his phrasing in sonnet 285, 'conosco or bene' (I now know well), after which Michelangelo speaks of turning his soul to Christ ('l'anima volta a quell'amor divino'; 285:13). And just as in that later poem, Michelangelo's error consists in having overestimated the value of his work. The artist 'now clearly sees' nothing but incongruity between what he can give, and what Christ or the earthly woman who is the dedicatee of 159 have already given him. This is only heightened by the presence of another echo in the lines above, for the failure of his memory, art, and *ingegno* alludes to *Paradiso* 33:56–57: 'memory fails when faced with such excess'.[32] The 'excess' is what Dante visually encounters ('il mio veder') when he turns his eyes on high following Bernard's prayer to the Virgin, at the culmination of his 100-canto journey. Michelangelo's failure of 'genius, art, and memory' is a response to a gift as well, Colonna's gift of friendship. Yet whereas Dante does not question his gift – nor, importantly, the ability of his *arte* to eventually represent that gift – Michelangelo declares in the opening line that he is unworthy of the 'don di vostra immensa cortesia' because he is unable to repay (*pagar*) Colonna for what she has given him. And if Dante asks for only a single *favilla* so that he might pass his poem on to others, Michelangelo is reduced by Colonna's overwhelming grace to asking for nothing – and so he has nothing to offer to 'la futura gente'.

Was Michelangelo putting Colonna in Mary's place – substituting one 'alta signora' for another? This becomes crucial when considering Colonna as someone whose questioning of popular devotional Catholicism has often been seen as influential for Michelangelo's attraction to certain tenets of Reformation belief – including its consignment of the Virgin to a less active posture, less

---

30   My translation; for the Italian text, ibidem 314: 'E veggio ben com'erra s'alcun crede / la grazia, che da voi divina piove, / pareggi l'opra mia caduca e frale. // L'ingegno, l'arte, la memoria cede: / c'un don celeste non con mille pruove / pagar del suo può già chi è mortale'.
31   Petrarca, *Petrarch's Lyric Poems* 36–37.
32   Dante, *Paradiso* 33:57: 'cede la memoria a tanto oltraggio'.

mediatrix than example of human obedience to the divine.[33] Many have speculated on Colonna's impact on Michelangelo's poetry, as well as on the theological implications of the several drawings he sent her as gifts.[34] That 159
along with the remaining poems to be addressed in this essay are all from a
gift manuscript that seems to have been intended for Colonna, suggests that
the dynamics of worth are deeply tied to Michelangelo's connection to this
'alta signora' who may come to serve in some ways for the sculptor as a substitute for Mary herself. This is the very Mary whose role was diminished by
the circle of reformers with whom Colonna was in direct contact, including
Reginald Pole, Bernardino Ochino, and Giovanni Morone.[35] While it would
require considerable space to assess Colonna's influence on Michelangelo in
detail, what can be addressed in this limited context is the extent to which
Michelangelo's sonnets for Colonna anticipate his later rejection of his art as
salvific as they return in intriguing ways to his forbears' appeals to Mary at the
moment of endings. In this light, Colonna can be seen as a figure onto whom
Michelangelo transfers his ambivalent reactions to his precursors' versions of
the mother of Christ – becoming as much a (failed) substitute for Mary as a
vehicle for expressing Michelangelo's uncertainties about Mary's role in the
vernacular tradition.

---

33 From the large bibliography of works that might be cited here, see Enrico Campi's thor-
ough study, *Michelangelo e Vittoria Colonna: Un dialogo artistico-teologico ispirato da
Bernardino Ochino* (Turin: 1994), as well as Abigail Brundin's edition of Vittoria Colonna,
Sonnets for Michelangelo (Chicago, IL: 2005) and the volume of essays she edited, *A Com-
panion to Vittoria Colonna* (Leiden: 2016). Also see Prodan S.R., *Michelangelo's Christian
Mysticism: Spirituality, Poetry and Art in Sixteenth-Century Italy* (Cambridge: 2017), and
her essay "Religious Desire in the Poetry of Vittoria Colonna: Insights into Early Modern
Piety and Poetics", in Cox V. – McHugh S. (eds.), *Vittoria Colonna: Poetry, Religion, Art,
Impact* (Amsterdam: 2022) 153–169.

34 On the question of the 'gift' in relation to Colonna and Michelangelo, see Alexander
Nagel's fundamental essay, "Gifts for Michelangelo and Vittoria Colonna", *Art Bulletin* 79
(1997) 647–668. More recently, see Maratsos J., "Michelangelo, Vittoria Colonna, and the
Afterlife of Intimacy", *Art Bulletin* 99 (2017) 69–101.

35 On Michelangelo's Mariology, see Campi, *Michelangelo e Vittoria Colonna* 55–76, as well
as his essay "Vittoria Colonna and Bernardino Ochino", in Brundin (ed.), *A Companion
to Vittoria Colonna* 371–398, particularly 391–395, where he addresses Colonna's prose
works and her role in extinguishing 'some of the brightest stars in the firmament of contemporary Marian spirituality' (394). Maria Forcellino suggests in the same volume that
Michelangelo's drawing of the *Pietà* for Colonna shows Mary as 'no longer the Mediatrix'
but an 'example of faith and humility': Forcellino, "Vittoria Colonna and Michelangelo:
Drawings and Paintings", in Brundin (ed.), *A Companion to Vittoria Colonna* 270–313, at
303. On the manuscript itself, see Brundin's edition of Colonna's *Sonnets for Michelangelo*,
and Fedi R., "'L'immagine vera': Vittoria Colonna, Michelangelo, e un'idea di canzoniere",
MLN 107 (1992) 46–73; see his final point about Michelangelo's inability to complete the
canzoniere after Colonna's death (69).

This seems to be the case with madrigal 149, which returns to the failure of *ingegno* and *arte*:

> I can't help seeming to lack talent and art
> to her who takes my life
> with such excessive help
> that one would get more out of much less mercy.
> Although my soul departs
> like an eye hurt by one who shines too much,
> and rises up above me
> to what's out of my reach, it doesn't raise me with it
> to make me equal to the smallest gift
> of my lofty, calm lady [...].[36]

The madrigal's final phrase pointedly describes this woman as abounding in grace ('di grazie piena'), a return to the Mary's of both *Paradiso* 33 and Petrarch's 'vergine santa, d'ogni grazia piena' (*Canzone* 366:39). But far from being open to receiving that grace, Michelangelo is tormented by his inadequacy, which is only heightened by the offerings of this 'donna alta e serena' (line 8). And here we see a striking difference with the Mary that Petrarch described as being of 'altissima umiltate' or 'highest humility' – the humility that enables Petrarch to hope in her pity. In his exhaustive analysis of Michelangelo's poetry, Glauco Cambon observes that 'this very saintliness [attached to Colonna's personal identity] is also what prevents fruition, a sometimes intolerable hardness (*durezza*), hence the pointed oxymora in the description of her impact on his tormented psyche'.[37] The 'excessive light' or *superchio lume* emanating from Michelangelo's lady – a phrase used in madrigal 113, one of the earliest poems to Colonna – can only reveal difference, rather than similarities, between her and the poet. The phrase 'superchio lume' is found in Dante and Petrarch too – although as Thomas Mussio suggests, Dante eventually adjusts to the excess of heavenly light, as it 'heal[s] the wound of his spiritual blindness', whereas

---

36 Buonarroti, *The Poetry of Michelangelo* 299: 'Non posso non mancar d'ingegno e d'arte / a chi mi to' la vita / con tal superchia aita, / che d'assai men mercé più se ne prende. / D'allor l'alma mie parte / com'occhio offeso da chi troppo splende, / e sopra me trascende / a l'impossibil mie; per farmi pari / al minor don di donna alta e serena, / seco non m'alza [...]'.

37 Cambon G., *Michelangelo's Poetry: Fury of Form* (Princeton, NJ: 1985) 70. The comment is elaborated with regard to sonnet 151, *Non ha l'ottimo artista alcun concetto*, about which Cambon says '*durezza* is attributed to Vittoria Colonna, who appears as the sphinx-like block of stone to be quarried for the good she hides inside; but the artist is unequal to the challenge and can only extract "death" from her' (76).

'for Michelangelo, grace threatens to dissolve his soul at the same time in which it dissolves his sin [...]'.[38] Such dissolution – or, perhaps more precisely, paralysis – prevents the noble, 'alta' Colonna from taking on Mary's humble role as loving mediator, and deprives the act of grace of being simply a free gift in the spirit of the Reformation's notion of *grazia*. Arguably distanced from a world in which Mary's centrality had presupposed the possibility of human dignity – *nobilitarsi* – and yet still inclined to believe in the Catholic doctrine of works, Michelangelo needs to invest his own works with a value worthy of making him the recipient of divine gifts. But what could those works ever be?

This was the good fortune of Dante, the Dante whom Michelangelo would give anything to become: 'Fuss'io pur lui!'. This line opens the climactic second terzina in one of Michelangelo's two sonnets for Dante, both written in the mid-late 1540s and included in the manuscript meant for Colonna. In 250, Michelangelo does not address the dead Dante directly. He is a distant, third person, whose life and poem are presented as one, as Michelangelo deliberately refuses to distinguish between the person and the narrator of the *Commedia*: '[Dante] descended to the just deserts of error / for our benefit, and then ascended to God' (250:5–6)[39] – a downward and upward motion that captures the narrative of the *Commedia* as well as of Dante's own life. Clearly Bernard of Clairvaux's prayer to the Virgin on Dante's behalf was answered, as Dante was enabled 'to contemplate God, in order to give us the true light of it all (*tutto il vero lume*)', as he writes in his other sonnet to Dante (248:3–4).[40] *Tutto* il vero lume: in Michelangelo's rendition, Dante gave us that light in its entirety, rather than a simple spark. Dante's systematic thoroughness in his writing merits the reward that only God can finally give, while the earthly reward he should have received was never forthcoming.

And that reward, as we learn in 248, was to become the 'lucente stella' or bright star whose rays from paradise brighten the nest where Michelangelo was born. This is what Dante receives for his words and his works, as seen in the moment of direct address spoken not to Dante, but to God, the 'Tu sol', who created Dante, and who alone can reward him for what he did. While Michelangelo considers himself 'indegno' of any gift he might receive, the only thing *indegno* about Dante was his exile – and his inability to have his works ('l'opre suo') recognized by an ungrateful people ('popolo ingrato'; 248). And

---

38   Mussio T.E., "The Augustinian Conflict in the Lyrics of Michelangelo: Michelangelo Reading Petrarch", *Italica* 74:3 (1997) 339–359, at 352. See Di Fenza A., "Excessive Poetry: The Use of *Superchio* in Michelangelo's Verses", MLN 132 (2017) 47–67 for a discussion of the word in Michelangelo.

39   Buonarroti, *The Poetry of Michelangelo* 424: 'Questo discese a' merti del fallire / per l'util nostro, e poi a Dio ascese'.

40   Ibidem 421: '[...] a contemplare Dio, / per dar di tutto il vero lume a noi'.

yet Dante received his 'gift' from God before he was born. The opening of 248 suggests that Dante descended directly from heaven – 'Dal ciel discese' – and then 'ritornò vivo', *returned there* in his mortal flesh to gaze on God, so as 'to give us the true light of it all'. Sent like Christ from heaven, he returns there not once, but twice.

Dante's lightness of being, which prompts recognition from God if not from his fellow Florentines, contrasts with the heaviness of Michelangelo and his works, a 'durezza' that has questionable value for Michelangelo's own purchase on heaven as conveyed in the late sonnet already considered, *Giunto è già 'l corso*. In madrigal 240, written in the same period as these sonnets to Dante, the stone or 'pietra' invoked in the madrigal's opening line is confined to earth alone, and can be valued only in human terms. And this is the case even if the stone is meant to represent the face of Mary's replacement, the divine Colonna:

> Art wills this lady's face
> to live down here as long
> as years go by, if only in living stone.
> Then what should God do for her,
> this being my handiwork, and she being his,
> not merely mortal but godly,
> and not only in my eyes?
> And yet she'll last but a short time and must leave;
> and her fortune will be hobbled on its right side
> if a rock remains and death still hurries her on.
> Who'll take revenge for her?
> Nature alone, since only her children's works
> last here below (*l'opra qui dura*), and time carries off her own (240).[41]

The closing phrase – 'l'opra qui dura' – seems to suggest the artist's triumph: nature's works are stolen by the passing of time, while those of the sculptor endure, a play on the doubleness of *dura* as both verb and adjective. Yet earlier in the madrigal Michelangelo pointedly contrasts his creation or *fattura* with that of God; and one is reminded once again of Bernard's depiction of Mary as the one who so ennobled human nature 'that its Creator did not disdain His being made its created' ('che 'l suo fattore / non disdegnò di farsi sua *fattura*').

---

41   Ibidem 406: 'Sol d'una pietra viva, / l'arte vuol che qui viva / al par degli anni il volto di costei. / Che dovria il ciel di lei, / sendo mie questo, e quella suo fattura, / non già mortal, ma diva, / non solo agli occhi mei? / E pur si parte e picciol tempo dura. / Dal lato destro è zoppa suo ventura, / s'un sasso resta e pur lei morte affretta. / Chi ne farà vendetta? / Natura sol, se de' suo nati sola / l'opra qui dura, e la suo 'l tempo invola'.

Michelangelo surely cannot intercede or compete with the deity who created Colonna as his 'fattura'. Given that a rock simply remains on earth – 's'un sasso resta' – while the now fragile, altogether too human Colonna is hurried along by death, Michelangelo can entertain no prospects of raising up anything, either the woman, 'diva' though she may seem, or his work. An even more despondent reading emerges when turning to the slightly different version of the poem found in the manuscript for Colonna: the alternate line for 'Dal lato destro è zoppa suo ventura', is 'Dal lato destro è zoppa *mio* ventura': *my* fortune must be hobbled on its right side if a rock remains and death still hurries her on.[42] If misfortune is Michelangelo's rather than nature's, then his hopes that his work will raise both himself and Colonna to heaven are inevitably shattered. Even if the heavy stone endures on earth, it can have no influence whatsoever on the heavenly force that crafted Colonna as its creature.

'L'opra qui dura'. Far from a triumph, the final line alludes to the limitations of the artist's works: they last *only here*. One does not have to look far to find other poems that insist on the 'qui', the earthly place where the sculptor's stones must remain, incapable of going elsewhere; and often with a sense of the lowliness and abjection of that place. Take, for example, fragment 282:

> In such slavery, and with so much boredom,
> and with false conceptions and great peril
> to my soul, to be here (*qui*) sculpting divine things.[43]

In the Italian the metrics of the third line accentuate the 'qui', literally giving it weight: 'a sculpir *qui* cose divine'. Michelangelo writes in another fragment (275) about the tragedy of a stone dragged from the highest mountains to places far less beautiful below, where the stone despondently speaks for itself:

> Once hidden and enclosed in a great rock (*d'un gran sasso*),
> I came down, against my will, from a great ravine
> in the high mountains to this lower place (*in questo basso*),
> to be revealed within this little stone.[44]

42   See the edition of the Colonna manuscript, Buonarroti Michelangelo, *Canzoniere*, ed. M.C. Tarsi (Rome: 2015) 152.
43   Buonarroti, *The Poetry of Michelangelo* 473: 'Con tanta servitù, con tanto tedio / e con falsi concetti e gran periglio / dell'alma, a sculpir qui cose divine'.
44   Ibidem 464: 'Dagli alti monti e d'una gran ruina, / ascoso e circunscritto d'un gran sasso, / discesi a discoprirmi in questo basso, / contr'a mie voglia, in tal lapedicina. // Quand'el sol nacqui, e da chi il ciel destina'.

'Discesi a discoprirmi in questo basso': Dante descended too, but it was to go up again, ascending to God. The stone can only go down, and in that lowly place – '*questo* basso' – we too reside, to read (or in the case of this fragment left incomplete, not read) the poem.[45]

Like the stone brought down and deprived of its former dignity, Michelangelo's sculptures are *here*, surrounded by the utter silence of the marble and of the dead whom the stones memorialize, unlike the words of Dante that easily ascended to the heavens along with their *fattore*.[46] Michelangelo allows for little back-and-forth between heaven and earth, nor is there any mediating fig-ure who can be approached so as to intervene. Here Michelangelo's curious allusion to a Dante who went not to hell and purgatory, but to what he calls in sonnet 248 'l'inferno giusto e 'l pio', the just hell and the compassionate one, is telling. His envy of Dante – his wish to be him – may extend to his desire to see in Dante someone who engaged not only with figures of mediation such as Mary, but with spaces of mediation: the 'inferno pio' or the merciful or com-passionate hell that is purgatory, a space that gives sinners a second chance and enables them to make up for what they failed to do while they were still on earth. Mary played a central role in Dante's 'inferno pio', as Dante invoked her on each of purgatory's seven terraces as the antithesis of the sin being purged, beginning in Canto 10 with a sculpted image of her humble acceptance of Gabriel and God's request as the antithesis of pride. (Moreover, those divine sculptures are endowed with life, as Dante seems to hear the angel speak: 'One would have sworn that he was saying, "Ave!"').[47] For Dante, the prayers in *purgatorio* still matter; negotiations between those on earth and those in the next world are still possible. Is Michelangelo's invocation of this 'inferno pio' marked by if not nostalgia – purgatory was very much alive in his day – then longing, despite his occasional sympathies with Colonna, Bernardino Ochino, and the Reformation more generally? Does he want to believe in the *pietà* that purgatory and Mary physically embody, in the possibility that one may have redemption through one's works – and in the mercy of a woman willing to be a good reader of one's words?

But this is not the Mary whom we see in Michelangelo's artwork. Michel-angelo's desperate Last Judgement, from the late 1530s and so contemporary

---

45   On the staircase leading from the Piazza to the church of St. Peter's in Rome, see Wölfflin H., *Renaissance and Baroque*, trans. K. Simon (Ithaca, NY: 1964) 45: 'There is no suggestion of ascent, only of downward movement'.

46   Agoston L., "Sonnet, Sculpture, Death: The Mediums of Michelangelo's Self-Imaging", *Art History* 20:4 (1997) 534–555, especially 541, speaks about the importance of sculpture for Michelangelo in 'engender[ing] the recognition of death' as articulated in sonnet 151.

47   Dante, *Purgatorio* 10:40: 'Giurato si sarìa ch'el dicesse "Ave!"'.

with some of the early writings for Colonna, conveys not a confident Mary in control but a cowering Mary shielding herself from her son's impatient gesture: not only is he not listening to her, but she is not even trying to speak [Fig. 11.1]. As Ambra Moroncini notes, preparatory drawings from around 1534 for the Sistine Chapel show that Michelangelo had earlier planned to depict Mary as an active intercessor with her son. Whether or not the shift is due to Michelangelo's association with Colonna, as Moroncini suggests, is not clear. But Michelangelo's alterations to the original design identify a growing ambivalence about an 'alta signora' protective of his and others' needs and prayers.[48] It is, of course, true that the Last Judgement features an apocalyptic moment when purgatory is no more. Arguably, the time for compassion is done. And it is also the case that, as Stefano de Fiores has argued, Michelangelo depicts Christ as less a figure of divine anger than of compassion.[49] But Mary's passivity is notable, as is Michelangelo's decision to change course.

Yet if the Sistine Chapel does not present Mary as a mediator it is also the case that Michelangelo never trafficked in the theme of her dormition and assumption. As in the drawing for Vittoria Colonna of a Mary with a dead Christ on her lap – perhaps the future gift Michelangelo promised in his letter – the majority of Michelangelo's sculpted works of Mary show her as a mother: of either a nursing child, or a dead adult son.[50] It is with one such Mary in stone – a Mary who stays *qui* – that this essay will close. Mary's failure to intervene with her son in the Sistine Chapel, modestly turning her head away from his forceful gestures, has a parallel in Mary's albeit very different posture in the New Sacristy in Florence's San Lorenzo, on which Michelangelo began work in the early 1520s, and never completed. Both Medici princes sit on their respective thrones, Lorenzo immersed in contemplation, Giuliano poised as though to shortly rise up from his seat. Yet both gaze in the direction of Mary, who is engaged in a contemplative act of her own, looking downward, her eyes barely

---

48   Moroncini A., *Michelangelo's Poetry and Iconography in the Heart of the Reformation* (London: 2019) 122 suggests that the change in Mary's posture was rethought in 'light of the "Christian friendship" with Colonna'.

49   De Fiores S., *La Madonna in Michelangelo: Nuova interpretazione teologico-culturale* (Vatican City: 2010) 202–203, suggests that Michelangelo moves toward a Christological perspective that 'prioritizes the Savior of the world in his infinite compassion and justice, and Mary as the *prima salvata*, profoundly sad for the sad fate of those who have obstinately persevered in their struggle against God' (202).

50   Stefano de Fiores (ibidem 191) argues persuasively that the drawing of Mary with the dead Christ on her lap before the cross now at the Isabella Stewart Gardner Museum in Boston, challenges interpretations of seeing in her gesture 'a function of a co-redentrix or an intercessory role', while he also discourages against seeing it as a straightforward defence of the doctrine of justification by faith alone.

FIGURE 11.1 Michelangelo Buonarroti, *Last Judgement*, 1538–1541. Detail of Christ and the Virgin. Fresco (pre-restoration). Rome, Vatican Palace, Sistine Chapel
IMAGE © SCALA / ART RESOURCE, NEW YORK

open, as she seems to gaze past the vigorous little body of the Christ child who sits astride her knee and turns around to grasp her breast [Figs. 11.2 and 11.3]. She bears striking similarities to the Madonna della Scala, given the somberness of her gaze in the much earlier work from 1491. There the boys playing on the stair look out to something in the distance, behind Mary and a Jesus who rests more comfortably against her body than the Jesus of the New Sacristy [Fig. 11.4]. But in both cases, she does not meet anyone's gaze – not that of the spectators, nor of the other sculpted figures nearby. Both Lorenzo and Giuliano turn their heads in her direction, but she acknowledges neither.

The statue of Mary and Jesus was meant to be part of the larger double tomb structure for Lorenzo di Piero de' Medici and Giuliano de' Medici, and like the complex of the sculptures as a whole, it was unfinished. It is doubtful that what we see today is what Michelangelo would have intended. Had he chosen to return at Cosimo's urging to Florence from Rome in the 1540s, or had he bothered to answer Vasari's insistent questions in the 1560s, the sacristy might look very different. Vasari claimed that Michelangelo had placed the three main figures in this configuration before he definitively left Florence in 1534, but Paul Joannides has cast doubt on Vasari's assertion. He argues that there would have been a Crucifixion placed in the sacristy's *cappelletta*, and that the dukes may well have been facing that instead – and thus would have been placed on the opposite sides of the chapel. This configuration, if correct, would have left Mary quite literally unremarked on, even as she too is positioned so that she would have been directly across from the scene from Calvary – and so she would have become what she appears to be, a figure in mourning, unable to take joy in the child on her lap because she is painfully aware of the man on the cross.[51] This is the situation of the Madonna della Scala as well, for whom the scala that she faces foreshadows the ladder on which Jesus is brought down from the cross. Even as it probably does not correspond to Michelangelo's final wishes, the Sacristy as it has remained for the past four and a half centuries, after Vasari

---

51   Joannides P., "Michelangelo's Medici Chapel: Some New Suggestions", *The Burlington Magazine* 114 (1972) 541–551: 'The *cappelletta* must have been intended to contain statuary, and marble statuary at that. The obvious subject would have been a Christ crucified; and a drawing in the Archivio Buonarroti confirms that Michelangelo planned a Calvary group in marble. [...] The Dukes would have had to face the Crucifixion, and would therefore have been placed, with their attendant allegories, on the opposite sides of the chapel' (551). For a contrary view regarding Mary's role as intercessor, see Ettlinger L.D., "The Liturgical Function of Michelangelo's Medici Chapel", *Mitteilungen des Kunsthistorischen Institutes in Florenz* 22 (1978) 287–304, who argues that the priest would have been 'looking toward the Madonna with ss. Cosmas and Damian' during his thrice-daily recitations of the Requiem Mass in which Mary is explicitly asked to intercede on behalf of the dead (299–300).

FIGURE 11.2   Michelangelo Buonarroti, *Tomb of Lorenzo de' Medici with Dawn and Dusk*, 1524–1531.
Florence, San Lorenzo, Medici Chapel

FIGURE 11.3   Michelangelo Buonarroti, *Medici Madonna*, 1521–1534. Florence, San Lorenzo,
                Medici Chapel
                IMAGE © ALINARI ARCHIVES (SERGE DOMINGIE)

FIGURE 11.4   Michelangelo Buonarroti, *Madonna della Scala* (Madonna of the Stairs),
1489–1492. Marble relief. Florence, Casa Buonarroti
IMAGE © ASSOCIAZIONE METAMORFOSI, ROME / PHOTO SCALA,
FLORENCE / ART RESOURCE, NEW YORK

and his associates finished what they could, accentuates a Madonna who does not and perhaps cannot respond to the two Medici dukes who sit above their tombs, immersed in her own grief.[52] She will not be an interlocutor for them in heaven. In this room dedicated to the lives of men whose lives ended too soon, to the sorrow of their mothers and relatives for whom the Medici lineage officially ended with their deaths,[53] perhaps Mary was never intended to be such a mediator.

"Grief" comes from the Old French *grever*, to burden or oppress, with roots in the Latin *gravis*. There is a heaviness to the Madonna's body in the Medici chapel, one that contrasts with the lightness and seeming ephemeralness of the many assumed Marys of early modern art, wafted up to heaven by the help of a few clouds and singing cherubim. Michelangelo's Mary remains earthbound, fixed to her own body as well as to the infant Christ's. If the sonnets to Vittoria Colonna speak of the burden and heaviness of debt on the recipient of Colonna's gifts, Mary of the New Sacristy is more like the oppressed Michelangelo than the generous Colonna. The four sculpted figures representing the hours lock us into earthly time, an effect that would have been highlighted with the addition of the four rivers originally planned by Michelangelo – whether or not they were meant as allusions to the rivers of the underworld. There is no vision of transcendence with Mary as our messenger, capable of carrying our works to God.

At best, perhaps, one might speculate that Michelangelo had in mind the phrase from Luke's gospel, shortly after Christ's birth when the shepherds had left, having been directed to find Jesus by the angels themselves: 'And Mary kept these things and pondered them in her heart'.[54] This is a Mary who is pondering the meaning of Jesus's future, and Michelangelo seems to show her in an act of reflection that contributes to her own heaviness, as though she were already burdened by grief. Such grief can be linked specifically to Mary's act of giving corporeal status to the divine, since Jesus suffers death only because

---

52   See, however, Carolina Mangone's fascinating essay, "Generation and Ruination in the Display of Michelangelo's Non-finito", in Jacobi L. – Zolli D.M. (eds.), *Contamination and Purity in Early Modern Art and Architecture* (Amsterdam: 2021), especially 63–68, where she argues that the chapel's incompleteness encourages the beholder to take an active role in its interpretation.

53   Rosenberg R., "Michelangelo's New Sacristy and Vecchietti's Criticism of the Missing Attributes of the *Times of the Day*", in Koja S. – Kryza-Gersch C. (eds.), *Shadows of Time: Giambologna, Michelangelo and the Medici Chapel* (Munich: 2018) 40: 'The family's hopes were dashed [...] when Lorenzo died without a male heir in May 1519'.

54   *Luke* 2:19: 'Maria autem conservabat omnia verba haec conferens in corde suo'.

he is the product of her flesh – the flesh that the tormented Michelangelo can do no more than sculpt, even as he craves escape from it. Hence his frequent desire to uncoil himself from his body, weighted down with years and with sin: 'carico d'anni e di peccati pieno', as he writes in Sonnet 293.[55] And while Mary is burdened neither by years nor by sin, Michelangelo depicts her too as weighted down by the stoniness of flesh. If Petrarch and Dante use the final stanzas of their works to confront oblivion or imminent death as a space where the divine brushes up against the earthly, Michelangelo's 'stanza' of the Medici Chapel remains closed, offering us no chance to move beyond the massive sculptures within. Despite the fact that masses would have been said in its space on a daily basis for the dukes, the cyclical turns that take us from Dawn through Dusk and Day to Night and the sombre gazes of the dead toward what may have been the cross accentuate this world of mourning.

What was Mary to Michelangelo? The above remarks have suggested the difficulties of weighing in unequivocally on Michelangelo's supposed Protestant sympathies even as he clearly found himself caught between new worlds and old. Before not only his sustained encounter with Colonna but the advent of the Reformation, he was preoccupied with the role his works could and should play in the Dantesque drama of redemption – the *real* meaning of Mary's centrality as a figure representing human *dignitas*. But his Mary is often *too* human – too heavy, rooted in stone, locked in her maternity and her foreknowledge that seems to stop with the torments of her son. Mary, that is to say, is too much like Michelangelo. And this may be why several of Michelangelo's major works – not only the New Sacristy, but the tomb for Julius II and his own tomb for Santa Maria Maggiore in Rome – were left incomplete; and why he even attempted to destroy the *Pietà* intended for his monument. The uncertainties involved in crossing thresholds in order to confront death suggest a larger fixation on states of incompleteness that characterize his canzoniere too. 'Memory yields to such excess'.[56] This is the oblivion that the vision of God produces for Dante, that Colonna with her 'superchia aita' (excessive help) produces for Michelangelo. But if Dante's silence coincides pointedly with the ending of the finished *Commedia*, Michelangelo's silence ushers in not a confident and ennobling close, but merely an interruption. Or perhaps, like Mary, he ponders: conserving within what he knows, and paralysed before what he does not yet know.

---

55 Buonarroti, *The Poetry of Michelangelo* 488.

56 *Paradiso* 33:57: 'e cede la memoria a tanto oltraggio', echoed in Buonarroti, *The Poetry of Michelangelo* 314: 'l'ingegno, l'arte, la memoria cede'.

Bibliography

Agoston L., "Sonnet, Sculpture, Death: The Mediums of Michelangelo's Self-Imaging", *Art History* 20.4 (1997) 534–555.

Alighieri Dante, *Rime*, ed. M. Barbi (Bologna: 1972).

Alighieri Dante, *The Divine Comedy of Dante Alighieri: Paradiso*, trans. A. Mandelbaum (Berkeley, CA: 1984).

Alighieri Dante, *Convivio*, ed. G. Inglese (Milan: 1999).

Alighieri Dante, *Rime Giovanili e della Vita Nuova*, ed. T. Barolini (Milan: 2009).

Alighieri Dante, *La Divina Commedia*, ed. E. Malato (Rome: 2018).

Brundin A. (ed.), *A Companion to Vittoria Colonna* (Leiden: 2016).

Buonarroti Michelangelo, *The Poetry of Michelangelo: An Annotated Translation*, ed. and trans. J.M. Saslow (New Haven, CT: 1991).

Buonarroti Michelangelo, *Canzoniere*, ed. M.C. Tarsi (Rome: 2015).

Cambon G., *Michelangelo's Poetry: Fury of Form* (Princeton, NJ: 1985).

Campi E., *Michelangelo e Vittoria Colonna: Un dialogo artistico-teologico ispirato da Bernardino Ochino* (Turin: 1994).

Campi E., "Vittoria Colonna and Bernardino Ochino", in Brundin A. (ed.), *A Companion to Vittoria Colonna* (Leiden: 2016) 371–398.

Casadei A., *Dante: Inno alla Vergine, Paradiso canto XXXIII* (Milan: 2021).

Cherchi P., *Verso la chiusura: Saggio sul Canzoniere di Petrarca* (Bologna: 2008).

Colonna Vittoria, *Sonnets for Michelangelo*, ed. and trans. A. Brundin (Chicago: 2005).

Daley B.E., *On the Dormition of Mary: Early Patristic Homilies* (Crestwood, NY: 1998).

Daley B.E., "At the Hour of Our Death: Mary's Dormition and Christian Dying in Late Patristic and Early Byzantine Literature", *Dumbarton Oaks Papers* 55 (2001) 71–89.

De Fiores S., *La Madonna in Michelangelo: Nuova interpretazione teologico-culturale* (Vatican City: 2010).

Di Fenza A., "Excessive Poetry: The Use of *Superchio* in Michelangelo's Verses", *MLN* 132 (2017) 47–67.

Eire C., *A Very Brief History of Eternity* (Princeton, NJ: 2009).

Ettlinger L.D., "The Liturgical Function of Michelangelo's Medici Chapel", *Mitteilungen des Kunsthistorischen Institutes in Florenz* 22 (1978) 287–304.

Fedi R., "'L'imagine vera': Vittoria Colonna, Michelangelo, e un'idea di canzoniere", *MLN* 107 (1992) 46–73.

Forcellino M., "Vittoria Colonna and Michelangelo: Drawings and Paintings", in Brundin A. (ed.), *A Companion to Vittoria Colonna* (Leiden: 2016) 270–313.

Joannides P., "Michelangelo's Medici Chapel: Some New Suggestions", *The Burlington Magazine* 114 (1972) 541–551.

Koslofsky C., *The Reformation of the Dead: Death and Ritual in Early Modern Germany, 1450–1700* (New York, NY: 2000).

Mangone C., "Generation and Ruination in the Display of Michelangelo's Non-finito", in Jacobi L. – Zolli D.M. (eds.), *Contamination and Purity in Early Modern Art and Architecture* (Amsterdam: 2021) 63–98.

Maratsos J., "Michelangelo, Vittoria Colonna, and the Afterlife of Intimacy", *Art Bulletin* 99 (2017) 69–101.

Marcozzi L., "Making the *Rerum vulgarium fragmenta*", in Ascoli A. – Falkeid U. (eds.), *The Cambridge Companion to Petrarch* (Cambridge: 2015) 51–62.

Martinez R., "Places and Times of the Liturgy from Dante to Petrarch", in Barański Z.G. – Cachey, Jr. T.J. (eds.), *Petrarch and Dante: Anti-Dantism, Metaphysics, Tradition* (Notre Dame, IN: 2009) 320–370.

Moroncini, A. *Michelangelo's Poetry and Iconography in the Heart of the Reformation.* (London: 2019).

Mussio T.E., "The Augustinian Conflict in the Lyrics of Michelangelo: Michelangelo Reading Petrarch", *Italica* 74.3 (1997) 339–359.

Nagel A., "Gifts for Michelangelo and Vittoria Colonna", *Art Bulletin* 79 (1997) 647–668.

Peraino J., *Giving Voice to Love: Song and Self-Expression from the Troubadours to Guillaume de Machaut* (Oxford: 2011).

Petrarca Francesco, *Petrarch's Lyric Poems: The Rime Sparse and Other Lyrics*, ed. and trans. R. Durling (Cambridge, MA: 1976).

Petrarca Francesco, *Res seniles*, ed. S. Rizzo, 5 vols. (Florence: 2017–2019).

Prodan S.R., *Michelangelo's Christian Mysticism* (Cambridge: 2017).

Prodan S.R., "Religious Desire in the Poetry of Vittoria Colonna: Insights into Early Modern Piety and Poetics", in Cox V. – McHugh S. (eds.), *Vittoria Colonna: Poetry, Religion, Art, Impact* (Amsterdam: 2022) 153–169.

Rosenberg R., "Michelangelo's New Sacristy and Vecchietti's Criticism of the Missing Attributes of the *Times of the Day*", in Koja S. – Kryza-Gersch C. (eds.), *Shadows of Time: Giambologna, Michelangelo and the Medici Chapel* (Munich: 2018) 39–55.

Rubin M., *Emotion and Devotion: The Meaning of Mary in Medieval Religious Cultures* (Budapest: 2009).

Rubin M., *Mother of God: A History of the Virgin Mary* (New Haven, CT: 2009).

Voragine Jacobus de, *The Golden Legend*, trans. W.G. Ryan, 2 vols. (Princeton, NJ: 1993).

Wallace W., "'Certain of Death': Michelangelo's Late Life and Art", *Renaissance Quarterly* 28 (2015) 1–32.

Wölfflin H., *Renaissance and Baroque*, trans. K. Simon (Ithaca, NY: 1964).

CHAPTER 12

The Calvinist Theatre of God as a Pleasure Garden at the Time of the First French War of Religion (ca. 1560)

Laurent Paya

Abstract

Circa 1560, in Calvinist culture, the theological concept of the Theatre of God replaces the idea of an Eden-like restoration occurring after the Fall. By using the theatre metaphor, Calvin pictured the earth as a generous gift of the Creator by which God shows his goodness. This idea was to counter millennialist beliefs and eschatological fears. The present essay shows how Calvinist garden architecture offered an allegorical transposition of this doctrine, which strongly correlated with the idea of an eschatological refuge for persecuted members of the Reformed Church community. Two examples allow us to make this clear: the 'Garden of Wisdom' portrayed by Bernard Palissy (1510–1590) in *La Recepte veritable* (1563) and the gardens of Duchess Renée de France in Montargis (1510–1574), drawn by Jacques Androuet du Cerceau (1511–1585/1586). Both gardens were refuges: the first, only anagogic; the second, also actual. In *La Recepte*, the garden is analogous to a sermon that partly consists of eschatological arguments. Its mineral and vegetal decorations are textual, visual, and material parts of a mnemonic rhetoric that rejected paganism and hermeticism, while praising humanism enlightened by the Reformed faith. The construction work on the garden of the castle of Duchess Renée de France, which accommodated between 300 and 600 refugees, necessarily destroyed a part of the cemetery where Catholic mourning rituals, condemned by the Huguenots, took place. Its architectural and decorative splendour, which derived from its overall geometry, extends to the surrounding landscape, while the *parterres de broderie* and monumental galleries or terraces can be interpreted as a way to reverse the *mundus inversus*, the world in which the natural order of things is 'upside-down'.

Keywords

pleasure garden – Theatre of God – Bernard Palisssy – Montargis – Jacques Androuet du Cerceau

During the French Wars of Religion – the armed conflicts between Catholics and Protestants that began in 1562–1563 – the proliferation of atrocities contributed to the emergence of an apocalyptic atmosphere.[1] It was against this backdrop that an important development in garden design took place: the medieval *hortus conclusus* was progressively transformed into a monumental pleasure garden, called *à la française*.[2] Members of the Reformed Church community, called Huguenots, were prominent contributors to, and witnesses of, this evolution.[3] Amidst this paradigm shift, one traditional element – the earthly paradise – survived but was transformed into the art of the garden.[4] This new type of garden, we suggest, has major relevance for the theme of the present volume, that is, space-time relations in the European eschatological imagination. Just like the archetypal Garden of Eden, which was part of an eschatological sequence – Creation, the Fall, redemption, and restoration – the pleasure garden with its reference to the biblical 'paradise of pleasure' (*Genesis* 2:8) was also a representation of an eschatological restoration.[5]

---

1 The history of the French Wars of Religion is detailed in Crouzet D., *Les guerriers de Dieu: La violence au temps des troubles de religion, vers 1525–vers 1610* (Seyssel: 1990). See also idem, *La genèse de la Réforme française: 1520–1560* (Paris: 1996) 546–547.

2 Guillaume J., "Le jardin mis en ordre: Jardin et château en France du XVe au XVIIe siècle", in Guillaume J. – Boudon F. (eds.), *Architecture, jardin, paysage* (Paris: 1999) 103–136; Paya L., "Jacques Androuet Du Cerceau, inventeur de jardins", in Latrémolière E. – Girault P.G. (eds.), *Jardins de châteaux à la Renaissance* (Montreuil: 2013) 125–133; idem, "Ideal 'Parquets' and 'Parquetages' by Jacques Androuet du Cerceau: Decorative Mannerism and the Art of Gardens in France in the Sixteenth Century", *Studies in the History of Gardens & Designed Landscapes: An International Quarterly* 34.1 (2014) 1–16; idem, "Les jardins des châteaux de Philibert", in *Philibert De l'Orme: Un architecte dans l'Histoire* (Turnhout: 2016) 121–136.

3 Randall C., *Building Codes: The Aesthetics of Calvinism in Early Modern Europe* (Philadelphia, PA: 1999) 33–43.

4 Comito T., "Renaissance Gardens and the Discovery of Paradise", *Journal of the History of Ideas* 32.4 (1971) 483–506; Fagiolo M., *Lo specchio del paradiso: Il giardino e il sacro dall'Antico all'Ottocento* (Cinisello Balsamo: 1998); Antoine E. (ed.), *Sur la terre comme au ciel: Jardins d'occident à la fin du Moyen-Âge* (Paris: 2002); Duport D., *Le jardin et la nature: Ordre et variété dans la littérature de la Renaissance* (Geneva: 2002) 123–124.

5 Stein A.B., "Thoughts Occasioned by the Old Testament", in Francis M. – Hester, Jr. R.T. (eds.), *The Meaning of Gardens* (Cambridge: 1966) 38–45; Levi Della Torre S., "The Anxiety of Eden", in Psaki R. (ed.), *The Earthly Paradise: The Garden of Eden from Antiquity to Modernity* (Cambridge: 1990) 5–13; Griswold M., "A History of the Sanctuary Garden", *Design Quarterly* 169 (1996) 1–10; Mukerji C., "Material Practices of Domination: Christian Humanism, the Built Environment, and Techniques of Western Power", *Theory and Society* 31.1 (2002) 1–34; Ribouillault D., "La villa Montalto et l'idéal rustique de Sixte Quint", *Revue de l'art* 173 (2011) 33–42.

However, Jean Calvin, theologian of the Reformation, never referred to the *Apocalypse* of John which, in the Bible, describes this restoration, that is to say, the coming of the Kingdom of God after the Last Judgement.[6] For Calvin, the glory of God in Genesis was never completely interrupted and the Kingdom of God already existed on earth, in a shape still incomplete but in continual emergence.[7] This ongoing emergence is called the Theatre of God.[8] In Calvinist garden culture, the Theatre of God replaces the idea of an Eden-like restoration, as several studies have shown.[9] Nevertheless, it is necessary to deepen them, for they do not consider the paradigms of artistic creation in the early modern period. In her monograph *Building Codes: The Aesthetics of Calvinism in Early Modern Europe*, Catharine Randall considers gardens in the context of Reformed architecture, pointing out that an 'architectural semantics' exists in Calvin's writings relative to the Kingdom of God, but she ignores the catachresis of the *theatrum mundi*.[10] We are indebted to Frank Lestringant for a fruitful parallel between the Theatre of God and cartography in connection with the contemporary meanings of the term *theatre*.[11] The Theatre of God could in fact be linked with the rhetoric of *energeia*, that is, the idea of 'a theatre in a broadly metaphorical sense, which appeals to sight and to the senses

---

6   See Quistorp H., *Calvin's Doctrine of the Last Things* (Richmond, VA: 1955) 158–162; Backus I., *Les sept visions et la fin des temps: Les commentaires genevois de l'Apocalypse entre 1539 et 1584* (Geneva: 1997).

7   Wyk J.H. van, "John Calvin on the Kingdom of God and Eschatology", *In die Skriflig* 35.2 (2001) 191–205.

8   For a comprehensive approach to this theological concept see, for example, Schreiner S., *Theater of His Glory: Nature and the Natural Order in the Thought of John Calvin* (Grand Rapids, MI: 1995).

9   Schaefer O., "'Théâtre de la gloire de dieu' et 'Droit usage des biens terrestres' Calvin, le calvinisme et la nature", in Varet J. (ed.), *Calvin, naissance d'une pensée* (Tours: 2012) 213–226; Carbonnier-Burkard M., "Le jardin et le désert, ou le 'théâtre sacré' des protestants français (XVIe–XVIIIe siècle)", *Diasporas* 21 (2013) 10–19.

10   Randall, *Building Codes* 33–43. According to Ann Blair, at the beginning of modern times, the *Theatrum mundi* was linked to three definitions which have in common the use of sight: the world as a scene of human tragedy, nature and her marvels animated by divine providence and a book (or a place) with an encyclopaedic intent: Blair A., *The Theater of Nature: Jean Bodin and Renaissance Science* (Princeton, NJ: 1997) 153. See the bibliography by Van Delft L., "L'idée de théâtre (XVIe–XVIIIe siècle)", *Revue d'histoire littéraire de la France* 101 (2001) 1349–1365.

11   Lestringant F., "Cartographie et théâtre au service de la Réforme: L'Exemple de la 'Mappe–Monde Papistique'", in Zinguer I.Y. – Yardeni M. (eds.), *Les deux réformes chrétiennes: Propagation et diffusion* (London: 2004) 216–235.

in order to be better anchored in one's intelligence and enter the soul'.[12] In this essay, we will first return to John Calvin's work and that of other Reformed theologians, to define better the eschatology of the Theatre of God in its relationship with the garden. On the basis of these observations, we shall next consider two gardens, one ideal and the other real. The first is the 'Garden of Wisdom' which Bernard Palissy (1510–1590) sketched in *La Recepte veritable* (1563), which, in spite of much research, still contains many obscure zones. With good reason, specialists have compared this garden to the earthly paradise, as well as to the Calvinist Theatre of God.[13] Other scholars have noted a relationship with the scheme of the celestial Jerusalem, strangely called 'city of refuge' in Calvinist writings, but have established no link with the theatre of God.[14] No link has been found either between this 'amphitheatre of refuge', saturated with images, and the rhetoric of the *theatrum mundi* combined with the *ars memoriae*, another art of space and time.[15] Second, we will examine the gardens of Duchess Renée de France in Montargis, as they appear in the drawings of Jacques Androuet du Cerceau, now in the British Museum, and the engravings in *Les plus excellents bastiments de France* (1576). According to

---

12   Ibidem 228: 'un théâtre au sens large et métaphorique, qui s'adresse à la vue et aux sens pour mieux s'ancrer dans l'intelligence et s'inscrire dans l'âme'. Translation by the author.

13   Palissy Bernard, *Recette véritable* (1563), ed. Lestringant F. – Barataud C. (Paris: 1996); Amico L., *Bernard Palissy: In Search of Earthly Paradise* (New York, NY: 1996) 172; Randall, *Building Codes* 44–77; Duport, *Le Jardin et la nature* 65; Giacomotto-Charra V., "Entre savoirs et imagination: Esthétique et symbolique du jardin dans les représentations édéniques de Du Bartas", in Peylet G. (ed.), *Les mythologies du jardin de l'Antiquité à la fin du XIXᵉ siècle* (Bordeaux: 2007) 73–83. Ferdinand J., *Artisan des réformes entre art, science et foi* (Berlin: 2019) 163–164; Lecoq A.M., "Le Jardin de la Sagesse de Bernard Palissy", in Mosser M. – Teyssot G. (eds.), *Histoire des jardins de la Renaissance à nos jours* (Paris: 2002) 65–73; Dyrness W.A., *The Origins of Protestant Aesthetics in Early Modern Europe: Calvin's Reformation Poetics* (New York, NY: 2019).

14   Palissy Bernard, *La Recepte veritable* (La Rochelle, Barthélémy Berton: 1563), fol. L ij v. Cf. idem, *Recette* 21–25. Lestringant F., "Le jardin des Origines: Palissy et Du Bartas", in Brunon H. (ed.), *Le Jardin, notre Double* (Paris: 1999) 113; Duport, *Le Jardin et la nature* 66; Ferdinand, *Bernard Palissy* 200.

15   Palissy, *La Recepte veritable*, fol. L lj v. See Yates F., *The Art of Memory* (Harmondsworth: 1969); Rossi P., *Clavis universalis* (Grenoble: 1993); Carruthers M. – Ziolkowski J.M. (eds.), *The Medieval Craft of Memory: An Anthology of Texts and Pictures* (Philadelphia, PA: 2002); Bolzoni L., *The Gallery of Memory: Literary and Iconographic Models in the Age of the Printing Press* (Toronto: 2001). More specifically in the context of the art of garden, Fagiolo M., "Il giardino come teatro del mondo e della memoria", in idem (ed.), *La città effimera e l'universo artificiale del giardino: La Firenze dei Medici e l'Italia del Cinquecento* (Rome: 1979) 125–141.

Catharine Randall, these drawings were meant to be decoded like texts, but the studies on the gardens of Montargis have not provided a key to a conclusive interpretation.[16] The new idea we will propose here will rely on the medieval history of agricultural planning, on the one hand, and emblem books, on the other. Our goal is to show that the art of gardens illustrated by Palissy and Du Cerceau consists in a confessional "reformation" of the *ars naturans*, which according to Michel Jeanneret is the art of representing nature in the process of its realization.[17] The point is to establish that the Reformed pleasure garden no longer produced a *locus amoenus* with a timeline fixed in eternal spring, but a space subject to an evolving process of reversibility of the *mundus inversus* discussed by Ernst Robert Curtius.[18] In the *mundus inversus*, the natural and divine order of things is 'upside-down', that is, corrupted and without order.

1   The Calvinist Theatre of God and the Restoration of Creation

In his visions predicting the end of the world, John of Patmos saw the Heavenly Jerusalem as described in the *Book of Revelation*. There the celestial city is a quadrangle whose perimeter of 'twelve thousand stades' (1370 miles) is enclosed by walls of one hundred and forty-four cubits high (76 yards) with twelve gates.[19] It is constructed from transparent glass, precious stones, pearls, and gold. It is not necessary to build temples there, for it is in itself the divine temple.[20] The Tree of Life grows in the middle near a river.[21] This tree was in the Garden of Eden before the Fall.[22] Therefore, in the sacred city Eden is

---

16   Randall, *Building Codes* 162–164. All French Calvinist architecture was built upon an 'inter-text', a conceptual interplay between the words of Scripture and Calvin's *Institutes*. On Montargis, see further Jarry L., *Renée de France à Montargis: Épisode des guerres religieuses* (Orléans: 1868); Rodocanachi E., *Une protectrice de la réforme en Italie et en France: Renée de France* (Paris: 1896); Androuet du Cerceau Jacques, *Les plus excellents bastiments de France* (Paris, s.n.: 1576) 85–87; Boudon C. – Mignot F. (eds.), *Jacques Androuet du Cerceau: Les dessins des plus excellents bâtiments de France* (Paris: 2010) 76–85; Cvetkovic C., "The Gardens of the Château de Montargis as an Expression of Renée de France's Identity (1560–1575)", in Peebles K.D. – Scarlatta G. (eds.), *Representing the Life and Legacy of Renée de France: From Fille de France to Dowager Duchess* (Basingstoke: 2021) 359–379.
17   Jeanneret M., *Perpetuum mobile: Métamorphoses des corps et des œuvres de Vinci à Montaigne* (Paris: 1997) 239.
18   Curtius E.R., *European Literature and the Latin Middle Ages*, trans. W.R. Trask (Princeton, NJ: 2013) 183–202 ("The Ideal Landscape").
19   *Revelation* 21:16, 21. Medieval representations show it, indiscriminately, round or square. The dimensions come from the 1566 edition of the Bible by Sébastien Honorat.
20   *Revelation* 21:18–21.
21   *Revelation* 22.
22   *Genesis* 3:24.

restored to its simplest essence.[23] Furthermore, as Lestrignant notes, 'Between the garden and the city there are many walkways. In medieval iconography paradise is often indistinguishable from the Heavenly Jerusalem [...]'.[24]

Between 1524 and 1535, during the early Reformation, the expectation of the Heavenly Jerusalem led millennial and Anabaptist sects to tragic defeats.[25] Likewise, during the French Wars of Religion, the belief in the coming Apocalypse was widespread. It was probably in order to avoid the harmful impacts of a literal reading of the *Book of Revelation* that Calvin did not comment on it. Denis Crouzet even goes so far as to suggest that Calvinist theology was 'anti-eschatological'.[26] For Jan Hendrick van Wyk, however, a Calvinist eschatology, based on New Testament texts, did exist.[27]

In the Institution de la religion Chrestienne (1560),[28] Calvin writes that providence predicts salvation.[29] But in his *Commentaire sur l'evangile selon saint Jean* (1553) he mentions that this salvation lies exclusively in the still and already present space-time of the Kingdom of God:

> Now we know that out of Christ there is nothing but confusion in the world; and though Christ had already begun to erect the Kingdom of God, yet his death was the commencement of a well-regulated condition, and the full restoration of the world.[30]

---

23   *Revelation* 21–22.
24   Lestringant F., "Le jardin des origines" 113: 'Entre le jardin et la ville, les passerelles sont multiples. Dans l'iconographie médiévale, le paradis est souvent mal distingué de la Jérusalem celeste [...]'. Translation by the author.
25   At the beginning of the German Reformation, the obsession with the end of days led to the disaster of the War of the Peasants of 1524–1525 and to the dramatic fall of Münster in 1535. See Cohn N., *The Pursuit of the Millennium* (Fairlawn, NJ: 1957); Barret P. – Gurgand J.N., *Le roi des derniers jours: L'exemplaire et très cruelle histoire des rebaptisés de Münster (1534–1535)* (Paris: 1981).
26   See especially Crouzet D., *Jean Calvin: Vies parallèles* (Paris: 2000) 189.
27   Van Wyk, "John Calvin on the Kingdom of God and Eschatology", 191–205. See, e.g., *Matthew* 13:24–53 (not mentioned by van Wyk).
28   In the first Latin edition of Calvin's *Institutes of the Christian Religion* in 1536, the doctrine of predestination is only briefly discussed. The final edition of the *Institutes* was published in Latin in 1559 and in French in 1560.
29   Calvin Jean, *Institution de la religion Chrestienne* (Geneva, Jean Crespin: 1560) 139–199.
30   Calvin Jean, *Commentaire sur l'evangile selon saint Jean* (Geneva, Jean Gérard: 1553) 716–717: 'Or nous savons qu'il n'y a que confusion au monde hors Jésus Christ. Et bien que le seigneur Jésus eut commencé à dresser le royaume de Dieu: toutefois sa mort a été le vrai commencement d'un état bien disposé, et la pleine restauration de ce monde'. English translation: idem, *Commentary on the Gospel According to John*, trans. W. Pringle, vol. 2 (Edinburgh: 1847) 36.

It is therefore not necessary to wait for the parousia, the Second Coming, for the coming of the Kingdom began as early as the resurrection, but the eschatological time is still to come. This doctrine, which may appear aporetic, is illustrated in particular in *Psalm* 104, on which Calvin commented, and which (as we will see) was also mentioned by Bernard Palissy. This sacred text makes no distinction between the creative work of God at the beginning and the present work of his providence. It is undoubtedly a question of temporal, spatial, and spiritual experience, offered to all Reformed Christians in the parts of the world where they live. For Calvin, the anticipation of the *eschata* does not wipe out a present full of calamities, but on the contrary, it stimulates and directs human activities and initiatives. This Christian activism must ensure an eschatological 'disanxiety', according to Denis Crouzet's expression.[31]

Calvin's *Commentaire* on *Psalm* 104 leads to the concept of Creation as a reassuring shelter and a protective Church intended for true Christians:[32]

> it is also intended to strengthen our confidence in regard to the future, that we may not live in the world in a state of constant fear and anxiety, as we must have done had not God testified that he has given the earth for a habitation to men [and] he has established it upon everlasting pillars.[33]

The Protestant refuge on earth, which refers to all the territories in which Protestants were protected, includes *de facto* an eschatological dimension associated with the Kingdom of God.[34] Calvin finds no conflict between these two kingdoms: spiritual and temporal; celestial, terrestrial, and political.[35] In

---

31   Crouzet D., *La genèse de la Réforme française, 1520–1560* (Paris: 1996) 571, 667; idem, *Dieu en ses royaumes: Une histoire des guerres de religion* (Paris: 2008) 10, 454.

32   There is a general agreement that Calvinist eschatology primarily concerns the individual rather than the world, and that the Kingdom of God refers to the Church: Birmelé A., "Eschatology", in idem (ed.) *Introduction à la théologie systematique* (Geneva: 2008) 385; Burns R., "Protestant Ecclesiology and Eschatology", *Angelicum* 54.1 (1977) 37; Holwerda D.E., "Eschatology and History: A Look at Calvin's Eschatological Vision", in idem (ed.), *Exploring the Heritage of John Calvin* (Grand Rapids, MI: 1976) 31–42.

33   Calvin Jean, *Commentaires sur le livre des psaumes* (Geneva, Conrad Baldius: 1561) 645: 'Et cela est un bénéfice singulier qu'il nous fait, quand il luy plaist que nous habitions sur la terre sans que nous soyons de rien espouvantez: d'autant qu'il l'a establie sur des appuis qui dureront à jamais'. English translation: idem, *Commentary on the Book of Psalms*, vol. 4, trans. J. Anderson (Edinburgh: 1847) 149.

34   Lestringant F., "Genève et l'Amérique: Le rêve du refuge huguenot au temps des guerres de religion (1555–1600)", *Revue de l'histoire des religions* 210.3 (1993) 335: 'one finds that the refuge haunts the policy of the Protestant party during the troubles and even once the peace returned'. Translation by the author.

35   Bouvignies I., "Qu'est–ce qu'un pouvoir légitime pour Calvin ?", *Rives nord–méditerranéennes* 19 (2004) 41–73; Bost H., "De la 'vraye Eglise' et du 'gouvernement civil':

several cases, devotional activism on earth led Calvinists to a reconciliation with political powers. He achieved this vision in Geneva, which became a Huguenot refuge.[36] In the *Institution*, Calvin mentions insistently the marvels of Creation which he compares to a 'beautiful masterpiece' or a 'bright mirror', using a vocabulary commonly applied to works of art.[37] Numerous researchers have drawn attention to the frequency with which his writings borrow from theatre terminology.[38] In his *Commentaires sur les Epistres de S. Paul* (1556) he writes that Creation is a 'beautiful theatre' or a 'spectacle of God's glory'.[39] Here, the Theatre of God, turned into a *topos*, is a variation of the *theatrum mundi*,

> this magnificent theatre of heaven and earth, which is replete with innumerable miracles, and from the contemplation of which we ought wisely to acquire the knowledge of God.[40]

In this space, the preferred site of the *magna sapientia* (God's wisdom), the marvellous works of the *arcanus agricola* are revealed to be admired. A link can be established with the parable of the hidden treasure (*Matthew* 13:44), which says that the Kingdom of Heaven is similar to a treasure hidden in a field, to be brought to fruition in faith and deeds by following the values defended by Jesus.

Human beings must take pleasure in these marvels. In the *Commentaires sur le premier livre de Moyse, dit Génèse* (1553–1554), Calvin writes: 'Here God is introduced by Moses as surveying his work, that he might take pleasure in it'.[41] In the Theatre of God, the pleasure depends on a marvellous beauty, derived not only from divine providence, but also from the human labour which brings

---

La démocratie serait–elle contagieuse ?", in Varet J. (ed.), *Calvin: Naissance d'une pensée* (Paris: 2012) 67–75.

36   Randall, *Building Codes* 29–32.

37   Calvin, *Institution* 3, 9.

38   Bouwsma W.J., *John Calvin: A Sixteenth-Century Portrait* (New York, NY: 1988) 177; Horton M., *Covenant and Eschatology: The Divine Drama* (Louisville, KY: 2002) 11, 15. Dyrness, *The Origins of Protestant Aesthetics* 83.

39   Calvin, *Institution* 11; idem, *Commentaires Genèse* 30, 366; idem, *Commentaire sainct Jean* 316; idem, *Commentaires sur les Epistres de S. Paul* (Geneva, Conrad Badius: 1556) 20; idem, *Institutes of the Christian Religion*, vol. 1, trans. J. Alley (Philadelphia, PA: 1843) 306; idem, *Institution* 10.

40   Calvin, *Institution* 139: 'ce théâtre du ciel et de la terre tant riche et excellent, et garni de miracles infinis, pour nous faire cognoistre Dieu par son regard avec jugement & prudence'. English translation: idem, *Institutes* 267.

41   Calvin Jean, *Commentaires sur le premier livre de Moyse, dit Genèse* (Geneva, Jean Gérard, 1554) 14: 'Moïse introduit ici Dieu considérant son œuvre, pour y prendre plaisir'. English translation: idem, *Commentaries on the First Book of Moses called Genesis*, trans. J. King, vol. 2 (Edinburgh: 1847) 77.

salvation.[42] Pleasure gardens embody this theological representation. In his *Commentaire* on *Psalm* 104, Calvin observes:

> It is no small honour that God for our sake has so magnificently adorned the world, in order that we may not only be spectators of this beauteous theatre, but also enjoy the multiplied abundance and variety of good things which are presented to us in it.[43]

In this theatre of the Creation everything is embellished and everything has its place. The most diverse and varied things are in visual relation to each other, as in a very 'formal' garden, as Calvin often writes, geometrically and functionally organized.[44] Calvin was the first theologian to formulate the concept of custody as a religious duty, in joining it metaphorically to gardening. In his *Commentaire sur la Genèse* he writes:

> The custody of the garden was given in charge to Adam, to show that we possess the things which God has committed to our hands, on the condition, that being content with a frugal and moderate use of them, we should take care of what shall remain [...] let everyone regard himself as the steward of God in all things which he possesses.[45]

As a promise of a new Eden which denotes 'the labour which men bestow in husbandry', the pleasure gardens are one version of the Theatre of God in *Psalm* 104.[46] In his *Commentaires sur la Génèse*, Calvin also renews the biblical map [Fig. 12.1], but his map only represents very general geographical

---

42 *Psalm* 104:10.

43 Calvin, *Commentaires sur le livre des psaumes* 652: 'Car ce n'est pas un petit honneur, que Dieu en fauveur de nous a si magnifiquement orné le monde, afin que nous n'ayons point seulement la veuë de ce beau théâtre, mais aussi que nous ayons la fruition de la diverse abondance et variété des biens qui nous sont exposéz en icelui'. English translation: idem, *Commentary on the Book of Psalms* 4:169.

44 The term 'theatre' is frequently used by Calvin. Calvin, *Institution* 114.

45 Calvin, *Commentaires sur le premier livre de Moyse* 35: 'Moyse adiouste qu'Adam fut ordonné gardien de ce jardin pour monstrer que nous possedons ce que Dieu nous a mis en main à telle condition, que nous nous contentions d'en user frugalement et modérément, gardans ce qui est de résidu. [...] que chacun pense qu'il est despensier de Dieu en tout ce qu'il possède'. English translation: idem, *Commentary on Genesis* 1:125.

46 Calvin, *Commentaires sur les psaumes* 641: 'la peine que prennent les hommes après le labeur de la terre'. English translation: idem, *Commentary on the Book of Psalms* 4:155.

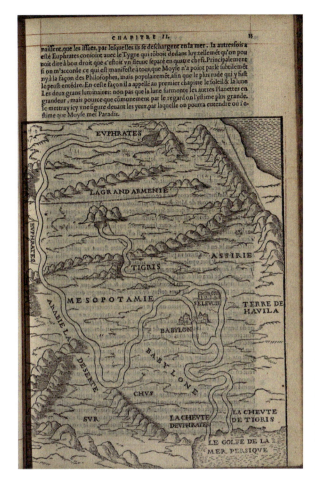

CHAPITRE II.

naissent, que les issues, par lesquelles ils se deschargent en la mer : la autresfois a esté Euphrates conioint auec le Tygre qui s'oboit dedans luy: tellemét qu'on pou noit dire à bon droit que c'estoit vn fleuue separé en quatre chefs. Principalement si on m'accorde ce qui est manifeste à tous, que Moyse n'a point parlé subtilemét ny à la façon des Philosophes, mais populairemét, afin que le plus rude qui y fust le peust entédre. En ceste façon il a appellé au premier chapitre le soleil & la lune Les deux grans luminaires: non pas que la lune surmonte les autres Planettes en grandeur, mais pource que cômunement par le regard on l'estime plus grande. Ie mettray icy vne figure deuant les yeux, par laquelle on pourra entendre ou i'e-stime que Moyse met Paradis.

FIGURE 12.1
Map of the area where
Calvin locates Eden. From:
John Calvin, *Commentaire
sur le premier livre de
Moyse, dit Genese* (Geneva,
Jean Gérard: 1554) 33
PUBLIC DOMAIN.
ARCHIVE.ORG

indications without exactly locating Eden.[47] After his death, the latter was added to the map, representing Adam and Eve in an outsized *hortus conclusus*, adopting the shape of an enclosed square orchard with a river crossing it. The same is the case, for example, in *La Sainte Bible* (1566) printed by Sébastien Honorat and prefaced by Jean Calvin.[48]

In the years from 1550 to 1560, several theologians close to Calvin wrote commentaries on the *Book of Revelation*.[49] They all mention that it is a parable.[50]

---

47   Calvin, *Commentaires sur le premier livre de Moyse* 33; Scafi A., *Maps of Paradise* (Chicago, IL: 2013) 112.

48   *La Saincte Bible* (Lyon, Sébastien Honorat: 1566).

49   Viret Pierre, *Le Monde à l'empire et le monde demoniacle, faict par dialogues* (Geneva, J. Berthet: 1561) 191.

50   See Backus, *Les sept visions et la fin des temps*.

In the *Exposition sur l'Apocalypse de Sainct Jean* (1543) by the humanist pastor Antoine Du Pinet (ca. 1510–ca. 1584), the celestial Jerusalem is a refuge whose twelve gates are guarded by angels who authorize access to the elect. Du Pinet also comes back to the sanctifying virtues of the number twelve, in particular those of the twelve precious stones which are the building material of the city.[51]

In the *Cent Sermons sur l'Apocalypse de Jesus Christ* (1564), Heinrich Bullinger (1504–1574) examines the luminosity emanating from the divine city built from precious stones:

> For the jasper is green and the crystal is clear, thus it seems [...] that this celestial clarity is perpetually verdant, that it never wilts, that is, the celestial light is eternal and in a certain way overly verdant. In being very green and shiny, it delights all the inhabitants of heaven.[52]

This 'reverdoyance' evokes the greenness of a perpetual *reverdie*, another name given to spring. Bullinger also says: 'In fact, we believe that there is one single gate, one single way, one single entrance, one single door to enter heaven, namely the one Lord Jesus, the only Son of God'.[53] This evokes the parable of the narrow door (*Luke* 13:24–28), one of the most important in Calvinist doctrine, according to which the path and the door leading to the Kingdom of God are narrow, and few find them. The brief mention of the Tree of Life in the celestial city serves to imagine a vast new Eden:

> there are fruit trees, which also offer great enjoyment. Also, the river flows down the middle of the streets, and on each side of the two shores one can see very beautiful trees bearing fruits of life.[54]

---

51 Du Pinet Antoine, *Exposition sur l'Apocalypse de sainct Jean* (Geneva, Jehan Girard: 1543) 373–400.

52 Bullinger Heinrich, *Cent Sermons sur l'Apocalypse de Jesus Christ* (Lyon, Sébastien Honorat: 1564) 1049–1050: 'Car le jaspe est vert et le cristal est clair. Il semble donc [...] que cette clarté céleste est perpétuellement verdoyante, qu'elle ne flétrit jamais, c'est à dire que la lumière céleste est éternelle et par manière de dire reverdoyante en elle-même, et en reverdoyant reluisant, et réjouissant tous les habitants du ciel'. Translation by the author.

53 Bullinger, *Cent Sermons* 1052: 'Au demeurant nous croyons qu'il y a une seule porte, une seule voie, une seule entrée, un seul huis pour entrer aux cieux, à savoir le seul Seigneur Jésus le Fils unique de Dieu'. Translation by the author.

54 Bullinger, *Cent Sermons* 1075: 'il y a des arbres fruitiers, mais aussi ces arbres y donnent grande recréation. Davantage la rivière coule par le milieu des rues, et d'un côté d'autre des deux rivages on voit de fort beaux arbres portant des fruits de vie'. Translation by the author.

Thus far the theological representations of the Theatre of God. Let us now examine the modes of its transposition in two early modern gardens.

2   Bernard Palissy's Theatre of God as Garden and Refuge

A committed follower of the Reformation, Bernard Palissy was a celebrated ceramist as well as a visionary encyclopaedist. In 1562, while imprisoned because of his faith, he wrote his book *La Recepte veritable*, in which he presents a model for a garden located below a hill and crossed by a brook. This garden has four parts. In the intersections of the paths, eight pavilions and an 'amphitheatre' are erected, four of which are made of masonry and five (including the 'amphitheatre') are planted. Religious texts from the Old Testament are carved above their gates.

There are clear similarities between Palissy's garden and the French translation by Jean Martin (d. 1553) of Francesco Colonna's *Hypnerotomachia Poliphili* (1499).[55] Nevertheless, for scholars like Gilles Polizzi, *La Recepte* is a 'counter-*Poliphile*', an experiment in revising Colonna's account based on an interweaving of different biblical texts.[56] The garden in the *Poliphile* is associated with erotic rituals and mythological images that are linked to the island of Cythera, the legendary birthplace of Venus. For Colonna, Eden and the celestial city probably constitute a model brought up to date. This garden forms a monumental circle with a one mile ('un mille') diameter and a three mile ('trois mille') perimeter.[57] It is surrounded by water, whereas the celestial city is surrounded by a wall and crossed by a river. The space of the garden in the *Poliphile* seems to be organized like the *negative* of the New Jerusalem, because in the periphery there is a compartmentalized area decorated with parterres, and in its centre stands an amphitheatre of rare and precious stones, bordered with a jasper colonnade.

---

55   Colonna Francesco, *Le Songe de Poliphile*, trans. Jean Martin (Paris: Jacques Kerver, 1546). On the link between *Le Songe de Poliphile* and *La Recepte*, see Palissy, *Recette*, ed. Lestringant 26, 32, 56; Duport, *Le Jardin et la nature* 68–83; Amico, *Bernard Palissy* 96–172; Polizzi G., "L'intégration du modèle: Le *Poliphile* et le discours du jardin dans la *Recepte véritable*", Albineana, *Cahiers d'Aubigné* 4 (1992) 65–92; Lestringant F., "De Francesco Colonna à Bernard Palissy: Du *Polifilo* au jardin de Refuge", *Studi di Letteratura Francese* 19 (1993) 453–467; Lecoq, "Le jardin de la Sagesse de Bernard Palissy" 65–73; Ferdinand, *Bernard Palissy* 121–159, 163.

56   Polizzi, "L'intégration du modèle" 66.

57   Colonna, *Le Songe de Poliphile*, fol. 111 r.

Now, for Palissy, the garden in the *Poliphile* expresses a paganism he disapproved of because of his religious convictions.[58] In order to restore this *mundus inversus*, or 'world turned upside-down', he passes geometrically from the radiocentric circle to the four-part square, which refers more to edenic geography.[59] Moreover, as the story unfolds, the 'amphitheatre' or 'palace' becomes the central green pavilion which has only its centrality and roundness in common with Colonna's amphitheatre. Then, he relates the previous mineral material of the garden to that of the New Jerusalem:[60]

> twelve rare stones that St. John in his Apocalypse describes as the foundations of the holy city of Jerusalem. For it must be understood that the twelve stones are hard and indissoluble, and that St. John considers them as the materials of an eternal construction.[61]

The 'Garden of Wisdom' is certainly a Theatre of God; in it, the characteristics of the Earthly Paradise and the New Jerusalem merge. According to Palissy, the conception of his garden is based on the message of *Psalm* 104; however, several specialists have pointed out a mismatch between the Creation landscape in the making, praised poetically by the psalmist, and the mannerist architecture of the garden in *La Recepte*.[62] Palissy's *ars naturans* is also based on gospel

---

58   Millet O. "Tradition de la révélation, exégèse biblique et autorité prophétique: Bible et culture profane selon Calvin", *Cahiers du GADGES* 4 (2006) 120.

59   Contemporaries, including Calvin, were fascinated by this *topos*. See particularly Bercé Y.M., "La fascination du monde renversé dans les troubles du XVIe siècle", in Lafond J. – Redondo A. (eds.), *L'image du monde renversé et ses représentations littéraires et para-littéraires de la fin du XVIe siècle au milieu du XVIIe siècle* (Paris: 1979) 9–15; Céard J., "Le thème du 'monde à l'envers' dans l'œuvre d'Agrippa d'Aubigné", in Lafond – Redondo (eds.), *L'image du monde renversé* 117–126; Millet O., "Calvin pamphlétaire", *Le Pamphlet en France au XVIe siècle*, special issue, *Cahiers V. L. Saulnier* 1.25 (1983) 18–19; Lestringant F., "De la *Première* à la *Dernière Semaine*, ou de la réversibilité du monde, selon Du Bartas, d'Aubigné, Augier Gaillard et Michel Quillian", in Ternaux J.-C. (ed.), *La Naissance du monde et l'invention du poème* (Paris: 1998) 435–453. On Palissy's garden and edenic geography see Ferdinand, *Bernard Palissy* 169.

60   Palissy's attraction to the *Apocalypse* is also expressed through vengeful millennialism when he claims that he wants to reveal to his enemies 'their destruction in the eighteenth [chapter] of the Apocalypse' (Palissy, *La Recepte*, fol. B ij v), or when he talks about simony (ibidem, fol. L iij r).

61   Ibidem, fol. G ij v: 'des douze pierres rares, lesquelles Saint-Jean en son Apocalypse, prend comme par une figure des douze fondements de la Sainte-Cité de Jérusalem. Car il faut entendre que les douze pierres sont dures et indissolubles, puis que Saint-Jean les prend par figure de perpétuel bâtiment'. Translation by the author.

62   Ibidem, fol. B iiij v: 'I want to base my garden on *Psalm* 104, where the Prophet describes the marvellous works of the Lord'. For Catherine Randall, this garden is effectively a

texts whose messages overlap and mix with that of *Psalm* 104. It concerns the already mentioned parable of the hidden treasure (*Matthew* 13:44) and the parable of the talents (*Matthew* 25:14–30), also linked to the Calvinist doctrine of double predestination, according to which God has entrusted us with talents that we are obliged to make fruitful.[63]

In his commentary on *Psalm* 104, Calvin compares the Creator to a 'farmer working in secret'.[64] Palissy is not satisfied to offer for contemplation, as in a naturalist landscape, the works of this divine labour in progress to which *Psalm* 104 refers: waters, mountains, wind, stones, plants, animals, etc. Thanks to the study of these 'secrets' (*arcana naturae*), he has developed talents necessary for a *techne* enabling the collection of treasures displayed on the scene of his garden-theatre (*theatrum mundi*).[65]

This way of taking advantage of the hidden properties of living materials and minerals is one form of recreative and devotional imitation of nature. Through this *mimesis*, which represents the Huguenot refuge as an allegorical garden-discourse, Palissy preaches the wisdom of the Theatre of God in progress. There is no contradiction between the production of this 'beautiful masterpiece' and the Protestant ethic, despite the lack of any external resemblance between the treasures of the garden and the divine Creation in *Psalm* 104. Here, the refuge, which combines the characteristics of Eden and the Celestial Jerusalem, results from human creativity applied to divine Creation.

The overall plan of the garden in the *Recepte* is oddly put together. There are in fact certain spatial and functional impossibilities.[66] The 'amphitheatre', presented 'as a refuge to receive Christians exiled in times of persecution', appears totally unsuitable for this function.[67] We agree with Gilles Polizzi when he writes that *La Recepte* displays 'non-congruent systems', and when he points

---

'psalmic paraphrase': see Randall C., "Realizing the Writings: Bernard Palissy's *Recepte Veritable* as Psalmic Paraphrase", *Romance Notes* 35.1 (1994) 101–106. For Polizzi, it is a 'paraphrase of *Psalm* 104, which evokes a landscape which has almost no relation to that of the garden' (Polizzi, "L'intégration du modèle" 92); for Amico, it serves only to describe the rural countryside which surrounds the garden (Amico, *Bernard Palissy* 104). Translations by the author.

63   This programme is made explicit in the complete title of Palissy's treatise, *Recepte verita ble par laquelle tous les hommes de la France pourront apprendre a multiplier et augmenter leurs thresors*. Lestringant notes that 'the two ways to "multiply and augment his treasures" appear closely inclusive of the temporal and the spiritual' (Lestringant, "L'Éden et les ténèbres extérieures" 120). Translations by the author.

64   Calvin, *Commentaires sur le livre des psaumes* 647.

65   Palissy, *La Recepte*, fols. L iiiij v, Q iij v.

66   Lestringant, "L'Éden et les ténèbres extérieures" 126.

67   Palissy, *La Recepte*, fol. B iij v; idem, *Recette* 15.

out that this garden, made of a series of pavilions and texts, is more linear than quadrangular. For Polizzi, Palissy's garden-refuge is above all a 'mental space',[68] a book without pictures, but many mental images. This underpins an unexplored aspect of *La Recepte*: its link with the *ars memoriae*. In the *Poliphile*, Colonna uses a mnemonic method based on the sequences of *imagines agentes* (sensitive or striking images), permeating the memory with a specific message or content.[69] Similarly, the surprising architectural images in *La Recepte* seem to be provided to surprise, in order to register gospel messages in the reader's memory. This hypothesis is reinforced by the fact that the *ars memoriae*, which was very much in vogue during this time, also made its way into Protestant literature.[70]

This garden, also called 'palace',[71] is apparently a 'memory palace', like the Temple of Solomon or the New Jerusalem used in the medieval mnemonic tradition. In this regard *La Recepte* may also be compared to *L'idea del teatro* (1550) by Giulio Camillo (ca. 1480–1544), who was the proponent of a mnemonic architecture in the shape of a Vitruvian theatre, created to transmit a universal hermetic wisdom.[72] Camillo's theatre includes in its centre a 'House of Solomon's wisdom'. It is also notable that the inscriptions in Palissy's 'Garden of Wisdom' were extracted from the *Wisdom of Solomon*, and from *Ecclesiasticus*, also called *The Wisdom of Jesus the Son of Sirach*, neither of which are part of the Calvinist canon. These lexical and programmatic analogies between Palissy's 'Garden of Wisdom' and Camillo's *Theatro della Sapientia* (Theatre of wisdom) do not seem to be accidental. *La Recepte*, which we already called a 'counter-*Poliphile*', is apparently also a 'counter-*Theatro della Sapientia*', the result of a reversal of the occult *mundus inversus* condemned by Calvin.[73]

---

68   Polizzi, "L'intégration du modèle" 73.

69   Jeannin-Corbin M., "Les 'vues imageantes', écho des *imagines agentes* rhétoriques? L'exemple du *Songe de Poliphile* de Francesco Colonna (1546)", in Voisin B. (ed.), *Fiction et vues imageantes: Typologie et fonctionnalités* (Tartu: 2008) 89–107. Connections have been established between the art of memory and other ideal gardens by Kuwakino K., *L'architetto sapiente: Giardino, teatro, città come schemi mnemonici tra il XVI e il XVII secolo* (Florence: 2011) 124, 174.

70   See Rossi, *Clavis universalis* 95–101; Banderier G., "Du Bartas et l'*ars memorativa*", in Winn C.H. (ed.), *Sens et enjeux de la mémoire dans la société moderne: De la Renaissance au seuil du siècle Classique*, special issue, *Tangence* 87 (2008) 31–45; Vérin H., "Olivier de Serres et son Théâtre d'agriculture", *Artefact* 4 (2016) 161–180.

71   Palissy, *La Recepte*, fol. B iij v.

72   Rossi, *Clavis universalis* 95.

73   In *De Scandalis* (1550) Calvin condemns especially Heinrich Cornelius Agrippa von Nettesheim.

3   Renée de France's Garden and Castellany in Montargis: a Theatre
      of God?

A confessional and historical proximity exists between Bernard Palissy and
Renée of France, Countess of Ferrara, Duchess of Chartres and Montargis,
the daughter of King Louis XII, and married to Ercole II d'Este since 1528.[74] In
Ferrara, as early as 1544, she was harassed, condemned, and then temporarily
imprisoned for her protection of numerous Protestants and for her ambiguous
religious behaviour.[75] Among her guests were Clément Marot and Jean Calvin,
whom she had met in 1536 and with whom she developed a regular correspondence. After the death of the Duke of Ferrara, in 1559, Renée left Ferrara
for Montargis in France.

Although not officially converted, Renée de France behaved like a Huguenot
on her land, but she did so inconsistently, depending on the circumstances.
Her political role was limited to that of a powerful patroness.[76] She invited
clergymen to spread the Reformation, sometimes sternly, throughout the province of Gâtinais. According to Jacques-Auguste de Thou (1553–1617), from 1562,
when the first War of Religion broke out, her château and gardens became
a place of refuge for persecuted reformers.[77] Apparently, it accommodated
between 300 and 600 refugees.[78]

A few literary and archival sources show, unsurprisingly, that Renée's
ideas developed in an intellectual environment marked by the *eschata*, and
they reveal the importance of her gardens.[79] However, these sources are too

---

74   Renée apparently met Palissy at the Tuileries: Rodocanachi, *Une protectrice de la
     réforme* 503.
75   Jarry, *Renée de France* 12–14.
76   Turias O., *Renée de France, duchesse de Ferrare, témoin de son temps (1510–1575)* (Ph.D. dis-
     sertation, University of Tours: 2004) 705–742.
77   These facts are related in part by the sixteenth-century historian Jacques-Auguste de
     Thou, *Histoire Universelle: Depuis 1543 jusqu'en 1607* (1560–1564), vol. 4 (London, s.n.: 1734)
     231, 275. See Jarry, *Renée de France*; Rodocanachi, *Une protectrice de la réforme* 219–382;
     Androuet du Cerceau J., *Les plus excellents bastiments de France*, ed. D. Thomson (Paris:
     1988) 85–87; Boudon – Mignot (eds.), *Jacques Androuet du Cerceau* 76–85; Cvetkovic, "The
     Gardens of the Château de Montargis" 359–379.
78   Rodocanachi, *Une protectrice de la réforme* 359, 386, 462.
79   An enigmatic poem by Clément Marot, dated 1535, evokes both the *Apocalypse* and
     Duchess Renée in the eschatological context of the refuge: Clément Marot, *Les Œuvres de
     Clément Marot* (Lyon, Guillaume Roville: 1561) 109–110. Renée does not reject the escha-
     tological texts of the canon, including the *Book of Revelation*, which she mentions in her
     will: Rodocanachi, *Une protectrice de la réforme* 550. The poet Agrippa d'Aubigné, who
     took refuge in Montargis in 1562, affirms the apocalyptic character of that period: Aubigné
     Théodore Agrippa d', *Les Tragiques* (Geneva, L.B.D.D.: 1606), fols. 8 v, 10 r, 372 v. For the

incomplete to find in them the programme for her garden projects. The main documentation at our disposal consists of Jacques Androuet Du Cerceau's drawings and prints. According to his own testimony and extant ledgers, Du Cerceau sought refuge at Montargis in 1563 and 1565, where he was commissioned to renovate the château and gardens; no further details are mentioned.[80] We know that contracts for work on the garden were recorded in 1561, thus one or two years before he arrived at Montargis, and that one of his functions was to distribute alms for the Duchess, which attests to their proximity.[81]

Renée's château was an imposing medieval fortress, reputedly invulnerable, which dominated the countryside it was meant to defend. Montargis was a large city for its period; it was located near Orléans, the capital of French Protestantism, and Châtillon-sur-Loing, the residence of the Huguenot military leader Gaspard de Coligny.[82] However, the Catholic population of Montargis was hostile to the Reformation. In this uncertain environment, the Duchess's priority was to fortify, arm, and live in her castle.[83]

The architecture and urbanization of Montargis were marked by the well-known process called castellation.[84] The *castrum* was too imposing to be reconstructed as an Italianate residence fit for a royal princess.[85] Thus, it was decided to consolidate its military architecture and to create new gardens on the north-western flanks of the natural promontory, both to embellish the complex and to feed the residents of the château.

The gardens comprised two semicircular sections, the 'upper gardens' and the 'great garden'. The upper terrace, over twenty-five metres wide and up to four or five metres high, featured a pleasure garden consisting of several

archival evidence, see Rodocanachi, *Une protectrice de la Reforme*; Jarry, *Renée de France à Montargis*; Cvetkovic, *The Gardens of the Château de Montargis*.

80   Androuet du Cerceau, *Les plus excellents bastiments de France* 76–85 ("Montargis"). According to Guillaume, Androuet du Cerceau settled at Montargis in 1563: Guillaume J., "Qui est Jacques Androuet du Cerceau ?", in idem (ed.), *Jacques Androuet du Cerceau* (Paris: 2010); Randall gives 1565 as the date (Randall, *Building Codes* 158).

81   Account books for the years 1567, 1568, 1571, 1573, 1574 are mentioned by Rodocanachi, *Une protectrice de la réforme* 425–477.

82   Ibidem 332. Today Châtillon-Coligny.

83   Jarry, *Renée de France à Montargis* 26.

84   Bazzana A. (ed.), *Guerre, fortification et habitat dans le monde méditerranéen au moyen âge*, Castrum 3 (Madrid: 1988); Hubert É., *L'"incastellamento" en Italie centrale* (Rome: 2002); Coulson C., *Castles in Medieval Society: Fortresses in England, France, and Ireland in the Central Middle Ages* (Oxford: 2004).

85   In 1697, a large part of the castle was destroyed to build a 'maison de plaisance': Androuet du Cerceau, *Les plus excellents bastiments de France*, ed. Thomson 87; Boudon – Mignot (eds.), *Jacques Androuet du Cerceau* 76.

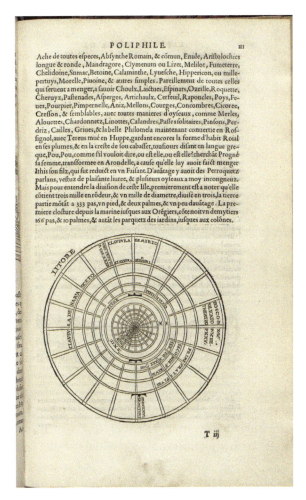

POLIPHILE. III

Ache de toutes efpeces,Abfynthe Romain, & cõmun, Enule, Ariftolochics
longue & ronde , Mandragore , Clymenum ou Lizet, Melilot, Fumeterre,
Chelidoine,Sumac,Betoine, Calaminthe, Lyuefche, Hippericon, ou mille-
pertuys,Morelle,Piuoine, & autres fimples . Pareillement de toutes celles
qui feruent a menger,a fauoir Choulx,Laictues,Efpinars,Ozeille,Roquette,
Cheruyz,Paftenades,Afperges, Artichaulx, Cerfeuil,Raponcles, Poys,Fe-
ues,Pourpier,Pimpernelle,Aniz,Mellons,Courges,Concombres,Cicoree,
Creffon, & femblables, auec toutes manieres d'oyfeaux, comme Merles,
Alouettes,Chardonnetz,Linottes,Calandres,Paffes folitaires,Pinfons,Per-
driz , Cailles , Griues,& la belle Philomela maintenant conuertie en Rof-
fignol,auec Tereus mué en Huppe,gardant encores la forme d'habit Roial
en fes plumes,& en la crefte de fon cabaffet,toufiours difant en langue gre-
que,Pou,Pou,comme s'il vouloit dire,ou eft elle,ou eft elle?cherchãt Progné
fa femme,transformee en Arondelle,a caufe qu'elle luy auoit faict menger
Ithis fon filz,qui fut reduict en vn Faifant.D'auãtage y auoit des Perroquetz
parlans,veftuz de plaifante liuree, & plufieurs oyfeaux a moy incongneuz.
Mais pour entendre la diuifion de cefte Ifle,premierement eft a noter qu'elle
cõtient trois mille en rõdeur,& vn mille de diametre,diuifé en trois,la tierce
partie mõtãt a 333 pas,vn pied,& deux palmes,& vn peu dauãtage . La pre-
miere cloflure depuis la marine iufques aux Orégiers,cõte noit vn demytiers
166 pas,& 10 palmes,& autãt les parquetz des iardins,iufques aux colónes.

T iij

compartments. There was a deer park in the moats and an aviary near the
noble dwelling. The walls around the upper terrace were decorated with high
merlons bordered by scrolls, evoking pinions 'in the antique style', placed in the
radiating axes formed by the alignment of the parterres. The lower part, probably kept for food production, was also organized in radial bands seventy-six
yards wide. A bushy hedge closed off this 'Grand Jardin'.

The spatial organization of the garden is extended into the surrounding
countryside by means of rows of elms which border the roads to Orléans and
Paris. This gives the monument a dramatic quality characteristic of Renaissance
architecture, obtained by recycling existing morphologies. Specialists have
noted the resemblance between the nearly circular and radial plan of Renée's
garden and the island of Cythera of the *Poliphile* [Fig. 12.2], but big differences

do exist.[86] Its elevation, which is adapted to the topography, is inverted compared to the scheme of the Vitruvian theatre: it is lower towards the exterior and higher towards the centre. At Montargis, the two terraces of the semicircular garden take the form of a *proscenium*.

There are also important differences with the garden in *La Recepte*, which do not come down to an opposition between circle and square, but which are evident in the choice of embellishments: pavilions, grottoes, and streams for Palissy, flower beds, galleries and panoramic views for Renée de France. Furthermore, and especially, the centre of the Montargis garden is a true refuge, with fortified walls and food resources, not an allegorical one. However, it seems that these dissimilarities express individual skills, more than a wish to reform with counter-models. This is confirmed by the almost simultaneous dates of the drafting of *La Recepte* and the planning of the gardens of Montargis.

According to Randall, Calvin considered the Church to be a tree subdivided into multiple branches and foliage attached to a trunk, a way to organize chaos, comparable to the architecture of Du Cerceau's gardens, and those of Montargis in particular.[87] Du Cerceau's iconoclastic aspirations apparently led him, in Randall's view, to a paradoxical art of 'overornamentation'.[88] It seems to us more convincing to link his art of ornate, compartmentalized knot gardens to the parable of the talents.[89] In this way, Renée's garden is an audacious and pragmatic recreation, materializing the heaven to come as a collection of *treasures*, which, like the garden of *La Recepte*, could also be connected with *Psalm* 104 and the parable of the talents. Moreover, this results in a display of *decorum*, whose function is not only the devout representation of the Theatre of God, but also – by way of this lavish art – the expression of the nobility and political power of the duchess.

We must rule out Cvetkovic's interpretation, which affirms: 'that none of the documents describing the gardens mentions any statuary could be the sign of an aesthetic adaptation to the Calvinist ideas'.[90] In fact, Calvin only encouraged the suppression of religious images from places of worship to eliminate idolatry, when he asserted: 'The true apostolic and early Church was without

---

86   Boudon – Mignot (eds.), *Jacques Androuet du Cerceau* 76–85; Cvetkovic, "The Gardens of the Château de Montargis" 359–379.

87   Randall, *Building Codes* 55, 160.

88   Ibidem, 167, 172.

89   Ibidem, 160.

90   Cvetkovic, "The Gardens of the Château de Montargis" 375.

images in her assembled saints'.[91] And: 'Today we have neither guilt nor qualms about reserving the temples contaminated by idols for a better use'.[92]

In addition, famous sixteenth-century sculptors such as Ligier Richer, Jean Goujon, and Barthélémy Prieur, were Huguenots, and the garden of Palissy contained several statues in the Mannerist style. The parable of the talents justifies this lavish art. In addition, in *Les Plus excellents bastiments de France*, the absence of sculpture in the gardens belonging to French Catholic patrons, such as the king at Blois and the constable of Montmorency at Chantilly and Ecouen, does not rest on any confessional logic. Conversely, in the German Protestant world, the Hortus Palatinus in Heidelberg of Prince-Elector Frederick V (1596–1632), created by the Huguenot Salomon de Caus (1576–1626), was dotted with statues and automata.

As specialists have pointed out, Du Cerceau, giving thanks to divine providence for having provided him with his artistic gifts, had a general tendency to embellish reality.[93] At Montargis he drew gardens that are rounder and more regular than in reality [Figs. 12.3 and 12.4]. This tendency was presumably based on a *theological agenda* in connection with the doctrine of the Theatre of God.[94]

In 1561, in order to develop this garden, about five hectares of land, one part of the cemetery was destroyed, certainly in order to increase the area, but also to make Catholic funeral rites invisible from the château. The Huguenots considered these rites superstitious and inherently derived from the *mundus inversus*.[95] For the followers of the Reformation, the 'papist' funeral rites are macabre and reprobate, as Pierre Viret (ca. 1510–1571) maintained.[96] For Catholics, as Florimond de Raemond (1540–1601) asserted, these customs are a

---

91   Calvin Jean, *Sermons sur le v livre de Moyse nommé Deutéronome* (Geneva, Thomas Courteau: 1567): 'La vraie Eglise apostolique et primitive a été sans images en ses saintes assemblées'. Translation by the author.

92   Calvin Jean, *Commentaire de Moïse* (Paris, Henri Estienne: 1564) 351: 'Nous ne ferons pas aujourd'hui conscience ni scrupule de réserver les temples qui ont été pollués d'idoles pour les appliquer à meilleur usage'. Translation by the author.

93   Androuet du Cerceau, *Les Plus excellents*, fol. A ii v.

94   Randall, *Building Codes* 164–165.

95   The funeral of Renée de France was solemn and without pomp.

96   Viret Pierre, *Disputations chrestiennes touchant l'estat des trepassez faites par dialogues* (Geneva: 1552) 31. See Koslofsky C., *The Reformation of the Dead: Death and Ritual in Early Modern Germany, 1450–1700* (Basingstoke – New York, NY: 2000); Grosse C., "Une mort déritualisée? Usages funéraires dans la tradition protestante réformée", in Boudet J.-F. (ed.), *Les rites et usages funéraires: essais d'anthropologie juridique* (Aix-en-Provence: 2019) 181–196.

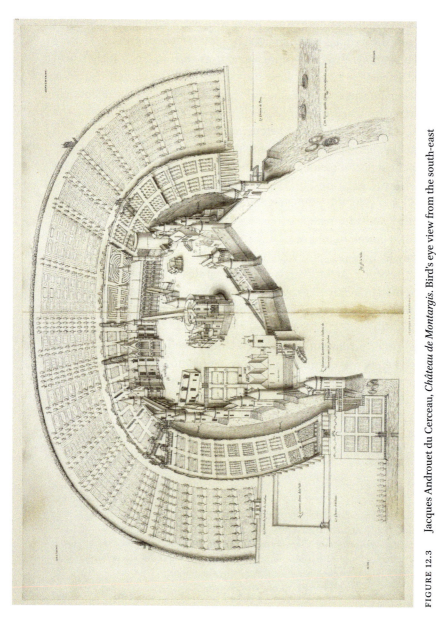

FIGURE 12.3   Jacques Androuet du Cerceau, *Château de Montargis*. Bird's eye view from the south-east showing the castle at the centre, with formal gardens and two mazes arranged in a semicircle around the moat, ca. 1570. Pen and black ink, with grey wash, on vellum, 512 × 744 mm. London, The British Museum, inv. no. 1972, U.817

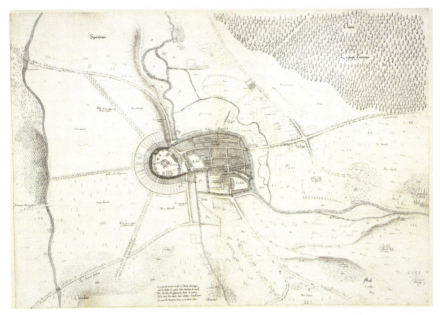

FIGURE 12.4   Jacques Androuet du Cerceau, *Château de Montargis*. Map of the area with
                 the castle at the centre, ca. 1570. Pen and black ink, with grey wash, on vellum,
                 515 × 740 mm. London, The British Museum, inv. no. 1972, U.815
                 IMAGE © THE TRUSTEES OF THE BRITISH MUSEUM

sign of 'irreligion' and 'ungodliness'.[97] The trimming of the cemetery enclosure
to extend the pleasure garden, in the midst of profound religious disagreement,
resulted in an uprising of the population, followed by a bloody crackdown.[98]
About ten years later, on a design of Montargis, Du Cerceau noted that near the
gardens was henceforth 'the shared cemetery of the city', undoubtedly referring to its interfaith use.

In 1563, that was still possible in theory thanks to the Edict of Amboise, but
in practice the Protestants experienced more and more difficulty in burying
their dead in communal cemeteries, where their graves were sometimes dug
up at night. Thus, Du Cerceau's drawing of the Montargis cemetery is probably another embellishment of reality, part of the restoration of the 'world
upside-down' inherent in the Calvinist Theatre of God. The garden, as an
image of the coming paradise, prevails over the cemetery, where a form of

---

97   Raemond Florimond de, *L'histoire de la naissance, progrès et décadence de l'hérésie de ce
      siècle* (Paris, Chez la Veuve Guillaume de la Noue: 1610) 1056.

98   Jarry, *Renée de France* 16–17; Rodocanachi, *Une protectrice de la réforme* 365.

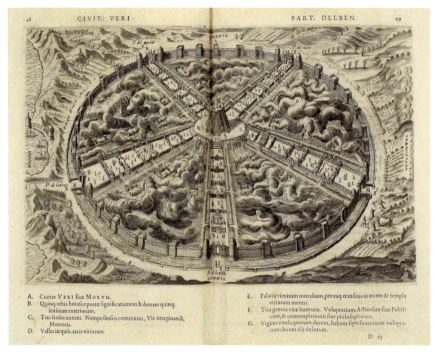

FIGURE 12.5   "The City of Truth or Ethics". Engraving. From: Bartholomeus Delbene, *Civitas veri sive morum* (Paris, Ambrosius and Hieronymus Drouart: 1609) 28–29
PUBLIC DOMAIN. ARCHIVE.ORG

condemned idolatry is practised. At the same time, this burial place is thought of as a symbol of religious reconciliation.

The noted resemblance between the Montargis gardens and the island of Cythera in the *Poliphile* can be extended to the radiocentric organization of several ideal cities designed at the beginning of modern times.[99] There is, in particular, a closeness between the gardens of the duchess and the *Civitas veri sive morum* (City of truth or ethics) by Bartolomeo Del Bene (1515–1595), printed in 1609 on the basis of a manuscript dated 1565, which describes a city planned to be a 'vero refugio de' veri christiani' ('true refuge of true Christians') [Fig. 12.5].[100] On a different scale, there are similarities with the theatrical and

99   This geometry reminds one of the ideal city of Sforzinda designed by Filarete (ca. 1400–ca. 1469), the island-landscape of Utopia created by Thomas More (1478–1535), or the "mondo savio" of Anton Francesco Doni (1513–1574).

100   See Balmas E., "Cité idéale, utopie et progrès dans la pensée française de la Renaissance", *Mélanges de littérature française offerts à M. René Pintard* (Paris: 1975) 47–57; Gorris

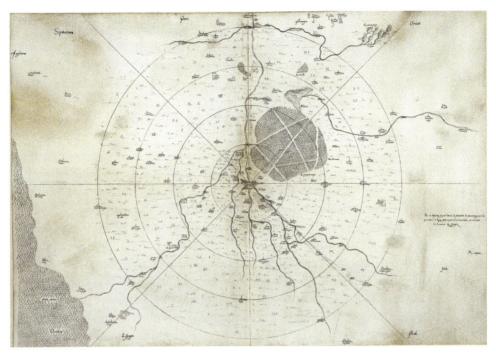

FIGURE 12.6   Jacques Androuet du Cerceau, *Château de Montargis*. Map from the south-west depicting
the castle with surrounding land, ca. 1570. Pen and black ink, with grey wash, on vellum,
518 × 751 mm. London, The British Museum, inv. no. 1972, U.814
IMAGE © THE TRUSTEES OF THE BRITISH MUSEUM

radial architecture of the Protestant church in heaven, constructed in wood in
Lyon in 1564.[101]

It is also necessary to take into account the ancient tradition of urbanization
and property planning centred on a *castrum*, examined by Armelle Querrien,
particularly in Issoudun and notably in Gâtinais, not far from Montargis.[102]
This plot-by-plot organization, evoking Renée de France's gardens in a striking way, extended very regularly, at times for several dozens of hectares. In Du

Camos R., *"La Città del Vero*, une ville en papier entre utopie et hétérotopie", *Seizième
Siècle* 9 (2013) 171–196.

101   Perrissin Jean, *Le Temple de Paradis*, ca. 1565, Musée International de la Réforme, Geneva,
inv. no. 179. See Reymond B., "D'où le 'temple Paradis' tenait–il son modèle?", *Bulletin de la
S.H.P.F.* (1999) 263–284.

102   Querrien A., "Les formes circulaires de l'espace bâti et agricole au Moyen Âge: Tracé,
mesure et partage", *Archéologie médiévale* 38 (2008) 123–158.

Cerceau's map of the Montargis lordship, the radiocentric geometry of the garden seems to be projected outwards along a radius of sixteen kilometres around the city [Fig. 12.6]. However, it is difficult to admit that this geometric layout belongs to a project to remodel long-held agricultural land. The context of the second half of the sixteenth century was very different from that of the birth of manor houses with radiocentric plots. This radial and concentric shape was apparently a form of graphical scale useful for at-a-glance evaluations of distances on a map.

Here, the project of rationalizing space is not specific to Protestant culture, but harmonizes with the concept of stewardship or custody as a religious duty, inherent in the doctrine of the Theatre of God. At this point, we can assume that the circle was allegorically incorporated into Calvinist theological discourse and transmitted through architecture and cartography, without thereby constituting an exclusive usage in landscapes fashioned during the Middle Ages or contemporary landscapes under Catholic control.[103]

The format of emblem books, just like the art of memory, was also applied to Calvinist reform.[104] Do these books illuminate Du Cerceau's plan for the gardens at Montargis? In the entire corpus of sixteenth-century books, it is in the *Emblèmes* (1580) by Théodore de Bèze that the circle is found by far the most frequently [Fig. 12.7]. The *figura perfectissima* takes on several meanings there, sometimes linked to eschatological themes: God's perfection, the course of life, eternal life, banishment or exile, the *urbs Christi*, that is, the Church as an institution in the form of a fortified circular celestial city.[105] Thus the form chosen for the plan of the Montargis garden could be interpreted on the basis of such allegorical readings provided by Bèze.

Specialists agree in attributing the project of the two parallel galleries built in the highest part of the garden to Du Cerceau [Fig. 12.8]. Their function was to cover, while enclosing it, a path leading to a panoramic view oriented along the axis of the way to Orléans. These two portals were raised on either side of an imposing door *à l'antique*, adorned with Graeco-Roman motifs. To reach

---

103   An old map of Porreta, near Bologna, shows a radiocentric organization of the county dating back to the fifteenth century (Archivio di Stato di Bologna, Ranuzzi, Istrumenti del feudo, Livre E n. 25). See also Ribouillault D., "Le vedute urbane di Girolamo Righettino: Le allegorie del principe cristiano, 1583–85", *IN_BO. Ricerche e progetti per il territorio, la città e l'architettura* 12.16 (2021) 50–65.

104   See Adams A., *Webs of Allusion: French Protestant Emblem Books of the Sixteenth Century* (Geneva: 2003).

105   See Stawarz-Luginbühl R., "Les *Emblemata/Emblemes chrestiens* (1580/1581) de Théodore de Bèze: Un recueil d'emblèmes humaniste et protestant", *Bibliothèque d'humanisme et renaissance* 67.3 (2005) 609.

FIGURE 12.7   *Emblema 1*. Engraving. From: Théodore de Beze, *Icones, id*
                est verae imagines virorum doctrina simul et pietate illustrium
                (Geneva, Jean Laon: 1580)
                PUBLIC DOMAIN. ARCHIVE.ORG

the château from that door, visitors had to climb a stairway, then cross a sloped
alley, which narrowed on the approach of an overpass suspended above the
moats. Thus, the most majestic access to the château is not found on the side
of the city, nor on the side of Paris or Fontainebleau where the king resided,
but on the road to Orléans, the religious epicentre of the Huguenot party.
A Reformed church, which even had a school of theology, was founded there

FIGURE 12.8   Jacques Androuet du Cerceau, *Château de Montargis*. Detail with
                 monumental gateway and galleries, ca. 1570. Pen and black ink, with grey
                 wash, on vellum, 512 × 744 mm. London, The British Museum, inv. no.
                 1972, U.819
                 IMAGE © THE TRUSTEES OF THE BRITISH MUSEUM

in 1557; yet in 1562 the Reformed cult was only tolerated there.[106] Thus, it was
probably through that doorway that the refugees coming from Orléans, such

106   Jouanna A., *La France du XVIᵉ siècle, 1483–1598* (Paris: 2012) 401–414.

as Du Cerceau himself, reached the gardens, then the château, and finally the refuge.

That grandiose portal, with its Orléanais orientation, could in this respect evoke the parable of the narrow door which gives access to the Kingdom of God, where a 'good tree bears good fruit'.[107] This parable is included allegorically on the frontispiece of numerous books of Reformed theology and in an important book, *Les Emblèmes ou devises chrestiennes* (1567/1571) by the Huguenot Georgette de Montenay (1540–1581), a cousin of Jeanne d'Albret.[108] In this book the emblem represents a monumental antique gate levitating in the sky, giving access to an invisible 'Celestial City' [Fig. 12.9].[109]

The particular way the Montargis labyrinths were drawn up seems to be another revision of a model condemned by Calvin. Numerous Renaissance gardens are decorated with labyrinths, or mazes, and there are many ways to interpret this iconic motif.[110] As Denis Crouzet recalled, for Calvin the labyrinth is the face of sin and fruitless soul-searching.[111] At Montargis, it is not necessary, in order to go through the maze, to follow its crooked path. One may simply cross it in a straight line, as the engraving shows [Fig. 12.10]. This example of 'reformation' of the labyrinth is unique in Du Cerceau's work and elsewhere. This suggests that the motif is meant to evoke Calvin's thinking.

In conclusion, the two gardens and landscapes considered in this essay, both in idealized and realized forms, became part of Calvinist culture during the 1560s. They were places of refuge implicitly or explicitly partaking of an imaginary world that linked the Garden of Eden to the Celestial Jerusalem. They can be connected to the eschatology of the Theatre of God, for the *ars naturans* which produced them was a *mimesis* of Creation in motion. In these gardens, the recreation of the world results from human labour and talent submitted to divine providence. They are no longer representations of the *locus amœnus*, temporarily motionless. They are the expression of a new paradise, developing in the early modern world, whereas the original Eden has not

---

107   *Matthew* 7:17; cf. *Luke* 6:43.

108   Joudrier P., *Un 'miroir' calviniste. 'Les Emblemes, ou Devises Chrestiennes' de Georgette de Montenay et Pierre Woeiriot, 1567/1571* (Geneva: 2021).

109   Montenay Georgette de, *Les Emblemes, ou Devises Chrestiennes* (Lyon, Jean Marcorelle: 1571), fol. 12 r.

110   Kern H., *Through Labyrinths* (Munich – London – New York, NY: 2000); Wright C., *The Maze and the Warrior: Symbols in Architecture, Theology, and Music* (Cambridge: 2001); Brunon H. (ed.), *Le Jardin comme labyrinthe du monde: Métamorphoses d'un imaginaire de la Renaissance à nos jours* (Paris: 2008).

111   See, for example, Calvin, *Institution* 13, 17, 52, 198, 369, 412, 453, 508, 512: Crouzet, *Jean Calvin* 62 and 211.

FIGURE 12.9
"Sed futuram inquirimus".
From: Georgette de
Montenay, *Emblèmes ou
Devises chrestiennes* (Zurich,
Christoph Froschauer: 1584),
fol. 12 r.
PUBLIC DOMAIN.
ARCHIVE.ORG

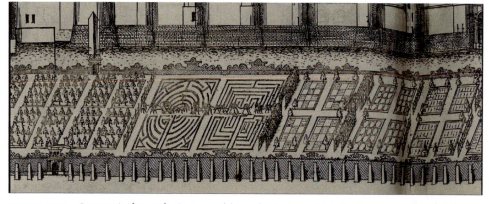

FIGURE 12.10   Jacques Androuet du Cerceau, *Château de Montargis*. Detail with mazes in the garden.
Engraving. From: *Les Plus excellents bastiments de France* (Paris, s.n.: 1607), originally
published in 1576

PUBLIC DOMAIN. ARCHIVE.ORG

totally disappeared. To achieve this, the designers of these gardens undertook to overturn the *mundus inversus*. The fact that these pleasure gardens, and others in Europe, created by Calvinists, are lavish works of art is in no contradiction with the Reformed Christian ethic, which is often mistakenly reduced to austerity. Through their vegetal and mineral decorations, influenced by psalms and gospel parables, they express the luxuriant diversity of Eden and the marvels to come in the New Jerusalem. They do so, even if the Calvinist theologians authorized only an allegorical – albeit at times highly imaginative – reading of *Revelation* 21.

Bibliography

Primary Sources

Androuet du Cerceau Jacques, *Les plus excellents bastiments de France* (Paris, s.n.: 1576).

Aubigné Théodore Agrippa d', *Les Tragiques* (Geneva, L.B.D.D.: 1606).

Bullinger Heinrich, *Cent Sermons sur l'apocalypse de Jesus Christ* (Lyon, Sébastien Honorat: 1564).

Calvin Jean, *Commentaire sur l'evangile selon sainct Jean* (Geneva, Jean Gérard: 1553).

Calvin Jean, *Commentaires sur le premier livre de Moyse, dit Génèse* (Geneva, Jean Gérad: 1554).

Calvin Jean, *Commentaires sur les Epistres de S. Paul* (Geneva, Conrad Badius: 1556).

Calvin Jean, *Institution de la religion Chrestienne* (Geneva, Jean Crespin: 1560).

Calvin Jean, *Commentaires sur le livre des psaumes* (Geneva, Conrad Baldius: 1561).

Calvin Jean, *Commentaires de M. Jean Calvin sur les cinq livres de Moyse; Genese est mis a part, les autres quatre livres sont disposez en forme d'Harmonie, avec cinq indices dont les deux contenans les passages alleguez et exposez par l'autheur sont adjoustez de nouveau en ceste traduction* (Geneva, François Estiene: 1564).

Calvin Jean, *Sermons sur le v livre de Moyse nommé Deutéronome* (Geneva, Thomas Courteau: 1567).

Calvin Jean, *Commentary on the Gospel According to John*, trans. W. Pringle, vol. 2 (Edinburgh: 1847).

Camillo Giulio, *L'idea del Teatro* (Venice – Florence, Lorenzo Torrentino: 1550).

Colonna Francesco, *Le Songe de Poliphile* (Paris, Jacques Kerver: 1546).

Du Bartas Guillaume de Salluste, *La seconde sepmaine* (Anvers, H. Mersmann: 1591).

Du Pinet Antoine, *Exposition sur l'Apocalypse de sainct Jean* (Geneva, Jehan Girard: 1543).

Marot Clément, *Les Œuvres de Clément Marot* (Lyon, Guillaume Roville: 1561).

Marot Clément – Bèze Theodore de, *Les Pseaumes mis en rime francoise* (Geneva, Thomas Courtaud: 1562).

Montenay Georgette de, *Les Emblemes, ou Devises Chrestiennes* (Lyon, Jean Marcorelle: 1571).

Palissy Bernard, *Recepte veritable par laquelle tous les hommes de la France pourront apprendre a multiplier et augmenter leurs thresors* (La Rochelle, Barthélémy Berton: 1563).

Raemond Florimond de, *L'histoire de la naissance, progrès et décadence de l'hérésie de ce siècle* (Paris, Chez la Veuve Guillaume de la Noue: 1610).

La Saincte Bible (Lyon, Sébastien Honorat: 1566).

Thou Jacques-Auguste de, *Histoire Universelle: Depuis 1543 Jusqu'en 1607*, 1560–1564, vol. 4 (London: 1734).

Viret Pierre, *Le Monde à Vempire et le Monde demoniacle, faict par dialogues* (Geneva, J. Berthet: 1561).

Secondary Sources

Adams A., *Webs of Allusion: French Protestant Emblem Books of the Sixteenth Century* (Geneva: 2003).

Amico L., *Bernard Palissy: In Search of Earthly Paradise* (Paris – New York, NY: 1996).

Androuet du Cerceau J., *Les plus excellents bastiments de France*, ed. D. Thomson (Paris: 1988).

Antoine E. (ed.), *Sur la terre comme au ciel: Jardins d'occident à la fin du Moyen-Âge* (Paris: 2002).

Backus I., *Les sept visions et la fin des temps: Les commentaires genevois de l'Apocalypse entre 1539 et 1584* (Geneva: 1997).

Backus I., "Calvin's Concept of Natural and Roman Law", *Calvin Theological Journal* 38.1 (2003) 7–26.

Bakker B., *Landscape and Religion from Van Eyck to Rembrandt* (London: 2016).

Balmas E., "Cité idéale, utopie et progrès dans la pensée française de la Renaissance", *Mélanges de Littérature française offerts à M. René Pintard* (Paris: 1975) 47–57.

Banderier G., "Du Bartas et l'*ars memorativa*", in Winn C.H. (ed.), *Sens et enjeux de la mémoire dans la société moderne: De la Renaissance au seuil du siècle classique*, special issue, *Tangence* 87 (2008) 31–45.

Barret P. – Gurgand J.N., *Le roi des derniers jours: L'exemplaire et très cruelle histoire des rebaptisés de Münster (1534–1535)* (Paris: 1981).

Bazzana A. (ed.), *Guerre, fortification et habitat dans le monde méditerranéen au moyen âge*, Castrum 3 (Madrid: 1988).

Bercé Y.M., "La fascination du monde renversé dans les troubles du XVIe siècle", in Lafond J. – Redondo A. (eds.), *L'image du monde renversé et ses représentations littéraires et para-littéraires de la fin du XVIe siècle au milieu du XVIIe siècle* (Paris: 1979) 9–15.

Birmelé A. (ed.), *Introduction à la théologie systématique* (Geneva: 2008).

Blair A., *The Theater of Nature: Jean Bodin and Renaissance Science* (Princeton, NJ: 1997).

Bolzoni L., *The Gallery of Memory: Literary and Iconographic Models in the Age of the Printing Press* (Toronto: 2001).

Bost H., "De la 'vraye Eglise' et du 'gouvernement civil': La démocratie serait-elle contagieuse ?", in Varet J. (ed.), *Calvin: Naissance d'une pensée* (Tours: 2012) 67–75.

Boudon F. – Mignot C. (eds.), *Jacques Androuet du Cerceau: Les dessins des plus excellents bâtiments de France* (Paris: 2010).

Bouvignies I., "Qu'est-ce qu'un pouvoir légitime pour Calvin ?" *Rives nord-méditerranéennes* 19 (2004) 41–73.

Bouwsma W.J., *John Calvin: A Sixteenth-Century Portrait* (New York, NY: 1988).

Brunon H. (ed.), *Le Jardin comme labyrinthe du monde: Métamorphoses d'un imaginaire de la Renaissance à nos jours* (Paris: 2008).

Burns R., "Protestant Ecclesiology and Eschatology", *Angelicum* 54.1 (1977) 36–54.

Carbonnier-Burkard M., "Le jardin et le désert, ou le 'théâtre sacré' des protestants français (XVIᵉ–XVIIᵉ siècles)", *Diasporas: Circulations, migrations, histoire* 21 (2013) 10–19.

Carruthers M. – Ziolkowski J. (eds.), *The Medieval Craft of Memory: An Anthology of Texts and Pictures* (Philadelphia, PA: 2002).

Céard J., "Le thème du 'monde à l'envers' dans l'œuvre d'Agrippa d'Aubigné", in Lafond J. – Redondo A. (eds.), *L'image du monde renversé et ses représentations littéraires et para-littéraires de la fin du XVIᵉ siècle au milieu du XVIIᵉ siècle* (Paris: 1979) 117–126.

Cohn N., *The Pursuit of the Millennium* (Fairlawn, NJ: 1957).

Comito T., "Renaissance Gardens and the Discovery of Paradise", *Journal of the History of Ideas* 32.4 (1971) 483–506.

Coulson C., *Castles in Medieval Society: Fortresses in England, France, and Ireland in the Central Middle Ages* (Oxford: 2004).

Crouzet D., *Les guerriers de Dieu: La violence au temps des troubles de religion, vers 1525–vers 1610* (Seyssel: 1990).

Crouzet D., *La genèse de la Réforme française, 1520–1560* (Paris: 1996).

Crouzet D., *John Calvin: Vies parallèles* (Paris: 2000).

Crouzet D., *Dieu en ses royaumes: Une histoire des guerres de religion* (Paris: 2008).

Curtius E.R., *European Literature and the Latin Middle Ages*, trans W.R. Trask (Princeton, NJ: 2013).

Cvetkovic C., "The Gardens of the Château de Montargis as an Expression of Renée de France's Identity (1560–1575)", in Peebles K.D. – Scarlatta G. (eds.), *Representing the Life and Legacy of Renée de France: From Fille de France to Dowager Duchess* (Basingstoke: 2021) 359–379.

Duport D., *Le jardin et la nature: Ordre et variété dans la littérature de la Renaissance* (Geneva: 2002).

Dyrness W.A., *The Origins of Protestant Aesthetics in Early Modern Europe: Calvin's Reformation Poetics* (New York, NY: 2019).

Fagiolo M., "Il giardino come teatro del mondo e della memoria", in idem (ed.), *La città effimera e l'universo artificiale del giardino: La Firenze dei Medici e l'Italia del Cinquecento* (Rome: 1979) 125–141.

Fagiolo M., *Lo specchio del paradiso: il giardino e il sacro dall'Antico all'Ottocento* (Cinisello Balsamo: 1998).

Ferdinand J., *Bernard Palissy: Artisan des réformes entre art, science et foi* (Berlin: 2019).

Giacomotto-Charra V., "Entre savoirs et imagination: Esthétique et symbolique du jardin dans les représentations édéniques de Du Bartas", in Peylet G. (ed.), *Les mythologies du jardin de l'Antiquité à la fin du XIXe siècle* (Bordeaux: 2007) 73–83.

Gorris Camos R., "La Città del Vero, une ville en papier entre utopie et hétérotopie", *Seizième Siècle* 9 (2013) 171–196.

Griswold M., "A History of the Sanctuary Garden", *Design Quarterly* 169 (1996) 1–10.

Grosse, C., "Une mort déritualisée? Usages funéraires dans la tradition protestante réformée", in Boudet J.F. (ed.), *Les rites et usages funéraires: Essais d'anthropologie juridique* (Aix-en-Provence: 2019) 181–196.

Guillaume J., "Le jardin mis en ordre: Jardin et château en France du XVe au XVIIe siècle", in Guillaume J. – Boudon F. (eds.), *Architecture, jardin, paysage* (Paris: 1999).

Guillaume J., "Qui est Jacques Androuet du Cerceau ?", in Guillaume J. (ed.), *Jacques Androuet du Cerceau* (Paris: 2010).

Holwerda D.E., "Eschatology and History: A Look at Calvin's Eschatological Vision", in Holwerda D.E. (ed.), *Exploring the Heritage of John Calvin* (Grand Rapids, MI: 1976) 31–42.

Horton M., *Covenant and Eschatology: The Divine Drama* (Louisville, KY: 2002).

Hubert É., *L'"incastellamento" en Italie centrale* (Rome: 2002).

Jarry L., *Renée de France à Montargis: épisode des guerres religieuses* (Orléans: 1868).

Jeanneret M., *Perpetuum mobile: Métamorphoses des corps et des œuvres de Vinci à Montaigne* (Paris: 1997).

Jeannin-Corbin M., "Les 'vues imageantes', écho des *imagines agentes* rhétoriques? L'exemple du *Songe de Poliphile* de Francesco Colonna (1546)", in Voisin B. (ed.), *Fiction et vues imageantes: Typologie et fonctionnalités* (Tartu: 2008) 89–107.

Jouanna A., *La France du XVIe siècle, 1483–1598* (Paris: 2012).

Joudrier P., *Un 'miroir' calviniste: 'Les Emblemes, ou Devises Chrestiennes' de Georgette de Montenay et Pierre Woeiriot, 1567/1571* (Geneva: 2021).

Kern H., *Through Labyrinths* (Munich – London – New York, NY: 2000).

Koslofsky C., *The Reformation of the Dead: Death and Ritual in Early Modern Germany, 1450–1700* (Basingstoke – New York, NY: 2000).

Kuwakino K., *L'architetto sapiente: Giardino, teatro, città come schemi mnemonici tra il XVI e il XVII secolo* (Florence: 2011).

Lecoq A.M., "Le jardin de la Sagesse de Bernard Palissy", in Mosser M. – Teyssot G. (eds.), *Histoire des jardins de la Renaissance à nos jours* (Paris: 2002) 65–73.

Lestringant F., "Genève et l'Amérique: Le rêve du Refuge huguenot au temps des guerres de Religion (1555–1600)", *Revue de l'histoire des religions* 210.3 (1993) 331–347.

Lestringant F., "De Francesco Colonna à Bernard Palissy: Du *Polifilo* au jardin de Refuge", *Studi di Letteratura Francese* 19 (1993) 453–467.

Lestringant F., "De la *Première* à la *Dernière Semaine*, ou de la réversibilité du monde, selon Du Bartas, d'Aubigné, Augier Gaillard et Michel Quillian", in Ternaux J.-C. (ed.), *La Naissance du monde et l'invention du poème* (Paris: 1998) 435–453.

Lestringant F., "Le jardin des Origines: Palissy et Du Bartas", in Brunon H. (ed.), *Le Jardin, notre Double* (Paris: 1999) 101–123.

Lestringant F., "Cartographie et théâtre au service de la Réforme: L'Exemple de la 'Mappe–Monde Papistique'", in Zinguer I.Y. – Yardeni M. (eds.), *Les deux réformes chrétiennes: Propagation et diffusion* (London: 2004) 216–235.

Levi Della Torre S., "The Anxiety of Eden", in Psaki R. (ed.), *The Earthly Paradise: The Garden of Eden from Antiquity to Modernity* (Cambridge: 1990) 5–14.

Millet O., "Calvin pamphlétaire", *Le Pamphlet en France au XVIe siècle*, special issue, *Cahiers V.L. Saulnier* 1.25 (1983) 18–19.

Millet O., "Tradition de la révélation, exégèse biblique et autorité prophétique: Bible et culture profane selon Calvin", *Cahiers du GADGES* 4 (2006) 117–129.

Mukerji C., "Material Practices of Domination: Christian Humanism, the Built Environment, and Techniques of Western Power", *Theory and Society* 31.1 (2002) 1–34.

Palissy Bernard, *La Recette véritable* (1563), ed. Lestringant F. – Barataud C. (Paris: 1996).

Paya L., *Jacques Androuet Du Cerceau, inventeur de jardins*, in Latrémolière E. – Girault P.-G. (eds.), *Jardins de châteaux à la Renaissance* (Montreuil: 2013) 125–133.

Paya L., "Ideal 'Parquets' and 'Parquetages' by Jacques Androuet Du Cerceau: Decorative Mannerism and the Art of Gardens in France in the Sixteenth Century", *Studies in the History of Gardens & Designed Landscapes: An International Quarterly* 34.1 (2014) 1–16.

Paya L., "Les jardins des châteaux de Philibert", in Pauwels Y. – Lemerle F. (eds.), *Philibert De l'Orme, Un architecte dans l'Histoire* (Turnhout: 2016) 121–136.

Polizzi G., "L'intégration du modèle: Le *Poliphile* et le discours du jardin dans la *Recepte véritable*", *Albineana, Cahiers d'Aubigné* 4 (1992) 65–92.

Querrien A., "Les formes circulaires de l'espace bâti et agricole au Moyen Âge: Tracé, mesure et partage", *Archéologie médiévale* 38 (2008) 123–158.

Quistorp H., *Calvin's Doctrine of the Last Things* (Richmond, VA: 1955).

Randall C., "Realizing the Writings: Bernard Palissy's *Recepte Veritable* as Psalmic Paraphrase", *Romance Notes* 35.1 (1994) 101–106.

Randall C., *Building Codes: The Aesthetics of Calvinism in Early Modern Europe* (Philadelphia, PA: 1999).

Reymond B., "D'où le 'temple Paradis' tenait-il son modèle?", *Bulletin de la S.H.P.F.* (1999) 263–284.

Ribouillault D., "La villa Montalto et l'idéal rustique de Sixte Quint", *Revue de l'art* 173 (2011) 33–42.

Ribouillault, D., "Le vedute urbane di Girolamo Righettino: Le allegorie del principe cristiano, 1583–85", *IN_BO. Ricerche e progetti per il territorio, la città e l'architettura* 12.16 (2021) 50–65.

Rodocanachi E., *Une protectrice de la réforme en Italie et en France: Renée de France* (Paris: 1896).

Rossi P., *Clavis universalis* (Grenoble: 1993).

Scafi A., *Maps of Paradise* (Chicago, IL: 2013).

Schaefer O., "'Théâtre de la gloire de dieu' et 'Droit usage des biens terrestres': Calvin, le calvinisme et la nature", in Varet J. (ed.), *Calvin, naissance d'une pensée* (Tours: 2012) 213–226.

Schreiner S., *Theater of His Glory: Nature and the Natural Order in the Thought of John Calvin* (Grand Rapids, MI: 1995).

Stawarz-Luginbühl R., "*Les emblemata/emblemes chrestiens* (1580/1581) de Théodore de Bèze: Un recueil d'emblèmes humaniste et protestant", *Bibliothèque d'Humanisme et Renaissance* 67.3 (2005) 597–624.

Stein A.B., "Thoughts Occasioned by the Old Testament", in Francis M. – Hester Jr. R.T. (eds.), *The Meaning of Gardens* (Cambridge: 1966) 38–45.

Turias O., *Renée de France, duchesse de Ferrare, témoin de son temps (1510–1575)* (Ph.D. dissertation, University of Tours: 2004).

Van Delft L., "L'idée de théâtre (XVIe–XVIIIe siècle)", *Revue d'histoire littéraire de la France* 101(2001) 1349–1365.

Vérin H., "Olivier de Serres et son *Théâtre d'agriculture*", *Artefact: Techniques, histoire et sciences humaines* 12 (2020) 161–180.

Wright C., *The Maze and the Warrior: Symbols in Architecture, Theology, and Music* (Cambridge: 2001).

Wyk J.H. van, "John Calvin on the Kingdom of God and Eschatology", *In die Skriflig* 35.2 (2001) 191–205.

Yates F., *The Art of Memory* (Harmondsworth: 1969).

PART 5

Sites of Purgation, Meditation, and Martyrdom

∴

CHAPTER 13

The Desert at the World's End: Eschatological Space in Van Hemessen's Hermit Landscapes

Anna-Claire Stinebring

Abstract

The desert in sixteenth-century Netherlandish hermit landscapes is a zone of relative visual simplicity. It mediates between enticing, often foregrounded terrains symbolizing sin and a visionary realm of heavenly splendour kept at a distance. In versions of the *Penitent St. Jerome in the Wilderness* by the Antwerp painter Jan Sanders van Hemessen (active 1524–after 1556), the bodily properties of the desert landscape are brought to the fore. These works prompt viewers to reflect on the material and affective dimensions of this eschatological space. The desert as it echoes the muscular topography of the saint's naked (or nearly naked) body models for original viewers the difficult process of emptying out worldly distractions in devotional meditation on the Last Things. Yet in these penitential landscapes the ascetic saint also models the ultimate sensory rewards of this ostensibly depriving devotional practice. Visionary vignettes promise a heavenly plenitude whose full visualization is intentionally withheld.

Keywords

affective devotion – Antwerp – desert – Jan Sanders van Hemessen – St. Jerome

In versions of St. Jerome in the wilderness by the sixteenth-century Antwerp painter Jan Sanders van Hemessen, the penitent's body and the rocky foreground landscape loom toward the viewer.[1] Particularly bold in this regard is a composition now in St. Petersburg, which is signed and dated 1543 [Fig. 13.1]. It reworks a subject already treated by Van Hemessen more than a decade

---

1 I am grateful to the volume editors, peer reviewers, and Eschatological Imagination working group members for their insights on this article. An earlier version was presented at the Historians of Netherlandish Art conference in Amsterdam (June 2022). This argument grows out of a portion of my dissertation: Stinebring A.-C., *Jan Sanders van Hemessen and Antwerp Painting before Bruegel* (Ph.D. dissertation, University of Pennsylvania: 2022).

earlier, in his ambitious *Penitent St. Jerome in the Wilderness* in Lisbon, signed and dated 1531 [Fig. 13.2].[2] Both the Lisbon and St. Petersburg panels contrast arid foregrounds and lush backgrounds. Patches of reds, browns, and ochres shape variegated rock. The eschatological implications of these desert foregrounds are revealed by a small vignette in the upper left corner of the St. Petersburg painting. Stone dissolves into clouds and an emblematic Last Judgement appears, with Christ as Judge on a rainbow and the Virgin and St. John the Evangelist kneeling in prayer. Standing before the painting the viewer is granted access to Jerome's interior vision of the end times, albeit in a remote and reduced form.

The large-scale works take part, in a self-aware manner, in what Christine Göttler has described as 'the paradoxical nature of all eschatological imagery', namely that the otherworldly must always be portrayed by artists through material means.[3] At stake is not only how to appropriately represent the unrepresentable but also how authentic, inward-looking devotional experience might be directed and obtained. Using the inventive output of Jan Sanders van Hemessen (active 1524–after 1556) as a case study and focusing on his paintings of Jerome, this chapter explores how an aesthetic of barrenness in hermit landscapes aided meditative devotional practice focused on the Last Things (death, judgement, hell, and heaven), with the aim of emptying out worldly distractions and preparing to encounter heaven's splendour. Furthermore, in Van Hemessen's renditions of Jerome, the bodily properties of the desert landscape are brought to the fore, prompting viewers to reflect on the material and affective dimensions of this eschatological space.

1   Jerome in Antwerp

A subject of sustained fascination for early modern artists and audiences, Jerome's retreat from society into the natural world attracted sophisticated

---

2   Special thanks to Joaquim Oliveira Caetano (Museu Nacional de Arte Antiga) for the opportunity to study the Lisbon painting closely. For previous literature on the St. Petersburg and Lisbon *Jerome* panels, Wallen B., *Jan van Hemessen: An Antwerp Painter between Reform and Counter-Reform* (Ann Arbor, MI: 1983) 37–45, 287–288, 301, cat. nos. 10, 26; Kaschek B., "Das kunsttheoretische Bordell: Metamalerei bei Jan van Hemessen", in Münch B.U. – Müller J. (eds.), *Peiraikos' Erben: Die Genese der Genremalerei bis 1550* (Wiesbaden: 2015) 360–363.

3   Göttler C., *Last Things: Art and the Religious Imagination in the Age of Reform* (Turnhout: 2010) 30. My thinking on depictions of the visionary in Netherlandish art has also been particularly influenced by Rothstein B., *Sight and Spirituality in Early Netherlandish Painting* (Cambridge – New York, NY: 2005).

FIGURE 13.1   Jan Sanders van Hemessen, *The Penitent St. Jerome in the Wilderness*, signed
                and dated 1543. Oil on panel, 102 × 83.5 cm. St. Petersburg, The State Hermitage
                Museum, inv. no. 451
                IMAGE © WIKIMEDIA COMMONS

FIGURE 13.2   Jan Sanders van Hemessen, *The Penitent St. Jerome in the Wilderness*, signed and dated 1531.
Oil on panel, 109 × 148 cm. Lisbon, Museu Nacional de Arte Antiga
IMAGE © AUTHOR

urban collectors from Antwerp to Venice.[4] In this robust visual tradition, wilderness terrain standing for the historical Jerome's time in the Syrian desert, whether dry or forested, is a place of extremes. It tests the anchorite and produces revelations. It is a site for wrestling with, and ultimately overcoming, the distractions and dangers of civilization.[5] Depictions of Jerome in the wilderness could also stand for retreats within city life – retreats into a scholarly study or via private meditation.[6]

Jerome was one of the most popular saints in sixteenth-century Antwerp art.[7] In addition to the Lisbon and St. Petersburg panels, Van Hemessen's workshop produced smaller-scale versions of Jerome in the wilderness as well as of Jerome in his study.[8] The latter was valued for its humanist focus on Jerome as a pious scholar and Bible translator with a deep knowledge of Latin, Greek, and Hebrew. Deriving from the influential prototype by Albrecht Dürer as well as a model by Quinten Massys, the subject was repeatedly taken up by Van Hemessen and his contemporaries. Pieter Coecke van Aelst, Joos van Cleve, Jan Massys, and Marinus van Reymerswaele all created variations on the theme.[9]

A consistent iconographic through-line in the Jerome in his study paintings made in Antwerp is the inclusion of a skull along with other *memento mori* imagery. The association in early modern art of Jerome with the Last

---

4   For this point concerning Venice: Belting H., "St. Jerome in Venice: Giovanni Bellini and the Dream of Solitary Life", *I Tatti Studies in the Italian Renaissance* 17.1 (2014) 5–33, which inspired the heading of this section.

5   Göttler C., "Realms of Solitude in Late Medieval and Early Modern European Cultures: An Introduction", in Enenkel K.A.E. – Göttler C. (eds.), *Solitudo: Spaces, Places, and Times of Solitude in Late Medieval and Early Modern Cultures* (Leiden – Boston, MA: 2018) 1–28.

6   Ibidem 8.

7   An equally popular saint in Antwerp was Mary Magdalene, herself a legendary repentant sinner who became an anchorite: Martens M.P.J. – Peeters N., "Paintings in Antwerp Houses (1532–1567)", in De Marchi N. – Van Miegroet H.J. (eds.), *Mapping Markets for Paintings in Europe 1450–1750* (Turnhout: 2006) 35–53.

8   Harth A. – Martens M., "Albrecht Dürer's Iconic Image of Saint Jerome: Making, Meaning, and Reception", in Foister S. – Brink P. van den (eds.), *Dürer's Journeys: Travels of a Renaissance Artist* (London – New Haven, CT: 2021) 262–264; Wallen, *Jan van Hemessen* 322–323, cat. no. 57 for the Rockox *Jerome* (incorrectly listed as a copy) and 288–289, 306, 311–312, 321, 324–325, 327, cat. nos. 12, 32, 39, 54, 60a–b, 64. Two altarpieces from Van Hemessen's workshop also feature penitent hermit saints: the *St. Sebastian Triptych with St. Roch and St. Onuphrius* (Paris, Petit Palais), a collaboration between Van Hemessen and the Master of Saints Paul and Barnabas; and the *Altarpiece with Scenes from the Old and New Testaments* (the *Tendila retablo*) (Cincinnati, Cincinnati Art Museum), which may have been a collaboration between Van Hemessen and his daughter, Catharina van Hemessen.

9   Harth – Martens, "Albrecht Dürer's Iconic Image of Saint Jerome" 253–264, with previous literature.

Judgement stemmed from a text apocryphally ascribed to Jerome, entitled 'The Fifteen Signs before Doomsday', widely published in Latin and in vernacular translations.[10] It foretold apocalyptic imagery of floods, fire, earthquakes, and astronomical anomalies. Adapted for the *Golden Legend*, it was condensed into a short devotional text attributed to Jerome, which acted as a reminder of how quickly quotidian existence could be overtaken by eschatological time and space. A variant of it is inscribed, for example, on a scrap of paper in front of the saint in a popular composition by Joos van Cleve: 'Whether I am drinking or eating or sleeping or doing anything else at all, I seem to hear that terrifying voice resound in my ears, saying, Arise ye dead and come to judgment'.[11]

Who was the audience for Van Hemessen's renditions of Jerome? While records of the original owners of almost all the artist's works have unfortunately not survived, one set of patrons is known, providing a picture of a well-to-do local clientele for the painter's highest-quality works.[12] In addition to commissioning a deluxe *Last Judgement Triptych* for their chapel in the Sint-Jacobskerk, the wealthy Antwerp couple Adriaan Rockox and Catharina van Overhoff owned a smaller *Penitent St. Jerome in His Study* by Van Hemessen or his workshop [Fig. 13.3].[13] The interior of the altarpiece features a central judgement scene flanked by family portraits. The *Jerome in His Study* brought the contemplation of the Last Things, made vividly present in the open view of the monumental altarpiece for the chapel, into the more intimate space of the home, serving personal devotional needs.[14] It directly relates to the altarpiece

---

10   Rice E.F., *Saint Jerome in the Renaissance* (Baltimore, MD: 1985) 161–162, with previous literature.

11   Translation from Rice, *Saint Jerome* 161–162, with original Latin at 161: 'Sive bibam sive comedam sive dormam/ Sive aliquid aliud faciam, semper videtur/ Michi illa vox terribilis sonare in auribus meis:/ Surgite mortui venite ad iudicium'. For Joos van Cleve's versions, Hand J., *Joos Van Cleve: The Complete Paintings* (London – New Haven, CT: 2004) 94 and 162–164, cat. nos. 79–79.10.

12   The original owners of the Lisbon and St. Petersburg panels are not known, although it is very possible that the Lisbon painting was made for an elite Portuguese patron who was either Antwerp-based or had close ties to the city, especially given the eighteenth-century provenance laid out by Wallen: Wallen, *Jan van Hemessen* 287–288, cat. no. 10.

13   Special thanks to Hildegard Van de Velde of the Snijders&Rockoxhuis for the opportunity to examine the Rockox *Jerome* up close. For the Rockox *Last Judgment Triptych*, still *in situ*, see most recently Stinebring A.-C., "Encountering Adam and Eve at the Apocalypse: Violence, Sensuality, and Hope in the Rockox *Last Judgment*", *Nederlands Kunsthistorisch Jaarboek* 72 (2022) 95–121. For the Sint-Jacobskerk chapel: Muller J., *St. Jacob's: Antwerp Art and Counter Reformation in Rubens's Parish Church* (Leiden – Boston, MA: 2016) 311–312, 570–571.

14   The Rockox *Jerome* appears in a ca. 1630 painting by Frans Francken II, *The Interior of Nicolaas Rockox's House*. While the setting is fictive, Francken's painting does record works

FIGURE 13.3   Jan Sanders van Hemessen, *The Penitent St. Jerome in His Study*, signed. Oil on panel,
103 × 81 cm. Antwerp, Snijders&Rockoxhuis, inv. no. 77.3

IMAGE © KBC BANK NV, ANTWERPEN, SNIJDERS&ROCKOXHUIS

FIGURE 13.4   Jan Sanders van Hemessen, *The Penitent St. Jerome in His Study*. Detail of
                Fig. 13.3, showing visionary Last Judgement vignette
                IMAGE © KBC BANK NV, ANTWERPEN, SNIJDERS&ROCKOXHUIS

in the Sint-Jacobskerk through the presence of the visionary Last Judgement
vignette seen through Jerome's study window. The vignette [Fig. 13.4] is a
slightly more extensive version of the same judgement vision that appears in
the St. Petersburg *Jerome*. Christ as Judge sits on a rainbow, his feet resting on
a globe. He is attended by the Virgin and St. John the Evangelist. Trumpeting
angels herald the decisive moment of judgement. Heaven is radiant.

In the versions of Jerome in his study by Quinten and Jan Massys as well
as Marinus van Reymerswaele, Jerome contemplates a full-page illuminated
Last Judgement scene in the Bible before him. A successful type by Marinus
[Fig. 13.5] even adapts Dürer's *Last Judgement* woodcut from the *Small Passion*
for the illumination.[15] In the Rockox *Jerome in His Study*, however, the fact

from the actual collection of the Antwerp burgomaster Nicolaas Rockox, the grandson
of Adriaan and Catharina. For Francken's painting: Filipczak Z., *Picturing Art in Antwerp,
1550–1700* (Princeton, NJ: 1987) 58–59.

15   Seidel C. (ed.), *Marinus: Painter from Reymerswale*, exh. cat., Museo Nacional del Prado
        (Madrid: 2021) 94–97, 114–119, 129–131, cat nos. 3, 9, 10, 14.

FIGURE 13.5   Marinus van Reymerswaele, *St. Jerome in His Study*, signed and dated 1541. Oil
on panel, 80 × 108 cm. Madrid, Museo Nacional del Prado, inv. no. P0026553
IMAGE © PHOTOGRAPHIC ARCHIVE MUSEO NACIONAL DEL PRADO

that the Last Judgement scene unfolds through the window, rather than being
illustrated in the book, makes it more emphatically present. Nevertheless,
the remoteness of the visionary vignette and its relative simplicity provide a
reminder of the necessarily translated nature of the vision. Framing the judgement scene through the window creates a picture-within-a-picture effect.[16]
Thick layers of clouds further insulate the visionary realm from the everyday
space of the audience.

It is the twisting body of the saint in the Rockox *Jerome in His Study* that
appears most emphatically and urgently present. Jerome holds out his hands
in fervent prayer and turns away from the window with an abstracted gaze,
further underlining the vision's interiority. Although the type of true visionary experience enacted by Jerome is reserved for exemplary sacred figures, the
Rockox family members were prompted by the devotional image – with its
nested scenes and inward-looking protagonist – to move beyond the visual

16   For the framing effect: Stoichita V.I., *The Self-Aware Image: An Insight into Early Modern
Meta-Painting*, trans. A.M. Glasheen (Cambridge: 1997).

FIGURE 13.6   Jan Sanders van Hemessen, *The Penitent St. Jerome in the Wilderness*. Oil on
               panel, 51 × 80 cm. Genoa, Musei di Strada Nuova (Palazzo Rosso)
               IMAGE © MUSEI DI STRADA NUOVA – PALAZZO ROSSO, GENOVA, ITALY

devotional realm toward more interiorized meditation ultimately designed to
occur independent of images. Following the model of Jerome, this meditative
practice is presented as an affective process that engages the whole body.

When compared to Marinus's focus on the still-life trappings of Jerome's
study, the focus on the dynamic pose in the Rockox *Jerome* magnifies the penitential rather than scholarly dimensions of the subject.[17] If cosmopolitan viewers like the Rockox family sought out hermit wilderness landscapes in part as
a metaphor for retreat *within* the city, including to a scholarly study, we might
therefore conclude that the more intensely penitential *Jerome in His Study* for
the Rockox family reverses this equation. It presents the study as a microcosm
of the desert. Jerome in the Rockox panel could easily be transposed to a cave
without major adjustments.

In fact, another successful Jerome composition by Van Hemessen, a *Penitent
St. Jerome in the Wilderness* in Genoa that is also in a bust-length portrait format, essentially enacts the substitution of the study for the desert [Fig. 13.6].[18]

---

17   For another interpretation: Harth – Martens, "Albrecht Dürer's Iconic Image of Saint
      Jerome" 264.
18   Wallen, *Jan van Hemessen* 311–312, cat. no. 39. Variants of this composition were par-
      ticularly popular within the Van Hemessen workshop. Additional versions not listed by
      Wallen include one in Berlin (Gemäldegalerie).

Standing in front of the Genoa painting, viewers find themselves in a rocky alcove in close quarters with the praying saint. Jerome's expression is once again abstracted. His gaze is on the Crucifix before him yet nevertheless remains unfocused. A halo of frizzy hair and long beard add to an overall impression of untamed intensity. A lusher landscape unfolds at right behind him. Its blues and greens entice the viewer, while Jerome keeps his back to it.[19] Has this larger vista fallen away from the saint's consciousness? Or does his turned back and the insistent focus of his prayer signal that he remains all too acutely aware of the world beyond his cell? The verdant background, while it may not seem like a site of temptation, conceptually fills that role. When compared to the craggy foreground it would have read as a place of ease and distraction, and thus sin. Before delving further into the portrayal of the desert in the Lisbon and St. Petersburg panels, it is instructive to look more closely at the painter's renderings of worldly, time-bound environments that contrast to it, through which the artist provocatively invites the viewers to travel.

2   Straying on the Pilgrimage of Life

Desolate regions routinely contrast more inhabitable terrains in Netherlandish depictions of Jerome in the wilderness. In Joachim Patinir's *The Penitence of St. Jerome* from ca. 1515 [Fig. 13.7], the saint resides in a panoramic Netherlandish landscape of supreme lushness and diversity, from a background harbour to a foreground riverbank decorated with mussel shells and coral. Yet he turns his back to this view as he positions himself between facing an outcropping and facing outward, toward the viewer. Taking a large rock from this landscape, he raises it to his chest, ready to strike.

As Reindert Falkenburg has argued, Patinir formulated landscapes that follow the structure of the medieval and early modern *topos* of the Wayfarer on the Pilgrimage of Life.[20] In this sixteenth-century Netherlandish landscape tradition it is the obstructed, circuitous path through rocky terrain that symbolizes the path away from temptation and toward salvation. Hieronymus Bosch inaugurated this new conceptual approach in which the world is figured as a

---

19   Originally this landscape passage would have been more sumptuous. There are now apparent condition issues in this part of the composition (abrasion and discoloration).

20   Falkenburg R.L., *Joachim Patinir: Landscape as an Image of the Pilgrimage of Life*, trans. M. Hoyle (Amsterdam – Philadelphia, PA: 1988). See also Ladner G.B., "Homo Viator: Medieval Ideas on Alienation and Order", *Speculum* 42.2 (1967) 233–259; Wenzel S., "The Pilgrimage of Life as a Late Medieval Genre", *Mediaeval Studies* 35 (1973) 370–388; Pinson Y., *The Fools' Journey: A Myth of Obsession in Northern Renaissance Art* (Turnhout: 2008) 125–148.

FIGURE 13.7   Joachim Patinir, *The Penitence of St. Jerome* (open view), ca. 1515. Oil on
              panel, 117.5 × 81.3 cm (center panel with frame). New York, The Metropolitan
              Museum of Art, inv. no. 36.14a–c
              IMAGE © THE METROPOLITAN MUSEUM OF ART

fallen paradise, shifting how naturalism operates in the art of fifteenth-century
predecessors, especially Jan van Eyck.[21] The Boschian lineage of Patinir's world
landscapes is evident in the fact that the verdant parts of the landscapes represent the fallen world instead of a paradise on earth.[22] It is the place of mistaken

---

21   The literature on Bosch is voluminous. For this point see most recently the essays in
      Tóth B. – Varga A. (eds.), *Between Hell and Paradise: The Enigmatic World of Hieronymus
      Bosch*, exh. cat., Museum of Fine Arts (Budapest: 2022). Other recent studies rele-
      vant for the context of my chapter include: Vandenbroeck P., *Utopia's Doom: The Graal
      as Paradise of Lust, the Sect of the Free Spirit and Jheronimus Bosch's So-Called Garden
      of Delights* (Louvain: 2017); Koerner J.L., *Bosch and Bruegel: From Enemy Painting to
      Everyday Life* (Princeton, NJ: 2016); Strickland D.H., *The Epiphany of Hieronymus Bosch:
      Imagining Antichrist and Others from the Middle Ages to the Reformation* (London: 2016);
      Falkenburg R.L., *The Land of Unlikeness: Hieronymus Bosch, The Garden of Earthly Delights*
      (Zwolle: 2011); Silver L., *Hieronymus Bosch* (New York, NY: 2006).
22   Along with Falkenburg, *Joachim Patinir*, see Silver L., "God in the Details: Bosch and
      Judgment(s)", *The Art Bulletin* 83.4 (2001) 626–650; Vergara A. (ed.), *Patinir: Essays and
      Critical Catalogue*, exh. cat., Museo Nacional del Prado (Madrid: 2007). For the world

identification, where the enticing path is confused for the right path, simply because it is the easy one.

Elck or *Elckerlijc* (Everyman), a personification of sinful yet potentially redeemable humankind, fulfils the role of the *homo viator* or pilgrim on the Pilgrimage of Life in manifold early modern Netherlandish morality plays. Fundamentally *Elck* is a type based in the *ars moriendi* (art of dying) tradition. A didactic figure designed to instruct the viewer in developing greater introspection and self-knowledge, *Elck* represents the irrefutability of death and its levelling power, irrespective of social rank. It also illustrates the inherent sinfulness of humankind, which requires repentance and penitence to achieve salvation. Life – or more aptly preparation for death – is indeed figured as a pilgrimage in the play *Elckerlijc*, which was published in Antwerp around 1525 by Willem Vorsterman (after a text from the later fifteenth century) and which was the source for the English play *Everyman*.[23] *Elckerlijc* must atone for what the personification of death characterizes at the play's outset as a life 'so beastly / outside of fear of God and too fleshly'.[24] He must do so through a journey in which he gradually unburdens himself of all his material and metaphorical possessions.

Another prime example of the staged journey of sin and redemption is *Acolastus* by Gulielmus Gnapheus, a Latin play of the Parable of the Prodigal Son that was first published in Antwerp in 1529.[25] Ignoring his father's council, the Prodigal Son arrives in the big city in Act II, Scene 2. Significantly, this is the start of a journey, and the Prodigal Son repeatedly refers to his arrival into the city as docking at a fortuitous harbour.[26] Throughout these early scenes, which mostly unfold in a brothel, the Prodigal Son unwittingly provides evidence of his false sense of self-knowledge. His confident self-presentation is immediately punctured for the audience by the asides of local characters who describe him,

landscape: Gibson W.S., *Mirror of the Earth: The World Landscape in Sixteenth-Century Flemish Painting* (Princeton, NJ: 1989).

23   For the original text: Ramakers B.A.M. – Wilmink W. (eds.), *Mariken van Nieumeghen and Elckerlijc: Zonde, hoop en verlossing in de late middeleeuwen* (Amsterdam: 1998) 152–225; Davidson C. – Walsh M.W. – Broos T.J. (eds.), *Everyman and Its Dutch Original, Elckerlijc* (Kalamazoo, MI: 2007) 15–77.

24   Davidson – Walsh – Broos (eds.), *Everyman and Its Dutch Original* 20, lines 59–60: '[...] so beestelic/ Buten Gods vreese ende alte vleeslick'. Translation mine.

25   Atkinson W.E.D. (ed.), *Acolastus: A Latin Play of the Sixteenth Century by Gulielmus Gnapheus* (London: 1964).

26   Ibidem 18–19, 128–129.

in turn, as a misfit – a 'peregrinus' (foreigner or pilgrim) – and as a prime target due to his full purse.[27]

Wayfarers or specifically labelled *Elck* figures appear in sixteenth-century Netherlandish visual art from Bosch to Pieter Bruegel the Elder.[28] Sinful straying on the Pilgrimage of Life is a leitmotif of early genre imagery innovated by Van Hemessen and his Antwerp peers.[29] The Brussels *Prodigal Son in the Brothel*, signed and dated 1536 reimagines the Gospel parable (*Luke* 15:11–32) by elaborating how, exactly, the Prodigal Son lost his fortune [Fig. 13.8]. While the background scenes framed by the brothel windows, painted by a collaborator (the Master of Saints Paul and Barnabas), do illustrate the main parable lessons centred on repentance, mercy, and salvation, they remain intentionally remote – almost like nested visionary vignettes. Meanwhile, the foreground scene of debauchery is immediate, absorbing, and very much of the world.[30] The male client stopping over in a brothel directly and negatively engages with the literary and visual *topos* of the Wayfarer or *homo viator* on the Pilgrimage of Life, once again envisioning the pilgrim's straying from the true path. This is true whether the client represents the Prodigal Son, in the case of the Brussels panel, or a generic Wayfarer in the cases of Van Hemessen's *Wayfarer in a Brothel* versions in Karlsruhe (ca. 1540) and Hartford (signed and dated 1543).[31]

For the purposes of this chapter's focus on eschatological space, what is key is that the Prodigal Son in the Brussels painting appears as a kind of antitype

27   Ibidem 130–131. For false self-knowledge see for instance 124–125, 128–133.
28   Rothstein B., "The Problem with Looking at Pieter Bruegel's *Elck*", *Art History* 26.2 (2003) 143–173; Sullivan M.A., "Bosch, Bruegel, Everyman and the Northern Renaissance", *Oud Holland* 121.2/3 (2008) 117–146; Pinson, *The Fools' Journey* 125–148.
29   Still foundational: Renger K., *Lockere Gesellschaft: Zur Ikonographie des verlorenen Sohnes und von Wirtshausszenen in der niederländischen Malerei* (Berlin: 1970) 34–37, 120–142. Recent relevant studies include: Rothstein B., "Beer and Loafing in Antwerp", *Art History* 35.5 (2012) 886–907; Rothstein B., "Jan van Hemessen's Anatomy of Parody", in Melion W.S. – Rothstein B. – Weemans M. (eds.), *The Anthropomorphic Lens: Anthropomorphism, Microcosm and Analogy in Early Modern Thought and Visual Arts* (Leiden: 2015) 457–479; Kaschek, "Das kunsttheoretische Bordell"; Ubl M., "Van hoerenhuis tot hoofse liefde: Jan Sanders van Hemessen, de Meester van de Vrouwelijke Halffiguren en Ambrosius Benson", in Coelen P. van der – Lammertse F. (eds.), *De ontdekking van het dagelijks leven*, exh. cat., Museum Boijmans van Beuningen (Rotterdam: 2015) 157–175. Also analysed in depth in Stinebring, *Jan Sanders van Hemessen* 269–369.
30   German printmakers Jörg Breu and Hans Sebald Beham, in their woodcuts of the Prodigal Son, also framed the background scenes through brothel windows: Renger, *Lockere Gesellschaft* 25; Kaschek, "Das kunsttheoretische Bordell" 365. Van Hemessen's collaboration with small figure specialists like the Master of Saints Paul and Barnabas are addressed in Stinebring, *Jan Sanders van Hemessen* 26–37, 93–110.
31   For the *Prodigal Son* and *Wayfarer* paintings see note 29, above. See also Wallen, *Jan van Hemessen* 53–66, 290–291, 294–295, 301–302, cat. nos. 15, 19, 27.

FIGURE 13.8   Jan Sanders van Hemessen and the Master of Saints Paul and Barnabas,
Prodigal Son in the Brothel, signed and dated 1536. Oil on panel, 140 × 198 cm.
Brussels, Musées royaux des Beaux-Arts
IMAGE © ROYAL MUSEUMS OF FINE ARTS OF BELGIUM, BRUSSELS /
PHOTO J. GELEYNS – ART PHOTOGRAPHY

of the penitent Jerome, because he has gone on a journey *to* the city, unwittingly seeking out sin through his lack of self-knowledge. Despite their location
in a spacious Renaissance loggia, the foreground figures are pressed together.
At lower left, the besotted Prodigal Son (dressed in the colourful costume of a
German *Landsknecht* or mercenary soldier) is smitten by the two women who
encircle him. Yet these intertwined foreground figures appear mostly caught
in a sequence of missed connections and blocked advances. Vacant gazes and
deflecting gestures signal self-absorption, or what might be characterized as negative interiority still focused on worldly things, in contrast to Jerome's intense,
abstracted gaze in the Rockox, Genoa, Lisbon, and St. Petersburg paintings.

Van Hemessen's *Prodigal Son* challenges viewers morally and intellectu-
ally rather than placing them at a comfortable remove.[32] Ultimately the portrayal guides attentive viewers to a positive interiority – the cultivation of

---

32   For this point with rich attention to the operations of Van Hemessen's compositional
structures, Rothstein, "Beer and Loafing". Another insightful recent essay on visual complexity in Van Hemessen's genre-inflected works is Lu H., "Games, Flirtation, and the Use

self-knowledge – albeit by circuitous means, mirroring a journey or pilgrimage. The novel compositional structure of the *Prodigal Son* not only trains the viewer in developing greater visual acuity and self-knowledge, but also prepares for the apprehension of visionary space through a guided process of moving from busy worldliness in the foreground toward spaces that are pared down or emptied out of worldly distractions in the background.

3   Traversing the Desert

When the historical Jerome withdrew into the Syrian desert near Chalcis in the fourth century CE, extending by several years his pilgrimage to the Holy Land and postponing his arrival in Jerusalem, he lived in a natural cave that was capacious enough for his library. Despite Jerome's literary self-styling as engaging in penitential extremes, he likely lived relatively comfortably compared to the Syrian anchorites whose model he followed. Since pilgrims, Jerome included, interrupted the practices of these legendary Syrian ascetics, the location was not entirely isolated.[33]

Jerome's letters, however, present a formidable and unforgiving landscape ideally suited for bodily punishment and purgation. At the same time, Jerome detailed his difficulty in truly escaping the city of the mind. In a passage widely known by medieval and early modern audiences, Jerome describes 'how often, when I was living in the sun-scorched solitude of the desert, which offers monks a savage hospitality, how often I imagined myself back among the pleasures of Rome'![34] In the same letter Jerome's cave and the surrounding desert take on a life of their own, seeming to apprehend his unclean thoughts and offering new forms of bodily torture beyond fasting. He proclaims: 'Wherever I found a deep valley or rough mountainside or rocky precipice, I made it my place of prayer and of torture for my unhappy flesh'.[35]

In his writings Jerome vividly describes the desert's eschatological dimensions, making clear that the desert is the best possible setting for repentance

---

of Interpretive Risk: Jan Sanders van Hemessen's *Portrait of Husband and Wife Playing Tables*", *Ludica: Annali di storia e civiltà del gioco* 28 (2022) 57–80.

33   Rice, *Saint Jerome in the Renaissance* 9–10.

34   Epistle 22. Translation from Rice, *Saint Jerome* 7. For the original Latin: Wright F.A. (ed.), *Select Letters of St. Jerome* (London – New York, NY: 1933) 66: 'O quotiens in heremo constitutus et in illa vasta solitudine, quae exusta solis ardoribus horridum monachis praestat habitaculum, putavi me Romanis interesse deliciis!'

35   Epistle 22. Translation from Rice, *Saint Jerome* 7. For the original Latin: Wright (ed.), *Select Letters* 68: 'Sicubi concava vallium, aspera montium, rupium praerupta cernebam, ibi meae orationi locus, illud miserrimae carnis ergastulum [...]'.

and thus for preparations for death. Time and again it is contrasted to the city life of his interlocutors. In another letter Jerome writes:

> Oh desert where Christ's flowers are blossoming! Oh solitude with whose stones the heavenly Jerusalem will be built according to the Apocalypse! [...] What do you, brother, seek in the world when you are greater than the world? [...] How long will you close yourself up in the smoky prison of such cities? [...] Does the infinite vastness of the hermitage terrify you? But you will walk there with a spirit already in paradise.[36]

Jerome contrasts the polluted, confining city to the desert's enormity. Acknowledging the fear that this vastness inspires for city-dwellers, Jerome promises that with fuller knowledge of this empty and isolated place it will become like paradise.

By Jerome's own report, self-denial in the desert brought ample rewards. In the same often-quoted letter where Jerome laments thoughts of 'the pleasures of Rome', he continues that after bodily torture 'I fixed my eyes on Heaven and seemed to find myself among the angelic hosts. Then, full of joy and happiness, I would sing out: "I run after you in the fragrance of your perfumes"'.[37] After depravations, in other words, the ascetic experiences a vision whose abundant, sensory nature Jerome suggests but does not attempt to recreate for his reader. It defies representation. He can only begin to express it through a quotation from the *Song of Songs* (1:3) that evokes the sense of smell and a garden in bloom.

In the 1531 Lisbon *Jerome* by Van Hemessen, the saint is naked except for a loincloth [Fig. 13.2]. His Cardinal robes lie crushed on the ground under him. Muscles flex and veins pop. His raised right leg rests somewhat awkwardly on an outcropping. This oddity of the pose draws attention to its reliance on a famous antique model, the *Laocoön*.[38] It also magnifies the pose's instability.

---

36 Epistle 14. Translation from Belting, "St. Jerome in Venice" 12. For the original Latin: Wright (ed.), *Select Letters* 48–50: 'O desertum Christi floribus vernans! O solitudo, in qua illi nascuntur lapides, de quibus in Apocalypsi civitas magni regis extruitur! [...] Quid agis, frater, in saeculo, qui maior es mundo? [...] Quam diu fumeus harum urbium carcer includit? [...] Infinita heremi vastitas terret? sed tu paradisum mente deambula'.

37 Epistle 22. Translation from Rice, *Saint Jerome* 7. For the original Latin: Wright (ed.), *Select Letters* 68: 'post caelo oculos inhaerentes nonnunquam videbar mihi interesse agminibus angelorum et laetus gaudensque cantabam: "Post te in odorem unguentorum tuorum currimus"'.

38 Van Hemessen adapted the *Laocoön* for other figures throughout his career, notably the two naked women at lower right in the *Last Judgement* triptych centre panel: Stinebring, "Encountering Adam and Eve at the Apocalypse" 112–114. For the Lisbon *Jerome* and the *Laocoön*: Wallen, *Jan van Hemessen* 38; Kaschek, "Das kunsttheoretische Bordell" 360.

In the 1543 St. Petersburg *Jerome*, Van Hemessen shows the penitent hermit almost on all fours [Fig. 13.1]. He is now entirely naked. The pose is once again precarious. Jerome's muscular back may derive in part from rotating the form of the *Belvedere Torso*, another antique sculptural fragment.[39] Yet the adaptation of the classical form is for a figure that is decidedly un-idealized and unheroic.

Van Hemessen's reworking of antique models galvanizes Jerome's own ambivalence concerning the place of classical knowledge in Christian scholarship. His famous dream in which Christ as Judge denounced Jerome as a Ciceronian precipitated his eventual pilgrimage. Jerome's ultimate stance that knowledge of classical literature could be harnessed for Christian causes made him a favourite saint of Renaissance humanists such as Erasmus.[40] Van Hemessen's choice of source material at once affirms how classical forms could serve Christian subjects and references this longstanding tension. He especially broadcasts the latter through the poses' theatricality and instability. Jerome's muscular back seemingly threatens to tip into our space in the case of the St. Petersburg painting. While this is a less obvious quotation of an antique sculptural fragment, it is precisely the striking, unusual vantage point that inspires viewers versed in classical forms to consider it for longer, perhaps debating whether the ambiguous reference is indeed intended.

In the desert Jerome had to fight not only his longing for the intellectual life of pagan Rome, but also sexual temptations.[41] The fact that the agitated fabric of the loincloth – and the potential delineation of what is underneath it – is something of a focal point in the Lisbon *Jerome* was designed to convey the Christian doctrine of Original Sin. In rendering this indecorous bodily detail, Van Hemessen drew from a long lineage of Christian thought on sexuality exemplified by the writings of St. Paul and Augustine as well as Jerome.[42] Jerome's ultimate success in this plight is affirmed by the tame lion who rests behind him.

---

39   Wallen, *Jan van Hemessen* 42; Kaschek, "Das kunsttheoretische Bordell" 360–361. The closest parallel to this view is found in a pen and ink drawing in the Roman sketchbook of the northern Netherlandish artist Maarten van Heemskerck (Berlin, Kupferstichkabinett), which depicts the fragmentary statue resting on its back, with its broken legs in the air: DiFuria A.J., *Maarten van Heemskerck's Rome: Antiquity, Memory, and the Cult of Ruins* (Leiden – Boston, MA: 2019) 20–22.

40   Rice, *Saint Jerome* 3–6 for a summary of the dream. For Erasmus and Jerome: Rice, *Saint Jerome* 116–136; Pabel H.M., *Herculean Labours: Erasmus and the Editing of St. Jerome's Letters in the Renaissance* (Leiden – Boston, MA: 2008).

41   Epistle 22. Rice, *Saint Jerome* 7–8 for visions of Roman 'dancing girls'.

42   Steinberg L., *The Sexuality of Christ in Renaissance Art and in Modern Oblivion* (Chicago, IL: 1996) 195–196. See also Brown P., *The Body and Society: Men, Women, and Sexual Renunciation in Early Christianity* (New York, NY: 2008).

Given that the classical reference would have been particularly apparent to viewers of the Lisbon *Jerome* due to the clarity of the *Laocoön* citation, I contend that the intuitive way that the lone muscular body in the Lisbon *Jerome* might be interwoven with other bodies suggests the stakes of Jerome's struggle to maintain his life as a hermit. The *Laocoön* was admired for how it communicated pathos through the elegant intertwining of the taut limbs of the Trojan priest Laocoön and his sons with the deadly serpents that attack them.[43] The Lisbon *Jerome* is a solitary figure, but a figure that seems to recall past entanglements with other bodies through its sinuous and outstretched pose, further dramatizing the saint's recall of the packed city within the desert. (Think of the interlaced bodies in the foreground of Van Hemessen's *Prodigal Son*.) The precariousness of the saint's pose reflects how, in his penitent state, Jerome is still poised between repentance and temptation. If this process of self-restraint is difficult and protracted for the erudite and ascetic Jerome, it is presented as even more challenging for original viewers, at home in an early modern urban centre.

With his crouching pose, the St. Petersburg *Jerome* reads less as a model of disciplined piety and more as a holy Wild Man, a type linked to period imaginings of prehistoric humans, mythological creatures like satyrs, and a longer medieval tradition of the inversion of the knight as courtly ideal.[44] The hunched pose along with the long beard and fully naked body place this Jerome in particularly close proximity to other images of holy Wild Men in early modern visual culture, such as the penitent St. John Chrysostom, who crawled on

---

43   For the early modern reception of the *Laocoön*: Haskell F. – Penny N., *Taste and the Antique: The Lure of Classical Sculpture, 1500–1900* (New Haven, CT: 1981) 243–247.

44   Bernheimer R., *Wild Men in the Middle Ages: A Study in Art, Sentiment, and Demonology* (New York, NY: 1970); Husband T., *The Wild Man: Medieval Myth and Symbolism*, exh. cat., Metropolitan Museum of Art (New York, NY: 1980); Silver L., "Forest Primeval: Albrecht Altdorfer and the German Wilderness Landscape", *Simiolus* 13:1 (1983) 4–43. Northern European images of hermit saints as holy Wild Men are connected to a renewed interest in the early sixteenth century in imaginatively reconstructing local prehistory, based in part on a reappraisal of classical sources. This interest in prehistory was inspired as well by European projections onto indigenous communities in the Americas. For a taxonomy of the Netherlandish Wild Man type that considers this question and the relationship of representations of marginalized groups within Netherlandish society, Vandenbroeck P., *Beeld van de andere, vertoog over het zelf: over wilden en narren, boeren en bedelaars*, exh. cat., Koninklijk Museum voor Schone Kunsten (Antwerp: 1987) 7–39. For the Wild Man (and nakedness more generally) and the colonial imaginary: Leitch S., *Mapping Ethnography in Early Modern Germany: New Worlds in Print Culture* (New York, NY: 2010) 37–62; Burke J., *The Italian Renaissance Nude* (New Haven, CT: 2018). For an important reversal of the colonial gaze in representations of the Last Things, Cohen Suarez [Cohen-Aponte] A., *Heaven, Hell, and Everything in Between: Murals of the Colonial Andes* (Austin, TX: 2016).

all fours for fifteen years to atone for impregnating – and then attempting to murder – a woman that he encountered while he was living as a hermit. Associations of Wild Men with unbridled carnality further heighten the sense of the saint's struggle against temptation in both works by Van Hemessen. The discarded cardinal robes draw attention to the saint's nakedness. As already seen in the Genoa painting, voluminous, even frizzy hair and beard contribute to the impression of animation. It suggests the Wild Man's untamed nature.[45]

What is crucial to clarify is that, for period viewers in cosmopolitan contexts, Jerome's wildness is shaped by his relationship to civilization and his difficulty in extricating himself from civilization's temptations and distractions, rather than from his complete lack of contact with it. That is, the self-inflicted work of 'taming' the flesh means embracing the uncharted terrain of the barren desert more fully, rather than escaping it. Jerome holds a stone aloft in the Lisbon panel, ready to beat his ribs until body and mind have reached a proper state of penitential devotional focus. In the St. Petersburg *Jerome*, with his right hand the saint raises a rock to pound his chest, while he leans on his left arm, covering his naked body.

It is tempting to draw a further analogy between the fragmented antique marble sculptures that the painter employed as source material and the stony foregrounds. Van Hemessen even carved his name into the cliff faces in both panels, heightening their materiality through this *trompe l'oeil* device [Fig. 13.9].[46] In so doing, he associated himself and his artistic skill with this area of the compositions, although his trademark focus across his oeuvre is decidedly on large-scale, muscular bodies. We might conjecture that Van Hemessen has to a certain extent imagined Jerome's body as its own penitential landscape that harmonizes with its surroundings. Bulging muscles rhyme with rugged outcroppings. Jerome's sloping back in the St. Petersburg painting, if flipped, could fill the concave outline of the cave wall, as if it had originally been hewn from the rock face. The sinuous S-curve of the Lisbon panel slopes away from the outcropping that he leans toward, resulting in a rough symmetry between the two contours [Fig. 13.10]. Through this visual analogy, viewers are invited to contemplate and become absorbed in the experiential and affective dimensions of the desert landscape.

The association of Jerome's body in Van Hemessen's paintings with uncultivated, difficult terrain, and its contrasting with a lusher, more populated

---

45   See discussion of hairy hermits in Jolly P.H., "Pubics and Privates: Body Hair in Late Medieval Art", in Lindquist S.C.M. (ed.), *The Meanings of Nudity in Medieval Art* (Farnham – Burlington, VT: 2011) 183–206.

46   The signature in the St. Petersburg *Jerome* is located directly above the saint's head. It is below the skull in the Lisbon *Jerome*.

FIGURE 13.9   Jan Sanders van Hemessen, *The Penitent St. Jerome in the Wilderness*. Detail of
                Fig. 13.2, showing signature
                IMAGE © AUTHOR

FIGURE 13.10   Jan Sanders van Hemessen, *The Penitent St. Jerome in the Wilderness*. Detail of
                Fig. 13.2, showing curve of saint's body
                IMAGE © AUTHOR

background, is in line with the approach taken by Patinir in his world land-scapes, following Bosch. Van Hemessen takes the approach a step further, how-ever, by having the saint more fully embody and internalize his surroundings. Jerome's desert with its relative suppression of visual complexity and visual interest was developed with a sophisticated urban audience in mind for its capacity to focus interior mediation. While showing Jerome's transforming of his own body into a kind of penitential landscape, it encourages original view-ers to cultivate a desert solitude of the mind. This interiority built toward a type of directed devotional imaginative abundance, inspired by Jerome's visionary experience that he can only express through quoting the *Song of Songs*: 'among the angelic hosts [...] I would sing out "I run after you in the fragrance of your perfumes"'. In other words, it offered an opening to glimpse infinite space and time of the afterlife, however indirectly, through visual and then progressively interiorized means.

4   Conclusion

As studied through depictions of the penitent Jerome by the Antwerp painter Jan Sanders van Hemessen, the desert in sixteenth-century Netherlandish art is a zone of relative visual simplicity. It mediates between, on the one hand, intentionally distracting genre-inflected foregrounds and verdant background terrains symbolizing sin, and, on the other hand, a visionary realm of heavenly splendour kept much less visually enticing and accessible to viewers. The fore-ground desert as it echoes the muscular topography of the saint's naked (or nearly naked) body in the Lisbon and St. Petersburg paintings of the *Penitent St. Jerome in the Wilderness* by Van Hemessen models for original viewers the difficult, extended process of emptying out worldly distractions in devotional meditation on the Last Things. While it is shown as an extended process fraught with difficulty, in these penitential landscapes the ascetic saint models the ultimate sensory rewards of this ostensibly depriving devotional practice, turning away from lush regions yet revealing visionary vignettes that hint at the potential plenitude of worlds promised beyond death.

Bibliography

Atkinson W.E.D. (ed.), *Acolastus: A Latin Play of the Sixteenth Century by Gulielmus Gnapheus* (London: 1964).

Belting H., "St. Jerome in Venice: Giovanni Bellini and the Dream of Solitary Life", *I Tatti Studies in the Italian Renaissance* 17.1 (2014) 5–33.

Bernheimer R., *Wild Men in the Middle Ages: A Study in Art, Sentiment, and Demonology* (New York, NY: 1970).

Brown P., *The Body and Society: Men, Women, and Sexual Renunciation in Early Christianity* (New York, NY: 2008).

Burke J., *The Italian Renaissance Nude* (New Haven, CT: 2018).

Cohen Suarez [Cohen-Aponte] A., *Heaven, Hell, and Everything in Between: Murals of the Colonial Andes* (Austin, TX: 2016).

Davidson C. – Walsh M.W. – Broos T.J. (eds.), *Everyman and Its Dutch Original, Elckerlijc* (Kalamazoo, MI: 2007).

DiFuria A.J., *Maarten van Heemskerck's Rome: Antiquity, Memory, and the Cult of Ruins* (Leiden – Boston, MA: 2019).

Falkenburg R.L., *Joachim Patinir: Landscape as an Image of the Pilgrimage of Life*, trans. M. Hoyle (Amsterdam – Philadelphia, PA: 1988).

Falkenburg R.L., *The Land of Unlikeness: Hieronymus Bosch, The Garden of Earthly Delights* (Zwolle: 2011).

Filipczak Z., *Picturing Art in Antwerp, 1550–1700* (Princeton, NJ: 1987).

Gibson W.S., *Mirror of the Earth: The World Landscape in Sixteenth-Century Flemish Painting* (Princeton, NJ: 1989).

Göttler C., *Last Things: Art and the Religious Imagination in the Age of Reform* (Turnhout: 2010).

Göttler C., "Realms of Solitude in Late Medieval and Early Modern European Cultures: An Introduction", in Enenkel K.A.E. – Göttler C. (eds.), *Solitudo: Spaces, Places, and Times of Solitude in Late Medieval and Early Modern Cultures* (Leiden – Boston, MA: 2018) 1–28.

Hand J., *Joos Van Cleve: The Complete Paintings* (London – New Haven, CT: 2004).

Harth A. – Martens M., "Albrecht Dürer's Iconic Image of Saint Jerome: Making, Meaning, and Reception", in Foister S. – Brink P. van den (eds.), *Dürer's Journeys: Travels of a Renaissance Artist* (London – New Haven, CT: 2021) 253–265.

Haskell F. – Penny N., *Taste and the Antique: The Lure of Classical Sculpture, 1500–1900* (New Haven, CT: 1981).

Husband T., *The Wild Man: Medieval Myth and Symbolism*, exh. cat., Metropolitan Museum of Art (New York: 1980).

Jolly P.H., "Pubics and Privates. Body Hair in Late Medieval Art", in Lindquist S.C.M. (ed.), *The Meanings of Nudity in Medieval Art* (Farnham – Burlington, VT: 2011) 183–206.

Kaschek B., "Das kunsttheoretische Bordell: Metamalerei bei Jan van Hemessen", in Münch B.U. – Müller J. (eds.), *Peiraikos' Erben: Die Genese der Genremalerei bis 1550* (Wiesbaden: 2015) 359–390.

Koerner J.L., *Bosch and Bruegel: From Enemy Painting to Everyday Life* (Princeton, NJ: 2016).

Ladner G.B., "Homo Viator: Medieval Ideas on Alienation and Order", *Speculum* 42.2 (1967) 233–259.

Leitch S., *Mapping Ethnography in Early Modern Germany: New Worlds in Print Culture* (New York, NY: 2010).

Lu H., "Games, Flirtation, and the Use of Interpretive Risk: Jan Sanders van Hemessen's *Portrait of Husband and Wife Playing Tables*", *Ludica. Annali di storia e civiltà del gioco* 28 (2022) 57–80.

Martens M.P.J. – Peeters N., "Paintings in Antwerp Houses (1532–1567)", in De Marchi N. – Van Miegroet H.J. (eds.), *Mapping Markets for Paintings in Europe 1450–1750* (Turnhout: 2006) 35–55.

Muller J., *St. Jacob's: Antwerp Art and Counter Reformation in Rubens's Parish Church* (Leiden – Boston, MA: 2016).

Pabel H.M., *Herculean Labours: Erasmus and the Editing of St. Jerome's Letters in the Renaissance* (Leiden – Boston, MA: 2008).

Pinson Y., *The Fools' Journey: A Myth of Obsession in Northern Renaissance Art* (Turnhout: 2008).

Ramakers B.A.M. – Wilmink W. (eds.), *Mariken van Nieumeghen and Elckerlijc: zonde, hoop en verlossing in de late middeleeuwen* (Amsterdam: 1998).

Renger K., *Lockere Gesellschaft: Zur Ikonographie des verlorenen Sohnes und von Wirtshausszenen in der niederländischen Malerei* (Berlin: 1970).

Rice E.F., *Saint Jerome in the Renaissance* (Baltimore, MD: 1985).

Rothstein B., "The Problem with Looking at Pieter Bruegel's *Elck*", *Art History* 26.2 (2003) 143–173.

Rothstein B., *Sight and Spirituality in Early Netherlandish Painting* (Cambridge – New York, NY: 2005).

Rothstein B., "Beer and Loafing in Antwerp", *Art History* 35.5 (2012) 886–907.

Rothstein B., "Jan van Hemessen's Anatomy of Parody", in Melion W.S. – Rothstein B. – Weemans M. (eds.), *The Anthropomorphic Lens: Anthropomorphism, Microcosm and Analogy in Early Modern Thought and Visual Arts* (Leiden: 2015) 457–479.

Seidel C. (ed.), *Marinus: Painter from Reymerswale*, exh. cat., Museo Nacional del Prado (Madrid: 2021).

Silver L., "Forest Primeval: Albrecht Altdorfer and the German Wilderness Landscape", *Simiolus* 13.1 (1983) 4–43.

Silver L., "God in the Details: Bosch and Judgment(s)", *The Art Bulletin* 83.4 (2001) 626–650.

Silver L., *Hieronymus Bosch* (New York, NY: 2006).

Steinberg L., *The Sexuality of Christ in Renaissance Art and in Modern Oblivion* (Chicago, IL: 1996).

Stinebring A.-C., "Encountering Adam and Eve at the Apocalypse: Violence, Sensuality, and Hope in the Rockox *Last Judgment*", *Nederlands Kunsthistorisch Jaarboek* 72 (2022) 95–121.

Stinebring A.-C., *Jan Sanders van Hemessen and Antwerp Painting before Bruegel* (Ph.D. dissertation, University of Pennsylvania: 2022).

Stoichita V.I., *The Self-Aware Image: An Insight into Early Modern Meta-Painting*, trans. A.M. Glasheen (Cambridge: 1997).

Strickland D.H., *The Epiphany of Hieronymus Bosch: Imagining Antichrist and Others from the Middle Ages to the Reformation* (London: 2016).

Sullivan M.A., "Bosch, Bruegel, Everyman and the Northern Renaissance", *Oud Holland* 121.2/3 (2008) 117–146.

Tóth B. – Varga A. (eds.), *Between Hell and Paradise: The Enigmatic World of Hieronymus Bosch*, exh. cat., Museum of Fine Arts (Budapest: 2022).

Ubl M., "Van hoerenhuis tot hoofse liefde: Jan Sanders van Hemessen, de Meester van de Vrouwelijke Halffiguren en Ambrosius Benson", in Coelen P. van der – Lammertse F. (eds.), *De ontdekking van het dagelijks leven*, exh. cat., Museum Boijmans van Beuningen (Rotterdam: 2015) 157–175.

Vandenbroeck P., *Beeld van de andere, vertoog over het zelf: over wilden en narren, boeren en bedelaars*, exh. cat., Koninklijk Museum voor Schone Kunsten (Antwerp: 1987).

Vandenbroeck P., *Utopia's Doom: The Graal as Paradise of Lust, the Sect of the Free Spirit and Jheronimus Bosch's So-Called Garden of Delights* (Louvain: 2017).

Vergara A. (ed.), *Patinir: Essays and Critical Catalogue*, exh. cat., Museo Nacional del Prado (Madrid: 2007).

Wallen B., *Jan van Hemessen: An Antwerp Painter between Reform and Counter-Reform* (Ann Arbor, MI: 1983).

Wenzel S., "The Pilgrimage of Life as a Late Medieval Genre", *Mediaeval Studies* 35 (1973) 370–388.

Wright F.A. (ed.), *Select Letters of St. Jerome* (London – New York, NY: 1933).

CHAPTER 14

'Abstracto igitur animo': Eschatological Image-Making in the Emblematic Spiritual Exercises of Jan David, s.j.

Walter S. Melion

Abstract

Designed and engraved by the Galle family of Antwerp, the extensive print series around which Jan David, s.j.'s innovative emblem books are organized all conclude with eschatological images having to do with the spiritual exercise of purgation – the freeing of one's bodily and spiritual senses from sinful impulses, in anticipation of one's imminent death and of final judgement. These emblems consistently turn on *paradoxa* that assist the votary visually and affectively to experience something beyond the realm of human experience, to see what cannot be seen, to partake in time of a state of salvation or damnation that is timeless. Having examined the eschatological cosmology adopted by David from Jerónimo Nadal, s.j.'s *Adnotationes et meditationes in Evangelia* (1595), I then turn to David's emblems focusing on the nature of the relation between present and future experience, between a prevenient and everlasting state of grace, and on the thoughts and emotions, texts and images that preview the eternal future of the embodied soul from the its present contingent circumstances. In particular, my essay looks closely at the images collaboratively designed by the Galles and David to represent how the end of the world and its perpetual aftermath may be imagined.

Keywords

occasio (God-given occasion) – oracle – parable – purgation – underworld

Designed and engraved by the Galle family of Antwerp, in collaboration with the Jesuit emblematist Jan David and his publishers Balthasar and Jan Moretus, the extensive print series around which David organized the majority of his innovative emblem books conclude with eschatological images having to do with the spiritual exercise of purgation – the freeing of one's bodily and spiritual senses from sinful impulses, in anticipation of one's imminent death

FIGURE 14.1   Theodore Galle, *Title-Page* of Jan David, S.J., *Veridicus*
Christianus (Antwerp, Ex officina Plantiniana, apud
Ioannem Moretum: 1601). Engraving, quarto. The
Newberry Library, Chicago

and of final judgement [Figs. 14.1–14.3]. David's epigrams and prose commentaries are centred on the emblematic *picturae* (pictorial images), and this suggests that Theodoor Galle, probably assisted by his younger brother Cornelis,
closely consulted with him, supplying the designs, either directly or through
the mediation of the Moretuses, which David then used to compose his *tit-*
uli (titles), *epigrammata* (epigrams, generally couplets, the first line a question, the second an answer), descriptive inscriptions (lettered and correlative
to specific scenes in the image, likewise marked with letters), and chapter-
length commentaries that expound, usually in great detail, upon the mutually

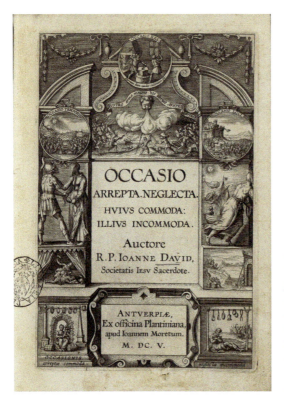

FIGURE 14.2
Theodore Galle, *Title-Page* of
Jan David, s.j., *Occasio arrepta,
neglecta; huius commoda, illius
incommoda* (Antwerp, Ex officina
Plantiniana, apud Ioannem
Moretum: 1605). Engraving,
quarto. Emory University,
Stuart A. Rose Manuscript,
Archives, and Rare Book Library

interpretative relation amongst the title, epigram, and *pictura*. Modelled on
the collaborative relation between the draughtsman Maarten van Heemskerck
and the author-engraver Dirck Volckertsz. Coornhert who invented the allegorical conceits that were converted into drawings by Van Heemskerck and
thereafter engraved by Coornhert, the relation between the Galles and David
involved his provision of a verbal image which, after being converted into a
pictorial one, was embedded within a fuller emblematic apparatus comprising
various species of text that read and are read by the picture. These emblems
consistently turn on *paradoxa* that assist the votary visually and affectively to
experience something beyond the realm of human experience, to see what
cannot be seen, to partake in time of a state of salvation or damnation that
exists outside time. Eschatological images of the last things – of death, salvation, and damnation in particular – feature at key points throughout several
of David's emblem books, where they serve to prompt reflection on the soul's
present condition and instigate the urgent desire for self-amendment. How and
why this occurs by way of proleptic *picturae*, and the reflexive nature of these
emblematic pictures, which call attention to the process of image-making and
its generative and / or purgative effects, are my chief topics.

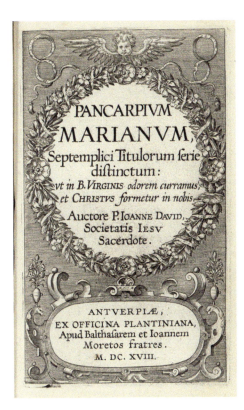

FIGURE 14.3
Theodore Galle, *Title-Page* of Jan
David, S.J., *Pancarpium Marianum,
Septemplici Titulorum serie distinctum:
ut in B. Virginis odorem curramus, et
Christus formetur in nobis* (Antwerp, Ex
officina Plantiniana, apud Balthasarem et
Ioannem Moretos: 1607; reprint ed., 1618).
Engraving, octavo. Emory University,
Stuart A. Rose Manuscript, Archives, and
Rare Book Library

My essay consists of five sections, the briefest of which, section 1, speculates
that the cosmological framework underlying David's musings on the afterlife
and its various zones – namely, heaven, purgatory, limbo, and hell – derives
from Jerónimo Nadal's *Adnotationes et meditationes in Evangelia* (Annotations
and meditations on the Gospels) (Antwerp, Martinus Nutius: 1595), especially
chapters I, XXVIII, XXXIX, and CIIII and their attendant *imagines*, executed by
a team of master engravers, above all, Jan, Hieronymus, and Antoon II Wierix
[Figs. 14.4–14.8].[1] I concentrate on chapters XXXIX and CIIII and their accompanying *imagines* 75 and 131, the organization of which provides a layered meditative image of the afterlife, which David, like all Jesuits, would have known
and memorized from Nadal, careful perusal of whose book had been enjoined
for all scholastics training to enter the Society of Jesus [Fig. 14.8].[2] Sections 2–4

---

1 Nadal Jerónimo, *Adnotationes et meditationes in Evangelia quae in sacrosancto Missae sacrificio toto anno leguntur cum eorunem Evangeliorum concordantia* (Antwerp, Martinus Nutius:
   1595; reprint ed., Ex Officina Plantiniana, apud Ioannem Moretum, 1607).
2 *Imago* 131 and its attendant annotations and meditation form part of a long sequence of
   chapters to be meditated during Holy Week.

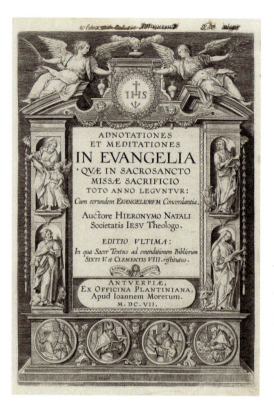

FIGURE 14.4
Jan and/or Hieronymus Wierix,
Title-Page of Jerónimo Nadal,
*Adnotationes et meditationes in
Evangelia quae in sacrosancto
Missae sacrificio toto anno leguntur*
(Antwerp, Martinus Nutius: 1595;
reprint ed., 1607). Engraving,
folio. Emory University, Stuart A.
Rose Manuscript, Archives, and
Rare Book Library

respectively discuss the eschatological emblems featured in three of David's
emblem books: *Veridicus Christianus* (The true Christian) (Antwerp, Ex officina
Plantiniana, apud Ioannem Moretum: 1601) [Fig. 14.1], *Occasio arrepta, neglecta*
(Occasion seized, shirked) (Antwerp, Ex officina Plantiniana, apud Ioannem
Moretum: 1605) [Fig. 14.2], and *Pancarpium Marianum* (Marian garland)
(Antwerp, Ex officina Plantiniana, apud Balthasarem et Ioannem Moretos: 1607)
[Figs. 14.3 and 14.8].[3] Whereas the *Veridicus* exploits the eschatological imaginary

---

3   David composed four major emblem books between 1601 and 1610 – *Veridicus Christianus*
    (ed. prin., 1601), *Occasio arrepta, neglecta* (Occasion seized, shirked, ed. prin., 1605), *Paradisus
    sponsi et sponsae et Pancarpium Marianum* (Paradise of the bridegroom and bride and
    Marian garland, ed. prin., 1607), and *Duodecim specula* (The twelve mirrors, ed. prin., 1610) –
    on which see Backer Aug. de – Backer Al. de – Sommervogel C., *Bibliothèque de la compagnie
    de Jésus*, 9 vols. (Brussels: 1890–1900; Paris: 1890–1932), vol. 2, cols. 1844–1853; Daly P.M. –
    Dimler G.R., s.j., *The Jesuit Series, Part One (A-D)* (Montreal et al.: 1991) 147–162; and Imhof D.,
    Jan Moretus and the Continuation of the Plantin Press, Bibliotheca Bibliographica Neerlandica,
    Series Major III, 2 vols. (Leiden: 2014), vol. 1, 221–223 (*Duodecim specula*), 224–227 (*Occasio*),
    227–229 (*Paradisus et Pancarpium*), 229–234 (*Veridicus Christianus*). My article focuses on
    the three emblem books that explicitly make use of eschatological imagery.

FIGURE 14.5   Jan Wierix after Bernardino Passeri, *What Things Shall Presently Precede the Universal Judgement*, in Jerónimo Nadal, S.J., *Adnotationes et meditationes in Evangelia* (Antwerp, Ex Officina Plantiniana, apud Ioannem Moretum: 1607), chapter I, *imago* 98. Engraving, folio. Emory University, Stuart A. Rose Manuscript, Archives, and Rare Book Library

FIGURE 14.6   Jan Wierix after Bernardino Passeri, *The Universal Judgement*, in
               Jerónimo Nadal, s.j., *Adnotationes et meditationes in Evangelia* (Antwerp,
               Ex Officina Plantiniana, apud Ioannem Moretum: 1607), chapter xxviii,
               imago 99. Engraving, folio. Emory University, Stuart A. Rose Manuscript,
               Archives, and Rare Book Library

FIGURE 14.7   Jan Wierix after Bernardino Passeri, *From out of Hell, the Reveller*
              Importunes Abraham in Vain, in Jerónimo Nadal, S.J., *Adnotationes et*
              meditationes in Evangelia (Antwerp, Ex Officina Plantiniana, apud Ioannem
              Moretum: 1607), chapter XXXIX, *imago* 75. Engraving, folio. Emory
              University, Stuart A. Rose Manuscript, Archives, and Rare Book Library

QVÆ GESSIT CHRISTVS DESCENDENS AD INFEROS. 131
Zach. ix. Eccle. xxiiij. ad Ephef. iiij.   ciiij

A. Chrifti anima nulla mora interpofita,
   venit in Limbum Patrum.
B. Omnium fanctorum Patrum animæ, animam IESV fupplices venerantur.
C. Anima latronis, paulo poft mortua, por-
   tatur ab Angelis ad Limbum.

D. In Limbo infantū nulla pars huius lætitiæ.
E. E Purgatorio multæ animæ liberantur,
   quod fignificant radij lucis inde ad
   limbum Patrum prodeuntes.
F. In inferno inferiori Lucifer cum fuis,
   ipfoque Iuda grauiter fremit.

FIGURE 14.8   Antoon II Wierix after Bernardino Passeri, *What Christ Accomplished on
his Descent into Hell*, in Jerónimo Nadal, S.J., *Adnotationes et meditationes
in Evangelia* (Antwerp, Ex Officina Plantiniana, apud Ioannem Moretum:
1607), chapter CIIII, *imago* 131. Engraving, folio. Emory University,
Stuart A. Rose Manuscript, Archives, and Rare Book Library

to foreclose on heresy, which David analogizes to trafficking in false images, the *Occasio* stages affective images of heaven and hell to sway the malleable hearts of schoolboy actors, and the *Pancarpium* purveys contemplative Marian images intended to shore up the votary as s/he sets about the task of securing salvation and averting damnation. In all three emblem books, images and the process of image-making are brought to consciousness as the chief means whereby eschatological concerns are articulated and anxieties addressed.

1   Mapping the Terrain of Death and Judgement in Nadal's
         Adnotationes et meditationes in Evangelia

Four of Nadal's *imagines* and their attendant *adnotationes* and *meditationes* centre on cosmological *imagines* – *imago* 98, chapter I, "What Things Shall Presently Precede the Universal Judgement" [Fig. 14.5]; *imago* 99, chapter XXVIII, "The Universal Judgement" [Fig. 14.6]; imago 75, chapter XXXIX, "From out of Hell, the Reveller Importunes Abraham in Vain" [Fig. 14.7]; *imago* 131, chapter CIIII, "What Christ Accomplished on his Descent into Hell" [Fig. 14.8] – in which eschatological themes are highlighted, and the votary's field of vision variously expands to encompass the nine heavenly spheres, the whole earth, and entire netherworld.[4] These images largely consist of elements inferred

4   On the form, function, and argument of the *Adnotationes et meditationes*, as they relate to Nadal's conception of the Jesuit vocation, see Fabre P.A., *Ignace de Loyola: le lieu de l'image* (Paris: 1992) 163–239, 263–295; Melion W.S., "The Art of Vision in Jerome Nadal's *Adnotationes et meditationes in Evangelia*", in *Jerome Nadal, Annotations and Meditations on the Gospels. Volume I: The Infancy Narratives*, trans. – ed. F.A. Homann, S.J. (Philadelphia, PA: 2003) 1–96; Smith J.C., *Sensuous Worship: Jesuits and the Art of the Early Catholic Reformation in Germany* (Princeton, NJ – Oxford: 2003) 40–46; Dekoninck R., '*Ad imaginem': status, fonctions et usages de l'image dans la littérature spirituelle jésuite du XVIIe siècle*, Travaux du Grand Siècle 26 (Geneva: 2005) 157–370 passim, esp. 234–37, 287–89, 303–205; Melion W.S., "*Mortis illius imagines ut vitae*: The Image of the Glorified Christ in Jerome Nadal's *Adnotationes et meditationes in Evangelia*", in *Jerome Nadal, Annotations and Meditations on the Gospels. Volume III: The Resurrection Narratives*, trans. – ed. F.A. Homann, S.J. (Philadelphia, PA: 2005) 1–32; Stroomberg H., "Introduction", in *The New Hollstein Dutch and Flemish Etchings, Engravings, and Woodcuts, 1450–1700: The Wierix Family, Book Illustrations*, 2 parts, comp. H. Stroomberg, ed. J. van der Stock (Ouderkerk aan den IJssel: 2007) 2: 3–7; Melion W.S., "*Haec per imagines huius mysterii ecclesia sancta [clamat]*: The Image of the Suffering Christ in Jerome Nadal's *Adnotationes et meditationes in Evangelia*", in *Jerome Nadal, Annotations and Meditations on the Gospels. Volume II: The Passion Narratives*, trans. – ed. F.A. Homann, S.J. (Philadelphia, PA: 2007) 1–73; Lazure G., "Nadal au Nouveau Monde: une traduction poétique des *Evangelicae historiae imagines*, Pérou, c. 1614", in Dekoninck R. – Guiderdoni-Bruslé A. (eds.), *Emblemata Sacra: rhétorique et herméneutique du discours sacré dans la littérature en image. The Rhetoric and Hermeneutics of Illustrated Sacred Discourse*, Imago Figurata 7 (Turnhout: 2007) 321–331; Bowen K. – Imhof D., *Christopher Plantin and Engraved Book Illustrations*

from scriptural prophecies that supplement Christ's prophecy of the Last Judgement in *Matthew* 23:27–33, *Mark* 13:24–29, and *Luke* 21:25–31. *Imago* 131 of chapter CIIII, for example, depicts the soul of Christ surrounded by angelic hosts, as he sets about the task of liberating the Fathers from limbo and many souls from purgatory, and laying siege to hell; engraved by Antoon II Wierix, the *imago* illustrates a cross-section of these zones or, better, experiential registers [Fig. 14.8]. The detailed image of hell and its environs has been plausibly inferred from scriptural prophecies in the Old Testament and allusions to the afterlife in the New. The stratigraphical image is thus more inferential than evidentiary, drawn only partially from the Gospels, and mainly from *Wisdom*, *Psalms*, the prophets, and the *Epistles*. The main biblical places are:

> *Ephesians* 4:8–10: 'Ascending on high, he led captivity captive [...]'.
> *Psalm* 23:7: 'Lift up your gates [...] and the king of glory shall enter in'.
> *Ecclesiasticus* 24:8 and 24:44–45: 'I alone have compassed the circuit of heaven, and have penetrated into the bottom of the deep [...]'.
> *Zechariah* 9:9 and 9:11–12: 'Thou also by the blood of thy testament hast sent forth thy prisoners out of the pit [...]'.
> and *Osee* 13:14: 'I will deliver them out of the hand of death [...]'.[5]

Working from a pen, ink, and wash drawing by Livio Agresti, Bernardino Passeri, designer of the modello on which Antoon II Wierix based his print, maps the underworld as a series of concentric layers, following the scheme introduced in *imago* 75 of chapter XXXIX, "From out of Hell, the Reveller Importunes Abraham in Vain", on the parable of Dives and Lazarus [Fig. 14.7].[6] In the

---

(Cambridge – New York, NY et al.: 2008) 50–51; and Melion W.S., "Parabolic Analogy and Spiritual Discernment in Jéronimo Nadal's *Adnotationes et meditationes in Evangelia* of 1595", in Stelling L. – Hendrix H. – Richardson T.M. (eds.), *The Turn of the Soul: Representations of Religious Conversion in Early Modern Art and Literature*, Intersections 23 (Leiden – Boston, MA: 2012) 299–338.

5   *The Holy Bible, translated from the Latin Vulgate and diligently compared with the Hebrew, Greek, and other editions in divers languages* (*The Old Testament* [...] *Douay, A.D. 1609 and The New Testament* [...] *Rheims, A.D. 1582*), ed. R. Challoner (New York: 1941; reprint ed., Fitzwilliam, NH: 2013).

6   On the protracted process of preparing the drawings and engravings for the plates of the *Adnotationes et meditationes in Evangelia*, see Wadell M.-B., *Evangelicae historiae imagines: Entstehungsgeschichte und Vorlagen*, Gothenburg Studies in Art and Architecture 3 (Gothenburg: 1985) 23–48, 51–54; Münch B.U., *Geteiltes Leid: Die Passion Christi in Bildern und Texten der Konfessionalisierung. Druckgraphik von der Reformation bis zu den jesuitischen Großprojekten um 1600* (Regensburg: 2009) 184–190; and Melion W.S., "'*Quis non intelliget hoc voluisse Christum*': The Significance of the Redacted Images in Jerónimo Nadal's *Adnotationes*

prefatory *adnotatio*, Nadal invites the votary to examine *imago* 75, paying close attention to the way it portrays four strictly demarcated zones, in the nearest of which Lazarus is situated, and in the farthest, Dives: 'In order that Lazarus be brought to view ("in conspectu poneretur") in the bosom of Abraham, the world has been designed skilfully ("commode factum est"), as if partitioned into four parts, a quadrant assigned to each, thus allowing all the underworld's holding places to be visualized ("pateant Inferni receptacula omnia")'.[7] The four spherical quadrants, visible at the earth's core, are stygian hell ('F'), respectively encircled by purgatory ('E'), the limbo of unbaptized children ('D'), and farthest from hell, the limbo of the Fathers ('B–C'), as it looked before the Anastasis ('Harrowing of Hell'). To emphasize that this is the underworld, Agresti surrounded the uppermost limbo with earthen escarpments, on the curved surface of which appear mountain ranges, a river, and cities and towns, with clouds drifting overhead. Passeri exaggerated the interval between heaven and hell by increasing the size and darkness of zone 'A': 'The space of earth that intercedes between the limbo of the Fathers and the earth's surface'.[8] In *imago* 75, giant serpents coil and slither along the ground, and burrow deep into the earth [Fig. 14.7]. They allude to the monstrous worms of hell that signify the fire of eternal punishment in *Mark* 9:46–47: 'It is better for thee with one eye to enter into the kingdom of God, than having two eyes to be cast into the hell of fire: where their worm dieth not, and the fire is not extinguished'. Similarly, they are adduced as an image of transgression in *Isaiah* 66:24: 'And they shall go out, and see the carcasses of the men that have transgressed against me: their worm shall not die, and their fire shall not be quenched, and they shall be a loathsome sight to all flesh'. The serpents are a pictorial amplification, added by reason of associative inference, to Nadal's annotative image of the spherically partitioned world comprising hell, purgatory, and the two limbos. In every other way, here and in *imago* 131, Passeri and Wierix punctiliously followed Nadal's annotations: for example, they carefully differentiate the twilit limbo of unbaptized children from the brighter light of the limbo of the Fathers and still brighter light of purgatory [Figs. 14.7 and 14.8].[9]

---

et meditationes in Evangelia of 1595", in *Jerome Nadal, s.j., Annotations and Meditations on the Gospels, Cumulative Index*, ind. J.P. Lea (Philadelphia, PA: 2014) 1–99.

7 Nadal, *Adnotationes et meditationes* 127: 'Ut in conspectu poneretur Lazarus in sinu Abrahae, commode factum est, ut quasi in quatuor partes diviso orbe terrarum in ascripto quadrante, pateant Inferni receptacula omnia'.

8 Ibidem 127, annotation A: 'Id spatium terrae, quod intercedit inter Limbum Patrum, et terrae superficiem'.

9 Ibidem 128, annotation C: 'Ad hos non pertingit lux Limbi Patrum, nec ignis Purgatorii ardor, etiamsi inter hos orbes collocatae sint infantium animae'.

FIGURE 14.9
Theodore Galle, *Title-Page* of
*Paradisus Sponsi et Sponsae:
in quo Messis myrrhae et
aromatum ex instrumentis
ac mysteriis Passionis Christi
colligenda, et Pancarpium
Marianum* (Antwerp, Ex
Officina Plantiniana apud
Ioannem Moretum: 1607;
reprint ed., 1618). Emory
University, Stuart A.
Rose Manuscript, Archives,
and Rare Book Library

In addition to extending and darkening the terrestrial zone, *imago* 131
drops the radiant aureole around Christ and his angels entirely beneath the
earth's surface, to emphasize how deeply Jesus descended to reach the Fathers
[Fig. 14.7]. In one significant respect, however, Passeri and Wierix diverge
from Nadal to bring their images closer to *Ephesians* 4:8–10. They portray the
risen Christ as he will appear in *imago* 134 of Chapter CVIII, "The Glorious
Resurrection of Christ", to emphasize that in now descending hellward, he is
'the same also' who 'ascending on high, led captivity captive', triumphing over
death at the Resurrection [Fig. 14.10]. Nadal, on the other hand, urges the votary
to layer onto the *imago* a somewhat different image of Christ, the spiritual
meaning of which may be inferred from its divergence from pictorial tradition:
'But Christ is described in human form, but without muscles, without hair on

his head or face, in order to signify that he is spirit, not body, but also by that bodily form to represent the spirit's inclination toward the body'.[10] This counterimage of Christ bald and muscleless may be seen to operate in tandem with the muscular, hirsute Christ of the *imago*: whereas the former is paradoxical, a body indicating that Christ is all spirit and no body, and also allegorical, a spiritual body signifying the soul's longing to be embodied, the latter is proleptic, in that it anticipates the form Christ shall take when he rises from the tomb. The complex image Nadal invites the votary to meditate – part *imago*, part imagined, part familiar, part unprecedented, partly paradoxical, allegorical, and proleptic – consists of multiple elements whose mutual relation he leaves it to the reader to infer.

The Society spared no expense to ensure that Nadal's book be published to the highest possible standard, hiring the finest draughtsmen and engravers, and retaining the services of the Antwerp publisher Martinus Nutius to produce a large folio edition more than 600 pages long. The fact that Ignatius of Loyola, founder of the Society, had himself delegated the task of producing a series of Gospel images and accessory spiritual exercises to Nadal, and Nadal's importance to the Society as the chief promulgator of the order's *Constitutiones* and the founder-propagator of its first teaching colleges, jointly explain why his fellow Jesuits lavished so much time and energy, and so many resources, on the *Adnotationes et meditationes*. The Society, by distributing the book worldwide to its vast network of houses and schools, thereby ensured that its students, novices, and professed priests would come intimately to know Nadal's words and images.[11] In musing on eschatological matters, Jan David could therefore rely on Nadal's images of the afterlife and their *loci particulares* as the armature upon which to construct his daedal meditations on death, judgement, salvation, and damnation.

---

10   Ibidem 395, annotation A: 'Describitur autem forma quidem humana Christus, verum absque musculis, et absque capillis, pilis vel barba; ut significetur anima illa esse, non corpus; repraesentari vero illa figura propensionem animae ad corpus'.

11   On the global circulation of the *Adnotationes et meditationes*, see Moffitt J.F., "Francisco Pacheco and Jerome Nadal: New Light on the Flemish Sources of the Spanish 'Picture-within-the-Picture'", *The Art Bulletin* 72 (1990) 631–638; Dekoninck R., "*Imagines peregrinantes*: The International Genesis and Fate of Two Biblical Picture Books (Hiël and Nadal) Conceived in Antwerp at the End of the Sixteenth Century", in Gelderblom A.J. – Jong L.J. de – Van Vaeck M. (eds.), *The Low Countries as a Crossroads of Religious Beliefs* (Leiden – Boston, MA: 2004) 49–64; Robin A., "El retablo de Zaltocán: Las *Imágenes* de Jerónimo Nadal y la monja de Ágreda", *Anales del Instituto de Investigaciones Estéticas* 88 (2006) 53–70; Lazure, "Nadal au Nouveau Monde"; and Hyman A.M., *Rubens in Repeat: The Logic of the Copy in Colonial Latin America* (Los Angeles, CA: 2021) 182–183.

RESVRRECTIO CHRISTI GLORIOSA. 134
Matth. xxviij.   Marc. xvi.   Luc. xxiiij.   Ioan. xx.   cviij

A. *Adest Chriſtus in anima ad ſepulcrum ex limbo cum Angelis, & animabus Patrum, ad finem crepuſculi primæ Sabbati.*
B. *Vnit animam corpori, & egreditur ſaluo ſepulcro; pronunciat; Vici mundum, conculcaui dæmonem, mortem interemi, viuo in æternum.*
C. *Sepulcrum obſignatum.*
D. *Milites duo agunt excubias; alij dormiunt, nemo quacquam omnino ſentit.*
E. *Ducit Chriſtus captiuum sathanam, mortem, &c.*
F. *Per totam Iudæam è ſepulchris apertis, ſanc̈ti excitantur, quorum animæ interfuerunt Chriſti reſurrec̈tioni, & apparent deinde multis.*

FIGURE 14.10   Hieronymus Wierix after Bernardino Passeri, *The Glorious Resurrection of Christ*, in Jerónimo Nadal, s.j., *Adnotationes et meditationes in Evangelia* (Antwerp, Ex Officina Plantiniana, apud Ioannem Moretum: 1607), chapter CVIIJ, *imago* 134. Engraving, folio. Emory University, Stuart A. Rose Manuscript, Archives, and Rare Book Library

2   Heresy and Death as Sources of the Eschatological Imaginary in
           David's *Veridicus Christianus*

Before embarking on a discussion of the eschatological images in David's
emblem books, it behoves us to consider the nature of his involvement with
Theodore Galle, designer and chief engraver of David's emblematic *picturae*.
Galle was the foremost designer-engraver in the print-publishing house
of his father Philips Galle, founder of one of Antwerp's premier engraving
workshops.[12] As Werner Waterschoot pointed out in a seminal article on
David's final emblem book, the *Duodecim specula* (Twelve mirrors) (Antwerp,
Ex officina Plantiniana, apud Ioannem Moretum: 1610), for the production
of which an extensive correspondence between David and his publisher
Balthasar Moretus survives, the lack of any single letter focusing at length on
the engraved illustrations strongly implies that detailed conversations, conducted in person, must have preceded publication of the book.[13] What does
occur frequently in the letters are passing yet telling remarks on Theodore's
plates. David looked very closely at proof impressions, asking for revisions and
amplifications: the addition of the holy name of Jesus to the mirror featured in
the frontispiece, for example, or the aggrandizement of the figure of the king's
son in mirror 11, to emphasize that this is the parable of the marriage-feast not
the wedding at Cana, and to accentuate the allegorical relation between the
bridegroom and Christ. As Waterschoot notes, every one of David's suggestions
was implemented.[14] With regard to composition of the Latin subscriptions, the

---

12   On the Galle workshop, see Bowen K.L. – Imhof D., "Reputation and Wage: The Case of
      Engravers Who Worked for the Plantin-Moretus Press", *Simiolus* 30.3/4 (2003) 161–195;
      Bowen K.L., "Workshop Practices in Antwerp: The Galles", *Print Quarterly* 26.2 (2009)
      123–142; and idem, "Declining Wages for the Printing of Book Illustrations: Arrangements
      between the Galle Family of Printmakers and the Managers of the Officina Plantiniana
      in Seventeenth-Century Antwerp", in Blondé B. – Munck B. de – Vermeylen F. (eds.),
      *Doodgewoon: mensen en hun dagelijks leven in de geschiedenis. Liber amicorum Alfons K.L.
      Thys* (Antwerp: 2004) 63–85.
13   See Waterschoot W., "Joannes David Editing 'Duodecim specula'", in Manning J. – Van
      Vaeck M. (eds.), *The Jesuits and the Emblem Tradition: Selected Papers of the Leuven
      International Emblem Conference, 18–23 August 1996*, Imago Figurata Studies 1a (Turnhout:
      1999) 353–364, esp. 360: 'With the elaborate illustrations in mind, David certainly had
      long talks in Dutch with Galle and his collaborators, the Latin texts being of course no
      help to these craftsmen. This very complicated matter was settled as a whole in Antwerp,
      since the subject and presentation of these enigmatic emblems are at no time discussed
      in the correspondence'.
14   Ibidem 359. On the close collaboration amongst David, Theodore Galle, and Balthasar
      Moretus, see Sors A.-K., *Allegorische Andachtsbücher in Antwerpen: Jan Davids Texte
      und Theodoor Galles Illustrationen in den jesuitischen Buchprojecten der Plantiniana*
      (Göttingen: 2015) 45–57.

images led the way: David asks Moretus to have Galle send the images (presumably proof states) as soon as possible, with capitals marking the scenes to be subscribed; once David knows which scenes have been selected, he can set about the task of writing the taglines.

An earlier instance of close collaboration between David and the Galles resulted in his first emblem book, *Veridicus Christianus*, which originated as a series of 100 Dutch distichs, *De wijsheyt der simpel christenen* (Brussels, Rutger Velpius: 1593); David then augmented this series, re-centring it on engraved images supplied by the Galles, for which he wrote extended emblematic commentaries. Known as the *Christeliicken waersegher* (Antwerp, Inde Plantijnsche Druckerije, by Ian Moerentorf: 1603), this text was in fact published after the Latin edition which, though organized around these same images, relied more heavily on scriptural exegesis to interpret them.[15] As "Admonitiuncula auctoris" (Author's little admonition [to the reader]) of the *Veridicus* concedes, it was the 'typorum aeneorum incisores', i.e., Philips and Theodore Galle, not Balthasar or Jan Moretus, who convinced David to translate his text into Latin and issue it first, in 1601.[16] David's prefatory remark attests the degree and intensity of his collaborative engagement with the Galles, just as his long association with them speaks to his profound interest in pictorial images and, above all, in emblematic *picturae*.

Unprecedented amongst emblem books focusing on sacred themes, the *Veridicus Christianus*, which consists of one hundred emblems, is catechetical in form and function [Fig. 14.1].[17] Each chapter commences with an opening,

---

15   On the *Christeliicken waersegher* and its relation to the *Veridicus Christianus*, see Waterschoot W., "*Veridicus Christianus* and *Christeliicken Waersegher* by Johannes David", in Dekoninckck – Guiderdoni-Bruslé (eds.), *Emblemata Sacra* 527–534; and Imhof, *Continuation of the Plantin Press* 1:234–235.

16   David Jan, S.J., *Veridicus Christianus* (Antwerp, Ex officina Plantiniana, apud Ioannem Moretum: 1601; reprint ed., 1606), fol. ++2v. On the Galles' role in spurring David to compose the *Veridicus Christianus*, see Imhof, *Continuation of the Plantin Press* 1:233–234. The reference to their decisive intervention perhaps suggests that they had the rudiments of Latin and were not *idiotae* (illiterate in Latin), pace Waterschoot.

17   On the book's production history, see Imhof, *Continuation of the Plantin Press* 1:234–236. On David's allegorical method in the *Veridicus*, as it relates to his three other emblem books, see Sors, *Allegorische Andachtsbücher* 58–83, 139–144. On David's image theory and practice, see Dekoninck, '*Ad imaginem*' 194–196, 286–297, 312–324, 339–349; Dekoninck – Guiderdoni-Bruslé – Van Vaeck, *Emblemata Sacra* 29–31, 55–62; Daly P.M., *The Emblem in Early Modern Europe: Contributions to the Theory of the Emblem* (Farnham, Surr. – Burlington, VT: 2014) 126, 192; Melion W.S., "Introduction: The Jesuit Engagment with the Status and Functions of the Visual Image", in De Boer W. – Enenkel K.A.E. – Melion (eds.), *Jesuit Image Theory*, Intersections 45 (Leiden – Boston, MA: 2016) 1–49; and Melion W.S., "*Ut pictura lex*: Jan David, S.J., on Natural Law and the Global Reach of Christian Images",

text at left, *pictura* at right, qualified by a title, and an epigram and corollary inscriptions, below. The epigrams take the form of a question and answer on an article of faith. Throughout the opening chapters, David imagines how sin – the sin of heresy above all – destabilizes the layered cosmology exemplified by Nadal, causing elements of eternity unseasonably to irrupt into human affairs. He further reflects on eschatological matters – principally on the four last things – in the closing chapters, which is to say that these concerns bracket the whole of his catechetical emblem book, functioning as one of the first and, appropriately, also the last things the catechumen ponders in meditating his obligations as *veridicus Christianus* (a true Christian). Eschatological imagery is marshalled to signal the dire consequences of heresy, which has damnation as its baleful effect. Take Emblem 6, "Haeresis, peste perniciosior" (Heresy, more baleful than the plague), which plays upon the imagery of leprosy in *Leviticus* 13:45, and of vulpine rapacity in *Matthew* 7:15 and *Acts* 20:28–29, to personify heresy as a hell on earth, whose effects on the heretic's body and soul are more fearful than the plague, in that they license an eternity of suffering [Fig. 14.11]. *Pictura* 6, in bodying forth Heresy ('B'), depicts her in a manner calculated to elicit horror, but also, by exposing her for what she truly is – toxic, rampant, hideous – strives to incite revulsion, thereby to inoculate the reader-viewer against the heretic's infectious distortions of the faith. On this account, the picture's eschatological elements can be characterized as both monitory and therapeutic, in the sense that they function to repel heresy by uncloaking its true nature.

Before closely reading Emblem 6, it should be set in the context of several prior emblems, especially Emblem 3, "Qui, spreto Deo, diabolo servit, desipit" (He who serves the devil, having scorned God, is void of understanding) [Fig. 14.12]. Here David persistently likens heretics to image-makers because he considers heresy an extreme form of idolatry. *Pictura* 3 contrasts Jesus, arms crossed, eyes raised heavenward, with an idolator who disdainfully spurns the Lord. Richly dressed, but draped with foolscap, the apostate reverences a

in Göttler C. – Mochizuki M. (eds.), *The Nomadic Object: The Challenge of World for Early Modern Religious Art*, Intersections 53 (Leiden – Boston, MA: 2017) 147–186. Also see Sors, *Allegorische Andachtsbücher* 217–223, on David's adaptation of the tripartite emblem, comprising a pictorial image, motto, and epigram, through the addition of polyglot epigrams, an extensive prose commentary, and Roman capitals correlating the picture's constituent scenes to explanatory passages in the commentary. On the joint involvement of the publisher Jan Moretus and printmaker Philips Galle in the production of the *Veridicus Christianus*, see Sellink M., "Joannes David, *Veridicus christianus*", in Imhof D. (ed.), *The Illustration of Books Published by the Moretuses*, exh. cat., Plantin-Moretus Museum, Antwerp (Antwerp: 1996) 88–89.

FIGURE 14.11   Theodore Galle, Emblem 6: "Haeresis, peste perniciosior"
(Heresy, more baleful than the plague), in Jan David, s.j.,
Veridicus Christianus (The True Christian) (Antwerp, Ex officina
Plantiniana, apud Ioannem Moretum: 1601; reprint ed., 1606).
Engraving, quarto. Emory University, Stuart A. Rose Manuscript,
Archives, and Rare Book Library

FIGURE 14.12 Theodore Galle, Emblem 3: "Qui, spreto Deo, diabolo servit, desipit" (He who serves the devil, having scorned God, is void of understanding), in Jan David, s.j., *Veridicus Christianus* (The True Christian) (Antwerp, Ex officina Plantiniana, apud Ioannem Moretum: 1601; reprint ed., 1606). Engraving, quarto. Emory University, Stuart A. Rose Manuscript, Archives, and Rare Book Library

chimeric idol set on a high pedestal, tenders a lit taper, and with his other hand, dismisses Christ. The epigram disparages him as a fool's fool: 'Who snatches folly's palm from these selfsame fools? He who prefers to exalt demons above God the thunderer'.[18] In the commentary, David's attention turns to the idolator's vices, which he compares to the sins of Solomon (3 *Kings* 11:4–10), Nabal (1 *Kings* 25:2–13), and Judas (*Luke* 22:3–6):

> One may behold, as in a mirror, an exemplum of such folly – king Solomon: who through wifely infatuation fell from great dignity of state before God, into vileness and blindness, giving himself over to the cult of demons, and publicly offering them sacrifice [...]. In this manner, fools do rave; however many they be, all live impiously, and by sinning arrive at the most iniquitous of follies. Of that ilk was Nabal, and [Judas], that least apostolic of apostles: and likewise whosoever soldiers on under the sign of these men ('sub istorum signis militant'): drunkards, gluttons, the irascible, the prideful, those whose avarice and sexual desire are insatiable, and men of most wicked life.[19]

Solomon appears between Christ and the apostate in *pictura* 3, accompanied by his wives whom he joins in kneeling before an idol ('B'). David asserts that the vices he and all idolators harbour, result from a refusal attentively to dwell on the image of God – more exactly, the image of the Holy Face – deeply impressed in every human heart. Instead of looking steadily at this image, all the while contemplating God's majesty, and conversely, his own baseness, the idolator obfuscates the *vultum Dei*, puts it out of sight, covers it over with the detritus of sin, and subordinates it to his unruly passions ('sed affectui soli indulgens, Dei vultum in anima sua, peccati faecibus obruit').[20] This is to say that idolatry, like heresy, indulgently layers a self-image – heedless, sinful, passion-led – over

---

18   David, *Veridicus Christianus* 10 and *pictura* 3: 'Stultitiae palmam stultis quis praeripit ipsis? / Daemona qui mavult Dominum, quam ferre Tonantem'.

19   Ibidem 12: 'Stultitiae huius exemplum in Rege Salomone velut in speculo, licet contueri: qui ex tantae dignitatis gradu apud Deum, in tantam, per mulierum infatuationem, vilitatem, caecitatemque delapsus est; ut se daemoniorum cultui dediderit, iisque publice litarit; templis etiam et aris idolorum coetui erectis. Hunc in modum insaniunt, quotquot impie vivunt, et ad nequissimam illam stultitiam peccando deveniunt. Talis stultus fuit et Nabal; talis et ille Evangelicus, minime Evangelicus: et quicunque sub istorum signis militant: bibones, epulones, iracundi, fastuosi, insatiatae libidinis et avaritiae, et id genus homines vitae nequioris'.

20   Ibidem.

the true image of God discernible from within. It operates under the sign, in the sense of 'under the image', of fools such as Solomon, a circumstance pictured, in episode 'A', by the idolator's turning away from the Lord's face.

Cognizant of the heretic's reliance on false images, Emblem 6 asseverates that God himself, in the Old Testament and the New, discloses how heresy may best be combatted – namely, by means of epideictic images founded on simile, metonymy, and hypotyposis [Fig. 14.11]. If heresy imposes itself through images, counter-images, especially eschatological ones, yet offer the most effective means of opposing it. *Pictura* 6 provides just such a potent image, modelled on these scriptural *loci textuales*, for defending against, even repelling the occasion of heresy and heresy's insidious effects. The epigram promulgates this newly fashioned image which, as cited above, David analogizes to the imagery of leprosy in *Leviticus* 13, and the ravenous wolf in *Matthew* 7 and *Acts* 20. Heresy is seen to repel and repulse no less forcefully than the plague: 'What deadly poison worse than the plague ought I to flee? Heresy, which the nest of Stygian Hydra incubates'.[21] The commentary supplies the reason why: since the soul is more precious than the body, heresy is more fatal than the plague, for it inflicts spiritual death ('tanto magis illius quam huius pestis et mors').[22] This is why the pesthouse ('A') in *pictura* 6 is smaller and more distant than the imposing personification *Haeresis* ('B'), who erupts from the jaws of hell ('D'), causing terrified men, women, and children to take flight. Heresy combines the attributes of Envy and a Fury: her face contorted with rage, snaky hair writhing, she clutches a cornucopia of lethal weaponry. The pestilential vapour exhaled from her mouth indicates that she is noxious like the plague; in this and other respects, as David points out, she embodies allusions to *Deuteronomy* 32:33 ('Their wine is the gall of dragons, and the venom of asps, which is incurable') and *Psalm* 13:3 ('Their throat is an open sepulchre: with their tongues they acted deceitfully; the poison of asps is under their lips').[23] That her profile repeats in small the gaping silhouette of hell signifies the virulence of Heresy's tongue / speech ('ipsorum virulentis linguis'); her emergence from Erebus reveals, in David's words, that that 'infernal serpent, and diabolical hydra', the devil himself, is the 'inventor, inciter, and originator of all heresies'.[24] Similarly, the weapons she furnishes are signs of the 'carnage'

---

21   Ibidem 18 and *pictura* 6: 'Peius letiferi vitem quid peste veneni? / Haeresin: Hanc Stygiae nidus confovit Echidnae'.
22   Ibidem 18.
23   Ibidem 18–19.
24   Ibidem 19.

wrought by heresy ('internecionis auctores'), and of the 'sectarian conspiracies' that heretics foment ('per conspirationes a vovis conflates').[25]

David presents these allegorical motifs as licensed by God who ensured the detestation of heresy when he first prefigured it in the guise of leprosy (*Leviticus* 13:45):

> God of old forewarned and solicitously fortified us with a marvelous example, to make this contagion more execrable and ensure that it be fled: when by law he decreed and admonished whomsoever leprosy had tainted to dress in loose garments, with head bare and face covered; and to cry out that they were defiled and unclean; and to live alone, outside the encampment, so that to the fullest extent possible, having been seen and made known, they might more safely be shunned, and infect no one with their fetid breath or too great proximity.[26]

This image of heresy, Christ and, in imitation of him, Paul rendered even more vivid when they renewed the Mosaic type, layering onto it the parabolic image of a ravening wolf in sheep's clothing, which deceives in order to devour its prey:

> In the present situation of danger, Christ himself renewed this warning in a manner fit to inspire terror, laying bare the latent virus, by saying (*Matthew* 7:15): 'Beware of false prophets, who come to you in the clothing of sheep, but inwardly they are ravening wolves'. The apostle reminded the Ephesians to be alert and take flight, with almost the same words (*Acts* 20:28–29): 'Take heed to yourselves, and to the whole flock. I know that, after my departure, ravening wolves will enter in among you, not sparing the flock'. What could be applied more efficaciously toward the diligent, scrupulous flight from heresy, than to expose to view the rapacity and ferocity of the wolf? Who should wish to traffic with wolves? Nay rather, having descried this, who would not presently take thought of himself and flee?[27]

---

25   Ibidem 21.

26   Ibidem 18: 'In maiorem huius contagii detestationem securioremque fugam, Deus nos mirabili olim praemonuit, et solicite praemunivit exemplo: quando lege lata cavit praecepitque; ut quicumque maculatus esset lepra, haberet vestimenta dissuta, caput nudum, os veste contectum; ac contaminatum se ac sordidum ipse clamaret; solusque extra castra habitaret: quae omnia ad hoc faciebant, ut noti et ad cutem usque perspecti, tutius vitarentur, neque quemquam foetido suo halitu, nimiave vicinitate inficerent'.

27   Ibidem: 'Hanc in tam praesenti periculo cautelam, propius vivaciorique adhuc terrendi modo Christus ipse renovavit, latensque virus aperte detexit, dicens: *Attendite a falsis*

These allegorical images of heresy – plague, leprosy, wolves – are complexly composite: by turns scriptural or pseudo-scriptural, they function jointly as similes, metonyms, and hypotyposes, and are vouchsafed to inspire fear and repugnance, as antidotes to the contagion they symbolically picture. Whereas the parable of the wolf and the flock originates with Christ, the typological image of leprotic heresy derives from exegetical tradition, and the specific analogy of plague to heresy, portrayed in *pictura* 6, is an exegetical image newly coined from *Deuteronomy* 32:33, *Psalms* 13:3, *Ecclesiasticus* 13:1, 1 *Timothy* 4:1–2, *Titus* 3:10, and *James* 3:15, as David explains in his commentary.[28] All three images are exempla, all share the same rhetorical function: they elicit the sort of negative emotions that it is the province of epideictic oratory to activate, for the purpose of adjuring the reader-viewer to detect and repudiate heresy.

The heretic's Luciferian fall from grace, a prolepsis of the final judgement that awaits idolators and other damnable sinners, constitutes the subject of Emblem 10, "Diaboli haereticique lapsus simillimus" (The most similar fall of the devil and the heretic) [Fig. 14.13]. The formal structure of *pictura* 10 is bipartite, with two distinct zones, marked 'A' and 'B' above, coalescing into the fiery zone of hell below, where, as a result of their fallen state, heretics and demons are seen to be veritably alike, if not indivisible. Just as the rebel angels were cast out of heaven, so, too, heretics are cast out of the protective ark of the Church ('D'), having succumbed to the devil's temptation of Christ in *Luke* 4:9, 'And he brought him to Jerusalem, and set him on a pinnacle of the temple, and he said to him: If thou be the Son of God, cast thyself from hence' ('C') – the difference being that the angels were ejected, whereas heretics have chosen to expel themselves. Emblem 10, then, narrates the originating source and inevitable end of the proud figure featured in Emblem 9, "Diabolici spiritus delineatio" (Drawing of the devilish spirit): viewed with an eye to the past, that figure, ever impenitent, can be seen to react bellicosely to its humiliating ejection from heaven and from the Church, which David calls heaven on earth ('in terris caelum'); viewed with an eye to the future, that figure's impenitence is predictive of its inevitable lapse into fiery oblivion.

---

prophetis, qui veniunt ad vos in vestimentis ovium; intrinsecus autem sunt lupi rapaces. Cuius attentionis et fugae etiam Apostolus Ephesios commonefecit iisdem fere verbis: *Attendite vobis, et universo gregi: Scio quod intrabunt lupi rapaces in vos, non parcentes gregi.* Quid posset ad diligentem accuratamque haereticorum fugam efficacius adhiberi; quam lupi rapacitatem ac ferociam obiicere? Quis cum lupo commercii aliquid habere velit? Immo quisnam eo conspecto non illico sibi fuga consulat?'.

28   On heresy as disease, see Moore R.I., "Heresy as Disease", in Lourdaux W. – Verhelst D. (eds.), *The Concept of Heresy in the Middle Ages* (Leuven: 1983) 1–11; and Marshall J., *John Locke, Toleration, and Early Enlightenment Culture*, Cambridge Studies in Early Modern British History (Cambridge – New York, NY: 2006) 212–218.

FIGURE 14.13 Theodore Galle, Emblem 10: "Diaboli haereticique lapsus simillimus" (The most similar fall of the devil and the heretic), in Jan David, s.j., *Veridicus Christianus* (The True Christian) (Antwerp, Ex officina Plantiniana, apud Ioannem Moretum: 1601; reprint ed., 1606). Engraving, quarto. Emory University, Stuart A. Rose Manuscript, Archives, and Rare Book Library

Inasmuch as [the devil] himself first raises them on high through prideful arrogance, and causes them to stand as if above the Church, until they convince themselves that they know more than priests and theologians, and look down upon every power and judge that all things lie prostrate beneath their feet. But just as he exalts them sublimely in their own eyes, so profoundly does he precipitate them into the abyss of perdition.[29]

Galle positions heaven and the rocky perch of the Church (cf. *Matthew* 16:18) at the level of the viewer's eyes, and does the same with the hell scene, so that both may be experienced at first hand, as if one were actually in these respectively sublime and abject places, looking with the eyes of the devil and the heretic, before and after their eventual collapse into fiery damnation.

The motto emphasizes that the heavenly expulsion of Lucifer and his fellow angels and the expulsion of the heretic from the Church are closely analogous ('lapsus simillimus'), a point upon which the Latin epigram enlarges: 'What accords duly to the devil and the heretic? / The one falls from heaven, the other from the sacred citadel of faith'.[30] Ironically, the rebel angel and the apostate are alike precisely in their refusal to see themselves as like their fellow beings; in his commentary, David credits this observation to Gregory's *Regulae pastoralis seu curae pastoralis liber* 2.6: 'Like unto an apostate angel is fashioned the man who disdains to be like [other] men'.[31] He then quotes *Isaiah* 14:12–13, reading it as a prophetic image of the devilish Luther: 'How art thou fallen from heaven, O Lucifer, who didst rise in the morning? [...] And thou saidst in thy heart: I shall ascend into heaven'.[32] The image of Luther, argues David, reveals how apt is the similitude of the devil and the heretic ('ut ostendatur quanta sit diaboli et haeretici similitudo').[33] Finally, he circles back to Gregory, this time the *Moralia in Job* (*praef.* 6.15), wherein the prophet vividly 'depicts after the life' ('ad vivum depingit') Job's three false friends and thereby represents all heretics, indicting them as 'fabricators of mendacity, and cultivators

---

29　David, *Veridicus Christianus* 32: 'Illos siquidem ipse primum in sublime rapit per superbiae fastum; et quasi supra Ecclesiam statuit: dum sibi se plusquam sacerdotes omnesque doctores sapere persuadent: omnemque quasi ab alto despectant potestatem; et iam omnia sub pedibus suis strata arbitrantur. Sed quo illos in suis oculis exaltat sublimius, eo profundius illos in damnationis voraginem praecipitat'.

30　Ibidem 30 and *pictura* 10: 'Daemoni et Haeretico, quid quadrat rite duobus? / Ille polo, hic fidei sacrata corruit arce'.

31　Ibidem 30: 'Apostatae angelo similis efficitur homo, qui hominibus esse similis dedignatur'. Cf. *Sancti Gregorii Papae I. Regula pastoralis*, ed. Congregatio de propaganda fide (Rome: 1849) 37. David here treats apostasy and heresy as complementary evils.

32　Cf. David, *Veridicus Christianus* 31: 'Quomodo cecidisti de caelo, Lucifer? (Luther, inquam) qui mane oriebaris: qui dicebas in corde tuo: Ascendam'.

33　Ibidem.

of perverse dogmas' ('ostenditque esse fabricatores mendacii, et cultores per-
versorum dogmatum').[34] David musters these exegetical comparanda to call
attention to the pictorial form, function, and meaning of his own efforts: like
Gregory, he fashions a telling image that turns on the paradoxical relation
between similitude and dissimilitude; like Isaiah he alludes to heresy in a proleptic image of Luther; and again, like Gregory, he pictures devils and heretics in the guise of mendacious artificers. His chief purpose in following their
lead is to frustrate and thwart the complacent self-image that devilish heretics
endeavour to cultivate in their unsuspecting victims.

3   Eschatological Image-Making at the Threshold of the Visible in the
       Occasio arrepta, neglecta

Jan David's third major emblem book, *Occasio arrepta, neglecta; huius commoda, illius incommoda* (Occasion seized, shirked; advantages of the former,
disadvantages of the latter) (Antwerp, Jan Moretus: 1605), consists of twelve
schemata (figured or figurative images) accompanied by mottoes (above)
and dialogic subscriptions (below), and followed by exegetical commentaries
(*explicationes*) focusing on the relation between the *schemata* and relevant
passages from Scripture [Fig. 14.2].[35] The *picturae* enact scenes from a Latin
school play authored by David and added here as an appendix, *Occasio. Drama*,
which adapts the deliberative mode of dialogic moral argument characteristic
of *rederijker* theatre. Roman capitals coordinate the conversational texts and

---

34   Ibidem 32. Cf. Migne J.-P. (ed.), *Patrologia latina*, vol. 75: *Gregorius I* (Paris: 1862), *praef.*,
      col. 0525C.

35   On the book's production history, see Imhof, *Continuation of the Plantin Press* 224–227; on
      David's innovative appropriation of the theatrical conventions of *rederijker* drama and
      his interpolation of personifications into scenes of everyday life, see Sors, *Allegorische
      Andachtsbücher* 84–101; and Melion W.S., "Figured Personification and Parabolic Embod-
      iment in Jan David's *Occasio arrepta, neglecta*", in Melion – Ramakers B. (eds.), *Personifi-
      cation: Embodying Meaning and Emotion*, Intersections 41 (Leiden – Boston, MA: 2016)
      371–432. On the staging of dialogue, debate, and disputation as a characteristic feature
      of Dutch rhetorical theatre, see Ramakers B., "Embodied Wits: The Representation of
      Deliberative Thought in Rhetoricians' Drama", *Renaissance Studies* 32.1 (2018) 85–105; and
      idem, "Dutch Allegorical Theatre: Tradition and Conceptual Approach", in Strietman E. –
      Happé P. (eds.), *Urban Theatre in the Low Countries, 1400–1625* (Turnhout: 2006) 127–147.
      On the epistemological functions of debate in plays staged by Dutch and Flemish cham-
      bers of rhetoric, see Vandommele J., "Mirroring God, Reflecting Man: Shaping Identity
      through Knowledge in the Antwerp Plays of 1561", in Ramakers B. (ed.), *Classicising the
      Popular, Popularising the Classic (1540–1580)* (Leuven – Paris – Walpole, MA: 2011) 173–196.

the pictured dramatis personae who give voice to these mutual utterances; the letters also tally with specific passages in the commentary. The first two plates introduce the cast of characters who variously interact in the successive ten *schemata*: *Schema* 1, "Tempus et Occasio sua explicant munia" (Time and Occasion explain their offices), introduces the personifications of *Tempus* (Time) with his attributes (a scythe, hourglass, and celestial globe) and *Occasio* (Occasion) holding the signs of worldly accomplishment in one hand (a sidereal and planetary sphere, laurel branch, crown, wreath, and book of history) and, in the other, further signs of temporal honours (a sceptre, palm of victory, chain of office, precious vessel, and bulging money bag) along with signs of spiritual attainment (a crucifix topped by the dove of the Holy Spirit, as well as the palm frond again, this time construed as a spiritual attribute, i.e., the palm of martyrdom) [Figs. 14.14 and 14.15]. *Schema* 2, "Ad frugem vocat Angelus, avocat Diabolus" ([Guardian] Angel calls to virtue, the Devil away from it), brings other key characters forward: *Angelus* ([Guardian] Angel), *Diabolus* (Devil) and his *Demoni* (diabolic minions), and the emblem book's ten central characters: five *Adolescentes prudentes* (prudent boys) who, alert to the ministrations of their Guardian Angel, learn over the course of the book how and why every occasion of serving God and one's fellow men must be seized, and five *Adolescentes imprudentes* (imprudent boys) who, failing to heed the Angel's call, instead foolishly fall prey to the Devil's seductions and the vain enticements of the material world.

As David explains in his brief second preface, "Ad candidum lectorem" (To the fair reader), the *Occasio arrepta, neglecta* grew out of an earlier, simpler emblem book, *Typus occasionis: in quo receptae commoda, neglectae vero incommoda, personat schemate proponuntur* (Image of Occasion: in which the advantages of [Occasion] received and true disadvantages of [Occasion] neglected are set before the eyes).[36] Designed by the engraver print-publisher Theodore Galle, with whom David collaborated closely on all his emblem books, the *Typus* consists of the twelve prints later incorporated into the *Occasio*. Working with David, Galle drew the modelli, engraved the plates, and published the *Typus* in 1603. The *subscriptiones* were excerpted from an allegorical school play written by David on the subject of Occasion received or rejected, titled *Occasio. Drama*. When he incorporated this *Drama* into the *Occasio*, adding the playscript as an appendix, David made every effort to integrate it into

---

36   See David Jan, S.J., *Occasio arrepta, neglecta; huius commoda, illius incommode* (Antwerp, Ex officina Plantiniana, apud Ioannem Moretum: 1605) 273. This preface introduces the book's second part, which consists of the playscript, titled *Occasio. Drama*, on which the emblems in the first part were based.

FIGURE 14.14   Theodore Galle, Schema 1: "Tempus et Occasio sua explicant munia"
(Time and Occasion explain their offices), in Jan David, s.j., *Occasio
arrepta, neglecta; huius commoda, illius incommoda* (Antwerp, Ex officina
Plantiniana, apud Ioannem Moretum: 1605). Engraving, quarto. Emory
University, Stuart A. Rose Manuscript, Archives, and Rare Book Library

FIGURE 14.15   Theodore Galle, Schema 2: "Ad frugem vocat Angelus, avocat Diabolus" ([Guardian] Angel calls to virtue, the Devil away from it), in Jan David, s.j., *Occasio arrepta, neglecta; huius commoda, illius incommoda* (Antwerp, Ex officina Plantiniana, apud Ioannem Moretum: 1605). Engraving, quarto. Emory University, Stuart A. Rose Manuscript, Archives, and Rare Book Library

the emblem book's image-text apparatus; as he states: 'For the present, I should wish you to be advised that this Dialogue has been subdivided not into *scenas* (scenes), as it was formerly, but into *schemata*, so that it might correspond exactly to the book's selfsame images and every single part, and they might thereby receive light reciprocally'.[37]

Occasio arrepta, neglecta models the by turns moral or immoral behaviour of two sets of boys, inviting the reader-viewer to identify fully with the *Prudentes* and, to the extent s/he sees her- / himself mirrored by the *Imprudentes*, to change course, to embrace every occasion for good works that comes her / his way, and to do so in full consciousness of what is ultimately at stake – eternal salvation or damnation. At the last judgement, as David intimates throughout the *Occasio* and explicitly demonstrates in *Schemata* 11 and 12, divine approbation is shown to be the wages of occasion embraced, divine disapprobation the wages of occasion forsaken [Figs. 14.16 and 14.17]. Eschatology is thus the touchstone or, better, bedrock upon which David constructs his emblematic edifice. The final two emblems are the most reflexive in the sequence in that they not only centre on images portraying heaven and/or hell but also examine the process of eschatological image-making, dwelling upon the form and function of such images.

Schema 12, "Captatae, neglectaeque Occasionis dispares exitus" (The disparate ends of Occasion seized and shirked), differs markedly from the preceding *schemata*: they tend to position the five circumspect boys or their five dissolute counterparts front and centre, where their interactive conversations with Time, Occasion, Guardian Angel, and/or the Devil are staged; by contrast, this *schema* depicts three men, not five boys, engulfed by hellfire and accosted by the Devil (at left) and two demons who rise from the base of the image as if it were coterminous with hell [Fig. 14.17]. Indeed, the monstrous gaping jaws that directly confront the viewer, threatening to devour her / him, position the lower two-thirds of the picture within the infernal environs it describes. No other *schema* subsumes the viewer in this way, virtually swallowing her / him whole. The three men gazing upward, the middle of whom holds his arms aloft, direct their attention toward the five boys kneeling in heaven; whereas the three large men are near us, the celestial figures, suffused with divine light and flanked by two music-making angels, are small, distant, and barely discernible.

Schema 12, in all these respects, visualizes the post-mortem, post-judgement antithesis distilled by the motto: above and below, the consequences of having prized or misprized the occasion of doing good in this life are set squarely

---

37   Ibidem: 'Hoc interim te monitum velim. Dialogum hunc non iam in Scenas ut ante, sed in Schemata digestum; ut iconibus ipsis singulisque libri partibus examussim respondeat, sicque ab invicem lucem accipiant'.

FIGURE 14.16   Theodore Galle, Schema 11: "Angelus Diabolo praedam extorquet
                poenitentiam" ([Guardian] Angel wrests away the devil's prey for the
                purpose of penitence), in Jan David, S.J., *Occasio arrepta, neglecta; huius
                commoda, illius incommoda* (Antwerp, Ex officina Plantiniana, apud
                Ioannem Moretum: 1605). Engraving, quarto. Emory University, Stuart A.
                Rose Manuscript, Archives, and Rare Book Library

FIGURE 14.17   Theodore Galle, Schema 12: "Captatae, neglectaeque Occasionis dispares exitus" (The disparate ends of Occasion seized and neglected), in Jan David, s.j., *Occasio arrepta, neglecta; huius commoda, illius incommoda* (Antwerp, Ex officina Plantiniana, apud Ioannem Moretum: 1605). Engraving, quarto. Emory University, Stuart A. Rose Manuscript, Archives, and Rare Book Library

against each other. The dialogic subscription heightens this contrast.[38] From heaven the boys proclaim the 'supreme love' and 'unfailing gift of joy' conferred by a 'forgiving God from whose font numberless delights pour forth' ('A'). Joyful beyond measure, they give voice to an apothegm: 'Happy are they to whom Occasion is dear of heart!'. The three damned men lament their former indifference to Occasion, the cause of their current, irreversibly dire circumstances; for example, the man labelled 'B' declares: 'Time has departed; while I lived, scorned Occasion did withdraw. Fit to be pitied, I now pay the unceasing penalty of [my] foolishness'. Meanwhile, the Devil taunts the trapped souls: 'You sing idle [songs]: weeping does ever redouble sorrows' ('D'). His fellow demon brings up the rear by issuing a final apothegm, minatory where the first was celebratory: 'The Phrygians come late to know that "Behind, Occasion is bald"' ('F').[39] (The Phrygians were an ancient byword for indolence and stupidity; Occasion's baldness is an allusion to the conceit that if her forelock is not plucked as she hastens by, her bald head will offer no purchase, no second chance.)

The unbridgeable divide between heaven and hell that every soul will discover to have opened due to occasion seized and occasion shirked, constitutes the key theme of Emblem 12, which urges the reader-viewer to fashion a climactic meditative image of this yawning gap, as a therapeutic against negligence. The noticeable disparity in the representation of heaven and hell in *schema* 12, the distance and miniaturization of the one, the presence and largeness of the other, correlates to David's emphasis in his commentary on the two zones' very different conditions of representability. Whereas the horrors of sin and of sin's punishments, as Scripture reveals, are visualizable as deterrents to the commission of sin, the heavenly rewards of a life well lived are so transcendent that they exceed the human faculty of description:

> Even if everything capable of pleasing sight greatly, and whatever is wont to caress the ears, and every kind of beautiful, useful, graceful, precious,

---

38   Ibidem 246: 'Captatae neglectaeque Occasionis dispares exitus'.
39   Ibidem: 'A. O pietas suprema, et inenarrabile donum
      Laetitiae! Deus alme, tuo quot fonte redundant
      Gaudia! Felices, quibus est occasio cordi!
      B. Tempus iit; dum vixi Occasio spreta recessit:
      Do nunc stultitiae poenas miseranda perennes.
      C. Hei quanti constas Occasio Perdita; quanti!
      D. Vana canis: duplicant semper lamenta dolores.
      E. Me miseram, quantas parit haec amentia clades!
      Propterea horribiles infelix incolo flammas.
      F. Sero Phryges sapiunt: Post est Occasio calva'.

and good thing representable by the human heart were to be conjoined into one, yet could the whole of it not represent even in outline the wealth, splendour, felicity, and glory of the blessed.[40]

This assertion follows from David's reading of *Ecclesiasticus* 11:17, 'The gift of God abideth with the just', which he takes to mean that the nature and scope of such a reward is known to them alone who have earned it, and of 1 *Corinthians* 2:9: 'That eye hath not seen, nor ear heard: neither hath it entered into the heart of man, what things God hath prepared for them that love him'. David underscores this point by citing the story of the Queen of Saba's visit to King Solomon, as told in 3 *Kings* 10:4–8: when she finally lays eyes on Solomon himself and on his house, ministers, and holocausts, she realizes that they exceed all she had expected to see; in truth, things that once beggared belief are now confirmed more abundantly than words could possibly convey. In avowing that 'we see expressed in the Queen every commendable thing that we desired in the whole of [this] treatise' – 'the seizing of occasion offered, the earnest effort to pursue it, [and] expense, labour, and requisite perseverance [applied] toward an intended end'[41] – he yet recognizes that her experience in the here and now is incommensurable with the eschatological experience for which her face-to-face encounter with Solomon serves as an adumbrative allegory:

> For even if she had come to Jerusalem with much of her court and wealth, with camels bearing spices and gold beyond measure, and precious gems; yet was everything she brought and bore of little worth [...] before that which she observed at first hand when she was admitted into the sight of Solomon. Certain, too, is that which we learned to know above from Paul, not only 'The eye hath not seen, etc.', but also that which he asserts elsewhere [*Romans* 8:18]: 'For I reckon that the sufferings of this time are not worthy to be compared with the glory to come that shall be revealed to us'.[42]

---

40 Ibidem 248: 'Etiamsi omnia quae ad visum maxime oblectandum pertinent, et quaecumque aures demulcere solent, quaeque cor humanum in omni genere pulchra, utilis, grati, pretiosi et boni, sibi possit effingere, in unum essent conflata; nihil tamen universa conficerent, ad opes, splendorem, felicitatem, et gloriam beatorum adumbrandam'.

41 Ibidem 249: 'Ecce ut singula in hac Regina videmus expressa, quae toto tractatu commendata cupivimus!'.

42 Ibidem: 'Ut, tametsi illa Ierosolymam venisset multo cum comitatu et divitiis, cum camelis portantibus aromata et aurum infinitum nimis, et gemmas pretiosas; tamen nihili fecit omnia quae attulit et sustinuit [...] prae his quae re ipsa deprehendit, quando in

Heavenly glory, on this account, is barely or not at all representable, and accordingly, *Schema* 12, even while purporting to represent a portion of the celestial sphere where the saved perpetually abide, strips it of much detail and nearly removes it from view.

David circles back to this point in the final section of his commentary on Emblem 12, where he compares the structure of *Schema* 12 to the parabolic image of Dives and Lazarus recounted by Christ in *Luke* 16:19–30. For his failure to embrace Lazarus as an occasion of doing good, Dives becomes an exemplum of 'deplorable ruination' ('deploratum divitis epulonis exitium') for all those 'negligent observers of Occasion' who 'train their eyes' upon him ('negligentes Occasionis observatores [...] oculos reflectunt').[43] David thus invites the reader-viewer to amplify the parabolic image, implicitly on the model of *Schema* 12, by inhabiting the subject position of Dives who having died 'was buried in hell' and witnessed 'Abraham afar off and Lazarus in his bosom'.[44] S/he must concentratedly see her- / himself there with Dives, all connection to terrestrial things severed and the sufferings of hell experienced at first hand:

> Therefore, with [their] spirit abstracted a while from thoughts of other things, let them imagine that they see themselves amidst the torments of hell, and hear [Dives] crying out and saying: 'Father Abraham, have mercy on me; send Lazarus, that he may dip the tip of his finger in water to cool my tongue, for I am tormented in this flame'.[45]

On the contrary, Lazarus's heavenly reward is mentioned merely in passing; distant and unattainable, it manifests only cursorily, as something covetable yet inaccessible, just as in *Luke* 16. Without 'hope of relief', *Metanoea* (inconsolable regret) is all that Lazarus and the Lazarus-identified reader-viewer are left to feel ('mansit Metanoea; non quae solatii spem daret').[46]

Conversely, the infernal scene that fills the foreground of *Schema* 12, projecting outward, not only co-opts the beholder's attention but even appears

---

conspectum Salomonis admissa est. Ita certum quoque, non solum quod supra ex Paulo didicimus, *Nec oculus vidit*, etc. sed etiam quod idem alibi asseverat: *Non sunt condignae passiones huius temporis, ad futuram gloriam, quae revelabitur in nobis*'.

43   Ibidem 267.

44   *Luke* 16:22–23.

45   David, *Occasio arrepta, neglecta* 267: 'Abstracto igitur parumper ab aliarum rerum cogitatibus animo, fingant se inter tormenta gehennae videre, audireque clamantem, dicentemque: *Pater Abraham, miserere mei; et mitte Lazarum, ut intingat extremi digiti sui in aquam, ut refrigeret linguam meam, quia crucior in hac flamma*'.

46   Ibidem.

to reach out and incorporate her / him. The eschatology of final damnation, unlike its antitype, the eschatology of final salvation epitomized by the Queen of Saba's indescribable vision of Solomon, demands to be visualized as if it were occurring at the present moment, a *hic et nunc* without end, its horror a function of its infinite protraction. David dwells on the particulars of what *Schema* 12 gives us to see: for instance, he emphasizes that the three young men are not to be confused with the five foolish boys portrayed earlier, most recently in *Schema* 11, "Angelus Diabolo praedam extorquet ad poenitentiam" ([Guardian] Angel wrests away the devil's prey for the purpose of penitence): these five, having felt the stirrings of *Metanoea*, seized the occasion to repent, veritably by the skin of their teeth, before that fleeting opportunity had finally vanished.[47] The violent circumstances that now engulf the other three are to be represented with an eye to affective evils such as contempt and rage:

> And so, the matter at hand must be thought to be exhibited as if malev-
> olent spirits, having been denied their prey by the [Guardian] Angel of
> the five imprudent youths, were sating their rage by calling to mind the
> punishments of the other three whom at another time they had seduced
> to feel contempt for Occasion, seeing that divine power had snatched
> from their jaws the haul much desired and hoped-for. I have said these
> things to prevent doubt from arising in the reader-viewer who sees only
> three [youths] in infernal torment, whereas the number of those using
> Occasion for good or ill has thus far been fixed at five.[48]

David cites *Apocalypse* 21:7–8, making clear that it underlies the amplified image he urges the reader-viewer to picture to her- / himself in response to Galle's *Schema* 12:

> He that shall overcome (namely, as we recall *supra*, he who shall have
> fought the good fight, and [done] that for the purpose of preserving those
> things fit to be preserved: which all carry out who observe the Occasion
> of doing good) will possess these things [...]. But the haughty, and

---

47   Ibidem 226. In this context, *Metanoea* signifies penitent regret.
48   Ibidem 265: 'Itaque res illa exhiberi censenda est, atque si maligni spiritus, praeda illa
       sua quinque imprudentium iuvenum ab Angelo ereptorum frustrati, in recognoscenda
       trium aliorum poena, quos aliquando ad Occasionis contemtum seduxissent, suam
       exsaturarent rabiem, quandoquidem tam optatus bolus in illis quinque speratus, ipsis e
       faucibus sit divina potentia ereptus. Haec dixerim, ne tribus tantum in inferni tormento
       conspectus, dubium Lectori Spectatorique oboriatur, eo quod hactenus quinario numero
       et bene et male Occasione utentes constiterint'.

unbelieving, and the abominable, and murderers, and whoremongers, and sorcerers, and idolaters, and all liars, they shall have their portion in the pool burning with fire and brimstone, which is the second death.[49]

Further, he invokes *Wisdom* 5:2–6, which describes the terrible fear to be felt by wicked men when they see the good souls they had once mocked now glorified in heaven, and realize that having erred from the way of truth, they have permanently lost the 'light of justice' and 'sun of understanding'.[50] *Schema* 12, by showing the three damned souls over-mantled by the mouth of hell and lit from the left, unlike the five saved souls who are lit from the right, indicates how altered their condition will be in the end-time when they are brought to perdition.

Why, we may ask, did David choose to conclude *Occasio arrepta, neglecta* on such an alarming note, centring his final emblem on an eschatological image unbridgeably divided into two zones, the lowermost of which engulfs the beholder? The answer has to do with his understanding of the psychology of the human soul. Humankind, as he explains in the penultimate section of his *explicatio* of *Schema* 12, is all too prone to confuse the occasion of doing good with the opportunity of doing evil. True occasion never leads to sin, whereas sinful men, when they seize the opportunity of committing a wicked deed, confuse *Opportunitas*, the mere image or semblance of *Occasio*, with God-given occasion. They exemplify the sort of behaviour condemned in *Romans* 7:8: 'But sin, taking occasion by the commandment, wrought in me all manner of concupiscence', and *Romans* 7:11: 'For sin, taking occasion by the commandment, seduced me: and by it killed me'. Moreover, they prove Ovid right when he says in *Amores* III.iv.17: 'We are ever striving after what is forbidden, and coveting what is denied us'.[51] Such sinners by their transgressions 'have seized the occasion of sin not given' ('occasionem [...] acceperunt non datam'). Like Judas, who complained, in *John* 12:4–6, about the Magdalene's extravagant use of spikenard to anoint the feet of Christ, or like the thief who sees money lying in an open place and takes it for a 'certain image of the occasion for theft' ('speciem quamdam occasionis furandi'), they are confounded by an image of something not inherently bad which they falsely construe as an

---

49   Ibidem: '*Qui vicerit* (hoc est, ut supra meminimus, qui bonum certamen certaverit, idque legitime servatis servandis: quod faciunt qui omnem bene agendi Occasionem observant) *possidebit haec* [...]. *Tumidis autem, et incredulis, et exsecratis, et homicidis, fornicatoribus, et veneficis, et idololatris, et omnibus mendacibus, pars illorum erit in stagno ardenti igni et sulphure, quod est mors secunda'.*

50   Ibidem 266.

51   Ibidem 261: 'Iuxta illud: *Nitimur in vetitum semper, cupimusque negata'.*

excuse for their own evildoing.[52] So, too, there are persons who, upon hearing what the ten commandments forbid, find themselves impelled to recall those very things as if they were being invited to enact them: 'but a man's evil proclivity to sin did illicitly receive the occasion to sin from the commandment: so that remembering sin, he might perpetrate by the selfsame law that which he saw was forbidden by the commandment'.[53] David thus emphasizes that the ease whereby the image of sin becomes in man an 'occasion' or, more precisely, an 'opportunity' to sin must be combatted by means of a counter-image having the power to move the proto-sinner in the direction of virtue. *Schema* 12 is the eschatological image he puts forward as a therapeutic counteragent: by blocking the impulse to confound true occasion with false opportunity, he attempts to prevent the delusory arrogation of the former and lays bare the exploitative use of the latter.[54]

Above all, as David asserts in section 2 of Emblem 12, the exercitant will prime her- / himself to seize virtuous occasion and neglect errant opportunity if s/he holds fast to the image of Christ in the flesh, bodied forth through the mystery of the Incarnation, and layers upon it the image of Christ the just judge who will come again to bestow salvation upon all who merit to be saved:

> Therefore, the delight in his advent will be the cause of the acquisition of glory for all those who have not neglected [occasion]; those who have held fast to the advent of Christ in the flesh as a great benefit vouchsafed to miserable, mortal men; those who in faith, with the whole of their heart have received him coming forth, and who with great charity have done him service as their soul's most dear guest; and those who by diligent preparation of a good life have come to meet him who shall come to offer judgement; they have done nothing but what they foreknew was according to his purpose.[55]

---

52   Ibidem.

53   Ibidem: 'sed malam hominis ad peccatum proclivitatem accepisse occasionem illegitime ex mandato: ut, quod videret in mandato prohiberi, hoc ipsa, quasi per mandatum memor peccati facta, perpetraret'.

54   See ibidem 263: 'Si arripit, occasio iusta non est, sed illicite usurpata'.

55   Ibidem 250–251: 'Dilectio igitur adventus eius, causa erit gloriae adipiscendae omnibus qui non neglexerint: qui adventum Christi in carnem pro magno beneficio miseris mortalibus concesso tenuerint, qui illum per fidem toto corde venientem susceperint, eique ut gratissimo animae suae hospiti magna serviverint caritate; quique venturo ad iudicium diligenti bonae vitae praeparatione occurrerint; nihil non fecerint eorum quae ex mente eius esse praesciverunt'.

The devil with weapons raised (a club and a grappling hook) and the two demons who join him in attacking the three trapped souls clearly allude to one of David's key themes, distilled from his reading of *Apocalypse* 2, 3, and 21: namely, that the effort to seize virtuous occasion, far from operating serendipitously, is analogous to mortal combat intentionally waged against the devilish forces that impede access to every such occasion or, alternatively, mask sinful opportunity under the guise of licit occasion. David has in mind passages such as *Apocalypse* 2:7: 'To him that overcometh I will give to eat of the tree of life which is in the paradise of my God'; *Apocalypse* 3:5: 'He that shall overcome shall thus be clothed in white garments'; and *Apocalypse* 21:7: 'He that shall overcome shall possess these things. And I will be his God'. In section 2, he sees through *Schema* 12 to these biblical excerpts, implicitly arguing that close perusal of the pictorial image enables the reader-viewer better to see the verbal images that *Apocalypse* 2, 3, and 21 place before her / his eyes. Salvation can be gained only by fighting the good fight against the forces of darkness that obscure the nature and scope of true occasion:

> If we direct the mind / heart to the preceding [passages], we shall see set before the eyes in almost every single word either the effort to seize salutary Occasion in the manner of men fighting for favour, or the reward of [Occasion] heeded. [...]
>
> For whenever struggles of this kind are adduced, so too, rewards and rules of engagement are divulged: nay rather, with great amplitude and by contemplative means things fit to be seen attentively by the eyes of all are exhibited. And what, I pray, is this other than sedulously to observe the due Occasion and opportunity of doing what ought to be done well and properly?[56]

Developing his argument, David contrasts the three lost souls for whom Occasion once spurned is now altogether lost (as the *subscriptiones* put it, 'Occasio spreta' has become 'Occasio perdita') with the Magdalene, the biblical figure who most fully and forcefully embraced Christ's call to sinners to reform

---

56 Ibidem 252: 'Si ad praecedentia mentem adverterimus, videbimus, in singulis fere dictionibus, vel Occasionis salutaris arripiendae stadium, certantium more commendari, vel praemium observatae proponi'. [...]

'Quandocumque enim eiusmodi certamina proponuntur, praemia quoque et leges certaminis evulgantur: immo magna cum amplitudine inspiciendique facultate oculis omnium conspicienda exhibentur. Et quid, quaeso, hoc aliud est, quam rerum omnium bene ac legitime gerendarum, debitam Occasionem et opportunitatem sedulo observare?'.

themselves.[57] 'She sought and found occasion at Christ's feet', states David, adding as further images of her hard-won struggle the analogy of a cart slid into the mire or of a draught animal stuck in mud, which it is incumbent upon the carter or herdsman to extricate.[58] In seizing the occasion of penitence, she not only beheld Occasion but made it, through her example, pellucidly visible for our benefit. David paraphrases *Luke* 7:37–38: 'And he went into the house of the Pharisee and sat down to meat. And behold (behold, I say, Occasion worthy of love, desired, divinely given) a woman that was in the city, when she knew that he sat at meat in the Pharisee's house, brought an alabaster box of ointment'. In a remarkable passage, David entirely conflates Occasion and the Magdalene, making the personification and the person indivisible:

> But what do we? Wherefore are we brought to account? While we our-
> selves strive with eyes intent upon Occasion offered for the purpose of
> noble deeds, we have left the same unnamed and almost unremarked.
> I confess that in narrating the real and speedy embrace of [Occasion],
> and in examining the good deeds that came thereafter, we have left that
> one herself unmentioned in her place, where she was presenting herself
> at first blush.[59]

The strategic conflation of Occasion and the Magdalene is a way for David to emphasize the theme of agency: the person who grabs hold of good occasion becomes, like the Magdalene, the agentive instrument through which salvation is secured; and in exemplifying this truth for us, the Magdalene converts her-self into the occasion for our own efforts, modelled on hers, to save ourselves. This being the case, occasion and agency are presented as mutually determina-tive. David underscores this point by admonishing the reader-viewer to follow the Magdalene in eschewing illusory social niceties: just as she paid no regard to the qualms of Judas or the Pharisees, so must we not let the fear of importu-nity or indecorum hold us back from taking advantage of every occasion that

---

57   See note 55 *supra*.

58   Ibidem 257: 'Occasionem ad Christi pedes quaerebat, et inveniebat'.

59   Ibidem: 'At, quid agimus? Quo delati sumus? Dum Occasionem ipsi ad tam praeclara
     oblatam intentis oculis consectamur, eamdem innominatam et vix notatam praeterivi-
     mus. Fateor, dum in reali festinantique eius amplexu narrando, bonisque inde subsecu-
     tis recensendis abripimur, illam ipsam suo loco non indicavimus, ubi se prima fronte
     offerebat'.

arises to achieve good things: such misgivings are like 'soot' ('fuliginem') and must be wiped away from wherever they obscure the face of Occasion.[60]

The eschatological theme of vanished agency is central, of course, to the manner and meaning of *Schema* 12 that features three damned souls for whom all occasion is now lost. Gone are the mediating personifications – *Tempus* or *Occasio* herself – whose presence had previously fortified the *prudentes* and reproached the *imprudentes*, urging them to do good. Gone, too, is the Guardian Angel who once guided and admonished. And most conspicuous by his absence is God the Father, who presided over Time, Occasion, Guardian Angel, and the two groups of five boys in *Schemata* 1, 4, 5, and 11: he has absconded from the souls' blinkered field of vision [Figs. 14.14, 14.16, and 14.18]. The theatrical format of the prior *schemata*, consisting of a kind of stage somewhat removed from its putative audience, upon which the players are seen to interact, coming and going as they recite their lines for the instructional benefit of a reader-viewer whose behaviour is thereby presumed to be amendable, has been displaced by a new format that fully implicates the beholder, placing her / him with the damned souls. By showing what it means to have lost occasion and with it all hope, *Schema* 12 itself offers, in a spirit of doleful irony, the occasion for changing oneself for the better, before the breach between the saved and the damned irremediably widens.

The difference between the eschatological final *schema* and the eleven *schemata* that precede it becomes all the more apparent if we look closely at *Schema* 11, "Angelus Diabolo praedam extorquet poenitentiam" [Fig. 14.17]. Emblem 11 deals with the kinds of affective power latent in David's eschatological imagery: he cautions the reader-viewer that images of hellfire and final damnation can function either positively or negatively, stirring feelings of penitential remorse that lead to acts of contrition or, adversely, feelings of despair and desperation that immobilize the soul, curbing the process of self-reformation. *Schema* 11 depicts the final decisive encounter between the five foolish boys and their ministering angel whose emphatic gesture of address indicates that he has summoned up, in their mind's eye, the lowering hell scene at right. Faced by the terrifying prospect of final damnation, they abruptly turn away, literally enacting the pivotal moment of conversion; God presides from on high, his arms extended in a gesture of blessing. Hastening toward the angel, the boys declare: 'My guardian angel, preserve, defend, and

---

60   See ibidem 258. David celebrates the Magdalene for doing precisely this: 'Ecce, ut a splendida Occasionis facie obscuram importunitatis et impudentiae fuliginem, qua obnubilari videbatur, abstergit!'.

FIGURE 14.18   Theodore Galle, Schema 4: "Stimulante Daemone, misere eluditur
Occasio" (By the Devil's urging, Occasion is pitiably mocked), in
Jan David, s.j., *Occasio arrepta, neglecta; huius commoda, illius
incommoda* (Antwerp, Ex officina Plantiniana, apud Ioannem
Moretum: 1605). Engraving, quarto. Emory University, Stuart A.
Rose Manuscript, Archives, and Rare Book Library

govern me entrusted to you by divine love'.[61] The chain with which the devil had lately bound them now lies broken on the ground. Despairing of his lost prey, Satan crouches at the threshold of hell, stopping his ears to muffle the sound of the Guardian Angel's voice, which commands: 'Hence, hence to Orcus, [you] odious plague of Erebus, with your wild beasts most evil: this food is not owed to your jaws so black' ('A'). Meanwhile, the boys entreat their angelic companion to look upon them as his clients ('clientes'), and to ensure that even after the occasion for material honours has passed, the occasion for the atonement of sins be still sufficient to prevent eternal death ('B'). Guardian Angel responds by adjuring the boys to let the dangers set before them make them duly circumspect ('A bis').[62] The *explicatio*, section 2 in particular, identifies *Metanoea* as the efficacious antidote to sinful negligence, alone capable of spiriting the sinner from the jaws of hell to safe harbour. Two eschatologies, eternal damnation and eternal glory, are to be visualized as if placed in the balance, their equivalent weights evenly distributed, with the sinner poised between them. If s/he exercises true contrition, the person holding the scales will find her- / himself empowered not merely to tip them but more importantly to transform the contents of one pan into that of the other, so that evil is turned into good, and sin becomes virtue. David, to drive his point home, invokes the image of the good thief upon the cross; by his newfound faith, the good thief ceases to be a criminal who suffers judicial punishment and instead becomes a 'just man, herald of the divine word, professor and confessor of the faith, and (as some of the Fathers said) is even made into a martyr'.[63] David enlarges upon this paradigmatic image of commutation, as follows:

> Inasmuch as enduring death freely in the name of Christ and for love of him, [a death] to which he had been condemned on account of [his] crimes and in such measure delivered, and making a virtue of necessity

---

61   Ibidem 226 (engraved on the banderole): 'Angele qui meus es custos, pietate superna / Me tibi commissum serva, defende, guberna'.

62   Ibidem: 'A. Hinc, hinc foeda lues Erebi, fera pessima, ad Orcum:
Non haec tam furvis debetur faucibus esca.
B. Angele, fide comes, nostraeque salutis amator,
Quaeso, tuere tuos deinceps hac lege clientes;
Ut, licet ad magnos posthac Occasio honores
Et Tempus miseris periit; tamen illa supersit
Ansa, patrocinio vestro, quae rite piandis
Commissis satis esse queat: ne morte luamus
Aeterna, et nunquam liceat sperare salutem.
A. Faxo, modo faciant praemissa pericula cautos'.

63   Ibidem 228: '[...] ut ex latrone non solum iustus, praeco verbi divini, fidei professor et confessor, verumetiam (ut nonnulli veterum locuti sunt) martyr effectus sit'.

in the tribunal of his conscience, he by a salutary resolution commuted guilt into merit, offence into reward, just and proper punishment into the palm of martyrdom.[64]

Citing Saint Cyprian's *Sermo de Coena Domini* (Sermon on the Lord's Supper), he adds that the thief's contrite heart, in converting capital punishment into martyrdom, also converted blood into baptism.[65] The good thief, mustered as a quintessential image of conversion, has the power to confront and over-throw the devil's stratagems, designed as they are to forestall compunction by deflecting persons from the path of virtue. Underlying David's remarks is the parabolic image of the two paths, in *Matthew* 7:13–14:

> And so, champions of both sexes have behaved prudently and laudably: well-nigh at life's end, having been seduced by the devil's wiles, having strayed through the lonely, steep places of vice, a thousand occasions of salvation and true glory having been ignored and scorned, they were finally touched interiorly by true sorrow of heart, stirred to compunction so great that in proportion as the road to life was longer and the space of time briefer, so with greater exertion of the spirit did they race more speedily through the [narrow] path of penitence and virtues.[66]

Most invidiously, Satan tricks by means of images strategically deployed to convince unwary victims that a change of heart is pointless; frozen by despair, they come to believe that the only 'salvation', in the sense of solace, available to those whom sin has vanquished is to give up all hope of salvation. On this view, resigned despair alone provides consolation, a sort of hollow peace, to the sinful heart: 'But the malign inciter places before their eyes and spirit solely that which, in the place of comfort most ready to hand, he whispers in both

---

64   Ibidem: 'Mortem siquidem, cui propter scelera fuerat adiudicatus, et eousque traditus, pro Christi nomine et amore libenter sustinens, faciensque in tribunali conscientiae suae de necessitate virtutem, ex culpa meritum, et praemium ex reatu, iustum debitumque sceleribus supplicium in martyrii palmam, salutari consilio commutavit'.

65   Ibidem 229: 'Sed cor contritum poenam mutavit in martyrium, et sanguinem in bap-tismum'. Cf. *S. Caecilii Cypriani opera*, ed. Joannis Fellus (Amsterdam, Apud Joannem Ludovicum de Lorme: 1700) 77.

66   David, *Occasio arrepta, neglecta* 229: 'Prudenter itaque ac laudabiliter omnes utriusque sexus Athletae fecerunt, qui ad finem ferme vitae, diaboli fraudibus illecti, mille salutis et verae gloriae neglectis irrisisque occasionibus, per devia et abrupta vitiorum erraverant, et tandem vero cordis dolore tacti intrinsecus, ad tantam emolliti sunt compunctionem, ut quo longior restaret via ad vitam et brevius spatium temporis, eo celerius maiorique contentione animi, per poenitentiae virtutumque semitam, properarent'.

ears of those so disposed'.[67] David marshals parabolic images as a corrective to the devil's sly susurrations; here as elsewhere in the *Occasio arrepta, neglecta* he laminates them onto his emblematic *schema*, construing his image-making as complementary to Christ's. As he puts it, just as a horse or rider, if they fall strive immediately to rise, and a cord or thread, if broken, is forthwith repaired with a strong knot, so a 'quill, small brush, or scalpel that has erred ought at once to be corrected'.[68] And so, too, must the devil's false images be remedied, and amended images set in their place: 'If something is lost, let it be found: for that reason, if you have sinned, fallen, rise again through penitence'.[69] The similes taken from the art of drawing, painting, or sculpting accentuate David's point that meditative image-making like his offers the best defence against the seductive properties of devilish false images. The reflexive indeed meta-discursive character of this kind of image-making becomes all the more apparent in the specific context of the *Occasio arrepta, neglecta*, whose *picturae* can be construed as doubly representational: *schemata* of twelve scenes from an erstwhile school play and, as such, pictures of performative enactments that model for the exercitant the nature of her / his engagement or disengagement with *Occasio*.

David invokes four further parables that have the power to shore up the penitent sinner by limning the mercy of an ever forgiving God: the parable of the unjust steward, in *Luke* 16:1–8, who weathered imminent disgrace and ruination, his resiliency finally earning his lord's commendation; the parable of the lost sheep, in *Matthew* 18:12–14, which represents, as if 'painted only lightly in outline by a small brush' ('penicillo solum leviter adumbravit'), the benignity of Christ toward sinners whom he finds ready to return to the fold; the parable of the old woman, in *Luke* 15:8–10, who searched unceasingly for a lost drachma until she finally found it;[70] and the parable of the prodigal son, in *Luke* 15:11–32, which depicts the love of God so forcefully that the parables just cited appear by comparison to be mere preliminary drawings ('praeviam delineationem'): 'But how does that most efficacious evidence of divine goodness in the prodigal son not mollify the sinner's heart, making it swerve into the orbit of grace when before, the other parabolic exempla did but exhibit the preliminary drawing of this living change of heart and return to grace?'.[71] In

---

67   Ibidem 231: 'sed hoc unum oculis animoque obversetur, quod taliter constitutis, loco solatii praesentissimi, in utramque insusurrat aurem malignus incentor'.

68   Ibidem: 'si penna, penicillum, vel scalpellum errarit, corrigatur extemplo'.

69   Ibidem: 'sic, si peccasti, lapsus es, resurge per poenitentiam'.

70   Ibidem 232.

71   Ibidem: 'Sed quomodo non efficacissimum illud in filio prodigo bonitatis divinae argumentum pectus peccatoris emolliat, ut in veniae ambitum inflectatur, cum reliqua

characterizing this final parable as a living image that brings fully to light what the prior parables have merely adumbrated, David evokes the tried-and-true comparison between a preparatory drawing and a finished painting. He thus strengthens his case that eschatological imagery, if properly handled and tempered by complementary scriptural images, especially images expressive of divine love, can transform their users, encouraging them to seize the occasion of penitence to remedy themselves.

4   Eschatological Image-Making and the Heart's Propagation of Christ in the *Pancarpium Marianum*

Produced two years after the *Occasio arrepta, neglecta,* David's next emblem book, the *Pancarpium Marianum, septemplici titulorum serie distinctum* (Marian garland, serially divided into sevenfold titles) (Antwerp, Jan Moretus: 1607) was designed to function in concert with its emblematic pendant, the *Messis myrrhae et aromatum, ex instrumentis ac mysteriis Passionis Christi colligenda* (Harvest of myrrh and aromatic herbs, gathered from the instruments and mysteries of the Passion of Christ) [Figs. 14.3 and 14.9].[72] The joint title of the *Messis* and *Pancarpium* together is *Paradisus Sponsi et Sponsae* (Paradise of the bridegroom and bride) [Fig. 14.9]. Having worked her / his way through the fifty Passion emblems comprised by the garden imagery of the *Messis*, the reader-viewer was expected to enter a second garden, this one consisting of fifty Marian emblems that focus on fifty aspects of her floriferous maternal relation to Christ. This second sequence of fifty emblems is in turn subdivided

---

praecedentium parabolarum exempla, vividae huius resipiscentiae et reditus in gratiam praeviam exhibuerint delineationem?'.

72 On the book's production history, see Imhof, *Continuation of the Plantin Press* 227–229. On the distinctive paired structure of the *Messis* and the *Pancarpium*, see Delfosse A., *La 'Protectrice du Païs-Bas': Stratégies politiques et figures de la Vierge dans les Pays-Bas espagnols* (Turnhout: 2009) 215–216; Melion W.S., "Meditative Images and the Portrayal of Image-Based Meditation", in Melion – Dekoninck R. – Guiderdoni-Bruslé (eds.), *Ut pictura meditatio: The Meditative Image in Northern Art, 1500–1700* (Turnhout: 2012) 7–60, esp. 32–60; idem, *The Meditative Art: Studies in the Northern Devotional Print, 1550–1625,* Early Modern Catholicism and the Visual Arts 1 (Philadelphia, PA: 2012) 334, 336–339; Sors, *Allegorische Andachtsbücher* 102–115; Melion W.S., "*Emblemata solitariae Passionis*: Jan David, s.j., on the Solitary Passion of Christ", in Enenkel K. – Göttler C. (eds.), *Spaces, Places, and Times of Solitude in Late Medieval and Early Modern Cultures,* Intersections 56 (Leiden – Boston, MA: 2018) 242–289; and idem, "*De Virgine natalitia ad rapientem*: Marian Maternity, Militancy, and Mimesis in the First Marian Emblem Book – Jan David, s.j.'s *Pancarpium Marianum* of 1607", *Emblematica: Essays in Word and Image* 4 (2021) 139–209.

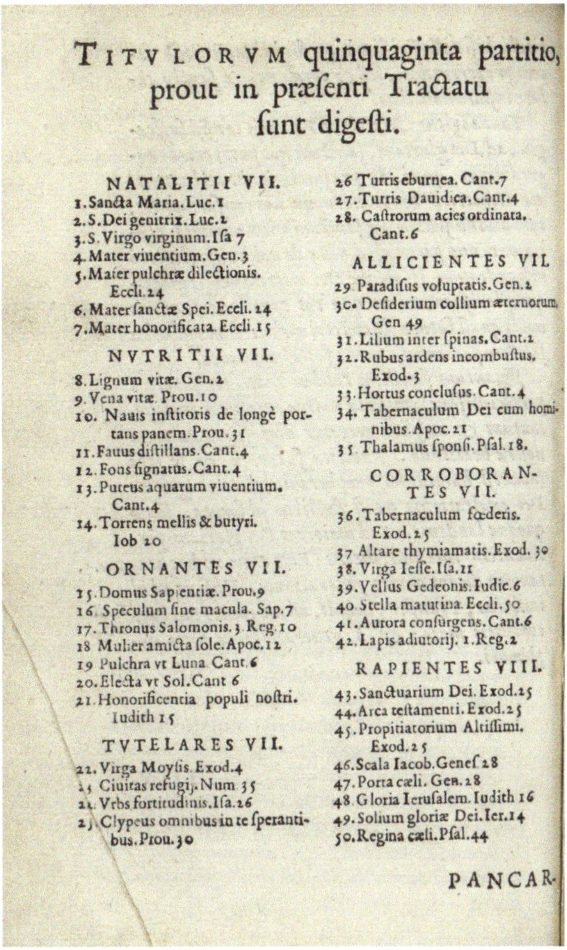

TITVLORVM quinquaginta partitio, prout in præfenti Tractatu funt digefti.

NATALITII VII.
1. Sancta Maria. Luc.1
2. S. Dei genitrix. Luc.1
3. S. Virgo virginum. Ifa 7
4. Mater viuentium. Gen.3
5. Mater pulchræ dilectionis. Eccli.24
6. Mater fanctæ Spei. Eccli.24
7. Mater honorificata. Eccli.15

NVTRITII VII.
8. Lignum vitæ. Gen.2
9. Vena vitæ. Prou.10
10. Nauis inftitoris de longè portans panem. Prou.31
11. Fauus diftillans. Cant.4
12. Fons fignatus. Cant.4
13. Puteus aquarum viuentium. Cant.4
14. Torrens mellis & butyri. Iob 20

ORNANTES VII.
15. Domus Sapientiæ. Prou.9
16. Speculum fine macula. Sap.7
17. Thronus Salomonis.3 Reg.10
18. Mulier amicta fole. Apoc.12
19 Pulchra vt Luna. Cant.6
20. Electa vt Sol. Cant 6
21. Honorificentia populi noftri. Iudith 15

TVTELARES VII.
22. Virga Moyfis. Exod.4
23. Ciuitas refugij. Num 35
24. Vrbs fortitudinis. Ifa.26
25. Clypeus omnibus in te fperantibus. Prou.30

26 Turris eburnea. Cant.7
27. Turris Dauidica. Cant.4
28. Caftrorum acies ordinata. Cant.6

ALLICIENTES VII.
29. Paradifus voluptatis. Gen.2
30. Defiderium collium æternorum. Gen 49
31. Lilium inter fpinas. Cant.2
32. Rubus ardens incombuftus. Exod.3
33. Hortus conclufus. Cant.4
34. Tabernaculum Dei cum hominibus. Apoc.21
35 Thalamus fponfi. Pfal.18.

CORROBORANTES VII.
36. Tabernaculum fœderis. Exod.25
37 Altare thymiamatis. Exod.30
38. Virga Ieffe. Ifa.11
39. Vellus Gedeonis. Iudic.6
40. Stella matutina. Eccli.50
41. Aurora confurgens. Cant.6
42. Lapis adiutorij. 1. Reg.2

RAPIENTES VIII.
43. Sanctuarium Dei. Exod.25
44. Arca teftamenti. Exod.25
45. Propitiatorium Altiffimi. Exod.25
46. Scala Iacob. Genef 28
47. Porta cæli. Gen.28
48. Gloria Ierufalem. Iudith 16
49. Solium gloriæ Dei. Ier.14
50. Regina cæli. Pfal.44

PANCAR-

FIGURE 14.19

"Titulorum quinquaginta partitio, prout in praesenti Tractatu sunt digesti" (Division of the fifty titles, as arranged in the present Treatise), in Jan David, s.j., *Pancarpium Marianum, Septemplici Titulorum serie distinctum: ut in B. Virginis odorem curramus, et Christus formetur in nobis* (Antwerp, Ex officina Plantiniana, apud Balthasarem et Ioannem Moretos: 1607; reprint ed., 1618), fol. + 8v. Engraving, octavo. Emory University, Stuart A. Rose Manuscript, Archives, and Rare Book Library

into seven groups of seven emblems (plus a concluding fiftieth), each group a celebration of one of seven kinds of relation between Mary and Christ incarnate: first, natal; second, nutritive; third, ornamental; fourth, tutelary; fifth, attractive; sixth, defensive; and seventh, capturing / captivating [Fig. 14.19]. The book returns to the format of the *Veridicus Christianus*: above the image, a motto; below, epigrams in Latin, Dutch, and French; in the image, Roman capitals that correlate to specified subsections of the four–five page commentaries anchored by the engravings. Throughout the *Pancarpium*, Christ, generally shown as a child, stands for the spiritual image of Jesus that the votary respectively imitates Mary in propagating; this 'spiritualis prolis' (spiritual offspring) is first carried to term, then nourished, adorned, instructed, attracted, defended, and held captive in proportion as he holds captive /

MELION

captivates.[73] Within the sequence, eschatological images are featured in two places: Emblem 18, "Mulier amicta sole" (Woman clothed by the sun), and Emblem 50, "Regina caeli" (Queen of Heaven) [Figs. 14.20 and 14.21].

Emblem 18 forms part of the seven titles that centre on ornamenting the image of Christ within [Fig. 14.20]. The emblematic *pictura* displays ('A') the woman clothed by the sun, ('B') radiant with dazzling light, ('D') constant unlike the inconstant moon, ('E') more bright than the sun, moon, and stars, ('C') prefigured by the burning bush from out of which God spoke to Moses, and ('F') by the visionary golden light of the Virgin and Child revealed by the sibyl to the emperor Augustus. The Latin subscription addresses the reader-viewer as if s/he were John, asking her / him to consider whom s/he sees on high: 'Clearer, greater than the splendour flashing in the sun, whom do you, placed on earth, see above the stars?'.[74] David explains in the preface to this subset of emblems that his topic is internal not external adornment, moral not superficial beauty, spiritual light not sunlight. Citing *Psalm* 44:14, 'All the glory of the king's daughter is within in golden borders, clothed round about with varieties', he compares the rays of light emanating from the Virgin to golden threads wisely worked in an orderly fashion to the highest degree of perfection; radiance is her spiritual raiment that supersedes actual cloth of gold.[75]

In Emblem 18, the vision of the woman clothed by the sun, whose presence inaugurates the events prophesied in *Apocalypse* 12, serves to represent the mystery of spiritual union that binds Jesus and Mary, presaging our own contemplative merger with Christ. As the entwinement of Virgin and Child enhances their beauty, so by uniting prayerfully with Christ in imitation of Mary, we and he are mutually embellished, we by his presence, he by our devotion. To put this another way, meditating upon the nature of this eschatological sign encourages us to clothe ourselves internally in the light of Christ, newborn within us; as she was clothed in the fiery splendour of the sun of justice, so we, through the spiritual exercise of meditating Emblem 18, endeavour to become luminously apparelled by Christ. The eschatological sign, seen in this

---

73   David expands upon his aim of rearing / fostering / educating the exercitant's spiritual offspring in the three preambles to the *Pancarpium*; see David Jan, s.j., *Pancarpium Marianum, Septemplici Titulorum serie distinctum: ut in B. Virginis odorem curramus, et Christus formetur in nobis*, in *Paradisus Sponsi et Sponsae: in quo Messis myrrhae et aromatum ex instrumentis ac mysteriis Passionis Christi colligenda, et Pancarpium Marianum* (Antwerp, Ex officina Plantiniana apud Ioannem Moretum: 1607; reprint ed., 1618), fols. t4 r–t8 r.

74   Ibidem 76 and *pictura* 18: 'Clarior, an maior, rutilo quae in sole coruscat, / In terris positus, quam super astra vides?'.

75   Ibidem 64: "In VII. Titulus ornantes argumentum".

FIGURE 14.20   Theodore Galle, Emblem 18: "Mulier amicta sole" (Woman
clothed by the sun), in Jan David, s.j., *Pancarpium Marianum,
Septemplici Titulorum serie distinctum: ut in B. Virginis odorem
curramus, et Christus formetur in nobis* (Antwerp, Ex officina
Plantiniana, apud Balthasarem et Ioannem Moretos: 1607;
reprint ed., 1618). Engraving, octavo. Emory University, Stuart A.
Rose Manuscript, Archives, and Rare Book Library

FIGURE 14.21   Theodore Galle, Emblem 50: "Regina caeli" (Queen of
                heaven), in Jan David, s.j., *Pancarpium Marianum, Septemplici
                Titulorum serie distinctum: ut in B. Virginis odorem curramus,
                et Christus formetur in nobis* (Antwerp, Ex officina Plantiniana,
                apud Balthasarem et Ioannem Moretos: 1607; reprint
                ed., 1618). Engraving, octavo. Emory University, Stuart A.
                Rose Manuscript, Archives, and Rare Book Library

way, signifies the exercitant's desire to be subsumed into Christ who yet lodges within her / him.

With reference to Moses and the burning bush, in *Exodus* 3, which David takes for a type of John's solar vison, the woman in the sun is interpreted as an heuristic instrument through whom Paul's account of the second coming of Christ in 1 *Timothy* 6:14–16 may be grasped, partially if not wholly:

> That thou keep the commandment without spot, blameless, unto the coming of our Lord Jesus Christ, which in his times he shall shew, who is the Blessed and only Mighty, the King of kings and Lord of lords: who only hath immortality and inhabiteth light inaccessible: whom no man hath seen, nor can see: to whom be honour and empire everlasting. Amen.

Visualizing Mary as the woman in the sun enables the votary better to imagine how a living creature can come indissolubly to dwell in that divine light, in the manner of Mary who dressed Christ in the substance of human flesh, and conversely, was dressed by him in ineffable glory:

> Wherefore, O Mary, bright light of the Church, singular solace of the afflicted, let it for a time be permitted me to discourse with the mellifluous words of your peerless friend (i.e., Saint Bernard) upon the majesty of this title. Just as it was granted you to be clothed by God, the sun of justice, you who entered most deeply into the abyss of divine wisdom, more even than can be believed, as much as the condition of a created being allows, short only of the union of personhood, so were you seen to be immersed in that inaccessible light. In truth, great [was] the familiarity, but altogether astonishing the closeness of the sun and the woman. For how is it that fragile [human] nature abides in such raging heat. Justly indeed, holy Moses, do you admire and curiously desire to observe [it]?[76]

---

76   Ibidem 76–77: 'Quapropter, o Maria, praeclarum Ecclesiae lumen, et afflictorum singulare solatium, liceat mihi aliquantisper singularis amici tui mellifluis verbis super huius tituli maiestate decurrere. Iure sole iustitiae, Deo, perhiberis amicta, quae profundissimam divinae sapientiae, ultra quam credi valeat, penetrasti abyssum; ut quantum sine personali unione creaturae conditio patitur, luci illi inaccessibili videaris immersa. Magna revera familiaritas, sed mira omnino vicinitas, solis et mulieris. Quomodo enim in tam vehementi fervore, tam fragilis natura subsistit? Merito quidem admiraris Moyses sancta, et curiosius desideras intueri'.

O sublime Virgin! You clothe Jesus, God of highest majesty, in the substance of flesh; and he himself clothes you in inenarrable glory. You clothe him in cloud, and you yourself are clothed by that sun.[77]

This reciprocal exchange of flesh and light, sun and cloud, terms so disparate that their combined effect is veritably catachrestic, compels the votary to reflect upon the mysteries of the Incarnation, Passion, Resurrection, and Final Judgement, as comprised by the great mystery of human salvation:

What is this, O my soul? What is this? What do you know? What do you grasp? Can it be that absorbed by wonder at such great things, you fail to train your sights on the secret mysteries within them?[78]

The answer is perforce a resounding 'no': the 'truly felicitous, sublime commutation of these garments [of flesh and light]' provides the basis for an interjected prayer of supplication that closely associates these entangled mysteries with Mary who is recognized as keeper of the mystery of our salvation.[79] The eschatological sign thus leads to an acknowledgement of her intercessory potency, yet another stratum of divine mystery: 'Would that by your patronage we might one day be vouchsafed such embellishing and holy changes of the raiment of grace and glory, O blessed and prudent Virgin, our Advocate'.[80]

The coalition of an apocalyptic image and a scriptural type, itself another kind of image, allows David to claim that the reciprocal adornment of Mary and Jesus has been excellently shown by various 'means and modes to the otherwise blind / obfuscatory world', both under the old dispensation and the new. The beautifying relation between Christ and the Virgin, being an eternal mystery, extends from the past to the future, encompassing all of time; likewise, the interpolation of an eschatological sign at this early stage of the sequence of fifty Marian emblems implicitly alludes to the supratemporal status of the titulus *ornans*. The nobility of Mary, mother of God, can thus be seen fittingly

---

77   Ibidem 77–78: 'O Virgo sublimis! Tu vestis Iesum, Deum summae maiestatis, carnis substantia; et ipse te ineffabili vestit gloria. Tu vestis eum nube, et sole ipsa vestiris ab illo'.

78   Ibidem 77: 'Quid est hoc, o anima mea? Quid est hoc? Quid sapis? Quid capis? An tota tantarum rerum admiratione sic absorberis, ut ad recondita in hisce mysteria non reflectas obtutum?'.

79   Ibidem 78: 'O felicem sublimemque plane indumentorum istorum commutationem!'.

80   Ibidem: 'Utinam, o benedicta et prudens Virgo, Advocata nostra, te patrocinante, mutatoriis tam ornantibus et beatis gratiae et gloriae aliquando donemur'.

to express the divinity of Jesus, son of the Virgin.[81] The 'means and modes' to which David refers are the various kinds of image bestowed upon humankind by a benevolent God for the purpose of meditating Mary's function of ornamenting Christ; in turn, these images stand for the internal image of Christ that David calls upon us to birth (tituli 1–7), nurture (tituli 8–14), and now embellish spiritually (tituli 15–21) [Figs. 14.19 and 14.20]. He further endorses meditative image-making by introducing a third species of image that he layers upon the sign and the type already discussed. This is where subsection 'F' of the *pictura* comes into play: here, as David puts it, the reader-viewer must 'attend to and see how Octavius [Caesar] Augustus, not without cause, is painted before your eyes, who admiring and reverent observes in the sky an aureole of gold encircling the sun, as if the sibyl were bringing it to view; and amidst the aureole a certain virgin, most beautiful, holding a boy at her breast [and] standing upon an altar'.[82] This is a fictive image, explains David, that signifies the modus operandi whereby Augustus came to visualize the Messiah born of a Virgin: he discovered the prophecy of the 'altar of heaven' amongst the sibylline oracles and, having 'read and seen it thus described, as if adverted to by a finger or pointer', he had a painter paint 'what that adumbration of the public icon placed before [his] eyes'.[83] This third kind of prophetic image, consisting of an icon elicited exegetically from close reading of a sibylline prophecy, functions as a mise en abyme of the collateral images called forth through close reading of David's exegetical commentary; as the emperor's reading of the oracles resulted in an icon, so images complementary to *pictura* 18 emerge from David's explication of its relation to the three kinds of divinely inspired text – Johannine, Mosaic, and sibylline – from which it can be thought to have issued.

The affective and transformative power of the image of the Virgin clothed by the sun is veritably boundless, avows David toward the close of Emblem 18: 'O celestial sign truly great, most admirable, which draws to itself the eyes of them who behold it, seizes [their] affections, inflames [their] hearts, adapts [their]

---

81   Ibidem 78: 'O providentiae divinae fulgorem, quae et matris Dei nobilitatem, et virginis filii divinitatem tam excellentibus mediis modisque mundo caecutienti monstravit!'.

82   Ibidem: 'attendite et videte, quam non sine causa vobis Augustus ille Octavius ante obtutum vestrum pingatur; qui quasi Sibylla monstrante, in caelo circulum aureum circum solem admirabundus iuxta ac venerabundus adspicit: et in medio circuli virginem quamdam pulcherrimam, puerum in gremio habentem'.

83   Ibidem: 'occasione pueri tantique Domini nascituri, quem in divinis illis vaticiniis sic descriptum legit atque suspexit, atque si digito vel radio indice ipsi in caelestibus fuisset ostensus: quod illa picturae communis adumbratio ob oculos statuit'.

hands to emulating it'.[84] He promises that no intercessory aid will be denied to any 'diligent and humble soul observant of the Virgin's solicitude' toward Christ, revealed by this image.[85] But why, asks David in his closing prayer of entreaty, was such a trifold image bestowed on us in the first place? His answer underscores the necessity of eschatological images that adapt the recondite mysteries of human salvation for human eyes, minds, and hearts congenitally unable, even partially, to apprehend such mysteries by any other means. By this adaptive device, the omnipotent, sempiternal God who resides in inaccessible light, made that light to some extent knowable through the analogy of the visible sun, for the use of the human race: 'you evinced the mother of your beloved Son, clothed by the sun, as a singular consolation to the world'. Having thereby alluded to Mary's relation to Christ, the sun of justice, God enjoins us to petition for the wherewithal 'to venerate her with a devout heart and imitate her in pious affection of virtues'.[86] On this account, the mediating power of images signifies the Virgin's intercessory potency; the Marian image works in concert with Mary herself to secure the salvation of whoever strives to see clearly the truths bodied forth in / through the "Woman Clothed by the Sun".

The *Pancarpium*'s fiftieth emblem, "Queen of Heaven", celebrates the eternal queenship of Mary who, as David asserts, is portrayed as the agent of every sovereign power Christ could confer, with the exception of his sole prerogative of final judgement [Fig. 14.21].[87] *Pictura* 50 situates her amongst the heavenly hosts, crowned by Christ the Son ('B') and God the Father ('C'), and venerated by angels ('D') and saints of the Old and New Testaments ('E' and 'F'). The subscription describes her as a merciful coadjutant of Christ: 'You the Ruler of Heaven adopted as partner of the Kingdom, that you might gladden the earth with a more favourable eye'.[88] David, in his *exposition* of the picture, states that it depicts the fulfilment of two eschatological prophecies: that of Mary's glorious apotheosis as the queen of heaven, in *Psalms* 44:9: 'The queen stood on thy right hand, in gilded clothing; surrounded with variety'; and that

---

84   Ibidem 78–79: 'O signum vere magnum in caelo, multumque admirabile, quod intuentium oculos ad se trahit, rapit affectus, mentes inflammat, et manus ad aemulandum accommodat!'.

85   Ibidem 79: 'quodque tibi non sit futurum auxilio, si diligens atque humilis ipsius obsequii fueris obervatrix'.

86   Ibidem: 'et dilecti Filii tui matrem, amictam sole, singulari mundo solatio praestitisti: da, ut quam devotae mentis veneramur officio, pio quoque virtutum imitemur affectu'.

87   Ibidem 207: 'ut quidquid salva iustitia concedi possit, id totum in potestate tua, ut Matris misericordiae, ac Reginae caeli, esset constitutum'.

88   Ibidem, *pictura* 50: 'Te Regni sociam Caeli Regnator adoptat; / Ut terras oculo dexteriore bees'.

of the divine mercy she embodies, in *Psalms* 30:20: 'O how great is the multitude of thy sweetness, O Lord, which thou hast hidden for them that fear thee; which thou hast wrought for them that hope in thee, in the sight of the sons of men'. Secreted miraculously in the person of Mary ('mirabiliter abscondisti'), the eternal principle of divine love is here made visible through her efforts as mediatrix of human salvation ('misericorditer ostendisti').[89] David indicates that Mary is commemorated both as Virgin of the Annunciation, who once bore Christ, and as Virgin of the Assumption, whom he bore aloft to preside for all future time over the kingdom of heaven. She also bears witness to *Ecclesiasticus* 25:8, 'I alone have compassed the circuit of heaven', for Christ who encompasses all things was contained in her, and through her he now and forever exercises universal dominion. The souls in purgatory, below, exemplify every person who pleaded with Mary to intercede on their behalf, from the moment of her Assumption onward; through service to her, their final end is assured:

> Therefore, all persons who are or have been servants of that Mistress; for that reason they can say [...], 'Whatever you command, we shall do'. O Mistress, O Mary, O Queen! Deservedly you say that you alone have encircled the circle of heaven [...]: for you encompassed the man in whom sky, earth, sea, deserts, and all things are contained.[90]

The theme of service freely indeed lovingly rendered connects to the status of Emblem 50 as the eighth and final of the 'tituli rapientes' (seizing / arresting / captivating titles). The term *rapiens* conveys Mary's ability to grab hold of human souls, enticing them to bind themselves to Christ with chains of affection and desire. By the same token, she wields pleasure as a spiritual power ('vis voluptatis'), displacing the material things and sensations that hold persons captive and alienate them from Christ; Mary instead enchains them to Jesus, thereby ensuring that their final end will be felicitous.[91] So, too, here as elsewhere in the *Pancarpium*, she personifies the condition of the exercitant's soul, measured by its relation to the spiritual offspring it bears internally, the living image of Christ nourished, adorned, defended, and cultivated within the

---

89   Ibidem 204.
90   Ibidem 205: 'Eapropter, omnes homines, qui sunt, et qui fuerunt, sunt servi istius Dominae; ideoque ipsi dicere possunt [...], quaecumque iusseris, faciemus. O Domina, o Maria, o Regina! Merito dicis; Gyrum caeli circuivi sola [...]; quia virum circumdedisti, in quo caelum, terra, mare, et arida, et universa continentur'.
91   Ibidem 176: '"In VIII. titulos rapientes argumentum": Quae delectant, alliciunt; sed tandem vi suae voluptatis, rapiunt quodammodo ad se corda amantium et desiderantium'.

heart. Having worked through the forty-nine prior spiritual exercises, the soul now finds itself nearly perfected, converted into a truly loving *socius* of Christ on the model of his supreme *socia* Mary. If Jesus has wholly seized / arrested / captivated the votary's soul, it is through the example and co-agency of Mary that this transformation has been effected:

> Therefore, let us commend our cause and ourselves, O my soul, to this Queen as to a more excellent Bathsheba, that she who in the first beginnings and auguries of our spiritual purpose / offspring was to us a singular patroness before the highest King, under the defensive form and type of that same heroine and Queen, may now also, in the consummation of the whole of [our] education, procure a happy and favourable end of all together; and that through her we may bring to a blessed outcome whatsoever with her assistance we have begun and to such an extent advanced.[92]

The happy outcome here envisaged, as the closing prayer of entreaty makes clear, involves carrying to term the fetal image of Jesus, first conceived with Mary's help and now brought to the highest degree of finish for the greater glory of his Holy Name. Accordingly, the *Pancarpium* concludes in the register of eschatology, calling upon the votary to complete her / his journey through the Marian *tituli* by visualizing the soul's final end:

> God, who in admirable order dispense the moments of human life, and ever multiply your Church with new offspring (*foetu*), grant us to bring more favourably to completion for the greater glory of your name the new life that we, aided by the defences and precedents of blessed Mary, favourably began.[93]

---

92   Ibidem 208: 'Huic ergo Reginae, ut excellentiori Bethsabeae, causam nostram, et nos ipsos, o anima mea, commendemus; ut quae nobis sub eiusdem heröinae et Reginae praesidio ac typo, in primis conceptus nostri spiritalis exordiis atque auspiciis, apud summum Regem patrocinio fuit singulari; nunc etiam in totius educationis consummatione, felicem faustumque cunctorum procuret finem; atque per eam beato exitu concludamus, quidquid eiusdem praesidio sumus exorsi, et hucusque produximus'.

93   Ibidem: 'Deus, qui miro ordine vitae humanae momenta dispensas, et Ecclesiam tuam novo semper foetu multiplicas; da, ut vitae novae, ceu prolis spiritalis exortum atque educationem hucusque productam, beatae Mariae praesidiis et exemplis adiuti, quemadmodum feliciter coepimus, ad maiorem tui nominis gloriam felicius absolvamus'.

5   Conclusion

Nadal's *Adnotationes et meditationes* furnished the cosmological template to which Jesuit emblematists such as David adverted, implicitly or explicitly, when considering the *novissima* – death, judgement, salvation, and damnation. This was surely the case for David, three of whose meditative treatises – the *Veridicus Christianus, Occasio arrepta, neglecta,* and *Pancarpium Marianum* – incorporate eschatological images pregnant with affective meaning [Figs. 14.1–14.3, 14.11–14.13, 14.14–14.18, 14.19–14.21]. Precisely and lavishly produced, these treatises in turn served as templates for the scores of Jesuit authors who, following David's lead, composed illustrated spiritual exercises in the form of emblems supplemented by extensive heuristic, exegetical commentaries. In centring his emblems on *picturae* bracketed by mottoes and subscriptions, he often stops to consider how and why *imagines*, especially eschatological ones, have the power to convert the wayward soul, impelling it more closely and punctiliously to follow Christ. Catechetical in format and function, the *Veridicus* utilizes images of hellfire and damnation to expose the dire effects of heresy, thereby to foreclose them [Figs. 14.11–14.13]. The irruption of eschatological prolepses into scenes of daily life serves as an apotropaic device that, if properly meditated, has the power to expose the devilish sting concealed behind the heretic's visual enticements. Admonitory images of this sort, argues David, must be used to countervail the deceptive and intensely seductive appeal of heretical images. Modelled on a Latin school play, the *Occasio's* last two emblems strive to reform the wayward soul by visualizing the disparity between salvation and damnation, and discoursing on the representability of the latter, the unrepresentability of the former [Figs. 14.16 and 14.17]. David layers multiple registers of eschatological imagery onto the final two emblematic *picturae*, develops an analogy between two kinds of image-making, eschatological and parabolic, and forewarns that images of human damnation, though they offer occasions for self-amendment, can also be devastating incitements to despair; such warnings against the consequences of spiritual negligence must therefore often be tempered by ready assurances of divine love. The *Pancarpium* adduces eschatological images of the Virgin to assist the exercitant to imagine how salvation is procured by cultivating the image of Christ brought forth within her / his heart like a spiritual offspring, on the model of Mary's maternal bond with Jesus [Figs. 14.19–14.21]. Various kinds of image – Johannine, Mosaic, and sibylline, which is to say, apocalyptic, typological, and oracular – are mustered to visualize, to the extent such a mystery can be discerned, the soul's indivisible, commutative relation to Christ as scion and Saviour. Together, the images of final things in the *Veridicus, Occasio,* and *Pancarpium* testify to the generative power of eschatological image-making within the Jesuit tradition of emblematic spiritual exercises founded by David. Produce these images, he counsels, and engage with them, reading them closely, if you wish to prepare yourself to meet your final end.

Bibliography

Backer Aug. de – Backer Al. de – Sommervogel C., *Bibliothèque de la compagnie de Jésus,* 9 vols. (Brussels: 1890–1900; Paris: 1890–1932) vol. II, cols. 1844–1853.

Bowen K.L., "Declining Wages for the Printing of Book Illustrations: Arrangements between the Galle Family of Printmakers and the Managers of the Officina Plantiniana in Seventeenth-Century Antwerp", in Blondé B. – Munck B. de – Vermeylen F. (eds.), *Doodgewoon: mensen en hun dagelijks leven in de geschiedenis. Liber amicorum Alfons K.L. Thys* (Antwerp: 2004) 63–85.

Bowen K.L., "Workshop Practices in Antwerp: The Galles", *Print Quarterly* 26.2 (2009) 123–142.

Bowen K.L. – Imhof D., "Reputation and Wage: The Case of Engravers Who Worked for the Plantin-Moretus Press", *Simiolus* 30.3/4 (2003) 161–195.

Bowen K. – Imhof D., *Christopher Plantin and Engraved Book Illustrations* (Cambridge – New York, NY et al.: 2008) 50–51.

Classen A., "Death, Sinfulness, the Devil, and the Clerical Author: The Late Medieval German Didactic Debate Poem *Des Teufels Netz* and the World of Craftsmanship", in Classen (ed.), *Death in the Middle Ages and Early Modern Time* (Berlin – Boston, MA: 2016) 277–296.

Daly P.M., *The Emblem in Early Modern Europe: Contributions to the Theory of the Emblem* (Farnham, Surr. – Burlington, VT: 2014).

Daly P.M. – Dimler G.R., S.J., *The Jesuit Series, Part One (A-D)* (Montreal et al.: 1991) 147–162.

David Jan, S.J., *Veridicus Christianus* (Antwerp, Ex officina Plantiniana, apud Ioannem Moretum: 1601; reprint ed., 1606).

David Jan, S.J., *Occasio arrepta, neglecta; huius commoda, illius incommode* (Antwerp, Ex officina Plantiniana, apud Ioannem Moretum: 1605).

David Jan, S.J., *Pancarpium Marianum, Septemplici Titulorum serie distinctum: ut in B. Virginis odorem curramus, et Christus formetur in nobis,* in *Paradisus Sponsi et Sponsae: in quo Messis myrrhae et aromatum ex instrumentis ac mysteriis Passionis Christi colligenda, et Pancarpium Marianum* (Antwerp, Ex officina Plantiniana apud Ioannem Moretum: 1607; reprint ed., 1618).

Dekoninck R., "*Imagines peregrinantes*: The International Genesis and Fate of Two Biblical Picture Books (Hiël and Nadal) Conceived in Antwerp at the End of the Sixteenth Century", in Gelderblom A.J. – Jong L.J. de – Van Vaeck M. (eds.), *The Low Countries as a Crossroads of Religious Beliefs* (Leiden – Boston, MA: 2004) 49–64.

Dekoninck R., '*Ad imaginem*': *status, fonctions et usages de l'image dans la littérature spirituelle jésuite du XVIIᵉ siècle*, Travaux du Grand Siècle 26 (Geneva: 2005).

Delfosse A., *La 'Protectrice du Païs-Bas': Stratégies politiques et figures de la Vièrge dans les Pays-Bas espagnols* (Turnhout: 2009) 215–216.

Fabre P.A., *Ignace de Loyola: le lieu de l'image* (Paris: 1992).

Hyman A.M., *Rubens in Repeat: The Logic of the Copy in Colonial Latin America* (Los Angeles, CA: 2021).

Imhof D., *Jan Moretus and the Continuation of the Plantin Press*, Bibliotheca Bibliographica Neerlandica, Series Major III, 2 vols. (Leiden: 2014).

Lazure G., "Nadal au Nouveau Monde: une traduction poétique des *Evangelicae historiae imagines*, Pérou, c. 1614", in Dekoninck R. – Guiderdoni-Bruslé A. (eds.), *Emblemata Sacra: rhétorique et herméneutique du discours sacré dans la littérature en image. The Rhetoric and Hermeneutics of Illustrated Sacred Discourse*, Imago Figurata 7 (Turnhout: 2007) 321–331.

Marshall J., *John Locke, Toleration, and Early Enlightenment Culture*, Cambridge Studies in Early Modern British History (Cambridge – New York, NY: 2006) 212–218.

Melion W.S., "The Art of Vision in Jerome Nadal's *Adnotationes et meditationes in Evangelia*", in *Jerome Nadal, Annotations and Meditations on the Gospels. Volume I: The Infancy Narratives*, trans. – ed. F.A. Homann, S.J. (Philadelphia, PA: 2003) 1–96.

Melion W.S., "*Mortis illius imagines ut vitae*: The Image of the Glorified Christ in Jerome Nadal's *Adnotationes et meditationes in Evangelia*", in *Jerome Nadal, Annotations and Meditations on the Gospels. Volume III: The Resurrection Narratives*, trans. – ed. F.A. Homann, S.J. (Philadelphia, PA: 2005) 1–32.

Melion W.S., "*Haec per imagines huius mysterij ecclesia sancta* [*clamat*]: The Image of the Suffering Christ in Jerome Nadal's *Adnotationes et meditationes in Evangelia*", in *Jerome Nadal, Annotations and Meditations on the Gospels. Volume II: The Passion Narratives*, trans. – ed. F.A. Homann, S.J. (Philadelphia, PA: 2007) 1–73.

Melion W.S., "Parabolic Analogy and Spiritual Discernment in Jéronimo Nadal's *Adnotationes et meditationes in Evangelia* of 1595", in Stelling L. – Hendrix H. – Richardson T.M. (eds.), *The Turn of the Soul: Representations of Religious Conversion in Early Modern Art and Literature*, Intersections 23 (Leiden – Boston, MA: 2012) 299–338.

Melion W.S., "Meditative Images and the Potrayal of Image-Based Meditation", in Melion – Dekoninck R. – Guiderdoni-Bruslé (eds.), *Ut pictura meditatio: The Meditative Image in Northern Art, 1500–1700* (Turnhout: 2012) 7–60.

Melion W.S., *The Meditative Art: Studies in the Northern Devotional Print, 1550–1625*, Early Modern Catholicism and the Visual Arts 1 (Philadelphia, PA: 2012).

Melion W.S., "'*Quis non intelliget hoc voluisse Christum*': The Significance of the Redacted Images in Jerónimo Nadal's *Adnotationes et meditationes in Evangelia* of 1595", in *Jerome Nadal, s.J., Annotations and Meditations on the Gospels, Cumulative Index*, ind. J.P. Lea (Philadelphia, PA: 2014) 1–99.

Melion W.S., "Figured Personification and Parabolic Embodiment in Jan David's *Occasio arrepta, neglecta*", in Melion – Ramakers B. (eds.), *Personification: Embodying Meaning and Emotion*, Intersections 41 (Leiden – Boston, MA: 2016) 371–432.

Melion W.S., "Introduction: The Jesuit Engagment with the Status and Functions of the Visual Image", in De Boer W. – Enenkel K.A.E. – Melion (eds.), *Jesuit Image Theory*, Intersections 45 (Leiden – Boston, MA: 2016) 1–49.

Melion W.S., "*Ut pictura lex*: Jan David, s.J., on Natural Law and the Global Reach of Christian Images", in Göttler C. – Mochizuki M. (eds.), *The Nomadic Object: The Challenge of World for Early Modern Religious Art*, Intersections 53 (Leiden – Boston, MA: 2017) 147–186.

Melion W.S., "*Emblemata solitariae Passionis*: Jan David, s.J., on the Solitary Passion of Christ", in Enenkel K. – Göttler C. (eds.), *Spaces, Places, and Times of Solitude in Late Medieval and Early Modern Cultures*, Intersections 56 (Leiden – Boston, MA: 2018) 242–289.

Melion W.S., "*De Virgine natalitia ad rapientem*: Marian Maternity, Militancy, and Mimesis in the First Marian Emblem Book – Jan David, s.J.'s *Pancarpium Marianum* of 1607", *Emblematica: Essays in Word and Image* 4 (2021) 139–209.

Migne J.-P. (ed.), *Patrologia latina 75: Gregorius I* (Paris: 1862).

Moffitt J.F., "Francisco Pacheco and Jerome Nadal: New Light on the Flemish Sources of the Spanish 'Picture-within-the-Picture'", *The Art Bulletin* 72 (1990) 631–638.

Moore R.I., "Heresy as Disease", in Lourdaux W. – Verhelst D. (eds.), *The Concept of Heresy in the Middle Ages* (Leuven: 1983) 1–11.

Münch B.U., *Geteiltes Leid: Die Passion Christi in Bildern und Texten der Konfessionalisierung. Druckgraphik von der Reformation bis zu den jesuitischen Großprojekten um 1600* (Regensburg: 2009).

Nadal Jerónimo, *Adnotationes et meditationes in Evangelia quae in sacrosancto Missae sacrificio toto anno leguntur cum eorunem Evangeliorum concordantia* (Antwerp, Martinus Nutius: 1595; reprint ed., Ex Officina Plantiniana, apud Ioannem Moretum, 1607).

Ramakers B., "Dutch Allegorical Theatre: Tradition and Conceptual Approach", in Strietman E. – Happé P. (eds.), *Urban Theatre in the Low Countries, 1400–1625* (Turnhout: 2006) 127–147.

Ramakers B., "Embodied Wits: The Representation of Deliberative Thought in Rhetoricians' Drama", *Renaissance Studies* 32.1 (2018) 85–105.

Robin A., "El retablo de Zaltocán: Las *Imágenes* de Jerónimo Nadal y la monja de Ágreda", *Anales del Instituto de Investigaciones Estéticas* 88 (2006) 53–70.

Sellink M., *Philips Galle (1537–1612): Engraver and Print Publisher in Haarlem and Antwerp*, 3 vols. (Gouda: 1993).

Sellink M., "Joannes David, *Veridicus christianus*", in Imhof D. (ed.), *The Illustration of Books Published by the Moretuses*, exh. cat., Plantin-Moretus Museum, Antwerp (Antwerp: 1996) 88–89.

Smith J.C., *Sensuous Worship: Jesuits and the Art of the Early Catholic Reformation in Germany* (Princeton, NJ – Oxford: 2003).

Sors A.-K., *Allegorische Andachtsbücher in Antwerpen: Jan Davids Texte und Theodoor Galles Illustrationen in den jesuitischen Buchprojecten der Plantiniana* (Göttingen: 2015).

Stroomberg H., "Introduction", in *The New Hollstein Dutch and Flemish Etchings, Engravings, and Woodcuts, 1450–1700: The Wierix Family, Book Illustrations*, 2 parts, comp. H. Stroomberg, ed. J. van der Stock (Ouderkerk aan den IJssel: 2007) 2:3–7.

Vandommele J., "Mirroring God, Reflecting Man: Shaping Identity through Knowledge in the Antwerp Plays of 1561", in Ramakers B. (ed.), *Classicising the Popular, Popularising the Classic (1540–1580)* (Leuven – Paris – Walpole, MA: 2011) 173–196.

Wadell M.-B., *Evangelicae historiae imagines: Entstehungsgeschichte und Vorlagen*, Gothenburg Studies in Art and Architecture 3 (Gothenburg: 1985).

Waterschoot W., "Joannes David Editing 'Duodecim specula'", in Manning J. – Van Vaeck M. (eds.), *The Jesuits and the Emblem Tradition: Selected Papers of the Leuven International Emblem Conference, 18–23 August 1996*, Imago Figurata Studies 1a (Turnhout: 1999) 353–364.

Waterschoot W., "*Veridicus Christianus* and *Christeliicken Waersegghen* by Johannes David", in Dekoninck R. – Guiderdoni-Bruslé A. (eds.), *Emblemata Sacra: rhétorique et herméneutique du discours sacré dans la littérature en image. The Rhetoric and Hermeneutics of Illustrated Sacred Discourse*, Imago Figurata 7 (Turnhout: 2007) 527–534.

CHAPTER 15

The Jesuit Martyrdom Landscape and the Optics of Death

Mia M. Mochizuki

Abstract

Death is everywhere, yet notoriously difficult to place. This is the riddle that vexed the minds of early modern Jesuits after globalization disrupted the *novissima*, or 'last things', with the fresh perspectives on *locus* and cross afforded by astronomy and Catholic mission. As the telescope extended the eye's reach, its capabilities captured the religious imagination and prompted the articulation of an environmental eschatology through the 'martyrdom landscape', as exemplified in the extra-European iteration of *The Martyrs of Japan*, ca. 1619–1650, three paintings attributed to the Jesuit Workshop of Japan presently displayed in the Gesù in Rome. When Crucifixion met *mundus*, Jesuits soldered the ambivalence of a body approaching death onto the making and un-making of the world through the slipstream between the sight and the site of a violence whose omnipresence could yet yield consolation. This essay pinpoints several overlooked sources for the *vista imaginativa* of death – the objective lens, the Ignatian 'composition of place' (*compositio loci*), the martyrdom landscape, and the violence and seriality of the cross – to unearth how Galileo's glimpse of *nova*, or 'new stars', contributed to the construction of a *novissima* whose history of the future could provide solace for the present.

Keywords

astronomy – Catholic mission – eschatology – geography – Society of Jesus

1 Galileo's *Lens*

When Galileo Galilei (1564–1642) first spied the moon through his telescope, he could not have suspected the merest act – a flicker, a squint, a blink of the eye – would come to register the coordinates of death.[1] Over the course of eight

---

1   I would like to express my gratitude to Wietse de Boer and Christine Göttler for their support during my own experiences with the optics of death. This essay is dedicated to John Endres,

crystalline nights, spread out between November 30 and December 18, 1609, Galileo conducted his first observations of the moon with a lens, outlining its topography with striking descriptions and precise drawings (eight still extant), so that his conclusions could be disseminated in the *Sidereus nuncius* (Starry messenger, 1610) the next year.[2] In contrast to the fictional 'moon worlds' of classical authors that captured the medieval imagination – as the location of another 'earth' in the *Vera Historia* of Lucian of Samosata (ca. 125–after 180), as the 'face on the moon' in the *Moralia* of Plutarch (ca. 46–119), complete with eschatological elements, or as the vantage point of the dream of the Roman general Scipio Aemilianus (185–129 BC) ('Somnium Scipionis') in the *De re publica* of Marcus Tullius Cicero (106 BC–43 BC) – Galileo's achievement was to empirically observe Jupiter's moons with his own eyes.[3] This *spectacle* of the moon was memorialized by a plano-convex *Objective Lens*, ca. 1609–1610, one of only two surviving lenses to be ground by Galileo, housed in an ornately carved ivory-on-ebony oval *Frame* by Vittorio Crosten, 1677, in the Museo Galileo in

---

S.J. (1946–2022), in memory of seeing the otherworldly Cappadocian plains from a hot-air balloon at dawn in 2008.

2   Bredekamp H., *Galileo's Thinking Hand: Mannerism, Anti-Mannerism, and the Virtue of Drawing in the Foundation of Early Modern Science*, trans. M. Cohen (Berlin – Boston, MA: 2019) 132–172, esp. 140–143, figs. 118–125; Galilei G., *Sidereus Nuncius or The Sidereal Messenger*, ed. and trans. A. van Helden (2nd ed. Chicago, IL: 2015 [1989]) xix, 10, 21, 41–59, 104; Galilei Galileo, *Sidereus nuncius, magna, longeque admirabilia spectacula pandens* (Venice, Thomas Baglioni: 1610); Reeves E., "Variable Stars: A Decade of Historiography on the *Sidereus Nuncius*", *Galilaeana* 8 (2011) 37–72; Saunders B., "Mapping the Moon", in Fineman M. – Saunders B. (eds.), *Apollo's Muse: The Moon in the Age of Photography*, exh. cat., The Metropolitan Museum of Art (New York, NY: 2019) 16–69, at 17; Winkler M.G. – Van Helden A., "Representing the Heavens: Galileo and Visual Astronomy", *Isis* 83.2 (1992) 195–217.

3   Cicero, "Dream of Scipio", in idem, *On the Republic; On the Laws*, trans. C.W. Keyes (Cambridge, MA – London: 1928) 256–283, bk. 6; Lucian of Samosata, "A True Story", in idem, *Lucian*, vol. 1, trans. A.M. Harmon (Cambridge, MA – London: 1913) 247–357, esp. 252–283; Nicolson M., *Voyages to the Moon* (New York, NY: 1948) 24; Plutarch, "Concerning the Face Which Appears in the Orb of the Moon", in idem, *Moralia*, vol. 12, trans. H. Cherniss – W.C. Helmbold (Cambridge, MA – London: 1957) 1–223, bk. 12, l. 920A–945D. For the earliest lunar drawings, both with and without the telescope, see: Brown H.I., "Galileo on the Telescope and the Eye", *Journal for the History of Ideas* 46.4 (1985) 487–501, esp. 499–501; Galilei, *Sidereus Nuncius* 4, 12, 22–23, 41–59; Göttler C., *Last Things: Art and the Religious Imagination in the Age of Reform* (Turnhout: 2010) 8; Sluiter E., "The Telescope before Galileo", *Journal for the History of Astronomy* 28.3 (1997) 225–226, 231–232; Montgomery S.L., *The Moon and the Western Imagination* (Tucson, AZ: 1999) 8–9, 95–113, 169–208, esp. 172–174; Reeves E., *Galileo's Glassworks: The Telescope and the Mirror* (Cambridge, MA – London: 2008); Saunders, "Mapping the Moon" 16–69, esp. 18; Whitaker E.A., "Selenography in the Seventeenth Century", in Taton R. – Wilson C. (eds.), *Planetary Astronomy from the Renaissance to the Rise of Astrophysics*, part A: *Tycho Brahe to Newton* (Cambridge – New York, NY – Melbourne: 1989) 119–143, at 119–120.

FIGURE 15.1   Galileo Galilei, *Objective Lens*, late 1609–early 1610, in Vittorio Crosten, *Frame*,
1677. Lens: glass, gilt brass; frame: ivory, ebony; lens: 5.8 cm (effective aperture
3.8 cm); frame: 41 × 30 cm. Florence, Museo Galileo / Istituto e Museo di Storia
della Scienza, Room VII: Galileo's New World, inv. no. 2429
IMAGE © MUSEO GALILEO, FIRENZE (PHOTO: SABINA BERNACCHINI)

Florence since 1841 [Fig. 15.1].[4] Interpretive attention has coalesced around the object of the telescope's gaze, the lunar surface, but the consequences of Galileo's telescope for this discussion reside in its challenge to vision, both physical, in its ability to transcend the limitations of the human eye alone, and perceptual, in its stimulus to mentally inhabit other worlds.[5] The viewing of the moon not only amended the contours of astronomy; it also transformed the *vista imaginativa*, or 'imagined landscape', of the newly standardized four 'last things' (death, judgement, heaven, and hell) as astronomer and artist, poet and priest, became increasingly engaged with the environs of the afterlife.[6]

Galileo's *Lens* would come to encapsulate what Nick Wilding has called a 'visually compelling argument about the potentialities of the visual', one enriched by semantic weight.[7] The *Lens* has been displayed beside Galileo's finger, and Horst Bredekamp and Beate Fricke have proposed that Galileo saw the telescope as an extension of his body, not simply as a metaphor for eyesight, thus elevating it, with its attendant truth claims, into this age's own *vera icon*.[8] The *Frame* of Galileo's *Lens* not only looks like a reliquary, as it marks the early modern valuation, borderline veneration, of this small piece of glass; the *Lens* functioned like a relic too, miraculously collapsing faraway distance with a glance, as the telescope's original Dutch name *verrekijker* (or *verkijker*) indicates.[9] In his first application for support to the Senate of Venice, on August 29, 1609, Galileo explained: 'The effect of this instrument is to represent

---

4 Bredekamp, *Galileo's Thinking Hand* 174; Bucciantini M. – Camerota M. – Giudice F., *Galileo's Telescope: A European Story*, trans. C. Bolton (Cambridge, MA – London: 2015) 1–3; Galilei, *Sidereus Nuncius* 18–20.

5 For the connection of optical devices to the religious inquiring mind, see: Göttler, *Last Things* 1–30, esp. 3–5, 8–9, 27; Mochizuki M.M., *Jesuit Art* (Leiden – Boston, MA: 2022) 115–116, 156–164.

6 Göttler, *Last Things* 13, 15–16, 162.

7 For the cross-pollination of astronomical and artistic ideas, see: Bucciantini – Camerota – Giudice, *Galileo's Telescope* 203–226; Galilei, *Sidereus Nuncius* 96–98, 114–15; Montgomery, *The Moon and the Western Imagination* 114–134, esp. 117, 122–123; Mochizuki, *Jesuit Art* 149, n. 282; Panofsky E., *Galileo as a Critic of the Arts* (The Hague – Dordrecht: 1954); idem, *Galileo Galilei und die Bildkünste*, ed. H. Bredekamp, trans. H. Jatho (Zurich: 2012); Reeves E., "Kingdoms of Heaven: Galileo and Sarpi on the Celestial", *Representations* 105.1 (2009) 61–84; idem, *Painting the Heavens: Art and Science in the Age of Galileo* (Princeton, NJ: 1997) 4–6, 138–225, esp. 152–154; Wilding N., *Galileo's Idol: Gianfrancesco Sagredo and the Politics of Knowledge* (Chicago, IL: 2014) 89–92, esp. 91.

8 Bredekamp, *Galileo's Thinking Hand* 19, 172–176; Fricke B., "Fingerzeig und Augenblick: Galileo Galileis Finger zwischen Fetisch und Reliquie", *Zeitschrift für Ideengeschichte* 3.1 (2009) 80–93, esp. 84–85, 90–91.

9 Göttler, *Last Things* 8–9.

Vtinam saperent et intelligerent ac nouiſſima
prouiderent ! Deuteron . 32.

14.

FIGURE 15.2   Boetius Bolswert, "Utinam saperent et intelligerent ac
                 novissima providerent! Deuteron[omy] 32[:29]" (Oh, that they
                 were wise, that they understood this, that they would consider
                 their latter end! *Deuteronomy* 32:29). Engraving, 15.2 × 9.4 cm.
                 From: Hugo Herman, s.j., *Pia desideria* (Antwerp, Hendrick
                 Aertssens: 1624), before 107, fig. 14. New York, The Metropolitan
                 Museum of Art, Harris Brisbane Dick Fund, 1939, inv. no. 39.33.1
                 IMAGE © THE METROPOLITAN MUSEUM OF ART

an object that is, for example, fifty miles away as large and near as if it were but five', and two days later, in another letter, he recounted, 'the new contrivance of glasses [*occhiale*] [...] which renders visible objects so close to the eye and represents them so distinctly that those that are distant, for example, nine miles appear as though they were only one mile distant'.[10] Artists were also attentive to the telescope's ability to play with the permutations of visual distance, with lenses that could make the 'furthest near' ('et remotissima prope') when pointed outward and the 'closest far away' ('propiora procul') when inverted, as in the telescope emblems of Giovanni Ferro's (1582–1630) *Teatro d'imprese* (1623).[11] The telescope's association with the emerging eschatological *vista imaginativa* was captured in an intriguing scene by Boetius Bolswert (ca. 1585–1633) – 'Utinam saperent et intelligerent ac novissima providerent! Deuteron[omy] 32[:29]' (Oh, that they were wise, that they understood this, that they would consider their latter end! *Deuteronomy* 32:29) – for the Jesuit Herman Hugo's (1588–1629) *Pia desideria* (1624) [Fig. 15.2].[12] Bolswert, a fascinating figure in his own right, depicted the Soul's sighting of death and the Last Judgement with a telescope down a symmetrical allée of cypress trees. However, true to Ferro's emblems, the surreal, pyrotechnic display at the end of nature's colonnade held no visual interest for the Soul; instead, sharply spotted by Christine Göttler, the Soul gazed deep within herself through a *reversed* telescope, when internal scrutiny (*sui ipsius cognitio*) was achieved by meditation on the 'last things'.[13] Self was interrogated by site, because Catholic eschatology paired looking inward with gazing outward by situating the end of a person's life within the apocalyptic termination of the world.

The optics of eschatology even became fodder for John Donne's skewering of St. Ignatius of Loyola (1491–1556) in his *Ignatius His Conclave* (1610/1611), begun the same year as the *Sidereus nuncius* pointedly referenced in his text.[14] Donne located hell on the moon, where Lucifer invited four sixteenth-century Catholic

---

10   Galilei, *Sidereus Nuncius* 7–9, 91.

11   Ferro Giovanni, *Teatro d'imprese* (Venice, Giacomo Sarzina: 1623) 522–524; Göttler, *Last Things* 18–22, figs. 4–5, n. 12.

12   Göttler, *Last Things* 1 30, esp. 5 8, 20 21, 29–30. For the impact of the telescope on terrestrial landscapes, see: Larsen E., "The Proof of the Use of the Inverted Telescope in Dutch 17th-Century Landscape Art", *Gazette des beaux-arts* 89.2 (1977) 172–174; Powell A., "Squaring the Circle: The Telescopic View in Early Modern Landscapes", *Art History* 39.2 (2016) 282–301.

13   Göttler, *Last Things* 2.

14   Bucciantini – Camerota – Giudice, *Galileo's Telescope* 146–147, n. 781; Donne J., *Ignatius His Conclave*, ed. T.S. Healy, s.j. (Oxford – New York, NY: 1969; reprint, Oxford – New York, NY: 2010) xxvi–xxix; Donne John, *Conclaue Ignati* (London, [William Hall]: 1611); idem, *Ignatius His Conclave* (London, N.O. [Nicholas Okes]: 1611); Hassel R.C., Jr., "Donne's 'Ignatius His Conclave' and the New Astronomy", *Modern Philology* 68.4 (1971) 329–337;

trailblazers – Nicolaus Copernicus (solar system, 1473–1543), Paracelsus (Theophrastus von Hohenheim, medicine, ca. 1493–1541), Niccolò Machiavelli (politics, 1469–1527), and Christopher Columbus (the New World, 1451–1506), as well as the playwright Pietro Aretino (1492–1556) and the founder of the Congregation of the Oratory Filippo Neri (1515–1595) – to debate an Ignatius 'more subtil then the *Devill*, and the verier *Lucifer* of the two'.[15] At last, '*Galilaeo the Florentine*' appeared:

> who by this time hath thoroughly instructed himselfe of all the hills, woods, and Cities in the new world, the *Moone*. And since he effected so much with his first *Glasses*, that he saw the *Moone*, in so neere a distance, that hee gave himselfe satisfaction of all, [...] when now being growne to more perfection in his Art, he shall have made new *Glasses*, and they received a hallowing from the *Pope*, he may draw the *Moone*, like a boate floating upon the water, as neere the earth as he will. And thither (because they ever claime that those imployments of discovery belong to them) shall all the Jesuites bee transferred, and easily unite and reconcile the *Lunatique Church* to the *Romane Church*; without doubt, after the Jesuites have been there a little while, there will soone grow naturally a *Hell* in that world also: over which, you *Ignatius* shall have dominion, and establish your kingdome and dwelling there. And with the same ease as you passe from the earth to the *Moone*, you may passe from the *Moone* to the other *starrs*, which are also thought to be worlds, and so you may beget and propagate many *Hells*, and enlarge your *Empire*, and come nearer unto that high seate, which I left at first.[16]

For the story's operatic finale, the moon was portrayed as the last frontier of Jesuit mission in neat antithesis to St. Ignatius's concurrent canonization campaign (beatified 1609, canonized 1622).[17] This galactic view of the eschatological landscape relied upon the association of cosmic and global exploration

---

Nicolson, *Voyages to the Moon* 50–51; Reeves E., "John Donne and the Oblique Course", *Renaissance Studies* 7.2 (1993) 168–83.

15   Donne, *Ignatius His Conclave* 88–89.

16   Ibidem 80–81.

17   Coffin C.M., *John Donne and the New Philosophy* (New York, NY: 1958) 207; Donne, *Ignatius His Conclave* 30–31, 88–89, 90–91, 94–97, 174–175 ("Appendix D: A Donne Discovery"). For Galileo's interest in hell, see: Bredekamp, *Galileo's Thinking Hand* 5–32, 60–67, esp. 60–62, fig. 42; Caspar M., *Kepler* (New York, NY: 1993) 352; Göttler, *Last Things* 142–151, esp. n. 77; Rosen E., *Kepler's Conversation with Galileo's Sidereal Messenger* (New York, NY: 1965) 27–28.

with the Society of Jesus. Their Roman College was home to some of astronomy's leading scholars, such as the Jesuits Christopher Clavius (1538–1612), Christoph Grienberger (1561–1636), Giovanni Paolo Lembo (ca. 1570–1618), and Odo van Maelcote (1572–1615); it was where the curious, both inside and outside the Church, turned to garner expert evaluation of Galileo's discovery, and where a dinner was hosted in his honour in mid-May 1611.[18] Besides Donne's comparison of the lunar landscape with the terra incognita of Jesuit missions (as the 'new *Indies*', the 'new world', and '*Empire*', so 'they ever claime that those imployments of discovery belong to them'), he named Jesuit whistle-blowers on Ignatius's miracles '*Acostas*' for the Jesuit missionary José d'Acosta (1539/1540–1600) in Panama, Peru, and New Spain.[19] Galileo's *Lens* portended a universe that if not quite infinite, certainly established the plurality of worlds that was a precondition for the crafting of a modern eschatology that sought to probe the terrains of death.[20]

2   The Jesuit *Locus* of Death

Much has been made of the famed Ignatian meditational practice of the 'composition of place', the locative visualization technique championed by

---

18   See, for example: letters from the Augsburg merchant Marc Welser (1558–1614) (March 12, 1611) and Cardinal Roberto Bellarmino (1542–1621) (March 19, 1611), then Dean of the College of Cardinals. Bucciantini – Camerota – Giudice, *Galileo's Telescope* 203–226; Campos Ribeiro L., "Jesuits and Astrology: Print versus Manuscript", *Journal of Jesuit Studies* 10.3 (2023) 438–455; Galilei, *Sidereus Nuncius* 92, 111–115; Reeves, *Painting the Heavens* 151–154; Reeves E. – Van Helden A., "Verifying Galileo's Discoveries: Telescope-making at the Collegio Romano", in Hamel J. – Keil I. (eds.), *Der Meister und die Fernrohre* (Frankfurt am Main: 2007) 127–141.

19   For other links between the exploration of new worlds and the moon, see: Álvarez M.-T., "Moon Shot: From Renaissance Imagination to Modern Reality", in Black C.V. – Álvarez M.-T. (eds.), *Renaissance Futurities: Science, Art, Invention* (Oakland, CA: 2020) 9–18, at 9–13, 17–18; Donne, *Ignatius His Conclave* 86–87; Fineman M., "Daydreams by Moonlight", in Fineman M. – Saunders B. (eds.), *Apollo's Muse: The Moon in the Age of Photography*, exh. cat., The Metropolitan Museum of Art (New York, NY: 2019) 70–103, at 71–74; Galilei, *Sidereus Nuncius* 18–20, 94–95; Montgomery, *The Moon and the Western Imagination* 9, 133, 140–148, 157–168, 198–204, esp. 141, 157; Nicolson, *Voyages to the Moon* (New York, NY: 1948); Rawson M., "Discovering the Final Frontier: The Seventeenth-Century Encounter with the Lunar Environment", *Environmental History* 20.2 (2015) 194–216.

20   Dick S.J., *Plurality of Worlds: The Origins of the Extraterrestrial Life Debate from Democritus to Kant* (Cambridge – New York, NY – Melbourne: 1982) 61–105, esp. 74–97; Koyré A., *From the Closed World to the Infinite Universe* (Baltimore, MD: 1957; reprint, Kettering, OH: 2016) 88–99.

St. Ignatius of Loyola in his *Exercitia spiritualia* (1548), or *Spiritual Exercises*.[21] Like Bolswert's eschatologically-oriented Soul, the *compositio loci* explicitly grounded spiritual reflection in place from the outset, with the First Prelude, of the First Exercise, of the First Week instructing the exercitant: 'to see in imagination the physical place where that which I want to contemplate is taking place'.[22] Yet the role of place in the order's approach to eschatology, the *compositio loci* as the point of transition between life and death, has been overlooked, even though the oft-quoted sensory invocation of the 'Meditation on Hell' was predicated upon a survey of its precincts: 'The *First Prelude*, the composition of place. Here it will be to see in imagination the length, breadth, and depth of hell'.[23] The requisite sketching of hellscapes, however, bore its

---

21   Fabre P.A., *Le lieu de l'image: Le probleme de la composition de lieu dans les pratiques spirit-uelles et artistiques jésuites de la seconde moitié du XVIᵉ siècle* (Paris: 1992); Ganss G.E., S.J. (ed. and trans.), *The Spiritual Exercises of Saint Ignatius: A Translation and a Commentary* (Chicago, IL: 1992); Ignatius of Loyola, S.J., *Exercitia spiritualia* (Rome, Antonio Blado: 1548); Mochizuki, *Jesuit Art* 61–99, esp. 80–84, n. 108; Standaert N., S.J., "The Composition of Place: Creating Space for an Encounter", *The Way* 46.1 (2007) 7–20.

22   Ganss, *Spiritual Exercises* 40, 43, v. 47, 56.

23   Besides four major primary sources for early modern Jesuit death practices, the Society of Jesus distinguished itself with a high number of manuals on the art of dying: Carlos Eire has calculated the publication of 20 treatises (1575–1620), 139 books (1621–1700), and at least 101 volumes (1701–1800). Eire C.M.N., *From Madrid to Purgatory: The Art and Craft of Dying in Sixteenth-Century Spain* (Cambridge – New York, NY – Melbourne: 1995) 28. Borja Francisco de, S.J., "Algunos remedios para que los siervos de Dios no teman la muerte (1568)", in Dalmases C. de, S.J. (ed.), *Tratados espirituales* (Barcelona: 1964) 461–469; Eire C.M.N., "The Good Side of Hell: Infernal Meditations in Early Modern Spain", *Historical Reflections* 26.2 (2000) 285–310; *Epistolae et monumenta P. Hieronymi Nadal*, vol. 5: *Commentarii de Instituto S.I.*, ed. M. Nicolau (Rome: 1962) 838–841; Ganss, *Spiritual Exercises* 46–47, v. 65–70, esp. v. 65; Göttler, *Last Things* 13–16, 273–317, esp. 275–278, n. 12; Hendrickson D.S., S.J., "Grave Matters: Juan Eusebio Nieremberg's *Partida a la eterni-dad* (1643) and Jesuit Approaches to Death in Early Modern Spain", *Journal of Jesuit Studies* 8.4 (2021) 638–659, esp. 639–644; Loarte Gaspar de, S.J., *Exercicio dela vida chris-tiana* (Cagliari, Vincencio Sembenino: 1567), fols. 130 r–143 v; O'Malley J.W., S.J., *The First Jesuits* (Cambridge, MA – London: 1993) 174–176; Pabel H.M., "Fear and Consolation: Peter Canisius and the Spirituality of Dying and Death", *Studies in the Spirituality of Jesuits* 45.1 (2013) 2–4, 7–12, 25–26, 30; Palmer M.E., S.J. (ed. and trans.), *On Giving the Spiritual Exer-cises: The Early Jesuit Manuscript Directories and the Official Directory of 1599* (St. Louis, MO: 1996) 127–130, 149–151; Polanco Juan Alfonso de, S.J., *Methodus ad eos adiuvandos, qui moriuntur* (Macerata, Sebastiano Martellini: 1575); Russell C., *Being a Jesuit in Renais-sance Italy: Biographical Writing in the Early Global Age* (Cambridge, MA – London: 2022) 146–172, esp. 163–166. For a visualization of the 'Meditation on Hell', see: Frederick II Bout-tats, Meditation on Hell, engraving, 8.3 × 12.7 cm (image), from: St. Ignatius of Loyola, S.J., *Geestelycke oeffeninghen vanden H. vader Ignatius van Loyola* (Antwerp, Michiel Cnob-baert: 1673), before 75, Brussels, Bibliothèque Royale de Belgique, Rare Books, call no. LP 11.979 A RP.

own dangers, for the persuasive 'imaginative faculty' of the soul, the *vis imaginativa*, could lead even the best-intentioned practitioner to sinful thoughts. To avoid this outcome, the Colloquy of a 'Meditation on the First, Second, and Third Sins' advised, 'Imagine Christ our Lord suspended on the cross before you, and converse with him in a colloquy'.[24] Comparable images – such as '[Quia et Christus] Passus est [pro nobis], vobis reliquens exemplum, ut sequamini: vestigia eius. 1 Pet[er] 2[:21]' (Because Christ suffered for us, leaving you an example, that you should follow in his steps. 1 *Peter* 2:21) by Frederick II Bouttats (1610–1676) to accompany 'On the Mystery of the Cross: *Matthew* 27, *Mark* 15, *Luke* 23, and *John* 19[:23–37]' in an illustrated edition of St. Ignatius's *Geestelycke oeffeninghen vanden H. vader Ignatius van Loyola* (1673) – positioned the Crucifixion as a shock to the universe: 'the sun was darkened, the rocks were split, the tombs were opened, the veil of the temple was torn in two from top to bottom' [Fig. 15.3].[25] Earlier Crucifixion scenes had depicted the sun and moon as flanking the cross, but in the *Exercises*, the event's time and place were accompanied by an eclipsed sun over an urban landscape whose skyline suggests Rome.[26] In the *Vestigatio arcani sensus in Apocalypsi* (1614), the Sevillan Jesuit Luis de Alcázar (1554–1613) maintained the apocalyptic imagery of *Revelation* 12 referred to a solar eclipse, where the moon acted as a Christ-like mediator between earth and heavens, man and God, and implicitly, sceptic and Christian.[27] It is no coincidence that the Crucifixion of Christ, spark and safeguard of the *compositio loci*, prepared Jesuit novices for mission.

---

24 Ganss, *Spiritual Exercises* 42, v. 53; Mochizuki, *Jesuit Art* 170.

25 Ganss, *Spiritual Exercises* 85–86, 115, v. 208, 297; Mochizuki, *Jesuit Art* 65–67; Salviucci Insolera L., "Le illustrazioni per gli Esercizi Spirituali intorno al 1600", *Archivum Historicum Societatis Iesu* 60, fasc. 119 (1991) 181.

26 For example: Jan van Eyck, *Crucifixion* and *Last Judgment*, ca. 1440–1441, oil on canvas, transferred from panel in 1867, 56.5 × 19.7 cm each, New York, Metropolitan Museum of Art, Fletcher Fund 1933, inv. no. 33.92ab. Montgomery, *The Moon and the Western Imagination* 85.

27 Alcázar Luis de, S.J., *Vestigatio arcani sensus in Apocalypsi* (Antwerp, Jan van Keerbergen: 1614); Reeves, *Painting the Heavens* 184–225, esp. 184–188. The subject of Christ on the Cross was a popular and well-circulated composition in seventeenth-century Antwerp: both painted and printed designs by Peter Paul Rubens (1577–1640) and Anthony van Dyck (1599–1641), potential sources for the Bouttats's image, also included an eclipse. For example: Peter Paul Rubens, *Christ on the Cross*, ca. 1592–1633, oil on canvas, 221 × 122.5 cm, Antwerp, Koninklijk Museum voor Schone Kunsten Antwerpen, inv. no. 313; Peter Paul Rubens, *Christ on the Cross*, 1631, engraving, 85 × 64 cm, Antwerp, Koninklijk Museum voor Schone Kunsten Antwerpen, inv. no. 10298; Anthony van Dyck, *Christ on the Cross*, ca. 1627, oil on canvas, 102.5 × 71.7 cm, Antwerp, Koninklijk Museum voor Schone Kunsten Antwerpen, inv. no. 406. I would like to thank Christine Göttler for this observation.

The vocation to place in thought and deed cemented the status of the *locus* of expiration in Jesuit martyrdom and established missionary martyrdom as the quintessential 'good death'. From an Ignatian perspective, death was a constant companion: from a scholastic practising a personal, *Exercises*-based contemplation of the Passion, to his petitioning to be sent on extra-European mission – the *indipetae* letters, derived from 'petere Indias' (to apply for the 'Indies'), and considered a baptism into sacred history by blood, some even using blood as ink – to the often perilous journey and its likely conclusion.[28] Jesuits had a special stake in a martyrdom defined by mission, as evidenced in the popularity of *litterae indipetae*, the frequency of overseas members' martyrdom, and their use of death masks and bodily remains for global canonization campaigns. The Flemish Jesuit Antoine Sucquet (1574–ca. 1627) even enlisted missionary metaphor when he distilled the goal of the thirty-two engraved 'pathways of eternal life' in his *Via vitae aeternae* (1620, 1625) as to 'capture [and] seize [...] the vanguard soul'.[29] After exposure to the religious cultures of other lands, opportunities for martyrdom multiplied around the world, honing a general directive to imitate the life of Christ (*imitatio Christi*) into an explicit desire to die for him, since Ignatius, adopting a Pauline theology of the cross, had prized sacrifice of the self as its highest expression.[30]

---

28   Colombo E. (ed.), *Digital Indipetae Database* [ca. 1560–1970], https://indipetae.bc.edu/bib liography (accessed 11.02.2024); idem, "Nel mezzo del cammino: *Indipetae* e racconti di vocazione", *Rivista Storica Italiana* 132.3 (2020) 990–1010; idem, "From Paper to Screen: The *Digital Indipetae Database*, a New Resource for Jesuit Studies", *Archivum Historicum Societatis Iesu* 177, fasc. 89.1 (2020) 213–230, esp. 214–218; Fabre P.A., "Les *Indipetae* comme exercice des *Exercise spirituels*", in Imbruglia G. – Fabre P.A. – Mongini G. (eds.), *Cinque secoli di Litterae indipetae: Il desiderio delle missioni nella Compagnia di Gesù* (Rome: 2022) 281–298; Imbruglia G. – Fabre P.A. – Mongini G. (eds.), *Cinque secoli di Litterae indipetae: Il desiderio delle missioni nella Compagnia di Gesù* (Rome: 2022); O'Malley, *First Jesuits* 175; Pabel, "Fear and Consolation" 24; Russell, *Being a Jesuit in Renaissance Italy* 52, 60–61, 84, 146–172, 206, esp. 163–166, n. 25.

29   Barbour C., "The Artist's Frame of Reference in Antoine Sucquet's *Via vitae aeternae*", in DiFuria A.J. – Melion W.S. (eds.), *Ekphrastic Image-making in Early Modern Europe, 1500–1700* (Leiden – Boston, MA: 2021) 93–119; Göttler, *Last Things* 292–302, esp. 293; Sucquet Antoine, s.j., *Via vitae aeternae* (vol. 1: Antwerp, Martin III Nuyts: 1620, vol. 2: Antwerp, Hendrick Aertssens: 1625) 2:498.

30   Daly R.J., s.j., *The Origins of the Christian Doctrine of Sacrifice* (Philadelphia, PA: 1978) 1–10, 53–83, esp. 59–61; Fabre P.-A., "Conclusion: The Narrow Road to Martyrdom", *Journal of Jesuit Studies* 9.1 (2022) 127; idem, "Vocation et martyre dans les *Vocationes illustres*", *Rivista Storica Italiana* 132.3 (2020) 1032–1048; Imbruglia G., "'Ad militandum': Sacrifice and the Jesuit Mode of Proceeding", in Lavenia V. – Pastore S. – Pavone S. – Petrolini C. (eds.), *Compel People to Come In: Violence and Catholic Conversion in the Non-European World* (Rome: 2018) 29–48, at 30; Gregory B.S., *Salvation at Stake: Christian Martyrdom in Early Modern Europe* (Cambridge, MA – London: 1999) 26–27, 73, 276–277; Marion J.-L., "Sketch of a Phenomenological Concept of Sacrifice", *Essential Writings*, ed. K. Hart (New

Andrés Pérez de Ribas, s.j. (1576–1655) recounted the deaths of eight Jesuits at the 'blood altar of the cross', at once site and symbol of Christ's death, during the Tepehuán Revolt on the eastern slopes of the Sierra Madre Occidental (present-day Durango, Mexico, 1616–1620) in his *Historia de los Triumphos de nuestra Santa Fee* (1645).[31] Fuelled by mission, martyrdom became a structural part of Ignatian identity, because, as Daniello Bartoli, s.j. (1608–1685) related, the first Jesuits took their vows on Montmartre, so the rock of martyrdom constituted a keystone in the order's legitimacy.[32]

The confessional compass of the missions dictated the mental coordinates of place. The term 'indiano' (pl. 'indiani') occasionally found in *indipetae*, could be used to refer to a vocation to go to the Indies for *missionari*, a place-oriented state of mind, or a *compositio loci* applied to one's own life, rather than a specific site of origin, destination, or race, in what Camilla Russell has dubbed a 'spiritual orientalism', as in 'east' of Europe, where a hermeneutics of place transmuted the physical Indies into the metaphysical realm.[33] This tendency was compounded by a sixteenth-century Christian cartography that situated

---

York, NY: 2013) 436–438; Motta F. – Rai E., "Jesuit Sanctity: Hypothesizing the Continuity of a Hagiographic Narrative of the Modern Age", *Journal of Jesuit Studies* 9.1 (2022) 10; Rai E., "Spargere il sangue per Cristo: La vocaziones al martirio missionario come elemento di identità gesuitica; il caso di John Ogilvie (1579–1615)", *Rivista Storica Italiana* 132.3 (2020) 1011–1031.

31   Ahern M., "Visual and Verbal Sites: The Construction of Jesuit Martyrdom in Northwest New Spain in Andrés Pérez de Ribas' *Historia de los Triumphos de nuestra Santa Fee* (1645)", *Colonial Latin American Review* 8.1 (1999) 23–25; Pérez de Ribas Andrés, s.j., *Historia de los Triumphos de nuestra Santa Fee* (Madrid, Alonso de Paredes: 1645); idem, *History of the Triumphs of Our Holy Faith amongst the Most Barbarous and Fierce Peoples of the New World: An English Translation Based on the 1645 Spanish Original*, ed. D.T. Reff, trans. D.T. Reff – M. Ahern – R.K. Danford (Tucson, AZ: 1999) 602–603, bk. 10, chap. 18, v. 607–608.

32   In the Society of Jesus, the taking of vows was deemed a 'white martyrdom' for the renunciation of personal matters and worldly possessions; the period from the Suppression of the Society of Jesus (begun by 1759, officially: July 21, 1773) through its Restoration (August 7, 1814) was also dubbed a 'martyrdom'. Ditchfield, "Baroque around the Clock: Daniello Bartoli s.j. (1608–1685) and the Uses of Global History", *Transactions of the Royal Historical Society* 31 (2021) 56; McAllen K., "Jesuit Martyrdom Imagery between Mexico and Rome", in Horodowich E. – Markey L. (eds.), *The New World in Early Modern Italy, 1492–1750* (Cambridge – New York, NY – Melbourne: 2017) 143–165, at 156; Motta F. – Rai E., "Martyrs and Missionaries: Strategies of Jesuit Sainthood between the Suppression and the Restoration", *Journal of Jesuit Studies* 9.1 (2022) 95, 123.

33   Mochizuki, *Jesuit Art* 106–113; Molina J.M., *To Overcome Oneself: The Jesuit Ethic and Spirit of Global Expansion* (Berkeley, CA: 2013); O'Malley J.W., s.j., "Early Jesuit Spirituality: Spain and Italy", *Religious Culture in the Sixteenth Century* (Aldershot – Burlington, VT: 1993) 18; Russell, *Being a Jesuit in Renaissance Italy* 62, 85–86.

FIGURE 15.4   Pirro Ligorio (designer) and Simone Moschino (sculptor), *Hannibal's Elephant Crushing a Roman Soldier*, *A Dragon Attacking a Lion and a Lioness*, and *The Mouth of Hell*, ca. 1547–1561, stone. Sacro Bosco, Orsini Castle, Bomarzo, Viterbo, Lazio
IMAGE © WIKIMEDIA COMMONS (CCO 1.0) (PHOTO: DADEROT)

the entrance to hell in the hazy eastern margins of the known world, as in the over-life-size, originally polychrome, stone *Mouth of Hell* in the phantasmago-ric *Sacro Bosco*, or 'Sacred Grove', of Pier Francesco (Vicino) Orsini (1523–1583), Duke of Bomarzo, beneath the Castle of Orsini in the northern Lazio region of Italy [Fig. 15.4].[34] Orsini's *The Mouth of Hell* shares real estate with *Hannibal's Elephant Crushing a Roman Soldier* and *A Dragon Attacking a Lion and Lioness*, two signs of a threatening, rampant East and its pantheon of real and imagined inhabitants: elephants, lions, and bears, but also ogres and dragons, so that the panoramas of the extant and the fantastic, the earthly and the mythological, melded into one *vista imaginativa*.[35] Stefania Tutino has underscored how the expanding reach of the early modern Catholic Church placed geography in its

---

34   The design of the *Sacro Bosco* (*Parco dei Mostri*, 'Park of the Monsters'), begun in 1547 and completed by 1561, has been attributed to Pirro Ligorio (ca. 1512–1583), and its sculp-tures to Simone Moschino (b. Simone Simoncelli, 1553–1610), Ippolita Scalza (1532–1617), and Fabiano Toti (fl. 1570–1607). Bredekamp H., *Vicino Orsini und der heilige Wald von Bomarzo: Ein Fürst als Künstler und Anarchist*, 2 vols. (Worms: 1991); Eire, "Good Side of Hell" 309; Göttler, *Last Things* 135–141.

35   Bredekamp, *Vicino Orsini* 1:105; Göttler, *Last Things* 137–139.

manifold expressions – actual, spiritual, and metaphorical – as the unexpected lynchpin of doctrinal truth, and thus also doubt, in the face of the need to nego-tiate the increasing gap between credibility and credulity.[36] Counterintuitive to modern inclinations, the early global missions focused the quest for histori-cal authenticity less on fact, and more on the place-based experience of death to create prime conditions for the flourishing of a Jesuit pictorial speciality, the 'martyrdom landscape'.

3   The Martyrdom Landscape

Three paintings of the Martyrs of Japan from the second quarter of the seven-teenth century have been attributed to the Jesuit Workshop of Japan founded by the Neapolitan Giovanni Cola (or Niccolò), s.j. (1560–1626), and are pres-ently displayed in the Gesù in Rome: *The Martyrdom of Leonardo Kimura, s.j. and Fourteen Companions* (*November 18, 1619*), *The Great Martyrdom of the Fifty-two Martyrs of Nagasaki* (*1622*), and the *St. Francis Xavier, s.j., Founder of the Mission to Japan, and the Jesuit Martyrs of Japan, 1617–1632* [Figs. 15.5–15.7].[37]

36   Tutino S., "Historical Authenticity and the Expanding Horizons of the Seventeenth-Century Catholic Church", *Journal of Modern History* 92.1 (2020) 1–39; idem, *The Many Faces of Credulitas: Credibility, Credulity, and Belief in Post-Reformation Catholicism* (Oxford – New York, NY: 2022) 54–57, 151–178.

37   Leonardo Kimura, s.j. (1575–1619). The Martyrs of Japan, who featured in at least ninety-one books published in pre-modern western Europe, have been grouped into six categories: (1) the Twenty-six Martyrs of Japan (February 5, 1597; beatified 1627, canon-ized 1862); (2) the Two Hundred and Five Martyrs of Japan (1598–1632; beatified 1867); (3) Justus Takayama Ukon (1552–1615; beatified 2017); (4) the Two Augustinian Recollects Martyrs (December 11, 1632; beatified 1989); (5) the Sixteen Martyrs of Japan (1633–1637; beatified 1981, canonized 1987); and (6) the One Hundred and Eighty-Eight Martyrs of Japan (1603–1639; beatified 2008); for a total of 438 beatified Martyrs of Japan of which forty-two were canonized. Blanco Perales J., *La imagen del martirio japonés en el periodo Namban: El cuadro del Gesù representando el Gran Martirio de Nagasaki y su función en la propaganda jesuítica de la misión* (Ph.D. dissertation, Universidad de Oviedo: 2019) 38–41, 59–65, 87–90, 109–196, 395–465, 521–528, esp. 397–404; Cañeque A., *Un imperio de már-tires: Religión y poder en las fronteras de la Monarquía Hispánica* (Madrid: 2020) 201–271; Ditchfield, "Baroque around the Clock 56, 68; Elison G., *Deus Destroyed: The Image of Christianity in Early Modern Japan* (Cambridge, MA – London: 1973); Garcés García, s.j., *Relacion de la Persecucion que huvo en la Iglesia de Iapon, y de los insignes martires que gloriosamente dieron sus vidas en defensa de nuestra Santa Fè, el añ̃o de 1622* (Madrid, Luis Sánchez: 1625), fols. 10 r–10 v; Mochizuki M.M., "Shock Value: The Jesuit Martyrs of Japan and the Ethics of Sight", in Promey S.M. (ed.), *Sensational Religion: Sensory Cultures in Material Practice* (New Haven, CT: 2014) 375–397; Omata Rappo H., *Des Indes loin-taines aux scènes des collèges: Les reflets des martyrs de la mission japonaise en Europe*

FIGURE 15.5   Jesuit Workshop of Japan, *The Martyrdom of Leonardo Kimura, s.j. and Fourteen Companions (November 18, 1619)*, ca. 1619–1650. Oil and ink on paper, later attached to canvas, 135 × 153 cm. Rome, Il Gesù, Casa Professa
IMAGE © ZENO COLANTONI

Although it is unlikely they were originally conceived as a set, they can be considered as a coherent body of work today, since they provide some of the earliest depictions of the Jesuit Martyrs of Japan to be produced under one imprimatur and use several pigments only seen in cultural encounter, such as carbon-copper-chromophore black, lead tin-yellow-copper green ('Niwa

(*XVIᵉ–XVIIIᵉ siècle*) (Munster: 2020) 83–183, 247–404, esp. 361–363; Roldán-Figueroa R., *The Martyrs of Japan: Publication History and Catholic Missions in the Spanish World (Spain, New Spain, and the Philippines, 1597–1700)* (Leiden – Boston, MA: 2021); Ruiz de Medina J., s.j., "Inventario cronológico de los martiros, 1558–1873", in idem, *El matirologio del Japón, 1558–1873* (Rome: 1999) 271–800, esp. 811; Tronu Montané C. – Zampol D'Ortia L. – Omata Rappo H., "Martyrs of Japan: Models, Emotions, and the Causes for Beatification and Canonisation", in Frei E. – Rai E. (eds.), *Profiling Saints* (Göttingen: 2023) 247–303.

FIGURE 15.6   Jesuit Workshop of Japan, *The Great Martyrdom of the Fifty-two Martyrs of
                Nagasaki (1622)*, ca. 1622–1650. Oil and ink on paper, later attached to canvas,
                127 × 170 cm. Rome, Il Gesù, Casa Professa
                IMAGE © ZENO COLANTONI

FIGURE 15.7   Jesuit Workshop of Japan, *St. Francis Xavier, S.J., Founder of the Mission to
                Japan, and the Jesuit Martyrs of Japan, 1617–1632*, ca. 1632–1650. Oil and ink on
                paper, later attached to canvas, 110 × 220 cm. Rome, Il Gesù, Casa Professa
                IMAGE © ZENO COLANTONI

Green'), and smalt (European vitreous blue pigment).[38] The two earliest paintings chronicle the first major martyrdom in Japan after the anti-Christian edict of the Shogun Tokugawa Ieyasu (1543–1616) in 1614 and the height of Christian persecution in the country in 1622. The third painting commemorates the Jesuit sacrifice for the cause through 1632, with the insertion of the first three Jesuit Martyrs of Japan from the 'Twenty-six Martyrs of Nagasaki' (February 5, 1597) – Sts. Diogo (Santiago) Kisai (1534–1597), Paulo Miki (ca. 1562–1597), and João (Soan) de Goto (1578–1597) – in the top row as the legacy of the 'Apostle of the East Indies', St. Francis Xavier (1506–1552), despite his dying peacefully on Shangchuan Island off the southern coast of China.[39] These paintings show how the Ignatian stress on the *compositio loci* of death became actualized in what could be classified as a 'martyrdom landscape', a subgenre of landscape imagery whose extra-European iteration came into its own when two sixteenth-century trends converged: Europe ceased to be a dominant arena for Roman Catholic martyrdom and an independent landscape tradition emerged.[40] Mission made the depiction of landscape central to martyrdom. Louis Richeome, s.j. (1544–1625) would capture the distinctive landmarks of Brazil, India, Japan, Ethiopia, and Mexico in the 102 portraits of martyrs that became so many places in the festive (ephemeral) canonization decorations of the Gesù for St. Ignatius of Loyola and St. Francis Xavier (1622).[41] According to Bartoli, a pupil of the Jesuit astronomer Giambattista Riccioli (1598–1671), geography and history completed one another: history was blind without the light (eyes) of geography and geography mute without the voice (tongue) of

---

38 Montanari R. – Alberghina M.F. – Schiavone S. – Pelosi C., "The Jesuit Painting *Seminario* in Japan: European Renaissance Technology and Its Influence on Far Eastern Art", *X-Ray Spectrometry* 51 (2022) 64–85, esp. 75–79, 83.

39 Despite the small number of Jesuits executed initially, the Society of Jesus was the order with the most martyrs in Japan during this early period, closely followed by the Dominicans. Blanco Perales, *Imagen del martirio japonés* 35–38, 56–57, 84–87, 106–107, graphs 1–3; Cañeque A., "In the Shadow of Francis Xavier: Martyrdom and Colonialism in the Jesuit Asian Missions", *Journal of Jesuit Studies* 9.3 (2022) 438–458; Frei E., "Through Daniello Bartoli's Eyes: Francis Xavier in *Asia* (1653)", *Journal of Jesuit Studies* 9.3 (2022) 398–414.

40 Gregory, *Salvation at Stake* 285; Mochizuki M.M., "*Waterland* and the Disquiet of the Dutch Landscape", in Göttler C. – Mochizuki M.M. (eds.), *Landscape and Earth in Early Modernity: Picturing Unruly Nature* (Amsterdam: 2023) 75–122, esp. 78–79.

41 Fabre, "Conclusion" 126, 130–131; Harpster G., "Illustrious Jesuits: The Martyrological Portrait Series *circa* 1600", *Journal of Jesuit Studies* 9.3 (2022) 378–397, esp. 382, 389–395, fig. 1; McAllen, "Jesuit Martyrdom Imagery between Mexico and Rome" 159–160; Richeome Louis, s.j., *La peinture spirituelle, ou l'art d'admirer, aimer, et louer Dieu* (Lyon, Pierre Rigaud: 1611) 225–240.

history.[42] History must be organized by place, not rhetorically or thematically, so the location of traumatic events would be fixed in the minds of audiences who may never set foot on those lands.[43]

But it would be a mistake to understand these tableaux of death as only, or even primarily, documentary; in these compositions, spatial confusion reigned supreme, where the elasticity of perspectives narrated by land was juxtaposed to convey a spiritual orientation, not modernity's fascination with topographical accuracy. So engravings such as 'The Martyrdom of Cornelis Beudin Godínez, s.j.' by Melchior Küsel (1626–1684) in *Societas Iesu usque ad sanguinis et vitae profusionem militans: in Europa, Africa, Asia, et America* (1675) by Matthias Tanner, s.j. (1630–1692) could feature three prominent pagodas peeking through robust cloud formations, akin to those in Japanese 'screens of foreigners' (*Namban byōbu*), rather implausibly in Tarahumara (Rarámuri) territory (present-day Chihuahua, Mexico), in order to communicate dying on mission to the East [Fig. 15.8].[44] And the polysemy of place and displacement in the *compositio loci* could manifest in the disjunction between figures represented in profile and a 'dove's eye' cityscape in *The Martyrdom of Leonardo Kimura*, or the omniscient, if inconsistent, kaleidoscopic lens applied in *The Great Martyrdom of Nagasaki* [Figs. 15.5 and 15.6].[45] Yet the verdant sloping hills, the groves of trees with leafy fronds, and the regular intervals of city streets in the *Martyrs of Japan* paintings could connect to European martyrdom landscapes and act as a catalogue of linked places, a pictorial complement to the Jesuit Republic of Letters.[46] The martyrdom landscape was never intended as a consistent ecology; it navigated dystopic vistas and apocalyptic

---

42   'Cieca dunque è l'Istoria, se a veder la terra le manca il lume della Geografia. Altresì la Geografia, se l'Istoria non le dà che parlare, da sè sola è mutola'. Bartoli Daniello, s.j., "La geografia trasportata al morale" (Rome, Egidio Ghezzi: 1664), in idem, *Delle opere del P. Daniello Bartoli, della Compagnia di Giesù: Le morali* (Rome, Lazzari Varese: 1684) 392; Ditchfield, "Baroque around the Clock" 60.

43   Bartoli, s.j., "La geografia trasportata al morale" 391; Bartoli Daniello, s.j., "Del modo di scrivere l'istoria della Compagnia", *Epistolae generalium ad nostros et nostrorum (et externorum) ad generalem (Epp. NN.)* 96, unpublished MS, Rome, Archivum Romanum Societatis Iesu, fols. 18 r–19 v; Ditchfield, "Baroque around the Clock" 49–73, esp. 60, 66–67.

44   Horodowich E. – Nagel A., *Amerasia* (New York, NY: 2023); McAllen, "Jesuit Martyrdom Imagery between Mexico and Rome" 162–164, fig. 9.4; Tanner Matthias, s.j., *Societas Iesu usque ad sanguinis et vitae profusionem militans: in Europa, Africa, Asia, et America, contra gentiles, Mahometanos, Judaeos, haereticos, impios, pro Deo, fide, Ecclesia, pietate* (Prague: Universitas Carolo-Ferdinandea, 1675) 543–545.

45   For the rhythm of place and displacement in Ignatian spirituality, see: Mochizuki, *Jesuit Art* 78–99; Standaert, "The Composition of Place" 7–20.

46   McAllen, "Jesuit Martyrdom Imagery between Mexico and Rome" 143–165.

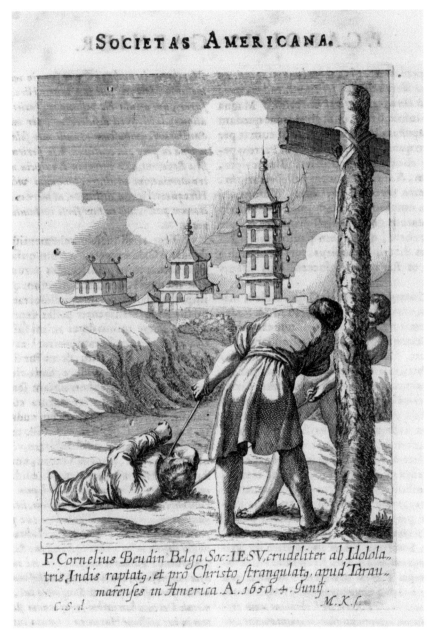

SOCIETAS AMERICANA.

P. Cornelius Beudin Belga Soc. IESV, crudeliter ab Idololatris Indis raptatꝗ, et pro Christo ſtrangulatꝗ, apud Tarau-
marenſes in America. A. 1650. 4. Junÿ.

C. S. d.   M. K. f.

FIGURE 15.8   Melchior Küsel, The Martyrdom of Cornelis Beudin Godínez, S.J. Engraving,
                30 × 18 cm. From: Tanner Matthias, S.J., *Societas Iesu usque ad sanguinis et
                vitae profusionem militans: in Europa, Africa, Asia, et America, contra gentiles,
                Mahometanos, Judaeos, haereticos, impios, pro Deo, fide, Ecclesia, pietate*
                (Prague, Universitas Carolo-Ferdinandea: 1675) 544. Boston, Boston College,
                John J. Burns Library, call no. BX3755 .T3 1675 Jesuitica Oversize
                IMAGE © HATHITRUST DIGITAL LIBRARY (PUBLIC DOMAIN)

worlds through the breaks in logic of an encounter, a journey, or a life in crisis to inscribe the visual assault on picture and person alike.[47]

For the *Martyrs of Japan* paintings depict grounds littered with corporeal remains that double as an archive of pain: flames surround the burning bodies of Jesuits and Japanese converts and pull the eye off-centre in *The Martyrdom of Leonardo Kimura and Fourteen Companions*, where Jesuits, Dominicans, Franciscans, and Augustinians were decapitated *and* incinerated to prevent the worship of relics [Fig. 15.5]. Three empty stakes raise the fear quotient by citing the cowardice of the Dominicans who reportedly tried to escape (in vain) during *The Great Martyrdom of Nagasaki* [Fig. 15.6].[48] And death by cringeworthy *anatsurushi*, men disoriented by being hung upside-down in fetid pits by the divergent poles of obscured sight and overtaxed smell, fills the bottom row of *The Jesuit Martyrs of Japan* [Fig. 15.7]. Bartoli itemized the range of miseries inflicted in his *Della vita e dell'istituto di S. Ignatio, fondatore della Compagnia di Giesù* (1650), the first vernacular portrayal of mission to enjoy official status:

> [Jesuits were martyred in Japan] by being slowly burned for two or three hours; drowned at sea; torn apart [i.e., quartered alive]; sliced up; pierced with spears; crucified; beheaded; killed by immersion in freezing or boiling water; poisoned; hanged or [killed] by means of the cruellest Japanese torture of being suspended upside down over a ditch until all one's blood had slowly drained out from incisions made behind each ear [i.e., *anatsurushi*].[49]

---

47   Bakhtin M.M., "Forms of Time and of the Chronotope in the Novel", in idem, *The Dialogic Imagination: Four Essays*, ed. M. Holquist, trans. C. Emerson – M. Holquist (Austin, TX: 1981) 243–250.

48   Hesselink R.H., *The Dream of a Christian Nagasaki: World Trade and the Clash of Cultures, 1560–1640* (Jefferson, NC: 2016) 201–207; Blanco Perales, *Imagen del martirio japonés* 37–38, 57, 66–69, 86–87, 107, 420–452, 529–532, esp. 425, n. 9, graph 4; Ruiz de Medina, *El matirologio del Japón* 217.

49   '[...] abbruciati lentamente a due e tre ore di fuoco, sommersi nel mare, squartati vivi, saettati, trafitti con lance, messi in croce, decapitati, uccisi col freddo delle acque gelate e col caldo delle bollenti, morti di veleno, di capestro, e del crudelissimo stento della fossa in Giappone [...]'. Bartoli Daniello, s.j., *Della vita e dell'istituto di S. Ignatio, fondatore della Compagnia di Giesù* (Rome, Domenico Manelfi: 1650) 177, as translated in Ditchfield, "Baroque around the Clock" 56. Daniello Bartoli's extensive catalogue of 'Tormenti straordinari dari a Christiani' (Extraordinary torments given to Christians [i.e., in Japan]) in the 'Tavola' (Index) of his *Dell'historia della Compagnia di Giesù: Il Giappone* (1660) also provided the basis for the illustrations of Asian martyrs in Tanner's *Societas Iesu usque ad sanguinis et vitae profusionem militans*. Bartoli Daniello, s.j., *Dell'historia della Compagnia di Giesù: Il Giappone, seconda parte dell'Asia* (Rome, Ignatio de' Lazzeri:

These unvarnished accounts of death furnished real-time equivalencies to the Jesuit Juan Alfonso de Polanco's (1517–1576) directions for practising the 'Meditation on Hell' in the *Spiritual Exercises*: 'Consider [...] the eternal punishment in hell called the pain of the senses; its bitterness should be weighed: horrible sights, hideous cries, unendurable stench, unending hunger and thirst, unquenchable flames'.[50] The martyrdom landscape distilled the *imago agens*, the dynamic 'driving image' that thrusts the viewer into the contemplative action of the bodying forth of ideals; its visual crystallization of *enargeia*, the 'vividness' of life force, elicited the application of the senses to transfigure the eyewitness into an engaged participant and convert mimesis into the miraculous.[51] By rehearsing the performance of primordial and ultimately providential pain, the *vista imaginativa* of martyrdom transformed the harrowing crucifixion of a Jesuit into a reenactment of the suffering Christ *in extremis*, as it retold the fulfilment of Old Testament messianic prophecies in the New Testament through the lens of the life-threatening costs of place.

4   The Violent Crucifixion

The key to the martyrdom landscape resided in violent Crucifixion, the excruciating 'bloodshed' of *cruor* so far from the life-giving 'blood circulation' of *sanguis*, cited by the 'blood altars of the cross' of Sts. Diogo Kisai, Paulo Miki, and João de Goto in *The Jesuit Martyrs of Japan* [Fig. 15.9].[52] In fact, these saints were executed by Japanese crucifixion (*haritsuke*, 'stringing up' on a middle perch with open legs), practised since at least the twelfth century.[53] But the

---

1660) 523; Ditchfield, "Baroque around the Clock" 50, 60, 69; Tanner, *Societas Iesu usque ad sanguinis et vitae profusionem militans* 207–432.

50   Palmer, *On Giving the Spiritual Exercises* 151.

51   De Boer W. – Enenkel K.A.E. – Melion W.S. (eds.), *Jesuit Image Theory* (Leiden – Boston, MA: 2016); Mochizuki M.M., "Jesuit Visual Culture in a Machine Age", in Županov I.G. (ed.), *The Oxford Handbook of the Jesuits* (Oxford – New York, NY: 2019) 449–486, at 449–456.

52   Nancy J.-L., "Image and Violence", in idem, *The Ground of the Image*, trans. J. Fort (New York, NY: 2005) 24.

53   *Haritsuke* also captured the attention of Luís Frois, s.J. (1532–1597), whose extensive description included the only image in his printed report. Frois Luís, s.J., "Letter", *Japonica-Sinica* (*Jap. Sin.*) 53, unpublished MS, Rome, Archivum Romanum Societatis Iesu, fols. 53 r–54 r; Frois Luís, s.J., *Relatione della gloriosa morte di XXVI* (Rome, Luigi Zannetti: 1599) 101. Botsman D.V., *Punishment and Power in the Making of Modern Japan* (Princeton, NJ: 2005) 16–18; Cooper M. (ed.), *They Came to Japan: An Anthology*

FIGURE 15.9   Jesuit Workshop of Japan, St. Francis Xavier, St. Diogo (Santiago)
               Kisai, St. Paulo Miki, and St. João (Soan) de Goto. Detail of Fig. 15.7

Relationes of the Roman Rota for their beatification imbued this method with Christological significance, including the phrase 'ex cruce, quam ex cathedra' that echoed the foremost martyrdom of Christianity, the Crucifixion of Christ, in a potent combination of spiritual message and political point during ongoing canonization campaigns.[54] Crucifixion and martyrdom were already visually linked in Niccolò Circignani's (ca. 1517/1524–after 1596) design for the opening fresco of the ambulatory of the Jesuit Church of San Stefano Rotundo, Rome: *Rex gloriose martyrum* (Christ as the glorious king of martyrs, 1582), where a towering cross, incised with 'Tu vincis in martiribus' (You conquer in martyrdom), referenced the prophesying of Christ's ordeals in *Isaiah* 53:10–12

---

of European Reports on Japan, 1543–1640 (Berkeley, CA: 1965) 151–168; Galdós Baertel R. (ed.), *Relación del martirio de los 26 cristianos crucificados en Nangasaqui el 5 febrero de 1597* (Rome: 1935) 100; Omata Rappo H., "Death on the Cross: The Beatification of the Twenty-six Martyrs of Nagasaki (1627) and the Iconography of the Crucifixion", in Quiles García F. – García Bernal J.J. – Broggio P. – Fagiolo Dell'Arco M. (eds.), *A la luz de Roma: Santos y santidad en el barocco iberoamericano*, vol. 3: *Tierra de santidad* (Seville: 2020) 129–150, at 131–137, 149.

54   Pope Benedict XIV, "De servorum Dei beatificatione et beatorum canonizatione", in idem, *Appendices ad quatuor libros de servorum Dei beatificatione et beatorum canonizatione*, vol. 7 (Rome, Niccolò Palearini – Marco Palearini: 1749) 430, bk. 3, app. 2; Coccino Giovanni Battista – Manzanedo de Quiñones Alfonso – Pirovano Filippo, "Sanctissimo domino nostro Urbano Papa VIII: Japoni, seu ordinis beati Francisci fratrum Discalceatorum canonizationis vigintisex martyrum", *Barberini latino* (*Barb. lat.*) 2777, unpublished MS, Vatican City, Biblioteca Apostolica Vaticana, fols. 1 r–1 v; Coccino Giovanni Battista – Manzanedo de Quiñones Alfonso – Pirovano Filippo, "Sanctissimo domino nostro Urbano Papa VIII: Japoni, seu ordinis beati Francisci fratrum Discalceatorum canonizationis vigintisex martyrum", *Barb. lat.* 2778, unpublished MS, Vatican City, Biblioteca Apostolica Vaticana, fols. 1 r–1 v; Omata Rappo, *Des Indes lointaines aux scènes des collèges* 157–163, 260–263.

[Fig. 15.10].[55] The Cologne Carthusian Laurentius Surius (Lorenz Sauer, 1523–1578) related martyr and crucified Christ thusly: 'Christ is the king of martyrs, the form of the martyrs, the strength of the martyrs, and the victory of the martyrs', such that 'the totality of the holy martyrs makes up the totality of Christ, from whom the nature of blessed martyrdom flows'.[56] This was the logic behind recycling the engravings of illustrated Jesuit martyrological calendars, such as those by Adriaen Collaert (ca. 1560–1618) in Bartolomeo Ricci, S.J.'s (1542–1613) *Triumphus Iesu Christi crucifix* (1608), into an index of crucifixions from Christ and St. Peter through the Jesuits in Japan for Pedro de Bivero, S.J.'s (1572–1656) *Sacrum sanctuarium crucis et patientiae crucifixorum et cruciferorum* (1634).[57] Through mission, the martyrdom landscape not only revised the late medieval *ars moriendi* tradition with place; it also updated the *technē* of a 'good death' with the *ars mechanica* of torture instruments employed in such works as the Oratorian Antonio Gallonio's (1556–1605) *Trattato degli instrumenti di martirio* (1591).[58] In the anguished Crucifixion, eschatology broached the 'folly of the cross', the *stultitia crucis*, where the supposed foolishness of 'God's chosen' justified St. Paul's rationale, 'to live is Christ and to die is gain' (*Philippians* 1:21).[59]

Only in Christian iconography did a person in pain, as De Polanco relayed in breathtaking detail, constitute the gateway to the next world: 'Reflect that at the hour of death, one's senses are most often dulled and one's mind so hindered

---

55   Monssen L.H., "*Rex Gloriose Martyrum*: A Contribution to Jesuit Iconography", *Art Bulletin* 63.1 (1981) 130–137, esp. 133–137, figs. 5, 14; idem, "*Triumphus* and *Trophaea Sacra*: Notes on the Iconography and Spirituality of the Triumphant Martyr", *Konsthistorisk Tidskrift* 51 (1982) 10–20, esp. 11–13; Noreen K., "*Ecclesiae militantis triumphi*: Jesuit Iconography and the Counter-Reformation", *Sixteenth Century Journal* 29.3 (1998) 689–715, esp. 689, 699–701, fig. 7, n. 4.

56   Gregory, *Salvation at Stake* 277–279, fig. 25; Surius Laurentius, O.Cart., *De probatis sanctorum historiis*, vol. 5 (Cologne, Gerwin Calenius – The Heirs of Johann Quentel: 1574) 982–983.

57   Bivero Pedro de, S.J., *Sacrum sanctuarium crucis et patientiae crucifixorum et cruciferorum* (Antwerp, Plantin Press under Balthasar Moretus: 1634) 439–445, esp. 444–445; Ricci Bartolomeo, S.J., *Triumphus Iesu Christi crucifix* (Antwerp, Plantin Press under Jan Moretus: 1608).

58   Fumaroli M., *L'École du silence: Le sentiment des images au XVIIᵉ siècle* (Paris: 1994) 371–374; Gallonio Antonio, C.O., *Trattato degli instrumenti di martirio* (Rome, Ascano Donangeli – Girolamo Donangeli: 1591); Touber J., *Law, Medicine, and Engineering in the Cult of the Saints in Counter-Reformation Rome: The Hagiographical Works of Antonio Gallonio, 1556–1605* (Leiden – Boston, MA: 2014) 200, 221, 231–232.

59   Gregory, *Salvation at Stake* 51–55, 276–277; Imbruglia G., "Sacrifice and the Missionary", in Imbruglia G. – Fabre P.A. – Mongini G. (eds.), *Cinque secoli di Litterae indipetae: Il desiderio delle missioni nella Compagnia di Gesù* (Rome: 2022) 428–438, at 429–430.

FIGURE 15.10   Monogrammist MP, "Rex gloriose martyrum" (Christ as the glorious
king of martyrs), ca. 1580–1630. Engraving, 27.1 × 17.4 cm. Copied
after: Cavalieri Giovanni Battista de', *Ecclesiae militantis triumphi*
(Rome, Bartolomeo Grassi: 1583), pl. 1. London, British Museum,
inv. no. 1869,0410.1561, asset no. 786043001

by pain or the vehemence of the illness that even practised persons are barely able to keep their minds concentrated on what is needful for their salvation'; 'Reflect upon the total sum of suffering in every limb, every sense, every power of the soul; one who finds it so hard to endure pain in a single limb: how will he be able to bear universal torments?'; 'Consider that this pain is continuous: without intermission, without alleviation, without end'.[60] The sheer agony of death was the focus of Bouttats's image '[Quia et Christus] Passus est [pro nobis]' accompanying the Mystery of the Cross, Christ's mouth agape as he gazes beseechingly upward in severe pain before shuffling off his 'mortal coil', and the last line of the first Colloquy of the *Exercises* that concludes with a visualization of Jesus's distress: 'In this way, too, gazing on him in so pitiful a state as he hangs on the cross, speak out whatever comes to your mind' [Fig. 15.3].[61] Jesuits in particular, with their sophisticated understanding of image operations, understood that the Crucifixion not only bore aesthetic, devotional, and historical import; it also functioned as an omnipresent and overdetermined picture of torture with 'the whole semaphoric language of the symmetrical spread-eagled body', in W.J.T. Mitchell's inimitable phrasing.[62] Unlike the late medieval stylized narrative of Passion-based Crucifixion, Jesuits coded candid pain into iconic depictions of Christ's death via the affective destruction of a human body.[63] The martyrdom landscape was the ongoing postscript to the sacrificial cross that would come to be seen, according to Michel de Certeau, s.j., as 'a body-theatre suffering "torments", where "tortures"' delimit a site, 'isolating suffering from the world, its surrounding landscape reduced to a barren shadow of its former self with no clear rationale, only disorientation and confusion'.[64]

Pain was crucial to theological reasoning because it fulfilled a fundamental purpose. Peter Canisius, s.j. (1521–1597) clarified, humankind 'should not fear death at all', because suffering is how 'we pass over to and arrive at eternal life and glory'; for he expounded, 'may the weakness of the crucified Jesus Christ be

60   Palmer, *On Giving the Spiritual Exercises* 149–151.

61   Fabre, *Le lieu de l'image* 36–38; Ganss, *Spiritual Exercises* 42, v. 53.

62   De Boer – Enenkel – Melion, *Jesuit Image Theory*; Mitchell W.J.T., "Foreword", in Terry-Fritsch A.   Labbie E.F. (eds.), *Beholding Violence in Medieval and Early Modern Europe* (Aldershot – Burlington, VT: 2012) xv–xxv, at xix; Mochizuki, "Shock Value" 384–390; Mochizuki, *Jesuit Art* 168–173.

63   Marrow J.H., "*Circumdederunt me canes multi*: Christ's Tormentors in Northern European Art of the Late Middle Ages and Early Renaissance", *Art Bulletin* 59.2 (1977) 167–181; idem, *Passion Iconography in Northern European Art of the Late Middle Ages and Early Renaissance: A Study of the Transformation of Sacred Metaphor into Descriptive Narrative* (Kortrijk: 1979) 44–67, 164–170; Pinkus A., *Visual Aggression: Images of Martyrdom in Late Medieval Germany* (University Park, PA: 2021).

64   Certeau M. de, s.j., "Stories of Passions", in idem, *The Mystic Fable*, vol. 2: *The Sixteenth and Seventeenth Centuries*, ed. L. Giard, trans. M.B. Smith (Chicago, IL: 2015) 135–138.

his strength, may Jesus's wounds be his medicine, may Jesus's agony be his joy, may Jesus's death be his life, may the shedding of Jesus's blood be the washing away of his sin and the obtaining of his eternal bliss'.[65] The *Official Directory of 1599* to the *Spiritual Exercises* counselled, 'In these meditations, the soul "conceives a holy fear of the Lord so as to bring forth a spirit of salvation"'.[66] Physical discomfort drove a personal tie to Christ, so that multiple editions of the *Spiritual Shugyo* were required from the Jesuit Press in Japan to sate demand.[67] Crucifixion was the moment when form became detached from spirit: the deterioration of the mortal body in the *Exercises* – 'consider my soul as imprisoned in this corruptible body' – had to be witnessed for the invisible soul to live and for the deceased to be distinguished from those merely sleeping, as earlier generations had represented the dead.[68] St. Augustine of Hippo (354–430) used the notion of the *Christus deformis* to capture the notion of Pauline *exinanitio*, or the emptying of Christ, in a sermon on *Philippians* 2:7–8: 'On the cross, therefore, hung the deformed Christ, but his deformity is our beauty. […] The way we follow is that of belief in Christ crucified. We are not ashamed of this deformity of Christ'.[69] It was the messy *dis*semblance of Crucifixion that broke through the limitations of mimetic Incarnation – *Christus deformis* to *imitatio Christi* – and consolidated a truly Baroque, provocative form, as noted by Valentin Groebner: 'When they [i.e., Crucifixion images] work, they go beyond

65   Begheyn P., s.j., "The Catechism (1555) of Peter Canisius, the Most Published Book by a Dutch Author in History", *Quaerendo* 36 (2006) 51–84; idem, *Petrus Canisius en zijn catechismus: De geschiedenis van een bestseller*, exh. cat., Museum Het Valkhof (Nijmegen: 2005); Flowers T., s.j., *The Reform of Doctrine in the Catechisms of Peter Canisius* (Leiden – Boston, MA: 2023); Pabel, "Fear and Consolation" 11, 16, 26–27; Canisius Peter, s.j., "Gebett, Underweisung und Fragstuck für sehr krancke und sterbende Menschen", *Betbuch und Catechismus: Nach rechter Catholischer Form und Weyss* (Dillingen, Sebald Mayer: 1568), fols. 372 r–v, 374 r–v, 383 r–v; idem, *De consolandis aegrotis* (Vienna, Michael Zimmermann: 1554), fol. ci verso; idem, *Summa doctrinae christianae* (Vienna, Michael Zimmermann: 1555).
66   Palmer, *On Giving the Spiritual Exercises* 316.
67   Certeau M. de, s.j., "L'institution de la pourriture: Luder (1977)", *Histoire et psychanalyse entre science et fiction*, ed. L. Giard (Paris: 1987) 148–167; Fabre, "Conclusion" 128; Shin J.M., *The Jesuits, Images, and Devotional Practices in China and Japan, 1549–1644* (Seoul: 2017) 149–164; idem, "The Passion and Flagellation in Sixteenth-Century Japan", *Renaissance and Reformation / Renaissance et Réforme* 36.2 (2013) 5–43, esp. 19–22.
68   Deleuze G., *Francis Bacon: The Logic of Sensation*, trans. D.W. Smith (Minneapolis, MN: 2003) 100–101; Ganss, *Spiritual Exercises* 40, v. 47; Mâle E., *L'art religieux après le Concile de Trente; Étude sur l'iconographie de la fin du XVIᵉ siècle, du XVIIᵉ, du XVIIIᵉ siècle: Italie – France – Espagne – Flandres* (Paris: 1932) 106–110; Russell, *Being a Jesuit in Renaissance Italy* 163–164.
69   St. Augustine of Hippo, "Sermon 27", in Migne J.-P. (ed.), *Patrologia Latina*, vol. 38 (Paris: 1845) 181, chap. 6.

the merely mimetic. Pictures of violence are intended to render invisible the difference between reflection and example, description and prescription'.[70]

For violence required visuality to signify a rupture with an established order.[71] Death bore a special significance for picture-making, not least, as Hans Belting has observed, since images of the dead modelled the core function of pictures: to present what is, by definition, absent.[72] The brutal Crucifixion built on this predilection to herald the conscious adoption of horror as a pictorial aid, the *terribilità* Giorgio Vasari (1511–1574) had advocated for arousing an instinctive reaction to a subject, where the unruly imagined world penetrated into lived experience, much like the Jesuit appropriation of Aristotelian *enargeia*.[73] Sixteenth-century crucifixes were constructed to 'induce no less fear than devotion', as Antonio de Beatis (fl. 1517), secretary to Cardinal Luigi d'Aragona (1474–1519), ascertained for the 'crucifixi revelatissimi e grandissimi' (the largest and most revelatory of the crucifixes) encountered by the roadsides from Trent onward during their journey through 'Upper Germany' (May 22–June 30, 1517).[74] The sight of profound distress, what Pedro Rueda Ramírez has named the 'pedagogy of fright', triggered responses to the *sacer*

---

70   Mochizuki, *Jesuit Art* 140–141; Groebner V., *Defaced: The Visual Culture of Violence in the Late Middle Ages*, trans. P. Selwyn (New York, NY: 2008) 35; Rahner H., s.j., *Ignatius the Theologian*, trans. M. Barry, s.j. (Freiburg im Breisgau: 1968) 133.

71   Clark T.J., *The Sight of Death: An Experiment in Art Writing* (New Haven, CT: 2006); Lavenia – Pastore – Pavone – Petrolini, *Compel People to Come In*; Mochizuki, *Jesuit Art* 171–173; Nancy, "Image and Violence" 15–26, esp. 17, 21–22; Perkinson S. – Turel N. (eds.), *Picturing Death, 1200–1600* (Leiden – Boston, MA: 2021); Sontag S., *Regarding the Pain of Others* (New York, NY: 2003); Pinkus, *Visual Aggression*; Terry-Fritsch – Labbie (eds.), *Beholding Violence in Medieval and Early Modern Europe*.

72   Belting H., "Image and Death: Embodiment in Early Cultures, with an Epilogue on Photography", *An Anthropology of Images: Picture, Medium, Body*, trans. T. Dunlap (Princeton, NJ: 2011) 84–124, esp. 84–88; Clark, *The Sight of Death* 235–236.

73   Göttler – Mochizuki (eds.), *Landscape and Earth in Early Modernity*; Gründler H., "*Orrore, terrore, timore*: Vasari und das Erhabene", in Eck C. van – Bussels S. – Delbeke M. – Pieters J. (eds.), *Translations of the Sublime: The Early Modern Reception and Dissemination of Longinus's Peri Hupsous in Rhetoric, the Visual Arts, Architecture, and the Theatre* (Leiden – Boston, MA: 2012) 83–116; Kim D.Y., "The Horror of Mimesis", *Oxford Art Journal* 34.3 (2011) 340–342, 353. The violence of Crucifixion was meant to shake a person to the core, as Fyodor Dostoevsky's fictional character Prince Myshkin declared on seeing Hans Holbein the Younger's *Dead Christ Entombed*, 1521–1522 (oil on panel, 30.5 cm × 200 cm, Basel, Kunstmuseum, Amerbach-Kabinett 1662, inv. no. 318): 'Why, some people may lose their faith looking at that picture!'. Dostoevsky F., *The Idiot*, trans. D. Magarshack (New York, NY: 1956) 236.

74   Groebner, *Defaced* 89; Hale J.R. (ed.), *The Travel Journal of Antonio de Beatis through Germany, Switzerland, the Low Countries, France, and Italy, 1517–1518*, trans. J.R. Hale – J.M.A. Lindon (London: 1979) 81.

horror of looking – the *pius horror*, the 'orrida bellezza' (Bartoli), and the *mysterium tremendum* (tremble-inducing mystery) that evoked involuntary screams, shudders, standing hair (*horripilatio*), and prickling of the flesh – as the colourful reverberations of terrible awe.[75] Canisius associated such 'horrendum' with the weeping and the gnashing of teeth of torture (*Job* 10:22).[76] And recently, Helen Langdon has assigned the *meraviglie* of Salvator Rosa's (1615–1673) turbulent painted landscapes to a grafting of terror onto an aesthetics of the infinite prompted by Bartoli's investigations of the earth and stars.[77] In the martyrdom landscape, Jesuits juxtaposed the corporeal agony of Crucifixion with a wide-angle lens on death to channel being transported 'outside the self' by gruelling physical distress and thereby suffuse the distanced objectivity of the sight of pain with the prophetic immediacy of a personal stake.[78] The body *in extremis* yielded a premonition of the future, to become, for De Certeau, 'the identification of the contingent act with the must be' and the 'atopia of an approaching event', where the looming aporia of Crucifixion trumped the past certainties of Incarnation.[79] When Christ was crucified, bodily decomposition consecrated the spaces of the conditional; the blood-red sun of *The Jesuit Martyrs of Japan* marked 'anything but a stable vanishing point' with a chorus of protagonists who staged the redundancy of the expiatory cross [Fig. 15.9].[80]

---

75   Bartoli Daniello, S.J., *Del ghiaccio e della coagulazione* (Rome, Lazzari Varese: 1681) 47; Dekoninck R. – Delfosse A., "*Sacer Horror*: The Construction and Experience of the Sublime in the Jesuit Festivities of the Early Seventeenth-Century Southern Netherlands", *Journal of Historians of Netherlandish Art* 8.2 (2016) 1–16, esp. 1–4, 7–8; Ditchfield, "Baroque around the Clock" 60–61; Hendrickson, "Grave Matters" 642; Kim, "The Horror of Mimesis" 338–342, esp. 339; Mochizuki, "Shock Value"; Otto R., *The Idea of the Holy: An Inquiry into the Non-rational Factor in the Idea of the Divine and Its Relation to the Rational*, trans. J.W. Harvey (London: 1923); Renaldo J.J., "Bacon's Empiricism, Boyle's Science, and the Jesuit Response in Italy", *Journal of the History of Ideas* 37.4 (1976) 693; Rueda Ramírez P., "Las artes de buena muerte en el comercio de libros con América: Aproximación a la circulación de la literatura devota en el Siglo de Oro", in Serrano Martín E. – Cortés Peña A.L. – Betrán Moya J.L. (eds.), *Discurso religioso y Contrarreforma* (Zaragoza: 2005) 141–159, at 151.

76   Pabel, "Fear and Consolation" 21–22.

77   Langdon H., "The Demosthenes of Painting: Salvator Rosa and the 17th-Century Sublime", in Eck C. van et al. (eds.), *Translations of the Sublime* 163–185, at 163–171.

78   Dekoninck – Delfosse, "*Sacer Horror*" 2–4, 7; Ditchfield, "Baroque around the Clock" 60; Göttler, *Last Things* 157–215; Mitchell, "Foreword" xix.

79   Certeau, "Stories of Passions" 135–138, 140–141; Grosse S., *Heilsungewissheit und Scrupolositas im späten Mittelalter: Studien zu Johannes Gerson und Gattungen der Frömmigkeitstheologie seiner Zeit* (Tübingen: 1994) 215–237; Pabel, "Fear and Consolation" 28.

80   Groebner, *Defaced* 120–123.

5   The Serial Cross

The cross was on repeat – as in Boetius Bolswert's 'Inspice, et imitare virtutis N. exemplar, quod tibi a Domino monstratum est' (Observe and imitate
the example of virtue N [i.e., the given virtue] shown to you by the Lord) for
Sucquet's *Via vitae aeternae* – where figures drag crosses, after Jesus's example ('C'), up to an illuminated, visceral Crucifixion ('E') [Fig. 15.11].[81] Christ
implores the viewer, 'Follow after me' ('Venite post me') and 'Look and make a
second example [after this]' ('Inspice et fac secun / dum exemplar'), recalling
Hugo Rahner, s.j.'s condensation of the *Exercises* into a refashioning of the
self on the basis of the crucified Christ.[82] Early modern Jesuits thought about
death through the magnification and multiplication of the cross: Francisco de
Borja (1510–1572), the third Superior General of the Society of Jesus, advocated
thinking about the Crucifixion as a way to confront the fear of mortality; Jacob
Gretser, s.j. (1562–1625) pondered the devotional ramifications of theological
disquisitions on the cross; and Justus Lipsius (1547–1606) penned the *De cruce
libri tres* (1593), a broad-based, illustrated antiquarian study of the etymologi-
cal, archaeological, and semantic values of Crucifixion that was popular among
Jesuit audiences.[83] Repetition of the cross mobilized the creative possibilities
print techniques had contributed to picture-making, so the martyrdom landscape could operate like Erwin Panofsky's 'reproductive optic', where the idea
of a work of art was rehabilitated in the performance of its intention, the plu-
ral collective of the cross as the foundation for its multi-directional 'hyperimage', to adopt Felix Thürlemann's term, that enabled its spread outward.[84]

81   Barbour C., "The Artist's Frame of Reference in Antoine Sucquet's *Via vitae aeternae*"
      104–107; Mochizuki, *Jesuit Art* 171–172; Sucquet, *Via vitae aeternae* 1:452–59; Zierholz S.,
      "*Conformitas crucis Christi*: Zum Motiv der Kreuzesnachfolge in der jesuitischen Druck-
      grafik des 17. Jahrhunderts im Licht der Vision von La Storta", *Archivum Historicum
      Societatis Iesu* 86, fasc. 171.1 (2017) 49–97; idem, *Räume der Reform: Kunst und Lebenskunst
      der Jesuiten in Rom, 1580–1700* (Berlin: 2019) 119–32, esp. 129–32.
82   Mochizuki, *Jesuit Art* 170; Rahner, *Ignatius the Theologian* 55, 101, 130–33.
83   Borja, "Algunos remedios para que los siervos de Dios no teman la muerte (1568)" 461–469,
      esp. 464–465; Catto M., "La scena pubblica della morte: L'istante ultimo e il compimento
      della vocazione gesuitica", *Rivista Storica Italiana* 132.3 (2020) 1068–1085, esp. 1082–1084;
      Gretser Jacob, s.j., *Opera omnia*, vols. 1–3: *De sancta cruce* (written ca. 1587–1625, pub-
      lished Regensburg, Johann Conrad Peetz – Emmerich Felix Bader: 1734); Lipsius Justus,
      De cruce libri tres (Antwerp, Plantin Press under Jeanne Plantin – Jan Moretus: 1593);
      O'Malley, *The First Jesuits* 176; Omata Rappo, "Death on the Cross" 138–141; Pabel, "Fear
      and Consolation" 3.
84   Thürlemann F., *Mehr als ein Bild: Für eine Kunstgeschichte des Hyperimage* (Munich:
      2013). Loh M.H., *Titian Remade: Repetition and the Transformation of Early Modern Italian*

FIGURE 15.11   Boetius Bolswert, "Inspice, et imitare virtutis N. exemplar, quod tibi a
                Domino monstratum est" (Observe and imitate the example of virtue N [i.e.,
                the given virtue] shown to you by the Lord). Engraving, 9.0 × 12.9 cm (image).
                From: Sucquet Antoine, S.J., *Via vitae aeternae*, vol. 1 (Antwerp, Martin III
                Nuyts: 1620), after 452, fig. 21. Brussels, Bibliothèque Royale de Belgique, Rare
                Books, call no. VB 1.999 A RP

In *The Jesuit Martyrs of Japan*, as in all group martyrdom imagery, the rows of not quite 'faceless' ('ungestalt'), generic figures, despite some names, titles, and dates of death, in large part dissolved the specifics of an individual life into a shared humanity, so the reproductive spectrum implied by the crosses of Sts. Kisai, Miki, and De Goto could invoke the chain of bodies and images to come [Figs. 15.7 and 15.9].[85] Søren Kierkegaard would later elaborate 'genuine repetition is recollected forward' in his didactic novel *Repetition* (1843), so the Aristotelian *kinesis* of the serial could transport a person to eternity.[86] The cross as multiple supplied a form of consolation forged in the double moment of giving up one world while receiving back another, so artists could cultivate the martyrdom landscape as a future-facing model for death.

The end was only the beginning, as Bolswert positioned a similarly composed landscape – 'Considera, o homo, finem tuum et vias tuas' (Consider, oh mankind, your end and your paths) – as a serial *avant la lettre* first image of Sucquet's *Via vitae aeternae* [Fig. 15.12].[87] In this *vista imaginativa*, a youth questions, 'En finis; quo, qua vado?' (For the end is near: where and which [i.e., path] am I taking?) ('A'), while the *globus cruciger* ('E'), the symbol of the ambition for a Catholic (and catholic) earth that prioritized the geography of the earth over an allegorical female figure, goes up in flames at his feet. The exhortative repetition of three routes to a 'good death' ('G') posit the landscape of choice so critical to the Jesuit determination of the 'last things': the left 'secular', 'tortuous [i.e., purgative]' trajectory of a couple; the middle 'ecclesiastical', 'oblique [i.e., illuminative]' way of a Jesuit; and the right (in every way) 'religious', 'direct [i.e., unitive]' road of the most advanced figures.[88] Above, the skies part to reveal their ultimate destination, the 'imminent future' of 'St. Paul, that philosopher of the third heaven', where numinous optics allowed that 'all places were seen in equally crisp detail regardless of distance', according to the Brazilian Jesuit António Vieira (1608–1697) in his *História do futuro* (1718).[89]

Art (Los Angeles, CA: 2007) 8; Panofsky E., "Original and Facsimile Reproduction (1930)", trans. T. Grundy, *Res: Anthropology and Aesthetics* 57/58 (2010) 330–338, esp. 332.

85   Groebner, *Defaced* 10–16.

86   Kierkegaard S., *Fear and Trembling; Repetition*, ed. and trans. H.V. Hong – E.H. Hong (Princeton, NJ: 1983) 125–231, esp. 131, 221, 229; Loh, *Titian Remade* 174, 178, n. 46; Mooney E.F., "*Repetition*: Getting the World Back", in Hannay A. – Marino G.D. (eds.), *The Cambridge Companion to Kierkegaard* (Cambridge – New York, NY – Melbourne: 1998) 282–307, at 287–289, 297.

87   Göttler, *Last Things* 296–300.

88   For the dynamics of personal choice in the *Spiritual Exercises*, see: Mochizuki, *Jesuit Art* 69–74.

89   Vieira António, s.j., *História do futuro* (written by 1649, published Lisbon: António Pedrozo Galram, 1718); Vieira A., s.j., *História do futuro*, ed. M.L. Carvalhão Buescu (Lisbon: 1982); idem, "History of the Future: The Hopes of Portugal and the Fifth Empire of the World",

FIGURE 15.12 Boetius Bolswert, "Considera, o homo, finem tuum et vias tuas" (Consider, oh
mankind, your end and your paths). Engraving, 9.1 × 13.4 cm (image). From:
Sucquet Antoine, s.j., *Via vitae aeternae*, vol. 1 (Antwerp, Martin III Nuyts:
1620), after 2, fig. 1. Brussels, Bibliothèque Royale de Belgique, Rare Books,
call no. vb 1.999 A rp

As in Bolswert's 'Utinam saperent et intelligerent' at the start of this essay, far-sight was integral to the development of eschatological foresight, in keeping with the *providere novissima* tradition of prophesy and the ocular mechanics, be it lens, mirror, or wheel, of 'remembering' future worlds through the sightlines of death [Fig. 15.2].[90] Vieira assessed the past and the future from the perspective of global panoramas: 'Time, like the World, has two hemispheres: one above and visible, which is the past, another below and invisible, which is the future. In between these hemispheres are the horizons of time, which are these moments of the present that we are living, where the past ends and the future begins'.[91] His sermons diagnosed this time-twisting phenomenon as 'a history of the future for present times', recognizable in the 'memories' of hell espied in the marvels of the moon or in the fanciful East, as opposed to the 'histories of the past for future times', so that in art, as in death, the 'reproductive optic' could be used to defy the seemingly impossible and 'paint a copy before there is an original'.[92]

In closing, the sequential cross was the summa bestowed by the virtuous artist in the lower right corner of 'Inspice, et imitare virtutis N. exemplar' and by St. Francis Xavier at the apex of *The Jesuit Martyrs of Japan*: the sacrificial landscape as the salvific medicine for impending loss [Figs. 15.9 and 15.11]. Walter Melion has asserted that the copious number of crosses dotting the graveyards of the *Veridicus Christianus* (1601) by Jan David, s.J. (1545–1613) alluded to the pivotal role of imagery in a 'good death'.[93] I would add, for Jesuits, new worlds reengineered the debt of place to Crucifixion not only as ethical domain and concrete earth, but also through the land as pictorial ground. The martyrdom landscape captured globalization's disruption of the *novissima* with the fresh perspectives on *locus* and cross afforded by astronomy and Catholic mission. As the telescope extended the eye's reach, its capabilities captured the religious imagination and prompted the articulation of an environmental eschatology

The Sermon of Saint Anthony to the Fish and Other Texts, trans. G. Rabassa (Dartmouth, MA: 2009) 77–78, 85–86. For the future in terms of worldly fame, posterity, and the foundation of the self, see: Álvarez, "Moon Shot" 9; Black C.V. – Álvarez M.-T., "The Future is Now: Reflections on Art, Science, Futurity", in idem (eds.), *Renaissance Futurities: Science, Art, Invention* (Oakland, CA: 2020) 1–8, at 1, 3; Derrida J., "Privilege: Justificatory Title and Introductory Remarks", in idem, *Who's Afraid of Philosophy? Right to Philosophy 1*, trans. J. Plug (Stanford, CA: 2002) 22.

90   Göttler, *Last Things* 11, 192–203.

91   Vieira, "History of the Future" 80–81.

92   Göttler, *Last Things* 111–155; Vieira, "History of the Future" 80.

93   David Jan, s.J., *Veridicus Christianus* (Antwerp, Plantin Press under Jan Moretus: 1601), pl. 81–100; Melion W.S., "*Coemeterium schola*: The Emblematic Imagery of Death in Jan David's *Veridicus Christianus*", in Perkinson – Turel (eds.), *Picturing Death* 311–354, esp. 314–330, figs. 14.2–14.3.

through the *vista imaginativa* of death. When Crucifixion met *mundus*, Jesuits soldered the ambivalence of a body approaching death onto the making and un-making of the world through the slipstream between the sight and the site of a violence whose omnipresence could yet yield consolation. In the martyrdom landscape, the repetition of suffering at one remove by the paradox of lifeless cadaver and organic landscape affirmed the dawning prospect of an afterlife, in keeping with Jean-Luc Nancy's formulation, of 'imminence infinitely suspended over itself'.[94] The insight of the Society of Jesus was to recruit the deferral of revelation that pictures signal so well – Jorge Luis Borges's recognition that 'a revelation as yet unproduced is, perhaps, the aesthetic fact' – to restructure the optics of eschatology, so the spectacle of its signature *nova*, its new stars, sites, and crosses, could shape a modern *novissima* whose history of the future leveraged the place of death as an investment in tomorrow.[95]

Bibliography

Ahern M., "Visual and Verbal Sites: The Construction of Jesuit Martyrdom in Northwest New Spain in Andrés Pérez de Ribas' *Historia de los Triumphos de nuestra Santa Fee* (1645)", *Colonial Latin American Review* 8.1 (1999) 7–33.

Alcázar Luis de, S.J., *Vestigatio arcani sensus in Apocalypsi* (Antwerp, Jan van Keerbergen: 1614).

Bakhtin M.M., *The Dialogic Imagination: Four Essays*, ed. M. Holquist, trans. C. Emerson – M. Holquist (Austin, TX: 1981).

Bartoli Daniello, S.J., *Della vita e dell'istituto di S. Ignatio, fondatore della Compagnia di Giesù* (Rome, Domenico Manelfi: 1650).

Bartoli Daniello, S.J., *Dell'historia della Compagnia di Giesù: Il Giappone, seconda parte dell'Asia* (Rome, Ignatio de' Lazzeri: 1660).

Bartoli Daniello, S.J., *La geografia trasportata al morale* (Rome, Egidio Ghezzi: 1664).

Bartoli Daniello, S.J., *Del ghiaccio e della coagulazione* (Rome, Lazzari Varese: 1681).

Bartoli Daniello, S.J., *Delle opere del P. Daniello Bartoli, della Compagnia di Giesù: Le morali* (Rome, Lazzari Varese: 1684).

Begheyn P., S.J., *Petrus Canisius en zijn catechismus: De geschiedenis van een bestseller*, exh. cat., Museum Het Valkhof (Nijmegen: 2005).

---

94   Nancy, "Image and Violence" 26.
95   Borges J.L., "The Wall and the Books (1950)", in idem, *Selected Non-fictions*, ed. E. Weinberger, trans. E. Allen – S.J. Levine – E. Weinberger (New York, NY – Toronto – London: 1999) 346; Galilei, *Sidereus Nuncius* xii.

Begheyn P., s.j., "The Catechism (1555) of Peter Canisius, the Most Published Book by a Dutch Author in History", *Quaerendo* 36 (2006) 51–84.

Belting H., *An Anthropology of Images: Picture, Medium, Body*, trans. T. Dunlap (Princeton, NJ: 2011).

Benedict XIV, Pope, *Appendices ad quatuor libros de servorum Dei beatificatione et beatorum canonizatione, Tomus Septimus* (Rome, Niccolò Palearini – Marco Palearini: 1749).

Bivero Pedro de, s.j., *Sacrum sanctuarium crucis et patientiae crucifixorum et cruciferorum* (Antwerp, Plantin Press under Balthasar Moretus: 1634).

Black C.V. – Álvarez M.-T. (eds.), *Renaissance Futurities: Science, Art, Invention* (Oakland, CA: 2020).

Blanco Perales J., *La imagen del martirio japonés en el periodo Namban: El cuadro del Gesù representando el Gran Martirio de Nagasaki y su función en la propaganda jesuítica de la misión* (Ph.D. dissertation, Universidad de Oviedo: 2019).

Borges J.L., *Selected Non-fictions*, ed. E. Weinberger, trans. E. Allen – S.J. Levine – E. Weinberger (New York, NY – Toronto – London: 1999).

Botsman D.V., *Punishment and Power in the Making of Modern Japan* (Princeton, NJ: 2005).

Bredekamp H., *Vicino Orsini und der heilige Wald von Bomarzo: Ein Fürst als Künstler und Anarchist*, 2 vols. (Worms: 1991).

Bredekamp H., *Galileo's Thinking Hand: Mannerism, Anti-Mannerism, and the Virtue of Drawing in the Foundation of Early Modern Science*, trans. M. Cohen (Berlin – Boston, MA: 2019).

Brown H.I., "Galileo on the Telescope and the Eye", *Journal for the History of Ideas* 46.4 (1985) 487–501.

Bucciantini M. – Camerota M. – Giudice F., *Galileo's Telescope: A European Story*, trans. C. Bolton (Cambridge, MA – London: 2015).

Campos Ribeiro L., "Jesuits and Astrology: Print versus Manuscript", *Journal of Jesuit Studies* 10.3 (2023) 438–455.

Cañeque A., *Un imperio de mártires: Religión y poder en las fronteras de la Monarquía Hispánica* (Madrid: 2020).

Cañeque A., "In the Shadow of Francis Xavier: Martyrdom and Colonialism in the Jesuit Asian Missions", *Journal of Jesuit Studies* 9.3 (2022) 438–458.

Canisius Peter, s.j., *De consolandis aegrotis* (Vienna, Michael Zimmermann: 1554).

Canisius Peter, s.j., *Summa doctrinae christianae* (Vienna, Michael Zimmermann: 1555).

Canisius Peter, s.j., *Betbuch und Catechismus: Nach rechter Catholischer Form und Weyss* (Dillingen, Sebald Mayer: 1568).

Caspar M., *Kepler* (New York, NY: 1993).

Catto M., "La scena pubblica della morte: L'istante ultimo e il compimento della vocazione gesuitica", *Rivista Storica Italiana* 132.3 (2020) 1068–1085.

Cavalieri Giovanni Battista de', *Ecclesiae militantis triumphi* (Rome, Bartolomeo Grassi:
1583).

Certeau M. de, s.j., *Histoire et psychanalyse entre science et fiction*, ed. L. Giard (Paris:
1987).

Certeau M. de, s.j., *The Mystic Fable*, vol. 2: *The Sixteenth and Seventeenth Centuries*, ed.
L. Giard, trans. M.B. Smith (Chicago, IL: 2015).

Cicero, *On the Republic; On the Laws*, trans. C.W. Keyes (Cambridge, MA – London:
1928).

Clark T.J., *The Sight of Death: An Experiment in Art Writing* (New Haven, CT: 2006).

Coffin C.M., *John Donne and the New Philosophy* (New York, NY: 1958).

Colombo E. (ed.), *Digital Indipetae Database* [ca. 1560–1970], https://indipetae.bc.edu
(accessed 11.02.2024).

Colombo E., "Nel mezzo del cammino: *Indipetae* e racconti di vocazione", *Rivista
Storica Italiana* 132.3 (2020) 990–1010.

Colombo E., "From Paper to Screen: The *Digital Indipetae Database*, a New Resource
for Jesuit Studies", *Archivum Historicum Societatis Iesu* 177, fasc. 89.1 (2020) 213–230.

Cooper M. (ed.), *They Came to Japan: An Anthology of European Reports on Japan,
1543–1640* (Berkeley, CA: 1965).

Dalmases C. de, s.j. (ed.), *Tratados espirituales* (Barcelona: 1964).

Daly R.J., s.j., *The Origins of the Christian Doctrine of Sacrifice* (Philadelphia, PA:
1978).

David Jan, s.j., *Veridicus Christianus* (Antwerp, Plantin Press under Jan Moretus: 1601).

De Boer W. – Enenkel K.A.E. – Melion W.S. (eds.), *Jesuit Image Theory* (Leiden – Boston,
MA: 2016).

Dekoninck R. – Delfosse M., "*Sacer Horror*: The Construction and Experience of
the Sublime in the Jesuit Festivities of the Early Seventeenth-Century Southern
Netherlands", *Journal of Historians of Netherlandish Art* 8.2 (2016) 1–16.

Deleuze G., *Francis Bacon: The Logic of Sensation*, trans. D.W. Smith (Minneapolis, MN:
2003).

Derrida J., *Who's Afraid of Philosophy? Right to Philosophy 1*, trans. J. Plug (Stanford, CA:
2002).

Dick S.J., *Plurality of Worlds: The Origins of the Extraterrestrial Life Debate from Democritus to Kant* (Cambridge – New York, NY – Melbourne: 1982).

DiFuria A.J. – Melion W.S. (eds.), *Ekphrastic Image-making in Early Modern Europe,
1500–1700* (Leiden – Boston, MA: 2021).

Ditchfield S., "Baroque around the Clock: Daniello Bartoli s.j. (1608–1685) and the Uses
of Global History", *Transactions of the Royal Historical Society* 31 (2021) 49–73.

Donne John, *Conclaue Ignati* (London, [William Hall]: 1611).

Donne John, *Ignatius His Conclave* (London, N.O. [Nicholas Okes]: 1611).

Donne J., *Ignatius His Conclave*, ed. T.S. Healy, s.j. (Oxford – New York, NY: 1969; reprint, Oxford – New York, NY: 2010).

Dostoevsky F., *The Idiot*, trans. D. Magarshack (New York, NY: 1956).

Eck C. van – Bussels S. – Delbeke M. – Pieters J. (eds.), *Translations of the Sublime: The Early Modern Reception and Dissemination of Longinus's Peri Hupsous in Rhetoric, the Visual Arts, Architecture, and the Theatre* (Leiden – Boston, MA: 2012).

Eire C.M.N., *From Madrid to Purgatory: The Art and Craft of Dying in Sixteenth-Century Spain* (Cambridge – New York, NY – Melbourne: 1995).

Eire C.M.N., "The Good Side of Hell: Infernal Meditations in Early Modern Spain", *Historical Reflections* 26.2 (2000) 285–310.

Elison G., *Deus Destroyed: The Image of Christianity in Early Modern Japan* (Cambridge, MA – London: 1973).

Epistolae et monumenta P. Hieronymi Nadal, vol. 5: *Commentarii de Instituto S.I.*, ed. M. Nicolau (Rome: 1962).

Fabre P.A., *Le lieu de l'image: Le probleme de la composition de lieu dans les pratiques spirituelles et artistiques jésuites de la seconde moitié du XVIᵉ siècle* (Paris: 1992).

Fabre P.A., "Vocation et martyre dans les *Vocationes illustres*", *Rivista Storica Italiana* 132.3 (2020) 1032–1048.

Fabre P.-A., "Conclusion: The Narrow Road to Martyrdom", *Journal of Jesuit Studies* 9.1 (2022) 125–135.

Ferro Giovanni, *Teatro d'imprese* (Venice, Giacomo Sarzina: 1623).

Fineman M. – Saunders B. (eds.), *Apollo's Muse: The Moon in the Age of Photography*, exh. cat., The Metropolitan Museum of Art (New York, NY: 2019).

Flowers T., s.j., *The Reform of Doctrine in the Catechisms of Peter Canisius* (Leiden – Boston, MA: 2023).

Frei E., "Through Daniello Bartoli's Eyes: Francis Xavier in *Asia* (1653)", *Journal of Jesuit Studies* 9.3 (2022) 398–414.

Frei E. – Rai E. (eds.), *Profiling Saints: Images of Modern Sanctity in a Global World* (Göttingen: 2023).

Fricke B., "Fingerzeig und Augenblick: Galileo Galileis Finger zwischen Fetisch und Reliquie", *Zeitschrift für Ideengeschichte* 3.1 (2009) 80–93.

Frois Luís, s.j., *Copia di due lettere annue scritte dal Giapone del 1589 e 1590* (Rome, Luigi Zannetti: 1593).

Frois Luís, s.j., *Relatione della gloriosa morte di XXVI* (Rome, Luigi Zannetti: 1599).

Fumaroli M., *L'École du silence: Le sentiment des images au XVIIᵉ siècle* (Paris: 1994).

Galdós Baertel R. (ed.), *Relación del martirio de los 26 cristianos crucificados en Nangasaqui el 5 febrero de 1597* (Rome: 1935).

Galilei Galileo, *Sidereus nuncius, magna, longeque admirabilia spectacula pandens* (Venice, Thomas Baglioni: 1610).

Galilei G., *Sidereus Nuncius or The Sidereal Messenger*, ed. and trans. A. van Helden (2nd ed. Chicago, IL: 2015 [1989]).

Gallonio Antonio, c.o., *Trattato degli instrumenti di martirio* (Rome, Ascano Donangeli – Girolamo Donangeli: 1591).

Ganss G.E., s.j. (ed. and trans.), *The Spiritual Exercises of Saint Ignatius: A Translation and a Commentary* (Chicago, IL: 1992).

Garcés García, s.j., *Relacion de la Persecucion que huvo en la Iglesia de Iapon, y de los insignes martires que gloriosamente dieron sus vidas en defensa de nuestra Santa Fè, el anõ de 1622* (Madrid, Luis Sánchez: 1625).

Göttler C., *Last Things: Art and the Religious Imagination in the Age of Reform* (Turnhout: 2010).

Göttler C. – Mochizuki M.M. (eds.), *Landscape and Earth in Early Modernity: Picturing Unruly Nature* (Amsterdam: 2023).

Gregory B.S., *Salvation at Stake: Christian Martyrdom in Early Modern Europe* (Cambridge, MA – London: 1999).

Gretser Jacob, s.j., *Opera omnia*, vols. 1–3: *De sancta cruce* (Regensburg, Johann Conrad Peetz – Emmerich Felix Bader: 1734).

Groebner V., *Defaced: The Visual Culture of Violence in the Late Middle Ages*, trans. P. Selwyn (New York, NY: 2008).

Grosse S., *Heilsungewissheit und Scrupulositas im späten Mittelalter: Studien zu Johannes Gerson und Gattungen der Frömmigkeitstheologie seiner Zeit* (Tübingen: 1994).

Hale J.R. (ed.), *The Travel Journal of Antonio de Beatis through Germany, Switzerland, the Low Countries, France, and Italy, 1517–1518*, trans. J.R. Hale – J.M.A. Lindon (London: 1979).

Hamel J. – Keil I. (eds.), *Der Meister und die Fernrohre* (Frankfurt am Main: 2007).

Hannay A. – Marino G.D. (eds.), *The Cambridge Companion to Kierkegaard* (Cambridge – New York, NY – Melbourne: 1998).

Harpster G., "Illustrious Jesuits: The Martyrological Portrait Series *circa* 1600", *Journal of Jesuit Studies* 9.3 (2022) 378–397.

Hassel, Jr., R.C., "Donne's 'Ignatius His Conclave' and the New Astronomy", *Modern Philology* 68.4 (1971) 329–337.

Hendrickson D.S., s.j., "Grave Matters: Juan Eusebio Nieremberg's *Partida a la eternidad* (1643) and Jesuit Approaches to Death in Early Modern Spain", *Journal of Jesuit Studies* 8.4 (2021) 638–659.

Hesselink R.H., *The Dream of a Christian Nagasaki: World Trade and the Clash of Cultures, 1560–1640* (Jefferson, NC: 2016).

Horodowich E. – Markey L. (eds.), *The New World in Early Modern Italy, 1492–1750* (Cambridge – New York, NY – Melbourne: 2017).

Horodowich E. – Nagel A., *Amerasia* (New York, NY: 2023).

Ignatius of Loyola, s.j., *Exercitia spiritualia* (Rome, Antonio Blado: 1548).

Ignatius of Loyola, s.j., *Geestelycke oeffeninghen vanden H. vader Ignatius van Loyola* (Antwerp, Michiel Cnobbaert: 1673).

Imbruglia G. – Fabre P.A. – Mongini G. (eds.), *Cinque secoli di Litterae indipetae: Il desiderio delle missioni nella Compagnia di Gesù* (Rome: 2022).

Kierkegaard S., *Fear and Trembling; Repetition*, ed. and trans. H.V. Hong – E.H. Hong (Princeton, NJ: 1983).

Kim D.Y., "The Horror of Mimesis", *Oxford Art Journal* 34.3 (2011) 335–353.

Koyré A., *From the Closed World to the Infinite Universe* (Baltimore, MD: 1957; reprint, Kettering, OH: 2016).

Larsen E., "The Proof of the Use of the Inverted Telescope in Dutch 17th-Century Landscape Art", *Gazette des beaux-arts* 89.2 (1977) 172–174.

Lavenia V. – Pastore S. – Pavone S. – Petrolini C. (eds.), *Compel People to Come In: Violence and Catholic Conversion in the Non-European World* (Rome: 2018).

Lipsius Justus, *De cruce libri tres* (Antwerp, Plantin Press under Jeanne Plantin – Jan Moretus: 1593).

Loarte Gaspar de, s.j., *Exercicio dela vida christiana* (Cagliari, Vincencio Sembenino: 1567).

Loh M.H., *Titian Remade: Repetition and the Transformation of Early Modern Italian Art* (Los Angeles, CA: 2007).

Lucian of Samosata, *Lucian*, vol. 1, trans. A.M. Harmon (Cambridge, MA – London: 1913).

Mâle É., *L'art religieux après le Concile de Trente; Étude sur l'iconographie de la fin du XVIe siècle, du XVIIe, du XVIIIe siècle: Italie – France – Espagne – Flandres* (Paris: 1932).

Marion J.-L., *The Essential Writings*, ed. K. Hart (New York, NY: 2013).

Marrow J.H., "*Circumdederunt me canes multi*: Christ's Tormentors in Northern European Art of the Late Middle Ages and Early Renaissance", *Art Bulletin* 59.2 (1977) 167–181.

Marrow J.H., *Passion Iconography in Northern European Art of the Late Middle Ages and Early Renaissance: A Study of the Transformation of Sacred Metaphor into Descriptive Narrative* (Kortrijk: 1979).

Migne J.-P. (ed.), *Patrologia Latina*, vol. 38 (Paris: 1845).

Mochizuki M.M., *Jesuit Art* (Leiden – Boston, MA: 2022).

Molina J.M., *To Overcome Oneself: The Jesuit Ethic and Spirit of Global Expansion* (Berkeley, CA: 2013).

Monssen L.H., "*Rex Gloriose Martyrum*: A Contribution to Jesuit Iconography", *Art Bulletin* 63.1 (1981) 130–137.

Monssen L.H., "*Triumphus* and *Trophaea Sacra*: Notes on the Iconography and Spirituality of the Triumphant Martyr", *Konsthistorisk Tidskrift* 51 (1982) 10–20.

Montanari R. – Alberghina M.F. – Schiavone S. – Pelosi C., "The Jesuit Painting *Seminario* in Japan: European Renaissance Technology and Its Influence on Far Eastern Art", *X-Ray Spectrometry* 51 (2022) 64–85.

Montgomery S.L., *The Moon and the Western Imagination* (Tucson, AZ: 1999).

Motta F. – Rai E., "Jesuit Sanctity: Hypothesizing the Continuity of a Hagiographic Narrative of the Modern Age", *Journal of Jesuit Studies* 9.1 (2022) 1–14.

Motta F. – Rai E., "Martyrs and Missionaries: Strategies of Jesuit Sainthood between the Suppression and the Restoration", *Journal of Jesuit Studies* 9.1 (2022) 95–124.

Nadal Jerónimo, s.j., *Evangelicae historiae imagines* (Antwerp, Society of Jesus: 1593).

Nadal Jerónimo, s.j., *Adnotationes et meditationes in Evangelia* (Antwerp, Martin II Nuyts: 1595).

Nancy J.-L., *The Ground of the Image*, trans. J. Fort (New York, NY: 2005).

Nicolson M., *Voyages to the Moon* (New York, NY: 1948).

Noreen K., "*Ecclesiae militantis triumphi*: Jesuit Iconography and the Counter-Reformation", *Sixteenth Century Journal* 29.3 (1998) 689–715.

O'Malley J.W., s.j., *Religious Culture in the Sixteenth Century* (Aldershot – Burlington, VT: 1993).

O'Malley J.W., s.j., *The First Jesuits* (Cambridge, MA – London: 1993).

Omata Rappo H., *Des Indes lointaines aux scènes des collèges: Les reflets des martyrs de la mission japonaise en Europe (XVIᵉ–XVIIIᵉ siècle)* (Munster: 2020).

Otto R., *The Idea of the Holy: An Inquiry into the Non-rational Factor in the Idea of the Divine and Its Relation to the Rational*, trans. J.W. Harvey (London: 1923).

Pabel H.M., "Fear and Consolation: Peter Canisius and the Spirituality of Dying and Death", *Studies in the Spirituality of Jesuits* 45.1 (2013) 1–32.

Palmer M.E., s.j. (ed. and trans.), *On Giving the Spiritual Exercises: The Early Jesuit Manuscript Directories and the Official Directory of 1599* (St. Louis, MO: 1996).

Panofsky E., *Galileo as a Critic of the Arts* (The Hague – Dordrecht: 1954).

Panofsky E., "Original and Facsimile Reproduction (1930)", trans. T. Grundy, *Res: Anthropology and Aesthetics* 57/58 (2010) 330–338.

Panofsky E., *Galileo Galilei und die Bildkünste*, ed. H. Bredekamp, trans. H. Jatho (Zurich: 2012).

Papa G., *Le cause di canonizzazione nel primo periodo della Congregazione dei Riti (1588–1634)* (Vatican City – Rome: 2001).

Pérez de Ribas Andrés, s.j., *Historia de los Triumphos de nuestra Santa Fee* (Madrid, Alonso de Paredes: 1645).

Pérez de Ribas A., s.j., *History of the Triumphs of Our Holy Faith amongst the Most Barbarous and Fierce Peoples of the New World: An English Translation Based on the 1645 Spanish Original*, ed. D.T. Reff, trans. D.T. Reff – M. Ahern – R.K. Danford (Tucson, AZ: 1999).

Perkinson S. – Turel N. (eds.), *Picturing Death, 1200–1600* (Leiden – Boston, MA: 2021).

Pinkus A., *Visual Aggression: Images of Martyrdom in Late Medieval Germany* (University Park, PA: 2021).

Plutarch, *Moralia*, vol. 12, trans. H. Cherniss – W.C. Helmbold (Cambridge, MA – London: 1957).

Polanco Juan Alfonso de, S.J., *Methodus ad eos adiuvandos, qui moriuntur* (Macerata, Sebastiano Martellini: 1575).

Powell A., "Squaring the Circle: The Telescopic View in Early Modern Landscapes", *Art History* 39.2 (2016) 282–301.

Promey S.M. (ed.), *Sensational Religion: Sensory Cultures in Material Practice* (New Haven, CT: 2014).

Quiles García F. – García Bernal J.J. – Broggio P. – Fagiolo Dell'Arco M. (eds.), *A la luz de Roma: Santos y santidad en el barocco iberoamericano*, vol. 3: *Tierra de santidad* (Seville: 2020).

Rahner H., S.J., *Ignatius the Theologian*, trans. M. Barry, S.J. (Freiburg im Breisgau: 1968).

Rai E., "Spargere il sangue per Cristo: La vocaziones al martirio missionario come elemento di identità gesuitica; il caso di John Ogilvie (1579–1615)", *Rivista Storica Italiana* 132.3 (2020) 1011–1031.

Rawson M., "Discovering the Final Frontier: The Seventeenth-Century Encounter with the Lunar Environment", *Environmental History* 20.2 (2015) 194–216.

Reeves E., "John Donne and the Oblique Course", *Renaissance Studies* 7.2 (1993) 168–183.

Reeves E., *Painting the Heavens: Art and Science in the Age of Galileo* (Princeton, NJ: 1997).

Reeves E., *Galileo's Glassworks: The Telescope and the Mirror* (Cambridge, MA – London: 2008).

Reeves E., "Kingdoms of Heaven: Galileo and Sarpi on the Celestial", *Representations* 105.1 (2009) 61–84.

Reeves E., "Variable Stars: A Decade of Historiography on the *Sidereus Nuncius*", *Galilaeana* 8 (2011) 37–72.

Renaldo J.J., "Bacon's Empiricism, Boyle's Science, and the Jesuit Response in Italy", *Journal of the History of Ideas* 37.4 (1976) 689–695.

Ricci Bartolomeo, S.J., *Triumphus Iesu Christi crucifix* (Antwerp, Plantin Press under Jan Moretus: 1608).

Riccioli Giambattista, S.J., *Almagestum novum* (Bologna, Heirs of Vittorio Benatio: 1651).

Richeome Louis, S.J., *La peinture spirituelle, ou l'art d'admirer, amimer, et louer Dieu* (Lyon, Pierre Rigaud: 1611).

Roldán-Figueroa R., *The Martyrs of Japan: Publication History and Catholic Missions in the Spanish World (Spain, New Spain, and the Philippines, 1597–1700)* (Leiden – Boston, MA: 2021).

Rosen E., *Kepler's Conversation with Galileo's Sidereal Messenger* (New York, NY: 1965).

Ruiz de Medina J., s.J., *El matirologio del Japón, 1558–1873* (Rome: 1999).

Russell C., *Being a Jesuit in Renaissance Italy: Biographical Writing in the Early Global Age* (Cambridge, MA – London: 2022).

Salviucci Insolera L., "Le illustrazioni per gli Esercizi Spirituali intorno al 1600", *Archivum Historicum Societatis Iesu* 60, fasc. 119 (1991) 161–217.

Serrano Martín E. – Cortés Peña A.L. – Betrán Moya J.L. (eds.), *Discurso religioso y Contrarreforma* (Zaragoza: 2005).

Shin J.M., "The Passion and Flagellation in Sixteenth-Century Japan", *Renaissance and Reformation / Renaissance et Réforme* 36.2 (2013) 5–43.

Shin J.M., *The Jesuits, Images, and Devotional Practices in China and Japan, 1549–1644* (Seoul: 2017).

Sluiter E., "The Telescope before Galileo", *Journal for the History of Astronomy* 28.3 (1997) 223–234.

Sontag S., *Regarding the Pain of Others* (New York, NY: 2003).

Standaert N., s.J., "The Composition of Place: Creating Space for an Encounter", *The Way* 46.1 (2007) 7–20.

Sucquet Antoine, s.J., *Via vitae aeternae* (vol. 1: Antwerp, Martin III Nuyts: 1620; vol. 2: Antwerp, Hendrick Aertssens: 1625).

Surius Laurentius, O.Cart., *De probatis sanctorum historiis*, vol. 5 (Cologne, Gerwin Calenius – The Heirs of Johann Quentel: 1574).

Tanner Matthias, s.J., *Societas Iesu usque ad sanguinis et vitae profusionem militans: in Europa, Africa, Asia, et America, contra gentiles, Mahometanos, Judaeos, haereticos, impios, pro Deo, fide, Ecclesia, pietate* (Prague, Universitas Carolo-Ferdinandea: 1675).

Taton R. – Wilson C. (eds.), *Planetary Astronomy from the Renaissance to the Rise of Astrophysics*, part A: *Tycho Brahe to Newton* (Cambridge – New York, NY – Melbourne: 1989).

Terry-Fritsch A. – Labbie E.F. (eds.), *Beholding Violence in Medieval and Early Modern Europe* (Aldershot – Burlington, VT: 2012).

Thürlemann F., *Mehr als ein Bild: Für eine Kunstgeschichte des Hyperimage* (Munich: 2013).

Touber J., *Law, Medicine, and Engineering in the Cult of the Saints in Counter-Reformation Rome: The Hagiographical Works of Antonio Gallonio, 1556–1605* (Leiden – Boston, MA: 2014).

Tutino S., "Historical Authenticity and the Expanding Horizons of the Seventeenth-Century Catholic Church", *Journal of Modern History* 92.1 (2020) 1–39.

Tutino S., *The Many Faces of Credulitas: Credibility, Credulity, and Belief in Post-Reformation Catholicism* (Oxford – New York, NY: 2022).

Vieira António, s.j., *História do futuro* (Lisbon, António Pedrozo Galram: 1718).

Vieira A., s.j., *História do futuro*, ed. M.L. Carvalhão Buescu (Lisbon: 1982).

Vieira A., s.j., *The Sermon of Saint Anthony to the Fish and Other Texts*, trans. G. Rabassa (Dartmouth, MA: 2009).

Wilding N., *Galileo's Idol: Gianfrancesco Sagredo and the Politics of Knowledge* (Chicago, IL: 2014).

Winkler M.G. – Van Helden A., "Representing the Heavens: Galileo and Visual Astronomy", *Isis* 83.2 (1992) 195–217.

Zierholz S., "*Conformitas crucis Christi*: Zum Motiv der Kreuzesnachfolge in der jesuitischen Druckgrafik des 17. Jahrhunderts im Licht der Vision von La Storta", *Archivum Historicum Societatis Iesu* 86, fasc. 171.1 (2017) 49–97.

Zierholz S., *Räume der Reform: Kunst und Lebenskunst der Jesuiten in Rom, 1580–1700* (Berlin: 2019).

Županov I.G. (ed.), *The Oxford Handbook of the Jesuits* (Oxford – New York, NY: 2019).

Index nominum